International Perspectives and Strategies for Managing an Aging Workforce

Fatma Ince
Mersin University, Turkey

IGI Global
PUBLISHER of TIMELY KNOWLEDGE

A volume in the Advances in Human Resources Management and Organizational Development (AHRMOD) Book Series

Published in the United States of America by
IGI Global
Business Science Reference (an imprint of IGI Global)
701 E. Chocolate Avenue
Hershey PA, USA 17033
Tel: 717-533-8845
Fax: 717-533-8661
E-mail: cust@igi-global.com
Web site: http://www.igi-global.com

Copyright © 2022 by IGI Global. All rights reserved. No part of this publication may be reproduced, stored or distributed in any form or by any means, electronic or mechanical, including photocopying, without written permission from the publisher. Product or company names used in this set are for identification purposes only. Inclusion of the names of the products or companies does not indicate a claim of ownership by IGI Global of the trademark or registered trademark.

Library of Congress Cataloging-in-Publication Data

Names: Ince, Fatma, 1983- editor.
Title: International perspectives and strategies for managing an aging workforce / Fatma Ince, editor.
Description: Hershey : Business Science Reference, 2022. | Includes bibliographical references and index. | Summary: "This book examines the organizational systems, processes and practices for managing older workers. It also analyzes the impact of an aging workforce on their retention, productivity, and wellbeing"-Provided by publisher"--
Identifiers: LCCN 2019039203 (print) | LCCN 2019039204 (ebook) | ISBN 9781799823957 (hardcover) | ISBN 9781799823964 (ebook)
Subjects: LCSH: Older people--Employment. | Personnel management. | Organizational behavior.
Classification: LCC HD6279 .H363 2022 (print) | LCC HD6279 (ebook) | DDC 658.30084/6--dc23
LC record available at https://lccn.loc.gov/2019039203
LC ebook record available at https://lccn.loc.gov/2019039204

This book is published in the IGI Global book series Advances in Human Resources Management and Organizational Development (AHRMOD) (ISSN: 2327-3372; eISSN: 2327-3380)

British Cataloguing in Publication Data
A Cataloguing in Publication record for this book is available from the British Library.

All work contributed to this book is new, previously-unpublished material. The views expressed in this book are those of the authors, but not necessarily of the publisher.

For electronic access to this publication, please contact: eresources@igi-global.com.

Advances in Human Resources Management and Organizational Development (AHRMOD) Book Series

Patricia Ordóñez de Pablos
Universidad de Oviedo, Spain

ISSN:2327-3372
EISSN:2327-3380

Mission

A solid foundation is essential to the development and success of any organization and can be accomplished through the effective and careful management of an organization's human capital. Research in human resources management and organizational development is necessary in providing business leaders with the tools and methodologies which will assist in the development and maintenance of their organizational structure.

The **Advances in Human Resources Management and Organizational Development (AHRMOD) Book Series** aims to publish the latest research on all aspects of human resources as well as the latest methodologies, tools, and theories regarding organizational development and sustainability. The **AHRMOD Book Series** intends to provide business professionals, managers, researchers, and students with the necessary resources to effectively develop and implement organizational strategies.

Coverage

- Disputes Resolution
- Employee Communications
- Executive Compensation
- Talent Identification and Management
- Upward Feedback
- Process Improvement
- Organizational Learning
- Outsourcing HR
- Collaborative Method
- Corporate Governance

IGI Global is currently accepting manuscripts for publication within this series. To submit a proposal for a volume in this series, please contact our Acquisition Editors at Acquisitions@igi-global.com or visit: http://www.igi-global.com/publish/.

The Advances in Human Resources Management and Organizational Development (AHRMOD) Book Series (ISSN 2327-3372) is published by IGI Global, 701 E. Chocolate Avenue, Hershey, PA 17033-1240, USA, www.igi-global.com. This series is composed of titles available for purchase individually; each title is edited to be contextually exclusive from any other title within the series. For pricing and ordering information please visit http://www.igi-global.com/book-series/advances-human-resources-management-organizational/73670. Postmaster: Send all address changes to above address. Copyright © 2022 IGI Global. All rights, including translation in other languages reserved by the publisher. No part of this series may be reproduced or used in any form or by any means – graphics, electronic, or mechanical, including photocopying, recording, taping, or information and retrieval systems – without written permission from the publisher, except for non commercial, educational use, including classroom teaching purposes. The views expressed in this series are those of the authors, but not necessarily of IGI Global.

Titles in this Series

For a list of additional titles in this series, please visit: http://www.igi-global.com/book-series/advances-human-resources-management-organizational/73670

Navigating the New Normal of Business With Enhanced Human Resource Management Strategies
Perfecto Gatbonton Aquino Jr. (Duy Tan University, Vietnam) and Revenio Cabanilla Jalagat Jr. (Al-Zahra College for Women, Oman)
Business Science Reference • © 2022 • 313pp • H/C (ISBN: 9781799884514) • US $195.00

Ergonomics and Business Policies for the Promotion of Well-Being in the Workplace
Mildrend Montoya-Reyes (Autonomous University of Baja California, Mexico) Ismael Mendoza-Muñoz (Autonomous University of Baja California, Mexico) Gabriela Jacobo-Galicia (Autonomous University of Baja California, Mexico) and Samantha E. Cruz-Sotelo (Autonomous University of Baja California, Mexico)
Business Science Reference • © 2022 • 303pp • H/C (ISBN: 9781799873969) • US $195.00

Gender Perspectives on Industry 4.0 and the Impact of Technology on Mainstreaming Female Employment
Shashi Bala (V. V. Giri National Labour Institute, India) and Puja Singhal (National Centre for School Leadership-NIEPA, India)
Business Science Reference • © 2022 • 325pp • H/C (ISBN: 9781799885948) • US $215.00

Handbook of Research on Key Dimensions of Occupational Safety and Health Protection Management
Snežana Živković (Faculty of Occupational Safety, University of Niš, Serbia) Bojan Krstić (Faculty of Economics, University of Niš, Serbia) and Tamara Rađenović (Faculty of Occupational Safety, University of Niš, Serbia)
Business Science Reference • © 2022 • 512pp • H/C (ISBN: 9781799881896) • US $295.00

Analyzing Telework, Trustworthiness, and Performance Using Leader-Member Exchange COVID-19 Perspective
Michael A. Brown Sr. (Right Fit Communications LLC, USA)
Business Science Reference • © 2022 • 263pp • H/C (ISBN: 9781799889502) • US $215.00

Future Advancements for CSR and the Sustainable Development Goals in a Post-COVID-19 World
Andrea Pérez (University of Cantabria, Spain)
Business Science Reference • © 2022 • 355pp • H/C (ISBN: 9781799880653) • US $225.00

Building Competencies for Organizational Success Emerging Research and Opportunities
Donta S. Harper (University of Washington, USA)
Business Science Reference • © 2021 • 217pp • H/C (ISBN: 9781799865162) • US $195.00

IGI Global
PUBLISHER of TIMELY KNOWLEDGE

701 East Chocolate Avenue, Hershey, PA 17033, USA
Tel: 717-533-8845 x100 • Fax: 717-533-8661
E-Mail: cust@igi-global.com • www.igi-global.com

Table of Contents

Preface xiv

Section 1
Workforce and Economy

Chapter 1
The Evolution of Aging Conceptualization and Its Effect on the Workforce 1
Maria C. Lamas, School of Health, Polytechnic of Porto, Portugal
Bruno de Sousa Lopes, University of Aveiro, Portugal
Vanessa Amorim, University of Aveiro, Portugal
Oscar Bernardes, Porto Accounting and Business School, Polytechnic of Porto, Portugal

Chapter 2
Indonesian Ageing Workforces in Rural and Urban Areas: Are They Similar or Not? 24
Deshinta Vibriyanti, The National Research and Innovation Agency, Indonesia
Sari Seftiani, The National Research and Innovation Agency, Indonesia
Vanda Ningrum, The National Research and Innovation Agency, Indonesia
Intan Adhi Perdana Putri, The National Research and Innovation Agency, Indonesia
Inayah Hidayati, The National Research and Innovation Agency, Indonesia
Luh Kitty Katherina, The National Research and Innovation Agency, Indonesia

Chapter 3
Senior Entrepreneurship: Agenda for a Youth Economy (Indian Perspective) 42
Shikha Aggarwal, Institute of Technology and Science, India
Vidhi Tyagi, Amity University, India

Chapter 4
LAD Regression Application: Factors Affecting Household Expenditures of Working Elderly in Turkey 68
Kübranur Çebi Karaaslan, Erzurum Technical University, Turkey

Chapter 5
A Knowledge-Based Recommender Framework to Recommend Destination Country for Human Migrants (KBRF): The Case of Ethiopia in Africa........ 84
Nilamadhab Mishra, VIT Bhopal University, India
Baye Yemataw, Debre Berhan University, Ethiopia
Kishore Kumar P. K., University of Technology and Applied Sciences, Oman

Section 2
Post-Pandemic New Normal

Chapter 6
Leader Competence Effectiveness........ 115
Paula Cristina Nunes Figueiredo, ULHT, Universidade Lusófona, Portugal

Chapter 7
Challenges for Higher Education Graduates in the Post-Pandemic Labor Market........ 144
Aslı Günay, Social Sciences University of Ankara, Turkey

Chapter 8
Managing the Remote Workforce in the New Normal........ 160
Dilek Esen, Dokuz Eylül University, Turkey

Chapter 9
COVID-19 Pandemic: The Impact of the Elderly Workforce on Social Security-Related Rights........ 178
Emre Kol, Anadolu University, Turkey

Section 3
Multigenerational Workforce

Chapter 10
Baby Boomers and Their Influence in the Colombian Organizational and Entrepreneurial Context. 201
Rafael Ignacio Pérez-Uribe, Universidad Santo Tomas, Colombia
David Ocampo-Guzmán, Universidad EAN, Colombia
Maria Pilar Ramirez-Salazar, Universidad EAN, Colombia

Chapter 11
Back to School: Mid-Life Adult Perspectives About Their Graduate Education........ 230
Özge Erdemli, Ankara University, Turkey
Nihan Demirkasımoğlu, Hacettepe University, Turkey
Tuğba Güner Demir, Ankara University, Turkey

Chapter 12
International Retirement Migration of European Baby Boomers: Retiring Knowledge Worker Perspectives and the Case of Turkey........ 252
Gülçin Bilgin Turna, Recep Tayyip Erdogan University, Turkey

Chapter 13
The Human Resources Perspective on the Multigenerational Workforce 274
Fatma Ince, Mersin University, Turkey

Compilation of References 298

About the Contributors 338

Index 344

Detailed Table of Contents

Preface..xiv

Section 1
Workforce and Economy

Chapter 1
The Evolution of Aging Conceptualization and Its Effect on the Workforce 1
Maria C. Lamas, School of Health, Polytechnic of Porto, Portugal
Bruno de Sousa Lopes, University of Aveiro, Portugal
Vanessa Amorim, University of Aveiro, Portugal
Oscar Bernardes, Porto Accounting and Business School, Polytechnic of Porto, Portugal

Increased life expectancy has resulted in improved health and quality of life, which has accelerated global demographic aging. This phenomenon is a significant source of concern for any country in the 21st century. Simultaneously, several policies have been implemented in a variety of areas, most notably the one advocated by the United Nations—Active Aging—which aims to maintain citizens' active participation in their communities for an extended period, as well as lifelong learning, health, and safety, including in the workforce context. In this chapter, the authors employed a research methodology consisting of two distinct phases, namely scientometrics and web-scraping, to analyze the predefined keywords "aging"/"ageing" and "work" in the context of a business environment. The results presented indicate that the interest in this theme has grown substantially. On the other hand, the keywords investigated are interconnected with other sub-areas, demonstrating the wide dissemination of this study area.

Chapter 2
Indonesian Ageing Workforces in Rural and Urban Areas: Are They Similar or Not? 24
Deshinta Vibriyanti, The National Research and Innovation Agency, Indonesia
Sari Seftiani, The National Research and Innovation Agency, Indonesia
Vanda Ningrum, The National Research and Innovation Agency, Indonesia
Intan Adhi Perdana Putri, The National Research and Innovation Agency, Indonesia
Inayah Hidayati, The National Research and Innovation Agency, Indonesia
Luh Kitty Katherina, The National Research and Innovation Agency, Indonesia

In 2020, Statistics Indonesia revealed that one of two older people is still working. Based on the region, the proportion of older people who are working in rural areas is higher than in urban areas. This chapter aims to describes the socio-demographic characteristics of the Indonesian older workers by region area. Data of this chapter were based on the research about the quality of older people life conducted by The

National Research and Innovation Agency and BPS data. The results show that the Indonesian older worker are vulnerable workers (both in urban and rural areas). The older workers in the rural areas have a worse condition due to lower wages, longer working hours, and lower health insurance ownership while the older workers in the urban mostly filled the service sector. Creating decent jobs for older people is an important thing to do considering that the older people in Indonesia still have the capacity and good physical condition to work.

Chapter 3
Senior Entrepreneurship: Agenda for a Youth Economy (Indian Perspective).................................... 42
Shikha Aggarwal, Institute of Technology and Science, India
Vidhi Tyagi, Amity University, India

The 50+ age group had made a significant contribution to the entrepreneurship and innovation agenda in the US. Similarly, entrepreneurs above the age of 50 constituted around 15% of all commercial startups in England. Senior entrepreneurship has been considered a promising way to manage the issue of aging population. Could India be the next destination for third-age entrepreneurship to find its calling? Should we acknowledge the advantages of senior entrepreneurship and sensitize the aging population and the governments toward it? In light of limited literature available for senior entrepreneurship, potential motivating factors or driving force are discussed. Furthermore, entrepreneurship in India is highlighted encompassing the status of entrepreneurship, policies and schemes promoting entrepreneurship, and opportunities and challenges for senior entrepreneurship. Finally, the chapter concludes with implications for practice in policy-making and in terms of encouraging senior entrepreneurship and its antecedents in the Indian context.

Chapter 4
LAD Regression Application: Factors Affecting Household Expenditures of Working Elderly in Turkey 68
Kübranur Çebi Karaaslan, Erzurum Technical University, Turkey

Household expenditures are important indicators in many aspects, especially in the economic growth of a country. One of the most important determinants of expenditures is the head of the household working within the framework of the household's income. From this point of view, the aim of the study is to determine the factors affecting the household expenditures of the heads of the household who are 60 years of age and older living in Turkey. In this framework, the data set of the Household Budget Survey of the Turkish Statistical Institute was used for the years 2015-2019. The least absolute deviation regression was used for the data set analysis. As a result of the study, it was determined that the gender of the head of the household, educational status, economic indicators, especially income, and social indicators were effective on the expenditures of the households. The results of the study provide valuable information to researchers, decision-makers, and policymakers who want to study this issue to understand the household spending patterns of working elderly household heads.

Chapter 5
A Knowledge-Based Recommender Framework to Recommend Destination Country for Human Migrants (KBRF): The Case of Ethiopia in Africa.. 84
Nilamadhab Mishra, VIT Bhopal University, India
Baye Yemataw, Debre Berhan University, Ethiopia
Kishore Kumar P. K., University of Technology and Applied Sciences, Oman

Human migration is a challenging process in Ethiopia, where special illegal human migrants cross different border countries without any basic information or knowledge. Due to this, there is the difficulty of getting a vast amount of information to know the destination countries. They go without any information, which also wastes more time, cost, violates their human rights, and endangers their lives. This study used a KBRF to assess the user input and compare them with the stored cases. For this, 75,920 cases were collected from MoLSA and central statistical agencies with and attributes selected for the query of users as well as for their solution. The best solutions are displayed for a user after the similarity calculation of the query and the stored cases. Then the users can decide on which similar cases satisfy their needs. KBRF has an average performance, recall, and precision score of 92% (4.60), 0.91 (91%), and 0.63 (63%), respectively, from domain experts and system performance.

Section 2
Post-Pandemic New Normal

Chapter 6
Leader Competence Effectiveness 115
Paula Cristina Nunes Figueiredo, ULHT, Universidade Lusófona, Portugal

The changes that have taken place over the last few decades have culminated in the existence of a workforce of different ages and experiences in the organizational context. This diversity of workforce is a challenge for the human resources management not only in the integration processes, but also in the development of competences and in the management of workers' careers. The aim of this research is to evaluate the effectiveness of the leader's competences following a model that integrates a great variety of competences grouped in four dimensions: intellectual competences, social competences, management competences, and emotional competences. The survey results show the validity and reliability of the integrative model of leader competence. With this model, organizations can identify the skills that need to be developed to improve leadership effectiveness.

Chapter 7
Challenges for Higher Education Graduates in the Post-Pandemic Labor Market................................ 144
Aslı Günay, Social Sciences University of Ankara, Turkey

The Covid-19 pandemic has brought widespread disruption to labor markets around the world. The pandemic has led to a dramatic shift in expected skill requirements, and it has forced people to acquire new demanded skills, including digital skills, to succeed in the workplace or find a job. Hence, the competition of higher education graduates in the labor market is now changing shape. Accordingly, young workers (15–24 years old) have a greater risk than older ones of being pushed out of the labor market since the current situation shows that higher education graduates do not have enough high-level digital skills in many countries. Although younger adults with a higher education degree are less likely to be unemployed than other educated adults, it is obvious the digital transformation in the workplace might affect them negatively if they cannot update their skills for the post-pandemic world.

Chapter 8
Managing the Remote Workforce in the New Normal 160
Dilek Esen, Dokuz Eylül University, Turkey

The purpose of this chapter is to determine how to manage the remote workforce in a period that covers during and after the COVID-19 pandemic called the new normal. According to this purpose, the content is as follows: the concept of new normal, remote working and hybrid work as a remote working model, advantages and disadvantages of remote working, managing the remote work and workforce. In this context, the author aimed to show remote working from all sides in the new normal and give an idea for researchers and practitioners about how to successfully manage the new normalization period post the COVID-19 pandemic.

Chapter 9
COVID-19 Pandemic: The Impact of the Elderly Workforce on Social Security-Related Rights 178
Emre Kol, Anadolu University, Turkey

The aim of this study is to evaluate and provide an overview of the significant impact of the increasing mean age of the communities on social insurance as well as the effects of COVID-19, which has turned into a pandemic, on social security rights of elderly. In this framework, strategies are suggested to minimize the negative effects of the issue on social security. This study aims to investigate the effects of aging of the population on social security systems in line with the reformist approach to social security systems, to seek an answer to the question of how social security systems will respond to this transition in the demographic structure and to suggest solutions against the effects of COVID-19. In addition, the authors discuss the implementation methods of a three-pillar social security model proposal, which is based on individual pension programs within the scope of social security reforms. Finally, flexible retirement plans developed in order to keep the aging workforce in employment for longer periods are discussed.

Section 3
Multigenerational Workforce

Chapter 10
Baby Boomers and Their Influence in the Colombian Organizational and Entrepreneurial Context. 201
Rafael Ignacio Pérez-Uribe, Universidad Santo Tomas, Colombia
David Ocampo-Guzmán, Universidad EAN, Colombia
Maria Pilar Ramirez-Salazar, Universidad EAN, Colombia

The Baby Boomers were a pivotal generation (1946 – 1964) for the Third Industrial Revolution (1945 – 2010), but with ages raging from 55 to 76, many are retirees and/or have entered the last stages of their productive lives. The last official census conducted in 2018 by Colombia's National Administrative Department of Statistics (DANE) concluded that there are 48,258,494 human beings living within Colombian soil, and out of the grand total, the Boomers accounted for 16,38%, which sums 7,904,742 (4,275,703 female and 3,629,039 male) raging between 55 to 75 years of age. The underlying question, and the one that the authors intend to answer, is Are Colombian Boomers like those in Europe and the US? In trying to answer this conundrum as best they can, an adaptation of the Rokeach's Personal Values Survey is employed, which is combined with another set of questions designed by the authors that identifies personal and familiar characteristics of the respondents by means of a non-probabilistic sample technique.

Chapter 11
Back to School: Mid-Life Adult Perspectives About Their Graduate Education 230
Özge Erdemli, Ankara University, Turkey
Nihan Demirkasımoğlu, Hacettepe University, Turkey
Tuğba Güner Demir, Ankara University, Turkey

This chapter aims to gain in-depth knowledge of the doctoral experience of older graduate students. For this purpose, a phenomenological study was conducted. Ten students aged 40 and older who are studying in graduate education were interviewed. Collected data were analyzed using descriptive and content analysis techniques. Findings revealed that being a doctoral student aged 40 and over has both advantages and disadvantages. Almost all of the participants try to complete their education simultaneously with their profession. In addition, they have heavier family responsibilities than the younger doctorants. This factor leads to a distraction and division in their motivation. However, it is clear that being in the university environment, acquiring new perspectives, and producing something new gives satisfaction to the participants despite the existing difficulties. On the other hand, young doctorants' insufficient professional experience makes older PhDs advantageous in terms of integrating their professional experience with doctoral education.

Chapter 12
International Retirement Migration of European Baby Boomers: Retiring Knowledge Worker Perspectives and the Case of Turkey 252
Gülçin Bilgin Turna, Recep Tayyip Erdogan University, Turkey

This chapter examines how retiring knowledge workers from Europe can carry their educational attainment, wealth, competencies, and experience with them to conduct their activities on a transnational scale. A qualitative approach is adopted consisting of observations and interviews with Dutch professors. What's more, a literature review was done about international retirement migration (IRM) and statistics about Europe and Turkey. IRM of thousands of baby boomers can be harnessed across borders through scientific, academic, volunteer, and educational (SAVE) activities, which can contribute to peace and prosperity in the host communities along with the knowledge workers' personal development and well-being. The propensity of retiring knowledge workers to engage in cross-border living, learning, and transition requires the analysis of Turkey's image as a temporary or permanent destination for IRM.

Chapter 13
The Human Resources Perspective on the Multigenerational Workforce 274
Fatma Ince, Mersin University, Turkey

It is a key issue how different generations coming together for a specific purpose of the business evaluate critical information. In information processing, HRM has critical roles in adapting to the diversity of the multigenerational workforce and fostering creativity. While managing a multigenerational workforce can provide a competitive advantage, ignoring the process can cause sustainability matters for the business. From this point of view, it is useful to consider the multigenerational workforce from different perspectives in terms of HRM. All efforts to understand employees are substantial as they contribute to creating an effective and synergic organization.

Compilation of References 298

About the Contributors 338

Index 344

Preface

Understanding diversity is one of the crucial dimensions of achieving sustainable leadership by making a difference with human capital in the global competitive environment. Detailed studies are needed to understand the thought and perception system of individuals who want to be directed towards a determined organizational goal and to motivate them in the desired direction. The way to correctly understand individuals and predict their behavior is to make classifications according to certain criteria and to make the psychological factors that affect the individual clear and understandable. From this point of view, one of the classifications used when interpreting individuals and their behaviors is the age factor. The classification of generations is also based on the age difference and the cultural evolution of each age (Ince, 2022a). Considering the age factor as one of the most basic demographic factors is one of the ways to reveal the benefits of diversity and avoid its disadvantages in multicultural business environments.

The experience gained with age in business life is one of the foundations of the value placed on the confidential knowledge of human capital, that is, seeing people as a resource. In an organization where technological development forces businesses to change on a global scale, trying to achieve success by ignoring this valuable resource is not a sustainable perspective. For this reason, the presence of the new generation, which is very good in technology, and the aging workforce in the same environment can contribute to the desired performance increase with a synergetic working environment (Ince, 2022b). Different age groups, which can provide high performance when managed effectively and efficiently, are the main source of creative and innovative solutions needed by changing business processes. While tangible items may be easier to replace, it may be more difficult to substitute the contribution of human capital, which is an important source of competition.

In addition, the fact that the aging workforce continues to contribute to the economy rather than being a burden is considered very beneficial in terms of sustainable resource management. Older employees should be seen as an opportunity and not as an obstacle for companies, especially regarding the transfer of knowledge and experience. Effective development and utilization of older professional and managerial employees is an important issue as most organizations are not prepared to tailor their training methods to the needs and preferences of these employees due to negative stereotypes. Managing a rapidly aging workforce and sustaining economic dynamism calls for systematic research to prevent age discrimination due to incomplete knowledge of older workers and politically challenging policy choices that require strong political commitments, robust management leadership, and social consensus (Doering et al., 1983). From this point of view, this book includes information on how to approach the employee with an international perspective, taking into account the age factor, and developing strategies suitable for this perspective.

Researchers and professors from different parts of the globe have generously provided their insights and knowledge. The book includes chapters hailing from Portugal, India, Indonesia, Ethiopia, Oman, Turkey, and Colombia, enriching the knowledge and perceptions.
The book itself is divided into three sections as described below:

- Workforce and economy: This section contains chapters that illustrate the contribution of the aging workforce to the economy as immigrants, households, and urbanites.
- Post-pandemic new normal: This section is devoted to the chapters covering the key aspects of the elderly workforce and business processes in the post-pandemic new normal.
- Multigenerational workforce: This section includes the chapters related to the concept of the generations and multigenerational workforce

The book is organized into thirteen chapters. A brief description of each of the chapters follows:

The first section, "Workforce and Economy," consists of five chapters.

Chapter 1, "The Evolution of Aging's Conceptualization and Its Effect on the Workforce," identifies the existing challenges in the management of the workforce in the twenty-first century. The chapter sets the scene for discussions presented by various authors and analyzes the predefined keywords "aging" and "work" in the context of a business environment. In particular, the chapter identifies the global orientation of the aging workforce and emphasizes the growing interest in the concept. It also identifies the importance of the aging workforce and its connection to other sub-areas of organizations.

Chapter 2, "Indonesian Ageing Workforces in Rural and Urban: Are They Similar or Not?" establishes the need for a new aging workforce policy and presents a comparison of urban and rural in terms of working conditions. The authors of this chapter argue that better conditions should be provided to exploit the potential of rural aging workers. They contend that it is possible to create added value to the economy by utilizing the existing potential only in this way. This section is important in terms of drawing attention to the working conditions of the elderly.

Chapter 3, "Senior Entrepreneurship: Agenda for a Youth Economy (Indian Perspective)," looks at the aging workforce from the perspective of entrepreneurs, showing countries in the 50+ age group that have contributed innovatively. Discussing that India's economic development can be achieved with senior entrepreneurs, the authors also touch on the challenges and opportunities created by the situation. Finally, the chapter provides implications for policymaking and implementation in promoting senior entrepreneurship and its predecessors in the Indian context.

Chapter 4, "LAD Regression Application: Factors Affecting Household Expenditures of Working Elderly in Turkey," examines the effect of the elderly workforce on household income and its reflections on budget management from a household perspective. According to the results of the research, the demographic characteristics of the elderly worker are effective on household expenditures. The chapter provides valuable information to researchers, decision-makers, and policymakers who want to examine this issue to understand the household spending patterns of working elderly household heads.

Chapter 5, "A Knowledge-Based Recommender Framework to Recommend Destination Country for Human Migrants (KBRF): The Case of Ethiopia in Africa," deals with the issue in terms of the transfer of knowledge through migration. The process of gathering, modeling, and presentation of information obtained in terms of many factors such as gender, age, region, zone, marital status means the preparation of an important data source. This information about people and the working population must be collected effectively and used in decisions that can shape the future. Therefore, the authors emphasize that integrating KBRF with transfer learning systems is critical for countries.

The second section, "Post-Pandemic New Normal," consists of four chapters.

Chapter 6, "Leader Competence Effectiveness," presents a competitive model that includes aging workers, taking the subject from a leadership perspective. According to the author, workforce diversity is a challenge for human resource management, not only in integration processes but also in the development of competencies and the management of employee careers. For this reason, there is a need for a leadership model that covers intellectual, social, managerial, and emotional competencies and competition from different perspectives. Research results showing the validity and reliability of the integrative leader competency model draw attention to the skills that need to be developed to increase leadership effectiveness.

Chapter 7, "Challenges for Higher Education Graduates in the Post-Pandemic Labor Market," emphasizes that while the elderly population can take their place in the labor market more easily with their work experience, the lack of digital skills, that need has increased after the pandemic, can lead to new employment challenges. Presenting different country comparisons according to OECD data, the author draws attention to the change in the labor market during and after the pandemic. The section, which deals with the working population in terms of age, education, and digital skills, states that in the future, organizations will include more algorithms in the selection of people and machines. For this reason, it is considered important for old and young employees to adapt to change with new skills.

Chapter 8, "Managing the Remote Workforce in the New Normal," refers to the impact of the pandemic on working systems. Discussing the disadvantages or challenges of remote working, the author emphasizes effective leadership while drawing attention to the hybrid working method. The chapter, which deals with change from the perspective of the social, organizational, individual, presents the arrangements that should be made according to the employees of different ages and qualifications from various perspectives such as HRM, leadership, and teamwork.

Chapter 9, "COVID-19 Pandemic: The Impact of the Elderly Workforce on Social Security-Related Rights," discusses the effects of the increasing average age of society on the social security system during and after the pandemic. Addressing flexible retirement plans developed to keep the aging workforce in employment for longer, the author states that ignoring the issue can put a great burden on the system. For this reason, a three-pronged social security model based on individual pension programs is mentioned within the scope of social security reforms in the chapter.

The third section, "Multigenerational Workforce," consists of four chapters.

Chapter 10, "Baby-Boomers and Their Influence in the Colombian Organizational and Entrepreneurial Context," discusses the Baby Boomer Generation working in the Third Industrial Revolution, with country comparisons. Authors analyze whether Colombian Boomers are like those in Europe and the Us with the data of Colombia's National Administrative Department of Statistics (DANE). The authors trying to answer the research question also use an adaptation of Rokeach's Personal Values Survey in the questionnaire they designed for the study. The results of the study are crucial in terms of revealing the contribution of aging workers to the economy by country comparison.

Chapter 11, "Back to School: Mid-Life Adults' Perspectives About Their Graduate Education," presents a phenomenological study by considering the age factor in terms of education. While the collected data is analyzed using descriptive and content analysis techniques, it is revealed that education has its own challenges after a certain age. Although focusing on education as well as family problems while at the center of business life creates some difficulties, the motivation to acquire new knowledge provides a driving force. The chapter is important in terms of showing that older workers with professional experience are advantageous in combining and integrating theoretical and practical knowledge.

Chapter 12, "International Retirement Migration of European Baby Boomers: Retiring Knowledge Worker Perspective and the Case of Turkey," examines how knowledge workers retired in Europe can bring their educational achievements, wealth, qualifications, and experience with them to run their activities on a transnational scale. Adopting a qualitative approach consisting of observations and interviews with Dutch professors, the study also includes comparative statistics about Europe and Turkey. The research is crucial in that it draws attention to the impact of retired knowledge workers' tendencies to engage in cross-border life, learning, and transition, on the image management of countries.

Chapter 13, "The Human Resources Perspective on the Multigenerational Workforce," considers the issue from a multigenerational perspective and sees the aging workforce as a resource for diversity management and presents this approach from a human resource management perspective. In the chapter that various classifications are made to understand the employees, it is emphasized that the investment to be made in the employee for sustainable competitive advantage can lead to organizational change and carry the business to the future. For this reason, the needs of five generations in the organization should be addressed simultaneously in all human resources practices that can shape the learning culture. This chapter is crucial in that it draws attention to the differences and the synergy they can create.

With the covering a range of topics such as the aging workforce, multigenerational workplace, and its economic effects, this reference work is ideal for researchers, academicians, practitioners, business owners, managers, human resource workers, instructors, and students. Surely, this collection of ideas and issues discussed by international authors will help you understand various aspects of an aging and multigenerational workforce, and provide valuable guidance in creating sustainable competitive advantage. Given the opportunity in an appropriate condition, the individuals fully achieve the potential of synergy in diversity.

I hope the book will contribute to your awareness and creativity.

Fatma Ince
Mersin University, Turkey

REFERENCES

Doering, M., Rhodes, S. R., & Schuster, M. (1983). *The Aging Worker: Research and Recommendations*. SAGE Publications.

Ince, F. (2022a). Leadership and Sustainability: From the First to the Second Generation of SMEs Ownership. In Research Anthology on Strategies for Maintaining Successful Family Firms (pp. 639-660). IGI Global. doi:10.4018/978-1-6684-3550-2.ch029

Ince, F. (2022b). Creative Leadership: A Multidisciplinary Approach to Creativity. In Z. Fields (Ed.), *Achieving Sustainability Using Creativity, Innovation, and Education: A Multidisciplinary Approach* (pp. 30–49). IGI Global. doi:10.4018/978-1-7998-7963-3.ch002

Section 1

Workforce and Economy

Chapter 1
The Evolution of Aging Conceptualization and Its Effect on the Workforce

Maria C. Lamas
School of Health, Polytechnic of Porto, Portugal

Bruno de Sousa Lopes
University of Aveiro, Portugal

Vanessa Amorim
University of Aveiro, Portugal

Oscar Bernardes
Porto Accounting and Business School, Polytechnic of Porto, Portugal

ABSTRACT

Increased life expectancy has resulted in improved health and quality of life, which has accelerated global demographic aging. This phenomenon is a significant source of concern for any country in the 21st century. Simultaneously, several policies have been implemented in a variety of areas, most notably the one advocated by the United Nations—Active Aging—which aims to maintain citizens' active participation in their communities for an extended period, as well as lifelong learning, health, and safety, including in the workforce context. In this chapter, the authors employed a research methodology consisting of two distinct phases, namely scientometrics and web-scraping, to analyze the predefined keywords "aging"/"ageing" and "work" in the context of a business environment. The results presented indicate that the interest in this theme has grown substantially. On the other hand, the keywords investigated are interconnected with other sub-areas, demonstrating the wide dissemination of this study area.

DOI: 10.4018/978-1-7998-2395-7.ch001

Copyright © 2022, IGI Global. Copying or distributing in print or electronic forms without written permission of IGI Global is prohibited.

INTRODUCTION

The most outstanding achievement of humanity is population aging (WHO, 2005). Obtained through an increase in life years and an improvement in the health of the elderly population, regardless of how far from ideal such achievements are, reaching old age is a common goal, even in underdeveloped countries. Unfortunately, this achievement has evolved into one of the century's most significant challenges.

The concept of aging and attitudes toward older people have evolved as a result of new knowledge gained about human physiology and anatomy, as well as about cultural determinants and social relationships, as well as a result of the accumulation of knowledge over time. In these days and times, which are ours, it is encouraged to associate aging with health, security, and social participation. Most notably, in the face of an active aging population, work plays an increasingly significant and even crucial role in the human life cycle. Changes in demographics are causing problems in many nations, with effects at the population level and in the structure of the workforce and the availability of labor-skilled personnel (Pinto et al., 2015).

Today's organizations will encounter issues related to the aging of their workforce, and it will be required to consider and implement new strategies that take into consideration age management for individuals to contribute to society at various phases of their life. A considerable literature has been committed to this subject to establish pillars that will enable better adaptation to the trends resulting from increased longevity, a higher average life expectancy, and declining birth rates over time.

This chapter uses scientometric tools to examine the evolution of the keywords "aging"/"ageing" and "work" in the Scopus database from 1975 to 2022. Combining this bibliometric analysis with a thorough assessment of the literature to map the terms linked with the keywords chosen, as well as co-citations by authors and responses to exposures to new and popular themes in this emerging field of inquiry, will produce interesting results.

BACKGROUND

All individuals are affected by aging, which is a constant and complex process that occurs throughout life. Although it exhibits distinct characteristics in specific organs and systems, it corresponds to anatomical and physiological changes caused by molecular and cellular alterations in all types of cells throughout the body (Seeley et al., 2008; Bernardes & Pinheiro, 2014).

Global population growth will be significant, according to various official sources, both international and national. The world's population is estimated to be around 7.9 billion people in 2021. According to the United Nations, the world's population will reach 11.2 billion by the end of this century. It is easiest to visualize this massive global transformation by analyzing Figure 1 (Ritchie & Roser, 2019). In particular, demographic aging in the United States is slower than in other developed economies, probably due to a higher fertility rate (Ferreira, 2014).

Figure 1. Population pyramid (1950-2100)
Source: Adapted from Ritchie & Roser (2019)

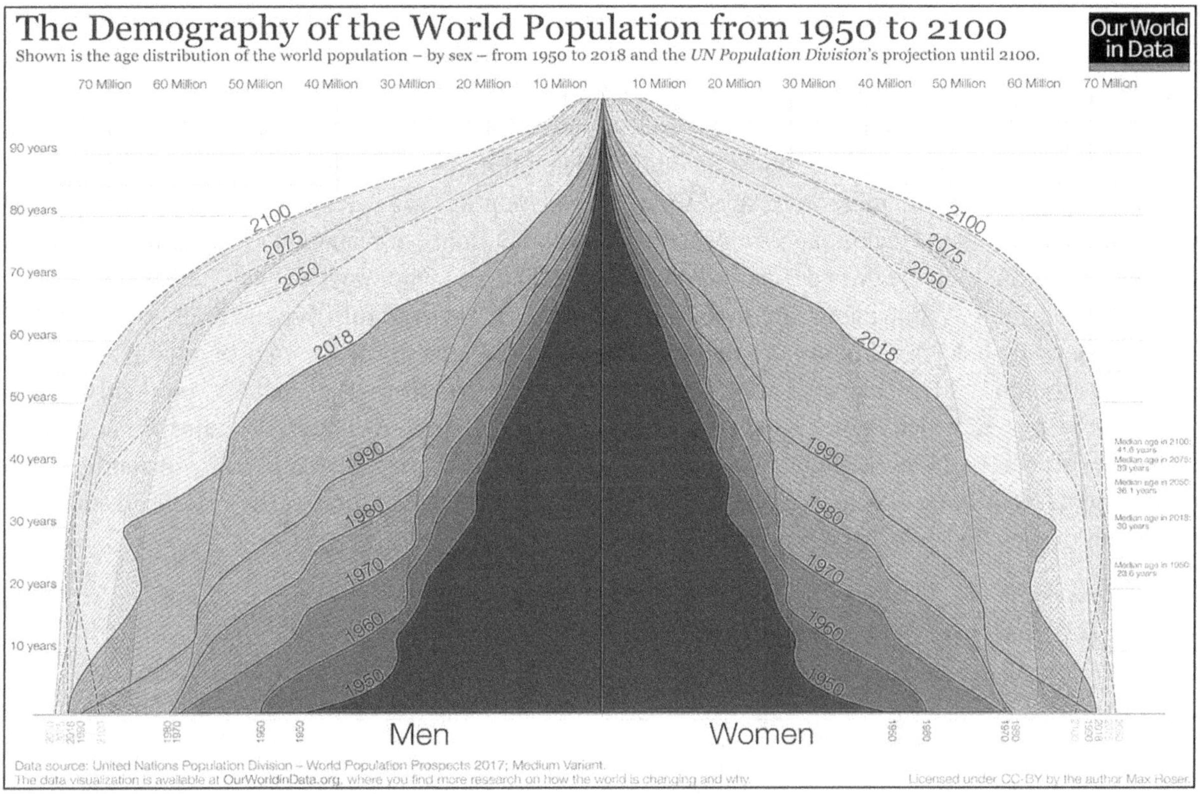

The elderly population is a highly heterogeneous group, with considerable variation in the aging process, i.e., some individuals experience a significant decline while others experience a less noticeable decline. Regardless of the various aging rhythms to which the body is subjected, additional factors contribute to the phenomenon, such as the influence of genetic, physical, psychological, social, and environmental factors (Bernardes & Pinheiro, 2014; Oliveira & Pinto, 2014).

The onset of aging is imprecise, and its progression is variable; so, it is generally divided into two categories: primary (normal aging) and secondary (pathological aging), the latter of which is characterized by a greater propensity to develop diseases (Bernardes & Pinheiro, 2014). At one age, the ability to repair oneself becomes more challenging until it becomes ineffective. As a result, aging is defined as a decline in the human body's adaptive capacity to deal with the challenges encountered throughout life. Thus, studying aging in its entirety enables us to intervene early and prevent functional decline in the human body, resulting in more active and healthy aging. It will be critical to delay vascular pathologies, metabolic syndrome, elderly frailty syndrome, sarcopenia, and neurodegenerative diseases as much as possible in this context (Oliveira & Pinto, 2014).

TEMPORAL PERSPECTIVES ON THE DEFINITION OF AGING

Population aging is a relatively recent demographic phenomenon that has been associated with significant biological, social, economic, and behavioral changes in addition to (naturally occurring) demographic changes. According to Rodrigues and Soares (2006) and Chalise (2019), the approach to the concept/definition of aging is a continuous process that involves analyzing cultural, political, and economic aspects, values, prejudices, and symbols that have existed throughout society's history.

Chronological age (the measurement of time in days, months, and years since birth) is a straightforward and frequently used technique for characterizing and obtaining information about an individual. On the other hand, biological age is defined by the organic changes - both physical and mental - that occur during human aging. While habits and social status define social age to fulfill social roles, psychological age is defined by behavioral patterns acquired throughout life that allow for environmental adaptation (Hoyer & Roodin, 2003; Chalise, 2019). Currently, it is understood as a normal and productive phase of human beings, in which the individual may have gains and losses. Although the gains are not always valued at this stage of life, they may allow the losses to be less experienced and a new meaning of life to be sought (Rodrigues & Soares, 2006). Table 1 summarizes the evolution of the definition and transformation of the concept of aging over time.

Table 1. Definitions of aging between 1959 and 2008

Year	Author	Definition
1959	Woltereck	"All the transformations that occur in all organisms in the course of their normal development and in the different forms of activities that accompany it. (...) the term aging covers the entire lifespan, from birth to death, (...) describing a chronological sequence or a defined period of time."
1975	Amâncio & Cavalcanti	"Aging represents a stage of individual development, the main characteristic of which is the marked loss of adaptive capacity."
1989	Magalhães	"In each society and in the same society, in different historical moments, (...) aging gain distinctive specificities, roles, and meanings depending on the environment, being rural or urban, the social class, the professional and kinship groups, the culture, the dominant ideology, and the economic and political power that influence the life cycle and the path of each individual, from birth to death."
1995	Fraiman	"Aging is not just a 'moment' in an individual's life, but an extremely complex and little-known process with implications both for those who experience it and for the society that supports or assists them."
1996	Bobbio	"(...) is a natural, complex, multidimensional phenomenon, clothed in individual and collective losses and acquisitions."
1996	Hayflick	"Aging is not the mere passage of time, but the biological manifestations that occur in the organism during the course of this time-space. Chronological aging is only a convention, and there is no influence of time on the organism."
1998	Langevin	Aging is "a construction made of obligatory passages, which delimit and guide the dynamics of the process."
1998	Costa	"Aging: evolutionary process, a continuous act, that is, without interruption, that happens from the birth of the individual until the moment of his death (...) is the constant process of transformation."
1999	Neri & Cachione	"The way we age depends on how the life course of each person, age group, and generation is structured by the constant and interactive influence of their historical-cultural circumstances, the incidence of different pathologies during the developmental and aging process, genetic factors, and the ecological environment."
1999	Erminda	A "process of organic and functional decline, not resulting from disease, happening inevitably over time."
2001	Neri	It is "a universal phenomenon, which affects all post-reproductive human beings, by force of genetic mechanisms typical of the species. It is progressive, that is, it gradually or cumulatively affects the whole organism, and is, therefore, a physiological process."

Continued on following page

Table 1. Continued

Year	Author	Definition
2002	Netto	"(...) is a dynamic and progressive process, in which there are morphological, functional, biochemical and psychological modifications that determine loss of the individual's ability to adapt to the environment, causing greater vulnerability and a higher incidence of pathological processes that eventually lead to death."
2002	Uchôa & Lima-Costa	"Aging is not a homogeneous process. Each person experiences this phase of life differently, considering their particular history and all the structural aspects related to their life: social class, gender, ethnicity."
2004	Coll et al.	Aging "is characterized by morphological and functional changes resulting from the transformations that the organism undergoes throughout life."
2004	Brito & Litvoc	"(...) is a phenomenon that affects all human beings, being characterized as a dynamic, progressive and irreversible process, closely linked to biological, psychic and social factors."
2005	Kertzman	"(...) it is a process that inscribes in the temporality of the individual, from the beginning to the end of life, a process composed of losses and gains (...)."
2005	Argimon & Stein	"(...) is a process in which, for each person, physical, behavioral and social changes develop at different rates, chronological age being only one of the aspects, among others, that may or may not affect the well-being of the elderly."
2007	Souza et al.	"A dynamic and progressive process, in which there are morphological, physiological, biochemical, and psychological modifications, which determine the progressive loss of the individual's ability to adapt to the environment, causing greater vulnerability and a higher incidence of pathological processes, which eventually lead to death".
2007	Salgado	"Multidimensional process that results from the interaction of biological, psycho-emotional and socio-cultural factors. Running the biological reason that has a procedural and universal character, the other factors are individual and social compositions, the result of visions and opportunities that each society assigns to its elderly". "Aging can also be a consequence of our society, and that in addition to the biological, chronological and psychological factors, the environment and the conditions in which one lives influence the aging process and how one reaches old age. Thus, the aging process is also influenced by society and the individual."
2008	Schneider & Irigaray	"Aging has intrinsic and extrinsic determinants, presenting a complexity of variables related to biological, psychological, intellectual, social, economic, and functional aspects. It is not something determined by chronological age, but is the consequence of past experiences, of the way one lives and manages his own life in the present, and of future expectations. It is an integration between personal experiences and the social and cultural context at a given time."

Source: Adapted from Dardengo & Mafra (2018)

As can be seen, there are no new definitions of aging after 2008. Indeed, there are few conceptual distinctions regardless of the dimension under consideration: chronological, biological, psychological, or social. As its dynamics become clearer, aging is being defined and assumed to be a natural biological process that occurs throughout the life cycle and manifests itself in various ways depending on the individual's way of life. As a complex and dynamic phenomenon characterized by morphological and functional changes, aging varies significantly between individuals, which significantly impacts both the individuals and social perceptions of the aging process (Dardengo & Mafra, 2018).

According to the WHO (2002), countries can afford aging if governments, international organizations, and civil society implement "active aging" policies and programs that improve older people's health, participation, and security based on their rights, needs, preferences, and abilities. On the assumption that the individual is also responsible for his or her aging, the term "active aging" enables us to envision aging as a process accompanied by opportunities for health, participation, and security to improve people's quality of life as they age.

The term "active" does not refer solely to the capacity for physical activity or participation in the labor force; it also refers to ongoing involvement in social, economic, cultural, spiritual, and civic affairs.

Thus, active aging aims to extend healthy life expectancy and improve the quality of life for all people, including frail, physically disabled, or in need of care. This model of active aging encompasses six groups of determinants, complemented by two cross-cutting determinants - gender and culture (Figure 2):

1. The availability and utilization of health and social services (e.g., health promotion and prevention; long-term care);
2. Behavioral determinants (e.g., physical activity and exercise; drinking and smoking habits; diet; medication);
3. Personal factors (e.g., biology, genetics, and psychological characteristics);
4. The physical environment (e.g., safe homes, low pollution levels);
5. Social determinants (e.g., education and social care); and
6. Economic determinants (e.g., salary and social security).

Figure 2. Active aging determinants
Source: Adapted from WHO (2002)

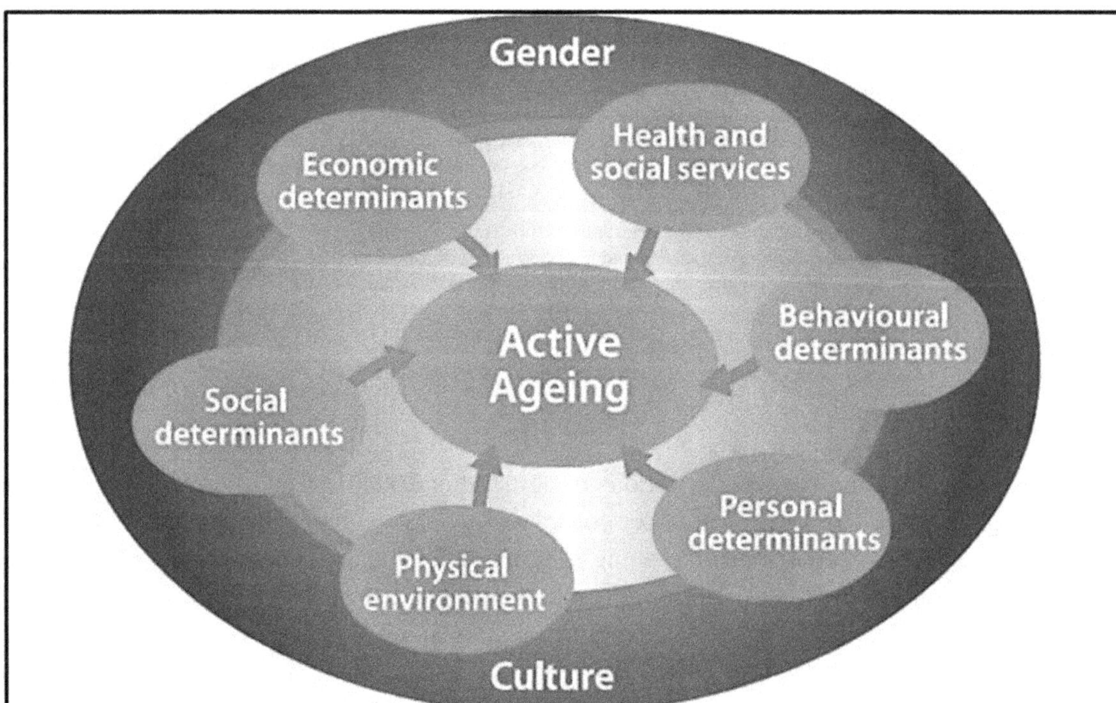

This forces individuals to recognize their potential for physical, social, and mental well-being throughout their lives and participate in society according to their wishes, needs, and abilities. Seniors, retirees, and those with a disability or illness can continue to play an active role in their families and other facets of local and national community life.

Currently, active aging manifests itself primarily due to several determinants that can be used to identify specific profiles that are more susceptible to active aging or, on the contrary, that are more favorable to active aging (Paúl et al., 2017).

AGING AND THE WORKFORCE

The increase in employment rates for older workers represents a reversal of a trend that began in the mid-1970s in Europe, the United States of America, Canada, and Japan. Early retirement of older labor, which was primarily encouraged by the state and businesses, allowed for creating jobs for the young unemployed. However, this result did not always translate into net job creation; instead, it resulted in a significant decline in employment among 55-64-year-olds, predominantly males (Kalwij et al., 2010). The labor force aging is a critical component of these dynamics (Lopes & Gonçalves, 2012).

Simultaneously, the early departure of workers in this age group is associated with temporally congruent organizational cultures: the decline of industry and growth of the tertiary sector, technological and organizational reconversion of businesses, geographical relocation of businesses, direct or indirect wage reductions due to a lack of regulation of labor relations, rejection of skilled labor but deemed unsuitable by employers, and company privatization, among others (Castells, 2002). Due to early retirement, it is possible to observe a depreciative culture among workers over the age of 55, during the second half of their professional careers. This status encourages social acceptance of "being old" to work at 40-50, especially in unskilled professions (Guillemard, 2003; Taylor, 2004). On the other hand, it is possible to observe a reduction in the total amount of time spent working during an individual's life cycle, which has lengthened due to the post-1980s increase in average life expectancy (Fernandes, 2008).

Only in the 1990s did the general public become aware of the consequences of this policy (OECD, 1998). The consequences of early retirement on the labor market, the long-term viability of the social security and pension systems, and the healthcare system are linked to the increase in demographic aging (Morel et al., 2004). Several economic and social asymmetries have been established in this context due to growing international economic and financial competitiveness.

During the same period, employment guidelines were issued to reverse this trend. For example, in the European Union, labor insertion is presumed within the context of the recommendation on active aging. Later that year, in 2001, the Stockholm European Council established the target of 50% employment for older workers by 2010. Another significant target was introduced the following year, in 2002, at the Barcelona Council: a gradual increase of approximately five years in the average effective retirement age by 2010. Furthermore, the European Union promoted generational solidarity in 2005 with the Lisbon Strategy (European Union, 2005). In retrospect, active aging policies have been implemented through the relationship between age and work and the restructuring of retirement and pension systems (Yvoire, 2010). The objective is to retain older workers and keep them in the labor force for a longer time. To this end, the extension of working life is primarily achieved by raising the legal retirement age and imposing restrictions on early retirement. This is possible only through flexible/progressive retirement plans that include the appropriate monetary reduction (Lopes & Gonçalves, 2012).

The dominant demographic aging in the 21st century is an irreversible characteristic of current societies and has raised multiple attention and concerns among various stakeholders, including the academic, scientific, social, and political communities (Luz, 2014). It is worthwhile to consider older workers as a subset of the broader field of active aging in this context. Extending one's working life entails reflecting on, delving deeper into, and debating a slew of unquestionably complex issues. As a result, there is a need to continue researching and developing knowledge about the nature and effectiveness of older workers' employment conditions.

AGING WORKFORCE AND HUMAN RESOURCES MANAGEMENT

According to Teixeira (2011), a value chain is a tool proposed by Porter, which allows the analysis of how the various activities that make up a company add value to the products/services they sell. The activity of a company constitutes a set of activities that have a link between them, with each activity contributing a part of the value that is consecutively added along the chain. Thus, the activities that constitute the value chain can be subdivided into primary activities and support activities.

Human Resources Management (HRM) integrates the support activities, including the "processes of recruitment, admission, development, and compensation concerning all types of people involved in the company" (Teixeira, 2011, p. 91). However, what is HRM's role in an aging workforce? HRM strategies directly impact the way people of different ages act in organizational contexts, regardless of their age (Pinto & Nunes, 2015).

As the demographic curve continues downward, age management is becoming an increasingly important strategy in combating it (Vranaková et al., 2021). It is stated by the authors Pedro et al., (2020) that age management "practices refer to the development and implementation of workplace strategies to support and improve the health and productivity of workers aged 45 years or older". The European Agency for Safety & Health at Work published an electronic guide in 2016, to assist organizations in implementing age management practices more effectively. In this context, it is necessary to comprehend the various dimensions within which age management is applicable. This concept is made of eight components, namely: job recruitment; learning, training, and lifelong learning; career development and progression; job redesign; redeployment; retirement planning; comprehensive approaches and the transition to retirement, as can be seen in Figure 3 (Pedro et al., 2020; Vranaková et al., 2021).

Figure 3. Age management dimensions
Source: Adapted from Vranaková et al. (2021)

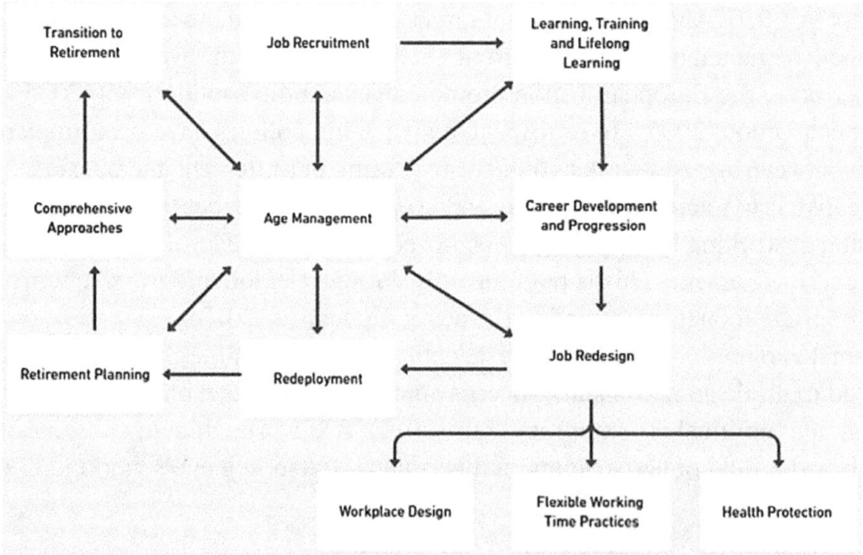

Furthermore, the age management concept is also founded on eight fundamental pillars that are intrinsically linked to one another in their many dimensions.

Table 2. Pillars of age management

Pillar	Application
Knowledge of age issue	Management inside the organization are conscious of challenges related to the future, including the future workforce, such as workforce aging, retirement plans, and a shortage of younger workers.
Accommodating attitude towards aging	Aging employees are viewed positively by managers, who recognize that their skills and understanding may be set to use for the advantage of both parties.
Management that understands individuality and differences	Individual approach to employees from all age categories and generations is something that managers are well conscious of, and they take responsibility for it.
Quality and functional measures of age management	The need of equality of opportunity for all employees in all sectors is growing in importance in the company. As a result, the age strategy is integrated into the personal goals of employees as well as the corporate policy.
Ensuring good work ability and motivation	Employee collaboration and a desire to continue working in the company until retirement are two outcomes of increased work capacity and motivation.
High level of competencies	Employers should be encouraged to participate in shared knowledge by their supervisors, who should be aware of the relevance of the idea. Managers should also guarantee that information is transferred from elderly to younger workers.
Quality work organization	The work structure, as well as working hours, are tailored to meet the demands of employees of varying ages and backgrounds.
Satisfied life	Workers may retire because of improvements in recognition, well-being, and overall quality of life, among other things.

Source: Adapted from Vranaková et al. (2021)

Employees and companies alike are benefiting from age management practices and policies. In this context, the following benefits are particularly advantageous to employees: greater motivation and job satisfaction, enhanced work-life balance, and the ability to maintain work capacity and employability throughout a career. On the other side, employing companies benefit from the program through the ability to retain experienced workers, reduce turnover, and lower hiring and training costs (Pedro et al., 2020).

METHODOLOGY

To provide a thorough understanding of aging in the context of work, the authors did a two-step method, first utilizing Scientometrics to identify the main clusters associated with this topic and the most prominent cited authors and journals. Following that, web-scraping was used to collect all articles relating to the topic.

First Stage – Scientometrics

Nalimov defined scientometrics for the first time in 1969 as a quantitative tool for analyzing science as an information process (Hood & Wilson, 2001). Significant research issues identified include the assessment of the quality and impact of research papers and academic journals, the comprehension of scientific citations, the mapping of scientific fields (Mingers & Leydesdorff, 2015), and the application of such measurements in policy and management contexts such as economics (Laverde-Rojas & Correa, 2019), education (Ramirez et al., 2019), health (Pakdel et al., 2019), environment (Zandi et al., 2019), and tourism (Jiang et al., 2014), among others.

The authors decided to use the Scopus database as a data source after comparing the primary abstract and citation databases. Scopus's extraordinary data collection includes an impressive 1.4 billion cited references stretching back to 1970, over 25,000 active titles, 16 million author profiles, and 7,000 publishers, all of which have been thoroughly validated and selected by an independent review board. As a result, the Scopus database is preferred for research assessment and evaluation by leading rating organizations such as Times Higher Education (THE), QS World University Rankings, MacLean's, and US News and World Report (Scopus, 2021).

The research was conducted in October 2021, throughout the Scopus search engine, applying the terms "aging"/"ageing" and "work" within article titles, abstracts, and keywords - TITLE-ABS-KEY (+aging AND work*) OR (+ageing AND work*) AND (LIMIT-TO (SUBJAREA, "BUSI")), subsequently filtering just articles.

Second Stage – Web-scraping

Academic databases contain enormous amounts of data; as a result, it is exceedingly challenging to summarize and reach a consensus on what has been discovered. As proposed in this chapter, machine learning and/or human wisdom could be used to ascertain the origins of the terms "aging"/"ageing" and "work", their evolution, and harmonize concepts. However, machine learning will be beneficial in the future, but it is still a very complex task; the research team must parametrize the algorithms and statistical models to avoid false positives (for example, non-definitions or incorrect quotes), and then thoroughly review all meanings.

To acquire human wisdom, authors must download and review all articles on a subject. However, the rate of growth of scientific data in these academic databases is increasing year after year. Furthermore, the data is mainly unstructured due to the various journals' frameworks and authors' autonomy, making this a time-consuming and complex task. As a result, the research authors must examine all articles for additional indexation, or else the meaning network will be disrupted, or an important path definition will be missed.

Putting together information is more difficult because of the different designations of "aging"/"ageing" and "work" in articles and the lack of specific data models for definitions. With the help of a software solution known as Web-scraping software, the first phase of the process, which is extraction and download, can be completed successfully.

Website content can be restructured quickly as part of various online research processes at different stages, according to the author Hassanien (2019), using the technique of web-scraping, which is performed in three distinct phases, namely: (1) site access, (2) HTML analysis and content extraction, and (3) generation of results.

The authors used Sequentum's CG enterprise web-scraping software, which was developed for businesses that rely heavily on structured data and includes advanced features not found in other software solutions, such as monitoring data extraction, legal compliance, and production fail-over. This solution downloaded all articles available in this database and then processed them using REGEX expressions to extract paragraphs containing the terms "aging"/"ageing" and "work". Following that, a thorough human analysis was conducted to identify the most relevant analysis for these terms.

RESULTS

It was possible to obtain a total of 1.361 articles that were distributed between 1975 and 2022 (Figure 4), 80.471 references, and 4.050 authors. As a result, one can conclude that there has been an increase in interest in the topic, and it is important to note that the year 2022 has not yet been determined due to the publication guidelines of the journal and the date of the authors' research.

Figure 4. Annual scientific production
Source: Own elaboration

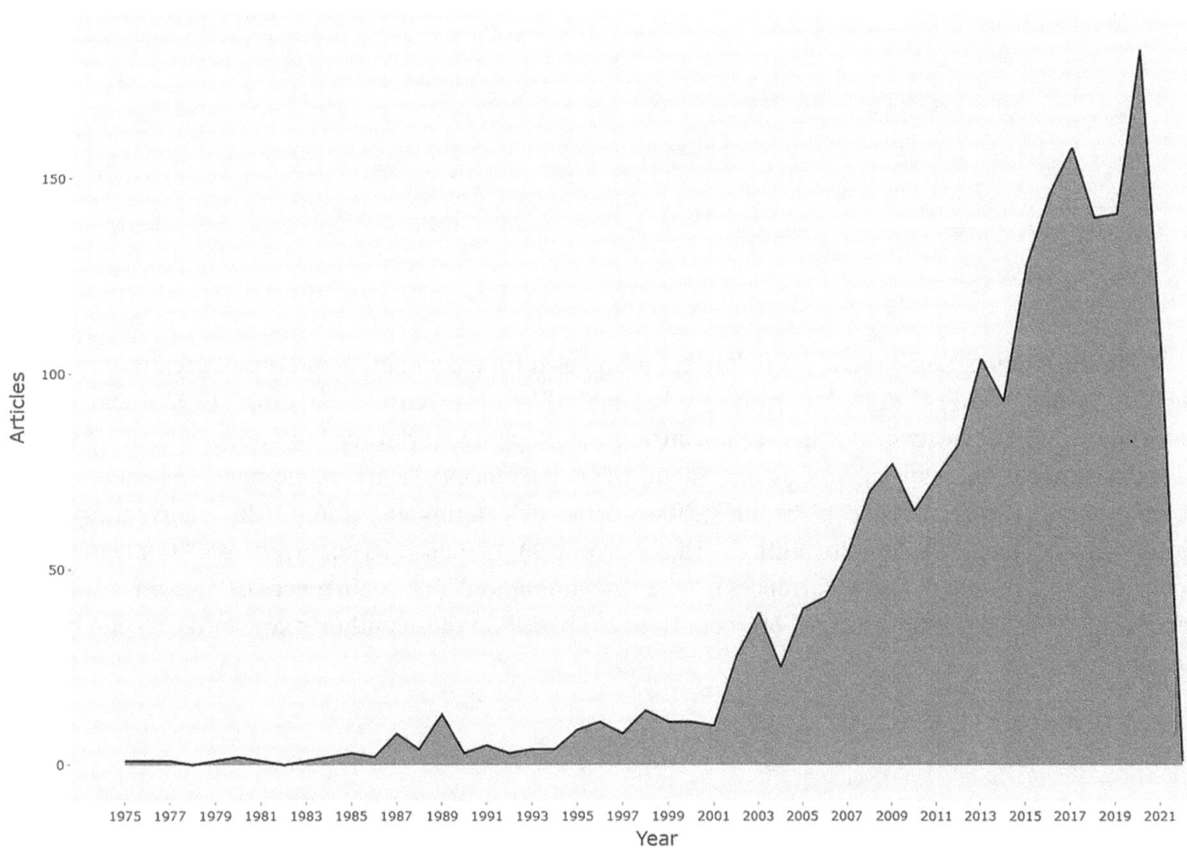

The cumulative occurrences of words associated with the authors' keywords have increased over time. Figure 5 demonstrates an increasing trend, particularly since 2009. In the year 2021, terms such as "older workers", "aging workforce", "aging", "retirement", and "age" remained relatively stable.

Figure 5. Word growth
Source: Own elaboration

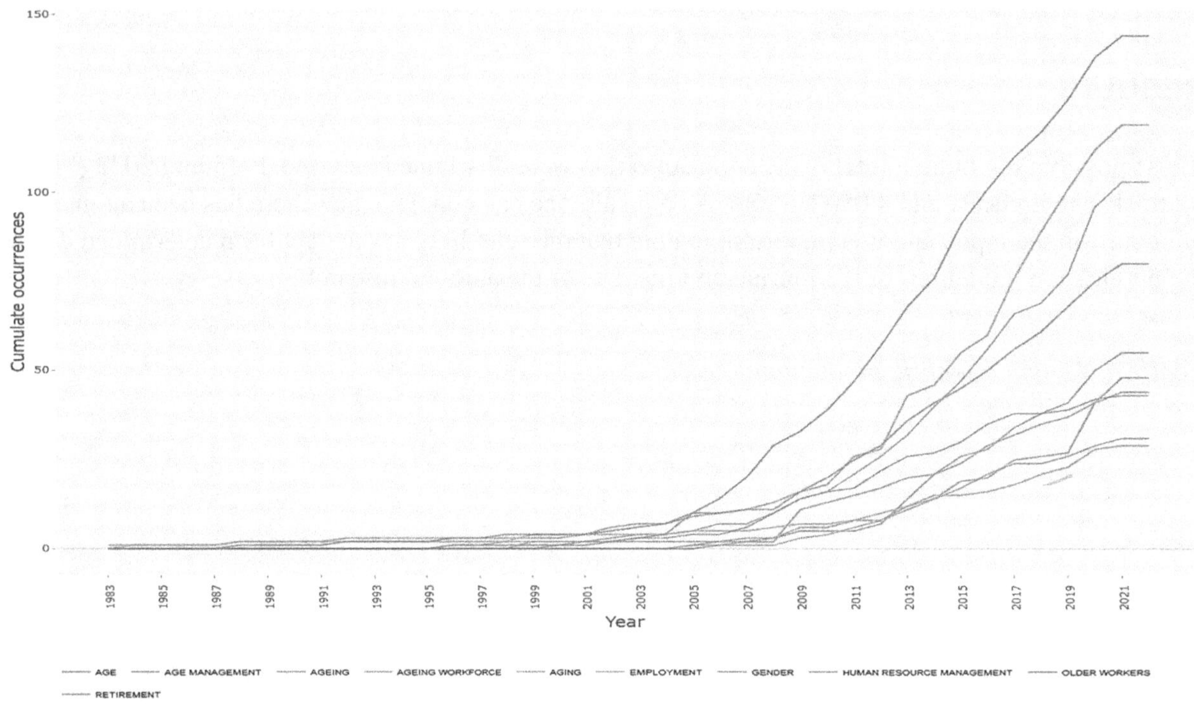

"Ageing"/"aging" and "work" also delivers a higher term frequency, trend topic, greater than terms such as "older workers" (144 occurrences), "aging" (119 occurrences), "ageing" (103 occurrences), "retirement" (80 occurrences), "age" (55 occurrences), "ageing workforce" (48 occurrences), "gender" (44 occurrences), "human resource management" (43 occurrences), "age management" (31 occurrences), "employment" (29 occurrences), "health" (29 occurrences), "aging workforce" (26 occurrences), "pensions" (22 occurrences), "employability" (18 occurrences), "Japan" (18 occurrences), "innovation" (17 occurrences), "training" (17 occurrences), "age discrimination" (16 occurrences), "ageism" (16 occurrences) and "demographic change" (16 occurrences) based on these author's keywords, as can be seen in Figure 6.

Figure 6. Trend topics
Source: Own elaboration

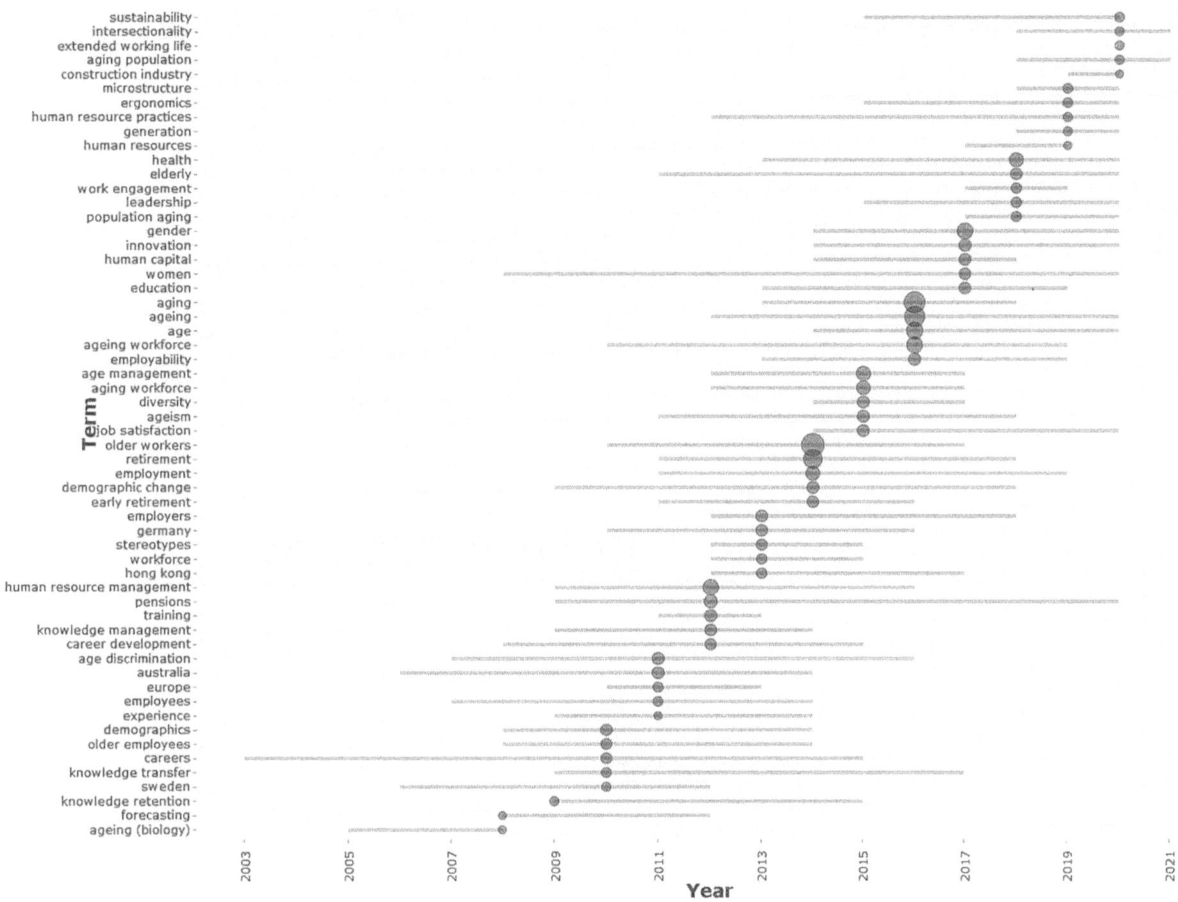

According to Saunders et al. (2019), clusters are linked together through hierarchical relationships, where each cluster is headed by a theme or subtheme. A population that is widely dispersed and large, requiring a significant amount of effort to gather the necessary information, makes the clustering strategy particularly effective (Robson & McCartan, 2016).

As shown in Figure 7, it is possible to determine the interrelation between the keywords “aging”/”ageing” and “work” with three main clusters, namely: “older workers”, “aging”, and “retirement”. Each cluster identified presents distinct sub-themes, which extend to a multitude of areas. The cluster “older works” presents subareas such as “motivation”; “job satisfaction”; “knowledge management” or “age discrimination”. On the other hand, the “aging” cluster is interrelated with sub-themes that address “gender”; “labor market”; “diversity”, or “productivity”. Finally, the “retirement” cluster is translated into subareas that integrate “employment”; “workability”; “career development”; “social security” or “women”.

It is possible to conclude from the analysis of the established clusters that the keywords defined by the authors over time have experienced widespread dissemination and extension to a variety of themes and sub-areas.

Figure 7. Clusters of keywords
Source: Own elaboration

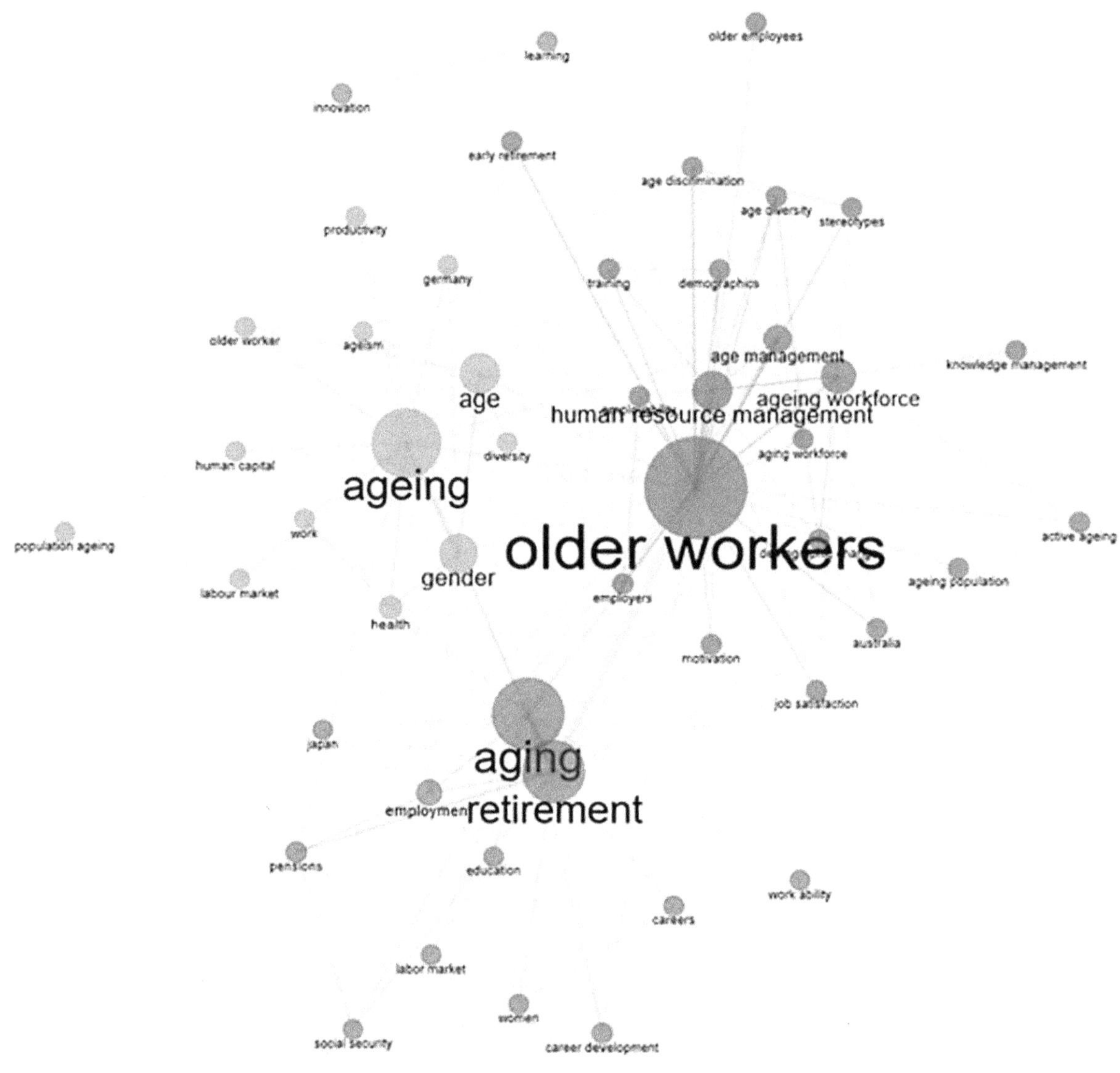

In Figure 8, it is possible to identify the authors who are the most relevant to the keywords under consideration, taking into account the number of documents that have been published. The following authors are found to be the most relevant in the study area, according to the results of this follow-up: Zacher, H. (21 documents); Kooij, D. (15 documents) and Henkens, K. (12 documents).

Figure 8. Most relevant authors
Source: Own elaboration

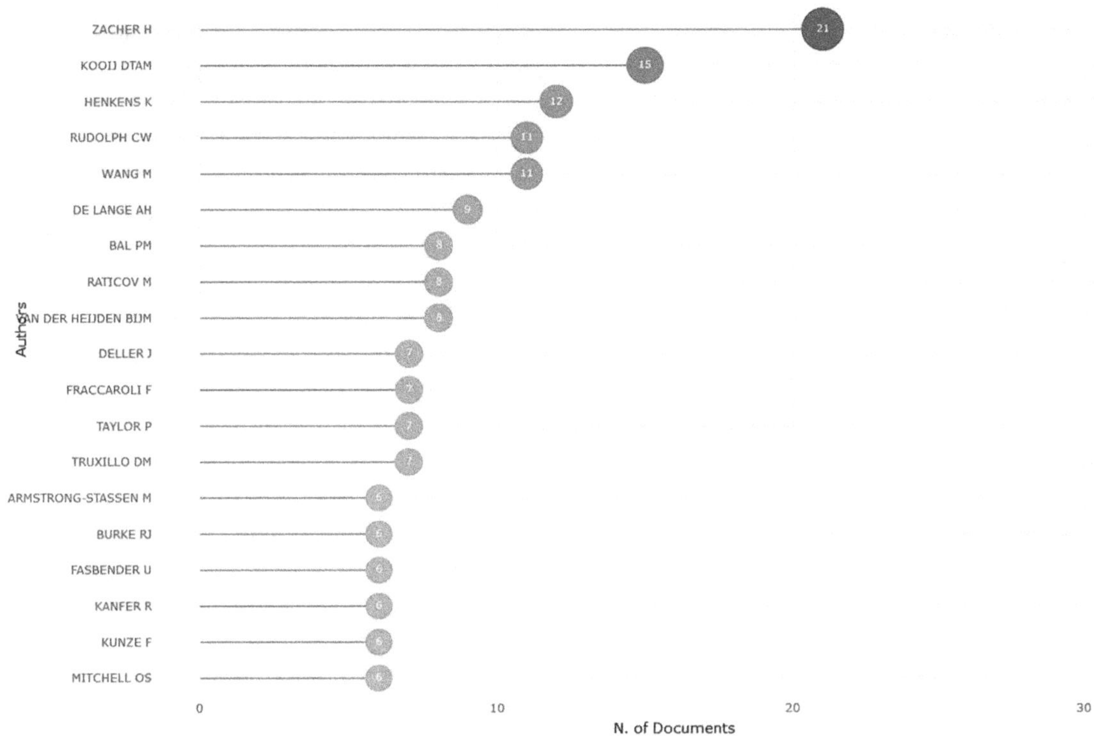

It is possible to establish a relationship between the most relevant authors and the production of the top authors over several years. In the first three positions of Figure 9, the authors who were considered most relevant previously are present. Thus, it can be established that author Zacher, H. (21 documents) comprises his research mainly between 2010 and 2021. The author, Kooij, D. (15 documents), focused on his publications between 2014 and 2021. Lastly, the author Henkens, K. (12 documents) has centered its research in the years between 2005-2019.

Figure 9. Top-authors' production between 1984-2022
Source: Own elaboration

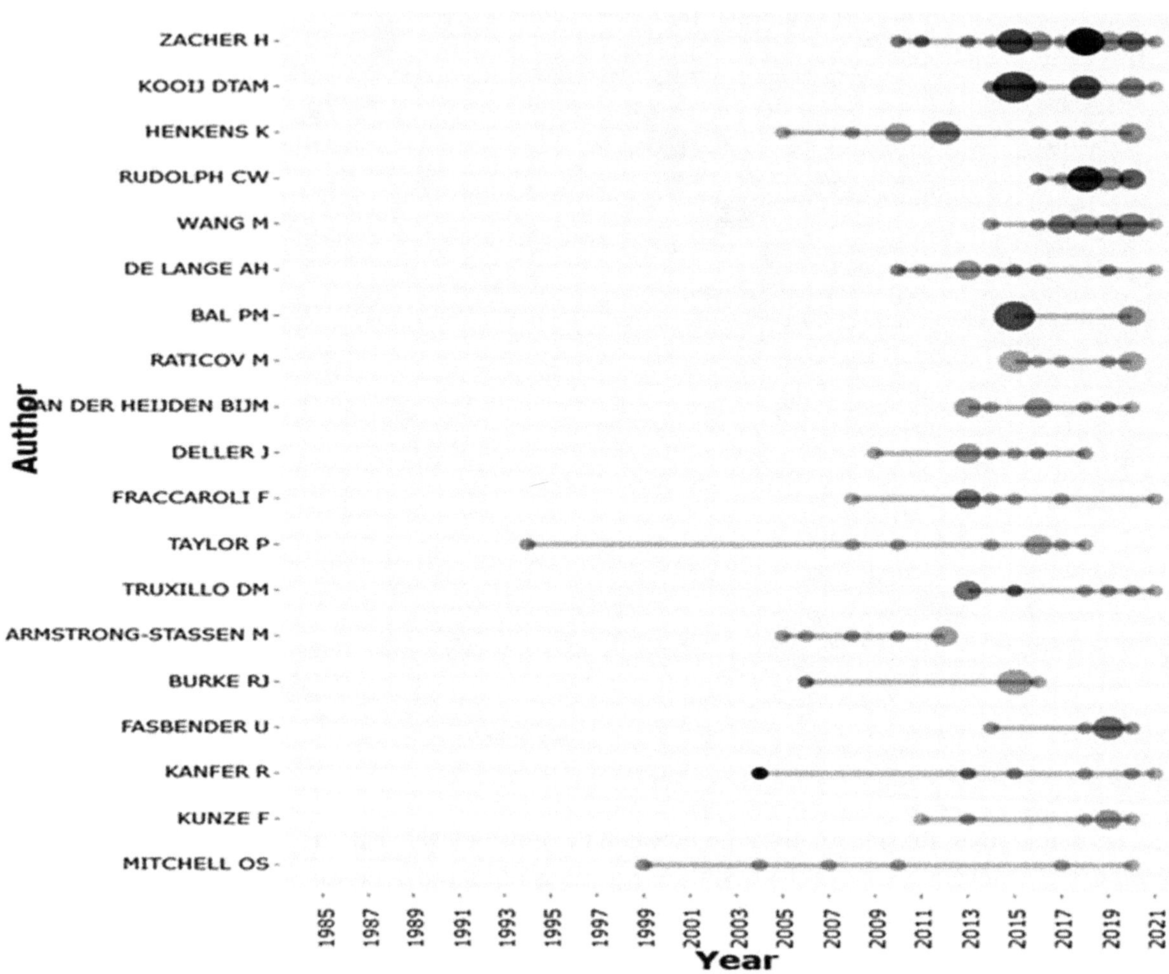

The keywords defined in the methodology also make it feasible to identify the sources that have the greatest number of documents in the study area. The most relevant sources are: Work Aging and Retirement (72 articles); Journal of Cleaner Production (33 articles); Retraite et Societe (28 articles); International Journal of Human Resource Management (26 articles); Extended Working Life Policies: International Gender and Health Perspectives (23 articles) and the International Journal of Manpower (23 articles), as can be seen in Figure 10.

Figure 10. Most relevant sources
Source: Own elaboration

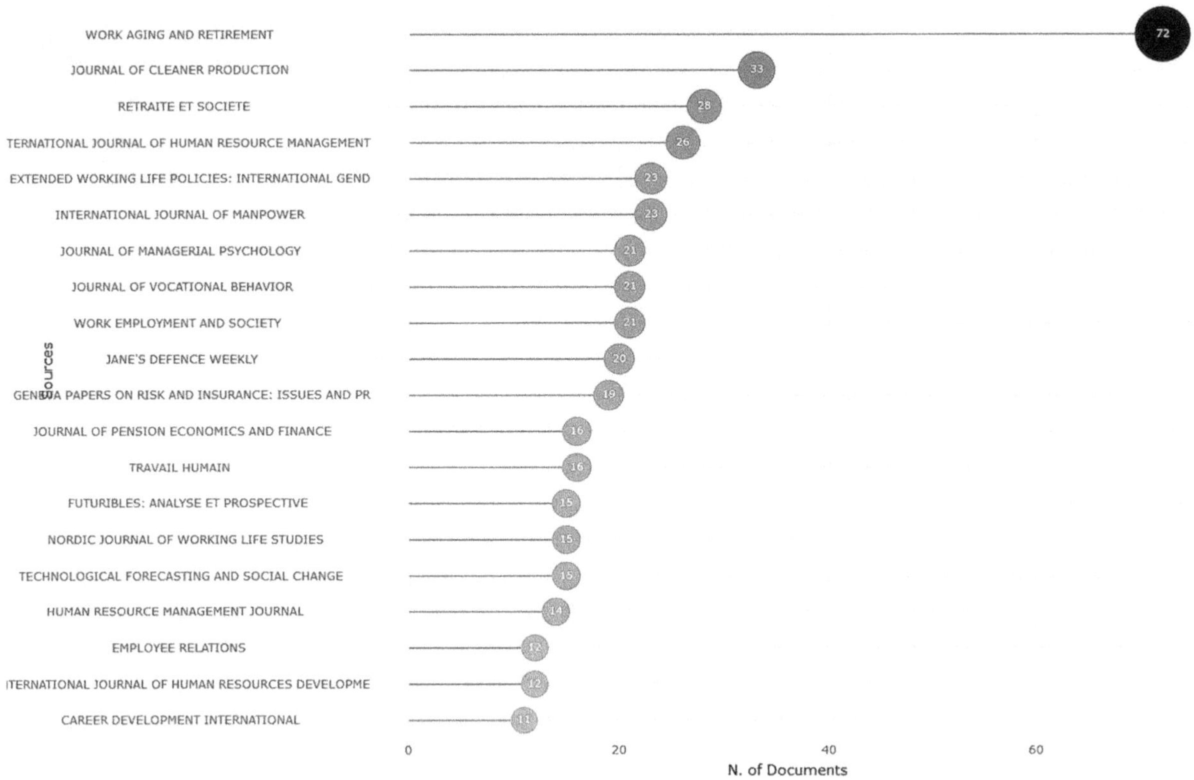

The H-index is a bibliometric indicator that is widely regarded as extremely valuable. According to Hirsch & Buela-Casal (2014), the H-index should:

- "Reflect elements of reality that are useful for evaluation and meaningful in a statistical sense and ideally have predictive power";
- "Not lead to undesirable incentives that are detrimental to the progress of science";
- "Not be too sensitive to small variations in bibliometric records that could be due to random events";
- "Be not too difficult to obtain from existing databases".

Considering the most relevant sources indicated previously, there is a direct relationship with the source local impact by H-Index (Figure 11). Three of the most relevant publications also have the highest H-Index, namely: Work Aging and Retirement (H-Index - 17), the Journal of Cleaner Production (H-Index - 16) and, by last, the International Journal of Human Resource Management (H-Index - 15).

Figure 11. Source local impact by H-Index
Source: Own elaboration

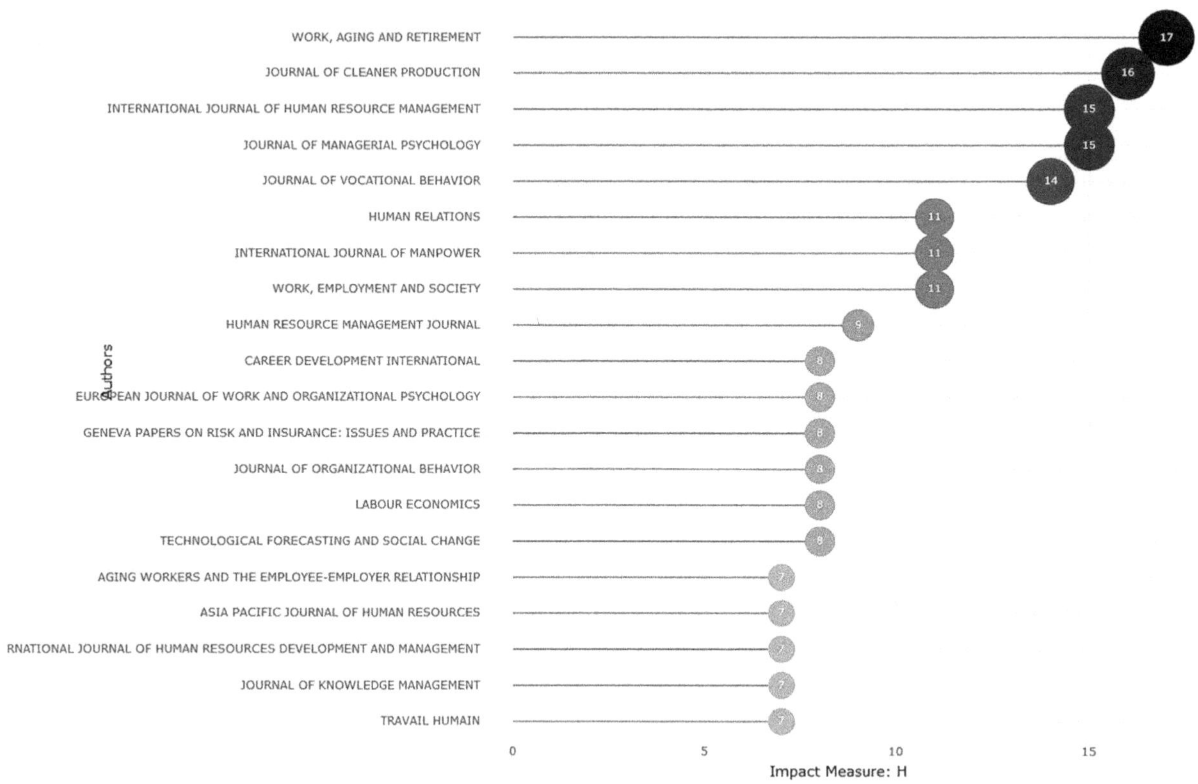

FUTURE RESEARCH DIRECTIONS

People will live longer and work for extended periods of time. This means that the age at which one retires will be higher than the chronological age to be considered elderly. In this framework, part of our active working life will take place in a phase of greater evidence and individual perception of the aging process. This and other issues addressed throughout the chapter invite the scientific community, organizations, and governments, among other stakeholders, to reflect and continue to develop studies to better understand and fit older workers into the labor market. Considering the importance of interdisciplinary research perspectives, the authors also consider that gender is a variable that should be introduced in this scope. Women live longer than men and have a very active role in society and the labor market. Even during her active life, she suffers the consequences of the aging of her reproductive system, which can be devastating. This biological change affects or may affect the relationship of women in the labor market, but on the other hand, it is possible to ask: To what extent does the labor market influence the aging of women, particularly during and after menopause?

Analyzing the role of technology in aging and the workforce will be another important dimension to include in future studies. Organizations will need to be prepared for an aging workforce, which involves designing and adapting jobs and people management. This brings us to another relevant area: assessing the importance of organizational cultures in human aging and the capacity that organizations have in their ability to include older workers and to what extent they use the intrinsic strength of intergenerational support and promote interaction between workers of all ages.

CONCLUSION

The interest in the aging workforce has been growing continuously. There have been numerous publications on this topic, however, the problem of trying to grasp a clear understanding of this theme leads to a dispersion of information. Most of the results obtained reference the aging workforce, either in the form of a sentence or a word. In the chapter results, it was possible to present the authors' most cited. However, in the articles obtained, not all are present. Thus, there are authors cited individually in the results; however, in the extracted articles these authors appear with other authors.

The authors' work also shows that when researching the aging workforce, other concepts emerge. It is also possible to ascertain which authors are most influential and so the most cited. The authors' contribution is essential for future researchers in this field since this work provides an extensive understanding of the definitions. Here, scholars find all the critical points about the aging workforce. Through a complete understanding of the topic, the authors hope that readers will gain more excellent knowledge about it.

Population aging cannot be addressed only by the needs of older and retired people. It must include the impacts (positive and negative) of an aging workforce, as aging will shape the future of work and impact various policies such as the labor market, health and quality of life, and social security.

REFERENCES

Amâncio, A., & Cavalcanti, P. C. U. (1975). *Clínica Geriátrica* [Geriatric Clinic]. Atheneu Publisher.

Argimon, I. L., & Stein, L. M. (2005). Habilidades Cognitivas em Indivíduos Muito Idosos: Um Estudo Longitudinal [Cognitive Skills in Very Elderly Individuals: A Longitudinal Study]. *Cadernos de Saude Publica*, *21*(1), 64–72. doi:10.1590/S0102-311X2005000100008 PMID:15692639

Bernardes, A., & Pinheiro, S. (2014). Anatomia do Envelhecimento [Anatomy of Aging]. In M. T. Veríssimo (Ed.), *Geriatria Fundamental, Saber e Praticar* [Fundamental Geriatrics, Know & Practice] (pp. 41–47). Ed. Técnicas, Lda.

Bobbio, N. (1996). *De Senectute*. Einaudi Publisher.

Brito, F. C., & Litvoc, J. (2004). Conceitos Básicos [Basic Concepts]. In F. C. Brito & J. Litvoc (Eds.), *Envelhecimento: Prevenção e Promoção de Saúde* [Aging: Prevention and Health Promotion]. Atheneu Publisher.

Castells, M. (2002). A Era da Informação: Economia [The Information Age: Economy, Society and Culture - Volume I]. *Society and Culture, I.*

Chalise, H. N. (2019). Aging: Basic Concept. *American Journal of Biomedical and Life Sciences*, *1*(1), 8–10.

Coll, C., Marchesi, A., & Palacios, J. (2004). *Desenvolvimento Psicológico e Educação* [Psychological Development and Education]. Artmed Publisher.

Costa, E. M. S. (1998). *Gerontodrama: A Velhice em Cena: Estudos Clínicos e Psicodramáticos sobre o Envelhecimento e a Terceira Idade* [Gerontodrama: Old Age on Stage - Clinical and Psychodramatic Studies on Aging and the Third Age]. Ágora Publisher.

Dardengo, C. F. R., & Mafra, S. C. T. (2018). Os Conceitos de Velhice e Envelhecimento ao Longo do Tempo: Contradição ou Adaptação? [The Concepts of Old Age and Aging over Time: Contradiction or Adaptation?]. *Revista de Ciências Humanas*, *18*(2), 1–23.

Erminda, J. G. (1999). Processo de Envelhecimento [The Aging Process]. In *O Idoso: Problemas e Realidade* [The Elderly: Problems and Reality]. Formasau Publisher.

European Union. (2005). *Livro Verde - "Uma nova solidariedade entre gerações face às mutações demográficas"* [Green Paper - "Confronting demographic change: a new solidarity between the generations"]. Academic Press.

Fernandes, A. (2008). *Questões Demográficas* [Demographic Issues]. Colibri Publisher.

Ferreira, A. J. (2014). Demografia e Epidemiologia do Envelhecimento [Demography and Epidemiology of Aging]. In M. T. Veríssimo (Ed.), *Geriatria Fundamental, Saber e Praticar* [Fundamental Geriatrics, Know & Practice] (pp. 59–64). Ed. Técnicas, Lda.

Fraiman, A. P. (1995). *Coisas da Idade* [Things of the Age]. Editora Gente.

Guillemard, A. (2003). *L'Âge de l'Emploi. Les Sociétés à l'Épreuve du Vieillissement* [The Age of Employment. The Societies to the Test of the Ageing]. Armand Colin Publisher.

Hassanien, H. (2019). Web Scraping Scientific Repositories for Augmented Relevant Literature Search Using CRISP-DM. *Applied System Innovation*, *2*(4), 37. doi:10.3390/asi2040037

Hayflick, L. (1996). *Como e Por Que Envelhecemos* [How and Why We Get Old]. Campus Publisher.

Hirsch, J. E., & Buela-Casal, G. (2014). The meaning of the h-index. *International Journal of Clinical and Health Psychology*, *14*(2), 161–164. doi:10.1016/S1697-2600(14)70050-X

Hood, W. W., & Wilson, C. S. (2001). The literature of bibliometrics, scientometrics, and informetrics. *Scientometrics*, *52*(2), 291–314. doi:10.1023/A:1017919924342

Hoyer, W. J., & Roodin, P. A. (2003). *Adult Development and Aging*. McGraw Hill Publisher.

Jiang, J., Woosnam, K., & Draper, J. (2014). Structural Elements of Articles and Diachronous Citation Analysis Among Top-ranking Tourism Journals (1990-2010). *Tourism Management Perspectives*, *12*, 48–56. doi:10.1016/j.tmp.2014.06.004

Kalwij, A., Kapteyn, A., & Vos, K. (2010). Retirement of Older Workers and Employment of the Young. *The Economist, 158*(4), 341-359.

Kertzman, O. F. (2005). Responsabilidade Social e Envelhecimento: O Que as Empresas Têm a ver com Isso? [Social Responsibility and Aging: What's in it for Companies?]. *A Terceira Idade*, 16.

Langevin, A. (1998). A Construção Social das Idades: Mulheres Adultas de Hoje e Velhas de Amanhã [The Social Construction of Ages: Today's Adult Women and Tomorrow's Older Women]. *Caderno CRH*, *29*, 129–149.

Laverde-Rojas, H., & Correa, J. C. (2019). Can Scientific Productivity Impact the Economic Complexity of Countries? *Scientometrics*, *120*(1), 267–282. doi:10.100711192-019-03118-8

Lopes, A., & Gonçalves, C. M. (2012). Envelhecimento Ativo e Dinâmicas Sociais Contemporâneas [Active Aging and Contemporary Social Dynamics]. In C. Paúl & O. Ribeiro (Eds.), *Manual de Gerontologia* [Gerontology Manual]. Ed. Técnicas, Lda.

Luz, H. R. A. (2014). Sociologia do Envelhecimento [Sociology of Aging]. In M. T. Veríssimo (Ed.), *Geriatria Fundamental, Saber e Praticar* [Fundamental Geriatrics, Know & Practice] (pp. 65–74). Ed. Técnicas, Lda.

Magalhães, D. N. (1989). *A Invenção Social da Velhice* [The Social Invention of Old Age]. Papagaio Publisher.

Mingers, J., & Leydesdorff, L. (2015). A Review of Theory and Practice in Scientometrics. *European Journal of Operational Research*, *246*(1), 1–19. doi:10.1016/j.ejor.2015.04.002

Morel, A., Joly, B., & Maigne, M. (2004). *Rapport sur la Gestion des Âges et les Politiques de l'Emploi dans l'Union Européenne* [Report on Labour Management and Employment Policies in the European Union]. IGAS.

Neri, A. L. (2001). *Memória e Sociedade: Lembranças de Velhos* [Memory and Society: Remembrances of Old People]. Companhia das Letras Publisher.

Neri, A. L., & Cachioni, M. (1999). Velhice Bem-sucedida e Educação [Successful Old Age and Education]. In A. L. Neri & G. G. Debert (Eds.), *Velhice e Sociedade* [Elderly and Society] (pp. 113–140). Papirus Publisher.

Netto, M. (2002). *Gerontologia: A velhice e o Envelhecimento em Visão Globalizada* [Gerontology: Old Age and Aging in a Global View]. Atheneu Publisher.

OECD. (1998). *Maintaining Prosperity in an Ageing Society*. OECD Publishing.

Oliveira, C. R., & Pinto, A. M. (2014). Biologia e Fisiopatologia do Envelhecimento [Biology and Pathophysiology of Aging]. In M. T. Veríssimo (Ed.), *Geriatria Fundamental, Saber e Praticar* [Fundamental Geriatrics, Know & Practice] (pp. 17–28). Ed. Técnicas, Lda.

Pakdel, F., Gharebaghi, R., & Ghazavi, R. (2019). Effect of Selenium on Thyroid Disorders: Scientometric Analysis. *Iranian Journal of Public Health*, *48*(3), 410–420. doi:10.18502/ijph.v48i3.883 PMID:31223567

Paúl, C., Teixeira, L., & Ribeiro, O. (2017). Active Aging in Very Old Age and the Relevance of Psychological Aspects. *Frontiers in Medicine*, *4*(181), 1–7. doi:10.3389/fmed.2017.00181 PMID:29164117

Pedro, D., Fracasso, N. V., Costa, R. G., Rossaneis, M. Â., Aroni, P., & Haddad, M. (2020). Age Management Practices Toward Workers Aged 45 years or Older: An Integrative Literature Review. *Revista Brasileira de Medicina do Trabalho*, *18*(2), 194–202. doi:10.47626/1679-4435-2020-536 PMID:33324461

Pinto, A., Ramos, S., & Nunes, S. (2015). Managing an Aging Workforce: What is the Value of Human Resource Management Practices for Different Age Groups of Workers? *TÉKHNE - Review of Applied Management Studies*, *12*, 58-68. doi:10.1016/j.tekhne.2015.01.007

Ramirez, M. C., Armando, R., & Devesa, R. (2019). A Scientometric Look at Mathematics Education from Scopus Database. *The Mathematics Enthusiast*, *16*(1), 37–46. doi:10.54870/1551-3440.1449

RitchieH.RoserM. (2019). *Age Structure*. https://ourworldindata.org/age-structure

Robson, C., & McCartan, K. (2016). *Real World Research* (4th ed.). John Wiley & Sons Ltd.

Rodrigues, L. S., & Soares, G. A. (2006). Velho, Idoso e Terceira Idade na Sociedade Contemporânea [Old, Elderly and Senior Citizens in the Contemporary Society]. *Revista Ágora*, *4*, 1–29.

Salgado, M. A. (2007). Os Grupos e a Ação Pedagógica do Trabalho Social com Idosos [The Groups and the Pedagogical Action of Social Work with the Elderly]. *A Terceira Idade, 18*(39), 1-96.

Saunders, M., Lewis, P., & Thornhill, A. (2019). *Research Methods for Business Students* (8th ed.). Pearson Education Limited.

Schneider, R. H., & Irigaray, T. Q. (2008). O Envelhecimento na Atualidade: Aspectos Cronológicos, Biológicos e Sociais [Aging in the Modern World: Chronological, Biological and Social Aspects]. *Estudos de Psicologia*, *25*(4), 585–593. doi:10.1590/S0103-166X2008000400013

Scopus. (2021). *Why choose Scopus*. https://www.elsevier.com/solutions/scopus/why-choose-scopus

Seeley, R. R., Stephens, T. D., & Tate, P. (2008). *Anatomia e Fisiologia - 8ª Edição* [Anatomy and Physiology - 8th Edition]. Lusociência Publisher.

Souza, J. A. V., Freitas, M. C., & Queiroz, T. A. (2007). Violência Contra os Idosos: Análise Documental [Violence Against the Elderly: A Documentary Analysis]. *Revista Brasileira de Enfermagem*, *60*(3), 268–272. doi:10.1590/S0034-71672007000300004 PMID:17684902

Taylor, P. (2004). Age and Work: International Perspectives. *Social Policy and Society*, *3*(2), 163–170. doi:10.1017/S1474746403001623

Teixeira, S. (2011). *Gestão Estratégica* [Strategic Management]. Escolar Publisher.

Uchôa, E., Firmo, J., & Lima-Costa, M. F. F. (2002). Envelhecimento e Saúde: Experiência e Construção Cultural [Aging and Health: Experience and Cultural Construction]. In M. C. S. Minayo & C. E. A. Coimbra (Eds.), *Antropologia, Saúde e Envelhecimento* [Anthropology, Health and Aging]. Fiocruz Publisher.

Vranaková, N., Gyurák Babel'ová, Z., & Chlpeková, A. (2021). Sustainable Human Resource Management and Generational Diversity: The Importance of the Age Management Pillars. *Sustainability*, *13*(15), 1–18. doi:10.3390u13158496 PMID:34804601

Woltereck, H. (1959). *Vida Nova Para os Velhos* [New Life for Old People]. IBRASA – Instituição Brasileira de Difusão Cultural S. A.

World Health Organization. (2002). *Active Aging: A Policy Framework*. World Health Organization.

World Health Organization. (2005). *Envelhecimento Ativo: Um Projeto de Política de Saúde* [Active Aging: A Health Policy Project]. World Health Organization.

Yvoire, A. (2010). *Les Systèmes de Retraite en Europe* [Retirement Systems in Europe]. https://www.futuribles.com/fr/revue/365/les-systemes-de-retraite-en-europe/

Zandi, S., Nemati, B., Jahanianfard, D., Davarazar, M., Sheikhnejad, Y., Mostafaie, A., Kamali, M., & Aminabhavi, T. M. (2019). Industrial Biowastes Treatment Using Membrane Bioreactors (MBRs) - A Scientometric Study. *Journal of Environmental Management*, *247*, 462–473. doi:10.1016/j.jenvman.2019.06.066 PMID:31254761

KEY TERMS AND DEFINITIONS

Active Aging: The process of maximizing opportunities for health, participation, and security, to improve quality of life as people age.

Aging: A natural process, characterized by specific biopsychosocial changes, associated over time, variable from individual to individual, and influenced by lifestyle, environmental factors, and health conditions.

Healthy Life Expectancy: Is a term generally used as a synonym for life expectancy without physical disabilities, corresponding to the length of time people can expect to live without needing special care.

Lifespan: The developmental period from birth to death. Individual development can be described as the succession of consecutive stages, in which the individual plays an active role in his development and to which he adjusts psychologically.

Population Aging: A process of the relative growth of the elderly population in relation to the total population.

Quality of Life: Is a very broad concept that integrates in a complex way a person's physical health, his psychological state, level of dependency, his social relations, his beliefs, and his relationship with environmental characteristics.

Web-Scraping: Is the process of collecting structured web data, gathering pages to create indices or collections, it is also called web data extraction.

Workforce: The ability of employees to generate value for organizations and society.

Chapter 2
Indonesian Ageing Workforces in Rural and Urban Areas: Are They Similar or Not?

Deshinta Vibriyanti
The National Research and Innovation Agency, Indonesia

Sari Seftiani
The National Research and Innovation Agency, Indonesia

Vanda Ningrum
The National Research and Innovation Agency, Indonesia

Intan Adhi Perdana Putri
The National Research and Innovation Agency, Indonesia

Inayah Hidayati
https://orcid.org/0000-0002-6646-6212
The National Research and Innovation Agency, Indonesia

Luh Kitty Katherina
The National Research and Innovation Agency, Indonesia

ABSTRACT

In 2020, Statistics Indonesia revealed that one of two older people is still working. Based on the region, the proportion of older people who are working in rural areas is higher than in urban areas. This chapter aims to describes the socio-demographic characteristics of the Indonesian older workers by region area. Data of this chapter were based on the research about the quality of older people life conducted by The National Research and Innovation Agency and BPS data. The results show that the Indonesian older worker are vulnerable workers (both in urban and rural areas). The older workers in the rural areas have a worse condition due to lower wages, longer working hours, and lower health insurance ownership while the older workers in the urban mostly filled the service sector. Creating decent jobs for older people is an important thing to do considering that the older people in Indonesia still have the capacity and good physical condition to work.

DOI: 10.4018/978-1-7998-2395-7.ch002

Copyright © 2022, IGI Global. Copying or distributing in print or electronic forms without written permission of IGI Global is prohibited.

INTRODUCTION

Indonesia is facing an aging population. The number of older people has continued to increase in the past five decades until it has doubled. BPS data shows that until 2020, the number of older people in Indonesia will reach 26.82 million or about 9.92 per cent of the total population in Indonesia. Given that the Indonesian population's life expectancy continues to rise, this statistic is expected to rise even further. In 1971, the life expectancy of the population. In 1971, the life expectancy of the Indonesian population only reached 55.1 years, then continued to increase until, in 2015, it reached 70.8 years (SUPAS, 2015). This figure is also projected to increase until it reaches 72 years in 2035 (Adioetomo & Mujahid, 2014). Currently, the characteristics of the older people population according to the age structure are dominated by young older people (60-69 years) as much as 64.29 per cent, followed by middle older people (70-79 years) as much as 27.23 per cent and old older people (80 years and over) as many as 8.49 per cent (Badan Pusat Statistik [BPS], 2020).

Along with the phenomenon of population aging, more and more older people are found who are still actively working. The participation of the older people population in the labor market reflects the level of economic independence of the older people (United Nations, Department of Economic and Social Affairs, Population Division, 2020). It can also be seen as a marker that the level of welfare of older people is still relatively low. Older people work because of a necessity to meet the needs of life, not just a desire for self-actualization. Economic needs are a driving factor for older people to work (Radl, 2013). In addition, the knowledge and understanding of the people in Indonesia regarding the pension program are still very minimal. It is considered natural to continue working until old age. Many older people in Indonesia still do not know and are not registered in the pension program. Retirement programs are known and owned, limited to employees in government or private. The Aging Asia series suggests that the decision to continue working in retirement is only one of the five main sources of income. In contrast, other sources include social security from the government, pension funds, family support, and income from household assets (Pusat Studi Kependudukan dan Kebijakan Universitas Gajah Mada, 2014).

On the other hand, it is undeniable that older people generally experience a decrease in work performance, which affects the availability of job opportunities. The older people also face the fact that their physical condition is also experiencing a decline which causes limited employment opportunities. Previous studies suggest that increasing age is also accompanied by an increasing prevalence of illness and disability (Christensen *et al.*, 2009; Gatimu *et al.*, 2016). According to Noone *et al.* (2018), several factors prevent older people from being involved in the labor market. These factors include physical and mental health, age, gender discrimination, limited skills and abilities, or family encouragement not to work.

However, BPS data for 2020 shows that 1 in 2 older people in Indonesia is still actively working (50.04%). This figure has increased by 2.67 per cent from 2016, which was only 47.37 per cent. Meanwhile, when compared by region, there are more older people who work in rural areas than those who live in urban areas (44.1%). This fact is in line with data showing that 54.81 per cent of the older people work in the agricultural sector. Characteristics of work, culture and ownership of pension insurance that differ between rural and urban areas influence the tendency of the older people in rural and urban areas to work or not (Sumarsono, 2015).

From employment status, as many as 85.83 per cent of the older people work in the informal sector. The labor literature generally defines informal workers as responsible for individuals who are not legal entities and only based on an agreement. Meanwhile, BPS categorizes informal workers as those who work with the self-employed status, trying to be assisted by temporary/unpaid workers, agricultural and non-agricultural workers, and family/unpaid workers. Therefore, the majority of the older people who work today are very vulnerable because they do not have social security, a legal basis for work, and decent work benefits. Job qualifications in the formal sector, which require a certain level of education and skills, result in fewer job opportunities for the older people in the formal sector (International Labour Organization [ILO], 2014).

In terms of business fields, there are differences between the older people who work in urban and rural areas. The older people in urban areas who work are concentrated in the service business field with 50 per cent. In comparison, the older people in rural areas are more concentrated in the agricultural sector (73.15 per cent) (BPS, 2020). Comparing the two characteristics and vulnerabilities of the older people who work in urban and rural areas is vital for formulating an employment policy, especially for the older people population group. As projected by BPS, the estimated working older people population in 2035 will reach around 11 per cent in the labour market. This proportion is expected to continue to increase in the following years.

BACKGROUND

According to Law no. 36 of 2009 concerning health, the definition of the older people is someone who, because of his age, undergoes biological, physical, psychological and social changes. In Indonesia, matters related to old age regulate in one law, namely Law No. 13 of 1998 concerning the Welfare of the Elderly. This law also explains that older people have reached the age of 60 years and over. The law also divides the characteristics of older people into two, namely, potential older people and non-potential older people. Potential older people are older people who can still do work and activities that can produce goods or services. Meanwhile, the older people who have no potential are the older people who are powerless to earn a living, so their lives depend on the help of others. According to WHO, older people are a group of people undergoing a gradual change process over a specific time. There are w4 categories of older people, namely 1) middle age, 45-59 years old; 2) older people (older people) 60-74 years; 3) Old older people, 75-90 years; and 4) very old age above 90 years.

The ongoing demographic transition in Indonesia, marked by a decline in fertility rates and an increase in life expectancy, is increasingly changing the structure of Indonesia's population. The proportion of the young population is decreasing, the proportion of the working-age population is increasing rapidly, and the proportion of the older population is moving up slowly. Indonesia is entering the phase of an old population country. In less than 50 years, the number of older people in Indonesia has now doubled. This number is projected to continue to increase until 2045 until it is estimated that 1 in five Indonesians is older people.

Figure 1. Projection of the number of older people in Indonesia (millions of people), 2010-2045
Source: Badan Perencanaan Pembangunan Nasional, Badan Pusat Statistik, United Nations Population Fund.(2018).

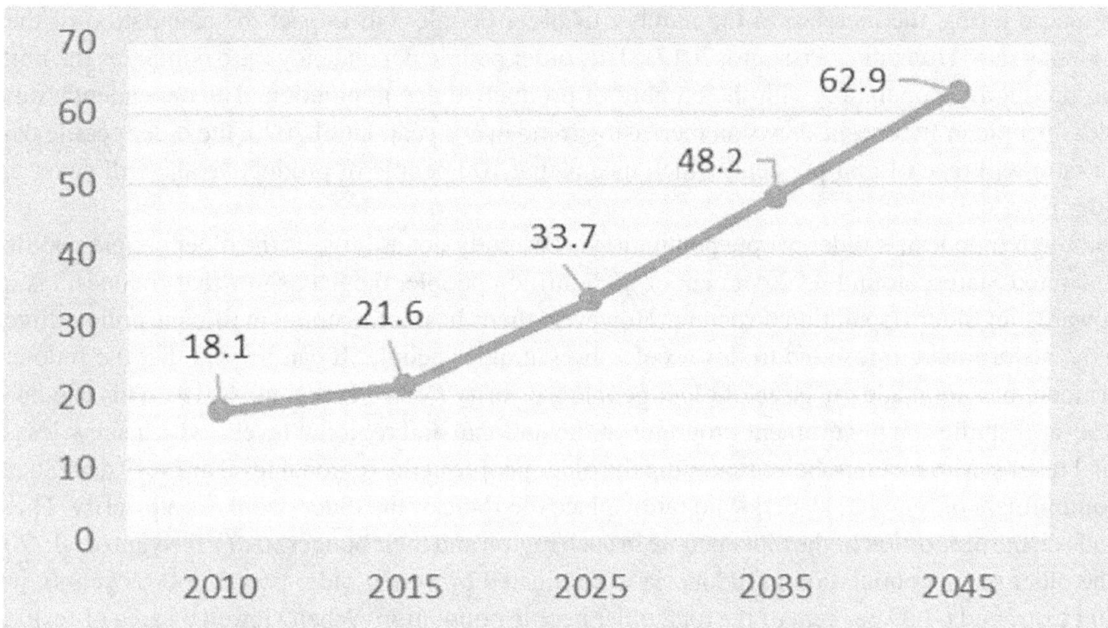

This condition can undoubtedly have implications for the direction of economic development policies. A large number of older people will affect the increasing needs of social security, care and health facilities for the older people population—an example of a developed country that has experienced an aging population phase in America. The number of older people in the United States is currently around 16 per cent or as many as 52 million people from the total population (Federal Interagency Forum on Aging-Related Statistics, 2020) The aging population directly impacts the burden on government budgets related to social security, health care, in-home caregiving, and assisted living facilities. Even economists say that the acceleration of the aging population also has a broader impact on macro-economic performance, especially related to the decline in productivity growth, employment participation and economic growth. In addition, the older people population is seen as having a small contribution tendency compared to the productive age group. The decline in performance in production activities impacts a slowdown in consumption and economic activities (Astrayuda, 2017). So that economists assess the condition of the aging population in a country in the long term has the potential to have a negative impact on economic performance and become a source of vulnerability.

In this regard, each country certainly has a different structure, regulation, capacity and capital. This is a determinant that determines the policy steps taken by each country in responding to the condition of the aging population. For developed countries with an established social security system and a good health system, extending the average retirement age above 65 is an alternative solution to reduce the burden on the state. Population aging that occurs in most developing countries, including Indonesia, is growing faster than in developed countries in the past (United Nations Department of Economic and Social Affairs [UNDESA], 2015). However, strategies and policies in developed countries are not necessarily suitable for countries like Indonesia, mainly because they do not yet have a robust social security system and adequate state capacity.

In macro terms, the increase in the number of older people will impact the calculation of the old dependency ratio (Junaidi & Prihanto, 2017). This older people dependency ratio compares the number of non-productive population with the number of productive age population. The dependency ratio of the older people in Indonesia shows an increasing trend every year. Until 2020, the older people dependency ratio will reach 15.54 per cent, which means that 100 people of productive age will cover about 15 older people.

Although Indonesia's older people population is currently not as large as the older people population in the United States, around 9.92 per cent or 26.6 million people, the data show that Indonesia is moving towards an older population structure. However, there has not been a significant policy direction from the government to respond to this acceleration in older people. It can be said that the Indonesian government has not made the issue of older people a priority (Vibriyanti et al., 2019). This can be seen from several studies on government programs at the national and regional levels, which show less than optimal results. Moreover, policies regarding the older people at the regional level are very dependent on the commitment of regional leaders who rarely place the issue of the older people as a priority. This one depends on the proportion of the older people in each region and their budget size (Vibriyanti et al., 2019).

The older people population in Indonesia is dominated by young older people (60-69 years), which amount to around 64.29 per cent of the total older people population. When viewed by area of residence, more Indonesian older people live in urban areas, namely 52.95, compared to those who live in rural areas (47.05%). The high number of older people living in urban areas is thought to be not solely due to an increase in the number of older people. However, it can also be driven by the increasing level of urbanization. The comparison of the characteristics of older people by gender is quite balanced. However, the number of older people women is more than that of older men (52.29% compared to 47.71%).

OLDER PEOPLE IN THE FAMILY AND REASONS TO WORK

Indonesia is one of the eastern countries that still adheres to the firm principle that caring for parents is the duty of children. This is why the older people in Indonesia, 87.46 per cent of the older people still live with their families (with a partner, with two generations or three generations). In the family, the older people can receive the attention, care, and social support needed in living their daily lives (Wang et al, 2012).

The data shown in Figure 2 shows that more older people in Indonesia live together with three generations, both in rural and urban areas. This shows that the extended family structure dominates families in Indonesia. The form of the relationship between the older people and their families can indirectly be a parameter to analyze the involvement of the older people in the labor market. Older people who become the Head of the Household (KRT) is proven to be found in the community, which is around 62.28 percent and is dominated by older people men. This means that with their role as head of household, six out of ten older people in Indonesia are allegedly still burdened with the responsibility to finance their household members economically. In addition, the high number of older people with the status of household heads can also be seen as an impact on the cultural values of the Indonesian people themselves. The perspective of family culture in Indonesia tends to be patrilineal, i.e., the head of the family will be in the older people male household member (in this case, the older people). Status in the household and marital status have the most significant influence on the possibility of older people working (Tusianti, 2019). Meanwhile, in calculating the odds ratio, the possibility of the older people being the head of the household to continue working is 3.3 times that of the older people who are not the head of the household. The probability of the older people who are married (still having a partner) to continue working is 2.7 times that of the older people who do not have a partner. (Vibriyanti et.al., 2017).

Figure 2. Percentage of Indonesian older people by living status, 2020
Source: BPS, 2020

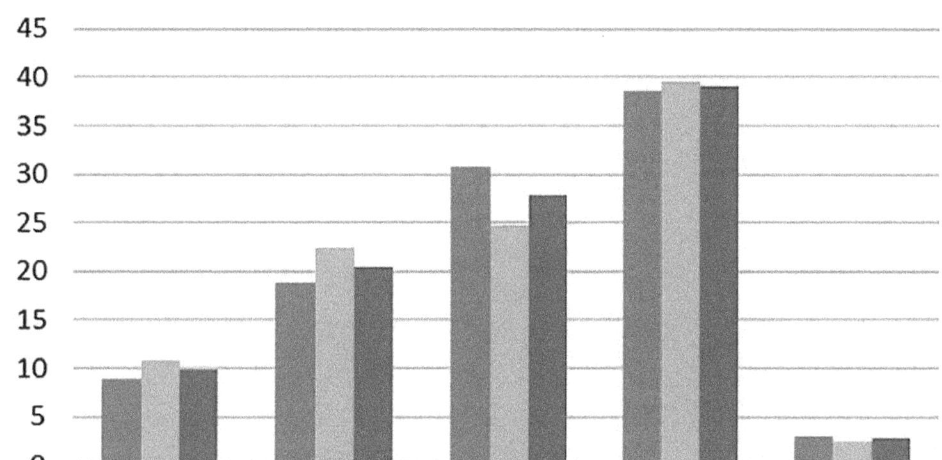

	living alone	with spouse	with 2 generations	with 3 generations	others
urban	8.91	18.77	30.69	38.59	3.04
rural	10.81	22.47	24.65	39.67	2.4
total	9.8	20.51	27.85	39.1	2.74

The classic problems of the old age group do not move from health, economic, psychological and social problems (Kwon, 2009). All of these problems are intertwined and affect each other. However, one crucial fact that can be the basis for how the author sees the condition of the older people population in Indonesia is that the majority of the older people (43.84%) are in households with the lowest 40% (poor) expenditure group (BPS, 2019). This is the answer to why many older people in Indonesia are still working. Work is one of the strategies to stay alive. Wirakartakusumah and Evi (1994) revealed at least three reasons that influence older people to work. First, many older people remain physically and mentally strong, so there is no reason to leave the job market. Second, the plunge of the older people into the job market due to economic pressure. Third, the reasons are not based on economic motives but instead based on self-actualization motives or emotions. A study proves that the tendency of the older people population to work is more significant in the older people male population, with married status, with relatively good health levels, and uniting as the head of the household. Meanwhile, the tendency of the older people population not to work is greater in the older people population who are getting older, with a higher level of education, with large household expenses, and living in urban areas (Sumarsono, 2015).

In general, we can be said that the majority of the Indoneisan older people live in households with the lowest 40 percent of the expenditure group (43.36 percent). There is no significant difference between the older poeple living in the urban and the rural. Meanwhile, when viewed from the largest source of income in older poeple families, the majority of income comes from the working family members (can be older poeple or other household members). This shows that the majority of the Indonesian older poeple do not have old-age insurance. Continuing to work or depend on children or other families is an economic strategy for the Indonesian older poeple to meet the needs of today's life.

Figure 3. Percentage of older people households by largest source of household financing and type of region, 2020
Source: BPS, 2020

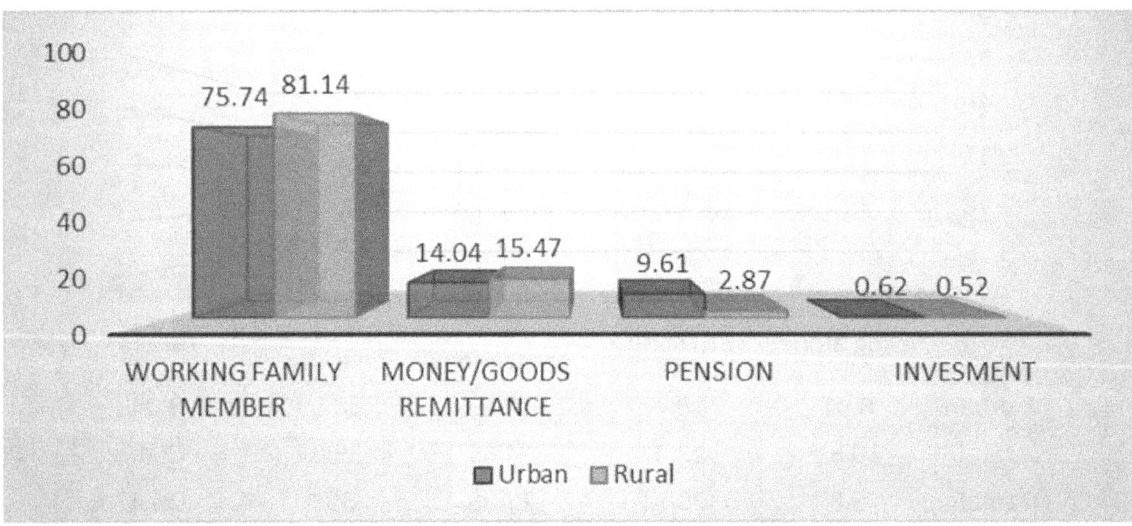

OLDER PEOPLE AND EMPLOYMENT IN A FRAMEWORK OF PRODUCTIVITY AND CULTURE

Concerning Human Resources (HR), the aging population is predicted to decrease productivity (Fougère et al., 2009, Bloom et al., 2010; Sharpe, 2011), whereas according to Elgin & Tumen (2010), total productivity will not decrease because a machine will replace human labor. However, productivity per worker will decrease even though productive labor can be substituted for old-age workers (Lisenkov et al., 2012). An analysis conducted by Tusiani (2019) proves that during the period 2010-2018, population aging has not seen its impact on productivity per worker in Indonesia.

Productivity is closely related to the quality of the workforce. When workers have high abilities and knowledge and good physical and mental health conditions, the work becomes effective and efficient (Kwon, 2009). At the macro level, the number of workers who have a high level of education affects a country's labor productivity (GDP per worker), as has been proven by Arshad & Malik (2015). People who have a high level of education can absorb new knowledge, including the latest technology. When entering an aging population, Indonesia's challenge is the low level of education of the population aged 40 years and over. The majority of them are still in junior high school and below. For the variable level of education, the tendency is that the higher the level of education, the fewer, the older people who choose to work. This is evident from the data showing that the older people who work the most are the older people with low education, namely those who did not finish primary school (38.34 per cent). Lanchimba et al. (2020) stated that older people with a high level of education would be less likely to work than those with a low level of education.

The phenomenon of the Indonesian older people with working status shows a trend that increases every year. Until 2020, the percentage of the older people who work reaches 51.04 per cent or one in 2 older people in Indonesia is currently still working. The increase of participation of older people in the labor market can signify the increasing empowerment of the older people in economic activities and an extension of their productive age. When viewed by area of residence, there are more older people living in rural areas than those working in urban areas (59.06 compared to 44.01 per cent). This difference in numbers is motivated by various factors. The pattern of work that is still traditional and does not require high qualifications and economic demands is the rationale for the high work participation of the older people in rural areas compared to urban areas. On the other hand, the older people in urban areas tend to choose still to work or not, and if they do work, the type of work tends to require specific qualifications.

A study on the quality of life of older people in urban areas proves that working older people status has proven to be a significant determinant of the quality of life of the older people. For the older people with a low quality of life, having a job or claiming to be economically active is proven to increase their quality of life. Meanwhile, at the level of quality of life from middle to high, the absence of involvement in the labor market increases the quality of life by 1.35 times compared to the low quality of life. Thus, having a job has a positive effect only on the poor-quality condition of older people (Vibriyanti et al., 2017). Interesting results from previous studies also show that working status in older people can only improve the quality of life for the low quality of life. Meanwhile, for older people that have a good quality of life consider work has a bad impact.

When viewed by gender, the older people who work are dominated by male older people as much as 65.05 per cent. Meanwhile, older people women are more likely to take care of the household, so participation in the labor market is only 38.28 per cent. This aligns with family norms in general in Indonesia, where men act as the main breadwinners while women take on domestic roles. Chang & Yen. (2011), stated that compared to women, the participation rate of older men is higher. Meanwhile, Lanchimba et al. (2020) stated that if the parent is a woman, then she will reduce the likelihood of working compared to men.

Table 1. Characteristics of older workers in Indonesia

Characteristics	Work (%)
Total	51,04
Region type	
Rural	59,06
Urban	44,01
Sex	
Male	65,05
Female	38,28
Age group	
Young (60-69 years)	60,17
Mid (70 -79 years)	40,20
Old (over 80 years)	18,34
Education	
Un-graduated from elementary school	38,34
graduated from elementary school	42,29
graduated from junior high school	8,66
graduated from senior high school	7,15
graduated from college	3,55

Source: BPS, 2020

However, working for older people still requires good physical condition and health. The health condition of the young older people tends to be better than the middle age group and the old older people, so, naturally, the most prominent work participation dominates by the young older people, which is as much as 60.14 per cent. Nasir et al. (2000) stated that the probability of older people participating in the labor market decreases with increasing age due to low mobility and health status associated with age. Similarly, Chang & Yen (2011) stated that age has a significant negative relationship with the supply of older people labor.

Figure 4. Percentage of Indonesian Aging Workforce Population 2016-2020
Source: BPS, 2020

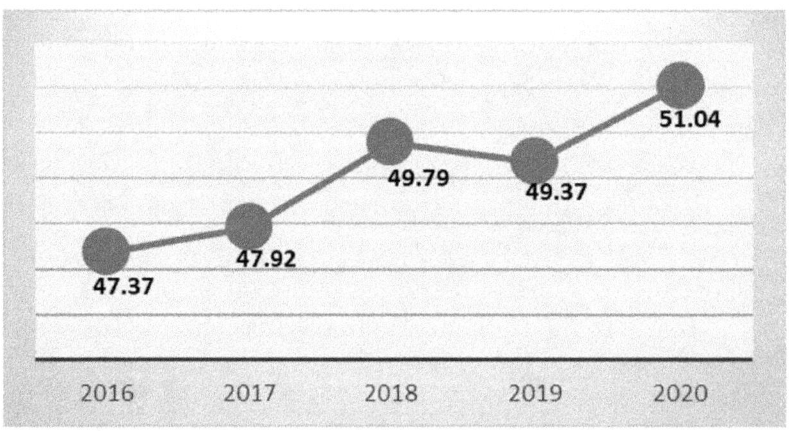

How Is an Older Urban or Rural Worker?

Data shows that one in two older people in Indonesia is still working. The facts show that there are more Indonesian older workers in the rural (59.06%) than in the urban (44.01%). Many research results prove that working olders are more valued by the need factor, not the aspect for self-actualization (Nasir et al, 2000; Tusianti, E., 2019). Characteristics of work, culture and ownership of pension insurance that differ between rural and urban areas influence the tendency of the older people in rural and urban areas to work or not (Sumarsono, 2015).

The employment opportunities availability for the elderly is one of the determining factors for the number of older working in an area. With the Indonesian olders characteristics, with low education and do not have special skills, the informal sector is a house to accommodate the elderly to keep working. According to Tursini (2019), the decision of the older people to keep working is influenced by several factors. In her research, Tursini proves that male older people, with the status of head of household, low education, household per capita expenditures below the average, and good health levels, are the older people who have the highest probability of still working.

Employment Sector for Older People

In line with the decline in productivity due to increasing age, older people will fill jobs according to their capacity. Similar to the employment pattern in general, most older people work in the agricultural sector, which is 54.81 per cent—followed by the service sector at 31.88 and manufacturing at 13.31. Most of the older people work in the agricultural sector, which typically has relatively low wages. Like informal work, the agricultural sector does not require special qualifications. Anyone, including the older people, can continue to work in this sector while having a relatively strong physique. Considering that agricultural land is generally located in rural areas, of course, most older people living in rural areas work in the agricultural sector (73.15%). Meanwhile, the working older people who live in the city mostly fill the service sector, for about 50 per cent.

Rural areas, especially the agricultural sector, are able to absorb older workers up to 73.15% higher than in the urban which is only 33.25% (see Figure.5). Availability of wider land and types of work that do not require special skills make the agricultural sector dominate in rural areas. Meanwhile, more older people in urban enter the service sector, which is around 50%, of course this is in accordance with urban characteristics which are dominated by the service sector. However, in general, the older worker in the urban and the rural both into the category of informal sector workers (older workers in the urban 79.33% and in the rural 91.36%). The definition of informal worker is someone who works with self-employed status, trying to be assisted by temporary/unpaid workers, agricultural and non-agricultural workers, and family workers/unpaid workers (BPS, 2020).

The involvement of the older people in the labor market in rural areas includes all household agricultural activities, such as rice cultivation, horticulture, plantations, fish cultivation, fishing, and others. For example, research results in North Lombok show that the older people work in cocoa plantations as harvesters. This is because the younger workers work on other agricultural land or migrate. In addition to the agricultural sector, the home industry sector is also filled by the older people group. For example, in the case of Kepuh village, Banguntapan sub-district, Bantul, there is a cracker industry center which is carried out by pre-and older people women who are members of the association. In addition to the chips industry center, the dent industrial center in Pelemadu Sriharjo Hamlet, Bantul also absorbs a lot of older people women. This small-scale food industry center in Bantul has multiplied after the 2006 earthquake due to the many assistance programs from the government.

Figure 5. Percentage of aging workforce by main employment, 2020
Source: BPS (2020)

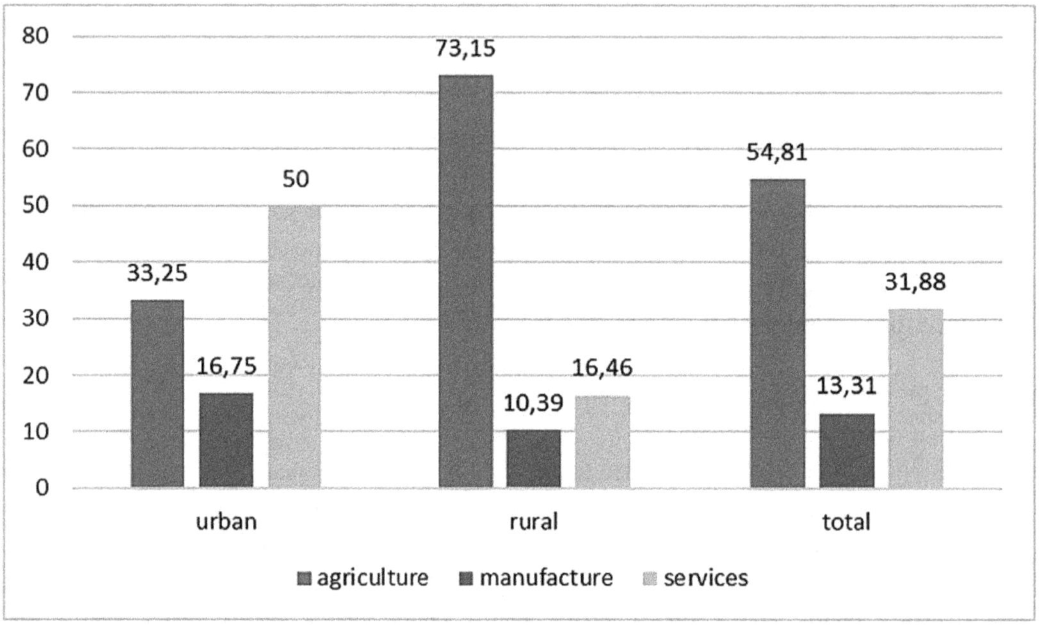

Meanwhile, the data shows that based on the status of the main job that is mostly done by the older worker in the urban is self-employment, which is 33.57% and the older people in the rural with the status of trying to be assisted by unpaid workers as much as 39.50%. From the description of the informal sector which is mostly filled by the elderly in the urban and the rural, it can reflect that the education level of the older worker is still low. (BPS, 2013).

A study on the quality of life of the older people in the Medan city showed that around 43 per cent of the older people work in trade, restaurants, and accommodation from the main occupations. Meanwhile, other types of employment that are also widely cultivated by the older people are community, social and individual services, which are 39.1 per cent. Then viewed from the primary job status, as many as 44.5 per cent of the older people who work are self-employed. This means that this condition indirectly illustrates that the older people who work in the city of Medan are mainly in the informal sector, which tend not to have old-age insurance. This analysis is supported by survey data which proves that as many as 77.80 per cent of the older people in Medan city do not have old-age insurance (Vibriyanti et.al., 2017)

Old Age Security and Pension Security Ownership

The basic idea of social security is to use social means to prevent deprivation and vulnerability and ensure sustainable human development over time (Dreze & Sen, 1999). In both developed and developing countries, social security supported by the state in protective or promotive social security aims to complement and replace the support provided by families, communities, or other charitable institutions (Gopal, 2003). So far, the government's attention to older people is still lacking. This can be seen from development policies that are more focused on older people who have problems. Meanwhile, the older people who are still healthy and active in the community do not receive proper attention according to their general condition.

The informal sector is synonymous with a high level of vulnerability of workers due to low wages, lack of social protection, and relatively long working hours. The average monthly income of the olders who work in the urban is higher than the olders who work in the rural (1,727,000 million rupiah compared to 1,110,000 million rupiah). However, ironically, there are fewer older workers in the rural have health insurance, 67.29% compared to the older worker in the urban 77.47%. There is 80.76% of the older worker in the rural are also more economically vulnerable groups than the older workers in the urban, which is 68.60%. The vulnerable category economically are do not have sufficient job opportunities, inadequate social protection, rights are not fulfilled in the workplace, and do not have the opportunity to express opinions about the work they do (BPS, 2020). Another similarity between the older workers in the urban and the rural is that they are both the precarious employment workers, which is as much as 10%. Precarious employment are free workers, workers with work contracts for a certain period of time, and workers with verbal work contracts (BPS, 2020).

On the one hand, older people need opportunities to actualize themselves, become independent, and participate in economic activities. But on the other hand, protection for the older people who primarily work in the informal sector is barely available (Chang & Yen, 2011). In most countries, the majority who engage in informal but productive activities do not enjoy social protection or cover only a part. Older people are a group that is vulnerable to risks of work safety and work continuity. The status of the older people as the head of the family can also reflect that the older people are still the backbone of the family economy. There are still many older people who pay for their children's needs even though they are married (Vibriyanti et.al., 2017). The vulnerability of the working older people can be seen from the low ownership of old-age security and pension insurance. According to PP No. 46 of 2015, Old Age Security is a cash benefit that is paid at once when the participant enters retirement age, dies, or experiences permanent total disability.

Meanwhile, pension insurance is social security that aims to maintain a decent standard of living for participants and/or their heirs by providing monthly income after the participant enters retirement age, experiences permanent total disability, or dies (https://www.bpjsketenagakerjaan.go.id/program-jaminan-pensiun.html).

Data for 2020 shows that only 10.76 per cent of the older people have pension insurance, and only 6.58 per cent of the total working older people have pension insurance. The older people in urban areas still have more old-age insurance and pension benefits than those in rural areas.

Working Hours

In general, Indonesian older people who work, including temporary workers, are 10.66 per cent. Based on the number of hours worked, out of every five older workers, at least one person works excessively (the number of working hours is more than 48 hours a week). Meanwhile, the average income of working older people is 1.45 million rupiahs per month (BPS, 2020). A study identified the characteristics of the older people who work full-time ($\geq$ 35 hours per week) and those who work part-time ($\leq$ 35 hours per week). The study proves that the tendency of older workers to work full-time is greater in older people male workers, older workers with married status, older workers with relatively good health levels of older workers, older workers united as heads of households, and older workers who live in urban areas. While the tendency of older workers to work part-time is greater in older workers who are getting older (Sumarsono, 2015). Economic factors are still why Indonesian older people work, although perhaps some of the older people work because they like to work and for the sake of life satisfaction. From the working hours of older people, on average, they are still in the range of 15-34 hours per week. Relatively long working hours for the physical older people. The older worker in the rural are more likely to work 15-34 hours per day (38.55%) than the older worker in the urban (29.57%).

OLDER WORKERS IN URBAN AND RURAL EXPERIENCES

The following discussion describes the experiences of the older people who are still working in urban areas and in rural areas and the problems they face from some research data from the research team at the Center for Population Research.

The Stories of Older Workers in Urban Conditions

This section will describe the condition of the older people who work in urban areas by using research data through a survey method for the Quality of Life for the Older people to 400 older people who live in Medan, Indonesia. One of the changes in living conditions when entering old age is related to the economic aspect. Approaching the age of 60 years, physically, the older people tend to experience a decline in performance and then known as retirement. However, not everyone who enters old age will simply stop working, especially for those who work in the informal sector. This is evidenced by the number of older people who are still working in this study, around 31.9 per cent. And if we look further, based on the main occupations, around 43 per cent of the older people work in trade, restaurants and accommodation.

Meanwhile, other types of employment that are also widely cultivated by the older people are community, social and individual services, which are 39.1 per cent. Meanwhile, when viewed from the main job status, 44.5 per cent of the older people who work are self-employed. This means that this condition indirectly illustrates that many older people in Medan work in the informal sector, and tends not to have old-age insurance.

The older people in the informal labor market are closely related to the level of education. The survey results prove that the education level of the older people in the city of Medan is mostly only at the basic education level and below, which is 58.60 per cent. The number of survey calculations in this study is still above the 2013 Susenas data, where the number of older people who occupy elementary school education and below is 47.9 per cent. In addition to information related to employment and education of the older people, the survey in this study also collected data related to the income earned by the older people with working status. The income of older people respondents who work per month ranges from 100,000 rupiah – 11,666,666 rupiah, or if the average income of the older people working in the city of Medan is 1,333,087 rupiah. The majority of the older people's income is above 750,000 rupiah, which is 50.80 per cent. As for the income of the older people per month by gender, there is a relatively similar pattern between male and female older people. Compared with the Sectoral Minimum Wage (SMW) issued through the Decree of the Governor of North Sumatra No. 188.44/33/KPTS/2017 concerning the 2017 Medan City Sectoral Minimum Wage, which is around 2,731,120 in the retail trade sector of various goods, mainly food, beverages or tobacco in supermarkets/minimarkets. The average income of older people is still below the SMW. This comparison is based on the assumption that 43% of the older people work in trade, restaurants and accommodation.

Meanwhile, a relatively large expenditure of the older people population is on health costs. The existence of health insurance for older people cannot be denied is very important for the lives of older people. This survey also asked 401 respondents about the ownership of health insurance. The survey results show that around 71 per cent of the older people have health insurance, and 29 per cent do not have health insurance. When viewed from the type of insurance, most older people respondents have BPJS PBI type health insurance (55%) and then BPJS Askes/PNS/Veterans, which is 26 per cent. This condition indirectly indicates that the socio-economic status of the older people respondents is classified as a group of poor and underprivileged people. Almost all respondents answered that they had experienced these diseases, and even the majority of respondents suffered from more than one kind of disease simultaneously. From the calculation results, the diseases suffered by the older people respondents in urban areas are gout (36.20%), rheumatism/arthritis (35.40%), high blood pressure (34.70%), digestive disorders (28.20%), cholesterol high (17.70%) and diabetes (13%).

Aging Farmers in Rural Agriculture

The description of the condition of the older people working in rural areas is the result of a separate study conducted in Central Java. In rural agriculture in Java, Indonesia, older workers are synonymous with agriculture, both rice fields and horticulture (Darmawan et al, 2006). The phenomenon of older people labor in agriculture is in line with the increasing migration of young people (Ministry of Youth and Sports defines youth as people aged 16-30 years) living in urban areas and the reduced interest of young workers to work in agriculture (Ningrum et al., 2016). However, there is a tendency towards the population of older farmers. The agricultural survey in 2013 showed that 60.79 per cent of Indonesian farmers were over 45 years old and only a small proportion of young farmers were less than 30 years old.

Aging of farmers also occurs in several agrarian countries in the world. Studies in Europe show a disparity in turnover rates between farmers leaving their farms and new farms run by young farmers. The average age of farmers in this area is 65 years (Tuscia, 2008). Other studies in other Asian countries show similar problems. In Japan, statistics reveal that older people now dominate the agricultural sector. In 2008, 46.8 per cent were aged 70 years or older, and 57.8 per cent of farmer households were farmers aged over 65 years (Yamashita, 2008).

The debate occurs when the agricultural workforce filled by older people farmers will be able to affect productivity. For example, the labor survey shows that 70 per cent of farmers in Indonesia only finish elementary school education, in such conditions, farmers will find it challenging to innovate and follow new technologies that can help them to increase agricultural productivity. Agricultural technology itself is used as a government strategy to increase agricultural productivity. However, with the characteristics of older people farmers, it becomes a problem in the process of learning and utilizing the technology. Although the youth agricultural movement has been found in several areas in Java, the number of older people farmers is still the mainstay of labor for the agricultural sector, especially rice fields in Java.

In the case of three villages in Central Java, small-scale rice farmers tend to be filled by parents. It is not easy to get young workers from family members because young people's interest in agriculture using the green revolution is considered not to provide economic or social benefits. However, for the older people farmers, farming is a source of livelihood for their families, although income from agriculture is unpredictable due to crop failure, soaring production input prices, natural disasters, and other risks.

Older workers in agriculture in Java can not only be seen from the farmers who own the land. They also occur in rice farming workers. Planting workers are dominated by older people women workers. The activities carried out by these older workers are planting traditionally and manually; usually, they do it in groups, their income is paid daily. The existence of female "tandur" workers is still the mainstay in the villages even though there are planting machines that are claimed to grow rice more efficiently than the traditional way. The long-standing relationship with the rice field owners has led to "tandur" workers, who are now old.

Small farmers see the cases of the older people in agriculture who are still working with limited land area and uncertain agricultural yields. Meanwhile, for female older workers, the available work cannot be done all the time and only gets paid according to the agreement with the landowner. These various types of work are still included in non-formal activities where there is no social protection in work—vulnerability increases when workers have to work physically hard without guaranteed income and adequate health insurance.

CONCLUSION

Indonesia is faced with an aging population increasing faster than the country's economic development. In this case, the welfare of older people must be prepared from an early age so that it does not become a burden in the future. More than 50 per cent of the older people population in Indonesia are still actively working. Viewed by region (urban-rural), most of the older people live in rural areas dominated by the agricultural sector. The agricultural sector which is included in the category of the informal sector shows that the Indonesian older workers have minimal access to social security, especially pension insurance. While, the older workers in the urban mostly filled the service sector. The older workers in urban areas, in terms of access to social security such as health insurance and old age, are much better than the older people who live in rural areas. Even though the average wage for the older workers in the rural is lower than in the urban. Therefore, it is important to consider regional aspects in policy making regarding older people.

In general, the motivation of the Indonesian older workers is due to economic pressure. From the study results, it can be concluded that there are still many older people who work as the head of the household in the family. Culture is one factor other than the demands to finance family members in the household why the older people still have to work. Unfortunately, the type or sector of work for older people is currently still in the category of low-income workers. Creating decent jobs for the older people is an important thing to do, considering that the older people in Indonesia still have the capacity and good physical condition to work. The wage differential for the older people that often occurs is one of the challenges for the government in ensuring the older people can work properly. The challenge of the aging population in the future is to create decent jobs for older people. As mentioned in the previous discussion, the estimated working older people population in 2036 is around 11 per cent of the labor market. This proportion is expected to continue to increase in the following years.

REFERENCES

Adioetomo, S. M., & Mujahid, G. (2014). *Indonesia on the threshold of population ageing (monograph series no. 1)*. UNFPA Indonesia. https://indonesia.unfpa.org/sites/default/files/pub-pdf/BUKU_Monograph_No1_Ageing_03_Low-res.pdf

Arshad, M. N. M., & Malik, Z. (2015). Quality of human capital and labor productivity: A case of Malaysia. *International Journal of Economics, Management and Accounting, 23*(1), 37-55. https://journals.iium.edu.my/enmjournal/index.php/enmj/article/view/289

Astrayuda, I. (2017, May 18). Mencermati fenomena aging population. *Investor.id*. https://investor.id/archive/mencermati-fenomena-aging-population

Badan Perencanaan Pembangunan Nasional, Badan Pusat Statistik, United Nations Population Fund. (2018). *Proyeksi penduduk Indonesia 2015-2045*. https://www.bps.go.id/publication/download.html?nrbvfeve=NzhkMjRkOTAyMDAyNmFkOTVjNmI1OTY1&xzmn=aHR0cHM6Ly93d3cuYnBzLmdvLmlkL3B1YmxpY2F0aW9uLzIwMTgvMTAvMTkvNzhkMjRkOTAyMDAyNmFkOTVjNmI1OTY1L3Byb3lla3NpLXBlbmR1ZHVrLWluZG9uZXNpYS0yMDE1LTIwNDUtaGFzaWwtc3VwYXMtMjAxNS5odG1s&twoadfnoarfeauf=MjAyMS0xMS0wOCAyMTozMzowMQ%3D%3D

Badan Pusat Statistik. (2013). *Sensus pertanian 2013*. https://st2013.bps.go.id/dev2/index.php

Badan Pusat Statistik. (2020). *Statistik penduduk lanjut usia 2020*. https://www.bps.go.id/publication/download.html?nrbvfeve=MGZjMDIzMjIxOTY1NjI0YTY0NGMxMTEx&xzmn=aHR0cHM6Ly93d3cuYnBzLmdvLmlkL3B1YmxpY2F0aW9uLzIwMjAvMTIvMjEvMGZjMDIzMjIxOTY1NjI0YTY0NGMxMTExL3N0YXRpc3Rpay1wZW5kdWR1ay1sYW5qdXQtdXNpYS0yMDIwLmh0bWw%3D&twoadfnoarfeauf=MjAyMS0xMS0wOCAyMTowMzoyNQ%3D%3D

Bloom, D. E., Canning, D., & Fink, G. (2010). Implications of population ageing for economic growth. *Oxford Review of Economic Policy*, *26*(4), 583–612. doi:10.1093/oxrep/grq038

Chang, H., & Yen, S. T. (2011). Full-time, part-time employment and life satisfaction of the older people. *Journal of Socio-Economics*, *40*(6), 815–823. doi:10.1016/j.socec.2011.08.008

Christensen, K., Doblhammer, G., Rau, R., & Vaupel, J. W. (2009). Ageing populations: The challenges ahead. *Lancet*, *374*(9696), 1196–1208. doi:10.1016/S0140-6736(09)61460-4 PMID:19801098

Darmawan, K., Saleh A., Subagjo, H., Masunaga, T., & Wakatsuki, T. (2006). The effect of green revolution technology during the period of 1970-2003 on sawah soils properties in Java, Indonesia; I. Carbon and nitrogen distribution under different land management practice and soils types. *Soil Science and Plant Nutrition, 52*(5), 634 - 644. doi:10.1111/j.1747-0765.2006.00075.x

Dreze, J., & Sen, A. (1999). India: Economic Development and social opportunity. Oxford University Press.

Elgin, C., & Tumen, S. (2010). Can sustained economic growth and declining population coexist? Barro-Becker children meet Lucas. *Economic Modelling*, *29*(5), 1899–1908. doi:10.1016/j.econmod.2012.06.004

Federal Interagency Forum on Aging-Related Statistics. (2020). *Older Americans 2020: Key indicators of well-being*. https://agingstats.gov/docs/LatestReport/OA20_508_10142020.pdf

Fougère, M., Harvey, S., Mercenier, J., & Mérette, M. (2009). Population ageing, time allocation and human capital: A general equilibrium analysis for Canada. *Journal Economic Modeling*, *26*(1), 30–39. doi:10.1016/j.econmod.2008.05.007

Gatimu, S. M., Milimo, B. W., & San Sebasti, M. (2016). Prevalence and determinants of diabetes among older adults in Ghana. *BMC Public Health*, *16*(1), 1174. doi:10.118612889-016-3845-8 PMID:27871259

Gopal, A. (2003). Disengaged employees cost Singapore $4.9 Billion. *Gallup Management Journal*. https://gmj.gallup.com/content/default.aspx?ci=1207

International Labour Organization. (2014). *World of work 2014: Developing with jobs*. https://www.ilo.org/wcmsp5/groups/public/@dgreports/@dcomm/documents/publication/wcms_243961.pdf

Junaidi., E., & Prihanto, P.H. (2017). Faktor-faktor sosial ekonomi yang mempengaruhi keterlibatan penduduk lanjut usia dalam pasar kerja di Provinsi Jambi. *Jurnal Masyarakat, Kebudayaan dan Politik*, *30*(2), 197-205. doi:10.20473/mkp.V30I22017.197-205

Kwon, D. B. (2009). *Human capital and its measurements*. OECD World Forum. https://www.oecd.org/site/progresskorea/44109779.pdf

Lanchimba, C., Quisnancela, J., & Méndez, Y. S. (2020). The choice of elderly labor: Evidence from Ecuador. *Revista de Análisis Económico*, *35*(1), 75–97. doi:10.4067/S0718-88702020000100075

Law on Health (Law No. 36/2009). https://peraturan.bpk.go.id/Home/Details/38778/uu-no-36-tahun-2009

Law on Welfare of the Elderly (Law No. 13/1998). https://peraturan.bpk.go.id/Home/Details/45509/uu-no-13-tahun-1998

Lisenkova, K., Mérette, M., & Wright, R. (2012). Population ageing and the labour market: Modelling size and age-specific effects. *Economic Modelling*, *35*, 981–989. doi:10.1016/j.econmod.2013.09.007

Nasir, Z. M., Ali, S. M., & Chaudhry, M. A. (2000). Labour market participation of the older people. *Pakistan Development Review*, *39*(4), 1075–1086. doi:10.30541/v39i4IIpp.1075-1086

Ningrum, V., Subroto, A., Widodo, Y. B., Aji, G. B., Harfina, G., Wiratri, A., & Suryanto, J. (2016). *Rural youth aspiration in agriculture: support or threaten food security?* [Presented Paper]. The 3rd Asia Future Conference.

Noone, J., Knox, A., O'Loughlin, K., McNamara, M., Bohle, P., & Mackey, M. (2018). An analysis of factors associated with older workers' employment participation and preferences in Australia. *Frontiers in Psychology*, *9*(2524), 1–16. doi:10.3389/fpsyg.2018.02524 PMID:30618949

Pusat Studi Kependudukan dan Kebijakan Universitas Gajah Mada. (2014). *Tinggi, angka pekerja lansia di Indonesia*. https://cpps.ugm.ac.id/ tinggi-angka-pekerja-lansia-di-indonesia/

Radl, J. (2013). Labour market exit and social stratification in western Europe: The effects of social class and gender on the timing of retirement. *European Sociological Review*, *29*(3), 654–668. doi:10.1093/esr/jcs045

Sharpe, A. (2011), Is ageing a drag on productivity growth? A review article on ageing, health and productivity: The economics of increased life expectancy, *International Productivity Monitor, 21*, 82-94. http://www.csls.ca/ipm/21/IPM-21-Sharpe.pdf

Sumarsono, F. S. (2015). Analisis partisipasi kerja penduduk lanjut usia di Indonesia. *Jurnal Ilmiah Mahasiswa FEB, 4*(1). https://jimfeb.ub.ac.id/index.php/jimfeb/article/view/2435/2217

Tuscia, U. (2008). *The generational turnover in agriculture : The ageing dynamics and the eu support policies to young farmers Anna Carbone and Giovanna Subioli* [Paper presentation]. 109th EAAE Seminar. https://www.researchgate.net/publication/23509051_The_Generational_Turnover_In_Agriculture_The_Ageing_Dynamics_And_The_Eu_Support_Policies_To_Young_Farmers

Tusianti, E. (2019). Penuaan penduduk dan tantangannya di masa depan dalam sudut pandang ketenagakerjaan. In W. Winardi & E. Tusianti (Eds.), *Analisis isi terkini 2019: penuaan penduduk dan tantangannya di masa depan dalam sudut pandang ketenagakerjaan*. https://www.bps.go.id/publication/2019/12/11/6749d130c7369027fd21df8c/analisis-isu-terkini-2019-.html

United Nations, Department of Economic and Social Affairs, Population Division. (2019). *World population ageing 2019: Highlights* (ST/ESA/SER.A/430). https://www.un.org/en/development/desa/population/publications/pdf/ageing/WorldPopulationAgeing2019-Report.pdf

United Nations Population Fund. (2014). *Indonesia on the Threshold of Population Ageing*. UNFPA Indonesia.

Vibriyanti, D., Harfina, D., & Widayatun. (2017). Pemetaan kondisi lansia dalam keluarga di era globalisasi. In *Keluarga dan globalisasi di Indonesia: Pemetaan data terkait remaja, ibu dan anak, serta penduduk lanjut usia (lansia).* Pustaka Sinar Harapan.

Vibriyanti, D., Harfina, D., Seftiani, S., & Sitohang, M. Y. (2019). *Lansia sejahtera tanggung jawab siapa?* Obor.

Wang, Z., Shepley, M., & Rodiek, S. (2012). Aging-inplace at home through environmental support of 654physical activity—An interdisciplinary conceptual framework and analysis. *Journal of Housing for the Elderly, 26*(4), 338–354. doi:10.1080/02763893.2011.625289

Wirakartakusumah, M.D., & Evi, H.A. (1994). *Aging in Indonesia: Demographic Characteristic*. Departement of Geography University of Adelaide.

Wiratri, A. (2017). Relasi petani, negara, dan swasta di Indonesia. In V. Ningrum & A. Wiratri (Eds.), *Pemuda & pertanian berkelanjutan: Dependensi, strategi, dan otonomi petani*. Pustaka Sinar Harapan.

Yamashita, K. (2008). *The Perilous Decline of Japanese Agriculture.* The Tokyo Foundation. http://www.tokyofoundation.org/en/articles/2008/the-perilous-decline-of-japanese-agriculture-1

Chapter 3
Senior Entrepreneurship: Agenda for a Youth Economy (Indian Perspective)

Shikha Aggarwal
Institute of Technology and Science, India

Vidhi Tyagi
Amity University, India

ABSTRACT

The 50+ age group had made a significant contribution to the entrepreneurship and innovation agenda in the US. Similarly, entrepreneurs above the age of 50 constituted around 15% of all commercial start-ups in England. Senior entrepreneurship has been considered a promising way to manage the issue of aging population. Could India be the next destination for third-age entrepreneurship to find its calling? Should we acknowledge the advantages of senior entrepreneurship and sensitize the aging population and the governments toward it? In light of limited literature available for senior entrepreneurship, potential motivating factors or driving force are discussed. Furthermore, entrepreneurship in India is highlighted encompassing the status of entrepreneurship, policies and schemes promoting entrepreneurship, and opportunities and challenges for senior entrepreneurship. Finally, the chapter concludes with implications for practice in policy-making and in terms of encouraging senior entrepreneurship and its antecedents in the Indian context.

INTRODUCTION

In the words of frivolous Mark Twain, Age is an issue of mind over matter. If you don't mind, it doesn't matter!

An entrepreneur is a person who schematize and synthesis business resources and operates with greater than normal financial risk and environmental uncertainties. Entrepreneurship is the intention and capability to develop, organize and manage a business undertaking, accompanied by its nasty risks, with an objec-

DOI: 10.4018/978-1-7998-2395-7.ch003

Copyright © 2022, IGI Global. Copying or distributing in print or electronic forms without written permission of IGI Global is prohibited.

tive to safeguard a profit interest. Entrepreneurship requires energy, attitude, inspiration, inventiveness as well as business acumen. Some argue that too much older workforce slows down entrepreneurship. Older workers occupying top position may also hinder younger workforces' opportunities to develop their skills and competences which increase with experience in high-level positions. While others believe that older workforce bring crucial resources (e.g., capital, networks etc.) in addition to their experience. Moreover, they tend to be well qualified, and keen to transform and innovate and view sustainable progress as a crucial business objective (Cannon, 2008). In one of the recent studies, it was found that there exist relatively weak but positive linear relationship between age and overall entrepreneurial success. At the same time, it does illustrate a U- shaped pattern, with the younger population having a negative relationship and the older population having positive relationship (Liang et al., 2018; Zhao et al., 2021). The model implies that entrepreneurship should display an inverted-U-shape relation to age. The very young do not possess the business skills necessary to start a business and the very old lack the creativity, energy, or willingness to engage in entrepreneurship.

In a developing youth- economy such as India, the age dependency ratio, old, in 2018 was recorded maximum to be 9.26%. Adding to that, steep surge in unemployment due to coronavirus pandemic-induced lockdowns was also observed throughout the country. Could India be the next destination for third- age entrepreneurship to find its calling? Should we acknowledge the advantages of senior entrepreneurship and sensitize the aging population and the Governments toward it? With an objective to answer the above questions, this chapter begins by highlighting the alternative perspective upon entrepreneurship triggered by changing circumstances world- wide. In light of limited literature available for senior entrepreneurship, potential motivating factors or driving force are discussed. Furthermore, entrepreneurship in India is highlighted encompassing status of entrepreneurship, policies and schemes promoting entrepreneurship and opportunities and challenges for senior entrepreneurship. Finally, the chapter concludes with implications for practice in policy- making and in terms of encouraging senior entrepreneurship and its antecedents in Indian context.

Entrepreneurship and Older Workforce

(Wiklund & Shepherd, 2003) suggests, studies of entrepreneurship to be largely associated with financial/ economic value creation for individuals. Recent developments in the entrepreneurship literature have confronted this money-centric approach, by presenting an alternative approach that suggests that entrepreneurship is driven by numerous factors which are likely to vary by geography, demography and even circumstances one encounter (Anderson, 2015; Galloway & Cooney, 2012) For instance, thousands of people losing their lives and annihilating economic buoyancy contributed to the devastating impact of Covid- 19 pandemic world- wide. Yet there happened some "magic" behind the entrepreneurial mindset across the globe, where entrepreneurs exhibited determination, strength, resilience and proficiency to recognize and pursue opportunity in chaos. With perfume companies producing sanitizers, toys and tech companies coming out with face shields, portable ventilators and masks, continued to contribute employment opportunities amidst the pandemic (Alex Maritz et al., 2020). In this regard, it is essential to broaden the scope of entrepreneurship related to stage, ethnicity, gender, age and even class. In the present times, when economies are suffering and public finances are getting reduced, entrepreneurship has conceivably emerged as the rising star and one of the means to countervail the situation and move towards some balance (Stypińska et al., 2019; Zhao et al., 2021). Interestingly, multiple evidence has shown many small businesses rebounding, transforming to the need and quickly adapting the product/

service offerings to continue their businesses. Creatively altering and recombining resources to utilize their existing facilities has also led to increase in bigger players in the markets. Some of the defining characteristics for such people include being open minded, optimistic, resilient, determined, able to manage uncertainty, visionary and resourceful, self- motivated, and calculated risk- taking capabilities. These abilities are essential for developing an entrepreneurial mindset and the aptitude to build something out of necessity within a short time, especially when instant results are required. It would not be entirely wrong to say that COVID- 19 has given rise to a new category of entrepreneurs – the necessity- opportunity entrepreneurs. Formerly, they were helping the community because they visualized opportunity aligned with the necessity. In future these people would be the ones to accelerate the economic lift off as and when situation eases and the "new normal" begins (Alex Maritz et al., 2020). Although, there exist a few research literatures on necessity entrepreneurs. They are certainly ignored by the media as well the policy-makers (Garcia, 2015). Policy-makers mostly aim to boost opportunity entrepreneurship rather than necessity entrepreneurship. However, research is there to assure that necessity entrepreneurship, especially at older ages, is found both in the Anglo-Saxon and the Southern European settings (Fonseca & Parker, 2019). Accordingly, entrepreneurship at older ages is one of the avenues to look for in the future.

The 50+ age group had made significant contribution to entrepreneurship and innovation agenda in the US. Similarly, entrepreneurs above the age of 50, constituted around 15% of all commercial startups in England (Cannon, 2008; Logan et al., 2009). Senior entrepreneurship has been considered a promising way to manage the issue of aging population. Especially in the developed economies of the world, where by 2031, the average age of population is expected to reach between 44 – 55 years, the focus is more towards, altering the very image of entrepreneurship to a more inclusive one, identifying barriers to entrepreneurship by diverse groups, building "entrepreneurial self- efficacy" and tailoring training and support programme, policies and incentives to encourage entrepreneurship in the country. The concept, however, is highly uncharted zone and there exists a dearth of systematized and organized literature support in the area (Fonseca & Parker, 2019; Zhao et al., 2021). There have been previous studies that explored and described various facets of senior entrepreneurship. Though, these studies are limited to very few parts of the world, mainly United Kingdom and the United States and Australia. Therefore, there exists huge scope of research on the subject with respect to other parts of the world including western and eastern European nations (Fonseca & Parker, 2019). In fact, many other upcoming and growing economies of Asia and Southeast Asian, unfamiliar with the concept, carry a good scope of research as well.

Age has been long recognized as a potential factor influencing entrepreneurship where enterprising has been perceived more of a young person's game. Contrary to the popular belief, Hisrich (2002) advocates the presence of innovative ideas, and entrepreneurial characteristics among diverse groups in all societies. However, the distinction in the level of business creation is largely supported by the economic and social infrastructure in the nation (Logan et al., 2009). The limited literature that there is on older workforce has even few sources exploring aging as a factor. Aging refers to the changes that happen biologically, psychologically and in social functioning over time and affects individual on physical, social and organizational levels (Kooij et al., 2008). Researchers investigating older workforce described the threshold at 40 and 45 years of age, contributing "old" to obsolescence of ideas, attitudes, knowledge and skills (Muijnck & Zwinkels, 2002). Alternatively, research also suggested that "chronological age" may be an inadequate factor for comprehending "age' in context of organizational settings (Avolio et al., 1984; Settersten & Mayer, 1997; Sterns and Alexander, 1987; Sterns & Miklos, 1995; Wolf et al., 1995).

Self-employment by aging workforce, especially over 50 years of age, is labeled under several names including gray (grey) entrepreneurship (Watkins- Mathys, 2012; Weber and Schaper, 2004), older entrepreneurship (Ratten, 2019; Singh, 2009; Stirzaker & Galloway, 2017), third age entrepreneurship (Botham & Graves, 2009; Lewis & Walker, 2013), senior entrepreneurship (Figueiredo and Paiva, 2019; Perenyi et al., 2018; Schøtt et al., 2017) and second career entrepreneurship (Baucus and Human, 1994) and silver entrepreneurship (Cannon, 2008). A tabular representation of various terminology used for self- employment by the aging workforce is present in Table 1. For the purpose of present chapter, we define self- employment of population aged 50 years or more as senior entrepreneurship (Hart et al., 2004). In studies conducted by HBR and MIT teams, it was suggested that the average age of founding entrepreneurs of successful business, in the USA, was 42 years and younger entrepreneurs had little chances of successful exit. Similar observations were also recorder by the Barclays Economic Reports, 2001. There are numerous examples to support these findings. For instance, the founders of the popular multinationals McDonald's, Coca- Cola and Kentucky Fried Chicken were all over 50 when they established their businesses. Entrepreneur Icons such as Steve jobs and Jeff Bezoz, however entered very young in their respective fields but even they cracked the fruit of success at middle- ages of 52 and 45 respectively. Having said that, these averages vary across industries as well. In some nations, the age group of 55 years – 64 years is one entrepreneurship segment that is growing the quickest (Mayhew, 2014).

There is continual increase in the number of businesses being ventured by people over the age of 50 years (Patel et al, 2006). The policy framework, Entrepreneurship 2020 Action Plan, 2013, highlighted senior entrepreneurship as an untapped capital which could be and should be utilized to make valuable contributions to the economy and society. Especially, in the present, post- pandemic world, entrepreneurship has emerged as a necessity-based outcome for many. Self- employment at a later stage not only extends the aging worker's career, generates savings in public pensions but also facilitates continued deployment of that human resource in the economy. It also had a significant positive change in the quality of life of older workforce in terms of satisfaction of the fundamental psychological needs of control, autonomy, self-realization, and pleasure (Kautonen et al., 2017). Besides the fact of increasing life expectancy, reworking of labor markets, conventional rules of employment and welfare systems linked workforce governance puts enhanced pressure, financially, on the welfare state. Adding to it, the underutilization of human capital throughout the society is expected to manifest as an outcome of declined economic growth by the year 2050 unless proper utilization and substitution of idle workforce happens (Bloom et al., 2010; Perenyi et al., 2018). On one hand where studies have found that "switchers", employed workers shifting to self- employment, are more likely to become self- employed for shorter periods of time and also their businesses might not add much value in the economic sense (Parker & Rougier (2007), other studies have explored societal benefits of late- career entrepreneurship, hence making it an attractive option for the aging individual. These benefits may include their experience, intellectual agility, knowledge and personal capabilities Kautonen et al. (2010).

Table 1. Different terminologies used for self-employment of aging workforce

S. No.	Terminology	Age (in years)	Authors
1	Gray Entrepreneurship	50 +	Weber and Schaper, 2004
		50 +	Watkins- Mathys, 2012
2	Older Entrepreneurship	55 +	Singh, 2009
		50 +	Stirzaker and Galloway, 2017
		50 +	Kautonen et al., 2008
		65 - 80	Schøtt et al., 2017
3	Third-age Entrepreneurship	50 +	Botham and Graves, 2009
		50 +	Lewis and Walker, 2013
4	Senior Entrepreneurship	50- 64	Schøtt et al., 2017
		50 +	Perenyi et al., 2018
		45 - 60	Figueiredo and Paiva, 2019
5	Second-career Entrepreneurship	39 - 60	Baucus and Human, 1994
6	Silver Entrepreneurship	50+	Cannon, 2008

THEORETICAL PERSPECTIVE ON SENIOR ENTREPRENEURSHIP

Theoretical approach to comprehend senior entrepreneurship has its roots in entrepreneurial motivations and cognitive developments forming entrepreneurial intentions. One of the most widely used psychological theories to predict human behavior is the Theory of Planned Behavior (TPB). Scholars of entrepreneurial studies argue that entrepreneurship is intentional. Ajzen (1991, p. 181) defines intentions as "indications of how hard individuals are willing to try, of how much of an effort they are planning to exert, to perform the behavior." The stronger the intention to involve in a certain behavior, the more conceivable should be its performance. Further, TPB posits three independent antecedents of intentions: attitude toward a certain behavior, subjective (social) norms and perceived behavior control. Using the Theory of Planned Behavior (TPB), Kautonen, & Kibler (2011), studied implications of perceived age norms on old- age entrepreneurial intentions and found that if individual perceives it socially acceptable or desirable to be active in entrepreneurial activity, then this perception has significantly positive impact on their entrepreneurial intention. Applying Shapero's Entrepreneurial Event Theory, Stirzaker & Galloway (2017), found that old- age circumstances contribute significantly to the decision to start one's own business. Vandemaele & Vancauteren (2015) and Schepers et al. (2014) explored entrepreneurship and socio- emotional wealth. Elsewhere, Baron and Tang (2011) theorized that affect stimuluses cognition. Cognition helps in shaping opportunity identification and motivation in individual, henceforth affect should also influence formation of opportunity processes. In the similar line of thought, Kato & Wiklund (2011) stated that starting one's own business can have positive emotional affect. Further, using Affective Events theory, Morris et al. (2006) examined entrepreneurial experience narrative and found that a temporal stream of emotional events effects the entrepreneurial process. (Baltes & Carstensen 1999; Carstensen, Fung, & Charles 2003; Carstensen, Isaacowitz, & Charles 1999), in their studies on and Socio- emotional Selectivity Theory (SST) found that younger adulthood is greatly invested to pursue a range of new involvements, information and associations to capitalize in future benefits, whereas as time perspective alters and one ages or matures, the motivations also become selective. This leads to investing in affective and purposeful goals and relationships.

METHODOLOGY

Present chapter is developed on the basis of reviews of literature. Webster & Watson, 2002, suggests literature reviews offer advanced knowledge through comprehensive conceptual and empirical study. Sengupta et al, (2017 p. 7) states "conceptual and literature review papers are of specific relevance to practitioners and researchers in an area which is in its nascent stage." It enables establishment of good foundational understanding for building research on the basis of critical analysis and synthesis (Tranfield et al, 2003). Literature review also provide a way of evaluating patterns and trends in the existing research (Torraco, 2005). It assists in finding research gaps or further scope of research and also highlights the areas which require more attention (Roehrich et al, 2014).

Keywords including "gray entrepreneurship", "older entrepreneurship", "third- age entrepreneurship", "late- career entrepreneurship", "entrepreneurship development schemes" and "entrepreneurial policies" were searched on Google Scholar. Majorly, journal articles from databases of Emerald, JSTOR, EBSCOhost, Wiley, Taylor & Francis, and ScienceDirect were used. In order to maintain the impact and credibility, mostly articles that were peer- reviewed were used as the sources of literature (Podsakoff et al, 2005). In addition to the limited literature published on senior entrepreneurship, especially in Indian context, content analysis of the government websites, databases, historical data, company case studies, and sector reports were performed to identify government schemes, policies, prospects of senior entrepreneurship in India and much other valuable information pertaining to our research.

SUMMARY OF FINDINGS

Drivers of Senior Entrepreneurship

There are numerous examples to highlight successful business ventures founded by people after they crossed 50 years of age. Certainly, there would be some driving factors or motivators that support the culture of senior entrepreneurship. Pinder, (1998; p. 11) quoted work motivation as "a set of energetic forces that originate both within as well as beyond an individual's being, to initiate work-related behavior, and to determine its form, direction, intensity, and duration". It is essential to comprehend drivers of senior entrepreneurship as "motivators to continue to work" as with aging the motivation to "continue to work" gets affected (Kooij et al., 2008). The popular American notion about entries into self- employment is associated with job losses ((Fonseca & Parker, 2019; Moulton & Scott, 2016). The International Labor Organization, in its flagship report in 2020, suggested that the absence of income or other means of financial support forces workers to engage in occupations that are informal, offer low pay and provide little or no access to social protection and rights at work. Wainwright et al. (2011) proposes senior entrepreneurship is driven by social and lifestyle influences such as roles, responsibilities, life stage and work in older age. For some people, entrepreneurship at later age in life, is a means of balancing interests, socio-emotional rewards and income. For others it appears that income is supplementary and entrepreneurship based on intrinsic social and emotional rewards and features of working for oneself, such as flexibility, autonomy and high ambition (Perenyi et al., 2018; Stirzaker et al., 2019). Kooij et al., 2008 suggested that senior entrepreneurship is motivated differently by both employment factors and specific age context. Moreover, people after a certain age, often have the skills, financial resources and time available to contribute to economic activity (A Maritz et al., 2015; Zhao et al., 2021). Table 2 presents various categories of motivation drivers for senior entrepreneurship.

Table 2. Types of drivers of senior entrepreneurship

On the basis of Entrepreneurial Motivation	On the basis of Classification of Age
Push & Pull Approach	Chronological Age
Intrinsic Motivators	Functional Age
Extrinsic Motivators	Psychological Age
	Organizational Age
	Life span Age

On the Basis of Entrepreneurial Motivation

The PPA suggested by many researchers broadly sorts entrepreneurs on the basis of their motivation for their enterprise. It describes two kinds of motivation factors: push factors, also regarded as negative factors as it forces one to move towards self- employment, and pull factors or positive factors as it attracts self- employment (Amit & Muller, 1995; Feeser & Dugan, 1989; Shapero & Sokol, 1982). Perceived social pressure and perceived behavioral control are also some of the anchoring factors for self- employment of the aging workforce (Harms et al., 2014).

Push factors may include long- term unemployment, insufficient incomes or low wages, dissatisfaction in current job and other stresses of salaries employment (Evans & Leighton, 1989; Fonseca & Parker, 2019; Parker & Rougier, 2007), increasing age discrimination in hiring/ or current employment, poor work environment, loss of job, premature retirement, high ambition and unwillingness to tolerated difficult work relationships, misfit of personal goals and working conditions, lack of perceived job security, job market discrimination and also fear of discrimination on the basis of age. Parker & Rougier (2007) suggested switches from paid employment to self- employment were prompted as being an "occupation of last resort" among less affluent workers with job histories of weak attachment to the labor market. Unresolved multigenerational challenges such as limited capacities of older workers to adapt to technological changes, unwillingness of the company to further invest in older workforce, differences among co- workers in multi- age work teams and limited resilience towards older workforce emerged out as crucial factors that pushed employees toward self-employment (Harms et al., 2014).

It has been observed, Harms et al., 2014, that gray entrepreneurs prefer flexibility in work schedules, are highly ambitious and tech- savvy people. Autonomy, purpose, enjoyment, flexibility, and financial incentives were identified as five key pull factors (Stirzaker et al., 2019). The opportunity to develop one's own abilities and experiences, flexible schedules, a wish to balance family and work life, take better advantage of business opportunity, desire of having fulfilling job, and of course better earning/ income opportunities does appear to be a lucrative deal with "being your own boss" being the cherry on top. Many studies with older workforce suggested that satisfaction with job is more closely related to intrinsic factors or internal rewards for that work in comparison to younger workers (Cohn, 1979; Gruenfeld, 1962; Kanfer & Ackermann, 2004; Schwab & Heneman, 1977; Saleh & Otis, 1964; Valentine et al., 1998; Vallerand et al., 1995). Many other studies have supported that self- employment at later age was driven by the need to prioritize intrinsic motivators such as spending time with spouse and children, enjoyment, happiness and helping others (Stirzaker et al., 2019). Availability of successor also has impact in going for self- employment at older stage in life (Brunetti, 2006; Fonseca & Parker, 2019; Grossman & Strulik, 2010). Experience was recognized as another crucial driver of self- employment. Being of more age seems to be an added advantage for pursuing entrepreneurial activity as one enjoys easy access to connections, communication and negotiation skills, professional network and other resources developed due to prior work experience. (Perenyi et al., 2018). However, at times when older entrepreneurs have only experience to bring at the table, their performance is bound to diminish. (Harms et al., 2014).

Perceived social norms refer to what one believes most other people typically do or approve of. Extant literature on social norms theory suggests that social norms are vital stimuluses and/ or can be used to encourage behavioral change that are meaningful (Robinson, E. (2015). The more positive a social norm is perceived to be towards a certain behavior, the more likely a person is to actually execute that behavior. Harms et al., 2014, suggests that perceived attitudes of co-workers may stimulate or inhibit self-employment motivations of senior employees. Also, perceived acceptability among different stakeholders including society, networks and family is great influence in shaping the decision to become an entrepreneur.

Economic Forces: In USA, the entrepreneurial decision of starting a new venture, by older people, is immensely affected by macroeconomic policies. The research done in context of the UK suggested that the institutional framework discouraged mature, older people from participating. In Finland, studies have supported that senior workforce was constrained by the lack of pull factors for entrepreneurship (Kautonen et al., 2008). In similar vein, in Australian studies on this topic, it was found that there existed very limited government programme that were effective towards encouraging senior entrepreneurship (Kautonen, 2013, Perenyi et al., 2018). Christelis & Fonseca (2015) also suggested that self- employment was immensely affected by government labor policies. For example, expenditures on employment incentives positively affected self- employment. Government policies for the labor market serves as a great motivation and also strengthen the quality of business startups. Institutional inflexibilities, rigidities in the labor market and more traditional economies with limited opportunities for flexible full-time working for older people are some other strong forces that pushes into self-employment observed in some countries (Fonseca & Parker, 2019). Likewise, other external enablers of new venture creation may include innovative technologies, economic or natural environments, or even pandemics like COVID-19 (Alex Maritz et al., 2020).

On the Basis of Classifications of Age

Age and Motivation factors have been recognized in many studies. However, there exists lack of consistency in conceptualization. For instance, age is conceptualized as a life stage in some studies, while in other as calendar age. Similarly, motivation is conceptualized as need in some studies and as intrinsic motivation in others. Using Sterns & Doverspike (1989) conceptualization of aging workers' Lange et al. (2006) extricates specific interrelated age- related factors that affect older workers' motivation to continue to work. They are described as following:

1. **Chronological age factors:** Calendar age can be a negative factor affecting motivation to continue to work, especially in organizational settings. Many companies in order to reduce training cost, although against the age- discrimination legislature, encourages such HR policies which impacts ones' intentions to continue working (Greller and Simpson, 1999; Kooij et al., 2008; OECD, 2005). It may not be entirely untrue to say that calendar age may have a negative impact on individuals' motivation to continue to work.
2. **Functional or performance- based age factors:** Functional age or performance-based age is highlighted by two types of ages categories: psychological age and biological age. Cognitive abilities (psychological age) alter with the effect of age. Intellectual abilities such as verbal comprehension and general knowledge get enhanced whereas fluid intelligence such as abstract reasoning, reacting speed and working memory, declines. In activities demanding more of fluid intelligence, the motivation to continue to work among older individual may diminish as the differences between comfortable effort levels and demands of the tasks perceives in. Nevertheless, studies have been inconclusive in depicting any significant association between motivation to work and psychological age as cognitive abilities can either have a positive or negative impact on motivation to continue to work (Kooij et al., 2008). Physical capabilities also decline with increasing age. Research establishes that with declining physical abilities, motivation also declines. Positive correlations are established between health and achievement motivation Holahan (1988) and self- determined external motivation factors Vallerand et al. (1995). Obsolescence of skills with increasing age is also possible. Employees having longer work histories may experience their knowledge and skills getting obsolete with changing time, also their increasing age and it becomes difficult to compete with the younger generation in the workplace (Čiutienė & Railaitė, 2014). They may not have had the time or opportunity to upgrade their skills pertaining to the changing requirements and may have less expectation of skill enhancement adding to any value addition or reward (Fossum et al., 1986; Gist et al., 1988). Apart from this, health conditions also contribute to limiting work in paid- employment (Anderson & Burkhauser, 1985; Higgs et al., 2003; Hayward et al. 1989) and thus aging workers may choose to self- enterprise (Fonseca & Parker, 2019).
3. **Psychosocial age factors:** Psychosocial factors are the one's forming self- perception of age and social perception of age. Self- perception of one's age is likely to affect self- efficacy. As individual age, the preference for activities that assist positive affect (emotional satisfaction), one's self concept and supporting one's own identity increases (Carstensen, 1995; Kanfer & Ackerman, 2004). Lang & Carstensen (2002) suggests that generativity motives increase with psychological aging. People find themselves more directed towards activities like teaching or mentoring (Farr et al., 1998; Pratt et al., 1999). It implies that older workers will be more motivated with tasks that have greater positive evolution and greater sense of identity. An altering view by Lévesque & Minniti (2006), is argued that one's self- perception of "old age" can negatively affect entrepreneurial activity. This may be because as people age, they perceive they have less time remaining which may not be sufficient to contribute towards long term exploitation of opportunities and realization of results that is an essential feature of entrepreneurial activity. Alternatively, they want to be associated with activities giving results comparatively faster and they consider generating profitable revenues as a limited opportunity from entrepreneurship. Stereotypical social perceptions such as unwillingness to learn new skills, having strong work ethic and not able to adapt changing times may also be observable in superiors, subordinates, peers prompting discriminatory decisions against older workers (Kooij

et al., 2008). The pressure arising from such social factors is likely to highly impact one's decision to continue work, especially in paid- employment.

4. **Organizational age factors:** Organizational age can be understood in terms of tenure (age of the service), and career stage. An individual's career is composed of different occupational stages (Hall & Nougaim, 1968; Super, 1984). Super (1984) proposed a career model which predicts that job attitude varies with career stage. London (1990) explains a model for understanding career motivations pertaining to later stages of career in terms of three dimensions i.e., career identity, career insight and career resilience. Identifying oneself with work roles and responsibilities explain career identity. Career insight, on the other hand, is the realistic perception of oneself and one's career. Career resilience is the limit to which people fight career barriers which in turn determines an individual's determination and perseverance in achieving career goals. Career resilience is found to be higher in late stages of career suggesting higher career motivation (Noe et al. (1990). However, any meaningful conclusions cannot be drawn in light of insufficient literature on association between motivation and career stage.
5. **Life-span factors:** The life- span concept characterizes age in terms of family status and life stage. Tamir and Antonucci (1981) studies motivation through seven distinct stages of family life cycle and found no significant difference in motivational choices among various stages of family life cycle. Nevertheless, health, wages, savings and personal desires of partner has greater impact on employee retirement decisions (Henkens & Tazelaar, 1997; Hayward et al., 1989; Saba & Guerin, 2005; Smith & Moen, 1998). As a worker ages, preference for more leisure time, pursuing hobbies and relaxation, deterioration of functional abilities, social perception, especially age norms and within- market discrimination may all be more prominent factors in a retirement decision and lessened motivation to continue to work in paid- employment.

ENTREPRENEURSHIP IN INDIA

Unemployment rates in India, according to recent data available from the Centre for Monitoring India Economy Pvt. Ltd., suggests steep rise in unemployment during the lockdown period in the first wave of coronavirus pandemic. During April- June 2020, taking it to a roaring 22.42% whereas during the second wave from April- May 2021 the rates of employment again rose as high as close to 12%, keeping it below the rates during first wave. According to an article in the Bloomberg quint, the significant downfall in these employment rates from the peaks seen after the Covid-19 pandemic is contributed to self- employment. On aggregate, self-employed workers rose to 41% as a percentage of persons working in the April-June 2020 quarter compared to 37.7% in the same quarter last year in India. Although many economists see it as disguised unemployment, could it carve the way towards a new perspective to entrepreneurship in India? With a lifespan of a little more than a decade, entrepreneurship in India is still a novice academic discipline. It has its own challenges leading to incongruence between the startup entrepreneurs' need and the availability of knowledge base and faculty and mentor expertise. In a country, like India, housing about 29% of Asia's population with more than 65% population below the age of 35 years (Misachi, J., 2021), the focus is inevitably to inculcate the culture of entrepreneurship more so focusing upon the youth. However, the world population structure has evolved tremendously in short span of time with changes impacting economy, social systems and healthcare systems. These changes have also led to increasing life span of human population or popularly, population aging (Čiutienė & Railaitė,

2014). It has also led to gradual increase in age dependency ratios around the world. Age dependency ratio, old, is the ratio of dependents more than the age of 64 years with respect to working age population aged between 15 – 64 years (indexmundi.com) It also implies that the employed population, probably, is to be subject to paying higher taxes in order to compensate for the non- working (children and retirees) ones (Mouraviev & Avramenko, 2020). In 2018, the age dependency ratio, old, in India was recorded maximum to be 9.26%. It was around 5.26% in 1960. With increasing life expectancy ratio y-o-y, it has become essential for older age people to find economic and social independence at least for an additional 15 – 20 years post- retirement. Senior entrepreneurship is a potential tool to provide self-reliance to aging individuals and the economy as well. In order to realize the huge potential of entrepreneurship both at societal and economic levels and its benefits to the aging and now post- pandemic unemployed workforce, it becomes equally important to create awareness about such schemes and develop entrepreneurship ecosystems encouraging senior entrepreneurship in India.

Role of Government in Senior Entrepreneurship

Many of the industries are meant for young people like gaming industry and social media. But there are many industries like healthcare where senior entrepreneurs bring more strength to the start-ups. Senior entrepreneurs have the opportunity to use their maturity, experience and patience while starting entrepreneurship. Many of the successful entrepreneurs have proven that age does not matters, it's all about the desire and passion. Many popular Indian entrepreneurs from time to time have supported entrepreneurship as an age- free concept. Ranjani Ayyar, Aparna Desikan and Shalina Pillai, a few, says that what drives them is their passion for new ideas and desire to keep working. "If you need execution, older entrepreneurs bring lot of strength," says Rajesh Sawhney, founder of GSF Accelerator. Starting up your own venture has nothing to do with age, it's all about the passion, says another serial entrepreneur and angel investor Ravi Gururaj. "You can't worry about being old. The person should be innovative and think out- of- the- box type of person. It becomes more about the mental age rather than the physical age," he quoted.

Today's start-up world raises up images of young doers with a positive attitude and ability to take risks. But there may be another kind of entrepreneur with full of energy and passion, just over the age of 50. It is evident from the history that Government of India has taken many initiatives to support entrepreneurship always. The support schemes of the Government can be broadly grouped into the following three periods:

During 1948-1991

Earlier, during the phase of 1948-1991, major emphasis was given to micro and small enterprises. Small and Cottage industries was a source of generating employment and developing national economy. Industrial Policy Resolution, New Delhi recommended to create cottage industries board in 1948 to strengthen the weak conditions of the artisans in India. Later on, the central government split the cottage industries into All India Handloom Board, All India Handicrafts Board, All India Khadi and Village Industries Board. In 1956, Khadi and Village Industries Commission Act was established to promote Khadi and Village Industries with the intention for rural development. Industrial Policy Revolution was adopted by Indian Parliament in 1956 to encourage the rural and small-scale industries along with other objectives like removing regional disparities and establishment of socialistic pattern of society. Industrial policy statement, 1973 gave preference to small scale industries and exempted them from licensing for expansion of business. Policy measures initiated till 1980's after Independence facilitated the development of various industries and broad infrastructure in India. The seventh five-year plan came up with the measures to uplift the Indian Industries through modern technology. This phase provided the supportive measures which were required to promote MSMEs. The support was provided in the form of reservation of products for their exclusive manufacturing, support was provided through access to bank credit under certain programmes of commercial banks, establishment of entrepreneurship development institutes and infrastructure development.

During 1991-1999

To rectify the distorts and weaknesses of the industrial set up of the country, the government has come up with new Industrial Policy on July 24, 1991. During 1990s, the entrepreneurship was promoted through campaigns and women were given training under the entrepreneurial development programmes. SIDBI was set up in 1990 to provide financial support to small scale enterprises. With the establishment of Industrial Policy of 1991, entrepreneurship promotion had taken a major shift with respect to changes in the approval procedures as the single window procedure was adopted for licensing and permissions to start new enterprises. Lot of investment have been done in research and development and to develop new technologies. This policy emphasised on government support in context of liberalization, the purpose of which was to promote enterprises in the face of foreign competition and open market. The focus was also given to improve quality and technology. Government came up with many developments after implementation of Industrial Policy, 1991 which could be seen by the emergence of Export Oriented Units (EOUs), Special Economic Zones (SEZs), Agri-export Zones and Export Processing Zones (EPZs) in order to increase exports from the country and promote export-oriented enterprises.

2000 Onwards

Government had expanded its support to incubation centres for the promotion of small- scale industry in the field of bio-technology, information technology, tele communications and electronics during 2001. Many schemes like credit linked capital subsidy (CLCS), credit guarantee scheme (CGS) was launched to provide easy credit to the entrepreneurs. Other issues of technology and marketing were also addressed through these schemes. Micro, Small and Medium Enterprises Development (MSMED) Act was established in the year 2006 for the promotion and development of micro, small and medium enterprises. Medium and small enterprises were protected from large enterprises through provision of rebates, and financial support under this Act. Government provided financial support to the enterprises registered under MSMED Act. Other schemes included overdraft interest rate rebate, protection against delayed payments, public procurement policy-SAMBANDH etc. In March 2007, for the promotion micro and small enterprises, schemes having direct impact on the promotion and development of the MSEs. Some of the other recent policy reforms targeted toward the growth and development of the MSME sector in India are as follows:

A Scheme for Promoting Innovation and Rural Entrepreneurship (ASPIRE)

ASPIRE was established with the aim to set up technology centres and incubation centres to support entrepreneurship and to encourage start-ups for innovation in Agri-industry. Under this scheme, provision for financial support is given to up Livelihood Business Incubators (LBI) or Technology Business Incubator (TBI). Various other objectives included creation of employment, Promote entrepreneurship and innovation.

Pradhan Mantri Mudra Yojana (PMMY) 2015

The Pradhan Mantri Mudra Yojana (PMMY), also known as "Shishu", "Kishore" and "Tarun" is a scheme run by the Government of India (GoI) through *MUDRA* (a subsidiary of SIDBI) that assists small company owners in obtaining microcredit up to Rs. 10 lakhs. The MUDRA scheme encourages financial intermediaries to lend to non-corporate, non-farm income-generating activities of micro and small businesses with credit needs of up to Rs. 10 lakhs. The scheme is available to any Indian citizen who requires credit up to Rs 10 lakh for a non-farm revenue generating activity such as manufacturing, processing, trading, or the service sector.

Shishu Scheme (Covering Loans up to Rs. 50,000/-)

This loan facility is for the entrepreneurs who are either in the early stages of their firms or want less capital to get them started. *Kishor* scheme (covering loans up to Rs. 5,00,000/-) category includes the loan facilities for individuals who have already launched a business and require more funding to expand it. *Tarun scheme* (Loans up to Rs. 10 lakhs) is for an entrepreneur who meets the required eligibility criteria, he or she may apply for a loan of up to Rs. 10 lakhs. The loan rates are set in accordance with the Reserve Bank of India rules, which is the central finance governing body, which are updated on a regular basis.

Atal Innovation Mission (AIM)-2016

Atal Innovation Mission (AIM) was set up in 2016, to create the culture of entrepreneurship in India. AIM has launched the Atal Tinkering Lab (ATL) program to create curiosity in young minds for creating innovative ideas through technologies like internet, Robotics, 3D Painting. The purpose was to establish Ata Tinkering Labs in the schools to develop the Creative mindset among the young children and till now this scheme has covered more than 7000 Schools and more than 2 million students have the access to ATLs.

Stand-Up India (SUI) Scheme- 2016

On August 15, 2015, the Hon'ble Prime Minister, Shri. Narendra Modi, launched the scheme "Start-Up India" to promote entrepreneurship for economic empowerment and employment creation. The Stand-Up India Scheme aims to utilize the institutional credit structure to provide opportunity to the underserved, such as scheduled caste, scheduled tribe, and women entrepreneurs. The scheme makes them enable to contribute to the national economic growth. The Government have received 137200 applications under this scheme out of which 118940 applications have been sanctioned. The SUI scheme aims to provide at least one scheduled caste (SC) or scheduled tribe (ST) borrower and at least one women borrower per bank branch with bank loans ranging from Rs.10 lakh to Rs.1 crore for the establishment of a firm.

SC/ST and/or female entrepreneurs over the age of 18 who wants to start greenfield projects are only eligible for this scheme.

Start-up India 2016

Through the scheme Start-up India, Government of India provided a common platform for startups to interact with Government and other institutions for all business needs. Since the launch of this scheme, Start-up India has come with several programs for promoting and supporting entrepreneurs. Start-up's program has developed Incubation Centres, facilitated easy procedures for IPR filing and patent filing. An online system known as Startup portal have been developed to bring all stakeholders like investors and entrepreneurs on common platform to collaborate with each other. Start-up India have facilitated with rebates in the Patent filing, Tax benefits in terms of Tax exemption in capital gains and removal of Angel Tax. This scheme has established various incubation centres, Research Parks and Labs. Under the umbrella of Startup scheme a variety of schemes have been established which includes Ucchatar Aavishkar Yojana, Startup India Yatra, Million Minds Augmenting National Aspirations and Knowledge Scheme (MANAK), NIDHI Yojana- National Initiative For Development And Harnessing Innovations. As per Start- up report 2018, 14036 applications were approved as Start-ups by Department of Industrial Policy and Promotion. 91 Start-ups got the approval for tax benefits Approval for availing tax benefits 91 Start-ups. Start-up India Hub was started in 2016 to resolve queries of start-ups and this hub has handled more than 10,00,000 queries till 2018. The hub has provided support through Incubation Centres and financing to more than 6000 start-ups (As per Start-up Report 2018).

PM Street Vendor's Atma Nirbhar Nidhi (PM SVANidhi)

The COVID-19 pandemic and subsequent lockdowns have had a negative influence on street sellers' livelihoods. They often work with a minimal capital basis, which they may have depleted during the lockdown. There was a pressing need to provide financing for operating capital to street vendors so that they can resume their operations. This scheme is a Central Sector Scheme, supported by the Ministry of Housing and Urban Affairs, is established to facilitate working capital loan up to 10,000 and to assist legitimize street sellers and provide new opportunities to advance up the economic ladder. The Scheme is open to all street vendors in metropolitan areas who start hawking on or before March 24, 2020. The Small Industries Development Bank of India (SIDBI) would be the implementation partner for scheme administration. For scheme implementation, SIDBI will rely on its network of lending institutions, which includes SCBs, RRBs, SFBs, Cooperative Banks, NBFCs, and MFIs.

Ambedkar Social Innovation Incubation Mission (ASIIM)

In 2014-15, the ministry of social justice, government of India, announced the venture capital fund for Scheduled Castes (VCF-SC) with the intention to encourage the entrepreneurship among the scheduled castes and people with disabilities "divyang" youth and enable them to create employment opportunities. Data reveals that approximately 117 enterprises led by SCs have received financial assistance through this scheme. This scheme has also encouraged entrepreneurship among students and provided assistance to establish successful commercial ventures, specifically the young entrepreneurs who were working on Innovative and technology-based business ideas. This scheme would also empower SC students to pursue innovation and business.

Pradhan Matri Kaushal Vikas Yojana (PMKVY)

The participants under this scheme get the support from e-skill India to access the digital learning resources. The digital resources are available in various sectors like automotive, beauty and wellness, construction, gems and jewelry, healthcare, etc. The interested candidates may access the resources of their choice through this scheme.

Make in India

Make in India was another initiative by the Government of India to encourage the entrepreneurs to manufacture products in India, develop modern infrastructure and open the doors for Foreign Capital. This scheme was established to promote the manufacturing sector, and create jobs in manufacturing sector.

PROSPECTS AND CHALLENGES FACING SENIOR ENTREPRENEURSHIP

Entrepreneurship helps in generating additional employment opportunities, enhances standards of living of weaker sections of society and involves participation of all sections of society in the progress of the economy. Governments of many countries have extended the working life of aging population by increasing retirement age. For instance, in Malaysia the retirement age has been increased from 55 to 60 years. Similarly in Indonesia, it has been increased from 56 to 65 years. At present, in India, retirement age in most states in 60 years, except Telangana, where it has been increased from 58 to 61 years recently. A report titled " *India's Demography at 2040: Planning Public Good Provision for the 21st Century*" recommends that increase in retirement age is "inevitable" and must be emphasized to prepare the workforce in advance. These recommendations refer to the state pension age instead of mandatory retirement form workplace. This would assist in curbing dependence on welfare benefits and pensions (Čiutienė & Railaitė, 2014). According to Charness & Czaja (2006), older groups today are much healthier and well educated than the previous generations. They are certainly more active, and intend to stay useful at work much longer.

Biological aging claims that individuals' performance on job and productivity diminishes with increasing age because of reduction in cognitive abilities. According Bal et al. (2011), it is common to think that older workers are less likely to adapt to new tasks, and resist change. More so, when technology and innovation form an essential part of that newly adopted task or job. Skills obsolescence is often related with increasing age and older workforce (Čiutienė & Railaitė, 2014). In this context, Beck (2009) emphasizes that productivity of older workers is not reduced by the age but obsolescence of skills. Unfortunately, no literature has been found that have examined or established the impact of obsolescence on work motivation. One's self- perception of aging can also have contributing effects to the decision of starting an entrepreneurial venture. There are different schools of thoughts on self- perception of age, where one finds its' positively linked with entrepreneurial intentions and the other presents a contradictory view. More empirical research on the subject is essential in order to derive to any conclusions. Another component of psychosocial age is social perception of age including age norms and stereotypes. Several studies have already established shared beliefs regarding age- specific career and type casted jobs for "older people" and "younger people". This social perception, especially in organizational environment among co-workers, superiors and peers may lead to age- discrimination and subsequently non- motivation to continue to work. Alternatively, community is inviting of older people coming into entrepreneurship because of their enhanced experience, networks and other resources (A Maritz et al., 2015; Perenyi et al., 2018).

Taking into consideration the significance of macro- environment factors such as the government policies and schemes, the GEM Report India, 2002 highlights the existence of significant gap between government's entrepreneurial policies planning and its implementation. Lack of coordination was experienced by the organizations delivering entrepreneurial knowledge and training. Perception about government official, inconsistency in plans and policies and ineffective administration were contributed to crucial factors in the gap between planning and implementation. It concludes that entrepreneurial opportunities and readiness certainly exist in India. However, social attitudes, inadequate infrastructure, lack of government support are the barriers towards realization of potential opportunities. Government should plan and focus on such initiative which would alter the present status and improve entrepreneurial environment and activity in the country.

PRACTICAL IMPLICATIONS

The times of crisis have been milestones for interventions and bringing change in the society. For example, as an impact of the 2008 global crisis, nearly 1 million people, in the UK, aged between 50 – 64 years became jobless. As a temporary solution to this problem, many public institutions in the country had begun promoting entrepreneurial activities to the older unemployed population (Garcia, 2015). In a similar vein, the Covid- 19 pandemic has also impacted developed and developing economies alike. Bread- earners of families losing their jobs, also losing their lives, healthcare systems failing, situations getting out of hands of governments. Indian continent was no exception to that. The government and policy makers are still struggling to bring the economy back on track since the lockdown periods are over. With little success, there is still a long and challenging path ahead. It is also observed that as people get older, they refrain from the idea of entrepreneurship, simply because of the fact that "realization of yield or return" is in the long- term. Decline health, levels of energy and reluctance to take financial risk also add on to the resistance towards starting their own enterprise (Garcia, 2015). Management of senior, aging workforce can be one of the tools to support their efforts. Especially focusing toward self- employment of aging workforce. Age management can be explored from macroeconomic labor policies, organizational as well as individual perspective. From a prospective policy point of view, creating awareness and promoting senior entrepreneurship can be one of the ways to engage senior (retired/ non- working) workforce to engage in entrepreneurship (Kautonen et al., 2014). The objectives of such policy could be to enhance entrepreneurial intentions; one's desire to start own business (Perenyi et al., 2018).

On organizational level, companies should device effective HRM systems to tackle age management issue. European union, 2012, p. 37 quotes "if people are to work for a longer period of time, then they will need to be in good physical and mental health, with access to more flexible working arrangements, healthy workplaces, lifelong learning and retirement schemes". In order to maintain competitiveness and enhance core competencies, non- discriminatory (age) recruitment, promotions and training, lifelong learning programme, health and safety programme, flexible form of employment and working hours can be some measures that can be adopted by organizations in order to retain and motivate older workforce (Fabisiak & Prokurat (2012). Technological solutions such as working from home, remote working devices and flexible work practices could be used as tools to encourage older workforce or age management in the organizations. However, since investing such measure especially, on older workforce seem a little riskier from organization point, it is suggested that such interventions must be applied to older workers with high entrepreneurial intentions and motivations (Harms & Ehrmann, 2002). Organizations should also focus on enhancing employees' skills and competencies irrespective of age, as many job-related characteristics are not dependent on age. Organizations should also inspire a culture that positively perceives "older employees" as it helps in enhancing health, work performance, work satisfaction and a willingness to share and disseminate their experience and knowledge (Čiutienė & Railaitė, 2014). Aaltio, Salminen and Koponen (2014) admit that it is incorrect to presume the existing connection between increasing age and deteriorating skills and abilities. As these misguided presumptions lead to encouraging discriminatory behavior amongst organization and the society. It is crucial to comprehend the entrepreneurial motivations of senior employees of an organization. If these motivations are managed and encouraged in the right manner, it may blossom and manifest successful intrapreneurship ventures. On the contrary, if these motivations are not harnessed properly, people may leave the organization with valuable insights and competence (Hatak et al., 2015). It is essential that organizations be the transformation and steer a positive attitudinal change toward the aging workforce. It would also help in altering the existing social perspective on aging and prejudices associated with that. One's self- perception of age as well a social norm associated with age can have huge impacts on decision to continue to work, it is essential that people should be made aware and encouraged about the benefits of self- employment after a certain age. Also, support and incentives from governments may be a huge motivating factor for older people to take up entrepreneurship.

CONCLUSION

It was suggested that chronological age might simply be a proxy or substitution for age- related processes that influence work- related outcomes directly or indirectly (Kanfer & Ackerman, 2004). Individuals of same chronological age may differ in respect to career stage, health, family status and many other factors. Notwithstanding the stereotype that claims that older employees tend to be less ambitious (Curran and Blackburn, 2001), Harms et al., 2014 found resonance with Helyer and Lee (2012), that older entrepreneurs do not exit a company because of insecurities of keeping up with younger co- workers. On the contrary, they are driven away because of non- ambitious and unenterprising employers. Although maximum number of gray entrepreneurs represent themselves as strong individuals, the societal norms toward entrepreneurial behavior does seem to have crucial impact on their decision for starting their own business. Furthermore, the decision to begin a new venture is largely dependent on government policies (macro- environment factor). Government policies not only provide incentives and subsidies to the business, but also technical, marketing and training assistance. Entrepreneurship has numerous advantages, especially for developing economies. The world economies hard- hit by the coronavirus-induced lockdown and economic stoppages, need innovative solutions to manage and come out of the reaping effects of the pandemic. Senior entrepreneurship, although has its own challenges, but cannot be completely overlooked as a measure to manage aging workforce and older population in a country. The governments should device policies and programme to increase awareness about the concept and inspire people to be more risk-taking keeping in mind their self- reliant future. Additionally, corporates should be encouraged to tackle the issue of age management with utmost sensitivity and awareness towards its benefitting outcomes. Human resource managers should focus on develop challenging positions and advancing career options for those who ask for them, regardless of age. Creating work-life balance for older personnel can be another important method of tackling aging workforce problems that must be carefully considered by employers. Lastly, social norms play a great role in motivating mature, older people to make a decision towards self- employment. Hence, social acceptance should systematically be orchestrated through awareness and education programme, training, support and incentives to boost senior entrepreneurship in the country.

Special Eurobarometer 378, 2012 report suggested that older workers arc willing to work after pensionable age. However, retaining older workforce in paid employment has its own problems including discrimination on the basis of age (Franck, 2010; Ainsworth and Hardy, 2013; Kibler et al., 2015; OECD, 2015; Stirzaker and Galloway, 2017), obsolete skills and knowledge, out- of- date work experience (Kenny and Rossiter, 2018) etc. It is, hence, suggested to explore senior entrepreneurship as a viable option which could provide flexible working hours, fulfil the need to be with one's family, and also tackle the issue of age discrimination at workplace. Although, Botham & Graves (2009) suggest that new ventures created before reaching the retirement age have higher changes of growth and survival. But that opinion is based on premise more focused on biological age only, and not inclusive of the wider perspective of aging. Countries can relish the significant advantages of entrepreneurship by encouraging a more diverse population toward self- employment. We suggest that additional research must be geared to address the unique avenues and challenges the older and mature entrepreneurs' encounter.

REFERENCES

Aaltio, I., Salminen, H. M., & Koponen, S. (2014). Ageing employees and human resource management–evidence of gender-sensitivity? *Equality, Diversity and Inclusion*, *33*(2), 160–176. doi:10.1108/EDI-10-2011-0076

Ajzen, I. (1991). The theory of planned behavior. *Organizational Behavior and Human Decision Processes*, *50*(2), 179–211. doi:10.1016/0749-5978(91)90020-T

Amit, R., & Muller, E. (1995). "Push" and "pull" entrepreneurship. *Journal of Small Business and Entrepreneurship*, *12*(4), 64–80. doi:10.1080/08276331.1995.10600505

Anderson, A. R. (2015). Conceptualising entrepreneurship as economic "explanation" and the consequent loss of "understanding.". *International Journal of Business and Globalisation*, *14*(2), 145–157. doi:10.1504/IJBG.2015.067432

Anderson, K. H., & Burkhauser, R. V. (1985). The retirement-health nexus: A new measure of an old puzzle. *The Journal of Human Resources*, *20*(3), 315–330. doi:10.2307/145884

Avolio, B. J., Barrett, G. V., & Sterns, H. L. (1984). Alternatives to age for assessing occupational performance capacity. *Experimental Aging Research*, *10*(2), 101–105. doi:10.1080/03610738408258551 PMID:6499889

Baltes, M. M., & Carstensen, L. L. (1999). Social-psychological theories and their applications to aging: From individual to collective. Handbook of Theories of Aging, 1, 209-226.

Barclays Economic Reports. (2001). *Third Age Entrepreneurs – Profiting from Experience*. Barclays PLC.

Baron, R. A., & Tang, J. (2011). The role of entrepreneurs in Firm-level innovation: Joint effects of Positive affect, Creativity, and environmental dynamism. *Journal of Business Venturing*, *26*(1), 49–60. doi:10.1016/j.jbusvent.2009.06.002

Baucus, D. A., & Human, S. E. (1994). Second-career entrepreneurs: A multiple case study analysis of entrepreneurial processes and antecedent variables, Entrepreneurship. *Theory into Practice*, *19*(2), 41–71.

Beck, V. (2009). *Older Workers–Older Learners: The Perspectives of Employers in the East Midlands*. Learning and Skills Council.

Bloom, D. E., Canning, D., & Fink, G. (2010). Implications of population ageing for economic growth. *Oxford Review of Economic Policy*, *26*(4), 583–612. doi:10.1093/oxrep/grq038

Botham, R., & Graves, A. (2009). *The Grey Economy: How Third Age Entrepreneurs Are Contributing to Growth*. National Endowment for Science, Technology and the Arts (NESTA).

Brunetti, M. J. (2006). The estate tax and the demise of the family business. *Journal of Public Economics*, *90*(10-11), 1975–1993. doi:10.1016/j.jpubeco.2006.05.012

Cannon, T. (2008). Silver entrepreneurship: New days, new ways. *Working with Older People (Brighton, England)*, *12*(2), 30–33. doi:10.1108/13663666200800029

Carstensen, L. L., Fung, H. H., & Charles, S. T. (2003). Socioemotional selectivity theory and the regulation of emotion in the second half of life. *Motivation and Emotion*, *27*(2), 103–123. doi:10.1023/A:1024569803230

Carstensen, L. L., Isaacowitz, D. M., & Charles, S. T. (1999). Taking time seriously: A theory of socioemotional selectivity. *The American Psychologist*, *54*(3), 165–181. doi:10.1037/0003-066X.54.3.165 PMID:10199217

Charness, N., & Czaja, S. J. (2006). *Older Worker Training: What We Know and Don't Know. #2006-22*. AARP.

ChristelisD.FonsecaR. (2016). Labor market policies and self-employment transitions of older workers. *Available at* SSRN 2837804. doi:10.2139/ssrn.2837804

Čiutienė, R., & Railaitė, R. (2014). Challenges of Managing an Ageing Workforce. *Procedia: Social and Behavioral Sciences*, *156*(April), 69–73. doi:10.1016/j.sbspro.2014.11.121

Cohn, R. M. (1979). Age and the satisfactions from work. *Journal of Gerontology*, *34*(2), 264–272. doi:10.1093/geronj/34.2.264 PMID:438481

Curran, J., & Blackburn, R. A. (2001). Older people and the enterprise society: Age and self-employment propensities. *Work, Employment and Society*, *15*(4), 889–902. doi:10.1177/095001701400438279

de Lange, A. H., Taris, T. W., Jansen, P. G. W., Smulders, P., Houtman, I. L. D., & Kompier, M. A. J. (2006). Age as a factor in the relation between work and mental health: results from the longitudinal TAS study. In J. Houdmont & S. McIntyre (Eds.), *Occupational Health Psychology: European Perspectives on Research, Education and Practice* (Vol. 1, pp. 21–45). ISMAI Publications.

Eurobarometer, S. (2012). Active Ageing–Report. European Commission, (378).

Europeia, C. (2013). *Entrepreneurship 2020 action plan*. Communication from the Commission to the European Parliament, The Council, The European Economic and Social Committee and the Committee of the Regions.

Eurostat. (2011). *Active ageing and solidarity between generations: A statistical portrait of the European Union 2012*. Publications office of the European Union.

Evans, D. S., & Leighton, L. S. (1989). The determinants of changes in US self-employment, 1968–1987. *Small Business Economics*, *1*(2), 111–119. doi:10.1007/BF00398629

Fabisiak, J., & Prokurat, S. (2012). Age management as a tool for the demographic decline in the 21st century: An overview of its characteristics. *Journal of Entrepreneurship Management and Innovation*, *8*(4), 83–96.

Farr, J. L., Tesluk, P. E., & Klein, S. R. (1998). Organizational structure of the workplace and the older worker. *Impact of Work on Older Adults*, 143-185.

Feeser, H. R., & Dugan, K. W. (1989). Entrepreneurial motivation: a comparison of high and low growth high tech founders. *Frontiers of Entrepreneurship Research, 9*(1), 13-27.

Figueiredo, E., & Paiva, T. (2019). Senior entrepreneurship and qualified senior unemployment: The case of the Portuguese Northern region. *Journal of Small Business and Enterprise Development*, *26*(3), 342–362. doi:10.1108/JSBED-01-2018-0006

Fonseca, R., & Parker, S. C. (2019). Entrepreneurship among older workers: International evidence. Handbook of Research on Entrepreneurship and Aging, 23–51. doi:10.4337/9781788116213.00007

Fossum, J. A., Arvey, R. D., Paradise, C. A., & Robbins, N. E. (1986). Modeling the skills obsolescence process: A psychological/economic integration. *Academy of Management Review*, *11*(2), 362–374. doi:10.2307/258466

Galloway, L., & Cooney, T. M. (2012). Introduction. *International Journal of Entrepreneurship and Innovation*, *13*(2), 77–79. doi:10.5367/ijei.2012.0080

Garcia, L. (2015). *Why do older entrepreneurs face unique challenges?* Academic Press.

Gist, M., Rosen, B., & Schwoerer, C. (1988). The influence of training method and trainee age on the acquisition of computer skills. *Personnel Psychology*, *41*(2), 255–265. doi:10.1111/j.1744-6570.1988.tb02384.x

Grossmann, V., & Strulik, H. (2010). Should continued family firms face lower taxes than other estates? *Journal of Public Economics*, *94*(1-2), 87–101. doi:10.1016/j.jpubeco.2009.10.005

Gruenfeld, L. W. (1962). A study of the motivation of industrial supervisors. *Personnel Psychology*, *15*(3), 303–315. doi:10.1111/j.1744-6570.1962.tb01625.x

Hall, D. T., & Nougaim, K. E. (1968). An examination of Maslow's need hierarchy in an organizational setting. *Organizational Behavior and Human Performance*, *3*(1), 12–35. doi:10.1016/0030-5073(68)90024-X

Harms, R., & Ehrmann, T. (2003). The performance implications of entrepreneurial management: linking Stevenson's and Miller's conceptualization to growth. In *Babson Kauffman Research Conference on Entrepreneurship*. Babson College.

Harms, R., Luck, F., Kraus, S., & Walsh, S. (2014). On the motivational drivers of gray entrepreneurship: An exploratory study. *Technological Forecasting and Social Change*, *89*, 358–365. doi:10.1016/j.techfore.2014.08.001

Hart, M., Anyadike-Danes, M., & Blackburn, R. (2004). Entrepreneurship and age in the UK: Comparing third age and prime age new venture creation across the regions. REnT xvIII, 25-26.

Hatak, I., Harms, R., & Fink, M. (2015). Age, job identification, and entrepreneurial intention. *Journal of Managerial Psychology*, *30*(1), 38–53. doi:10.1108/JMP-07-2014-0213

Hayward, M. D., Grady, W. R., Hardy, M. A., & Sommers, D. (1989). Occupational influences on retirement, disability, and death. *Demography*, *26*(3), 393–409. doi:10.2307/2061600 PMID:2529146

Helyer, R., & Lee, D. (2012). The twenty-first century multiple generation workforce: Overlaps and differences but also challenges and benefits. *Education + Training*, *54*(7), 565–578. doi:10.1108/00400911211265611

Henkens, K., & Tazelaar, F. (1997). Explaining retirement decisions of civil servants in the Netherlands: Intentions, behavior; and the discrepancy between the two. *Research on Aging*, *19*(2), 139–173. doi:10.1177/0164027597192001

Higgs, P., Mein, G., Ferrie, J., Hyde, M., & Nazroo, J. (2003). Pathways to early retirement: Structure and agency in decision-making among British civil servants. *Ageing and Society*, *23*(6), 761–778. doi:10.1017/S0144686X03001326

Holahan, C. K. (1988). Relation of life goals at age 70 to activity participation and health and psychological well-being among Terman's gifted men and women. *Psychology and Aging*, *3*(3), 286–291. doi:10.1037/0882-7974.3.3.286 PMID:3268271

India-Age dependency ratio. (n.d.). *Indexmundi*. https://www.indexmundi.com/facts/india/age-dependency-ratio

Kanfer, R., & Ackerman, P. L. (2004). Aging, Adult Development, and Work Motivation. *Academy of Management Review*, *29*(3), 440–458. doi:10.2307/20159053

Kato, S., & Wiklund, J. (2011). Doing Good to Feel Good—A theory of entrepreneurial action based in Hedonic Psychology. *Frontiers of Entrepreneurship Research*, *31*(4), 123–137.

Kautonen, T., Down, S., & Minniti, M. (2014). Ageing and entrepreneurial preferences. *Small Business Economics*, *42*(3), 579–594. doi:10.100711187-013-9489-5

Kautonen, T., Kibler, E., & Minniti, M. (2017). Late-career entrepreneurship, income and quality of life. *Journal of Business Venturing*, *32*(3), 318–333. doi:10.1016/j.jbusvent.2017.02.005

Kautonen, T., Luoto, S., & Tornikoski, E. T. (2010). Influence of work history on entrepreneurial intentions in 'prime age'and 'third age': A preliminary study. *International Small Business Journal*, *28*(6), 583–601. doi:10.1177/0266242610368592

Kautonen, T., Tornikoski, E. T., & Kibler, E. (2011). Entrepreneurial intentions in the third age: The impact of perceived age norms. *Small Business Economics*, *37*(2), 219–234. doi:10.100711187-009-9238-y

Kelly, R., Hayward, C., Avolio, A., & O'rourke, M. (1989). Noninvasive determination of age-related changes in the human arterial pulse. *Circulation*, *80*(6), 1652–1659. doi:10.1161/01.CIR.80.6.1652 PMID:2598428

Kooij, D., de Lange, A., Jansen, P., & Dikkers, J. (2008). Older workers' motivation to continue to work: Five meanings of age: A conceptual review. *Journal of Managerial Psychology*, *23*(4), 364–394. doi:10.1108/02683940810869015

Lang, F. R., & Carstensen, L. L. (2002). Time counts: Future time perspective, goals, and social relationships. *Psychology and Aging*, *17*(1), 125–139. doi:10.1037/0882-7974.17.1.125 PMID:11931281

Lévesque, M., & Minniti, M. (2006). The effect of aging on entrepreneurial behavior. *Journal of Business Venturing*, *21*(2), 177–194. doi:10.1016/j.jbusvent.2005.04.003

Lewis, K., & Walker, E. (2013). Third age self-employment: A business assistance perspective. *Journal of Small Business and Enterprise Development*, *20*(2), 399–419. doi:10.1108/14626001311326798

Liang, J., Wang, H., & Lazear, E. P. (2018). Demographics and entrepreneurship. *Journal of Political Economy, 126*, S140–S196. doi:10.1086/698750

Logan, J., Hendry, C., Brown, J., & Courtney, N. (2009). *Barriers and pathways to entrepreneurship and innovation*. Academic Press.

Logan, J., Hendry, C., Courtney, N., & Brown, J. (2008). *Unlocking the potential of the UK's Hidden Innovators*. Cass Business School.

London, M. (1990). Enhancing career motivation in late career. *Journal of Organizational Change Management*, *3*(2), 58–71. doi:10.1108/09534819010001351

Maritz, A., Perenyi, A., de Waal, G., & Buck, C. (2020). Entrepreneurship as the unsung hero during the current COVID-19 economic crisis: Australian perspectives. *Sustainability (Switzerland)*, *12*(11), 4612. Advance online publication. doi:10.3390u12114612

Maritz, A, Zolin, R., De Waal, G., Fisher, R., Perenyi, A., & Eager, B. (2015, Sept.). Senior entrepreneurship in Australia: Active ageing and extending working lives. *International Journal of Organizational Innovation,* 1–39.

Mayhew, W. (2014). Seniorpreneurs are the fastest growing segment of entrepreneurship. *PivotMagazine.* http://www.pivotmagazine.ca/2014/seniorpreneurs/

Misachi, J. (2021). The population of India. *Worldatlas.* https://www.worldatlas.com/geography/the-population-of-india-an-overview.html

Moulton, J. G., & Scott, J. C. (2016). Opportunity or necessity? Disaggregating self-employment and entry at older ages. *Social Forces*, *94*(4), 1539–1566. doi:10.1093fow026

Mouraviev, N., & Avramenko, A. (2020). Senior Entrepreneurship: Ageing, Entrepreneurial Identity, Behaviour and Challenges. *Entrepreneurship for Deprived Communities*, 67–93. doi:10.1108/978-1-78973-985-520201005

Muijnck, J. A., & Zwinkels, W. S. (2002). Older Employees in SME's: A Literature Review on the Use of Older Employees. In Onderzoek voor Bedrijf & Beleid, Zoetermeer. EIM.

Noe, R. A., Noe, A. W., & Bachhuber, J. A. (1990). An investigation of the correlates of career motivation. *Journal of Vocational Behavior*, *37*(3), 340–356. doi:10.1016/0001-8791(90)90049-8

OECD. (2017). *Social security contributions (indicator)*. doi:10.1787/3ebfe901-en

Parker, S. C., & Rougier, J. C. (2007). The retirement behaviour of the self-employed in Britain. *Applied Economics*, *39*(6), 697–713. doi:10.1080/00036840500447807

Parker, S. C., & Rougier, J. C. (2007). The retirement behaviour of the self-employed in Britain. *Applied Economics*, *39*(6), 697–713. doi:10.1080/00036840500447807

Patel, S. H., & Grey, C. (2006). *Grey Entrepreneurs in the UK; IKO Working Paper No. 18.* Open University Research Centre on Innovation, Knowledge and Development. Milton Keynes: Open University.

Perenyi, A., Zolin, R., & Maritz, A. (2018). The perceptions of Australian senior entrepreneurs on the drivers of their entrepreneurial activity. *International Journal of Entrepreneurial Behaviour & Research*, *24*(1), 81–103. doi:10.1108/IJEBR-12-2016-0424

Pinder, C. (1998). *Work motivation in organizational behavior*. Prentice Hall.

Pratt, M. W., Norris, J. E., Arnold, M. L., & Filyer, R. (1999). Generativity and moral development as predictors of value-socialization narratives for young persons across the adult life span: From lessons learned to stories shared. *Psychology and Aging*, *14*(3), 414–426. doi:10.1037/0882-7974.14.3.414 PMID:10509696

Ratten, V. (2019). Older entrepreneurship: A literature review and research agenda. *Journal of Enterprising Communities: People and Places in the Global Economy*, *13*(1/2), 178–195. doi:10.1108/JEC-08-2018-0054

Robinson, E. (2015). Perceived social norms and eating behaviour: An evaluation of studies and future directions. *Physiology & Behavior*, *152*, 397–401. doi:10.1016/j.physbeh.2015.06.010 PMID:26072177

Robinson, E. (2015). Perceived social norms and eating behaviour: An evaluation of studies and future directions. *Physiology & Behavior*, *152*, 397–401. doi:10.1016/j.physbeh.2015.06.010 PMID:26072177

Roehrich, J. K., Lewis, M. A., & George, G. (2014). Are public–private partnerships a healthy option? A systematic literature review. *Social Science & Medicine*, *113*, 110–119. doi:10.1016/j.socscimed.2014.03.037 PMID:24861412

Saba, T., & Guerin, G. (2005). Extending employment beyond retirement age: The case of health care managers in Quebec. *Public Personnel Management*, *34*(2), 195–214. doi:10.1177/009102600503400205

Saleh, S. D., & Otis, J. L. (1964). Age and level of job satisfaction. *Personnel Psychology*, *17*(4), 425–430. doi:10.1111/j.1744-6570.1964.tb00077.x

Schepers, J., Voordeckers, W., Steijvers, T., & Laveren, E. (2014). The entrepreneurial orientation-performance relationship in private family firms: The moderating role of socioemotional wealth. *Small Business Economics*, *43*(1), 39–55. doi:10.100711187-013-9533-5

Schøtt, T., Rogoff, E., Herrington, M., & Kew, P. (2017). *GEM Special Report on Senior Entrepreneurship 2017*. Global Entrepreneurship Research Association.

Schwab, D. P., & Heneman, H. G. III. (1977). Age and satisfaction with dimensions of work. *Journal of Vocational Behavior*, *10*(2), 212–220. doi:10.1016/0001-8791(77)90058-6

Sengupta, S., Sahay, A., & Croce, F. (2018). Conceptualizing social entrepreneurship in the context of emerging economies: An integrative review of past research from BRIICS. *The International Entrepreneurship and Management Journal*, *14*(4), 771–803. doi:10.100711365-017-0483-2

Settersten, R. A. Jr, & Mayer, K. U. (1997). The measurement of age, age structuring, and the life course. *Annual Review of Sociology*, *23*(1), 233–261. doi:10.1146/annurev.soc.23.1.233

Shapero, A., & Sokol, L. (1982). *The social dimensions of entrepreneurship. University of Illinois at Urbana-Champaign's Academy for Entrepreneurial Leadership Historical Research Reference in Entrepreneurship*. Prentice Hall.

Singh, R. (2009). The aging population and mature entrepreneurs: Market trends and implications for entrepreneurship. *New England Journal of Entrepreneurship*, *12*(1), 45–53. doi:10.1108/NEJE-12-01-2009-B004

Smith, D. B., & Moen, P. (1998). Spousal influence on retirement: His, her, and their perceptions. *Journal of Marriage and Family*, *60*(3), 734–744. doi:10.2307/353542

Sterns, H. L., & Alexander, R. A. (1987). Industrial gerontology: the aging individual and work. In K. W. Schaie (Ed.), *Annual Review of Gerontology and Geriatrics* (Vol. 7, pp. 243–264). Springer Publishing Company.

Sterns, H. L., & Doverspike, D. (1989). Aging and the retraining and learning process in organizations. In I. Goldstein & R. Katze (Eds.), *Training and Development in Work Organizations* (pp. 299–332). Jossey-Bass.

Sterns, H. L., & Miklos, S. M. (1995). The aging worker in a changing environment: Organizational and Individual Issues. *Journal of Vocational Behavior*, *47*(3), 248–268. doi:10.1006/jvbe.1995.0003

Stirzaker, R. J., & Galloway, L. (2017). Ageing and redundancy and the silver lining of entrepreneurship. *International Journal of Entrepreneurship and Innovation*, *18*(2), 105–114. doi:10.1177/1465750317706441

Stypińska, J., Franke, A., & Myrczik, J. (2019, April). Senior Entrepreneurship: The Unrevealed Driver for Social Innovation. *Frontiers in Sociology*, *4*, 1–16. doi:10.3389/fsoc.2019.00030 PMID:33869354

Super, D. E. (1984). Career and life development. In D. Brown & L. Brooks (Eds.), *Career Choice Development*. Jossey-Bass.

Torraco, R. J. (2005). Writing integrative literature reviews: Guidelines and examples. *Human Resource Development Review*, *4*(3), 356–367.

Tranfield, D., Denyer, D., & Smart, P. (2003). Towards a methodology for developing evidence-informed management knowledge by means of systematic review. *British Journal of Management*, *14*(3), 207–222.

Valentine, S., Valentine, W. R., & Dick, J. (1998). Intrinsic and extrinsic motivators and older employees' attitudes towards their current jobs. *Perceptual and Motor Skills*, *87*(2), 407–410.

Vallerand, R. J., O'Connor, B. P., & Hamel, M. (1995). Motivation in later life: Theory and assessment. *International Journal of Aging & Human Development*, *41*(3), 221–238.

Vandemaele, S., & Vancauteren, M. (2015). Nonfinancial goals, governance, and dividend payout in private family firms. *Journal of Small Business Management*, *53*(1), 166–182.

Wainwright, T., Kibler, E., Blackburn, R., & Kautonen, T. (2011). Who are you calling old?: revisiting notions of age and ability amongst older entrepreneurs. *34th Institute for Small Business and Entrepreneurship (ISBE) Annual Conference: Sustainable futures: enterprising landscapes and communities.*

Watkins-Mathys, L. (2012). Age and grey entrepreneurship. In *Lessons on Profiting from Diversity* (pp. 94–113). Palgrave Macmillan.

Weber, P., & Schaper, M. (2004). Understanding the grey entrepreneur. *Journal of Enterprising Culture*, *12*(2), 147–164.

Webster, J., & Watson, R. T. (2002). Analyzing the past to prepare for the future: Writing a literature review. *Management Information Systems Quarterly*, xiii–xxiii.

Wiklund, J., & Shepherd, D. (2003). Knowledge-based resources, entrepreneurial orientation, and the performance of small and medium-sized businesses. *Strategic Management Journal*, *24*(13), 1307–1314. https://doi.org/10.1002/smj.360

Wolf, G., London, M., Casey, J., & Pufahl, J. (1995). Career experience and motivation as predictors of training behaviors and outcomes for displaced engineers. *Journal of Vocational Behavior*, *47*(3), 316–331.

Zhao, H., O'Connor, G., Wu, J., & Lumpkin, G. T. (2021). Age and entrepreneurial career success: A review and a meta-analysis. *Journal of Business Venturing*, *36*(1), 106007. https://doi.org/10.1016/j.jbusvent.2020.106007

KEY TERMS AND DEFINITIONS

Age Dependency Ratio: Ratio of the population not included in working force, usually ages 0 to 14 years and 65 years and older and those which constitutes the typical working population, usually ages 15 to 64 years.

Aging Workforce: Part of workforce over and above 40 years of age.

GEM Report: Global Entrepreneurship Monitor report was prepared as a result of a comprehensive survey conducted covering 37 countries and 3/5th of total world's population. The report presented assessment about the entrepreneurial activities covering about 460 million adult entrepreneurs worldwide.

HRM: Human resource management.

OECD: Organization for Economic Co-operation and Development

SST: Socio-economic selectivity theory.

TPB: Theory of planned behavior.

Chapter 4
LAD Regression Application: Factors Affecting Household Expenditures of Working Elderly in Turkey

Kübranur Çebi Karaaslan
https://orcid.org/0000-0001-9288-017X
Erzurum Technical University, Turkey

ABSTRACT

Household expenditures are important indicators in many aspects, especially in the economic growth of a country. One of the most important determinants of expenditures is the head of the household working within the framework of the household's income. From this point of view, the aim of the study is to determine the factors affecting the household expenditures of the heads of the household who are 60 years of age and older living in Turkey. In this framework, the data set of the Household Budget Survey of the Turkish Statistical Institute was used for the years 2015-2019. The least absolute deviation regression was used for the data set analysis. As a result of the study, it was determined that the gender of the head of the household, educational status, economic indicators, especially income, and social indicators were effective on the expenditures of the households. The results of the study provide valuable information to researchers, decision-makers, and policymakers who want to study this issue to understand the household spending patterns of working elderly household heads.

INTRODUCTION

Consumption is the sum of households' expenditures on goods and services to meet their needs. Consumption, that is, household expenditures, covers a significant part of the gross domestic product (Türkbal, 2005; Ünsal, 2013). In addition to showing the welfare level of the society where the households live, the expenditures of the households also affect many important economic issues such as economic development and policy planning. Any information on the expenditure values of households is undoubtedly of great importance for policymakers and decision-makers. Household expenditures are affected by many factors such as the age of the head of the household, in other words, the life cycle stage that is considered to be in the first place, the structure of the household, and the income level. Likewise, the

DOI: 10.4018/978-1-7998-2395-7.ch004

Copyright © 2022, IGI Global. Copying or distributing in print or electronic forms without written permission of IGI Global is prohibited.

relationship between the ages of individuals and their expenditures has been a remarkable phenomenon in terms of economics. The life cycle hypothesis of Franco Modigliani and his student, which has a very important place in the economic literature, was formed on the basis of the idea of how much people want to spend at what age (Deaton, 2005). Therefore, in the study, all the variables that are thought to affect the household expenditure values were determined with the help of the literature, and it was progressed on the focus of the variables of age and working status in terms of the dependent variable.

Studies in recent years have focused on online spending, and in this case, it means having information at the level of the young population where technological literacy is high. Although Turkey is in a country where the young population is higher compared to the elderly population, creating an econometric perspective that takes into account the expenditures of the elderly population has been the main motivation source of the study in order not to overlook a remarkable expenditure value. In the literature, individuals aged 60 and 65 are classified as elderly (Axelson and Penfield 1983; Host et al., 2016; Moehrle, 1990). Working elderly individuals are not passive consumers.

The aim of this study is to determine the factors that affect the household expenditures of the heads of the household aged 60 and over living in Turkey. In this framework, the Household Budget Survey data set of the Turkish Statistical Institute was used. When households are mentioned, it should be considered that each member of the household is considered. In order to make the data set suitable for econometric analysis, first, the total consumption values of the individual in each household were calculated, and then the consumption values of the individuals in the same household were summed to obtain the total consumption expenditures of the relevant household. Subsequently, from the data set obtained, considering the working status and age values of the household heads, the data belonging to the household heads who are working and at the same time aged 60 and over were filtered and the data set to be used for analysis was created. After the introduction part of the study, a literature summary is involved in section 2. In section 3, the methodology and data set used in the study are described. section 4 contains the findings, and, finally, in section 5, the conclusions are included.

LITERATURE REVIEW

There are many studies on household expenditure items from past to present (Bellante and Foster, 1984; Bryant, 1988; Cook et al, 1995; Jacobs et al, 1989; Koelln et al, 1995; Paulin, 2000; Rubin and Koelln, 1996; Strober and Weinberg, 1977; Yen, 1993; Weinberg and Winer, 1983). In this section, summaries of some of these studies will be presented.

Expenditure patterns of elderly individuals were examined by Chung and Magrabi (1990). The data set of the study was obtained through the 1986 Consumer Expenditure Survey. Multiple regression analysis was applied in the study. As a result of the study, it was determined that age is an important factor in expenditures, compared to younger households, older households spend more on public services, care, and domestic services, and less on clothing, housing, and entertainment. In addition, it has been identified that there is no statistically significant difference between old and young individuals in terms of eating at home and making food expenditures outside.

Factors affecting household expenditures were examined by Soberon-Ferrer and Dardis (1991). Data obtained from the United States Consumer Expenditure Surveys were used in the study. As a result of the study, it was determined that households with full-time and part-time working spouses have significant differences in their expenditures on childcare, dining out, and total services, and that the effects of other variables such as family life cycle, education, race, and geographical location do not differ from according to the service category and employment status of the spouse.

A study was conducted by Abdel-Ghany and Sharpe (1997) on the consumption patterns of elderly individuals. The data set of the study was obtained from the Consumer Expenditure Survey in the United States. The multivariate tobit regression model was used in the study. In the study, households with people aged 65-74 and people aged 75 and over were divided into two groups. As a result of the study, it has been determined that there are significant differences in expenditures for food at home, eating out, alcohol and tobacco, housing, clothing, transportation, entertainment, and self-care.

The examination related to the household expenditures of men and women was made by Phipps and Burton (1998). The study uses microdata from the 1992 Statistics Canada Family Expenditure Survey. As a result of the study, it has been determined that traditional gender roles are important, expenditures for childcare increase only with the increase in women's income, and spouses are more likely to use their own income for private consumption items.

A study was conducted by Denton et al. (2002) on the consumption expenditures of the elderly population. Canada Family Expenditure Surveys were used to collect data in the study. As a result of the study, it has been determined that the changes observed in the budget allocations of elderly individuals are mostly associated with decreases in income.

Ong et al., (2008) examined the expenditure patterns of elderly consumers. 1500 elderly individuals were included in the study. As a result of the study, it has been determined that the elderly spend the most on food, followed by rent, fuel, and electricity, these expenditure items make up 67% of their monthly expenditures, leaving relatively little usable income for other potential purchasing decisions.

A review of household expenditures was made by Song (2008). Survey data collected by the Institute of Economics of the Chinese Academy of Social Sciences were used in the study. According to the results of the study, it was determined that women's bargaining abilities changed their expenditure patterns, and young men were more sensitive to household health expenditures compared to young girls.

Çağlayan and Astar (2012) investigated the determinants of household consumption expenditures in Turkey. The data set of the study was obtained from the household consumption expenditures survey of the Turkish Statistical Institute in 2009. As a result of the study, regardless of the rural-urban distinction, the consumption expenditures of men are lower than the consumption expenditures of women, the consumption expenditures increase as income increases, the consumption expenditures in urban areas are higher than in rural areas, and the variables of age, income, marital status, insurance, and household size in rural areas are statistically significant, and it has been determined that as age increases, while consumption expenditures increase in urban areas, consumption expenditures decrease in rural areas.

A study was conducted by Ong (2012) on the grocery shopping of elderly individuals. In the study, the household survey covering Peninsular Malaysia was conducted in urban and rural areas. 537 individuals were included in the study. As a result of the study, it was determined that the elderly tend to shop in supermarkets and weekend/night markets alone or with their spouses, the most important criterion for purchasing decisions is quality, the least important criterion is brand, leisure activities are watching television, reading books, gardening, and exercising.

Socioeconomic determinants of household expenditures were investigated by Sekhampu and Niyimbanira (2013). In the study, a survey was conducted in Bophelong, South Africa. Multiple regression analysis was applied in the study. According to the results of the study, it was determined that household income, household size, number of working people in the household, employment status, and education level of the head of the household create a strong positive effect on household expenditures. In addition, the marital status of the head of the household was associated with a negative impact on household expenditures. It was detected that the gender and age of the head of the household had no effect on the differences in household expenditures.

A study on the household expenditures of working spouses was conducted by Bodur and Avcı (2015). The data set of the study was obtained from the 2003 Household Budget Survey of Turkey. The Tobit regression model was used in the study. As a result of the study, it has been determined that while the wage rates of the spouses have no statistically significant effect on food away from home, processed food, and entertainment-culture expenditures, they have a statistically significant effect on personal care expenditures. Besides, while the age of women did not have a statistically significant effect on expenditures, it was also determined that the education level of women increased their food away from home, personal care, and entertainment-culture expenditures.

The out-of-pocket expenditures of individuals during the COVID-19 pandemic were examined by Erişen and Yılmaz (2020). In the study, 484 people were surveyed and SPSS 20 package program was used to analyze the data. Mann Whitney U and Pearson Correlation analysis were used to analyze the data. As a result of the study, it was determined that 436.1 TL for health, 1011.9 TL for other expenditure items, and a total of 1163.3 TL was spent on average, and the expenditures differed according to age, marital status, gender, and the status of being diagnosed with COVID-19.

Household consumption expenditures were analyzed by Topal and Çağlayan Akay (2021). The data set of the study was obtained through the 2018 Turkey Household Budget Survey. In the study, the least-squares method, least absolute deviation, least absolute reduction, and selection operator methods were used. According to the results of the study, income, savings, and household size increase household consumption expenditures for all models, and it has been determined that in the LAD-LASSO model, various variables such as kitchen, bathroom floors, heating, air conditioning preferences, energy sources used, detached house, apartment, summer house, credit card usage, internet shopping habits are the determinants of household consumption expenditures.

MATERIALS AND METHODS

Data

In this study, the data set obtained from the Household Budget Survey conducted by the Turkish Statistical Institute between 2015-2019 was used. The geographical scope of the data set covers all settlements within the borders of the Republic of Turkey. In the study, those included in the institutional population and the nomadic population were excluded. The main sampling framework applied in the selection of blocks, which is the primary step sampling unit in the Household Budget Survey, is the National Address Database. Blocks were determined with probability, proportional to the size of the settlement from urban areas, rural areas with a municipal organization and villages, and the households from each block were systematically selected. The stratified two-stage cluster sampling method was used as the sampling method. In addition, the sampling structure was created in accordance with the purpose of giving estimates based on Turkey. The head of the household in the definition of the dependent variable in the study is the individual who is responsible for the income and expenses of the household, manages the household, can make legal, social, and economic decisions on behalf of the household, and plays a superior and active role than other individuals (TUIK, 2021). From the data set for the years 2015-2019, 4644 household heads aged 60 and over who were currently working were included in the study.

Measure and Variables

The dependent variable of the study is the household's total monthly expenditure. Since the inflation rate changes over the years, inflation adjustments have been made to the expenditure and income variables.

Factors related to demographic, economic, and social characteristics that may affect the total expenditure values of the households are considered as independent variables. The demographic factors are the gender (male, female), educational status (did not finish a school-primary school; secondary school; high school; the university), marital status (never married; married; widowed/divorced) of the household responsible person and household size variables.

Annual disposable inflation-adjusted income of the household, type of house (detached house; apartment), second home ownership (yes; no), number of automobiles, saving status (yes; no), inflation-adjusted lighting expenditure, inflation-adjusted heating and kitchen expenditure and inflation-adjusted fuel expenditure for vehicle variables are economic factors.

Social factors are whether there is a person who has the habit of using a credit card (yes; no), whether there is an individual who has the habit of going to the farmer market (yes; no), whether there is an individual who has a habit of smoking (yes; no), whether there is an individual who has a habit of using alcohol. (yes; no), whether there is a person who has the habit of eating out, (yes; no), whether there is an individual who has the habit of going to places such as a coffee house, cafe, local, internet cafe etc. (yes; no), and whether there is an individual who has the habit of buying daily newspapers (yes; no) as variables.

Research Method

The data set of the study was made ready for statistical analysis through the Microsoft Excel program and then Stata 14.1 program was used to make the necessary analysis.

In the study, in which the factors affecting the expenditures of the households were investigated, first of all, the variables and descriptive statistics used for the households participating in the research were investigated. Then, by applying Least Absolute Deviation (LAD) regression analysis, the factors affecting the total expenditures of the households were identified.

RESULT

Descriptive Statistic

The independent variables that may have an impact on the total expenditures of households in Turkey were selected based on the available literature and the availability in our data set. The category definitions and descriptive statistics of the independent variables used in the econometric analysis are presented in Tables 1 and 2.

Table 1. List and description of the modeled variables

Variables		n (%)	Frequency
Demographic indicators			
Gender			
1	Male	93.26	4331
2	Female	6.74	313
Education Status			
1	Did Not Finish A School-Primary School	42.59	1978
2	Secondary school	39.51	1835
3	High school	6.35	295
4	University	11.54	536
Marital status			
1	Never Married	0.78	36
2	Married	89.04	4135
3	Divorced - Widowed	10.19	473
Economic indicators			
House Type			
1	Detached	72.03	3345
2	Apartment	27.97	1299
Second Home Ownership			
1	Yes	15.44	717
2	No	84.56	3927
Saving Status			
1	Yes	40.09	1862
2	No	59.91	2782
Social indicators			
The Habit of Using a Credit Card			
1	Yes	36.50	1695
2	No	63.50	2949
The Habit of Going to the Farmer Market			
1	Yes	64.13	2978
2	No	35.87	1666
The Habit of Smoking			
1	Yes	42.53	1975
2	No	57.47	2669
The Habit of Using Alcohol			
1	Yes	5.51	256
2	No	94.49	4388
The Habit of Eating Out			
1	Yes	25.58	1188

Continued on following page

Table 1. Continued

Variables		n (%)	Frequency
2	No	74.42	3456
The Habit of Going to the Cafe			
1	Yes	33.12	1538
2	No	66.88	3106
The Habit of Buying Daily Newspapers			
1	Yes	5.25	244
2	No	94.75	4400

The majority (93.26%) of the heads of the household working at the age of 60 and over are male, 11.54% of them are university graduates, and 89.04% of them are married. 72.03% of the participants, who attended the study, live in a detached house, 15.44% have a second home, 40.09% of them practice economy, and 36.41% of them use credit cards. 63.50% of the household heads have the habit of going to the farmer market, 42.53% have the habit of smoking, 5.51% have the habit of alcohol use, 25.58% have the habit of eating out, 33.12% have the habit of going to the cafe, 5.25% have the habit of buying daily newspapers.

Table 2. List and description of the modeled variables

Variables	Mean	Standard Deviation
Household Expenditure (₺)	4326.549	4149.042
Number of Automobiles	0.482	0.574
Household Size	2.955	1.831
Income	66588.820	67165.480
Lighting Expenditure	109.782	127.952
Heating and Kitchen Expenditure	168.864	167.750
Fuel Expenditure for Vehicle	182.181	270.882

Households with household heads aged 60 and over have an average monthly expenditure of 4326.549₺, lighting expenditure an average of 109.782₺, heating and kitchen expenditure an average of 168.864₺, fuel expenditure for vehicle an average of 182.181₺ and monthly annual income an average of 66588.82₺. In addition, the number of cars in the households is an average of 0.482, and the average household size is 2.955.

Figure 1 indicates the distribution of household expenditures in Turkey with an average of 4326.549₺, and a standard deviation of 4149,042₺. We can observe that the distribution is asymmetrical and indicates a right-skewed average household expenditure.

Figure 1. Histogram curve showing total expenditure distribution

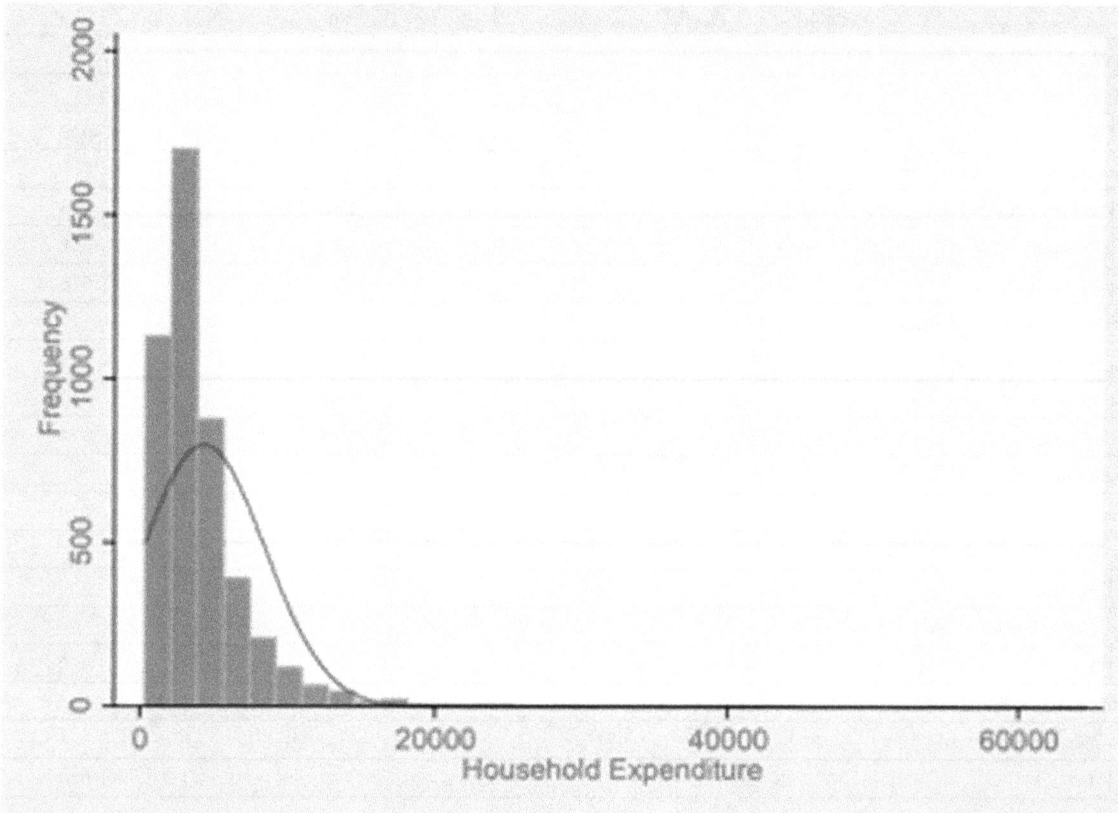

Estimation of Models

The ordinary least squares (OLS) method was primarily applied to determine the factors affecting the expenditures of the households included in the study. Then, the assumptions of the ordinary least squares method were tested. First, a multicollinearity test was performed. The variance inflation factor (Vif) being less than 5 indicates that there is no multicollinearity problem (Çebi Karaaslan, Oktay & Alkan, 2022). Table 3 exhibits the Vif values of the independent variables. When the Vif values of the independent variables used in the study are examined, they are all less than 5. Thus, there is no independent variable that causes the multicollinearity problem.

Table 3. Variance inflation factor

Variables		Vif	1/Vif
Demographic indicators			
Gender (reference: female)			
	Male	1.70	0.59
Education Status (reference: university)			
	Did Not Finish A School-Primary School	3.82	0.26
	Secondary School	3.58	0.28
	High School	1.52	0.66
Marital Status (reference: married)			
	Never Married	1.05	0.96
	Divorced - Widowed	1.68	0.59
Household Size		1.19	0.84
Economic indicators			
Income		1.66	0.60
House Type (reference: detached house)			
	Apartment	1.36	0.74
Second Home Ownership (reference: no)			
	Yes	1.11	0.90
Number of Automobile		1.82	0.55
Saving Status (reference: no)			
	Yes	1.12	0.89
Lighting Expenditure		1.16	0.86
Heating and Kitchen Expenditure		1.07	0.93
Fuel Expenditure for Vehicle		1.93	0.52
Social indicators			
The Habit of Using a Credit Card (reference: no)			
	Yes	1.43	0.70
The Habit of Going to the Farmer Market(reference: no)			
	Yes	1.09	0.92
The Habit of Smoking(reference: no)			
	Yes	1.12	0.89
The Habit of Using Alcohol(reference: no)			
	Yes	1.11	0.90
The Habit of Eating Out (reference: no)			
	Yes	1.20	0.83
The Habit of Going to the Cafe (reference: no)			
	Yes	1.14	0.88
The Habit of Buying Daily Newspapers (reference: no)			
	Yes	1.14	0.88
Mean Vif		1.55	

For the assumption tests, the normal distribution assumption test and the heteroscedasticity assumption test were performed. The heteroscedasticity problem was tested with Breusch-Pagan / Cook-Weisberg test (P<0.000) and the normal distribution was tested with the Jarque-Bera test (P<0.000) respectively. As a result of the assumption tests, it was determined that the data set contained extreme values and did not show a normal distribution. For the data with extreme values, robust regression models, which are resistant to the presence of extreme values, are used instead of the OLS method. The reasons why the OLS method cannot be used when there is extreme value in the data set: the detection of extreme values and the estimation stage of parameters, it is mostly not possible to distinguish them; even if the raw observation values consist of normal observations with large errors, the extracted data is not normal and the performance of the best exclusion methods does not reach the performance of the robust method sufficiently (Huber, 1981; Türkay, 2004).

To overcome these inconveniences, LAD regression was used in the study. LAD regression parameters estimate by minimizing the sum of the absolute values of the errors, rather than the square of the errors (McGreevy et al., 2009).

Table 4 includes the LAD regression estimation results regarding the factors affecting the household expenditures of household heads aged 60 and over.

Table 4. LAD regression model estimation results

Variables	β	Robust Std. Error	P	95% Conf. Interval	
				LL	UL
Demographic indicators					
Gender (reference: female)					
Male	-149.817	77.406	0.053	-301.569	1.936
Education Status (reference: university)					
Did Not Finish A School-Primary School	-701.751	126.045	0.000	-948.859	-454.642
Secondary School	-581.689	125.325	0.000	-827.386	-335.992
High School	-635.318	143.428	0.000	-916.505	-354.130
Marital Status (reference: married)					
Never Married	-52.887	140.149	0.706	-327.646	221.871
Divorced - Widowed	-72.438	73.371	0.324	-216.279	71.403
Household Size	138.583	17.100	0.000	105.060	172.107
Economic indicators					
Income	0.024	0.001	0.000	0.021	0.027
House Type (reference: detached house)					
Apartment	433.351	60.464	0.000	314.813	551.889
Second Home Ownership (reference: no)					
Yes	151.310	73.533	0.040	7.150	295.471
Number of Automobile	53.831	64.983	0.407	-73.567	181.228
Saving Status (reference: no)					
Yes	-444.639	44.154	0.000	-531.203	-358.075

Continued on following page

Table 4. Continued

Variables		β	Robust Std. Error	P	95% Conf. Interval	
					LL	UL
Lighting Expenditure		2.341	0.256	0.000	1.840	2.843
Heating and Kitchen Expenditure		1.589	0.180	0.000	1.237	1.942
Fuel Expenditure for Vehicle		2.260	0.209	0.000	1.850	2.671
Social indicators						
The Habit of Using a Credit Card (reference: no)						
	Yes	162.510	57.116	0.004	50.536	274.485
The Habit of Going to the Farmer Market (reference: no)						
	Yes	146.670	40.952	0.000	66.384	226.956
The Habit of Smoking(reference: no)						
	Yes	284.230	42.942	0.000	200.043	368.418
The Habit of Using Alcohol(reference: no)						
	Yes	250.194	71.487	0.000	110.044	390.343
The Habit of Eating Out (reference: no)						
	Yes	322.968	63.885	0.000	197.723	448.214
The Habit of Going to the Cafe (reference: no)						
	Yes	159.711	45.097	0.000	71.299	248.122
The Habit of Buying Daily Newspapers (reference: no)						
	Yes	446.175	145.134	0.002	161.643	730.708
Cons		1097.631	160.739	0.000	782.505	1412.756
	N: 4644					
	Pseudo R^2: 0.3448		Prob: 0.000			

When Table 4 is examined, the gender of the household head, educational status, household size, annual disposable income of the household, type of housing, second home ownership, saving status, lighting expenditure, heating and kitchen expenditure, fuel expenditure for the vehicle, use of credit card, going to farmer market, smoking, alcohol use, eating out, going to a cafe and buying daily newspapers were found to be statistically significant.

In terms of demographic factors, male household heads have a lower median household expenditure compared to female household heads. Household expenditure median is lower for those who have not completed school, those who have graduated from secondary school and high school, compared to those who have graduated from university. As the household size increased by 1 unit, the median household expenditure increased by 138,583₺.

In terms of economic factors, as the household income level increased, the median household expenditure increased. Those who practice the economy have a lower median household expenditure than those who do not. A 1-unit increase in lighting expenditure increases the household expenditure median by 2,341₺, a 1-unit increase in heating and kitchen expenditure increases the household expenditure median by 1,589₺, and a 1-unit increase in fuel expenditure for the vehicle increases the household expenditure median by 2,260₺.

In terms of social indicators, those who use credit cards have a higher median household expenditure compared to those who do not. The household expenditure median is higher for those who have the habit of going to the farmer market compared to those who do not have the habit of going to the farmer market. Households with an individual, who has a smoking habit, have a higher median household expenditure than those who do not have a smoking habit. Households with an individual who has a habit of drinking alcohol have a higher median household expenditure than those who do not. Households with an individual, who has a habit of eating out, have a higher median household expenditure than those who do not. Households with a habit of going places such as coffeehouses, cafes, local, internet cafes have a higher median household expenditure than those without. Households with the habit of buying daily newspapers have a higher median household expenditure than those without.

CONCLUSION

In this study, the factors affecting the household expenditure of actively working household heads aged 60 and over in Turkey were examined. As a result of the study, it was determined that the gender of the head of the household, educational status, economic indicators, especially income, and social indicators were effective on the expenditures of the households. The results have a qualification to support the economic literature. The results of this study contribute to understanding the spending patterns of elderly working individuals by analyzing the factors associated with household expenditures.

First, it was determined that the gender factor had a statistically significant effect on the household expenditure value. According to the econometric model, male household heads have less household expenditure than female household heads.

In terms of the educational status of household heads, university graduates have the highest household expenditure value. It is possible to explain this situation by the fact that educated and qualified individuals tend to spend more as a natural consequence of earning more.

As the household size increased, the household expenditure value increased. This situation may be related to the increase in the number of people in the household, and the increase in many expenditure items, especially the kitchen, lighting, education, and transportation expenses.

As the household income level increased, the household expenditure value increased as expected. Households that save have a lower household expenditure value than those that do not save. This situation comes from the definition of saving. Saving is the portion that individuals separate from their income to spend (Keynes, 1936). As a result, those who save spend less money than those who do not.

The increase in Lighting Expenditure increased the value of household expenditure, the increase in Heating and Kitchen Expenditure increased the value of household expenditure, and the increase in Fuel Expenditure for Vehicle increased the value of household expenditure. All of these are important expenditure items for households. Fuel Expenditure for Vehicle has the largest coefficient of these increases. This situation is related to the high costs as a result of high taxes on fuel prices in Turkey.

Households that use credit cards have a higher household expenditure value than those that do not. This situation may be related to the fact that credit cards provide many spending conveniences such as not having cash, being able to shop online, and so on.

Households with a habit of going to the farmer market have a higher household expenditure value than those without. Households with an individual who has a smoking habit have a higher median household expenditure than those who do not have a smoking habit. Households with an individual who has a habit of drinking alcohol have a higher median household expenditure than those who do not. Households with an individual, who has a habit of eating out, have a higher median household expenditure than those who do not. Households with a habit of going places such as coffeehouses, cafes, local, internet cafes have a higher median household expenditure than those without. Households with the habit of buying daily newspapers have a higher median household expenditure than those without. These variables can be regarded as socio-cultural variables, and it is appropriate for the economic realities to have higher expenditure values for the responsible person in the household with more socialization.

FUTURE RESEARCH DIRECTIONS

The study has several limitations. A cross-sectional dataset was used in the study. The dependent variable is based on expenditures reported by household heads, and, therefore may be affected by excessive values due to incorrect reporting. There is no rural/urban distinction in the study. The impact of these limitations as a whole does not invalidate the policy significance of the findings yielded in this study. Working with econometric models that will allow comparing the spending characteristics of certain age groups, as well as a wider year range for future studies, can be carried to a more valuable point.

ACKNOWLEDGMENT

No specific funding was received from a funding agency for this research. The author expresses his sincere thanks to the Turkish Statistical Institute for the data. The views expressed in this article solely belonged to the author and may not represent the views and official policy of the Turkish Statistical Institute.

REFERENCES

Abdel-Ghany, M., & Sharpe, D. L. (1997). Consumption patterns among the young-old and old-old. *The Journal of Consumer Affairs*, *31*(1), 90–112. doi:10.1111/j.1745-6606.1997.tb00828.x

Altunöz, U. (2014). Tüketim Fonksiyonu ve Türkiye için Gelir-Tüketim İlişkisinin Ampirik Analizi. International Conference of Eurasian Economies.

Axelson, M. L., & Penfield, M. P. (1983). Factors associated with food expenditures of elderly persons living alone. *Home Economics Research Journal*, *12*(2), 228–236. doi:10.1177/1077727X8301200213

Bellante, D., & Foster, A. C. (1984). Working wives and expenditure on services. *The Journal of Consumer Research*, *11*(2), 700–707. doi:10.1086/209006

Bodur, F. B., & Avcı, G. M. (2015). Household Expenditure Patterns: Evidence from Working-Couple Households in Turkey. *International Review of Economics and Management*, *3*(2), 85–108. doi:10.18825/irem.23503

Bryant, W. K. (1988). Durables and wives' employment yet again. *The Journal of Consumer Research*, *15*(1), 37–47. doi:10.1086/209143

Çağlayan, E., & Astar, M. (2012). A microeconometric analysis of household consumption expenditure determinants for both rural and urban areas in Turkey. *American International Journal of Contemporary Research*, *2*(2), 27–34.

Çebi Karaaslan, K., Oktay, E., & Alkan, Ö. (2022). Determinants of Household Saving Behaviour in Turkey. *Sosyoekonomi*, *30*(51), 71–90. doi:10.17233osyoekonomi.2022.01.04

Chung, Y. S., & Magrabi, F. M. (1990). Age-related changes in expenditure patterns. In *The 36th Annual Conference of the American Council on Consumer Interests* (pp. 200-206). Academic Press.

Cook, F. L., & Settersten, R. A. (1995). Expenditure Patterns by Age and Income Among Mature Adults: Does Age Matter? *The Gerontologist*, *35*(1), 10–23. doi:10.1093/geront/35.1.10 PMID:7890194

DeatonA. (2005). Franco Modigliani and the life cycle theory of consumption. *Available at* SSRN 686475. doi:10.2139/ssrn.686475

Denton, F. T., Mountain, D. C., & Spencer, B. G. (2002). *Age, retirement and expenditure patterns: An econometric study of older Canadian households* (No. 82). McMaster University.

Erişen, M. A., & Yılmaz, F. Ö. (2020). COVID-19 Pandemisi Döneminde Bireylerin Harcamalarının İncelenmesi. *Gaziantep Üniversitesi Sosyal Bilimler Dergisi, 19*, 340-353. doi:10.21547/jss.787849

Host, A., McMahon, A. T., Walton, K., & Charlton, K. (2016). Factors influencing food choice for independently living older people—A systematic literature review. *Journal of Nutrition in Gerontology and Geriatrics*, *35*(2), 67–94. doi:10.1080/21551197.2016.1168760 PMID:27153249

Huber, P. J. (1981). *Robust Statistics*. John Wiley. doi:10.1002/0471725250

Jacobs, E., Shipp, S., & Brown, G. (1989). Families of working wives spending more on services and nondurables. *Monthly Labor Review*, *112*, 15–23.

Keynes, J. M. (2018). *The general theory of employment, interest, and money*. Springer. (Original work published 1936) doi:10.1007/978-3-319-70344-2

Koelln, K., Rubin, R. M., & Picard, M. S. (1995). Vulnerable elderly households: Expenditures on necessities by older Americans. *Social Science Quarterly*, 619–633.

McGreevy, K. M., Lipsitz, S. R., Linder, J. A., Rimm, E., & Hoel, D. G. (2009). Using median regression to obtain adjusted estimates of central tendency for skewed laboratory and epidemiologic data. *Clinical Chemistry*, *55*(1), 165–169. doi:10.1373/clinchem.2008.106260 PMID:19028825

Moehrle, T. (1990). Expenditure Patterns of the Elderly Workers and Nonworkers. *Monthly Labor Review*, *113*, 34–41.

Ong, F. S. (2012). Older consumers in Malaysia: Spending pattern, leisure activities and consumption preferences. *International Journal of Ageing and Later Life*, *2*(1), 85–117. doi:10.3384/ijal.1652-8670.072185

Ong, F. S., Kitchen, J. P., & Jama, A. T. (2008). Consumption patterns and silver marketing: An analysis of older consumers in Malaysia. *Marketing Intelligence & Planning*, *26*(7), 682–698. doi:10.1108/02634500810916663

Paulin, G. D. (2000). Expenditure patterns of older Americans, 1984-97. *Monthly Labor Review*, *123*, 3–28.

Rubin, R. M., & Koelln, K. (1996). Elderly and nonelderly expenditures on necessities in the 1980s. *Monthly Labor Review*, *119*, 24–31. PMID:10162467

Sekhampu, T., & Niyimbanira, F. (2013). Analysis Of The Factors Influencing Household Expenditure In A South African Township. *International Business & Economics Research Journal*, *12*(3), 279–284. doi:10.19030/iber.v12i3.7671

Soberon-Ferrer, H., & Dardis, R. (1991). Determinants of household expenditures for services. *The Journal of Consumer Research*, *17*(4), 385–397. doi:10.1086/208565

SongL. (2008). In search of gender bias in household resource allocation in rural China. *Available at* SSRN 1136265. doi:10.2139/ssrn.1136265

Strober, M. H., & Weinberg, C. B. (1977). Working wives and major family expenditures. *The Journal of Consumer Research*, *4*(3), 141–147. doi:10.1086/208689

Topal, K., & Çağlayan Akay, E. (2021). Hanehalkı Tüketim Harcamalarının Mikroekonometrik Analizi: LAD-LASSO Yöntemi. *Ekoist: Journal of Econometrics and Statistics*, (33), 13–31. doi:10.26650/ekoist.2020.33.843564

TUİK. (n.d.). *Household Budget Survey*. Retrieved March 3, 2021, from https://www.tuik.gov.tr/Kurumsal/Mikro_Veri

Türkay, H. (2004). Doğrusal Regresyon Analizinde M Tahminciler ve Ekonometrik Bir Uygulama. *Doğu Anadolu Bölgesi Araştırmaları*, 106-115.

Türkbal, A. (2005). *Makro İktisat*. Aktif Yayınevi.

Ünsal, E. M. (2013). *Makro İktisat*. İmaj Yayınevi.

Weinberg, C. B., & Winer, R. S. (1983). Working wives and major family expenditures: Replication and extension. *The Journal of Consumer Research*, *10*(2), 259–263. doi:10.1086/208965

Yen, S. T. (1993). Working wives and food away from home: The Box-Cox double hurdle model. *American Journal of Agricultural Economics*, *75*(4), 884–895. doi:10.2307/1243976

ADDITIONAL READING

Alakır, E. (2010). *Tüketim Harcamalarına Yönelik Talep Analizi: Konya Örneği*. Yayınlanmamış Yüksek Lisans Tezi, Selçuk Üniversitesi, Sosyal Bilimler Enstitüsü.

Çalmaşur, G., & Kılıç, A. (2018). Türkiye'de Hanehalkı Tüketim Harcamalarının Analizi. *Erzurum Teknik Üniversitesi Sosyal Bilimler Enstitüsü Dergisi*, *3*(5), 61–73. doi:10.29157/etusbe.45

Giles, D. E. A., & Hampton, P. (1985). An Engel Curve Analysis of Household Expenditure in New Zealand. *The Economic Record*, *61*(1), 450–462. doi:10.1111/j.1475-4932.1985.tb01997.x

Nişancı, M. (2002). Gelir Grupları İtibariyle Harcama Kalıpları: 1987-1994 Türkiye Kentsel Kesim Verileri. *Dokuz Eylül Üniversitesi İ.İ.B.F. Dergisi*, *17*(1), 127–139.

Oflaz, V. E. (2007). *Türkiye Tüketim Harcaması Esneklik Tahminleri, 2003*. Yayınlanmamış Yüksek Lisans Tezi, İstanbul Teknik Üniversitesi, Sosyal Bilimler Enstitüsü.

Özer, H. (1992). *Erzurum'da Tüketim Harcamalarının Ekonometrik Analizi*. Yayınlanmamış Yüksek Lisans Tezi, Atatürk Üniversitesi, Sosyal Bilimler Enstitüsü.

Şenesen, Ü., & Raziye, S. (1995). Consumption Patterns of Turkish Urban and Rural Households in 1987. *ODTÜ Gelisme Dergisi*, *22*(2), 207–220.

Sizege, Ç. (2012). *Türkiye'de Hanelerin Tüketim Harcamaları: Panel Verilerle Talep Sisteminin Tahmini*. Yayınlanmamış Yüksek Lisans Tezi, Çukurova Üniversitesi, Sosyal Bilimler Enstitüsü.

Stigler, G. J. (1954). The Early History of Empirical Studies of Consumer Behavior. *Journal of Political Economy*, *62*(2), 95–113. doi:10.1086/257495

Tansel, A. (1986). An Engel Curve Analysis of Household Expenditure in Turkey 1978- 1979. *ODTÜ Gelisme Dergisi*, *13*(3), 239–257.

KEY TERMS AND DEFINITIONS

Cross-Sectional Data: Data collected from different units at a certain time is called cross-sectional data.

Dependent Variable: The basic variable whose value is determined in the model, which is thought to be affected by other variables, is called the dependent variable.

Heteroscedasticity: It means that error terms do not have constant variance. Thus, the variance of the error terms will change with the independent variable.

Independent Variable: The variable whose value, which is thought to have an effect on the dependent variable, is determined outside the model is called the independent variable.

Least Absolute Deviation Regression: It is an estimation method that aims to obtain estimators that minimize the sum of the absolute values of the errors.

Normal Distribution Assumption: It is an assumption that the error terms are normally distributed.

Ordinary Least Squares Method: It is an estimation method that aims to obtain estimators that minimize the sum of squares of error.

Chapter 5
A Knowledge-Based Recommender Framework to Recommend Destination Country for Human Migrants (KBRF):
The Case of Ethiopia in Africa

Nilamadhab Mishra
https://orcid.org/0000-0002-1330-4869
VIT Bhopal University, India

Baye Yemataw
Debre Berhan University, Ethiopia

Kishore Kumar P. K.
University of Technology and Applied Sciences, Oman

ABSTRACT

Human migration is a challenging process in Ethiopia, where special illegal human migrants cross different border countries without any basic information or knowledge. Due to this, there is the difficulty of getting a vast amount of information to know the destination countries. They go without any information, which also wastes more time, cost, violates their human rights, and endangers their lives. This study used a KBRF to assess the user input and compare them with the stored cases. For this, 75,920 cases were collected from MoLSA and central statistical agencies with and attributes selected for the query of users as well as for their solution. The best solutions are displayed for a user after the similarity calculation of the query and the stored cases. Then the users can decide on which similar cases satisfy their needs. KBRF has an average performance, recall, and precision score of 92% (4.60), 0.91 (91%), and 0.63 (63%), respectively, from domain experts and system performance.

DOI: 10.4018/978-1-7998-2395-7.ch005

Copyright © 2022, IGI Global. Copying or distributing in print or electronic forms without written permission of IGI Global is prohibited.

INTRODUCTION

According to UN Migration Agency (IOM), "no commonly conventional definition for migration exists". In reality, there are a lot of definitions of human migration, and it defines differently. It can be defined as "a process of moving, either across different border countries, or within a state; it is a peoples movement, nearby any kind of movement of peoples, whatever its length, composition, and causes; it includes migration of refugees, displaced persons, uprooted people, and economic migrants" (Fiorini, A., 2016). On the other hand, Encyclopedia Britannica defines the term 'migration' as being "a permanent change of residence by an individual or group; it excludes such movements as migrant labor, travel, and tourism, all of which are transitory in nature". Finally, defines migration as being a long-term movement of an individual people or group of peoples outside their place of migrant's source. In general, these processes are it may be illegal or legal.

"Since the dawn of human progress, more than 70,000 years ago, humans have migrated across different border countries to search for food, shelter, safety, and hospitable climate". The movement is continuing in the beginning of the 21st century (Hristoski, I., & Sotiroski, K., 2012), but new reasons for human migration are arising too, such as job-related movement (Boubakri, H., 2013). Due to the great technological advances in electronic communications and transportation, the scale of modern human migration is even bigger and more dynamic than ever before. It is a global problem of huge strength, involving people from various countries, of different ages, gender, and race, belonging to various nationalities and religions, and having various social, economic and political background problems (Yemisrach, F., 2015).

As stated in (Yemisrach, F., 2015) illegal migration front multiple challenges or problems to countries of source, bridge, and destination, as well as to migrants themselves. Migrants in the illegal situation are particularly open to bias, exploitation, and violence. Such migrants are also in danger of being exploited by crime organizations involved in human trafficking and migrant smuggling crimes that constitute a serious violation of the human rights of its sufferers.

Basic Information about unrecorded migrants in the illegal situation is often difficult to put a figure on. Estimates vary greatly from one source to another. As described in IOM, "has approximate that 10–15% of the world's 214 million international migrants in 2010 were unrecorded and also the UNDP has estimated that around one-third of all migration flows in developing countries were unrecorded" and also both the UNDP and the OECD include unrecorded migrants in their estimation of the migrant database, but the accurate amount of migrants in the illegal situation are unknown.

According to the central statically agency and MoLSA office, from 2000-2014 years, there are around 84, 000 and 459, 810 young people in Ethiopia living outside their place of birth, in different regions by legally system was recorded about 459, 810 respectively. The main origins of Ethiopian migrants are from the populated regions, such as Amhara, Oromiya, SNNPR, Addis Ababa, Gambela, Dire Dawa, Harari, Tigray, Somali, and Beshangul Gumuz region. These areas are also the same that belong to the poorest regions in Ethiopia, with low per capita incomes. Central statically agency and MoLSA Office clearly defines the number of migrants in each year in different regions as shown, in Table 1 and 2.

Table 1. Human migration numbers of record from 2000-2014

Name of Region	Gender		Total
	Male	Female	
Addis Ababa	5622	8430	14052
Oromiya	6324	7098	13322
Tigray	8242	9354	17596
Afar	3523	1363	4886
Amhara	13022	21122	34144
Total			***84,000***

(Salem, A. B. M., Roushdy, M., & Hodhod, R. A., 2005)

The main destinations countries for migrant's area are Saudi Arabia, Kuwait, Dubai, Israel, Peru, Japan, Denmark, Qatar, Italy, and India countries with the highest per capita income as stated by center statically agency and MoLSA office.

The current practices to control illegal migration of Ethiopia Government made to control illegal migration the first option was to prevent human trafficking, by coordinating both regional and national policy to make awareness the dangers of illegal migration in Ethiopia, by creating TV program. The government monitored the activities of labor staffing agencies and closed in a different agency that was facilitating the migration for a dangerous condition. And also, make labor migration right discussion in the previous reporting period with Jordan, Kuwait, and Qatar stay in place, the government discuss new agreements in 2013 with the Governments of Djibouti, Sudan, the UAE, and Kenya. However, these agreements did not explicitly contain provisions to protect workers, such as by outlining mandatory rest periods, including grounds for filing grievance, and prohibiting recruitment fees.

One of the challenging problems in the world to control illegal migrants is the absence of (Arione, E., Barone, G., Holsten, M., & Weber, F., 1999) recorded information for analysis purposes. Ethiopia also faces this problem, since most young Ethiopian migrant follows an illegal system. As a result, the country loses its young human power every year. Therefore law enforcement bodies like police need to learn the factors that constitute human migration. To control migration, there should be a need for careful migration prevention strategies and policies.

Table 2. Human migration status in Ethiopia from 2009-2013

Name of Region	Gender		Total
	Male	Female	
Amhara	7959	134985	142944
Oromiya	5501	148437	153938
Tigray	3076	20086	23162
Afar	619	1374	1993
SNNPR	2482	56041	58523
Addis Ababa	6167	70365	76532
Gambela	8	90	98
Harari	19	238	257
Somali	11	11	22
Benshangul Gumuz	44	749	789
Dire Dawa	100	1356	1456
Total			***459, 810***

(Moore, C. J., Lehane, M. S., & Price, C. J., 1994, March)

The challenging problem in Ethiopia is that most of the migrants cross the border of the countries in an illegal system. They move across different life cycles to arrive at the destination countries. Amid illegal migration, with the hope of finding better jobs, a considerable pack of nationals leaves Ethiopia with the help of human traffic, and their preferred destinations are European countries. It requires pure luck to reach the destination crossing the Mediterranean Sea often; this dangerous journey of life takes the lives of many on the barren desserts or the seas. "In the aftermath of the brutal ISIS massacre of 30

Ethiopian migrants in Libya, citizens have started to talk seriously about the dangers of illegal migration". Human trafficking has become an immense problem in Ethiopia. As a result of poverty, large numbers of Ethiopians are voluntarily trafficked, through illegal 'desert routes and they are mainly trafficked for household labor purposes (Watson, I., 1998).

The challenge these migrants face during the journey is not the end but the beginning of the disturbance. Even in the case, they succeed to reach their destination and get a job, they are subjected to abuses such as long working hours, unbearable workload, restricted movement, isolation, inability to change employers, lack of leisure, denial of wages, and irregular payment of wages.

Metema-Galabat, a 'desert route' of human trafficking from Ethiopia to Sudan, is a place of suffering for many illegal migrants from Ethiopia, and also the migrants physical and emotional abuse, torture, imprisonment, threats, beatings, and even death are just some of the horrors the majority of trafficked women face while passing through this route. The magnitude of "illegal migration in Ethiopia is becoming significant the view of the MoLSA, around 1.5 million Ethiopians left the country illegally between the years 2008 and 2014". However, the illegal migrants travel around with the aid of organized smugglers across the borders and the deserts of Yemen and Libya. The time between going away and arrival may vary from some days to several months or even years (Iqbal, N., & Ashraf, M. H., 2006).

Very often, the illegal travels take place under inhuman conditions: the migrants are overcrowded in trucks, with minimal or no food and drink for extended hours, and fatal accidents occur commonly. After they arrive in the destination country, their illegal status puts them at the mercy of their smugglers, who often force the migrants to work for years in the illegal labor market to pay off the debts incurred as a result of their transportation.

Smuggling is mostly done by land and sea, high pressure and low economy in the illegal migration work are the big factors that make not as good as these situations (Van Meteren, R., & Van Someren, M., 2000, May).

Since in Ethiopia, there is no local research to recommend destination countries for human migrants to give basic information about the migrant where they go and also make awareness for illegal migrants. So, we design a prototype KBRF system to solve those problems in Ethiopia.
Based on the above-stated problems, the study addresses the followings research problems:

- What are the factors of human migration in Ethiopia?
- How to identify variables that help to recommend the destination country?
- How to recommend?
- To what extent the recommender system gets users' acceptance?

LITERATURE REVIEW

Recommender systems are a special type of information filtering system. Information filtering deals with the delivery of items selected from a large collection that the user is likely to find interesting or useful and can be seen as a classification task (Al-Wakel, E., 2014).

Recommender systems provide advice to users about items they might wish to purchase or examine. Recommendations made by such systems can help users navigate through large information spaces of product descriptions, news articles, or other items. As online information and e-commerce burgeon, recommender systems are an increasingly important tool (Ekstrand, M. D., Riedl, J. T., & Konstan, J. A., 2011).

Recommender systems are a special type of information filtering system. Information filtering deals with the delivery of items selected from a large collection that the user is likely to find interesting or useful and can be seen as a classification (Sun, S. H., & Chen, J. L., 2007, June).

Collaborative filtering (CF) is a popular recommendation algorithm that bases its predictions and recommendations on the ratings or behavior of other users in the system. The fundamental assumption behind this method is that other users' opinions can be selected and aggregated in such a way as to provide a reasonable prediction of the active user's preference (El-Sappagh, S. H., & Elmogy, M., 2015).

The main advantage of this type of recommender system is that they are more effective when it comes to customer satisfaction as they recommend the most appropriate items to users which are personalized at the same time. The collaborative filtering algorithms are designed such that the accuracy of their prediction increases tremendously over time as more user preferences are added to the database, irrespective of the size of the database. It has the same problem as with a content-based system. To make accurate recommendations, the system must first learn the user's preferences from the ratings that the user gives. New items are added regularly to recommender systems. Collaborative systems rely solely on users' preferences to make recommendations. Therefore, until the new item is rated by a substantial number of users, the recommender system would not be able to recommend it (Salem, A. B. M., 2007).

Content-based recommendation systems try to recommend items similar to those a given user has liked in the past. Indeed, the basic process performed by a content-based recommender consists in matching up the attributes of a user profile in which preferences and interests are stored, with the attributes of a content object (item), to recommend to the user new interesting items.

Disadvantages of Content-Based Recommender Systems

Limited Content Analysis

Content-based techniques have a natural limit in the number and type of features that are associated, whether automatically or manually, with the objects they recommend. Domain knowledge is often needed, e.g., for movie recommendations, the system needs to know the actors and directors, and sometimes, domain ontology is also needed. No content-based recommendation system can provide suitable suggestions if the analyzed content does not contain enough information to discriminate items the user likes from items the user does not like. Some representations capture only certain aspects of the content, but many others would influence a user's experience. For instance, often there is not enough information in the word frequency to model the user interest's in-jokes or poems, while techniques for affective computing would be most appropriate. Again, for Web pages, feature extraction techniques from the text completely ignore aesthetic qualities and additional multimedia information.

Over-specialization

Content-based recommenders have no inherent method for finding something unexpected. The system suggests items whose scores are high when matched against the user profile; hence the user is going to be recommended items similar to those already rated. This drawback is also called the serendipity problem to highlight the tendency of the content-based systems to produce recommendations with a limited degree of novelty. To give an example, when a user has only rated movies directed by Stanley Kubrick, she will be recommended just that kind of movie. A "perfect" content-based technique would rarely find anything novel, limiting the range of applications for which it would be useful.

Case-Based Reasoning System

The objective for computer systems being able to support human experts during the complex problem-solving task is a usual topic of AI research. To enable a computer system to give rational support when solving problems in a complex application domain, it is essential to provide it with specific knowledge within that domain. Several methodologies to realize such knowledge knowledge-based systems have been developed, such as the rule-based approach and KBRF approach. KBRF means "adapting earlier solutions to meet new demands, using earlier cases to account for new situations, using earlier cases to evaluate new solutions, or reasoning from precedents to understand a new situation" (Mishra, N., Lin, C. C., & Chang, H. T., 2015). KBRF is easier to make better decisions in a dynamically changing environment. People learn from their success and wrong activities to handle similar situations in the right manner and not to repeat their mistakes of the past. KBRF approach is more compatible to reuse earlier solved problems and learn from experiences for future decisions. Similarly, KBRF is an approach to incremental learning. Once a problem has been solved, KBRF approaches use the solution to solve future problems (Mishra, N., Lin, C. C., & Chang, H. T., 2014, December) (Chang, H. T., Mishra, N., & Lin, C. C., 2015).

Knowledge-Based Reasoning Techniques

There are different types of knowledge-based reasoning techniques. Some of them are semantic networks, neural networks, fuzzy logic, rule-based reasoning, and case-based reasoning techniques. From those types of techniques, the researcher discusses rule-based and case-based techniques. Rule-based reasoning is a system whose knowledge representation is in a set of rules and facts. Symbolic rules are one of the most popular knowledge representation and reasoning methods. This popularity is mainly due to their naturalness, which facilitates comprehension of the represented knowledge. The basic forms of a rule, if <condition> then <conclusion> where <condition> represents premises and <conclusion> represents associated action for the premises as described. The condition of rules is connected between each other with logical connectives, such as AND, OR, NOT, etc. When sufficient conditions of a rule are satisfied, then, the conclusion is derived and the rule is said to be fired.

The case based on earlier history understanding is that it can be used for coming problems solving, and can refer to the past case, stored or retained case Express reasoning by reusing earlier cases is the most strong and common applied way to find or to solve the problem of humans. In other words, KBRF is a group of occurrences that happens in a particular order, one following the other, which are often repeated and process of two or more combined cases that become more effective for problem-solving. Similarly, the new case or unsolved is a description of a new problem that is to be solved. Problem-solving is not needed to achieve a particular correct result of an application problem; it may be expressed by the user. The term solving a problem is used in the wide sense, a set of ideas or plans within the area of knowledge base system in general.

KBRF SYSTEM CYCLE

The problem-solving cycle of KBRF consists of four main methods.

- Retrieving: the majority of similar history experience cases were retrieved for the similar unsolved problem.
- Reusing: the cases from history retrieved cases by joining together and copying.
- Revising: the future (proposed) solution from the attempt to solve new (cases) problem or adopt a new (future) proposed solution.
- Retaining: when the new solution was confirmed, then the newly proposed solution was retained.

The nearest-neighbor retrieval technique is to measure the "similarity between a source case and case which we are searching" according to and if the case is not matched with the KBRF library. Then, the KBRF system will return the nearest match. The nearest match corresponds to the following equation.

$$\text{Similarity}(T, S) = \sum_{i=1}^{n} f(Tj, Si) * Wi \text{ ----} \quad (1)$$

Where

T= target case
S= source case
n= number of attributes in each case
I= individual attribute from 1 to n
f= similarity function for attributes I in cases T and S
w= importance weighting of attribute I

To inductive retrieval, use history experienced cases to construct decisions or extract rules. Inductive retrieval is used to retrieve a set of matched cases and then nearest-neighbor retrieval rank these cases according to their similarity with the target case. Study the effects of migration on the economic condition of the moving country. Thus, an investigation of the current trends in migration has been done, to improve the understanding of this occurrence, and a model based on growth accounting was developed and applied on aggregated data for 131 countries. From this study, the researchers used the geographic instrument technique, often employed in practice. Differences in the economic condition of the countries have been accounted for by dividing the countries according to the value of average income per person. Also, a model variable has been used to divide the effects of the different countries with migration rates of highly skilled from the rest. The results show that migration rates have a positive effect on the GDP per capita growth rate and also on employment and capital stock growth rates and income. Finally, from these study, "countries, where migration charge is of very much educated, exceed 30% there is less economic growth and a lower increase in wages, compared to the others, as predicted by the economic theory". The study recognizes the major causes of migration of educational intellectuals from Addis Ababa University to the "industrial world and to compare and contrast the brain drain from Imperial regime up to FDRE (1974-1993)".

The researcher also used both narrative and survey research designs are used and the researchers "divided the sampling frame into commonly selected strata (groups) of five Colleges and two institutes arranged by strata". In the selection process, respondents were selected from each college and research institutes using stratified random sampling techniques. The data were gathered from Addis Ababa University educational intellectuals, analyzed by using percentage, average (mean), descriptive words, and the documents were incorporated to substitute the qualitative information. Finally, from this study, some recommendations are forward: Policymakers to control this issue promote on adjusting housing, salary, creating a conducive environment, attracting foreign intellectuals and both are should know university is not political and it is an area of academic, avoid conflict, take the responsibility on political issues, social situation and in democratic principles for the realization of better development. Gudetu Wakgari, human migration is a movement of people from one geographic area to the other for a better life in different developed countries. Ethiopia is not exceptional to this challenges problem where migration is initiated by both pull and push reasons. But this time it is categorized by mass migration of women to the Middle East Arabic countries, among which the majority are illegal humans. Illegal humans in Ethiopia are causing several serious problems, turning the hope of many young girls into disaster. This study attempts to assess the causes and consequences of an illegal human taking women in the Middle East Arabic Countries as a case study. The researchers used qualitative research this study concludes that in addition to poverty and unemployment several interrelated factors cause trafficking.

Migration Patterns in the Horn of Africa

According to IOM in 2012, there are now about "192 million people" who migrate to developed countries, which is "about 3% of the world's population". The most common challenges in the horn of Africa, are especially in Ethiopia in the past years. "The political overthrow of the Ethiopian Imperial Government in 1974, the independence struggle of Eritrea, the war between Ethiopia and Somalia 1978, and the civil conflict in Sudan and Somalia in the 1980". These are the major cause of people migrating across different border countries. In general, the causes of the migration pattern in the Horn of Africa, especially in Ethiopia is complex because there are so many factors, including "ethnic and religious conflicts, irredentist and separatist-inspired violence, an international war between countries in the region, and intervention in domestic conflicts by external powers" (Mishra, N., Chang, H. T., & Lin, C. C., 2015).

Until the early 1990s, Ethiopia was one of the largest producers of migrants in Africa, and also to some scholar migration flows in the Horn Africa and Ethiopia is presented in Table 3. As this table shows, the movement or migration number in Ethiopia increased from "55,000 in1972 to over a million in 1992". Even though Ethiopia has experienced migratory flows throughout its history, the movement of Ethiopian civilians became greater in the late 1960 and 1970 as described.

Table 3. Migrants in the Horn of Africa and Ethiopia: 1972-1992

Year	Refugees in the Horn of Africa	Refugees from Ethiopia	Percentage of Refugees from in Ethiopia
1972	55, 000	55,000	100.00
1977	102,000	91,000	89.22
1982	1,091,000	1,081,500	99.13
1987	1,343, 300	1,122,300	83.55
1992	1,676,800	752,400	44.87

(Van Meteren, R., & Van Someren, M., 2000, May)

Here in this section, the researcher discusses different research papers that are related to case-based reasoning in different areas conducted locally in Ethiopia which helps to understand how to solve and develop case-based reasoning to recommend destination countries for human migrants. Application of case-based recommender system has been instigated in the field of study selection in the case of higher education in Ethiopia". The objective of the study was to develop a prototype case base recommender system that assists the students in their field of study selection process. That helps and recommends to the students based on previously solved cases and new queries given by the users/students. With the collection of 105 cases that are collected from successful students. For the implementation, the author uses JCOLIBRI as an implementation tool to develop the prototype recommender system. Queries from users are used as input for the system to provide a recommendation. After accepting the input the system calculates the similarity between existing cases and new queries that are provided by the students and provides solutions or recommendations by taking best cases to the new query this helps the students to make decisions easily. After developing the prototype of the system, testing of the prototype for case base recommender system was done to evaluate the performance of the system. Based on user acceptance of prototype testing, the average performance of the system was 77.2% and 80.2% by the domain experts and students respectively.

Research studies that are titled "application of case-based reasoning for anxiety disorder diagnosis" to develop a prototype case-based reasoning system that can give decision support for anxiety disorder diagnosticians at a different level of expertise. The investigation of the research paper is based on limitations of a rule-based knowledge base system such as incremental learning and specific knowledge acquisition. The implementation tool used to develop the prototype is the JCOLIBRI case-based framework and for the implementation of the prototype, successfully solved cases were acquired from Amanuel Mental Specialized Hospital. In addition, the main parameter was identified in consultation with anxiety disorder experts. Testing of the prototype case-based reasoning system was done to evaluate the performance of the system. The testing of the prototype was performed from two sides. The first one was testing in terms of precision and recall and registered 71% and 82% respectively. In addition to this, the average solution similarity using methods Leave One Out evaluator and Hold Out evaluation achieved performance of 73% and 75.5% respectively. The second one was the performance of the system was evaluated by the potential users of the system and achieved 83.2% performance. The research study that is titled "application of recommender system in investment activity selection in the case of Ethiopia" develop a Case-Based Recommender System that can give recommendations on the selection of investment sectors and investment activity in Ethiopia to foreign and domestic investors. The prototype system also provides a recommendation to new investors based on previously solved cases and new queries given by the investor. 1344 cases were used which are collected from the successful investor as a case base. In this study, the author also uses the JCOLIBRI case-based development framework for the implementation of the prototype system. Finally, testing of the prototype for case base recommender system was done to evaluate the performance of the system, and Based on user acceptance of prototype testing; the average performance of the system was 82% and 84% by the domain experts and investors respectively.

DATA PREPARATION FOR KBRF

This study is based on data collected from the central statistical agency and the MoLSA office. Before implementing the Knowledge-base (KBRF) system, the researcher clearly understands the migrant's factors and has worked closely with the two dataset sources. To understand the migrant's factors to migrate legally, the first step is identifying the migrant's causes to understanding the characteristics of migration that determines migrant's goals and DM goals were set to identify and prepare data required for the study. Next, the KBRF system task is ready for retrieve, retain, revision, and also to recommend destination country for human migrants in Ethiopia. Migration can be defined as a process of moving, either across different border countries or within a State. Migration is part of human history since its very beginning. People have migrated from one continent to the other, from country to country or internally, inside the same country. Currently, IOM states that there are "about one billion migrants around the world". This number includes "214 million international migrants and 740 million internally displaced persons". The business understanding was carried out on pertinent issues giving due emphasis on the following parameters as noted in. Observing domain experts work to define clearly the problem and determine the goal. Secondly, organizing the migrants' cases and learning about the current solutions to the problem. We are processing the dataset to make it useable for experimentation, and also how to make the dataset useable for the KBRF.

In the activity of the DM process, data gathering and understanding of the data was the first task to get useful information for the knowledge discovery. The migrants' dataset was collected from MoLSA and the central statistical agency office. But, the study preprocessing the dataset was held to make it suitable for the intended purpose. From 2000-to 2014, the offices recorded the migrants' data and information in an unorganized format. Originally, the dataset consists of 11 attributes from the MoLSA office: Gender, Age, Region, Zone, Marital Status, Education Levels, Year of Migrants, Length Of Stay, Income Level, Kebele and Migrants Destination with 459, 810 records, and also 10 attributes Gender, Age, Region, Zone, Werda, Marital Status, Education Levels, Year of Migrants, Income Level and Migrants Destination countries with 84, 000 records from central static agency office, which include the relevant information relating to migrants.

Description of the Initial Data

The data collected from MoLSA and central static agency offices are using the same standard paper format and they are not directly collected for this study. Initially, the data were in record file format. The data in a record file format are then exported to Microsoft Excel for further preparation and ready for input to WEKA 3.6.9 data mining tool. This initial dataset is described and visualized using Microsoft excel. Then data preprocessing is performed to verify the quality of the dataset such as missing values, error values, and to obtain high-level information regarding the data mining questions. Table 4 shows the dataset information which is collected from the MoLSA and central static agency office.

Table 4. Description of the initial dataset

Data source	Categories	Total
MoLSA office	No of Instances	459, 810
	Number of Attributes	11
Central statically agency office	No of Instances	84,000
	Number of Attributes	10

As shown in Table 4 the initial data collected from MoLSA and central static agency office have 11 and 10 attributes respectively. One important feature of WEKA, which may be crucial for some learning schemes, is the opportunity of choosing a smaller subset from all attributes. As a result of the dataset from the two data sources as business process analysis, relevant attributes are selected, DM techniques such as discretization or categorization are used to summarize the low level too many distinct values into high-level values. The following Figure 1 shows the selected attributes for this study after being discussed with the two data source domain experts.

Figure 1. Dataset before experimentation

1	Gender	Age	LevelOfQualification	Marital_status	Region	Zone	YearOfMigration	IncomeLevel	Destination
2	Male	young	College Level	Unmarried	Amhara	South Gondar	2000	Low	Israel
3	Male	young	College Level	Unmarried	Amhara	South Gondar	2000	Low	Israel
4	Male	young	College Level	Unmarried	Amhara	South Gondar	2000	Low	Israel
5	Male	young	College Level	Unmarried	Amhara	South Gondar	2000	Low	Israel
6	Male	young		Unmarried	Amhara	South Gondar	2000	Low	Israel
7	Male	young	College Level	Unmarried	Amhara	South Gondar	2000	Low	
8	Male	young	College Level	Unmarried	Amhara	South Gondar	2000	Low	Israel
9	Male		College Level	Unmarried	Amhara		2000	Low	Israel
10	Male	young	College Level	Unmarried	Amhara	South Gondar	2000	Low	Israel
11	Male	young	College Level	Unmarried		South Gondar	2000	Low	Israel
12	Male	young	College Level	Unmarried	Amhara	South Gondar	2000	Low	Israel
13	Male	young	College Level	Unmarried	Amhara	South Gondar	2000	Low	
14	Male	young	College Level	Unmarried	Amhara	South Gondar	2000	Low	Israel
15	Male	young	College Level		Amhara	South Gondar	2000	Low	Israel
16	Male	young	College Level	Unmarried	Amhara	South Gondar	2000	Low	Israel
17	Male	young		Unmarried	Amhara	South Gondar	2000	Low	Israel
18	Male	young	College Level	Unmarried		South Gondar	2000	Low	Israel
19	Male	young	College Level	Unmarried	Amhara	South Gondar	2000	Low	
20	Male	young	College Level	Unmarried	Amhara	South Gondar	2000	Low	Israel
21	Male	young	College Level	Unmarried	Amhara	South Gondar	2001	Low	Israel
22			College Level	Unmarried	Amhara		2002	Low	Israel
23	Male	young	College Level		Amhara	South Gondar	2003	Low	Israel
24	Male	young	College Level	Unmarried	Amhara	South Gondar	2004	Low	Israel

Organizing data is a significant pre-processing step for data analysis not only as part of data warehousing but also for DM. The main reason is that the quality of the input data strongly influences the quality of the analysis results. Data pre-processing is a DM technique that involves transforming raw data into an understandable format. Real-world data is often "incomplete, inconsistent, and/or lacking in certain behaviors or trends, and is likely to contain many errors" (Mishra, N., Chang, H. T., & Lin, C. C., 2014). Data pre-processing is a proven method of resolving such issues. Data pre-processing prepares raw data for further processing. Pre-processing the data helps to fill some missing values; to detect some outliers that may put the data at risk, and remove or correct some noisy data. In general, data preparation comprises several subtasks: selection, transformation, cleaning as well as reduction and/or discretization of data. Often, these tasks are very expensive.

Data Selection

The whole dataset has not been taken for the KBRF cycles task. Before that, by using DM unnecessary instances and attributes are removed before starting the actual KBRF function. After removing the instance and attributes, an only total of 75, 920 records and 9 attributes were used for conducting this study from the two central statically agency and MoLSA data sources. The following are the initial sets of attributes, which are further preprocessed to select the final attributes used in the study. GENDER, AGE, REGION, ZONE, MARITAL STATUS, EDUCATION LEVEL, MIGRANTS YEAR, INCOME LEVEL, and MIGRANTS DESTINATION were the initial set of attributes that are selected. But we remove LENGTH OF STAY and KEBLE attributes from the data source MoLSA, and also the WERDA attribute from the data source central statically agency because it is difficult to integrate the two data sources using different attributes. After removing uncommon attributes we make the dataset used for the extermination of the two data sources.

Data Cleansing

There were numerous inconveniences in thc original dataset which need additional pre-processing of the migrants' data. These are:

- Attributes have so many missing values. For example, the attribute migrants region has a missing value of 51187, 8426 from MoLSA and central static agency office respectively. The researcher removes each instance from the dataset because had enough instances in the dataset.
- Discretize or organize an instance filter that discretizes a range of numeric attributes in the dataset into nominal attributes.
- In the original dataset, there was an error in changing the attribute values from attribute to attribute. For instance, some records had age value in the sex attribute and sex value in the age attribute. Like the attribute age had a value of "M" at someplace "F" in another place. Whereas, the attribute sex had a value of the number in some places.
- Another problem in the dataset was that there was inconsistency or irregularity in writing, way of attributes i.e. some attributes were written in abbreviation format and some attributes in standard form. For example, in the attribute migrants region, one of its attribute regions was written as reg. in some places and the full name region in other places. These are simple tasks for the researcher to full fill these problems.

Some attribute names are different in different places. For instance, the attribute name "sex" in some places is and "gender" in another place. In Table 2 below, the total missing instance from the Ethiopian MoLSA dataset. The next task of the study is to rewrite each instance. It must be reprocessed manually system by filtering each missing attribute value, in Table 5 it shows the number of missing after ignoring missing values. After removing, then the researcher imported the data to Microsoft Office Excel 2007 and changed it to with appropriate ways as indicated in Figure 2.

For this reason, the study takes time to correct and normalize the above-stated problem of the migrants' dataset sequentially by the manual system, using Microsoft Excel. After removing the missing values in the dataset, the dataset MoLSA decreased from 405, 810 rows data to 354623 rows and also decreased the dataset central statically agency from 84,000 instances to 75574 instances as indicated in above Table 5.

Figure 2. Before preprocessing some missing attribute value MoLSA office dataset

Gender Nominal	Age Nominal	LevelOfQualification Nominal	Marital_status Nominal	Region Nominal	Zone Nominal	YearOfMigration Numeric	IncomeLevel Nominal	**Destination** Nominal
Male	Adult	College Complete	Married	Amhara	East G...	2010.0	Low	Saudi Arabia
		College Complete	Married	Amhara	East G...	2010.0	Low	Saudi Arabia
Male	Adult	College Complete	Married	Amhara	East G...	2010.0	Low	Saudi Arabia
Male	Adult		Married	Amhara	East G...	2010.0	Low	Saudi Arabia
Male	Adult	College Complete	Unmarried	Amhara	East G...	2010.0	Low	Saudi Arabia
	Adult	College Complete	Married	Amhara	East G...	2010.0	Low	Saudi Arabia
Male	Adult		Married	Amhara	East G...	2010.0	Low	Saudi Arabia
Male	Adult	College Complete	Unmarried		East G...	2010.0	Low	
	Adult		Unmarried	Amhara	East G...	2010.0	Low	Peru
Male	Adult	College Complete	Unmarried	Amhara	East G...	2010.0	Low	Saudi Arabia
	Adult	College Complete	Married	Amhara	East G...	2010.0	Low	Dubai
Male	Adult		Married	Amhara	East G...	2010.0	Low	Saudi Arabia
Male	Adult	College Complete	Married	Amhara	East G...	2010.0	Low	Saudi Arabia
Male	Adult	College Complete	Unmarried		East G...	2010.0	Low	
	Adult			Amhara	East G...	2010.0	Low	Saudi Arabia
Male	Adult	College Complete	Married	Amhara	East G...	2010.0	Low	Saudi Arabia
Male	Adult	College Complete	Married	Amhara	East G...	2010.0	Low	Peru
Male	Adult		Married	Amhara	East G...		Low	Saudi Arabia
	Adult	College Complete	Married	Amhara	East G...	2010.0	Low	Saudi Arabia
Male		College Complete	Married	Amhara	East G...	2010.0	Low	
Male	Adult		Unmarried		East G...	2010.0	Low	Saudi Arabia
Male	Adult	College Complete	Married	Amhara	East G...	2010.0	Low	Saudi Arabia
Male	Adult	College Complete	Married	Amhara	East G...	2010.0	Low	Saudi Arabia
Male	Adult	College Complete	Unmarried	Amhara	East G...	2010.0	Low	Saudi Arabia
Male	Adult	College Complete	Unmarried	Amhara	East G...	2010.0	Low	Saudi Arabia
Male	Adult	College Complete	Unmarried	Amhara	East G...	2010.0	Low	Saudi Arabia
Male	Adult	College Complete	Married	Amhara	East G...	2010.0	Low	Saudi Arabia

Table 5. Missing values in the dataset

Name of Region	Gender		Total
	Male	Female	
Addis Ababa	5622	8430	14052
Oromiya	6324	7098	13322
Tigray	8242	9354	17596
Afar	3523	1363	4886
Amhara	13022	21122	34144
Total			***84,000***

Figure 3. The dataset after cleansing

Gender Nominal	Age Nominal	LevelOfQualification Nominal	Marital_status Nominal	Region Nominal	Zone Nominal	YearOfMigration Numeric	IncomeLevel Nominal	**Destination** Nominal
Female	young	College Complete	Unmarried	Amhara	Bahir Dar	2012.0	Low	Kuwait
Female	young	College Complete	Unmarried	Amhara	Bahir Dar	2012.0	Low	Kuwait
Female	young	College Complete	Unmarried	Amhara	Bahir Dar	2012.0	Low	Kuwait
Female	young	College Complete	Unmarried	Amhara	Bahir Dar	2012.0	Low	Kuwait
Female	young	College Complete	Unmarried	Amhara	Bahir Dar	2012.0	Low	Kuwait
Female	young	College Complete	Unmarried	Amhara	Bahir Dar	2012.0	Low	Kuwait
Female	young	College Complete	Unmarried	Amhara	Bahir Dar	2012.0	Low	Kuwait
Female	young	College Complete	Unmarried	Amhara	Bahir Dar	2012.0	Low	Kuwait
Female	young	College Complete	Unmarried	Amhara	Bahir Dar	2012.0	Low	Kuwait
Female	young	College Complete	Unmarried	Amhara	Bahir Dar	2012.0	Low	Kuwait
Female	young	College Complete	Unmarried	Amhara	Bahir Dar	2012.0	Low	Kuwait
Female	young	College Complete	Unmarried	Amhara	Bahir Dar	2012.0	Low	Kuwait
Female	young	College Complete	Unmarried	Amhara	Bahir Dar	2012.0	Low	Kuwait
Female	young	College Complete	Unmarried	Amhara	Bahir Dar	2012.0	Low	Kuwait
Female	young	College Complete	Unmarried	Amhara	Bahir Dar	2012.0	Low	Kuwait
Female	young	College Complete	Unmarried	Amhara	Bahir Dar	2012.0	Low	Kuwait
Female	young	College Complete	Unmarried	Amhara	Bahir Dar	2012.0	Low	Kuwait
Female	young	College Complete	Unmarried	Amhara	Bahir Dar	2012.0	Low	Kuwait
Female	young	College Complete	Unmarried	Amhara	Bahir Dar	2012.0	Low	Kuwait
Female	young	College Complete	Unmarried	Amhara	Bahir Dar	2012.0	Low	Kuwait
Female	young	College Complete	Unmarried	Amhara	Bahir Dar	2012.0	Low	Kuwait
Male	young	College Level	Unmarried	Amhara	South ...	2000.0	Low	Israel
Male	young	College Level	Unmarried	Amhara	South ...	2000.0	Low	Israel
Male	young	College Level	Unmarried	Amhara	South ...	2000.0	Low	Israel
Male	young	College Level	Unmarried	Amhara	South ...	2000.0	Low	Israel
Male	young	College Level	Unmarried	Amhara	South ...	2000.0	Low	Israel
Male	young	College Level	Unmarried	Amhara	South ...	2000.0	Low	Israel
Male	young	College Level	Unmarried	Amhara	South ...	2000.0	Low	Israel
Male	young	College Level	Unmarried	Amhara	South ...	2000.0	Low	Israel
Male	young	College Level	Unmarried	Amhara	South ...	2000.0	Low	Israel
Male	young	College Level	Unmarried	Amhara	South ...	2000.0	Low	Israel
Male	young	College Level	Unmarried	Amhara	South ...	2000.0	Low	Israel
Male	young	College Level	Unmarried	Amhara	South ...	2000.0	Low	Israel
Male	young	College Level	Unmarried	Amhara	South ...	2000.0	Low	Israel
Male	young	College Level	Unmarried	Amhara	South ...	2000.0	Low	Israel
Male	young	College Level	Unmarried	Amhara	South ...	2000.0	Low	Israel

KBRF- KNOWLEDGE ACQUISITION, CONCEPTUAL MODELING, AND REPRESENTATION

Firstly, the study organized migrant cases and conceptual models by applying a hierarchical structure concept system before designing a prototype KBRF system. The knowledge for this study is acquired from relevant documents by using the document analysis technique which was employed to purify the acquired knowledge. As discussed by the different researchers (Mishra, N., Lin, C. C., & Chang, H. T., 2014) (Chang, H. T., Li, Y. W., & Mishra, N., 2016) (Chang, H. T., Liu, S. W., & Mishra, N., 2015), the most significant steps that the knowledge engineer follows to carry out during the knowledge acquisition process are:

1. Eliciting data and information from the domain experts and relevant documents.
2. Read the acquired data and information to be aware of human expert reasoning processes.
3. Construct a conceptual knowledge model to represent the expert's knowledge.
4. Repeating step I-III as the knowledge-based system involves a functional system.

In general, the knowledge engineers to develop the knowledge-based system use two main steps in the knowledge acquisition process: these are knowledge elicitation and knowledge structuring. This involves extracting knowledge from human experts, and/or written documents to build a knowledge-based system. In this study, the knowledge required to build a knowledge-based system was elicited from both tacit and explicit sources of knowledge. Tacit knowledge is collected from eight experts in the domain area from MoLSA and central static agency by using semi-structured interviews. Here, the number of experts to gather the needed knowledge was determined as eight because there were about 8 domain experts at MoLSA, central statically agency office and also we, interviewing all of them is challenging and time taking for both the experts and the researcher. And it can be the representative of them. Domain experts are chosen purposely for wide-ranging discussion using semi-structured interviews to understand the domain knowledge Architecture of the Knowledge Base System.

Figure 4. KBS architecture

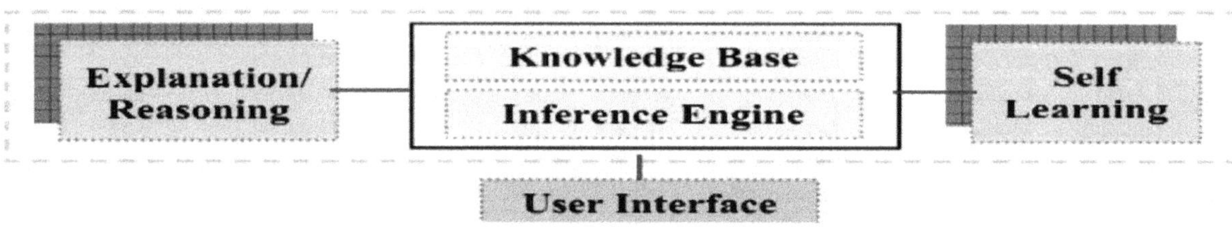

During the knowledge elicitation process, we build a conceptual knowledge model or representation of the relevant document knowledge. In this study, we focused on building the knowledge-based system by extracting the knowledge from the relevant documentation regarding migrant cases. The main process of knowledge acquisition of this research covered some basic actions such as gathering the relevant document knowledge, analyzing the document knowledge, identifying a migrant destination, and lastly modeling the knowledge by applying a hierarchical structure concept system.

Migrants' Knowledge Acquisition From Relevant Document

There are numerous sources of explicit knowledge. Document analysis involves gathering knowledge from existing documentation. For this reason, document analysis has been carried out to acquire explicit knowledge which is found in various secondary sources of knowledge. To elicit explicit knowledge, relevant documents which are related to migrant destination countries and migrant factors have been reviewed. The most important documents used for this study are published books and journal articles, research papers, etc. As a consequence, relevant document knowledge was extracted and structured in a manner that is suitable for conceptual knowledge modeling and lastly knowledge representation. As a result, the challenges and difficulties confronted in the transfer of knowledge acquisition have been shown as the obstruction of Knowledge-Based Systems Development. Accordingly, this study gathers and analyzes the basic domain knowledge regarding migrants' characteristic, and that help to develop the proposed prototype knowledge-based (KBRF) system. The knowledge engineer collects migrants' destination countries; the study explores the applicability of KBRF.

Knowledge Representation

The next task after knowledge acquisition is representing the elicited knowledge in such a way that the computer can understand it. It refers to expressing knowledge explicitly in a computer-tractable way such that the agent can reason out (Mishra, N., Chang, H. T., & Lin, C. C., 2018) (Mishra, N., 2018) (Mishra, N., 2017) (Patnaik, B. C., & Mishra, N., 2016). Acquired knowledge is organized so that it will be ready for use, in an activity called knowledge.

A case in case-based reasoning is a contextualized piece of experience, which can be represented in various forms and that teaches a lesson fundamental to archiving the goal of the reasoned. The issue of case representation involves deciding the type and the structure of the domain knowledge within the cases. Case representation is one of the main components of a case-based reasoning system because it is the process of representing the case in a way that, the programming language (jCOLIBRI) can easily understand or interpret. Case representation in case-based reasoning (KBRF) makes use of familiar knowledge representation formalisms from AI to represent the experience contained in the cases for reasoning purposes.

Conceptual Knowledge Modelling

As noted in (Mishra, N., 2011) (Priyadarsini, K., Mishra, N., Prasad, M., Gupta, V., & Khasim, S., 2021) (Mishra, N., Alebachew, K., & Patnaik, B. C., 2018) (Mishra, N., Chang, H. T., & Lin, C. C., 2018), conceptual modeling of domain knowledge implies capturing the static structure of information and knowledge types. Models are applied to express the important characteristics of real-time systems to understand simply by dividing them into small parts. Models are more related to the problem domain they represent. Models assist individuals to weigh up and know such complications by supporting them to explore every specific area of the system. They are applied in the construction process of systems to draw the architecture of the system and to simplify the exchange of information between several individuals in the group at various levels of abstraction. Individuals have numerous thoughtful of the system and models can help them to know these understandings in a coordinated way. After the knowledge acquisition stage, the next job is modeling the knowledge. According to, the modeling process builds conceptual models of knowledge-intensive activities. During the knowledge acquisition process, the knowledge engineer will attempt to understand the explicit form of knowledge and then use visual tools to make an exchange of views among end-users. This exchange of views produces concepts and understandings concerning how the acquired knowledge is applied, how judgments are made, and so on. The knowledge engineer should build the knowledge model from the acquired exchange of views with end-users. This helps the knowledge engineer to transfer the knowledge model into functional computer-machine programs (Mishra, N., 2010) (Mishra, N., & Samuel, J. M., 2021) (Mishra, N., Thangavel, G., & Samuel, J. M., 2020)

(Mishra, N., 2019). As noted by conceptual knowledge modeling is extremely significant for knowing the functioning means in the development process of a knowledge-based system. It is also a vital stage of the knowledge engineering process. It can provide a means to without difficulty recognize the source of knowledge, the inputs and outputs of knowledge, and the designation of other parameters. After the knowledge acquisition phase is completed from the previous migrant case, domain experts, and relevant documents, the next task is modeling the knowledge. As noted by Schreiber, *et al*, the modeling process builds conceptual models of knowledge-intensive activities. During the knowledge acquisition process, the knowledge engineer will attempt to understand both the tacit and explicit form of knowledge and then use visual tools to make an exchange of views between domain experts and end-users. This exchange of views produces concepts and understandings concerning how the acquired knowledge is applied, how judgments are made, and so on. And the knowledge engineer should build the knowledge model from the acquired exchange of views with domain experts and end-users. This helps the knowledge engineer to transfer the knowledge model into functional computer machine programs. According to Schreiber et al., Knowledge modeling is very significant for knowing the operational means in the development process of a knowledge-based system (Mishra, N., Alebachew, K., & Patnaik, B. C., 2018) (Dandu, S., Rage, K., Sundar Raj, M., Mishra, N., Sivakumar, D., & Mohan, S., 2021). It is also a vital stage of the knowledge engineering process. This model starts from the main concept at the highest level of the hierarchy and other sub-concepts that can affect or be affected by the highest level concept put next to downzone in the hierarchy as shown in Table 6.

Table 6. Problem context solution

Problem	Human migrants in Ethiopia may face the problem of finding the right information about destination countries at the right time.
Context	Makes human migrants choose the best destination countries which satisfy their need
Solution	The recommender system enables human migrants to save their information gap on finding the destination countries.

- Identifying knowledge: Relevant cases and attributes were collected using documents. Next to that, the following input attributes were selected.

Input-- Gender; Age; Educational Level; Region; Zone; Marital status; Year of Migrant; Income Level. The selected output attributes are also Migrants' Destination Countries.

KBRF- DESIGN AND IMPLEMENTATION

To recommend destination country for human migrants by design prototype KBRF system to create knowledge-base, in addition, KBRF provides recommend and add a new migrant' cases or problems into the knowledge-base (KBRF) system. As shown in Figure 5-1, the structural design prototype indicates how to recommend a destination country for human migrants by using the KBRF.

Figure 5. Architecture of migrants KBRF system

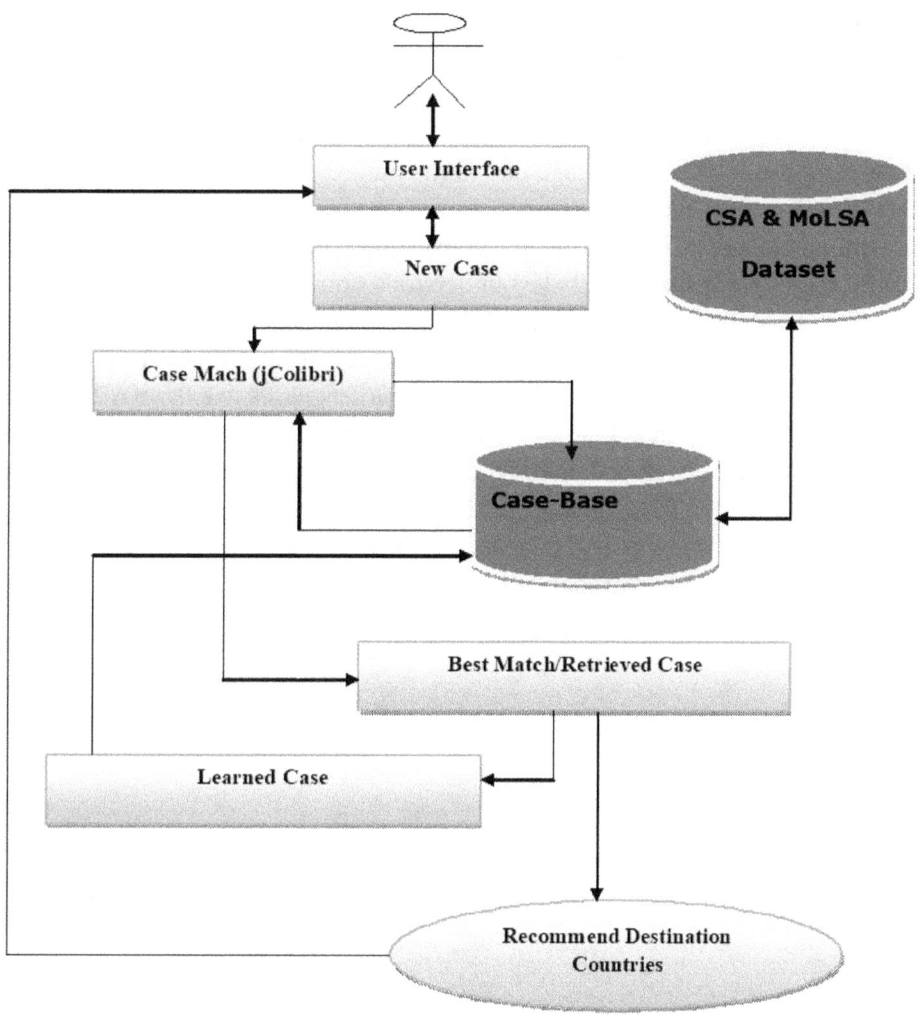

As shown in Figure 5, the developed prototype system functions by selecting the migrant cases from the user interface. It starts by selecting migrant cases from the user interface, after this, the system generates historical migrants cases (retrieve), similarity cases (revision), recommend destination countries, and retain (conformed to the solution) and also the system visualizes the migrants with gender and destination countries to make clear the numbers of migrants in Ethiopia. The user interface is a means of communication with the end-users that enables them to interact easily with the designing prototype KBRF system. It must translate the KBRF knowledge of the prototype to its representation in the KBRF system. The end-users of the system can start by clicking the executive file, after starting the window, the system displayed migrant attributes with selected options. Then it gives general basic information about migrants' attributes for retrieving, revision, and retaining, recommends the destination countries for each migrant. KBRF is a methodology for solving problems by utilizing previous experiences. It involves retaining a memory of previous problems and their solutions and, by referencing these, solves new problems. Generally, a case-based reasoned will be presented with a problem. It may be presented by either a user or another program or system. The case-based reasoned then searches its memory of past cases (the case base) and attempts to find a case that has the same problem specification as the current case. If the reasoned cannot find an identical case in its case base, it will attempt to find the case or cases in the case base that most closely match the current query case. Case-based reasoning systems are an alternative in many situations to rule-based systems. In many domains and processes, referring to cases as a means of reasoning can be an advantage due to the nature of this type of problem-solving. One of the most time-consuming aspects when developing a rule-based system is the knowledge acquisition task. Acquiring domain-specific information and converting it into some formal representation can be a huge task and, in some situations, especially less understood domains the formalization of the knowledge cannot be done at all. Case-based systems usually require significantly less knowledge acquisition as it involves collecting a set of past experiences without the added necessity of extracting a formal domain model from these cases. In many domains, there are insufficient cases to extract a domain model. There is another benefit to KBRF, which is that a system can be created with a small, or limited, amount of experience and incrementally developed, adding more cases to the case base as they become available. After creating the case base, the query dialog, as shown in Figure 6, appears. The user has to fill in the appropriate inputs in the selected options. This information presents in the case base, as our application is dependent on real-time data as stated in chapter four, the study clearly describes the migrants' attributes.

Figure 6. To create the new migrant user interface

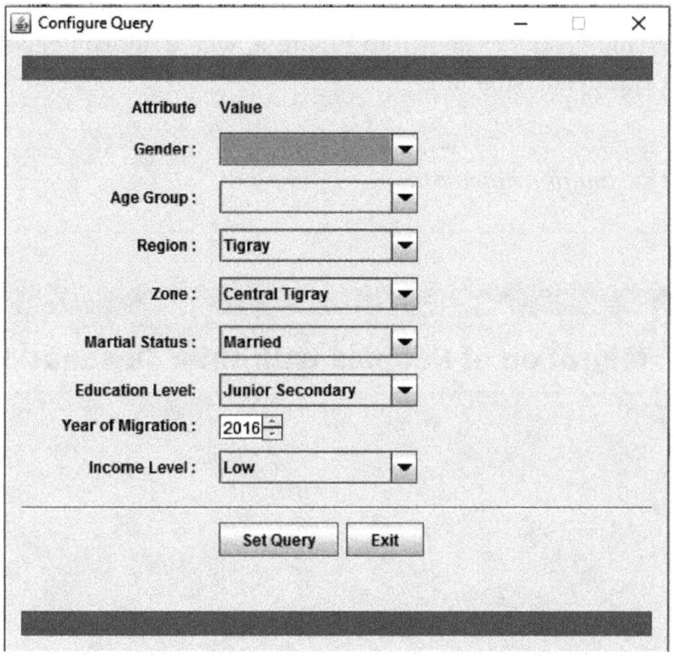

The default similarity function of the case attributes is set according to the recommended values. The similarity dialog is shown in the figure below. The resulting dialog shows the top similar cases as presented as shown in Figure 7. It also includes the evaluation of cases in a range between 0 and 1.

Cases are selected and retrieved in a ranked order based on their similarity for the given new case query. For this research nearest neighbor retrieval algorithm is used to measure the similarity of input cases with cases in the case base.

Figure 7. Similarity migrant case configuration

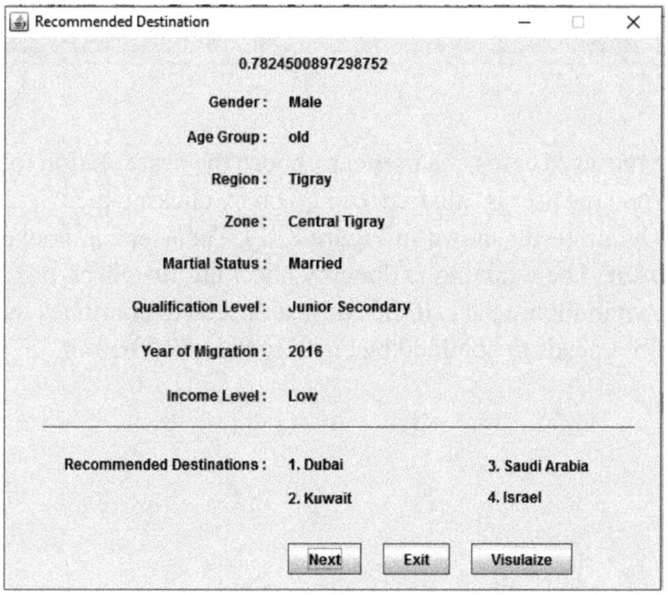

The similarity number is also shown here; closer to "1" is more similar. A destination countries factor of either: Saudi Arabia, Dubai, Kuwait, Others countries. The end-user can also choose to visualize the destination countries and gender as shown in Figure 8, where domain experts need to see the total destination countries of Ethiopian Migrants.

Figure 8. Total migrant destination countries

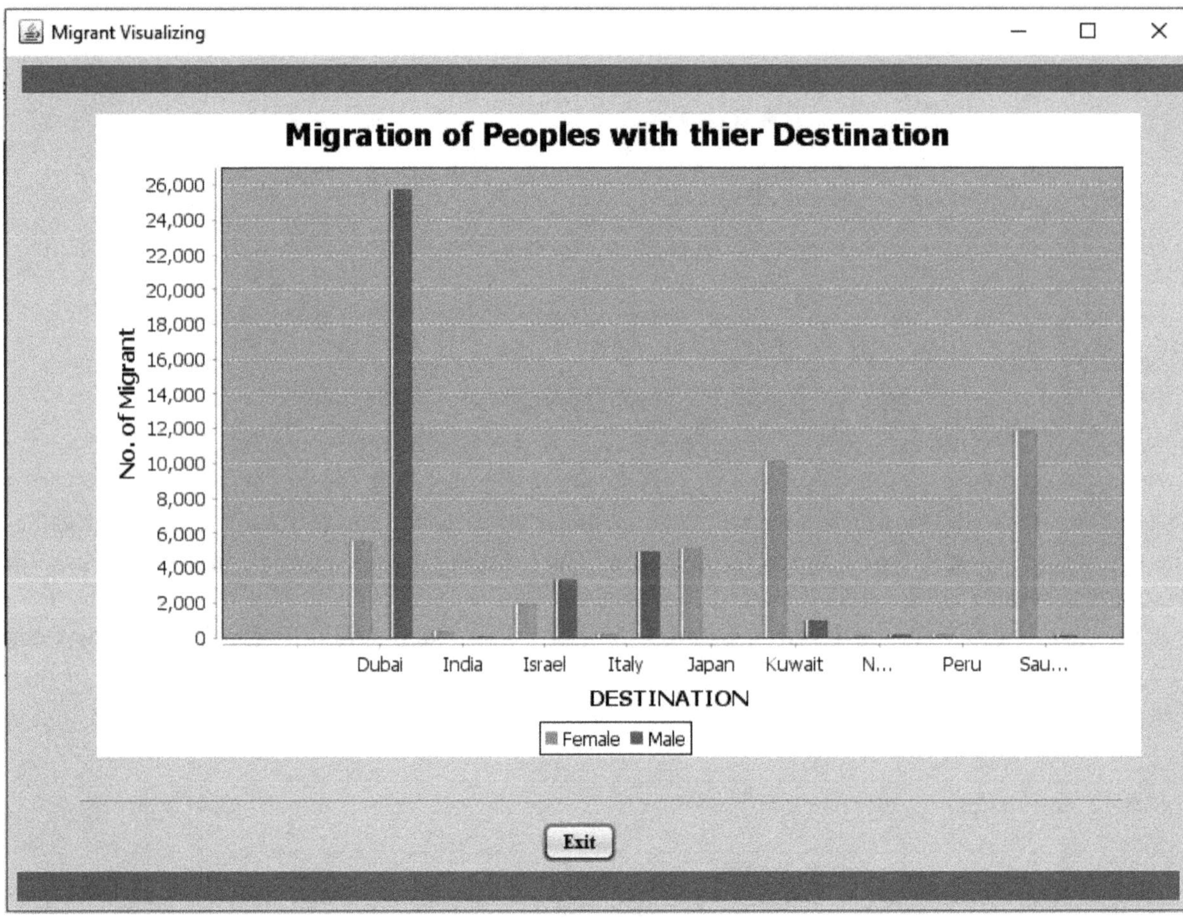

User after having the retrieved cases, the user can choose the best solution to the user query and click on the "Next" button. When the user is satisfied, can go on by clicking the "Set Revision" button, which will take him/her to the retain result shown in Figure 8.-11 The user can now decide to retain the case for later use or to discard it. The retaining is done by checking the check box and clicking the "save" button. And also, as shown in Figure 8-11, if the end-user needs to continues there is the option to click the "Yes" button, and if not needs to continue by clicking the "No" button.

Figure 9.The revise migrant cases

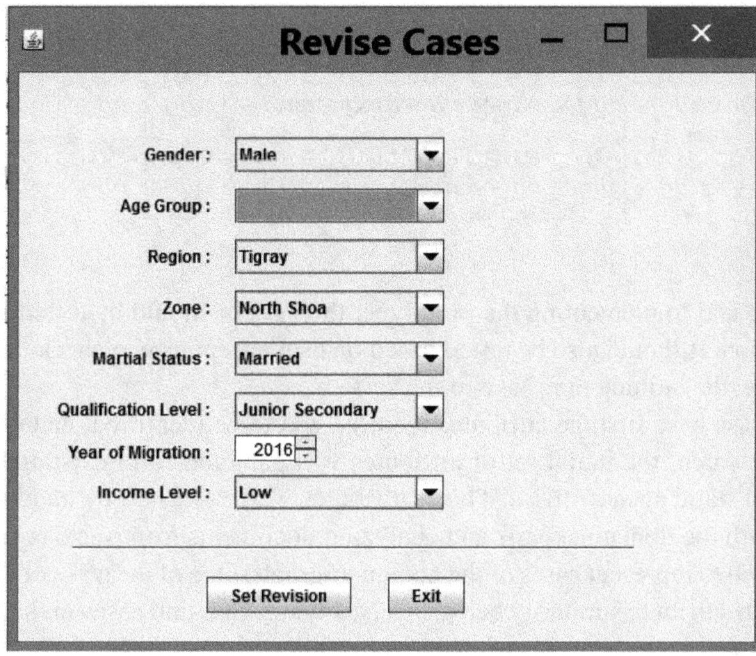

Figure 10. The retain migrant case

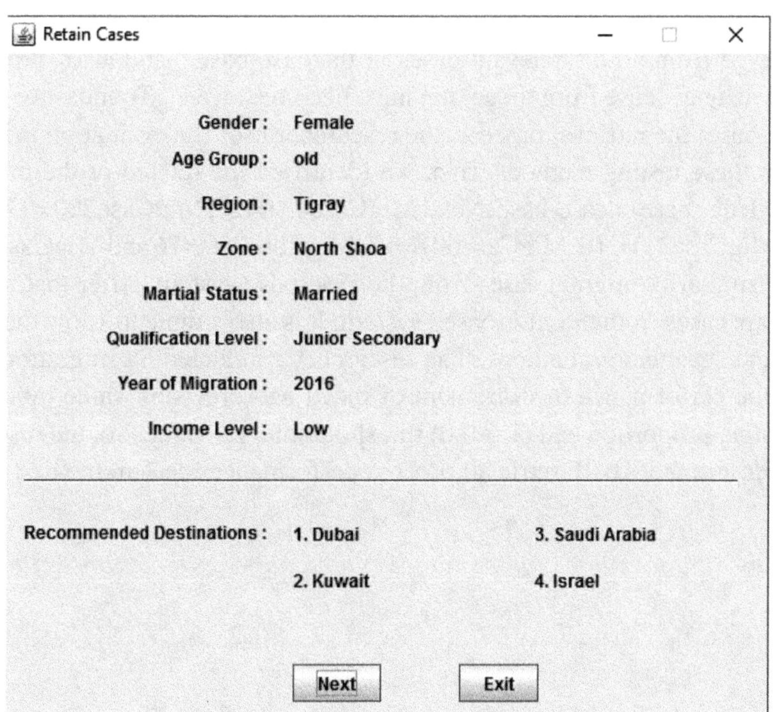

Figure 11. If the end-user needs to continue and exit

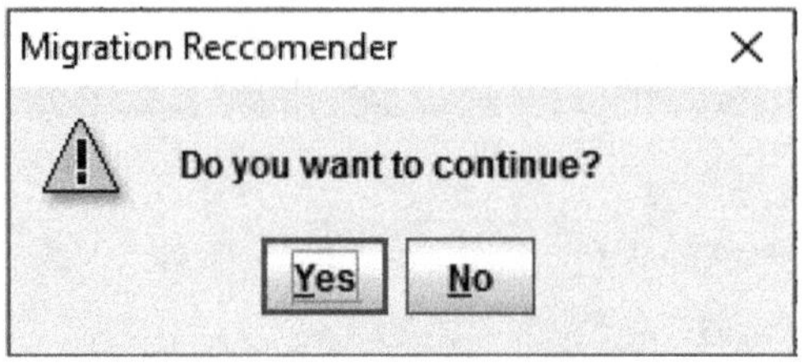

After developing and implementing the prototype, the system should be tested against the requirement of its expectation. It should also be tested based on user acceptance to check that the end-users are satisfied and to know the attitude they have to the system.

To develop the case base first the attributes required had to be identified, including their similarity functions. In this research, the initial set of attributes was gathered from existing documents of each MOLSA and central static agency office. Those attributes were reviewed by undertaking a qualitative type of interview with the domain experts and analyzing documents from various sources. Therefore 9 attributes were chosen to represent cases of the human migrants. One of the tasks of a case-based recommender is to calculate attribute similarity between a new query case and cases in the case base, and then to show the most similar cases. For this research, the similarity function to be used for each identified attribute had to be decided. The most similar cases were retrieved using a k-nearest neighbor algorithm. To find a solution for a query case, instead of recommending just the solution of the nearest neighbor or the k-nearest neighbors, a mechanism in which the k-nearest neighbor's vote was implemented. To measure the significance of KBRF system cycles, the researcher applied recall and precision methods. The researcher explores the most commonly used to measure the performance of KBRF system cycles and also stated the test values are between (1.0 – 0). "Recall tests the relevant cases to a given new case that has been retrieved from all the relevant cases in the case-base", and also "precision measure the relevant cases to give a new case from those that have been retrieved". To measure the performance of KBRF (knowledge-base) the retrieval process, the researcher uses the evaluation methods of recall and precision. To begin these tasting methods, first, we identified the related or the most similar migrant cases from the knowledge base or case-base. Next, MigCase431=20, MigCase200=17, MigCase219=16, MigCase300=18, MigCase311=16, MigCase601=17, MigCase700=16 and MigCase719=22 identified the most related or similarity migrant cases from the case-base system. After that, the domain experts assign related migrant cases from the case-based system. It is also simple to know the value of recall and precision performance evaluation methods. The researcher conducted 82 migrant cases query experiments to measure the performance measurement of recall and precision value by using leave-one-out cross-validation testing proportion and (1.0-0.0) threshold interval value. So, the researcher applies this interval value to measure the KBRF retrieval process performance measurement.

Table 7. KBRF retrieval process performance measurement by using recall and precision

Test Case Query	Recall Value	Precision Value
MigCase431	0.80	0.71
MigCase200	0.94	0.60
MigCase219	1.0	0.57
MigCase300	0.89	0.64
MigCase311	1.0	0.57
MigCase601	0.94	0.60
MigCase700	1.0	0.57
MigCase719	0.73	0.79
Total Average	***0.91***	***0.63***

As per the investigation in Table-7, the researcher scores the recall threshold interval value which becomes 0.80(80%). Similarly, already calculate precision values like the recall concept. That is the researcher calculates the precision threshold interval values from the number of most related migrant cases dividing by the sum of the retrieved cases from the test cases. So, the precision threshold value becomes 0.71(71%). The researcher also calculated the rest of the migrant case's precision threshold interval value in the same way. From these results, the system registers the average and promising result the recall and precision are 0.91 (91%) and 0.63 (63%) respectively. As shown in Table 6-2 above, in general, the researcher can say that the system score is a good result. To compare and contrast the two performance measurements the result of recall and precision threshold interval value, the recall registers is a better result than the precision. This is because the numbers of migrant cases are not enough. From this result, the researcher concludes the number of recall results registered in the system is higher than the precision result, so most of the migrant solution cases can retrieve the most similar migrant destination countries. On the other hand, the knowledge-based or case-based system retrieved most related or similar migrant cases for the end-user with a 0.63 (63%) precision threshold interval value.

CONCLUSION AND FUTURE RESEARCH DIRECTION

The objective of this research was to solve the problems faced by human migrants to know basic information about human migrants for destination countries. In this case, case-based reasoning would be more suitable. A case-based system stores previously solved and successful cases, reasons by comparing a problem case to solved cases and retrieving human factors or causes. The solution of a KBRF system can be revised by testing its success in the real world or by giving it to domain experts. It also increments its knowledge by learning from its own solving experience. Recommender systems are tools and techniques providing suggestions aimed at supporting users in decision making. In this research, a case-based recommender system uses case-based reasoning to suggest the destination countries for human migrants. To undertake the from section stated problems, the researcher initiated to conduct research having the main goal of developing a prototype KBRF system to recommend destination country for human migrants. The KBRF system uses the well-known KBRF cycles (Retrieval, Revise and Retain) to perform different tasks. In this recommender system, the first task is the retrieval of cases by entering a new problem description (case) by using the query window. Next case similarity computation is performed and retrieves most similar cases. The retrieval task of the prototype used in this study is the Nearest Neighbor retrieval algorithm. Regarding the evaluation process of the system, the recommender system registers encouraging retrieval performance which is an average value of 91% recall and 63% precision. The system was also evaluated from the users' side which is called user acceptance testing. Then domain experts the average user acceptance evaluation registered 92% performance by domain experts. To make the system effective and accurate, it is important integrating KBRF with transfer learning systems for further research.

REFERENCES

Al-Wakel, E. (2014). *Ontology-based recommendation of academic papers* (Doctoral dissertation). University of New Brunswick.

Arione, E., Barone, G., Holsten, M., & Weber, F. (1999). *Capitalisation of Existing Approaches*. Academic Press.

Boubakri, H. (2013). *Revolution and international migration in Tunisia*. Robert Schuman Centre for Advanced Studies. (MPC RR 2013/01)

Chang, H. T., Li, Y. W., & Mishra, N. (2016). mCAF: A multi-dimensional clustering algorithm for friends of social network services. *SpringerPlus*, *5*(1), 1–15. doi:10.118640064-016-2420-1 PMID:27386242

Chang, H. T., Liu, S. W., & Mishra, N. (2015). A tracking and summarization system for online Chinese news topics. *Aslib Journal of Information Management*, *67*(6), 687–699. doi:10.1108/AJIM-10-2014-0147

Chang, H. T., Mishra, N., & Lin, C. C. (2015). IoT big-data centred knowledge granule analytic and cluster framework for BI applications: A case base analysis. *PLoS One*, *10*(11), e0141980. doi:10.1371/journal.pone.0141980 PMID:26600156

Dandu, S., Rage, K., Sundar Raj, M., Mishra, N., Sivakumar, D., & Mohan, S. (2021). Practical Approach to the Defect Prediction Model for Software Testing. *J Nucl Ene Sci Power Generat Techno, 10*(9), 2.

Ekstrand, M. D., Riedl, J. T., & Konstan, J. A. (2011). *Collaborative filtering recommender systems*. Now Publishers Inc. doi:10.1561/9781601984432

El-Sappagh, S. H., & Elmogy, M. (2015). Case based reasoning: Case representation methodologies. *International Journal of Advanced Computer Science and Applications*, *6*(11), 192–208.

Fiorini, A. (2016). *The Protection of the Best Interests of Migrant Children-Private International Law Perspectives. Migrant Children in the XXI Century. Selected Issues of Public and Private International Law, Series" La ricerca del diritto*. Editoriale Scientifica.

Hristoski, I., & Sotiroski, K. (2012). Conceptual data modelling of modern human migration. *Management Information Systems*, *7*(4), 3–12.

Iqbal, N., & Ashraf, M. H. (2006). *Evaluation of jCOLIBRI. Master*. Malardalen University.

Mishra, N. (2010). *Art of Software Defect Association & Correction Using Association Rule Mining. Academic Press.*

Mishra, N. (2011). A Framework for associated pattern mining over Microarray database. *Journal of Global Research in Computer Science*, *2*(2).

Mishra, N. (2017). In-network distributed analytics on data-centric IoT network for BI-service applications. *International Journal of Scientific Research in Computer Science, Engineering and Information Technology*.

Mishra, N. (2018). Internet of Everything Advancement Study in Data Science and Knowledge Analytic Streams. *International Journal of Scientific Research in Computer Science and Engineering, 6*(1), 30-36.

Mishra, N. (2019). Data Science and Knowledge Analytic Contexts on IoE Data for E-BI Application Case. In Edge Computing and Computational Intelligence Paradigms for the IoT (pp. 100-126). IGI Global. doi:10.4018/978-1-5225-8555-8.ch007

Mishra, N., Alebachew, K., & Patnaik, B. C. (2018). Knowledge Analytics in Cloud Centric IoT Vicinities. *International Journal on Computer Science and Engineering*, *6*(1), 385–390.

Mishra, N., Alebachew, K., & Patnaik, B. C. (2018). Data Organization and Knowledge Inference from Sensor Database for Smart Wear. International Journal of Scientific Research in Computer Science. *Engineering and Information Technology*, *3*(1), 1039–1044.

Mishra, N., Chang, H. T., & Lin, C. C. (2014). Data-centric knowledge discovery strategy for a safety-critical sensor application. *International Journal of Antennas and Propagation*, *2014*, 2014. doi:10.1155/2014/172186

Mishra, N., Chang, H. T., & Lin, C. C. (2015). An Iot knowledge reengineering framework for semantic knowledge analytics for BI-services. *Mathematical Problems in Engineering*, *2015*, 2015. doi:10.1155/2015/759428

Mishra, N., Chang, H. T., & Lin, C. C. (2018). Sensor data distribution and knowledge inference framework for a cognitive-based distributed storage sink environment. *International Journal of Sensor Networks*, *26*(1), 26–42. doi:10.1504/IJSNET.2018.088387

Mishra, N., Chang, H. T., & Lin, C. C. (2018). *Sensor Data Distribution and Distributed Knowledge Inference Systems*. LAP LAMBERT Academic Publishing.

Mishra, N., Lin, C. C., & Chang, H. T. (2014, December). A cognitive oriented framework for IoT big-data management prospective. In *2014 IEEE International Conference on Communiction Problem-solving* (pp. 124-127). IEEE. 10.1109/ICCPS.2014.7062233

Mishra, N., Lin, C. C., & Chang, H. T. (2014). Cognitive inference device for activity supervision in the elderly. *TheScientificWorldJournal, 2014*, 2014. doi:10.1155/2014/125618 PMID:25405211

Mishra, N., Lin, C. C., & Chang, H. T. (2015). A cognitive adopted framework for IoT big-data management and knowledge discovery prospective. *International Journal of Distributed Sensor Networks, 11*(10), 718390. doi:10.1155/2015/718390

Mishra, N., & Samuel, J. M. (2021). Towards Integrating Data Mining With Knowledge-Based System for Diagnosis of Human Eye Diseases: The Case of an African Hospital. In Handbook of Research on Disease Prediction Through Data Analytics and Machine Learning (pp. 470-485). IGI Global.

Mishra, N., Thangavel, G., & Samuel, J. M. (2020). A Case Assessment Of Knowledge-Based Fit In Frame For Diagnosis Of Human Eye Diseases. *Journal of Critical Reviews, 7*(6), 754–763.

Moore, C. J., Lehane, M. S., & Price, C. J. (1994, March). Case based reasoning for decision support in engineering design. In *IEE Colloquium on Case Based Reasoning: Prospects for Applications* (Digest No. 1994/057) (pp. 4-1). IET.

Patnaik, B. C., & Mishra, N. (2016). A Review on Enhancing the Journaling File System. *Imperial Journal of Interdisciplinary Research, 2*(11).

Priyadarsini, K., Mishra, N., Prasad, M., Gupta, V., & Khasim, S. (2021). Detection of malware on the internet of things and its applications depends on long short-term memory network. *Journal of Ambient Intelligence and Humanized Computing*, 1–12. doi:10.100712652-020-02823-0

Salem, A. B. M. (2007). Case based reasoning technology for medical diagnosis. *World Academy of Science, Engineering and Technology, 31*, 9–13.

Salem, A. B. M., Roushdy, M., & HodHod, R. A. (2005). A case based expert system for supporting diagnosis of heart diseases. *AIML Journal, 5*(1), 33-39.

Sun, S. H., & Chen, J. L. (2007, June). *Knowledge representation and reasoning methodology based on CBR algorithm for modular fixture design. Journal of the Chinese Society of Mechanical Engineers.*

Van Meteren, R., & Van Someren, M. (2000, May). Using content-based filtering for recommendation. In *Proceedings of the machine learning in the new information age: MLnet/ECML2000 workshop* (Vol. 30, pp. 47-56). Academic Press.

Watson, I. (1998). *Applying case-based reasoning: techniques for enterprise systems*. Morgan Kaufmann Publishers Inc.

Yemisrach, F. (2015). *Experience of eight deported women Ethiopians who returned from Kingdom of Saudi Arabia* (Unpublished Master's thesis). Addis Ababa University. Retrieved from http://hdl. handle. net/123456789/8056

KEY TERMS AND DEFINITIONS

Artificial Intelligence: It's a mechanism to transform man-made Cognition and insights for the stated application.

Case Base System: It's a part of the knowledge base expert system that consists of a set of cases and heuristics, which are accumulated from both primary and secondary resources to generate expert solutions for migrant cases.

Conceptual Knowledge Modelling: It is described through a rational structure that transforms both tacit and explicit knowledge into some sort of logical and structural representation to further enable the development of knowledge-based applications.

Data Elicitations: It consists of a set of tools to accumulate data from both primary and secondary resources.

Data Mining: It consists of a set of processes to extract knowledge and insights from the data associated with real-world application, i.e. human migrant recommendation application.

KBRF: It's a knowledge-based recommender framework that suggests artificial intelligence-inspired cognitive solutions following the human migrant's domain.

Knowledge Base: It's the structured representation of an expert system that integrates knowledge and insights with inference engine and user's interfaces with a set of explanation facilities.

Recommender System: It's associated with a search engine along with a knowledge base to recommend a set of cognitive solutions based on the user's inputs.

Rule-Based: It's a part of the knowledge base expert system that consists of a set of rules and heuristics, which are accumulated from both primary and secondary resources to generate expert solutions.

Section 2
Post-Pandemic New Normal

Chapter 6
Leader Competence Effectiveness

Paula Cristina Nunes Figueiredo
https://orcid.org/0000-0002-5267-546X
ULHT, Universidade Lusófona, Portugal

ABSTRACT

The changes that have taken place over the last few decades have culminated in the existence of a workforce of different ages and experiences in the organizational context. This diversity of workforce is a challenge for the human resources management not only in the integration processes, but also in the development of competences and in the management of workers' careers. The aim of this research is to evaluate the effectiveness of the leader's competences following a model that integrates a great variety of competences grouped in four dimensions: intellectual competences, social competences, management competences, and emotional competences. The survey results show the validity and reliability of the integrative model of leader competence. With this model, organizations can identify the skills that need to be developed to improve leadership effectiveness.

INTRODUCTION

In the digital transformation context accelerated by the COVID-19 pandemic situation, younger generations and older workers coexist within organizations. The aging workforce has significant implications for people, human resource management, organizations and societies (Ciutienė & Railaitė, 2014; Hertel & Zacher, 2018). This scenario reinforces the relevance in the implementation of competence management processes in organizations. The new generations are culturally different and have a greater technological domain. Older workers have the knowledge and experience. "Training is less effective for older than for younger employees. Training effectiveness is measured with respect to key aspects such as career development, earnings, adoption of new skills, flexibility and job security" (Zwick, 2012).

The pandemic has had a major impact on the lives of people, organizations, and societies. Researchers are concerned with understanding the role of leaders and human resource development in the pandemic and post-pandemic contexts (Dirani et al., 2020). Competence development is critical to business success.

DOI: 10.4018/978-1-7998-2395-7.ch006

Copyright © 2022, IGI Global. Copying or distributing in print or electronic forms without written permission of IGI Global is prohibited.

Sometimes, there is a greater concern with younger workers in order to provide them with knowledge and experience. Although older workers are retiring later, it is necessary to prepare the transfer of knowledge to younger ones. In the leadership context, we are witnessing the reform of the baby boomer generation and it is essential to prepare the succession within organizations (Behan et al., 2009; Brant et al., 2008; Giambatista et al., 2005; Groves, 2007; Kowalewski et al., 2011). An individual development plan for workers who can succeed leaders is essential. Organizations must timely plan the succession of their leaders. The pandemic and working in virtual environments are also a challenge for leaders (Chen & Sriphon, 2021), and the need for a "task- and relation-oriented leadership behavior to maintain service employees' work performance in a virtual environment during crisis situations" (Bartsch et al., 2021).

Competence Management is the HRM practice that ensures an internal policy of continuous promotion of the development of competences that guarantee the business sustainability. The big challenge is to find a model and identify which competences need to be developed by workers. Researchers' concern with the effectiveness of competences has already been identified in studies carried out in the last decades of the last century. Yukl referred that there is a segmentation of research through theoretical approaches and sought a frame of reference that would integrate the various contributions (Yukl, 1989). In the 21st century, work has an intellectual rather than a physical component and the subject of competences continues to be on the agenda both at the organizational and research levels (Boyatzis, 2008). Therefore, the researchers' greatest concern on how to develop the competences of leaders is evident.

As a result of the critical analysis of the competence models found in the literature, some weaknesses were highlighted – the wide range of competences; the selection of competences following different focuses (e.g., emotional intelligence, problem solving); and the difficulty in perceiving or measuring the effectiveness of these models and the competences identified, due to lack of knowledge and lack of external validity/generalization (Figueiredo, 2019). Through an integrative model of leader competences presented by Figueiredo (2019), this research aims to understand how leaders and the followers evaluate the effectiveness of the leader's competences. Considering a broader range of competences, the intention is to make a diagnosis of the competence's development needs of leaders. It is believed therefore be possible to identify the competences of aging leaders, contributing to the implementation of more appropriate development plans to their needs.

LITERATURE REVIEW

Theoretical Concept: Competence

Several differences are found in the use of 'competence', 'competency', 'competencies' and 'competences' in the literature. Mulder and Collins (2007) consider 'competence' as a general capacity and 'competencies' as components of competence. From a European perspective, the concept of 'competence' is seen in an orientation towards holistic or professional development and 'competences' as its components. The term 'competency' maintains a specific or behavioral perspective. Different concepts are associated with the research carried out in the countries. In the US, functional and cognitive competences are increasingly being added to behavioral competences, while in the UK, cognitive and behavioral competences are being added to the occupational functional competence model. In European countries (France, Germany, and Austria), more holistic approaches were adopted (Delamare-Le Deist & Winterton, 2005).

In 1973, McClelland discussed the concept of competence or individual characteristics regarding them as significant predictors of workers' performance and success (McClelland, 1973). Over time, new concepts have emerged in the literature. "Competences are descriptions of clusters or groupings of behaviors, motivations, and knowledge related to job success or failure under which data on motivation, knowledge, or behavior can be reliably classified" (Byham, 1996, 2). According to Byham and Moyer, it is difficult to define a concept because there are three different meanings: i) "Organizational Competencies - Unique organizational factor that are key to competitiveness; ii) Job/Role Competencies - Things individuals must demonstrate to be effective in a job or role; iii) Personal Competencies - Skills or abilities possessed by an individual at an adequate level" (Byham & Moyer, 1996, 6). The first meaning is based on the definition of Core Competences by Prahalad and Hamel – "provides potential access to a wide variety of markets, make a significant contribution to the perceived customer benefits of the end product, and are difficult for competitors to imitate" (Prahalad & Hamel, 1990, 7). The second meaning refers to what the individual should be able to do in the context of their role in the organization and, lastly, 'personal competences' are different from the others because they refer to the individual's development efforts. Another way of grouping the competence' concept is through three different approaches: - 'The Educational approach, the Psychological approach and the Business approach' (Markus et al., 2005). The first approach is more related to the competence development and the search for patterns; the second approach is more focused on the studies of McClelland and Boyatzis, on the identification of competences through specialized behavioral repertoires; and the last one has a more entrepreneurial vision and based on 'core competences'. "A competency is defined as a capability or ability. It is a set of related but different sets of behavior organized around an underlying construct, which we call the 'intent'" (Boyatzis, 2008, 6). The behaviors are alternate manifestations of the intent. Through the concepts it is possible to describe competence as a combination of personal characteristics and competences and reinforce the idea of this approach arising from the theory of personality (Boyatzis, 2009). This approach can also arise from behaviors that translate into actions and high performance when acting on problem solutions in line with the organization's strategy. All concepts contribute to demonstrate the scope of the theme. This paper follows a more behavioral approach in which competence is seen as a set or group of organized behaviors as referred by Boyatzis (2008) and motivations and knowledge as mentioned by Byham (1996). Competence and behavior are not autonomous concepts; behaviors are the effective manifestation of a certain competence, the result of learning the competence.

The competency approach can follow several paths, however, in the organizational context, the focus can be on the competences of workers (in general) or leaders. Boyatzis sought to distinguish the role of the leader and contributed to the leadership development approach in organizations. The researcher says that being a leader is an individual's choice. "Many people in leadership positions do not demonstrate leadership and frustrate members of their organizations and their stakeholders, even though they possess many of the competencies necessary to be an effective leader" (Boyatzis, 1993, 6). One of the aspects that can influence the choice of developing competences and being a leader is the moment in the individual's career and life. Boyatzis presents three modes of growth that can occur at different times in life - Performance, Learning and Development. With the integration of research by Kolb that focused on learning and Boyatzis that focused on performance, a new theoretical framework emerged regarding learning styles and the theory of experiential learning (Boyatzis & Kolb, 1995). In a competence approach, it is important to consider that when defining the competences to be developed by leaders, it is essential to consider the moment of each person's career and life.

Competency Models

The competence model emerges as a trend after the researchers found that the analysis of functions wasn't enough for the new challenges of organizations (Schippmann et al., 2000). "The competency approach to human resource management is based on identifying, defining and measuring individual differences in terms of specific work-related constructs, especially the abilities that are critical to successful job performance" (Vakola, Soderquist, & Prastacos, 2007, 260). The relevance of the models is visible in terms of benefits for organizational leaders and human resources development professionals, providing the basis on which training programs can be created to encourage superior performance, maintaining a strong link with strategy and direction of the organization (Stevens, 2012). There are also criticisms of the models. "Competency modeling has typically been fraught with issues of conceptual ambiguity, lack of methodological rigor, and dubious psychometric quality" (Stevens, 2012, 102). Several researchers present the evolution of competence model, highlighting competency-based human resource management (Ratnawat, 2018).

At the end of the last century, there was a greater mobility of the workforce and the retirement of leaders of the baby boomer's generation. In this scenario, competence models associated with training, 'assessment', people development and succession planning proliferate (Ennis, 2008). Competences models have become a fashion in the organizational context due to the demands of leadership development. The need for leaders available and prepared to assume leadership roles has become a priority in organizations. The need to complement the analysis of functions, more precisely the description of a worker's work activities with organizational strategies and objectives also contributed to the adoption of competence management models (Stevens, 2012). Their use results in a conceptual ambiguity due to the lack of methodological rigor in the development of the system and to psychometric issues (Stevens, 2012).

Like some competence concepts, some competence model definitions are defined as a set of behaviors among other aspects such as traits, skills and characteristics that need to be effective in the work context. "A competency model is a descriptive tool that identifies the competencies needed to operate in a specific role within a job, occupation, organization or industry" (Ennis, 2008, 3). Other construct "competency development or competency modeling, refers to the process of identifying a set of competences representative for job proficiency" (Burnett & Dutsch, 2006, 141). Regarding leadership, "competency models that define what leaders know and how they behave have become common in most organizations" (Burns, Smith, & Ulrich, 2012, 17). A more recent literature review reports that, "managerial competency models located in the literature capture business skills, intra–personal skills, interpersonal skills, and leadership skills as important competencies for effective performance" (Manxhari et al., 2017, 187). Some studies refer to the mapping of competences in organizations and their role in organizational success. "The competency mapping process helps the organization in developing a clear strategy for developing competencies of their workforce. It supports successful performance of the employees within the organization" (Chouhan & Srivastava, 2014, 14).

Competence models seek to know what competences and behaviors are necessary for the effectiveness of functions and roles performed within organizations. In the light of complexity theory, it is necessary to know how many times competence must be demonstrated to be regarded enough for performance (Boyatzis, 2006). Most human resource management practices are not published because companies are afraid to disclose the data, considering it a competitive advantage (Boyatzis, 2006). This was the main difficulty in analyzing the several competence models in literature. In Appendix, several models and the competences associated with each of them are identified.

Katz was one of the first researchers to show concern for grouping technical, human, and conceptual skills. More recently, through the emotional intelligence approach, competences are defined by Goleman (1998), Boyatzis, Goleman and Rhee (2000) e Dulewicz & Higgs (2003, 2004) and Hawkins & Dulewicz (2007). The model developed by Mumford, Zaccaro, Harding et al (2000) seeks to integrate personal attributes and skills and see the impact on leadership results, through career experience and environmental influence. Skills are related to problem solving. Mumford and his team, established the requirements for leadership skills according to the hierarchical level of the leader/manager (Mumford et al., 2007). Researchers identified four groups: - 'Cognitive skills' are the foundations of leadership skills, 'Interpersonal skills' and 'Business skills' make up the model and 'Strategic skills' are the most important skills for the senior level. The study concludes that when the hierarchical level of the leader/manager increases, the need for these competences increases too. These competence groups are described by the researchers as 'Leadership Skills Requirements' (Mumford et al., 2007). Hogan and Warrenfeltz propose another model with four competence domains that are made up of lists - Intrapersonal skills, Interpersonal skills, Business skills, Leadership skills). The content of the domains is defined through 'management education' where intrapersonal skills are the first to be developed and the most difficult to develop. Leadership skills are developed later and are less difficult to learn. The remaining competences are essential for effective leadership (Hogan & Warrenfeltz, 2003). Following the trend of creating a competency taxonomy, Chin, Gu, and Tubbs created the Global Leadership Competences model. Its identification arises from a pyramidal hierarchy that represents the phase of development similar to Maslow's hierarchy of needs (Bueno & Tubbs, 2004). At the base of the pyramid is the cognitive level, represented by the Ignorance phase and at the top of the pyramid is the behavioral level, represented by the Transformation phase. Bueno and Tubbs tested this model by conducting a qualitative study of several international leaders and established some of the most important leadership competences: i) "communication competences; ii) motivation to learn; iii) flexibility; iv) open-mindedness; v) respect for others; e, vi) sensitivity" (Bueno & Tubbs, 2004). The search for a competency taxonomy is found in other researchers who establish a set of generic behaviors and competences associated with leadership and management (Hamlin, 2002; House et al., 2002; Tubbs & Schulz, 2006; Yukl et al., 2002).

Researchers in the social sciences field have often been focused on what makes the leader most effective regardless of the several leadership approaches (Burns et al., 2012). Ulrich, Smallwood & Sweetman created the 'The Leadership Code' with the idea that it is possible to simplify what makes leaders more effective and efficient. This model also derives from several competences models and presents five domains – 'Strategist; Executor; Talent Manager; Human Capital Developer; Personal Proficiency' -, each one has specific competences (Burns, Smith, & Ulrich, 2012). At the organizational level, there are the competences related to Strategist and Executor, the first is framed in the long-term view and the second is more operational, so a short-term view. At the individual level, there are the competences related to the role of Human Capital Developer and Talent Manager, the first framed in the long-term view and the second is more operational, therefore, a short-term view. In the Personal Proficiency domain are the competences related to the leader's self-knowledge, character and integrity and the concerns with himself (balance work and life) and his results (Burns et al., 2012). Organizations have been concerned with the work and personal life balance of their workers, as their impact is direct on productivity and performance. Managers, leaders, CEO, executives should be aware of these issues in their beliefs and decision making (Eversole et al., 2007).

Conger and Ready have three limitations to the competence management models. Competences are complicated, conceptual and built through current realities leading to a tendency for models with too many dimensions (Conger & Ready, 2004). This is the first limitation and the second refers that competence models are based on an idealized concept of leadership - the concept of a leader capable of working in all situations. This results from extensive research to identify competences. The last limitation states that competence models focus on current leadership behaviors, that is, they are developed using today's high-performance leaders as a reference. Models tend to stabilize within organizations and the competences that have contributed to the identification and development of current leaders may not be appropriate for the next leaders generation (Conger & Ready, 2004). It is possible that leaders are being evaluated using outdated models.

In short, competency-based management models have characteristics and specificities, and it is difficult to evaluate which is more complete and best suits the current reality, as well as the competences that contribute to increasing the effectiveness of leaders. Some theoretical models are developed and implemented in organizations (e.g., army or multinational companies) (Mcevoy et al., 2005; Mumford, Zaccaro, Harding, et al., 2000; Rodriguez et al., 2002; Rouco, 2015; Rouco & Sarmento, 2012), therefore, it is not possible to obtain relevant information for a good analysis. It is also complicated to assess the effectiveness of each of them, not only because of the lack of information, but because the models are implemented in organizations with specific contexts. It is necessary to replicate them in other organizations with different characteristics to validate and generalize the results of the models and the associated competences. Through this analysis, it is concluded that some focus only on emotional competences and others on competences associated with problem solving. This demonstrates that there is no integrated view of competences.

Integrative Model of the Leader Competence

In an attempt to integrate the competences of the leader in a model, Figueiredo (2019) presented the Integrative Model of the Leader Competence. According to the author, through this integration, four dimensions of competences are identified – Intellectual Competences (CMPE_I), Management Competences (CMPE_I), Emotional Competences (CMPE_I) and Social Competences (CMPE_I). These dimensions arise from the analysis of various models and types of competences found in the literature (Table 1).

Table 1. Relationship between the four dimensions of the model and the other competence models

Authors	Intellectual Competences	Management Competences	Emotional Competences	Social Competences
Katz, 1974	*Conceptual Skills*	*Technical Skills*	-	*Human Skills (interpersonal)*
Goleman, 1998	-	-	*Self-awareness, Self-regulation, Motivation, Empathy, Social skills*	*Motivation, Empathy, Social skills*
Mumford et al., 2000	*Knowledge*	*Problem-solving*	-	*Social Judgement*
Analoui et al., 2000	*Analytical and self-related skills*	*Task-related skills People-related skills (Problem-solving)*	*Analytical and self-related skills*	*People-related skills Analytical and self-related skills*

Continued on following page

Table 1. Continued

Authors	Intellectual Competences	Management Competences	Emotional Competences	Social Competences
Goleman, Boyatzis, McKee, 2001	-	-	*Self-awareness, Self-management, Social awareness, Relationship management*	*Social awareness, Relationship management*
Dulewicz, Higgs, 2003	*Intellectual Competencies*	*Intellectual Competencies, Managerial Competencies*	*Emotional Competencies*	*Managerial Competencies Intellectual Competencies*
Hogan & Warrenfeltz, 2003	*Leadership Skills Intrapersonal Skills*	*Technical Skills*	*Intrapersonal Skills Leadership Skills*	*Leadership Skills Interpersonal Skills*
Tubbs, 2005	*META COMPETENCY I: Understanding the Big Picture META COMPETENCY II. Attitudes are Everything META COMPETENCY III: Leadership, The Driving Force META COMPETENCY IV: Communication, The Leader 's Voice*	*META COMPETENCY IV: Communication, The Leader 's Voice META COMPETENCY V: Innovation and Creativity*	*META COMPETENCY II. Attitudes are Everything META COMPETENCY III: Leadership, The Driving Force META COMPETENCY IV: Communication, The Leader's Voice*	*META COMPETENCY III: Leadership, The Driving Force META COMPETENCY IV: Communication, The Leader 's Voice META COMPETENCY VI: Leading Change META COMPETENCY VII: Teamwork and Followership*
Boyatzis, 2006b	*Cognitive Cluster*		*Self-motivation cluster, Self-regulation cluster*	*People management cluster*
Mumford et al., 2007	*Cognitive skills Strategic skills*	*Business skills Strategic skills*	-	*Cognitive skills Interpersonal skill*
Boyatzis, 2009, 2011	*Cognitive Competencies*	-	*Emotional Intelligence Competencies*	*Social Intelligence Competencies*
Burns, Smith, & Ulrich, 2012	*Personal Proficiency*	*Strategist, Executor Talent Manager Human Capital Developer*	-	*Talent Manager Human Capital Developer*

The dimension of Intellectual Competences includes Conceptual Skills (Katz), Cognitive Skills/competences (Mumford et al., 2007), Intrapersonal Skills (Boyatzis and Hogan and Warrenfeltz) and Intellectual Competencies (Dulewicz and Higgs). This dimension refers to the leader's intrapersonal competences, that is, knowledge for the role and a vision of the change-oriented future. Today, knowledge about digital transformation and artificial intelligence is crucial for the future. Intellectual Competences distinguish the leader from other team members, for their vision and knowledge of the organization and the market. Knowledge of each person's culture (specific and linguistic information) is essential in the context of globalization.

Management Competences include Technical Skills (Katz and Hogan and Warrenfeltz), Business/Strategic Skills (Mumford et al., 2007), Managerial Competencies (Dulewicz and Higgs) and Task-related skills and Problem-solving Analoui et al. (2000) and Mumford et al., 2000). This dimension refers to the competences related to strategy and problem solving such as setting goals, planning, and monitoring activities and evaluating results. These competences are task-oriented. Management Competences focus on strategy and on solving the day-to-day problems.

Social Competences include Human Skills (Katz), Social Judgment (Mumford et al., 2000), People-related skills, (Analoui et al, 2000), Leadership Skills and Interpersonal Skills (Hogan and Warrenfeltz and Mumford et al, 2007), People management cluster and Social Intelligence Competencies (Boyatzis). Social Competences are people-oriented. These refer to the leader's interpersonal competences such as the competences linked to the way the leader listens and speaks to others, how he communicates and shares information, his relationship with others, the creation of bonds, empathy, and concern for others, both personally and professionally. Social Competences contribute to good people management as they seek to build and maintain the relationship between the leader and the team members. Following Goleman's model of emotional intelligence, a study carried out highlighted social competences, namely Relationship Management as those that leaders and followers perceive as less practiced by leaders (Figueiredo & Sousa, 2016). It is important to understand whether this is due to the need to develop such competences.

Emotional Competences are found in models that only focus on that type of competence or are included in Intrapersonal, Leadership and Interpersonal Competences. Emotional Competences are found both at a personal and social level as suggested by the model of Goleman, Boyatzis and Mckee (2007). Emotional Competences allow to understand and use the emotional knowledge of the leader and others to achieve high performances.

With the view to understand the leader's competences in the context of 4.0 Industry, the researchers used the model of Mumford et al. (2007). They concluded that only Business Skills were not identified. Regarding the remaining 3 groups, it was found that the most important Cognitive Skills, in descending order, are active learning, speaking, active listening and critical thinking; the most important Interpersonal Skills in descending order are negotiation, persuasion and social perceptiveness; and, the most important Strategic Skills in descending order are visioning, identification of key causes, solution appraisal and systems perception (Guzmán et al., 2020). In another study, there are 3 competences that 4.0 industrial revolution leaders must have: (1). Having the basic ability to be a leader (2). Quick decision (3). Choosing and building your own team (Tulasi et al., 2019). More than defining the competences of the 4.0 leader, some researchers reinforce the concept of training – "promotes the qualification of the participants with regard to leadership competencies and provides specific methods and tools which support transferability to the participants' everyday work" (Helming et al., 2019). Other researchers refer to the lack of digital culture and competences in the organization that they need to develop (Oberer & Erkollar, 2018, 411). Thus, it is considered that the competences for the 4.0 leader are already included in the dimensions of the presented model.

This model follow the assumption of orientation for change, task and people defended by Yukl et al. (2002) and is presented in Figure 1 and is described in more detail in Appendix.

Figure 1. Integrative model of the leader competences
(Figueiredo, 2019)

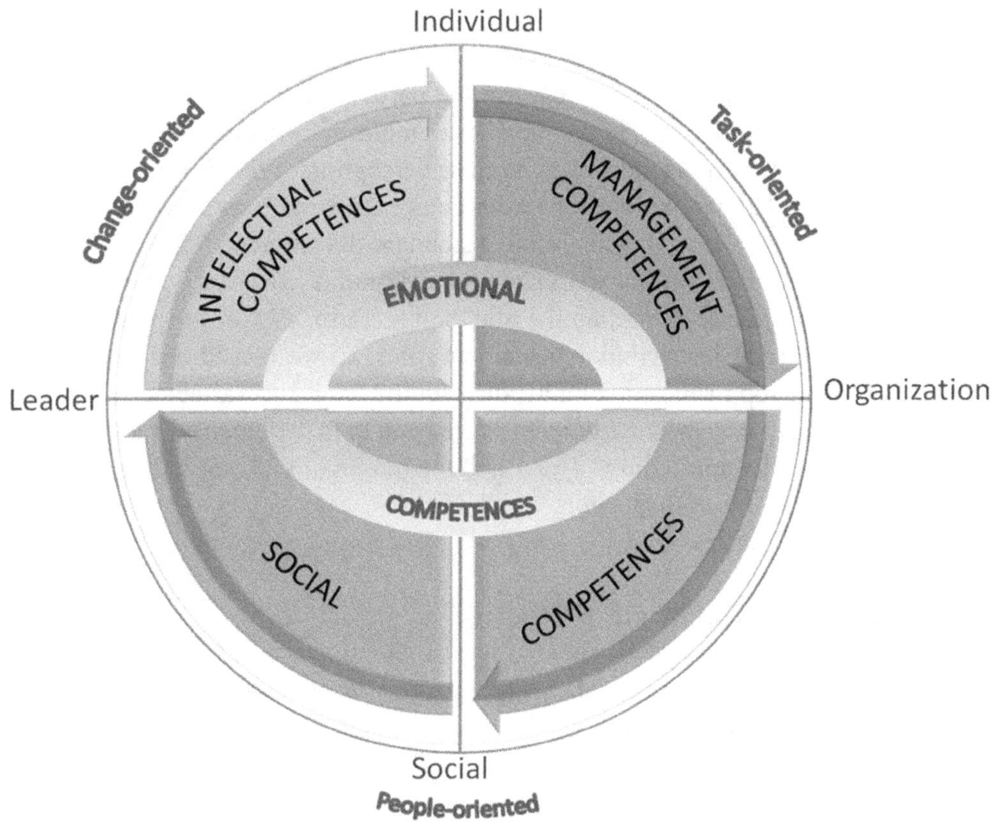

This model makes it possible to diagnose the competences that need to be developed by the leaders according to the perception of their own and the followers. These dimensions help human resources professionals to prepare training and leadership development programs according to the organization's needs. The model enables leaders to make a self-assessment to prepare their own personal and professional development.

RESEARCH METHODOLOGY

The research follows a quantitative and non-experimental research methodology (Creswell, 2009) and the research strategy adopted is by questionnaire (Yin, 2009). The main objective is to evaluate the effectiveness of the leader competences identified in the integrative model according to the leaders and followers' perceptions. The quantitative methodology also aims to verify the issues of validity and reliability of the model's constructs that resulted from the integrative literature review and the critical analysis of existing models. This methodology uses various statistical techniques and allows us to validate or not certain results. In this sense, in addition to the descriptive analysis of the variables, an Exploratory Factor Analysis is carried out to ensure the validity of the model's constructs.

The questionnaire emerged from the Integrative Model of Leader competences (Appendix) and allows evaluating each competency as to the effectiveness perceived by leaders and followers, using an ordinal Likert scale, where 1 means Not Effective, 2 means Little Effective, 3 means Effective and 4 means Very Effective.

This study was carried out in a company and had the participation of 92 workers of the 157 workers of the department based in Lisbon. The online questionnaire setting only allowed a single response per worker and asked them to respond according to their perception of the direct supervisor's behavior and not according to what they would like. The average age of workers is 38 years and there is some dispersion around the average, which translates into a standard deviation of 7.553, due to the amplitude of the interval between the minimum (24 years) and the maximum (57 years). The sample has 51% of participants female and 49% male. Regarding the role they perform, 47% of the participants are middle managers, 39% do not perform leadership/management roles, so we considered them in the study as non-managers and 14% are top managers. Finally, through the Seniority variable, the average tenure in the organization is 6 years, that is, most participants have been in the company for less than 6 years. The range of the range is large; the minimum is 1 year and the maximum 34 years. The standard deviation (6.363) shows the existence of data dispersion.

ANALYSIS AND DISCUSSION OF RESULTS

At this point of the research, an analysis of the metric qualities is made through the Exploratory Factor Analysis and a descriptive analysis of the variables related to the leader competences.

Analysis of Metric Qualities

The analysis of metric qualities is performed at subscales through the analysis of validity, reliability, and sensitivity. Validity is "the degree to which a measure accurately represents what i tis supposed to" (Hair Jr. et al., 2010). To ensure validity it is necessary to understand what is to be measured and then the measurement must be 'correct' and accurately. Validity analysis is performed using Exploratory Factor Analysis and allows the verification of correlations between the original variables in order to estimate common factors and structural relationships between factors and variables. "Factor analysis is an interdependence technique whose primary purpose is to define the underlying structure among the variables in the analysis" (Hair Jr. et al., 2010). This analysis uses the observed correlations between the original variables to estimate the common factor and the structural relationships that link the latent factor to the variables (Marôco, 2011). Factor extraction requires that the variables have a multivariate normal distribution. The most used method is the Kaiser-Meyer-Olkin test (KMO). The KMO measures the homogeneity of the variables and compares the simple correlations with the partial correlations observed between the variables. According to several authors (Marôco, 2011; Pestana & Gageiro, 2014), KMO can have the value from 0 to 1 and is unacceptable when the index is less than 0.5; between 0.5 and 0.6, the index is considered bad but still acceptable; between 0.6 and 0.7, the index is considered mediocre; between 0.7 and 0.8, the index is considered average; between 0.8 and 0.9, the index is considered good; and, between 0.9 and 1, the index is considered excellent.

With the Exploratory Factor Analysis, only the minimum number of factors that allow explaining the phenomenon under study is retained. The KMO criterion and the eigenvalue rule greater than 1 explain that factors with greater variance should be retained, that is, that explain more information than the standardized information of the original variable, whose value is 1. As for the variance extracted by each factor and the total variance extracted, it is to retain the factors that extract at least 5% of the total variance or to extract a minimum number of factors that explain at least 50% of the total variance of the original variables. Exploratory Factor Analysis is not always able to properly interpret the factor weights in common factors, so the Varimax Rotation Method is used. The objective is to obtain a factorial structure in which one and only one of the original variables is strongly associated with a single factor, and little associated with the remaining factors (Marôco, 2011).

Reliability is "the degree to which the observed variable measures the 'true' value and is 'error free'" (Hair Jr. et al., 2010). The researcher's role is to assess the reliability indicators of the variables and choose those that are more reliable. This analysis is done using Cronbach's Alpha. This coefficient varies between 0 and 1, and represents the scale's internal consistency, evaluating the ratio between the variance of each item with the entire scale. A value equal to or greater than 0.70 is acceptable (Pestana & Gageiro, 2014).

Sensitivity is analyzed through measures of dispersion, asymmetry, and kurtosis, as they explain the ability of an item to discriminate subjects. For this purpose, the median, asymmetry, flatness, maximum and minimum of each item were analyzed. Items must not have the median at any of the extremes, the absolute values of asymmetry and flatness must be less than 3 and 7 respectively, and must have answers at all points (Kline, 2011). Sensitivity must discriminate subjects according to the factor being evaluated. For this purpose, the average of the sum of the items of each of the scales used is calculated.

The leader's competences are measured based on a new scale composed of twenty-eight items, classified using the Likert scale with four points ranging between "Not Effective" (1) and "Very Effective" (4). These items are distributed in four dimensions of competences - Intellectual Competences (CMPE_I), Management Competences (CMPE_M), Social Competences (CMPE_S) and Emotional Competences (CMPE_E). Validity analysis is performed using Exploratory Factor Analysis at four subscales.

Intellectual Competences (CMPE_I) - Through the KMO and Bartlett tests, it is possible to assess the quality of the correlations between items. The KMO test is a measure that allows you to analyze the adequacy of data. The KMO test has a value of 0.884, which can be considered good. Through the Bartlett test, it is verified that a significance level of 0 is associated, so there is a correlation between some pairs of items (Table 2).

Table 2. KMO and Bartlett test - CMPE_I

	Kaiser-Meyer-Olkin Measure test					0.884
	Bartlett Test		Approx. Qui-quadrado			360.734
			Sig.			0.000

	Initial Eigenvalues			Extraction of squared loadings		
Component	Total	% de variance	% cumulative	Total	% de variance	% cumulative
1	4.594	57.421	57.421	4.594	57.421	57.421

	Component 1	Communalities
CMPE_I1	**0.827**	0.684
CMPE_I2	**0.838**	0.701
CMPE_I3	**0.838**	0.701
CMPE_I4	**0.759**	0.576
CMPE_I5	**0.704**	0.495
CMPE_I6	**0.717**	0.514
CMPE_I7	**0.625**	0.391
CMPE_I8	**0.729**	0.531

Factor extraction allows obtaining a factorial structure in which one and only one of the original variables is strongly associated with a single factor and little associated with the other factors. The result was to obtain a single factor that explains about 57.42% of the variance. While the commonality matrix shows the percentage of variance explained jointly by the retained factor, the component matrix explains the correlation per item in each factor. Each component is a linear combination, that is, the correlation between the item and the component. The weight of the items is greater than 0.7, except for item CMPE_I7. Since all factor weights are greater than 0.60, it is not necessary to remove any item. All items are accepted, as they measure what is intended to be studied – Intellectual Competences.

Management Competences (CMPE_M) - Through exploratory factor analysis, the KMO criterion has a value of 0.853 and is considered a good indicator. The KMO test shows that the items are homogeneous (Table 3).

Table 3. KMO and Bartlett test - CMPE_M

Kaiser-Meyer-Olkin Measure test						0.853
Bartlett Test					Approx. Qui-quadrado	412.793
					Sig.	0.000

	Initial Eigenvalues			Extraction of squared loadings		
Component	Total	% de variance	% cumulative	Total	% de variance	% cumulative
1	4.732	59.147	59.147	4.732	59.147	59.147

	Component 1	Communalities
CMPE_M1	**0.742**	0.551
CMPE_M2	**0.843**	0.711
CMPE_M3	**0.745**	0.555
CMPE_M4	**0.786**	0.617
CMPE_M5	**0.801**	0.641
CMPE_M6	**0.758**	0.575
CMPE_M7	**0.702**	0.493
CMPE_M8	**0.767**	0.589

After extracting the factors, a single factor is obtained that explains about 59.15% of the variance. All items have weights greater than 0.7 in the component matrix, so it is not necessary to remove any item from the Management Competences; all items measure the same construct.

Social Competences (CMPE_S) - The KMO test presents a value considered good (0.879), demonstrating that the items are homogeneous (Table 4).

Table 4. KMO and Barlett test - CMPE_S

Kaiser-Meyer-Olkin Test						0.879
Bartlett test					Approx. Qui-quadrado	309.351
					Sig.	0.000

	Initial Eigenvalues			Extraction of squared loadings		
Component	Total	% de variance	% cumulative	Total	% de variance	% cumulative
1	4.151	59.293	59.293	4.151	59.293	59.293

	Componente 1	Communalities
CMPE_S1	**0.792**	0.628
CMPE_S2	**0.871**	0.759
CMPE_S3	**0.801**	0.641
CMPE_S4	**0.688**	0.474
CMPE_S5	**0.719**	0.516
CMPE_S6	**0.784**	0.614
CMPE_S7	**0.720**	0.518

Table 5. KMO and Barlett test - CMPE_E

	Kaiser-Meyer-Olkin test					0.857
	Bartlett test		Approx. Qui-quadrado			240.379
			Sig.			0.000
	Initial Eigenvalues			**Extraction of squared loadings**		
Component	Total	% de variance	% cumulative	Total	% de variance	% cumulative
1	3.389	67.776	67.776	3.389	67.776	67.776

	Component 1	Communalities
CMPE_E1	**0.702**	0.492
CMPE_E2	**0.794**	0.630
CMPE_E3	**0.864**	0.747
CMPE_E4	**0.871**	0.759
CMPE_E5	**0.872**	0.760

After the extraction method, it appears that a single factor is also obtained that explains about 59.29% of the explained variance. The weight of each item is also greater than 0.7 in the component matrix, so the validity of the construct is accepted, with no need to remove any item from the Social Competences.

Emotional Competences (CMPE_E) - The KMO test presents the value of 0.857. It can be concluded that there is a good correlation between the items (Table 5).

With the extraction method, it appears that a single factor is obtained that explains about 67.78% of the explained variance. Compared to previous analyses, this is the one with the greatest explained variance. As for the weight of the items, it is verified that they are greater than 0.7 in the component matrix, so the validity of the construct is accepted. There is no need to remove any item, as they measure what is intended to be studied - Emotional Competences.

Reliability analysis allows to analyze internal consistency through Cronbach's Alpha. However, this indicator is heavily influenced by the correlation between the items. Cronbach's Alpha indicator if the item is excluded is used. This analysis was performed at subscales, considering the types of competences. The outputs are presented in Table 6.

Table 6. Reliability statistics

Scale Dimension	Items	Initial Cronbach's Alpha	Cronbach Alpha if Item Is Deleted
Intellectual Competences	CMPE_I1	0.892	0.870
	CMPE_I2		0.869
	CMPE_I3		0.869
	CMPE_I4		0.878
	CMPE_I5		0.885
	CMPE_I6		0.883
	CMPE_I7		0.891
	CMPE_I8		0.882

Continued on following page

Table 6. Continued

Scale Dimension	Items	Initial Cronbach's Alpha	Cronbach Alpha if Item Is Deleted
Management Competences	CMPE_M1	0.900	0.890
	CMPE_M2		0.878
	CMPE_M3		0.89
	CMPE_M4		0.885
	CMPE_M5		0.883
	CMPE_M6		0.888
	CMPE_M7		0.894
	CMPE_M8		0.887
Social Competences	CMPE_S1	0.885	0.865
	CMPE_S2		0.851
	CMPE_S3		0.864
	CMPE_S4		0.879
	CMPE_S5		0.875
	CMPE_S6		0.865
	CMPE_S7		0.874
Emotional Competences	CMPE_E1	0.880	0.884
	CMPE_E2		0.862
	CMPE_E3		0.841
	CMPE_E4		0.838
	CMPE_E5		0.837

Through the reliability statistics, it is verified that Cronbach's Alpha always presents good or very good internal consistency (greater than 0.88); if any of the items in each dimension were excluded, the value of Cronbach's Alpha would not be higher. The dimension of the Management Competences scale (CMPE_M) are those that present a higher Cronbach's Alpha (0.9) as opposed to Emotional Competences (CMPE_E). Thus, it is chosen to include all items in each dimension.

Sensitivity is analyzed using measures of dispersion, asymmetry, and kurtosis. In Table 7, it is verified that the items do not have the median at any of the extremes, the absolute values of asymmetry and flatness are less than 3 and 7 respectively, and all items have answers at all points. In this regard, it appears that the items meet the established criteria and are important for the analysis of the phenomenon under study.

Table 7. Sensitivity statistics

	N		Median	Asymmetry	Standard Asymmetry Error	Kurtosis	Standard Kurtosis Error	Min.	Max.
	Válid	Missing							
CMPE_I1	92	0	3.00	-0.470	0.251	-0.063	0.498	1	4
CMPE_I2	92	0	3.00	-0.363	0.251	-0.229	0.498	1	4
CMPE_I3	92	0	3.00	-0.473	0.251	-0.494	0.498	1	4
CMPE_I4	92	0	3.00	-0.429	0.251	-0.199	0.498	1	4
CMPE_I5	92	0	3.00	-0.374	0.251	1.064	0.498	1	4
CMPE_I6	92	0	3.00	-0.429	0.251	-0.215	0.498	1	4
CMPE_I7	92	0	3.00	-0.286	0.251	0.234	0.498	1	4
CMPE_I8	92	0	3.00	-0.069	0.251	-0.276	0.498	1	4
CMPE_M1	92	0	3.00	-0.348	0.251	0.116	0.498	1	4
CMPE_M2	92	0	3.00	-0.400	0.251	-0.535	0.498	1	4
CMPE_M3	92	0	3.00	-0.623	0.251	0.871	0.498	1	4
CMPE_M4	92	0	3.00	-0.483	0.251	-0.472	0.498	1	4
CMPE_M5	92	0	3.00	-0.245	0.251	-0.349	0.498	1	4
CMPE_M6	92	0	3.00	-0.207	0.251	-0.135	0.498	1	4
CMPE_M7	92	0	3.00	-0.619	0.251	-0.124	0.498	1	4
CMPE_M8	92	0	3.00	-0.545	0.251	0.454	0.498	1	4
CMPE_S1	92	0	3.00	-0.414	0.251	-0.101	0.498	1	4
CMPE_S2	92	0	3.00	-0.169	0.251	-0.589	0.498	1	4
CMPE_S3	92	0	3.00	-0.396	0.251	-0.583	0.498	1	4
CMPE_S4	92	0	3.00	-0.318	0.251	-0.243	0.498	1	4
CMPE_S5	92	0	3.00	-0.424	0.251	-0.223	0.498	1	4
CMPE_S6	92	0	3.00	-0.463	0.251	0.041	0.498	1	4
CMPE_S7	92	0	3.00	-0.221	0.251	-0.346	0.498	1	4
CMPE_E1	92	0	3.00	-0.442	0.251	0.147	0.498	1	4
CMPE_E2	92	0	3.00	-0.564	0.251	0.446	0.498	1	4
CMPE_E3	92	0	3.00	-0.295	0.251	-0.559	0.498	1	4
CMPE_E4	92	0	3.00	-0.255	0.251	-0.074	0.498	1	4
CMPE_E5	92	0	3.00	0.039	0.251	-0.633	0.498	1	4

Descriptive Analysis

After verifying the validity and reliability of the data, a descriptive analysis of the leader competences is carried out. Twenty-eight of the Integrative Model of the Leader Competence items follow an ordering (Likert scale), so they are ordinal qualitative variables; these do not assume quantitative values and are defined by several categories that represent a classification of individuals (McClave et al., 2014). These are grouped into four dimensions

- Intellectual Competences (CMPE_I), Management Competences (CMPE_G), Social Competences (CMPE_S) and Emotional Competences (CMPE_E). These dimensions are quantitative variables. Analyzing the frequencies of the variables presented in Appendix, it is concluded that:
- Regarding Intellectual Competences (CMPE_I), respondents perceive the following competences as less effective, in descending order: - CMPE_I2 - Imagination, Creativity and Innovation, an open and confident approach to new solutions (40%); CMPE_I6 - Leadership by example, practicing and defending the principles, rules, and good practices (33%); e, CMPE_I3 - Creating an inspiring and attractive mission that motivates all team members (32%). More than 30% of respondents rated these competences as 'Not Effective' and 'Little Effective'. Management and personal development, promoting improvements in their performance (CMPE_I5) is considered by respondents as the competence in which direct supervisors demonstrate greater effectiveness (90% considered 'Effective' and 'Very Effective').
- It appears that the Management Competences (CMPE_G) perceived by respondents as being the least effective are as follows in descending order: - CMPE_G2 - Timely resource management (materials, technical, financial, and human) (36%); CMPE_G5 - Analysis, planning and timely work organization (36%); and, CMPE_G6 - Monitoring and evaluating of activities and results and constructive feedback (35%). More than 60% of respondents perceive these competences as 'Effective' and 'Very Effective' by the supervisor.
- It is observed that the Social Competences (CMPE_S) perceived as the least effective by respondents are as follows, in descending order: - CMPE_S2 - Active listening and negotiating power (39%); CMPE_S1 - Effective and frequent communication (verbal and non-verbal) according to the motivations, needs, attitudes and feelings of others (37%); CMPE_S3 - Influence and people management (direction, motivation, and development) (33%); CMPE_S7 - Monitoring, coaching, support, and direction according to the needs of each one (33%); e, CMPE_S4 - Creation and management teams encouraging participation, team spirit and confidence (32%). Personal and professional development of the team and future leaders (CMPE_S5) is a competence that respondents perceived as the most effective by their supervisors (about 79% of respondents rated it as 'Effective' and 'Very Effective').
- Finally, it is shown that the Emotional Competences (CMPE_E) perceived by respondents as the least effective are as follows, in descending order: - CMPE_E5 - Relationship management, inducing desirable responses in others, through teamwork, conflict management, inspiration, and influence (41%) e CMPE_E3 - Confidence in oneself and in one's abilities (39%). On the contrary, Awareness of one's emotions and the effect of the emotional state on others (CMPE_E1) is the competence perceived in which direct supervisors demonstrate greater effectiveness compared to other competences (about 87% rated it as 'Effective' and 'Very Effective').

In summary, Table 8 presents the ranking of competences perceived by respondents.

Table 8. Ranking of competences

5 competences Perceived With Greater Effectiveness	5 Competences Perceived With Lower Effectiveness
90% - Management and personal development, promoting improvements in their performance (CMPE_I5)	41% - Relationship management, inducing desirable responses in others, through teamwork, conflict management, inspiration, and influence (CMPE_E5)
87% - Awareness of one's emotions and the effect of the emotional state on others (CMPE_E1)	40% - Imagination, Creativity and Innovation, an open and confident approach to new solutions (CMPE_I2)
82% - Management of own emotional states, impulses, and internal resources (CMPE_E2)	39% - Confidence in oneself and in one's abilities (CMPE_E3)
79% - Personal and professional development of the team and future leaders (CMPE_S5)	39% - Active listening and negotiating power (CMPE_S2)
78% - Involvement of everyone in decision making and problem solving (CMPE_G3)	37% - Effective and frequent communication (verbal and non-verbal) according to the motivations, needs, attitudes and feelings of others (CMPE_S1)

Integrative Model of the Leader Competence arises from the integration of competences from the various theoretical models to obtain a more up-to-date and comprehensive list of competences. Analyzing the data in isolation, the intellectual competence related to personal and career management and development, promoting improvements in their performance is the competence with the greatest effectiveness according to the participants' perception (CMPE_I5). This result demonstrates the leaders' concern with their personal and professional development. Considering Boyatzis and Kolb's theory of experimental learning, this result can be explained by the moment in the individual's career and life that influence the development of competences (Boyatzis, 1993; Boyatzis & Kolb, 1995). If we look at the profile of respondents, it appears that more than 60% are under 40 years of age. From the findings, it is believed that they are now at a career stage where performance is very important, hence the need for constant updating of knowledge and competences. The remaining competences of the model with greater effectiveness in each of the dimensions are: - Involvement of everyone in decision making and problem solving (CMPE_M3); Personal and professional development of the team and future leaders (CMPE_S5); Awareness of one's emotions and the effect of the emotional state on others (CMPE_E1); and Management of own emotional states, impulses, and internal resources (CMPE_E2).

These results are in line with the emotional intelligence approach of Dulewicz & Higgs (2003), who claim that emotional and intellectual competences are most responsible for leadership performance (36% and 27%, respectively) in relation to management competences (16%). One of the explanations for the competence of 'Personal and professional development of the team and future leaders' being considered as one of the most effective, may be due to the development experience. According to several researchers, influences the development of leaders (DeRue & Myers, 2009; Mumford, Marks, et al., 2000; Mumford, Zaccaro, Connelly, et al., 2000). The focus on developing the team and future leaders should be highlighted.

According to the descriptive analysis of the integrative model's leadership competences, it is possible to outline them following the respondents' perception of effectiveness. Table 9 summarizes the results.

Table 9. Leader competences effectiveness

	Greater Effectiveness	Lower Effectiveness
Intellectual Competences CMPE_I	Management and personal development, promoting improvements in their performance (CMPE_I5)	Imagination, Creativity and Innovation, an open and confident approach to new solutions (CMPE_I2) Leadership by example, practicing and defending the principles, rules, and good practices (CMPE_I6) Creating an inspiring and attractive mission that motivates all team members (CMPE_I3)
Management Competences CMPE_M	Involvement of everyone in decision making and problem solving (CMPE_M3)	Timely resource management (materials, technical, financial, and human) (CMPE_M2) Analysis, planning and timely work organization (CMPE_M5) Monitoring and evaluation of activities and results and constructive feedback (CMPE_M6)
Social Competences CMPE_S	Personal and professional development of the team and future leaders (CMPE_S5)	Active listening and negotiating power (CMPE_S2) Effective and frequent communication (verbal and non-verbal) according to the motivations, needs, attitudes and feelings of others (CMPE_S1) Influence and people management (direction, motivation, and development) (CMPE_S3)
Emotional Competences CMPE_E	Awareness of one's emotions and the effect of the emotional state on others (CMPE_E1) Management of own emotional states, impulses, and internal resources (CMPE_E2)	Relationship management, inducing desirable responses in others, through teamwork, conflict management, inspiration, and influence (CMPE_E5) Confidence in oneself and in one's abilities (CMPE_E3)

CONCLUSION AND IMPLICATIONS

The context of the labor market shows that the nature of work has changed, so it is necessary to identify and assess the effectiveness of the competences of leaders. In addition, there are workers from different generations within organizations. Young workers need to develop competences not only when they are integrated into organizations, but also for career advancement. On the other hand, it is necessary to provide working conditions and career development suitable for the perspectives of aging workers. Yukl (1989) demonstrated the existence of a segmentation of research through the various competency approaches. He created a framework for integrating the various contributions. As for the models after Yukl, some of them continue to show weaknesses regarding the wide variety of competences that are selected in each model, following different focuses – emotional intelligence, problem solving, for example. Thus, we chose a model that is an attempt to integrate various types of leader competences (Figueiredo, 2019) and that provides a more comprehensive list of competences.

The originality of this research is present in the analysis of the effectiveness of the leader's competences according to a theoretical model that integrates several types of competences. Through this study, the validity and reliability analysis of the model is also promoted. The analysis of the metric qualities of the scales through the analysis of validity, reliability, and sensitivity, validate the constructs of the Integrative Model of the Leader Competence. This model diagnoses the gap in leader competences at any point in their professional career, with the aim of promoting their development.

More important than the research findings are its implications for the management and development of human resources. The implications of research at the Management level consist fundamentally in the issues of the connection between the strategy and the business itself. The most important and required competences evolve, that is, they are not the same over time. It is not only competences that become obsolete in the face of work demands, but development methods also must be suited to the type of competences and the profile of leaders that organizations need. Without jeopardizing the organization's objectives, strategy, and business growth, it is important to diagnose the competences that leaders need to develop. This model can thus be adopted by organizations. This process of identifying competences that contributes to perceived effective leadership is an ongoing process that must be updated considering the context and needs of organizations. Developing leaders' competences is crucial to business strategy.

The challenge of human resource development is to accelerate the development of leadership in organizations, improving the performance of leaders and creating a talent management channel to 'feed' the training of leaders internally. The identification of competences thus contributes to the effectiveness of leadership as it has direct implications for the development of human resources. In terms of human resource development, this research has implications for the process of selecting people, training management, talent management and retention, and career management within the organization. In practice, the identification of competences is a reference for the design of training programs and the development of human resource management techniques, such as 360º performance evaluation. With the identification and assessment of competences, it is possible to create individual development plans suited to the organization's requirements and review the competency management models, thus increasing their relevance and the usefulness of the evaluation criteria used in the selection of leaders and in the measurement of its performance.

RECOMMENDATIONS FOR FUTURE STUDIES

This is a first study using the integrative model of leader competences and the need to apply it in other contexts and business realities is clear. Other studies make it possible to introduce improvements and make the model more robust and adequate to organizational needs. The use of the questionnaire in other organizations with different characteristics will be an asset to compare the results obtained and improve the model and the questionnaire. The context and development of society and organizations lead to the emergence of new critical competences, so competency models must keep pace with these changes.

The training and development programs for new leaders are essential tools for managing and retaining talent within the organization. In operational terms, it is also essential to understand which leadership development practices are most appropriate for each leader profile. Thus, organizations are looking to increasingly value their human capital, adding more value to it. Competences impact leadership effectiveness and create value for organizations, contributing to performance and bottom-line results.

Leadership development is indisputably essential for organizations' survival. Studies related to leadership competences and effectiveness seek to encourage and stimulate the development processes of leaders in organizations. However, competences are not enough to guarantee this effectiveness, as leader development programs can be great in acquiring competences, but without translating into results in the organization. It is necessary to study the impact of these programs and measure their effectiveness in terms of performance. The leader's motivation for the development of competences is also an important factor that needs to be deepened. On the other hand, a greater perception by leaders of what others think about their behavior and competences is crucial for management and leadership in organizations. This type of research is thus an asset for a continuous valorization of human capital in the organizational context.

REFERENCES

Analoui, F., Labbaf, H., & Noorbakhsh, F. (2000). Identification of clusters of managerial skills for increased effectiveness: The case of the steel industry in Iran. *International Journal of Training and Development*, *4*(3), 217–234. doi:10.1111/1468-2419.00109

Bartsch, S., Weber, E., Büttgen, M., & Huber, A. (2021). Leadership matters in crisis-induced digital transformation: How to lead service employees effectively during the COVID-19 pandemic. *Journal of Service Management*, *32*(1), 71–85. doi:10.1108/JOSM-05-2020-0160

Behan, B. A., Kirschner, J., & Snyder, S. M. (2009). Succession in PRACTICE. *Chief Executive*, *239*(Mar/Apr), 28.

Boyatzis, R. (1993). Beyond competence: The choice to be a leader. *Human Resource Management Review*, *3*(1), 1–14. doi:10.1016/1053-4822(93)90007-Q

Boyatzis, R. (2006). Using tipping points of emotional intelligence and cognitive competencies to predict financial performance of leaders. *Psicothema*, *18*(SUPPL.1), 124–131. PMID:17295969

Boyatzis, R. (2008). Competencies in the 21st century. *Journal of Management Development*, *27*(1), 5–12. doi:10.1108/02621710810840730

Boyatzis, R. (2009). Competencies as a behavioral approach to emotional intelligence. *Journal of Management Development*, *28*(9), 749–770. doi:10.1108/02621710910987647

Boyatzis, R. (2011). Managerial and Leadership Competencies: A Behavioral Approach to Emotional, Social and Cognitive Intelligence. *Vision: The Journal of Business Perspective*, *15*(2), 91–100. doi:10.1177/097226291101500202

Boyatzis, R., Goleman, D., & Rhee, K. (2000). Clustering competence in emotional intelligence: Insights from the Emotional Competence Inventory (ECI). In R. Bar-On & J. D. A. Parker (Eds.), *Handbook of Emotional Intelligence* (pp. 343–362). Jossey-Bass.

Boyatzis, R., & Kolb, D. (1995). From learning styles to learning skills the exec skills profile. *Journal of Managerial Psychology*, *10*(5), 3–17. doi:10.1108/02683949510085938

Brant, J., Dooley, R., & Iman, S. (2008). Leadership succession: An approach to filling the pipeline. *Strategic HR Review*, *7*(4), 17–24. doi:10.1108/14754390810880499

Bueno, C. M., & Tubbs, S. L. (2004). Identifying Global Leadership Competencies: An Exploratory Study. *The Journal of American Academy of Business, Cambridge*, *5*(1/2), 80–87.

Burnett, M., & Dutsch, J. (2006). Competency-based training and assessment center: Strategies, technology, process, and issues. *Advances in Developing Human Resources*, *8*(2), 141–143. doi:10.1177/1523422305279687

Burns, E., Smith, L., & Ulrich, D. (2012). Competency Models with Impact. *People & Strategy*, *35*(3), 16–23.

Byham, W. (1996). *Developing dimension / competency based Human Resource Systems*. Development Dimensions International, Inc.

Byham, W., & Moyer, R. (1996). *Using competencies to build a successful organization*. Development Dimensions International, Inc.

Chen, J. K. C., & Sriphon, T. (2021). Perspective on COVID-19 pandemic factors impacting organizational leadership. *Sustainability*, *13*(3230), 1–21. doi:10.3390u13063230

Chouhan, V. S., & Srivastava, S. (2014). Understanding Competencies and Competency Modeling— A Literature Survey. *IOSR Journal of Business and Management*, *16*(1), 14–22. doi:10.9790/487X-16111422

Ciutienė, R., & Railaitė, R. (2014). Challenges of Managing an Ageing Workforce. *Procedia: Social and Behavioral Sciences*, *156*(April), 69–73. doi:10.1016/j.sbspro.2014.11.121

Conger, J., & Ready, D. (2004). Rethinking leadership competencies. *Leader to Leader*, *2004*(Spring), 41–48. doi:10.1002/ltl.75

Creswell, J. W. (2009). Research Design: Qualitative, Quantitative and Mixed Approaches. In Research Design: Qualitative, Quantitative, and Mixed Methods Approaches (3rd ed.). Sage Publication, Inc.

Delamare-Le Deist, F., & Winterton, J. (2005). What Is Competence? *Human Resource Development International*, *8*(1), 27–46. doi:10.1080/1367886042000338227

DeRue, D., & Myers, C. (2009). Leadership Development: A Review and Agenda for Future Research. *Journal of Selection and Assessment*, 832–855.

Dirani, K. M., Abadi, M., Alizadeh, A., Barhate, B., Garza, R. C., Gunasekara, N., Ibrahim, G., & Majzun, Z. (2020). Leadership competencies and the essential role of human resource development in times of crisis: A response to Covid-19 pandemic. *Human Resource Development International*, *00*(00), 1–15. doi:10.1080/13678868.2020.1780078

Dulewicz, V., & Higgs, M. (2003). Leadership at the top: The need for emotional intelligence in organizations. *The International Journal of Organizational Analysis*, *11*(3), 193–210. doi:10.1108/eb028971

Dulewicz, V., & Higgs, M. (2004). Can Emotional Intelligence be developed? *International Journal of Human Resource Management*, *15*(1), 95–111. doi:10.1080/0958519032000157366

Ennis, M. (2008). *Competency models: A review of the literature and the role of the Employment and Training Administration (ETA)*. Academic Press.

Eversole, B., Gloeckner, G., & Banning, J. H. (2007). Understanding differential organizational responses to work/life issues: The role of beliefs and decision-making styles of chief executive officers. *Journal of European Industrial Training*, *31*(4), 259–273. doi:10.1108/03090590710746423

Figueiredo, P. (2019). *Competências para uma liderança percebida como eficaz - Líderes e liderados* [PhD Thesis in Management]. Universidade Europeia.

Figueiredo, P., & Sousa, M. J. (2016). Leaders and followers: The leadership style perceived in modern organizations. In G. L. Jamil, J. Poças-Rascão, F. Ribeiro, & A. Malheiro da Silva (Eds.), *Handbook of Research on Information Architecture and Management in Modern Organizations*. IGI Global. doi:10.4018/978-1-4666-8637-3.ch009

Giambatista, R., Rowe, W., & Riaz, S. (2005). Nothing succeeds like succession: A critical review of leader succession literature since 1994. *The Leadership Quarterly*, *16*(6), 963–991. doi:10.1016/j.leaqua.2005.09.005

Goleman, D. (1998). What makes a leader? *Harvard Business Review*, 82–91. PMID:10187249

Goleman, D., Boyatzis, R., & Mckee, A. (2001). Primal Leadership: The Hidden Driver of Great Performance. *Harvard Business Review*, (December), 42–51.

Goleman, D, Boyatzis, R., & Mckee, A. (2007). *Os Novos Líderes – A Inteligência Emocional nas Organizações* (3ª edição). Gradiva.

Groves, K. S. (2007). Integrating leadership development and succession planning best practices. *Journal of Management Development*, *26*(3), 239–260. doi:10.1108/02621710710732146

Guzmán, V. E., Muschard, B., Gerolamo, M., Kohl, H., & Rozenfeld, H. (2020). Characteristics and Skills of Leadership in the Context of Industry 4.0. *Procedia Manufacturing*, *43*, 543–550. doi:10.1016/j.promfg.2020.02.167

Hair, J. Jr, Black, W., Babin, B., & Anderson, R. (2010). *Multivariate Data Analysis* (7th ed.). Pearson Education Inc.

Hamlin, R. (2002). *Towards a Generic Theory of Managerial Effectiveness: a meta-level analysis from organisations within the UK public sector*. Academic Press.

Hawkins, J., & Dulewicz, V. (2007). *The relationship between performance as a leader and emotional intelligence, intellectual and managerial competences.* Academic Press.

Helming, S., Ungermann, F., Hierath, N., Stricker, N., & Lanza, G. (2019). Development of a training concept for leadership 4.0 in production environments. *Procedia Manufacturing*, *31*, 38–44. doi:10.1016/j.promfg.2019.03.007

Hertel, G., & Zacher, H. (2018). Managing the Aging Workforce. In C. Viswesvaran, N. Anderson, D. S. Ones, & H. K. Sinangil (Eds.), The SAGE Handbook of Industrial, Work and Organizational Psychology: Personnel Psychology and Employee Performance (2nd ed., vol. 3). SAGE Publications Ltd. doi:10.4135/9781473914964.n19

Hogan, R., & Warrenfeltz, R. (2003). Educating the Modern Manager. *Academy of Management Learning & Education*, *2*(1), 74–84. doi:10.5465/amle.2003.9324043

House, R., Javidan, M., Hanges, P., & Dorfman, P. (2002). Understanding cultures and implicit leadership theories across the globe: An introduction to project GLOBE. *Journal of World Business*, *37*(1), 3–10. doi:10.1016/S1090-9516(01)00069-4

Kline, R. B. (2011). Principles and practice of structural equation modeling. In Structural Equation Modeling (3rd ed.). The Guilford Press.

Kowalewski, S., Moretti, L., & McGee, D. (2011). Succession Planning: Evidence from "Best Companies in New York.". *International Journal of Management and Marketing Research*, *4*(2).

Manxhari, M., Veliu, L., & Jashari, J. (2017). Developing Models of Managerial Competencies of Managers : A Review. *International Journal of Economics. Commerce and Management*, *V*(4), 186–200.

Markus, L. H., Cooper-Thomas, H., & Allpress, K. N. (2005). Confounded by Competencies? An Evaluation of the Evolution and Use of Competency Models. *New Zealand Journal of Psychology*, *34*(2), 117–126.

Marôco, J. (2011). *Análise Estatística com o SPSS Statistics* (5ª ed.). ReportNumber, Lda.

McClave, J., Benson, P., & Sincich, T. (2014). *Statistics for Business and Economics* (12th ed.). Pearson Education Inc.

McClelland, D. C. (1973). Testing for competence rather than for "intelligence". *The American Psychologist*, *28*(1), 1–14. doi:10.1037/h0034092 PMID:4684069

Mcevoy, G. M., Hayton, J. C., Warnick, A. P., Mumford, T. V., Hanks, S. H., & Blahna, M. J. (2005). A competency-based model for developing human resource professionals. *Journal of Management Education*, *29*(3), 383–402. doi:10.1177/1052562904267538

Mulder, M., & Collins, K. (2007). Competence Development in Organisations : Its Use in Practice. Paper Presented at the *Annual Meeting of the AERA*.

Mumford, M., Marks, M., Connelly, M., Zaccaro, S., & Reiter-Palmon, R. (2000). Development of leadership skills: Experience and timing. *The Leadership Quarterly*, *11*(1), 87–114. doi:10.1016/S1048-9843(99)00044-2

Mumford, M., Zaccaro, S., Connelly, M., & Marks, M. (2000). Leadership skills: Conclusions and future directions. *The Leadership Quarterly*, *11*(1), 155–170. doi:10.1016/S1048-9843(99)00047-8

Mumford, M., Zaccaro, S., Harding, F., Jacobs, T., & Fleishman, E. (2000). Leadership skills for a changing world: Solving complex social problems. *The Leadership Quarterly*, *11*(1), 11–35. doi:10.1016/S1048-9843(99)00041-7

Mumford, T., Campion, M., & Morgeson, F. (2007). The leadership skills strataplex: Leadership skill requirements across organizational levels. *The Leadership Quarterly*, *18*(2), 154–166. doi:10.1016/j.leaqua.2007.01.005

Oberer, B., & Erkollar, A. (2018). Leadership 4.0: Digital Leaders in the Age of Industry 4.0. *International Journal of Organizational Leadership*, *7*(4), 404–412. doi:10.33844/ijol.2018.60332

Pestana, M. H., & Gageiro, J. N. (2014). Análise de dados para ciências sociais - A complementaridade do SPSS (6a ed.). Academic Press.

Prahalad, C., & Hamel, G. (1990). The core competence of the corporation. *Harvard Business Review*, (May-June), 1–15.

Ratnawat, R. K. (2018). Competency Based Human Resource Management : Concepts, Tools, Techniques, and Models : A Review. *International Journal of Multidisciplinary*, *3*(5), 119–124.

Rodriguez, D., Patel, R., Bright, A., Gregory, D., & Gowing, M. K. (2002). Developing competency models to promote integrated human resource practices. *Human Resource Management*, *41*(3), 309–324. doi:10.1002/hrm.10043

Rouco, C. (2015). Identification of Leadership Competences in the Different Organizational Levels: Military Context. *Journal of Business and Economics*, *6*(4), 709–721. doi:10.15341/jbe(2155-7950)/04.06.2015/008

Rouco, C., & Sarmento, M. (2012). Development model of leadership skills in the military context. *Proceedings of the 13th UFHRD International Conference on Human Resource Development Research and Practice across Europe*, 1–17.

Schippmann, J. S., Ash, R. A., Carr, L., & Hesketh, B. (2000). The practice of competency modeling. *Personnel Psychology*, *53*(3), 703–740. doi:10.1111/j.1744-6570.2000.tb00220.x

Stevens, G. W. (2012). A Critical Review of the Science and Practice of Competency Modeling. *Human Resource Development Review*, *12*(1), 86–107. doi:10.1177/1534484312456690

Tubbs, S., & Schulz, E. (2006). Exploring a taxonomy of global leadership competencies and meta-competencies. *The Journal of American Academy of Business, Cambridge*, *8*(2), 29–35.

Tulasi, D., Sigit, R., Pradana, D. W., & Ellitan, L. (2019). The Role of Leadership in Industrial Revolution 4.0. *International Journal of Trend in Research and Development*, *6*(5), 97–100.

Vakola, M., Soderquist, K. E., & Prastacos, G. P. (2007). Competency management in support of organisational change. *International Journal of Manpower*, *28*(3/4), 260–275. doi:10.1108/01437720710755245

Yin, R. (2009). *Case study research: Design and methods* (4th ed.). Sage Publication, Inc.

Yukl, G. (1989). Managerial Leadership : A Review of Theory and Research. *Journal of Management*, *15*(2), 251–289. doi:10.1177/014920638901500207

Yukl, G., Gordon, A., & Taber, T. (2002). A Taxonomy of Leadership Behavior: Integrating a Half Century of Behavior Research. *Journal of Leadership & Organizational Studies*, *9*(1), 15–32. doi:10.1177/107179190200900102

Zwick, T. (2012). Training effectiveness - Differences between younger and older employees. In Working and ageing - The benefits of investing in an ageing workforce (pp. 36–55). Academic Press.

ADDITIONAL READING

Boyatzis, R. (2011). Managerial and Leadership Competencies: A Behavioral Approach to Emotional, Social and Cognitive Intelligence. *Vision: The Journal of Business Perspective*, *15*(2), 91–100. doi:10.1177/097226291101500202

Galvin, T., Gibbs, M., Sullivan, J., & Williams, C. (2014). Leadership Competencies of Project Managers: An Empirical Study of Emotional, Intellectual, and Managerial Dimensions. *Journal of Economic Development, Management, IT. Finance and Marketing*, *6*(March), 35–60.

Kjellström, S., Stålne, K., & Törnblom, O. (2020). Six ways of understanding leadership development: An exploration of increasing complexity. *Leadership*, *16*(4), 434–460. doi:10.1177/1742715020926731

Moreira, A., Cesario, F., Chambel, M., & Castanheira, F. (2018). Competences development and affective Commitment: Mediation through employability and moderation by generation. *European Journal of Management Studies*, *23*(2), 123–149. doi:10.5455/EJMS/289312/2018

Naquin, S., & Holton, E. III. (2006). Leadership and Managerial Competency Models: A Simplified Process and Resulting Model. *Advances in Developing Human Resources*, *8*(2), 144–165. doi:10.1177/1523422305286152

Rakowska, A., & Babnik, K. (Eds.). (2015). *Human Resources Management Challenges: Learning & Development*. ToKnow Press.

Rowe, W., & Guerrero, L. (2013). Leadership Skills Approach. In *Cases in Leadership* (3rd ed., pp. 81–99). Sage Publication, Inc.

Yukl, G. (2010). *Leadership in organizations* (7th ed.). Pearson Prentice Hall.

KEY TERMS AND DEFINITIONS

Competence: It is a set of attitudes, skills, abilities, and knowledge that are acquired by the individual throughout life.

Competence Management: Is a human resource management practice that aims to develop skills according to the individual's profile and the organization's needs.

Effectiveness: Is a combination of quality and quantity of performance of a group or unit of work managed by a responsible/leader.

Human Resource Management: Is a strategic area made up of several practices and techniques that are implemented not only to achieve the organization's goals, but also to manage human relations, ensuring people's satisfaction and fulfillment.

Leader: Is someone who has the ability to influence, share and inspire their vision on others; others live and feel this vision as their own.

Leader Competence: Are skills that prepare a leader to effectively manage people.

Leadership: Is the art of influencing people, attracting followers and promoting the development of positive mindsets and behaviors in order to achieve goals.

APPENDIX 1: TYPES OF COMPETENCES IDENTIFIED IN THE COMPETENCE MODELS

Table 10.

Competences	Authors
- Technical Skills *- Human Skills* *- Conceptual Skills*	Katz, 1974
- Self-awareness *- Self-regulation* *- Motivation* *- Empathy* *- Social Skill*	Goleman, 1998
- Problem solving *- Social judgment* *- Knowledge*	Mumford, Zaccaro, Harding, Jacobs, & Fleishman, 2000
- Analytical and self-development *- People-related skills* *- Task-related skills*	Analoui, Labbaf, & Noorbakhsh, 2000
- Self-awareness *- Self-management* *- Social awareness* *- Relationship management*	Goleman, Boyatzis, & Mckee, 2001
- Intellectual skill (IQ) *- Managerial skill (MQ)* *- Emotional skill (EQ)*	Dulewicz & Higgs, 2003
- Intrapersonal Skills *- Interpersonal Skills* *- Technical Skills (work skills)* *- Leadership Skills*	Hogan & Warrenfeltz, 2003
- METACOMPETENCY I: Understanding the Big Picture *- METACOMPETENCY II. Attitudes are Everything* *- METACOMPETENCY III: Leadership, The Driving Force* *- METACOMPETENCY IV: Communication, The Leader 's Voice* *- METACOMPETENCY V: Innovation and Creativity* *- METACOMPETENCY VI: Leading Change* *- METACOMPETENCY VII: Teamwork and Followership*	Tubbs & Schulz, 2006
- Self-motivation cluster *- Self-regulation cluster* *- People Management cluster* *- Cognitive Cluster*	Boyatzis, 2006b
- Cognitive skills *- Interpersonal skills* *- Business skills* *- Strategic skills*	Mumford, Campion, & Morgeson, 2007
Cognitive competencies *Emotional intelligence competencies - Self-Awareness cluster; Self-Management cluster* *Social intelligence competencies - Social Awareness cluster; Relationship Management*	Boyatzis, 2009, 2011
- Strategist *- Executor* *- Talent Manager* *- Human Capital Developer* *- Personal Proficiency*	Burns, Smith, & Ulrich, 2012

APPENDIX 2: DIMENSIONS OF THE INTEGRATIVE MODEL OF THE LEADER COMPETENCES

Table 11.

Dimensions	Competences
Intellectual Competences (CMPE_I)	1. Vision, perspective of 'helicopter', 'the big picture'. 2. Imagination, Creativity and Innovation, an open and confident approach to new solutions. 3. Creating an inspiring and attractive mission that motivates all team members. 4. Analysis and organization of information, through its knowledge and critical thinking. 5. Management and personal development, promoting improvements in their performance. 6. In-depth knowledge of the contexts, role and impact of culture and other worldviews 7. Leadership by example, practicing and defending the principles, rules, and good practices. 8. Stress management at work. 9. Creating an environment for learning and change.
Management Competences (CMPE_M)	1. Definition of an effective business strategy and objectives according to the available resources. 2. Timely resource management (materials, technical, financial, and human). 3. Involvement of everyone in decision making and problem solving. 4. Definition and development of necessary rules and procedures. 5. Analysis, planning and timely work organization. 6. Monitoring and evaluating of activities and results and constructive feedback. 7. Delegation and allocation of resources. 8. Coordination and performance evaluation.
Social Competences (CMPE_S)	1. Effective and frequent communication (verbal and non-verbal) according to the motivations, needs, attitudes and feelings of others. 2. Active listening and negotiating power. 3. Influence and people management (direction, motivation, and development). 4. Creation and management teams encouraging participation, team spirit and confidence. 5. Personal and professional development of the team and future leaders. 6. Concern about the personal and professional life of the team members. 7. Monitoring, coaching, support, and direction according to the needs of each one.
Emotional Competences (CMPE_E)	1. Awareness of one's emotions and the effect of the emotional state on others (Leader). 2. Management of own emotional states, impulses, and internal resources (Leader). 3. Confidence in oneself and in one's abilities (Leader). 4. Awareness of the feelings, emotions, needs and concerns of others and the power of relationships between team members (Organization). 5. Relationship management, inducing desirable responses in others, through teamwork, conflict management, inspiration, and influence (Organization).

APPENDIX 3: FREQUENCY ANALYSIS OF VARIABLES

Table 12.

Intellectual Competences

	CMPE_I1			CMPE_I2			CMPE_I3			CMPE_I4			CMPE_I5			CMPE_I6			CMPE_I7			CMPE_I8		
	Abs. Frequency	Rel. Frequency (%)	Cumulative Rel. Freq. (%)	Abs. Frequency	Rel. Frequency (%)	Cumulative Rel. Freq. (%)	Abs. Frequency	Rel. Frequency (%)	Cumulative Rel. Freq. (%)	Abs. Frequency	Rel. Frequency (%)	Cumulative Rel. Freq. (%)	Abs. Frequency	Rel. Frequency (%)	Cumulative Rel. Freq. (%)	Abs. Frequency	Rel. Frequency (%)	Cumulative Rel. Freq. (%)	Abs. Frequency	Rel. Frequency (%)	Cumulative Rel. Freq. (%)	Abs. Frequency	Rel. Frequency (%)	Cumulative Rel. Freq. (%)
1. Not Effective	6	7%	7%	9	10%	10%	10	11%	11%	6	7%	7%	1	1%	1%	8	9%	9%	2	2%	2%	1	1%	1%
2. Little Effective	20	22%	28%	28	30%	40%	19	21%	32%	21	23%	29%	8	9%	10%	22	24%	33%	21	23%	25%	24	26%	27%
3. Effective	48	52%	80%	47	51%	91%	42	46%	77%	46	50%	79%	60	65%	75%	47	51%	84%	55	60%	85%	52	57%	84%
4. Very Effective	18	20%	100%	8	9%	100%	21	23%	100%	19	21%	100%	23	25%	100%	15	16%	100%	14	15%	100%	15	16%	100%

Management Competences

	CMPE_M1			CMPE_M2			CMPE_M3			CMPE_M4			CMPE_M5			CMPE_M6			CMPE_M7			CMPE_M8		
	Abs. Frequency	Rel. Frequency (%)	Cumulative Rel. Freq. (%)	Abs. Frequency	Rel. Frequency (%)	Cumulative Rel. Freq. (%)	Abs. Frequency	Rel. Frequency (%)	Cumulative Rel. Freq. (%)	Abs. Frequency	Rel. Frequency (%)	Cumulative Rel. Freq. (%)	Abs. Frequency	Rel. Frequency (%)	Cumulative Rel. Freq. (%)	Abs. Frequency	Rel. Frequency (%)	Cumulative Rel. Freq. (%)	Abs. Frequency	Rel. Frequency (%)	Cumulative Rel. Freq. (%)	Abs. Frequency	Rel. Frequency (%)	Cumulative Rel. Freq. (%)
1. Not Effective	3	3%	3%	12	13%	13%	4	4%	4%	6	7%	7%	6	7%	7%	4	4%	4%	6	7%	7%	5	5%	5%
2. Little Effective	21	23%	26%	21	23%	36%	16	17%	22%	20	22%	28%	27	29%	36%	28	30%	35%	16	17%	24%	20	22%	27%
3. Effective	52	57%	83%	44	48%	84%	58	63%	85%	39	42%	71%	44	48%	84%	48	52%	87%	43	47%	71%	55	60%	87%
4. Very Effective	16	17%	100%	15	16%	100%	14	15%	100%	27	29%	100%	15	16%	100%	12	13%	100%	27	29%	100%	12	13%	100%

Social Competences

	CMPE_S1			CMPE_S2			CMPE_S3			CMPE_S4			CMPE_S5			CMPE_S6			CMPE_S7		
	Abs. Frequency	Rel. Frequency (%)	Cumulative Rel. Freq. (%)	Abs. Frequency	Rel. Frequency (%)	Cumulative Rel. Freq. (%)	Abs. Frequency	Rel. Frequency (%)	Cumulative Rel. Freq. (%)	Abs. Frequency	Rel. Frequency (%)	Cumulative Rel. Freq. (%)	Abs. Frequency	Rel. Frequency (%)	Cumulative Rel. Freq. (%)	Abs. Frequency	Rel. Frequency (%)	Cumulative Rel. Freq. (%)	Abs. Frequency	Rel. Frequency (%)	Cumulative Rel. Freq. (%)
1. Not Effective	8	9%	9%	7	8%	8%	8	9%	9%	5	5%	5%	2	2%	2%	6	7%	7%	4	4%	4%
2. Little Effective	26	28%	37%	29	32%	39%	22	24%	33%	24	26%	32%	17	18%	21%	21	23%	29%	26	28%	33%
3. Effective	49	53%	90%	39	42%	82%	39	42%	75%	46	50%	82%	46	50%	71%	50	54%	84%	45	49%	82%
4. Very Effective	9	10%	100%	17	18%	100%	23	25%	100%	17	18%	100%	27	29%	100%	15	16%	100%	17	18%	100%

Emotional Competences

	CMPE_E1			CMPE_E2			CMPE_E3			CMPE_E4			CMPE_E5		
	Abs. Frequency	Rel. Frequency (%)	Cumulative Rel. Freq. (%)	Abs. Frequency	Rel. Frequency (%)	Cumulative Rel. Freq. (%)	Abs. Frequency	Rel. Frequency (%)	Cumulative Rel. Freq. (%)	Abs. Frequency	Rel. Frequency (%)	Cumulative Rel. Freq. (%)	Abs. Frequency	Rel. Frequency (%)	Cumulative Rel. Freq. (%)
1. Not Effective	1	1%	1%	3	3%	3%	11	12%	12%	3	3%	3%	4	4%	4%
2. Little Effective	11	12%	13%	14	15%	18%	25	27%	39%	24	26%	29%	34	37%	41%
3. Effective	51	55%	68%	52	57%	75%	42	46%	85%	50	54%	84%	38	41%	83%
4. Very Effective	29	32%	100%	23	25%	100%	14	15%	100%	15	16%	100%	16	17%	100%

Chapter 7
Challenges for Higher Education Graduates in the Post-Pandemic Labor Market

Aslı Günay
Social Sciences University of Ankara, Turkey

ABSTRACT

The Covid-19 pandemic has brought widespread disruption to labor markets around the world. The pandemic has led to a dramatic shift in expected skill requirements, and it has forced people to acquire new demanded skills, including digital skills, to succeed in the workplace or find a job. Hence, the competition of higher education graduates in the labor market is now changing shape. Accordingly, young workers (15–24 years old) have a greater risk than older ones of being pushed out of the labor market since the current situation shows that higher education graduates do not have enough high-level digital skills in many countries. Although younger adults with a higher education degree are less likely to be unemployed than other educated adults, it is obvious the digital transformation in the workplace might affect them negatively if they cannot update their skills for the post-pandemic world.

INTRODUCTION

Globally, the rise of the knowledge-based economy has a critical role in a long-term competitive advantage for all sectors, including higher education. Hence, competition between countries in the era of the knowledge-based economy has become the driving force for higher education expansion since the 1980s (Liu et al., 2016). Therefore, human capital development for a knowledge-based economy has become a central component of economic and social policies for international competition worldwide in the last few decades (Organisation for Economic Co-operation and Development [OECD], 1996; Sum and Jessop, 2013).

National and international competition in higher education has led to a massive expansion in enrolment over the last decades. Today, the total number of higher education students globally has reached more than 227 million (United Nations Educational, Scientific, and Cultural Organization [UNESCO],

DOI: 10.4018/978-1-7998-2395-7.ch007

Copyright © 2022, IGI Global. Copying or distributing in print or electronic forms without written permission of IGI Global is prohibited.

2021). In recent years, the early cohorts of higher education students have experienced massification, flooding into the labor market and boosting the proportion of higher education degrees workers (Mok and Jiang, 2018). Higher education enrolments are less typical among the older population as students graduate and transition to the labor market. For example, the OECD average enrolment rate in all levels of education reached 16% among 25–29 years old, which is higher than 6% among 30-39 years old (OECD, 2021a). However, the increasing number of higher education graduates has negatively affected the labor market and national economic competitiveness since there are unemployment problems for many graduates (Mok and Wu, 2016; Mok and Jiang, 2018).

However, the Covid-19 pandemic, which emerged in December 2019 in China, has affected everyone worldwide. Globally, as of September 20, 2021, there have been 228.394.572 confirmed cases of Covid-19, including 4.690.186 deaths. As of September 19, 2021, a total of 5.776.127.976 vaccine doses have been administered (World Health Organization [WHO], 2021). It is not just a global health crisis; it has triggered the most severe economic recession in nearly a century and is causing enormous damage to people's jobs and well-being, along with their health. The global economy has been experiencing the deepest recession since the Great Depression in the 1930s, with GDP declines of more than 20% and a surge in unemployment in many countries in the early stages of the pandemic (OECD, 2020). The OECD projects that global output will rise by nearly 6% in 2021, an impressive surge after the 3.5% contraction in 2020. Although the OECD states that recovery will return most of the world to pre-pandemic GDP levels by the end of 2022, many OECD countries may not return to pre-pandemic levels as quickly as expected due to high unemployment rates (OECD, 2021b). Hence, the recovery will be long-lasting due to the unprecedented uncertainty characteristics of the pandemic (Altig et al., 2020; Açıkgöz & Günay, 2021).

The International Labor Organization (ILO) confirms that the pandemic caused massive disruptions in the labor market throughout 2020. At the end of 2020, globally, 114 million jobs disappeared compared to 2019. In contrast to previous crises, the bulk of employment losses in 2020 translated into rising inactivity rather than unemployment, leading to an additional 81 million people shifting to inactivity alongside 33 million additional unemployed (ILO, 2021a). In particular, workers like those in the hospitality, retail, service, travel, and tourism sectors, who have been displaced from their jobs in the short term and potentially in the future, have been affected most negatively by the Covid-19 pandemic (World Economic Forum [WEF], 2020a). The pandemic has accelerated digital transformation and automation in the workplace while widening wage disparities. Many jobs are fully or partially transformed into digital jobs, expanding the digital economy and related activities (OECD, 2021c).

The application of digital technology has already changed or destroyed many work environments, industries, and business activities (Nyiri, 2002). Also, while there is uncertainty about the speed of these changes, technology-intensive working life is spreading and constantly transforming. Also, the types of jobs that are being created are not the same as those that are being lost (OECD, 2018). As new technologies are adopted by enterprises globally, skills shortages for the jobs of tomorrow are set to become more pronounced as populations have switched to remote work during the Covid-19 pandemic. The WEF's Future of Jobs Report 2020 estimated that by 2025, 85 million jobs may be displaced by a shift in the division of labor between humans and machines, while 97 million new roles may emerge that are more adapted to the new division of labor between humans, machines, and algorithms (WEF, 2020a). This situation has also led to a dramatic shift in expected skill requirements, and it has forced people to have new skills to succeed in the workplace or find a job. Hence, this new transformation is a big challenge for all the workforce, including higher education graduates. Only a higher education degree is not enough to survive in the new post-pandemic world.

In this regard, this study aims to address the transformation in the labor market after the Covid-19 pandemic, especially for higher education graduates. In other words, how the Covid-19 pandemic has characterized the labor market for higher education graduates is the main focus of this study. Thus, the objective of this study is to characterize the current state of higher education graduates in the labor market concerning the pandemic circumstances, to synthesize the findings on available data, particularly in OECD countries, and to make some recommendations for new demanded skills, such as critical thinking, problem-solving, and digital skills, acquisition and improvement. However, this study mainly focuses on digital skills since they will probably be the most in-demand skills in the long-term labor market due to the rapid digital transformation in the workplace. Therefore, OECD data, analysis, and surveys can be used as a good proxy for evaluating digital skills among higher education graduates worldwide, along with other resources such as the ILO and WEF, providing information about unemployment and the prospects of the job market. This study comprehensively analyzes existing databases and other sources to identify the current state of higher education graduates for the post-pandemic labor market, especially in terms of digital skills.

In this context, the paper's organization is as follows: The following section provides some background and literature review about the topic. While the third section discusses the current situation of youth and higher education graduates in the labor market during the pandemic, the following are related to newly demanded skills in the labor market during the pandemic and the current digital skills level of higher education graduates, respectively. The next section is about future research directions, and finally, the study is concluded.

BACKGROUND

In recent decades, the massive expansion of higher education has resulted in many higher education graduates, making the labor market highly competitive. Existing research consistently suggests that recent cohorts of higher education graduates have had difficulty finding jobs that match their skill sets, while employers claim they are unable to find people with the skills they require (Bai, 2006; Kim and Lee, 2006; West, 2000; Teichler, 1997; Walker, 2007; Wu, 2011; Vedder et al., 2013; Lauder and Mayhew, 2020; Mok and Jiang, 2018). This is simply characterized as a skill mismatch in the labor market, where a skill mismatch is commonly defined in terms of an individual's excess or deficiency of skills in comparison to job skill requirements (McGuinness and Pouliakas, 2016). Studies of skill mismatch tend to focus on two of four central measures: over-qualification, under-qualification, over-skilled, and under-skilled. Although terms like "over-qualification" and "over-skilled" are often used interchangeably, they refer to different situations in the labor market. Over-qualification or under-qualification occurs when individuals take jobs that do not match their qualifications. People are over-skilled or under-skilled when whatever their qualification level, their skills do not match the job (European Centre for the Development of Vocational Training [CEDEFOP], 2015). As a result of the misalignment of supply and demand for various talents, unemployment rates in the labor market have risen.

Prior to the Covid-19 pandemic, evidence from several advanced economies showed that skill mismatch is a common occurrence, affecting approximately one-third of the higher-educated employed population (McGuinness and Pouliakas, 2016). Several research studies have also cautioned in recent years that, as a result of the 2008 economic crisis, there has been a tendency towards higher over-qualification rates across Europe (Pouliakas, 2012; ILO, 2014). As a result, higher education graduates may secure employment by accepting jobs that are typically reserved for those with less education. In other words, for many higher education graduates, their degree serves as a credential or signal for admittance into jobs that formerly required only high school diplomas (Lauder and Mayhew, 2020; Dolado et al., 2000; Mayhew et al., 2004; Chan and Lin, 2016; Mok and Jiang, 2018). Furthermore, policymakers predict that there will be an ever-increasing demand for a highly skilled workforce, which should meet by mass higher education graduates (Lauder and Mayhew, 2020). For example, CEDEFOP's skill supply forecast for Europe up to 2020 suggested a substantial further increase in the proportion of the adult labor force with high-level qualifications acquired by a higher education degree. The European labor force aged 25 and over with a high level of qualification will represent 34% of the entire labor force in 2020 (CEDEFOP, 2010). From this perspective, the proportion of people with high levels of qualification has risen steadily in recent years in most countries due to the massification of higher education worldwide. In addition, firms had strong incentives to invest in automation to remain competitive in a changing world of work. Such motives will be stronger in the post-pandemic period, as businesses will aim to gain a competitive edge by offering pandemic work environments, services, and products. Hence, high-level qualifications, in other words, higher education degrees, will be more critical than in the pre-pandemic world.

The pandemic has brought widespread disruption to labor markets around the world. Unlike the previous crisis, the pace and depth of the Covid-19 crisis have been unprecedented, with no country spared from the sharp deterioration in labor market conditions (Dewan and Ernst 2020; Lee et al., 2020; ILO, 2021b). Those who lost their jobs gave up looking for work or were unavailable due to the pandemic, resulting in more people leaving the labor force and becoming inactive rather than unemployed. As a result, many previously inactive workers will enter the labor force during the pandemic but might not find a job. It is expected that employment growth will reach 100 million jobs in 2021, followed by a further 80 million in 2022. However, this rebound will not be sufficient to accommodate those who have lost their jobs and new labor market entrants, given the growth of the working-age population. As a result, the pandemic-induced shortfall in jobs is projected to amount to 75 million in 2021 and 23 million in 2022, which exacerbates the precarious labor market situation before the Covid-19 pandemic. While economic recovery will induce more individuals to reenter the labor force, the lack of available jobs will increase global unemployment, reaching 205 million people (ILO, 2021b). Hence, it is evident that a significant share of graduates might struggle to find good jobs in the post-pandemic world due to the lack of available jobs or newly demanded skills because of digital transformation in the workplace during the pandemic.

YOUTH AND HIGHER EDUCATION GRADUATES IN THE LABOR MARKET DURING THE PANDEMIC

Table 1 displays the world's actual and estimated unemployment rates according to country groups based on income levels before and during the pandemic. The unemployment rate is projected to fall from 6.3% to 5.7% in 2022, slightly higher than the pre-pandemic value (5.4%). Even before the pandemic, unemployment rates were nearly three times higher for youth (between 15 and 24 years) than for adults (aged 25 years and above). The rise in the unemployment rate among youth would be driven by young people in employment being more likely to lose their jobs and new entrants to the labor market finding it challenging to secure entry-level jobs with hiring rates down. Alongside new large numbers of young higher education graduates, youth unemployment rates will likely remain elevated for some time to come. Young workers who lose their jobs have been more likely than their adult counterparts to become inactive, which further impairs their labor market prospects (ILO, 2021b). Table 1 shows that the number of unemployed youth increased only 1.1% between 2019 and 2020 worldwide, compared to the 1.2% rise in adult unemployment because many young people without a job have stopped looking for one or have delayed their entry into the labor market. Moreover, other studies showed that the pandemic has a more adverse impact on younger workers than older workers since the effects could be more fiscally costly for older workers due to the spillovers onto social security (Bui et al., 2020; Gupta et al., 2020; Goda et al., 2021).

On the other hand, Table 1 shows that unemployment is projected to be high in countries at all income levels in 2022, with upper-middle-income countries being the most affected. The unemployment rate is forecasted to be 6.4% in upper-middle-income countries, higher than the world unemployment rate (5.7%). Indeed, the recovery will be relatively faster in high-income countries. The unemployment rate is forecasted to be 5%, probably due to unprecedented policy support and privileged access to vaccines in those countries. In low and lower-middle-income countries, the more limited access to vaccines and more significant constraints on fiscal spending will probably dampen the employment recovery. The unemployment rate is projected to be 5.2% and 5.5% in those countries, respectively. Also, upper-middle-income countries have a higher young unemployment rate, with a 16.2% value in 2020, above the 14.6% world rate. However, higher-income countries have the highest adult unemployment rate, most probably due to their effective labor support income policies.

Table 1. Unemployment Rate (%)

	Total (15+)				Youth		Adult	
	2019	2020	2021	2022	2019	2020	2019	2020
World	5.4	6.5	6.3	5.7	13.5	14.6	4	5.2
Low-income countries	4.8	5.3	5.3	5.2	8	8.7	3.7	4.1
Lower-middle-income countries	5.1	6.5	5.9	5.5	15.1	15.4	3	4.6
Upper-middle-income countries	6	6.7	7	6.4	15.1	16.2	4.7	5.5
High-income countries	4.8	6.8	5.8	5	10.9	14.9	4.1	5.9

Source: (ILO, 2021b)

In many OECD and partner countries, younger adults with a higher education degree are less likely to be unemployed compared to those with upper secondary or post-secondary non-higher education as their highest attainment. While the OECD average for unemployment rates as a percentage of 25–34-years old (younger adults) with a higher education degree in the labor force was 5% in 2019, this ratio jumped to 7% in 2020. In addition, the positive effect of higher education attainment on unemployment rates is exceptionally high in the United Kingdom (UK) and the United States (US), since the unemployment rate as a percentage of 25–34-years old with a higher education degree is 3%. However, countries like Spain (15%), Italy (11%), and Greece (21%) have a higher unemployment rate among younger adults with higher education attainment (OECD, 2021a). Furthermore, higher education graduates are now in a more difficult situation than before when it comes to finding a job due to the pandemic. The fact that they have not found the jobs they expected after graduation. It is predicted that the youth unemployment rate will increase further in the next few years. Hence, there will be some possible adverse impacts on higher education graduates.

Figure 1. Unemployment rates of higher education graduates as a percentage of 25-34 years old in the labor force (%)
Source: (OECD, 2021a)

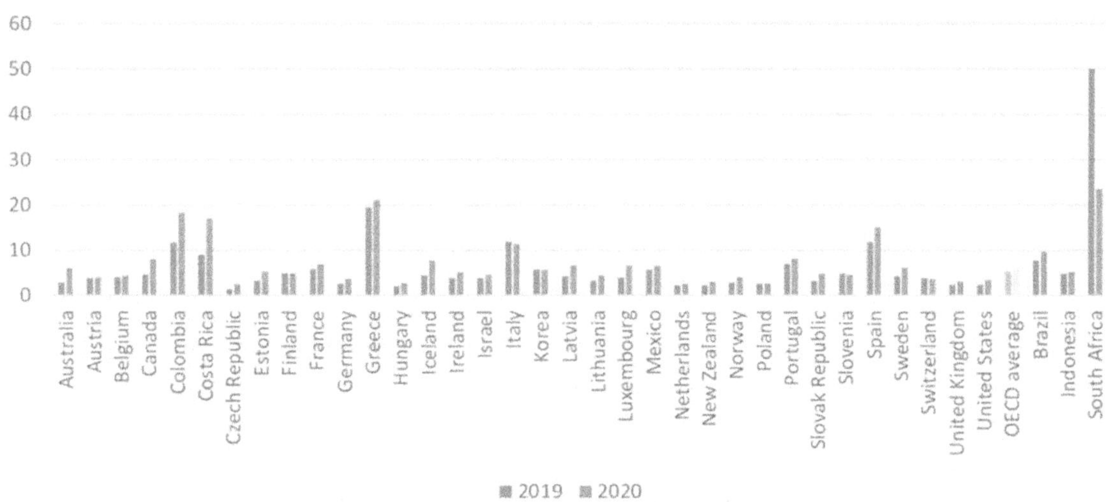

NEW DEMANDED SKILLS IN THE LABOR MARKET DURING THE PANDEMIC

Figure 2 shows that high-skilled workers accounted for the lowest share of employment worldwide among all the occupational categories in 2019, namely 20.6%, but as a group, they also exhibited the lowest decline in employment relative to the pre-pandemic period, at 3%. In other words, high-skilled "white-collar" workers (managers, professionals, and technicians) were far more likely to be able to work from home during the pandemic than "blue-collar" workers (middle-skilled occupations in production, construction, or manufacturing) and workers in low-skilled service occupations involving manual tasks and personal interaction (ILO, 2021b). Job loss among high-skilled workers differs from that of low- and middle-skilled workers, implying that technological change affects workers differently depending on the skill content of their occupation (Autor et al., 2003; Goos et al., 2014). Suppose high-skilled workers are associated with higher education graduates. In that case, it might be said that adults with higher education degrees are less affected when compared to other degree graduates during the pandemic.

Figure 2. Distribution of employment by occupational skill level (%)
Source: (ILO, 2021b)

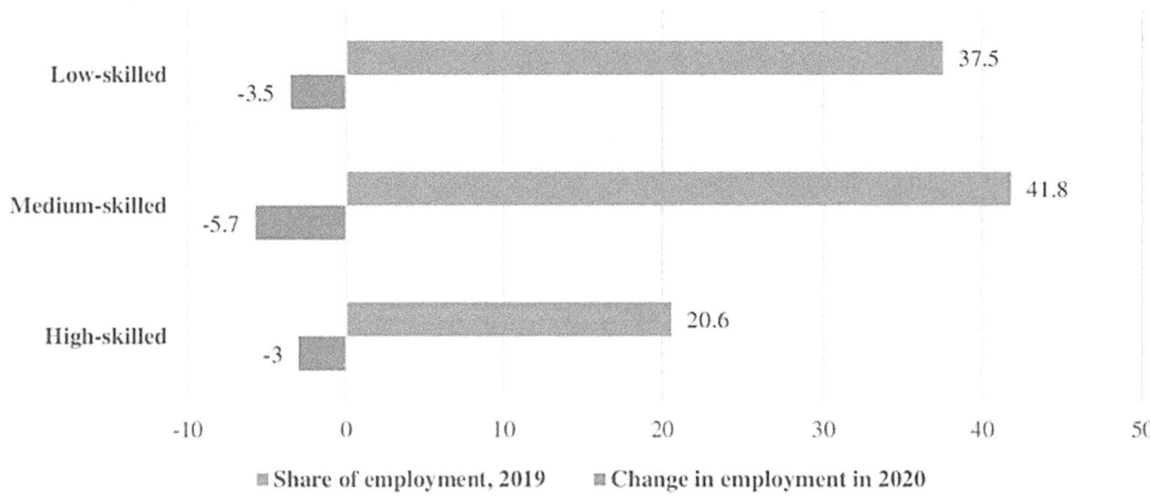

According to the survey results conducted by WEF in 15 major developed and emerging economies and regional economic areas, more than one-third (36%) of all jobs across all industries are expected to require problem-solving skills as one of their core skills. Also, the WEF's Future of Jobs Report 2020 is projected that technological change is set to displace a range of skills in the labor market while driving greater demand for a new set of core demand skills such as critical thinking and analysis, problem-solving, in addition to digital skills (WEF, 2020a). In this context, Figure 3 displays that employers set to accelerate their job automation and augmentation agendas, raising the possibility of a jobless recovery. Among the business leaders surveyed, just over 80% report accelerating the automation of their work processes and expanding their use of remote work. A significant 50% also indicate that they set to accelerate the automation of jobs in their companies. In addition, nearly 30% of employers expect to reduce their workforce temporarily, and nearly 15% expect to do so permanently. Hence, digital skills will be more critical than ever before to survive in the labor market during the pandemic and after that.

Figure 3. Planned business adaptation in response to the pandemic
Source: (WEF, 2020a)

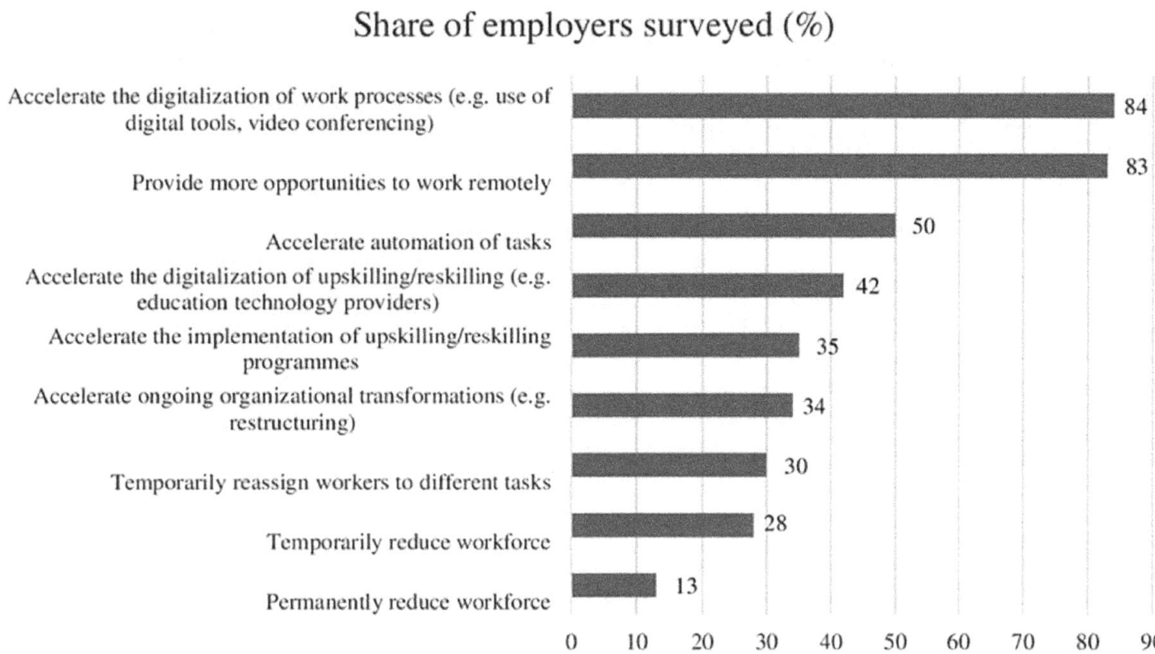

DIGITAL SKILLS LEVEL OF HIGHER EDUCATION GRADUATES

The OECD defines problem-solving in technology-rich environments as "using digital technology, communication tools and networks to acquire and evaluate information, communicate with others and perform practical tasks" (PIAAC Expert Group in Problem Solving in Technology-Rich Environments, 2009). Problem-solving in technology-rich environments does not measure the cognitive skills required to solve problems. Instead, it measures both problem-solving and basic computer literacy skills, like the capacity to use Information and Communications Technology (ICT) tools and applications. That is done by assessing how well adults can use ICT tools and applications to assess, process, evaluate, and analyze information in a goal-oriented way (OECD, 2019a). Therefore, OECD's data on problem-solving in technology-rich environments might be used as a proxy variable to measure the digital skills of higher education graduates.

Programme for the International Assessment of Adult Competencies (PIACC) is conducted every 10 years and has had two cycles so far. For the PIAAC 1st Cycle, 39 countries participated between 2011-2018, and data were collected in three different rounds: Round 1 (2011-2012), Round 2 (2014-15), and Round 3 (2017). Under the supervision of trained interviewers, the survey was administered to the respondents. The respondents completed the assessment test on a laptop computer or a paper version using printed test booklets, depending on the respondents' computer skills. On average, it took 50 minutes to complete the assessment tests. The results from the assessment are analyzed based on a 500-point scale. However, each participating country had a substantial proportion of adults who could not display any proficiency in problem-solving in technology-rich environments since they took the assessment in the paper-based format. Three separate groups of adults fall into this category: those with no computer experience, those who failed the ICT core test and thus did not have the basic computer skills needed for the computer-based assessment, and those who opted to take the paper-based version of the assessment even though they reported having ICT experience. Overall, around one in ten adults (11.7%) reported having no prior computer experience. A further 4.7% of adults did not have the basic ICT skills assessed by the ICT core test, such as the capacity to use a mouse or scroll through a web page across OECD countries (OECD, 2019a).

Figure 4. Percentage of higher education graduates having no computer experience (adults aged 25-65)
Source: (OECD, 2019a)

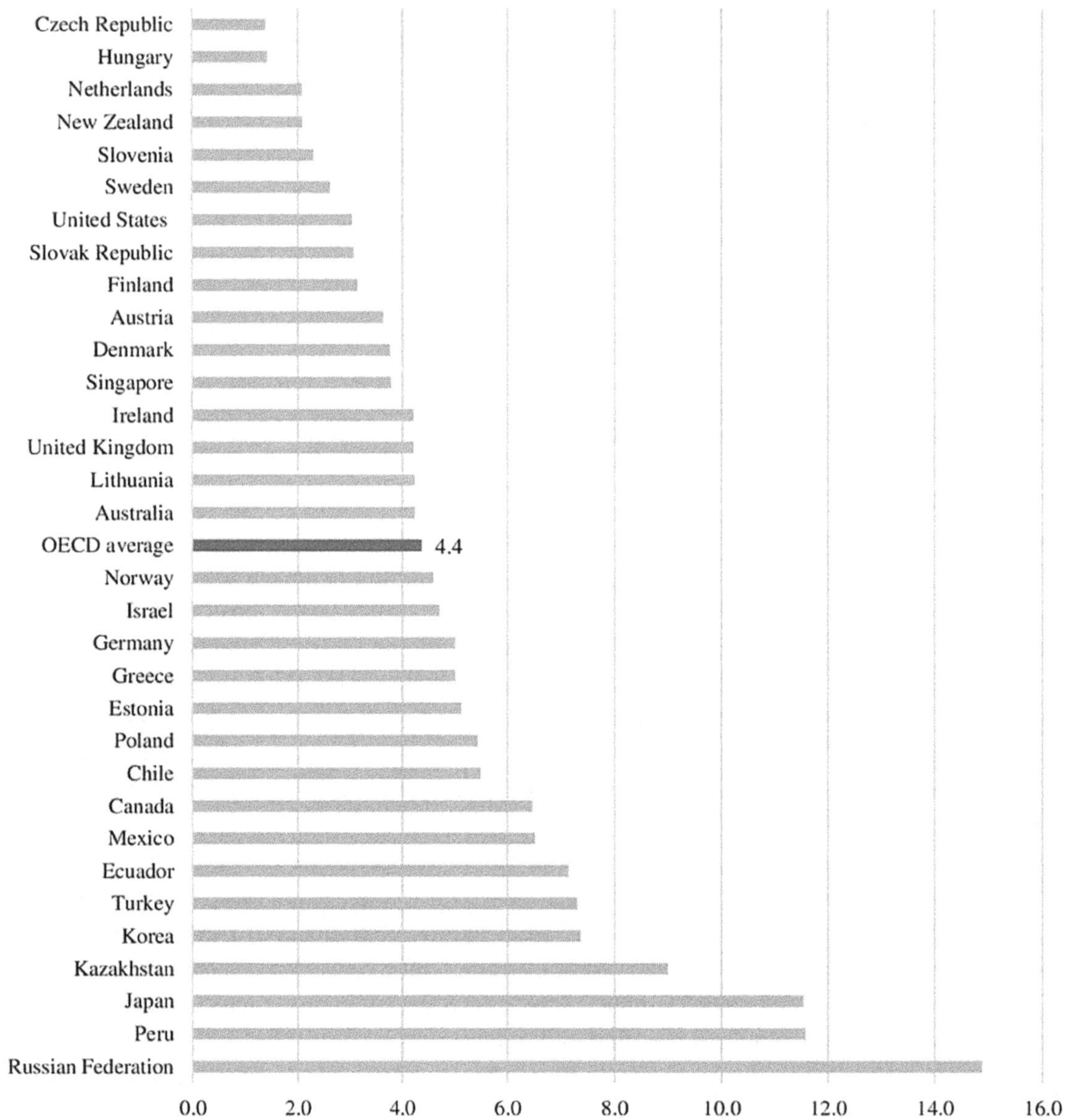

On the other hand, Figure 4 shows that among higher education graduates across OECD countries, only 4.4% of adults in this group were not able to participate in the problem-solving assessment due to the lack of computer experience. Moreover, the shares of higher education graduates having no computer experience were slightly higher in Ecuador, Mexico, and Turkey (7%), Kazakhstan (9%), and Peru and Japan (12%). On the other hand, the Russian Federation, on the other hand, is a leader, with a 15% higher percentage of higher education graduates who have no computer experience. The share of higher education graduates without basic digital skills or computer experience reflects these countries' levels of economic development and ICT penetration. Although internet users have doubled since 2010, surpassing 50% of the world population worldwide (WEF, 2020b), the share of higher education graduates having no computer experience is higher in many OECD countries. However, the pandemic most probably would raise the digital divide around the world.

Mainly, educational attainment positively affects the proficiency levels of adults' problem-solving in technology-rich environments (OECD, 2016; Xiao et al., 2019). In other words, it can be said that adults with higher education diplomas probably have higher-level digital skills than others if problem-solving skills in technology-rich environments is used as a proxy for digital skills. Hence, Figure 5 shows the proficiency levels of digital skills for higher education graduates. The total shares of higher education graduates are 46.6% scored at higher proficiency level in digital skills on average across OECD countries. In other words, 46.6% of higher education graduates can at least use both generic and more specific technology applications in their typically required tasks. Some navigation across pages and applications is required to solve the problem (OECD, 2019a). This share was much lower in some countries, including Peru (13.7%) and Mexico and Turkey (26.2%). In contrast, the shares in countries like the Netherlands, Norway, Germany, and the UK is higher than the 50% in digital skills. Therefore, countries with lower digital skills proficiency levels for higher education graduates should focus on equipping higher education students with digital skills for the post-pandemic labor market.

Figure 5. Proficiency level of higher education graduates in problem-solving technology-rich environments (%) (aged 16-65)
Source: (OECD, 2019a)

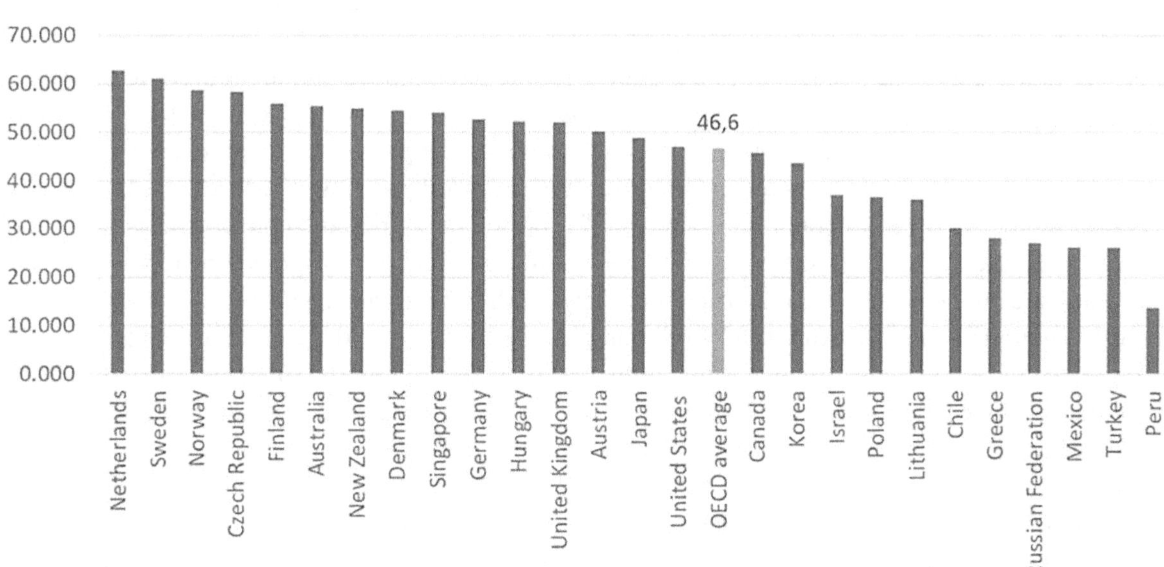

FUTURE RESEARCH DIRECTIONS

Since this study focused on the indirect measure of digital skills or currently employed, there is a need to investigate alternative measurements to more objectively examine the impact of the Covid-19 pandemic on higher education graduates. For example, how the highly educated 25–64 age group that has been affected by the pandemic might be investigated. Another study might answer how the new demanded skills like digital skills of young and older higher education graduates can be improved. Measurement of other new demanded skills like problem-solving or critical thinking is open to debate. Finally, it is pretty problematic to collect homogeneous and reliable data to examine the skill gaps and unemployment levels for young and old due to the pandemic's unprecedented uncertainty structure. Because countries' economic recovery is now uneven, labor market conditions might change according to the new paths of the Covid-19 pandemic. Researchers should focus more on higher education and labor market studies.

CONCLUSION

Globally and across all countries, the pandemic has affected employment losses. As vaccination continues and some countries begin to loosen pandemic restrictions, economic growth is expected to accelerate. The unprecedented levels of assistance that countries have provided through job retention schemes and income support have saved up to 21 million jobs and helped many households make it through the pandemic (OECD, 2021c). However, the Covid-19 pandemic has deepened existing social and economic divides, between those with high skills and those without, between generations, between those with good jobs and those with precarious jobs or no jobs at all. Unemployment is high, and jobs are not expected to make a rapid recovery. Reaching pre-pandemic employment rates may take several years.

Along with the mass number of higher education students, higher education graduates have also increased. Although the supply in the labor market has expanded, many jobs have started to vanish or transform even before the pandemic. However, the pandemic has accelerated this process, and digitalization and automation have expanded in the workplace.

In OECD countries, younger adults with a higher education degree are less likely to be unemployed compared to other levels of graduates. Many graduates, especially older ones, have weak basic digital skills, and lifelong training opportunities are limited for the unemployed and the low-skilled. Despite a robust labor market, and in order to accelerate job transition, it will be essential to strengthen the training and skills of these groups through lifelong learning activities, help displaced workers with job placement measures, and facilitate the reallocation of resources toward growing industries (OECD, 2021b).

Furthermore, the WEF's "Youth Recovery Plan" reported the hopes and concerns of young people between the ages of 20 and 30 worldwide about their skills and readiness for jobs. The report was based on responses to an online survey and virtual interviews with immigrants, heads of state, and public figures in 187 countries in 2021. Almost 50% of young people surveyed said they felt inadequately skilled, and only 16% of respondents said they were "fully confident" in their skills' sufficiency to find a decent job for the next five to ten years (WEF, 2021). Therefore, higher education institutions should focus on academic courses and guidance lessons to raise students' confidence.

Young people have a greater risk of being pushed out of the labor market than older ones. While today's youth are the most educated compared to the past, they are also debt-ridden and suffer from unemployment. Unemployment has increased, especially for low-skilled and young workers, calling for strengthening the capacity of public employment services to provide job search support and training (OECD, 2021a). Younger workers are more likely to have transitioned to new roles during these uncertain times. Hence, higher education institutions are required to upgrade their curricula with the express function of job acquisition in a rapidly digitalized world (WEF, 2021). For instance, students and academicians should be equipped with digital skills to assist students in developing or improving their basic digital skills or other newly demanded skills in the workplace. Besides, university-industry relations should be improved to provide more vocational education in workplaces for students. So they can more easily acquire the skills employers demand. In other words, the higher education institutions need to reinvent themselves to give people greater ownership over what they learn, how they learn, when they learn, and where they learn to meet tomorrow's demand for skills' (OECD, 2019b).

Adult employees with a higher education degree are also affected by the disruption because training providers are forced to close, causing disruptions in work-based learning, professional development, and other sorts of education, all of which significantly impact human potential. It is critical to upgrade or update workers' skills to remain competitive in the job market. Unsurprisingly, digital-based work will become more prevalent in the digital economy. More jobs will be formed by technological disruption, labor automation, and more flexible and fluid employment, all of which will include significant involvement with technology. As a result, there will be greater demand for lifelong learning in the post-pandemic world. Despite the current economic recession, most employers understand the need to invest in human capital. It is time to think about the future and solve the underlying structural challenges wreaking havoc on the labor market. Briefly, national policies that lead to the rapid changes in the higher education landscape are required to digitalize higher education institutions' infrastructures. Also, countries should increase their budget for employment policies of higher education graduates.

REFERENCES

Açıkgöz, Ö., & Günay, A. (2021). Short-term impact of the Covid-19 pandemic on the global and Turkish economy. *Turkish Journal of Medical Sciences*, *51*(SI-1), 3182–3193. doi:10.3906ag-2106-271 PMID:34365782

Altig, D., Baker, S., Barrero, J. M., Bloom, N., Bunn, P., Chen, S., Davis, S. J., Leather, J., Meyer, B., Mihaylov, E., Mizen, P., Parker, N., Renault, T., Smietanka, P., & Thwaites, G. (2020). Economic uncertainty before and during the COVID-19 pandemic. *Journal of Public Economics*, *191*, 104274. doi:10.1016/j.jpubeco.2020.104274 PMID:32921841

Autor, D. H., Frank, L., & Richard, J. M. (2003). The skill content of recent technological change: An empirical exploration. *The Quarterly Journal of Economics*, *118*(4), 1279–1333. doi:10.1162/003355303322552801

Bai, L. (2006). Graduate unemployment: Dilemmas and challenges in China's move to mass higher education. *The China Quarterly*, *185*, 128–144. doi:10.1017/S0305741006000087

Bui, T., Button, P., & Picciotti, E. G. (2020). Early evidence on the impact of coronavirus disease 2019 (COVID-19) and the recession on older workers. *The Public Policy and Aging Report*, *30*(4), 154–159. doi:10.1093/ppar/praa029 PMID:34191898

CEDEFOP. (2010). *Future skill supply in Europe. Medium-term forecast up to 2020.* Luxembourg: Publications Office of the European Union. https://www.cedefop.europa.eu/files/3052_en.pdf

CEDEFOP. (2015). *Matching skills and jobs in Europe: Insights from Cedefop's European skills and jobs survey*. Luxembourg: Publications Office. https://www.cedefop.europa.eu/files/8088_en.pdf

Chan, S. J., & Lin, J. W. (2016). Aiming for better employment: A holistic analysis from admission to labor market. *Journal of Higher Education Policy and Management*, *38*(3), 282–296. doi:10.1080/1360080X.2016.1174405

Dewan, S., & Ernst, E. (2020). Rethinking the world of work. *Finance & Development*, *57*(4), 22–25.

Dolado, J. J., Felgueroso, F., & Jimeno, J. F. (2000). Youth labor markets in Spain: Education training and crowding-out. *European Economic Review*, *44*(4-6), 943–956. doi:10.1016/S0014-2921(99)00050-1

Goda, G. S., Jackson, E., Nicholas, L. H., & Stith, S. S. (2021). *The impact of Covid-19 on older workers' employment and social security spillovers.* NBER Working Paper, 29083. https://www.nber.org/papers/w29083

Goos, M., Manning, A., & Salomons, A. (2014). Explaining job polarization: Routine-biased technological change and offshoring. *The American Economic Review*, *104*(8), 2509–2526. doi:10.1257/aer.104.8.2509

GuptaS.MontenovoL.NguyenT. D.Lozano-RojasF.SchmutteI. M.SimonK. I.WeinbergB. A.WingC. (2020). *Effects of social distancing policy on labor market outcomes.* NBER Working Paper, w27280. https://ssrn.com/abstract=3615476

ILO. (2014). *Skill mismatch in Europe: Statistics Brief.* International Labor Organisation.

ILO. (2021a). *ILO monitor: COVID-19 and the world of work. Seventh edition.* https://www.ilo.org/global/topics/coronavirus/impacts-and-responses/WCMS_767028/lang--en/index.htm

ILO. (2021b). *World employment and social outlook. Trends 2021.* https://www.ilo.org/global/research/global-reports/weso/trends2021/WCMS_795453/lang--en/index.htm

Kim, S., & Lee, J. H. (2006). Changing facets of Korean higher education: Market competition and the role of the state. *Higher Education*, *52*(3), 557–587. doi:10.100710734-005-1044-0

Lauder, H., & Mayhew, K. (2020). Higher education and the labor market: An introduction. *Oxford Review of Education*, *46*(1), 1–9. doi:10.1080/03054985.2019.1699714

Lee, S., Schmidt-Klau, D., & Verick, S. (2020). The labor market impacts of Covid-19: A global perspective. *Indian Journal of Labor Economics*, *63*(1), 11–15. doi:10.100741027-020-00249-y

Lewis, S. (2021). *Why age inclusive workforces play a crucial role in building back a better society post-COVID.* https://www.weforum.org/agenda/2021/09/why-age-inclusive-workforces-play-a-crucial-role-in-building-back-a-better-society-post-covid/

Liu, Y., Green, A., & Pensiero, N. (2016). Expansion of higher education and inequality of opportunities: A cross-national analysis. *Journal of Higher Education Policy and Management*, *38*(3), 242–263. doi:10.1080/1360080X.2016.1174407

Mayhew, K., Deer, C., & Dua, M. (2004). The move to mass higher education in the UK: Many questions and some answers. *Oxford Review of Education, 30*(1), 65–82. doi:10.1080/0305498042000190069

McGuinness, S., & Pouliakas, K. (2017). Deconstructing theories of overeducation in Europe: A wage decomposition approach. In S. W. Polachek, K. Pouliakas, G. Russo, & K. Tatsiramos (Eds.), *Research in labor economics, skill mismatch in labor markets* (pp. 81–127). Emerald Publishing Ltd. doi:10.1108/S0147-912120170000045003

Mok, K. H., & Jiang, J. (2018). Massification of higher education and challenges for graduate employment and social mobility: East Asian experiences and sociological reflections. *International Journal of Educational Development, 63*, 44–51. doi:10.1016/j.ijedudev.2017.02.003

Mok, K. H., & Wu, A. (2016). Higher education, changing labor market and social mobility in the era of Massification in China. *Journal of Education and Work, 29*(1), 77–97. doi:10.1080/13639080.2015.1049028

Nyiri, L. (2002). Knowledge-based society and its impact on labor-market values. *Society and Economy, 24*(2), 201–218. doi:10.1556/SocEc.24.2002.2.3

OECD. (1996). *The knowledge-based economy*. OECD Publishing.

OECD. (2016). *Skills matter: Further results from the survey of adult skills*. Paris: OECD Publishing. https://www.oecd.org/skills/piaac/Skills_Matter_Further_Results_from_the_Survey_of_Adult_Skills.pdf

OECD. (2018). *Transformative technologies and jobs of the future*. Paris: OECD Publishing. https://www.oecd.org/innovation/transformative-technologies-and-jobs-of-the-future.pdf

OECD. (2019a). *Skills matter: Additional results from the survey of adult skills*. OECD Publishing., doi:10.1787/1f029d8f-

OECD. (2019b). *Speech at launch of OECD's: Education at a glance 2019: OECD indicators*. https://www.hepi.ac.uk/2019/09/10/hepi-hosts-the-launch-of-education-at-a-glance-2019-oecd-indicators%EF%BB%BF-the-worlds-best-source-of-education-data/

OECD. (2020). *OECD economic outlook 2020*. OECD Publishing. doi:10.1787/0d1d1e2e-

OECD. (2021a). *Education at a glance 2021: OECD indicators*. OECD Publishing. doi:10.1787/b35a14e5-

OECD. (2021b). *OECD economic outlook 2021*. OECD Publishing., doi:10.1787/edfbca02-

OECD. (2021c). *OECD employment outlook 2021: Navigating the Covid-19 crisis and recovery*. OECD Publishing. doi:10.1787/5a700c4b-

PIAAC Expert Group in Problem Solving in Technology-Rich Environments. (2009). PIAAC problem solving in technology rich environments: A conceptual framework. *OECD Education Working Papers*, 36. doi:10.1787/19939019

Pouliakas, K. (2012). The skill mismatch challenge in Europe. *Employment and Social Developments in Europe*, 351-394.

Sum, N. L., & Jessop, B. S. (2013). Competitiveness, the knowledge-based economy, and higher education. *Journal of the Knowledge Economy*, *4*(1), 24–44. doi:10.100713132-012-0121-8

Teichler, U. (1997). Graduate employment: Challenges for higher education in the twenty-first century. *Higher Education in Europe*, *22*(1), 75–84. doi:10.1080/0379772970220109

UNESCO. (2021). *Institute of statistics*. http://data.uis.unesco.org/

Vedder, R., Denhart, C., & Robe, J. (2013). *Why are recent college graduates underemployed? University enrollments and labor-market realities*. https://files.eric.ed.gov/fulltext/ED539373.pdf

Walker, P. (2007). System transition in Japanese short-term higher education: What future for the Japanese junior college in crisis? *Compare: A Journal of Comparative Education*, *37*(2), 239–255. doi:10.1080/03057920601165603

WEF. (2020a). *The future of jobs report 2020*. Geneva: World Economic Forum https://www3.weforum.org/docs/WEF_Future_of_Jobs_2020.pdf

WEF. (2020b). *The global competitiveness report 2020*. Geneva: World Economic Forum. https://www.weforum.org/reports/the-global-competitiveness-report-2020

WEF. (2021). *Davos Lab: Youth Recovery Plan*. Geneva: World Economic Forum https://www3.weforum.org/docs/WEF_Davos_Lab_Youth_Recovery_Plan_2021.pdf

West, J. (2000). Higher education and employment: Opportunities and limitations in the formation of skills in a mass higher education system. *Journal of Vocational Education and Training*, *52*(4), 573–588. doi:10.1080/13636820000200148

WHO. (2021). *WHO coronavirus (Covid-19) dashboard*. https://covid19.who.int/

Wu, C. C. (2011). High graduate unemployment rate and Taiwanese undergraduate education. *International Journal of Educational Development*, *31*(3), 303–310. doi:10.1016/j.ijedudev.2010.06.010

Xiao, F., Barnard-Brak, L., Lan, W., & Burley, H. (2019). Examining problem solving skills in technology-rich environments as related to numeracy and literacy. *International Journal of Lifelong Education*, *38*(3), 327–338. doi:10.1080/02601370.2019.1598507

ADDITIONAL READING

Abad-Segura, E., González-Zamar, M. D., Infante-Moro, J. C., & García, G. R. (2020). Sustainable management of digital transformation in higher education: Global research trends. *Sustainability*, *12*(5), 2107. doi:10.3390u12052107

Antonopoulou, H., Halkiopoulos, C., Barlou, O., & Beligiannis, G. N. (2021). Transformational leadership and digital skills in higher education institutes: During the Covid-19 pandemic. *Emerging Science Journal*, *5*(1), 1–15. doi:10.28991/esj-2021-01252

Bayerlein, L., Hora, M.T, Dean, B.A., & Perkiss, S. (2021). Developing skills in higher education for post-pandemic work. *Labour & Industry: A Journal of the Social and Economic Relations of Work*. do i:10.1080/10301763.2021.1966292

Brown, P., Lauder, H., & Cheung, S. Y. (2019). *The death of human capital?* Oxford University Press.

Grishin, V. I., Domashchenko, D. V., Konstantinova, L. V., Koshkin, A. P., Ustyuzhanina, E. V., Shtykhno, D. A., & Shubenkova, E. V. (2020). Life after the pandemic: Economic and social sonsequences. *Vestnik of the Plekhanov Russian University of Economics*, *3*(3), 5–18. doi:10.21686/2413-2829-2020-3-5-18

Kalantzis, M., & Cope, B. (2020). After the COVID-19 crisis: Why higher education may (and perhaps should) never be the same. *Access: Contemporary Issues In Education*, *40*(1), 51–55. doi:10.46786/ac20.9496

Lauder, H., Brown, P., & Cheung, S. Y. (2018). Fractures in the education–Economy relationship: The end of the skill bias technological change research programme? *Oxford Review of Economic Policy*, *34*(3), 495–515. doi:10.1093/oxrep/gry008

Piopiunik, M., Schwerdt, G., Simon, L., & Woessman, L. (2020). Skills, signals, and employability: An experimental investigation. *European Economic Review*, *123*, 103374. doi:10.1016/j.euroecorev.2020.103374

KEY TERMS AND DEFINITIONS

COVID-19 Pandemic: A disease caused by a new coronavirus, which has not been previously identified in humans, discovered in China in 2019.

Digital Skills: Ability to use, access, filter, evaluate, create, program, and share digital content.

Graduate: A person who has finished their school, college, or university education.

Higher Education: Educational qualification awarded upon successful completion of specific educational programs in universities and equivalent institutions.

Labor Market: Place where workers and employees interact with each other.

PIACC: A program of assessment and analysis of adult skills.

Problem Solving in Technology-Rich Environments: Using digital technology, communication tools, and networks to acquire and evaluate information, communicate with others, and perform practical tasks.

Unemployment: Individuals who are employable and actively seeking a job but cannot find a job.

Chapter 8
Managing the Remote Workforce in the New Normal

Dilek Esen
Dokuz Eylül University, Turkey

ABSTRACT

The purpose of this chapter is to determine how to manage the remote workforce in a period that covers during and after the COVID-19 pandemic called the new normal. According to this purpose, the content is as follows: the concept of new normal, remote working and hybrid work as a remote working model, advantages and disadvantages of remote working, managing the remote work and workforce. In this context, the author aimed to show remote working from all sides in the new normal and give an idea for researchers and practitioners about how to successfully manage the new normalization period post the COVID-19 pandemic.

INTRODUCTION

After understanding that Covid 19 is a pandemic, several regulations were made by governments or decision-makers. Several industry sectors started functioning partially, some of them completely closed for some time. In this process, while companies had to continue their economic activities, they also had to keep the employees healthy and safe. At the same time, the necessity of sustaining economic activities and ensuring the health and safety of employees has made working remotely the best solution. Because of Covid-19, many people have to change many habits related to both their work and daily life routines approximately in 3 months.

Although remote working is seen as the best solution for companies, the most important problem is for companies and employees to be caught unprepared for remote working processes. Lack of supportive infrastructure for large-scale work, mixed emotions and feelings about remote working, lack of experiences for the remote working process, are some of the problems.

In the traditional management approach, cooperation, teamwork, large offices were seen as important values. Remote or flexible working was only preferred to maintain the work-life balance of the employees. However, with Covid 19, issues such as where, how, with whom and, when we work, were

DOI: 10.4018/978-1-7998-2395-7.ch008

Copyright © 2022, IGI Global. Copying or distributing in print or electronic forms without written permission of IGI Global is prohibited.

constructed from the beginning. On the other hand, remote and flexible working, required simultaneous adaptation to the work and personal lives of employees, rather than balancing between them (Patil & Gopalakrishnan, 2020).

This process, which covers the period of Covid-19 and "new normals", has been the focus of many researchers and practitioners to monitor the current situation and make the necessary improvements. Therefore so many researches published about the Covid-19 pandemic and its effect on companies, employees, effective management alternatives, etc. In these processes, workplace isolation, social distances, work-life balance, remote working, multiple roles for employees (Prasad & Mangipudi, 2020), burnout, remote working topics are the popular subjects for business management.

In this section, the author aimed that determine remote working with all sides in the new normal and give an idea for researchers and practitioners about how to manage the new normalization period with successfully post Covid-19 pandemic.

BACKGROUND

When the literature is determined, it is possible to come across many studies about remote work or the economic world on the Covid-19 and the pandemic process (Hamblin, 1995; Kurland & Bailey, 1999; Kırpık, 2020; Koirala & Acharya, 2020; Petzer, 2020; Ting et al., 2020). Among these researches, besides academic publications, it is possible to find articles published in popular journals, reports published by various human resource management companies (Entrust, 2021; Levenson, 2020; Phillips, 2020; Prasad & Mangipudi, 2020; PwC, 2021; Zeegen et al., 2020). Although these studies are important for the formation of a general judgment on the subject in the literature, it can be stated that this area is still in the discovery phase. In other words, it is seen that there is no consensus about managing the remote working and workforce in the literature. Therefore, it is thought that new studies in this field will be important in terms of the cumulative progress of the process and gaining new perspectives.

Buheji and Buheji's research (2020) is about employability competency in post- the COVID-19 pandemic. According to research results, employability competencies are called, "proactiveness", "preparedness", "pulling-together", "problem-solving", "publishing and publicizing". These competencies may help employees to overcome the challenges in the new normal.

Koirala and Acharya (2020) stated in their study that the Covid-19 pandemic is a turning point for the workplace concept. It has been mentioned that this transformation, will force human resources management units to change their policies and strategies. The concept of "social distance" draws attention as an important concept in this transformation process. While remote working is seen as a more suitable working method for the service sector, it is not seen as a suitable working method for many production sectors.

Bonacini and others (2020) conducted a study on Italian employees. In this study, the authors explored the potential results in the employee income distribution related to a long-lasting increase in remote work. The results showed that in remote working, an increase in the income of the employees will not be evenly distributed among the employees. It is stated that this increase mostly supports male, elderly, highly paid and, highly educated workers.

According to the results of the research conducted by Deloitte (2020), it is revealed that remote working is preferred by both employees and employers. While motivation and the factors related to motivation are effective factors in the preference of employees to work remotely; financial gains are effective in employers who prefer to work remotely. It is stated that the variables that may be effective in preferring to work remotely are affected by the age and personal characteristics of the employees. According to another finding of the research, there are important cyber security problems of enterprises in remote working processes.

In their research, Ware and Grantham (2020) questioned the reasons why businesses choose to work remotely, what tools and methods are used for remote work in successful companies, and what are the suggestions of successful leaders for companies that are just starting to work remotely. As a result, it is stated that the most important motivation in the adaptation of companies to new ways of doing business is to save costs. In addition, leaders state that remote working is an important strategy for attracting talented employees to the companies and ensuring their continuity.

However there is a lot of research in the literature, it is thinking that this book section will be helpful, both organizations decide to adjust remote working strategies, choosing between office or remote, scheduling employees time, workplaces or decide to a hybrid model and gain perspective about advantages-disadvantages for companies, decision-makers, employees.

MAIN FOCUS OF THE CHAPTER

Concept of New Normal

Since the Covid-19 pandemic has been seen around the world, nothing is going on the same. All around the world lots of things, such as social relationships, the education systems, the working processes, commerce, have been changed and these changes seem to be going on. All of these changes are called "new normal". New normal is defined in Oxford Dictionary ("as an event or status or era that was unfamiliar, atypical situation that has become standard, or usual, or expected"(2007).

The meaning of the new normal can be expressed, in simpler terms, as "not going back to the old one again". This means that "don't want to waste time during the commuting", "don't want to long office hours", "want to flexible time management", "want to use time with our family", e.t.c. (Oxford Dictionary, 2007)

New normal is an era full of demanding situations and instability, wherein agility, curiosity, threat mitigation, learning by exploring, learning by doing, however with focus, will be the norm for both survival and competitiveness (Levenson, 2020). Besides these meanings, in this paper, new normal was used to explain the indispensables of people's life routines after the Covid-19 pandemic.

The remote work is called the new normal during the Covid-19 pandemic for companies (Patil & Gopalakrishnan, 2020). When the threat of the Covid-19 pandemic diminishes, organizations will decide whether to bring employees back to the office or continue working remotely. (Hershkowitz, 2020). At this point, some researchers should provide data to guide decision-makers. PwC's research report can be evaluated such as a guiding document.

According to PWC's research report by July 2021, in the United States, After the Covid-19 pandemic, 61% of the employees do not want to go back to the office. (PwC, 2021). And now it's known that (PwC, 2021; PwC, 2020), remote work has become more precious for employees. And both employers and employees, remote work has been an overwhelming success (83% employers, 71% employees). Because during the pandemic by trying new methods in working styles, both employers and employees have gained enough knowledge to have an idea about the advantages and disadvantages of these methods. In other words, it could be said that employees explain a preference for remote working after the Covid-19 pandemic. At the same time, employers and employees say that they have been more productive, their organizations have been better performing such as collaborating on new projects and customer services, now than they were before the Covid-19 pandemic. Also, remote working is been making a norm rather than a passing phase by government decision-makers (Entrust, 2021).

Remote Working and as a Remote Working Model Hybrid Work

Remote work is a flexible working arrangement that allows employees to work from a flexible location outside of offices. Remote work is also known as telecommuting or work from home (WFH) (Gartner Glossary).

Remote work (telecommuting) has been applied in different years for different purposes. In the 1970s, remote work was used as an alternative working method to solve problems in areas where traffic congestion and air pollution are intense. In the 1980s, it became a preferred working method to reduce costs by reducing office areas and also to attract senior employees to the companies, to ensure their continuity in the following years. With the development of technology and internet providers, computer-based technologies such as "satellite work centers", "neighborhood work centers", "mobile work" have reduced the need for physical travel and home-based telecommunication. The concepts of "teleworking" or "remote working" are used to express all of these alternative working methods (Kurland & Bailey, 1999).

Figure 1. From the traditional office to hybrid work
Source: (Gratton, 2021)

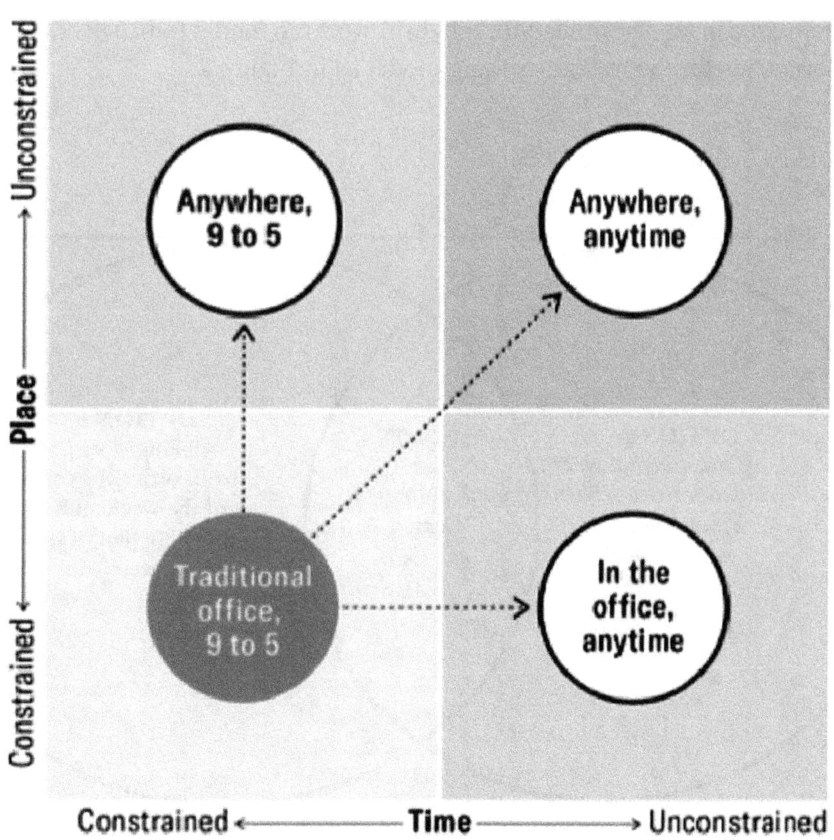

The pandemic has also been an important breaking point in the content, importance, and scope of remote work applications. Before the pandemic, going to the office for working and spending working hours in the office was the norm; time-flexibility and place-flexibility were very limited. During the pandemic, managers and employees have realized that employees can be productive by working anywhere, at any time. Thus the constrained understanding about time and place has shifted to the unconstrained understanding. So it has been possible for employees to work independently of time and place (Gratton, 2021).

When the literature is reviewed, the studies which are conducted about new normal, indicate that especially employees include future talent, give importance to flexibility, acknowledge and that it is thought to continue to be implemented in the post-pandemic period (Flood, 2019; Larson et al., 2020; Ware & Grantham, 2010). According to the PwC research report (PwC, 2021), employees who have the least experience need the office more than the other employees. In general, over half of employees prefer to working remotely at least three days a week. For example, at Fujitsu, before the pandemic, more than 74% of all employees considered the office is the best place to work, but by May, only %15 of all employees considered the office is the best place to work, 30% said the best place was their home and 55% favored a hybrid model which is a mix of home and office (Gratton, 2021). Because pandemic turns all understanding about working style upside down.

Hybrid working is a "blended working", that's combining work on-site or working remotely. This is a kind of flexible working, that employees can work wherever they want such as the home, company, warehouse. So employees were allowed to split their time between working remotely or attending the workplace (Peace, 2021; Rosencrance, 2021; Simpson, 2021). In the hybrid work model, while offices keep on going remain, their roles are changing.

Various alternatives can be determined for a hybrid working model to be successful. Fowell (2021) expressed the alternatives for the hybrid working model as in Figure 2.

Figure 2. Alternatives hybrid working models
Source: (Fowel, 2021)

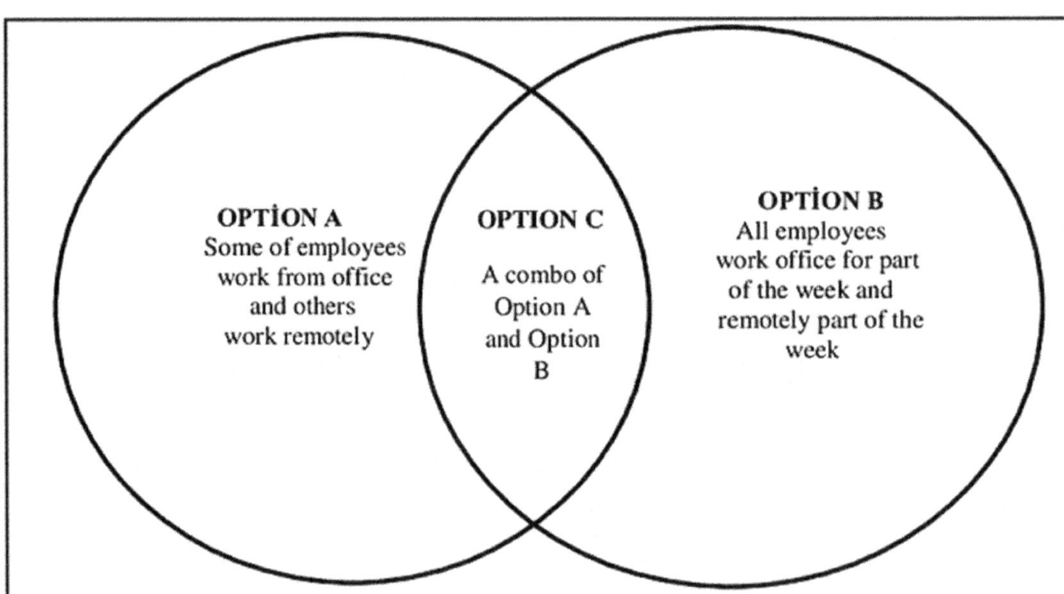

In Fowell's hybrid work model first option is, some employees work on-site and the other part of employees work remotely. The second option is, on exact days of week employees working remotely, on the other days of the week, employees are expected to work on the office. The third option is, some employees have the flexibility to work office on some days and remotely on others. The remaining employees work fully remote or fully office (Fowell, 2021). Companies can choose any hybrid work model, which is suitable for their production field, and apply it in their companies.

It is possible to count many reasons for the preference of hybrid working models. Saving office costs and reducing transfer costs are among the most important driving forces that direct businesses to hybrid working models (Ware & Grantham, 2020). The growth and complexity of businesses, the development of technology, transform the needed employee profile into qualified white-collar employees, and the number of contracted employees from wide geographies is increasing. In addition, the demographic structure of the workforce is changing, which weakens the influence of businesses on employees' career decisions. Accordingly, young female employees with young children, dual-career spouses and, employees with strong individual life preferences can be examples of the changing structure of the workforce.

Although some of the research results show that after the Covid-19 pandemic, working remotely is highly preferable (Fowell, 2021; PwC, 2021), employees and employers also mention the necessity of being in the workplace for some reasons. The reasons, that make it necessary to work from the office, are "increasing employee productivity", "providing a space to meet with clients", "enabling collaborate effectively", "enabling company culture", "accessing equipment or documents securely", "training and career development", etc. There is a paradox that assumes that remote working leads to incompatible results: on the one side, it enhanced work-life balance and perceived autonomy, on the other side it negatively impacts the quality of work relationships and career (Gajendran & Harrison, 2007). So hybrid work models are recommended as the best solution method to use the advantages of working remotely and to get rid of the disadvantages caused by working remotely.

Sustaining a company's culture, providing a collaborative environment for employees, relationship-building with colleagues, managers, or clients, planning for the right office space model, scheduling teams, evaluating performance, and other human resources management topics are the questions that have to be answered in the hybrid work model for successful management (PwC, 2021). In other words, in the hybrid work model, it is important to be scheduled who, when, and for how long to be in the office and what is expected to accomplish by employees.

Advantages of Remote Working

There are lots of opinions about the advantages of remote working. According to these opinions, remote work suggests a "win-win" concept for both employers and employees. Remote working provides employees flexibility. So employees work where and when they are more productive, thereby increasing employee productivity (We Work Remotely [WWR], 2021). At the same time, lost time for commuting to the office every day is eliminated and employees can use their time more effectively by remote work. In addition, remote work facilitates increasing levels of job satisfaction and organizational commitment (Felstead & Henseke, 2017; Rowan, 2021), improvements in performance, saving organizational resources (Barbuto et al., 2020; Thulin et al., 2020), decreasing work-role stress, work exhaustion, turnover intent (Sardeshmukh et al., 2021; Gajendran & Harrison, 2007). The flexibility provided by remote working increases the perception of control, and the increased perception of control leads to a decrease in stress (Duxbury et al., 2014).

If a company wants to keep talented employees, the company should prepare itself to work remotely. Because especially after the Covid-19 pandemic employees want flexibility in their jobs (PwC, 2021; Fowell, 2021) and remote work can be a good strategy to attract talented employees. On the other side, opening the positions for global candidates will provide an advantage both in bringing together employees with different skills and in providing candidates who can work in different time zones (Fowell, 2021).

Remote working facilitates employment and increases the life comforts of employees with disabilities. It is also among the advantages of working remotely that infectious diseases such as the flu, cold, and COVID spread in the workplace and reduce the risk of increased absenteeism due to these reasons (Fowell, 2021).

After the Covid-19 pandemic, it's estimated that, as a result of social distancing needs, increasing working areas per employee to become a necessity (PwC, 2021). This necessity that having larger working areas or moving cheaper working areas will lead to significant costs for employers. So working remotely can be considered as an important alternative in reducing these costs. Also, working remotely saves the company costs (Felstead & Henseke, 2017) by reducing the use of energy resources and lower overheads. From a macro and long-term perspective, working remotely will reduce air pollution by reducing the commutes to work (Rowan, 2021).

Work-life balance is defined as 'satisfaction and good functioning of work and home, with a minimum of role conflict (Clark, 2000). In the literature, there are different opinions on the effects of remote work on maintaining a work-life balance. According to one opinion, while remote working has positive effects on the work-life balance of employees (Gajendran & Harrison, 2007); another opinion argues the opposite (Felstead & Henseke, 2017). According to the second opinion, it is argued that remote workers work more, the borders between home and work are blurred (Aborg et al., 2002; Baruch et al., 1997,; Marsh & Musson, 2008).

Table 1. Advantages of remote work

Societal	Organizational	Individual
Less traffic congestion	Greater productivity	Less time commuting
Less pollution	Lower absenteeism	Cost-saving
Greater community involvement	Better morale	Less stress
	Greater openness	No need for relocation
	Fewer interruptions at the office	More Autonomy
	Reduced overhead	Schedule flexibility
	Wider talent pool	Comfortable work environment
	Lower turnover	Fewer distractions
	Regulation compliance	Absence of office politics
	Customer proximity	Work-family balance
		Workplace fairness
		More job satisfaction

Source:(Compiled from Kurland & Bailey pages 56-59)

Disadvantages or Challenges of Remote Working

Besides of advantages of remote working, it has some disadvantages or challenges. The most striking issues, among these disadvantages or challenges, are communication, sustaining corporate culture, security problems, continuing collaboration among employees, enhancing productivity (Entrust, 2021, p. 8; PwC, 2021), lack of access to information, social isolation, distractions at home (Larson et al., 2020).

Beyond fulfilling organizational duties, going to the office means that, socializing, chatting, eating together, sharing information, and developing social networks. So employees may feel isolated and left out when they work remotely instead of coming to the office. Sometimes time differences can become a challenge and communication get an extra effort for remote employees (WWR, 2021). Therefore, going to the workplace is an important factor for the formation and maintenance of a corporate culture that is increasing productivity and organizational commitment. In the opposite situation, that is, in virtual workplaces, employees may be more negative, distracted, more reluctant to cooperate, share information, and listen to different ideas (Patil & Gopalakrishnan, 2020, p. 3912).

High workload, uncertain boundaries of work and life, burnout, mental and physical health, and occupational safety can be counted among other challenges. Lack of concentration, depression, anxiety, insomnia, loneliness, apprehension may be among the most common physical and mental health problems (Patil & Gopalakrishnan, 2020, p. 3912). It is estimated that the reasons for these problems are that people stay away from their loved ones while under quarantine, their routines are disrupted, all family members have to work from home at the same time, and the increased responsibilities related to child care and home. Also, "non stop going on at work", exceeding organizational demands normal working hours may be caused physical and mental health problems (Molino et al., 2019, p. 446).

Another problem with remote work is some injustices that may occur in the wage and performance evaluations, promotions, of those who work remotely. Office workers can move up the career ladder faster than remote workers as they will interact more with decision-makers (WWR, 2021). So decision-makers or leaders may be incapable of observing the performance of their employees (Kurland & Bailey, 1999, p. 56). According to the results of the research conducted by the Rensselaer Polytechnic Institute before the coronavirus started, it had been founded that employees who are working at home regularly complain about lower wages than employees who work in the company (Rowan, 2021).

Another important challenge related to remote working is system security, network stability, and data security. These risks, which already exist, can increase with working remotely. While many businesses are willing to embrace remote working, few of these businesses have a cybersecurity infrastructure. With the epidemic, phishing scams and other attacks are increasing, trying to take advantage of existing system vulnerabilities, targeting employees who continue their work from home, from any open network. To take precautions against all these attacks and risks, providing cyber security for the remote management of the working day, protecting networks and data is one of the main agendas of companies in this and the next period (Deloitte, 2020, p. 2).

Technical infrastructure may be another challenge. Employees may have some difficulties, having an office, quiet workspace, video cameras, high-speed connectivity, e.t.c. or skills to manage all of them (Rowan, 2021). And another challenge working from home for employees is juggling their children or other housework while keep on working. According to the World Economic Forum reports, in the long term juggling can be caused a serious risk of increased levels of burnout and stress-related outcomes (Schawbel, 2020).

Table 2. Challenges of remote work

Societal	Organizational	Individual
Remote work culture	Performance monitoring	Social isolation
Loss of ability interact with others	Performance measurement	Professional isolation
	Managerial control	Reduced office influence
	Mentoring	Work-family balance
	Informal interaction	İnformal interaction
	Organizational culture	Conductive home environment
	Organizational loyalty	Focusing on work
	Schedule maintenance	Longer working hours
	Work coordination	Access technology, internet, other resources
	Communication	

Source: (Compiled from Kurland & Bailey, 1999)

There has not been a clarified concept in the literature about the advantages and disadvantages of remote work. Because remote work is a new topic both in theory and practice. As Felstead & Hense (2017) has been mentioned, these advantages and disadvantages may be changeable according to the working area and working sector. In this context, it seems like the best approach to consider these issues in the context of contingency, instead of clearly distinguishing the advantages and disadvantages of remote working.

Managing the Remote Work and Workforce

Although Covid-19 is seen as a crisis, it is also possible to evaluate this situation as an opportunity to reset existing working methods and processes. In this process; hybrid work offices, digital literacy, digital leadership, scheduling, work-life balance, virtual teams, etc. draw attention as important topics. Therefore, it is very important to organize all these changes simultaneously for the effective management of remote work. Managing remote work and workforce, it should be mentioned three contexts which are called; organizational context, employers-leaders context, and employees context, for successful management.

In an organizational context, a few methods can be mentioned to achieve remote work successfully. These methods can be stated as in shortly; "establishing goals", "good at employee communication", "providing workspace and virtual tools for employees", "maintaining an accessible connection between employees and IT support", "establishing deepen trust and connection" (Rowan, 2021; Lester, 2020).

In the employers-leaders context, employers-leaders should establish and agree upon goals that are important for employee's resiliency, positivity, and psychological safety. Also so that maintain employee's motivation, employers-leaders should establish weekly priorities and milestones. Because of giving the sense of being part of a whole even though employees are working physically alone, virtual meetings should be done frequently (Rowan, 2021). In other words for successful management, there should be no communication gaps between employers-leaders and employees.

In the employee's context, employees gain new competencies in the new normalization period (Meister, 2020). According to Buheji and Buheji (2020), these competencies are defined as, imagination, curiosity, creativity, and resilience. Harvey (2001) mentions that in the new normalization period, employees must react, realize, resolve, reshape and be resilient to be employed.

Shortly for both companies, employers-leaders and employees to adapt to dynamic, changing, and non-predictive environmental conditions in the pandemic and the post-pandemic period, companies should be more involved in processes as education and training. And the employees should manage to change continuously (Buheji & Buheji, 2020).

Another view should be mentioned for successful management of managing remote work and workforce, it is recommended to consider the following points (Adapted from Patil & Gopalakrishnan, 2020; Kurland & Bailey, 1999; Gratton, 2021):

Regulations on Working Infrastructure

These may be among the first considered topic when managing remote work and workforce. According to new business (remote work, hybrid work) priorities, communication-related studies, scheduling, technical infrastructure, etc. can be counted in this context.

It is important that which channels will be preferred for internal and external communication (e-mail, Whatsapp groups, telephone), the infrastructure of the program to be used, the necessary agreements with the internet service provider, and all communication channels open for users. For all these, it should be decided whether new tools are needed or whether existing tools will be used in new ways (Fowell, 2021). In other words, it should be ensured that employees do not have any problems with accessing technical infrastructure (Kurland & Bailey, 1999). A blockage in communication or access to technical infrastructure will mean that all business processes will stop so it is necessary to manage this process very well.

Scheduling is another important topic in regulations on working infrastructure. In the hybrid working model, organizations can offer different working hours alternatives to their employees, as well as completely give employees flexibility in working hours, especially in project-oriented works. In this process, organizations could decide employees will work office on certain days or weeks (Fowell, 2021). While some organizations set the working schedule from 8 to 5 to coordinate with other office workers. However, this working schedule may not be suitable for all positions in the organization. For example, working in the hours determined by the organization may be suitable for customer service, but it may not be an efficient method for an architect (Kurland & Bailey, 1999). So, the infrastructure related to working hours should be designed according to the types of work in the organization.

Regulations Regarding Employees

Another important issue to consider in managing the remote work and workforce is, employees. It is necessary to consider issues related to the protection of physical and mental health such as anxiety, stress, and excessive workload, ensuring the work-life balance of employees, creating socialization opportunities for the employees. So companies should offer employees training or proactive, family-friendly strategies and some instruments to cope with the challenges of remote work on work-life balance (Molino et al., 2020).

While designing remote working, employees should be informed about their personal preferences regarding their working models, which hours of the day are more preferable to work, whether their home offices are efficient, what they need in terms of cooperation, coordination, and focus on work (Gratton, 2021), and what difficulties they face. Various surveys may be applied to the employees by the management to better determine the employee preferences and the difficulties they face.

Regulations on Leadership

Studies on leadership are another important topic in the success of remote work. Although working remotely has advantages such as selecting candidates from a wider talent pool, dividing time into 24-hour periods, and bringing remote employees closer to external customers, but leading employees in this process carry some challenges. So much so that, remote work is characterized as the inability of the leaders to observe the work processes of the employees (Kurland & Bailey, 1999).

Leaders and managers take an important responsibility through; identify technostress problems and implementing solutions, developing suitable human resource management programs, policy changes, and take preventive measures (Atanasoff & Venable, 2017). While employees are working remotely, leaders have to manage all of these responsibilities also remotely. But remotely managing employees is difficult because of great distances and greater concern (Kurland & Bailey, 1999).

The roles of leaders for this context are, coaching, encouraging, motivating and engaging, etc. employees. Leaders should help employees about work-private life balance, designing of the conducive home. At the same time, leaders should be able to coaching and mentoring employees about clear communication skills, emotional support, the way to relax and get involved with employees (Koirala & Acharya, 2020; Kurland & Bailey, 1999).

Regulations on Human Resources Management Processes

After Covid-19, many businesses are planning to maintain remote work in different business lines. In this direction, each country or state develops methods related to remote working and carries out the necessary studies for the legalization of these procedures. Human resources management units are primarily obliged to act by the procedures and principles of remote working, which covers them according to the regions in which they operate. In this context, these regulations are binding on agreements to be made between companies and employees on issues such as providing the necessary office environment, tools, and equipment and meeting their maintenance and breakdown costs, working hours, occupational health and safety, and remote working data.

Apart from the legally binding issues, it can be seen as a necessity for the human resources units to go digital in the functions of human resources such as recruiting, orientation, performance evaluation, training and development of employees, personnel rights, and ensuring job security. In this direction, businesses need to redesign their human resources processes, such as Artificial Intelligence, Robotic Process Automation, Machine Learning (Patil & Gopalakrishnan, 2020), by digitalizing them.

The pandemic process, which is seen as a crisis, can create an opportunity for employees to participate in various certification programs, to become digitally literate, to manage many human resources functions such as recruitment and performance evaluation in digital environments, and for human resources units to become strategic business partners of enterprises.

Regulations for Projects, Virtual Teams, and Workflows

To be successful in remote working, workflow processes need to be effectively coordinated. In remote working models, coordination between projects and virtual teams or follow workflows is more difficult than coordination between office works. Because employees participate from different organizational or geographical environments. Also, team or project members may consist of employees with different levels of authority and responsibility, partners, business owners, or people outside the business. In remote work, communication between team/project members depends on digital tools such as e-mail, video conferencing, or audioconferencing (Kurland & Bailey, 1999). If there is effective coordination between digital communication tools and team/project members, then unnecessary work (meetings) will be eliminated, time will be used more efficiently thanks to asynchronous work, tasks will be automated, done remotely and more easily, and as a result, the value of the work will increase (Gratton, 2021).

During the remote working process, communication problems, adoption of corporate culture, loneliness, inability to focus, and lack of motivation are among the issues that employees complain about most frequently. To reduce these problems and challenges that can be experienced in teams and workflows and also increase productivity, various workspace alternatives can be offered. As workplace alternatives; hubs that maximize collaboration, satellites that increase coordination, and shared offices that enable focus (Gratton, 2021).

Hub means "centre of all the activities" or "the center of everything that is happening" (Market Business News [MBN], 2021). Head offices of institutions are accepted as hub offices. A satellite is a small space which is in a different location from the company's main office. Reaching an underserved area, the employees' life quality and expanding market share should be reasons for opening satellite spaces (Kenton, 2021). The biggest advantages of satellite offices are that they reduce the problems of loneliness and isolation by enabling employees to come face to face and provide coordination among employees (Gratton, 2021).

Shared workspaces (coworking spaces) are workstations rented by anyone else like remote workers, freelancers, gig workers, consultants, who may not have a central office. A shared workspace could be shared at different times by many different people. The purpose of these shared workspaces is to work together (Sheynkman, 2021). Also, these areas could be located around train stations, that's what, easily get to, reduce commuting time. There are internet connections and desks, allowing employees undisturbed, attend meetings, online meetings, work independently (Gratton, 2021).

Minimizing Challenges of Remote Working

As known that since the beginning of the Covid-19 pandemic, management processes have been discovered by trial and error. So there has been a lot of challenges for remote working. But as remote working is being seen as new normal, it is important to systematize and standardize new processes for successful management. By taking some of the tasks, organizations, employers-leaders, and employees are responsible for systematizing and standardizing the post-pandemic and remote working processes.

Minimizing the challenges of remote working, companies should guide their leaders and employees by preparing, remote working guides, regulations, policy decisions, etc. These guides should support employees both physically, technically, financially, and emotionally. Therefore, guidelines will cover topics such as education, consultancy, performance expectations, communication process, scheduling, preparation of technical infrastructure, expense, salary policies, maintain the organizational culture, reduce stress, work-life balance (Kurland & Bailey, 1999). As a result, it is expected that, while affecting the employees' well-being positively, increasing cooperation and organizational commitment and also reducing burnout (Gratton, 2021; Kniffin et al., 2020; Rudolph et al., 2020).

Business culture is one of the most important challenge areas for remote working. To successfully manage this challenge, companies can apply various tactics. For example, companies may require remote workers to work in the office for a certain amount of time. Visiting customers face-to-face, holding some meetings and face-to-face communion (Kurland & Bailey, 1999), celebrating important dates for the institution with face-to-face organizations, and ensuring employee participation in managerial processes can be considered as other alternatives.

SOLUTIONS AND RECOMMENDATIONS

The Covid-19 pandemic, which has affected the whole world since 2020, has necessitated significant changes in the methods of doing business. Although this change is a necessity, it also required to be fast. While it is easier to adapt this change, which use digital processes in business; it is more difficult to adapt this change, which are unfamiliar with digital processes.

In the quarantine period, remote working methods are seen as a temporary solution to prevent interruptions in their work, but in the new normalization period, it has been seen that remote working methods are a preferred working model by both employers and employees. As mentioned in detail in the previous sections, remote working is preferred by qualified workforce because of the advantages it provides such as flexibility, autonomy, increased productivity, facilitating work-life balance, decreased commuting, and preventing unnecessary time losses. In terms of employers, reasons such as providing cost advantages, preventing epidemics, decreasing absenteeism rates, increasing organizational commitment, and increasing employee motivation, make working remotely preferable.

However, although remote working is seen as a highly preferable working model, some challenge areas need to be effective managed in this process. In particular, organizational culture, isolation of employees, communication problems, lack of clear boundaries between work and private life, problems with internet infrastructure, cyber security, and some inequality problems that can be experienced in the evaluation of employees are the leading ones.

To manage remote working processes more successfully, there may be some precautions that organizations should take. Preparations and investments related to remote working infrastructure can be counted among these. Also, all technical and hardware infrastructure that remote workers will need, necessary satellite offices or shared offices are within the scope of these issues. It is another issue for organizations to take the necessary security measures against possible cyber-attacks and to ensure service continuity in a secure infrastructure.

Organizations should inform their employees about remote working policies and procedures. Not every economic activity or business segment is suitable for remote work. In these policies and procedures, it should be stated which economic activity is suitable for remote working, what time and day alternatives are available for remote working. Also, the performance evaluation and promotion proceeding of remote workers should be specified in these processes. Employees should be asked about their preferences regarding remote working hours and days.

All employees in the organization need to be supported emotionally, physically, technically and, financially. In this process, it is important to provide training on topics such as digital literacy, digital communication tools, solving technical problems. And also ensure that employees participate in certification programs and follow change, open to learning is another important thing for successful management of remote working

Leaders-managers also have some responsibilities in remote working. It is very important for the success of remote working that the leaders-managers are in constant communication with the employees, providing emotional support to the employees, being inclusive and equidistant to the employees, providing supportive motivation, and coaching-mentoring.

Hybrid working models can be seen as an important alternative to support organizational culture, increase organizational commitment, reduce feelings of loneliness and alienation, increase the advantages of remote working and reduce its disadvantages. Thus, employees will be at work on certain days of the week and will have the opportunity to work from home or remotely on certain days. In addition, choosing satellite offices or shared offices as an alternative to the head offices will be an application that reduces both the commuting time and office costs for businesses.

FUTURE RESEARCH DIRECTIONS

Especially in the last two years, the issue of remote working and managing remote workers has attracted the attention of many researchers. In addition to scientific studies on this subject, it is also frequently encountered in the form of columns, blogs, conversations, to which practitioners contribute. Among these studies, it has been observed that the remarkable topics are generally gathered around the results of remote working for businesses and employees, advantages and disadvantages of remote working, alternatives to a remote working model, and minimizing the challenges of remote working. In the literature, although it is seen that there is a consensus about remote working in the literature, it has been determined that there is no consensus on the results of remote working.

In this context, it can be advised to researchers that to conduct regional comparisons in which individual and organizational outcome variables such as subjective well-being, job satisfaction, organizational commitment, the individual and organizational performance, productivity of remote work will be revealed through quantitative research.

CONCLUSION

With the Covid 19 pandemic, there have been significant changes in our lives, including working life. The pandemic process has dragged businesses into a crisis that requires rapid response, and in this process, it has become necessary to transition to new business operations and methods. Issues such as remote working, remote workers, flexible working hours, teleconferences, remote meetings, interactive applications (Zoom, Skype, Microsoft Teams, etc.), internet infrastructure, digital literacy are at the center of our lives. In addition to the threats created by the crisis period, the most important opportunity offered by the pandemic to businesses is the discovery that many jobs can be done with remote working methods.

Remote working is an alternative working model that focuses on the concept of "flexibility" and enables the fulfillment of duties and responsibilities regardless of time and place, without being in the workplace. Although remote working is practiced before Covid-19, it can be considered as an opportunity by the Pandemic that it has become widespread to cover almost all sectors and business lines.

While there are many advantages offered by remote working, there are also some challenges for both companies and employees. While it is relatively easy to adapt to remote working for some companies which are located in regions with high digital literacy, having developed network infrastructure, having sufficient technological equipment, and using technology; other companies have had more challenges with remote working. To overcome these challenges and benefit more from the advantages of remote working models, hybrid working models are recommended. The hybrid working model is a working model that proposes to work from the office for certain periods (day-hours) and to work remotely for certain periods.

To achieve success in remote working and managing remote workers, both companies, leaders-managers and, employees have important responsibilities. Providing the necessary technical and hardware infrastructure for remote working, meeting the technical and hardware needs of the employees, supporting all employees in this process technically, financially, emotionally and, administratively, being in constant communication with the employees, coaching-mentoring the employees, increasing their emotional motivation, good scheduling, providing equal opportunities to employees, fair treatment of employees, participation of employees in necessary certification programs, and being open to continuous learning and development can be counted among these.

REFERENCES

Aborg, C., Fernström, E., & Ericson, M. (2002). *Telework Work Environment and Well-Being: Longitudinal Study*. Technical Report 2002-031, Uppsala University, Department of Information Technology, Uppsala, Sweden.

Atanasoff, L., & Venable, M. A. (2017). Technostress: Implications for adults in the workforce. *Career Development*, *65*(4), 326–338. doi:10.1002/cdq.12111

Barbuto, A., Gilliland, A., Peebles, R., Rossi, N., & Shrout, T. (2020). *Telecommuting: smarter workplaces.* http://hdl.handle.net/1811/91648

Baruch, Y., & Nicholson, N. (1997). Home, sweetwork: Requirements for effective homeworking. *Journal of General Management*, *23*(2), 15–30. doi:10.1177/030630709702300202

Bonacini, L., Gallo, G., & Scicchitano, S. (2021). Working from home and income inequality: Risks of a 'new normal' with COVID-19. *Journal of Population Economics*, *34*(1), 303–360. doi:10.100700148-020-00800-7

Buheji, M., & Buheji, A. (2020). Planning competency in the new normal– employability competency in post- covıd-19 pandemic. *International Journal of Human Resource Studies*, *10*(2), 237–251. doi:10.5296/ijhrs.v10i2.17085

Clark, S. C. (2000). Work/Family border theory: A new theory of work/family balance. *Human Relations*, *53*(6), 747–770. doi:10.1177/0018726700536001

Deloitte. (2020, 1 August). *COVID-19: Çalışanlara ve Çalışma Hayatına Olası Etkileri*. https://www2.deloitte.com/content/dam/Deloitte/tr/Documents/human-capital/covid-19-calisanlara-vecalisma-hayatina-olasi-etkileri.pdf

Dictionary, O. (2020, April 11). *Meaning of the New Normal in English*. https://www.lexico.com/definition/the_new_normal

Duxbury, L., & Halinski, M. (2014). When more is less: An examination of the relationship between hours in telework and role overload. *Work (Reading, Mass.), 2014*(48), 91–103. doi:10.3233/WOR-141858 PMID:24763352

Entrust, J. G. (2021). Securing the remote workforce in the new normal. *Computer Fraud & Security, 2*, 8–11.

Flood, F. (2019). Leadership in the remote, freelance, and virtual workforce era. *Global Encyclopedia of Public Administration, Public Policy, and Governance*. https://link.springer.com/referenceworkentry/10.1007%2F978-3-319-31816-5_3825-1

Fowell, T. (2021). *Hybrid work: What is hybrid work and why do employees want it?* https://envoy.com/blog/what-is-a-hybrid-work-model/

Gajendran, R. S., & Harrison, D. A. (2007). The good, the bad, and the unknown about telecommuting: Meta-analysis of psychological mediators and individual consequences. *The Journal of Applied Psychology, 92*(6), 1524–1541. doi:10.1037/0021-9010.92.6.1524 PMID:18020794

Glossary, G. (2021, 23 August). *Remote work*. https://www.gartner.com/en/information-technology/glossary/remote-work

Hamblin, H. (2001). Employees' perspectives on one dimension of labour flexibility: Working at a distance. *Work, Employment and Society, 9*(3), 473–498. doi:10.1177/095001709593003

Harvey, L. (2001). Defining and measuring employability. *Quality in Higher Education, 7*(2), 97–109. doi:10.1080/13538320120059990

Henseke, G., & Felstead, A. (2017). Assessing the growth of remote working and its consequences for effort, well-being and work-life balance. *New Technology, Work and Employment, 32*(3), 195–212. doi:10.1111/ntwe.12097

Hershkowitz, M. (2020). *The new normal balancing act. How to manage both remote and on premises teams*. https://www.cio.com/article/3587592/the-new-normal-balancing-act-how-to-manage-both-remote-and-on-premises-teams.html

James, W. & Grantham, C. (2010). Managing a remote workforce: proven practices from successful leaders. *The Work Design Collaborative*, 1-23.

Kenton, W. (2021). *Satellite Operation, Investopedia*. https://www.investopedia.com/terms/s/satellite-operation.asp

Kırpık, G. (2020). COVID-19 pandemisinin insan kaynakları üzerindeki etkisinin akademi, medya ve iş dünyası perspektifinden incelenmesi. *Manas Sosyal Araştırmalar Dergisi, 9*(4), 2393–2406. doi:10.33206/mjss.757777

Kniffin, K. M., Narayanan, J., Anseel, F., Antonakis, J., Ashford, S., Bakker, A. B., Bamberger, P., Bapuji, H., Bhave, D. P., Choi, V. K., Creary, S. J., Demerouti, E., Flynn, F. J., Gelfand, M. J., Greer, L. L., Johns, G., Kesebir, S., Klein, P. G., Lee, S. Y., ... Vugt, M. (2020). COVID-19 and the workplace: Implications, issues, and insights for future research and action. *The American Psychologist, 76*(1), 63–77. doi:10.1037/amp0000716 PMID:32772537

KoiralaJ.AcharyaS. (2020). Dimensions of Human Resource Management Evolved with the Outbreak of COVID-19. https://ssrn.com/abstract=3584092or doi:10.2139/ssrn.3584092

Kurland, N. B., & Bailey, D. E. (1999). Telework: The advantages and challenges of working here, there, anywhere, and anytime. *Organizational Dynamics*, *28*(2), 53–68. doi:10.1016/S0090-2616(00)80016-9

Larson, B. Z., Vroman, S. R., & Makarius, E. E. (2020). A Guide to managing your (newly) remote workers. *Harvard Business Review*. https://hbr.org/2020/03/a-guide-to-managing-your-newly-remote-workers

Lester, R. (2020), *Support Remote Work Durıng The Pandemıc & Beyond*. https://blog.bold360.com/ai-insights/the-new-normal-4-steps-to-support-remote-work-during-the-pandemic-beyond/

Levenson, A. (2020). A long time until the economic new normal, leaders must learn from the pandemic now to position their companies to thrive in the next crisis. *Sloan Review*. https://sloanreview.mit.edu/article/a-long-time-until-the-economic-new-normal/McArdle

Market Business News (MBN). (2021, July 23). *Hub – definition and meaning*. https://marketbusinessnews.com/financial-glossary/hub-definition-meaning/

Marsh, K., & Musson, G. (2008). Men at work and at home: Managing emotion in telework. *Gender, Work and Organization*, *15*(1), 31–48.

Meister, J. (2020). The impact of the coronavirus on HR and the new normal of work. *Forbes*. https://www.forbes.com/sites/jeannemeister/2020/03/31/the-impact-of-the-coronavirus-on-hrand-the-new-normal-of-work/#178b9d232b60

Molino, M., Cortese, C. G., & Ghislieri, C. (2019). Unsustainable working conditions: The association of destructive leadership, use of technology, and workload with workaholism and exhaustion. *Sustainability*, *11*(2), 446. doi:10.3390u11020446

Molino, M., Ingusci, E., Signore, F., Amelia, M., Amelia, G., Maria, L., Russo, V., Zito, M., & Cortese, C. G. (2020). Wellbeing costs of technology use during covid-19 remote working: An investigation using the italian translation of the technostress creators scale. *Sustainability*, *12*(5911), 1–20. doi:10.3390u12155911

Patil, R., & Gopalakrishnan, G. (2020). A study on employee experience with respect to remote working during the covid 19-pandemic. *Journal of Critical Reviews*, *7*(11), 3910–3918.

Peace, J. (2021). *Hybrid work model: 4 best practices for fairness, The Enterprisers Project*. https://enterprisersproject.com/article/2021/6/hybrid-work-model-4-best-practices

Petzer, M. (2020). *Coronavirus and the Workforce: How Can We Limit Redundancies?* http://researchonline.ljmu.ac.uk/iFd/eprint/12960/1/coronavirus-workforce redundancies _2020 0402T170659.pdf 31.

Phillips, S. (2020). Working through the pandemic: Accelerating the transition to remote working. *Business Information Review*, *37*(3), 129–135. doi:10.1177/0266382120953087

Prasad, K. D. V., & Mangipudi, M. R. (2020). Post-Covid19 pandemic back to workplace policies and procedures: A case study with reference to agricultural research sector. *Hyderabad. European Journal of Business and Management Research*, *5*(4), 1–5. doi:10.24018/ejbmr.2020.5.4.421

PwC. (2020, May 8). *TMT companies well-prepared for hybrid work model.* https://www.pwc.com/us/en /industries/tmt/library/companies-prepared-for-hybrid-work-model.html

PwC. (2021, January 12). *PwC's US Remote Work Survey. It's time to reimagine where and how work will get done.* https://www.pwc.com/us/en/library/covid-19/us-remote-work-survey.html

Rosencrance, L. (2021). *Hybrid Workforce.* https://whatis.techtarget.com/definition/hybrid-workforce

Rowan, L. (2021). *Remote Work: The New Normal?* https://www.15five.com/blog/remote-work-the-new-normal/

Rudolph, C. W., Allan, B., Clark, M., Hertel, G., Hirschi, A., Kunze, F., Shockley, K., Shoss, M., Sonnentag, S., & Zacher, H. (2020). Pandemics: Implications for research and practice in industrial and organizational psychology. *Industrial and Organizational Psychology: Perspectives on Science and Practice*, 1–82.

Sardeshmukh, S. R., Sharma, D., & Golden, T. D. (2012). Impact of telework on exhaustion and job engagement: A job demands and job resources model. *New Technology, Work and Employment*, *27*(3), 193–207. doi:10.1111/j.1468-005X.2012.00284.x

Schawbel, D. (2020). How to put people at the heart of your company's COVID-19 response, *World Economic Forum*. https://www.weforum.org/agenda/2020/10/covid19-remote-working-burnout-business-response/

Sheynkman, A. (2021). *SpaceIQ.* https://spaceiq.com/blog/what-is-shared-workspace/

Simpson, S. (2021). Writing a hybrid working policy: A guide for HR. *Personnel Today.* https://www.personneltoday.com/hr/hybrid-working-policy-hr-guide/

Thulin, E., Vilhelmson, B., & Johansson, M. (2020). New telework, time pressure, and time use control in everyday life. *Sustainability*, *11*(11), 3067. doi:10.3390u11113067

Ting, H., Ling, J., & Cheah, J. H. (2020). Editorial: It Will Go Away!? Pandemic crisis and business in asia. *Asian Journal of Business Research*, *10*(1), 1–7. doi:10.14707/ajbr.200072

Ware, J., & Grantham, C. (2010). Managing a remote workforce: proven practices from successful leaders. *The Work Design Collaborative*, 1-27. https://pdfslide.net/reader/f/managing-a-remote-workforce-proven-practices-from-successful-leaders

We Work Remotely (WWR). (2021, July 15). *Hybrid Work From Home Work Model: Here's How to Make it Work.* https://weworkremotely.com/hybrid-wfh-work-model-here-s-how-to-make-it-work

Zeegen, E. N., Yates, A. J., & Jevsevar, D. S. (2020). COVID-19 pandemic: Returning to normalcy or returning to a new normal. *The Journal of Arthroplasty*, *35*(7), 537–541. doi:10.1016/j.arth.2020.04.040 PMID:32376171

Chapter 9
COVID-19 Pandemic:
The Impact of the Elderly Workforce on Social Security-Related Rights

Emre Kol
https://orcid.org/0000-0002-3242-6925
Anadolu University, Turkey

ABSTRACT

The aim of this study is to evaluate and provide an overview of the significant impact of the increasing mean age of the communities on social insurance as well as the effects of COVID-19, which has turned into a pandemic, on social security rights of elderly. In this framework, strategies are suggested to minimize the negative effects of the issue on social security. This study aims to investigate the effects of aging of the population on social security systems in line with the reformist approach to social security systems, to seek an answer to the question of how social security systems will respond to this transition in the demographic structure and to suggest solutions against the effects of COVID-19. In addition, the authors discuss the implementation methods of a three-pillar social security model proposal, which is based on individual pension programs within the scope of social security reforms. Finally, flexible retirement plans developed in order to keep the aging workforce in employment for longer periods are discussed.

INTRODUCTION

Developments in modern life and medical technology prolong life expectancy and consequently elderly population is gradually increasing today. The share of the population aged 65 and over is increasing faster than any other age group all over the world (United Nations, 2019). The number of elderly people in the world is expected to reach 1.4 billion as of 2030, 2.1 billion as of 2050 and 3.1 billion as of 2100 (United Nations, 2017: 11).

The number of the population aged 65 and over in our country, which is referred to as the elderly, was 6 million 192 thousand 962 people as of 2014, whereas this figure increased by 21.9% over the last five years and reached 7 million 550 thousand 727 people as of 2019. Hence, the share of the elderly

DOI: 10.4018/978-1-7998-2395-7.ch009

Copyright © 2022, IGI Global. Copying or distributing in print or electronic forms without written permission of IGI Global is prohibited.

in the total population which was 8.0% as of 2014, increased to 9.1% as of 2019. As of 2019, 44.2% of the elderly population is male and 55.8% is female. Population-based projections reveal that the share of elderly population will be 10.2% by 2023, 12.9% by 2030, 16.3% by 2040, 20.8% by 2050, 22.6% by 2060 and 25.6% by 2080 (Turkish Statistical Institute [TURKSTAT], 2020a). However, it is expected that the rate of young population will decrease to 11.8% by 2060 (TURKSTAT, 2020b), whereas the rate of the population is expected to reach out to 22.6% by 2060 (TURKSTAT, 2020a).

This change in the demographic structure, which is generally defined as the elderly-aging population problem due to lower birth rates and longer life expectancy has a multi-dimensional negative effect on the functioning of social insurance, which is the most common technique of the social security system. First of all, when the labor force participation rate of individuals decreases, the number of active insured workforce paying social security premiums will decrease which subsequently will result in a decrease in income. It is accepted that there is an agreement between generations in society as such: The working generation provides care for children and youth; when they get older, they are entitled to be cared for by the generation whom they had previously taken care of (Tufan, 2016: 125).

Secondly, as the average life expectancy prolongs and the elderly population increases, the passive population that social insurance pays salaries, thus their monthly expenses will increase accordingly. The most important expense item among the total expenditures of social security systems is expenditures for the elderly, with a ratio of nearly 60%. In brief, aging population will disrupt the income-expenditure balance of the social security system and a structure that will make the financial sustainability of the system difficult will emerge (Arıcı and Alper, 2018: 220).

Demographers refer to this new century as the century in which the population will age rapidly. The aging population is attributed to two main reasons: The first is the decrease in birth rates while the second is the increase in life expectancy. The average age of the world's population, which was 23.6 in 1950, will rise to 26.5 by 2000 and to 36.2 by 2050. For developed regions such as Europe and North America, this figure is even higher. While the share of child population (0-14 years old) in the world, which was 34% as of 1950, decreased to 30% in 2000, the share of the elderly population (60 years and older) increased from 8% to 10%. Over the next 50 years, the rate of child population is estimated to decrease by 21% while the share of the elderly population is estimated to double, i.e., increase to 21% (Gündoğan, 2001: 97).

Older population reduces the productivity of the economy to the extent that it reduces the labor force participation rate. The aging of the population is not a problem that concerns only the social security system, so raising the retirement age alone will not be sufficient to solve this problem. The problem of change in the demographic structure and aging of the population is the common problem as of the 21st century of all countries independent of their level of development and it is not possible to limit their effects only to the social security system (Arıcı and Alper, 2018: 220).

The region mostly affected by the aging of the population in the world is Europe. The share of people aged 60 and over in the total population in Europe was 20% in 1998 and this rate is estimated to increase to 35% as of 2050. In other words, one out of every three people will be in the 60 and above age group of by 2050. Southern Europe, where the number of older people made up 20% of the population as of 1998, is today the oldest region in the world. This rate is expected to further increase to 39% by 2050. The share of the child population in Europe, which was 17% in 2000, is estimated to decrease to 14% by 2050 while the share of the elderly thereof will rise from 20% to 37%. Thus, it is expected that there will be 1 child for every 2.6 elderly people in Europe. Furthermore, average age is projected to increase from 37.5 to 49.5 by 2050. The country with the oldest population in the world today is Japan. Japan is followed by Italy, Switzerland, Germany and Sweden with an average age of 40. Estimates reveal that the country with the oldest population in the world as of 2050 will be Spain, with an average age of 55. Spain will be followed by Italy, Slovenia and Austria. Moreover, there will be 4 elderly people for every 1 child in Spain and Italy as of 2050 (Gündoğan, 2001: 98).

Any change in the demographic structure is reflected in the structure of employment and the labor market. Particularly in developed countries; aging of the population also refers to an increase in the share of the elderly workforce in the workforce. The increase in life expectancy combined with the decrease in birth rates, in many developed countries, result in the inevitable aging of the population and therefore the workforce. This ongoing change is perceived as a sign pointing out a continuing increase in the elderly population (Özen and Özbek, 2017: 549-550).

Aging population increases the number of elderly employees in the total labor supply and decreases the number of young people therein, which further causes the aging of the workforce. Today, the labor force participation rates of elderly individuals tend to decrease in all regions of the world. This may indicate a decrease in the total labor supply (Gündoğan, 2001: 99). An approach claiming an increase in the elderly population, the increase in expenses as a result of the decrease in the ratio of the elderly population in production, the fact that the elderly population only consumes and further increases social expenditure finally raises the danger of "the elderly consuming the system". This situation has caused pressures on the social security systems of countries and an increase in the age of entitlement to retirement (Özen and Özbek, 2017: 550).

RESEARCH METHODOLOGY

Along with the globalization process, social security systems have faced challenges all over the world. In order to respond to these challenges, social security systems began to evolve from a two-pillar structure to a three-pillar structure in which private pension systems are also included in addition to public pension systems. The problem of the aging of the population, which may also be referred to as the crisis of the social security systems, has brought with it the increase of the retirement age and the decrease in the rates of pensions. Globalization and all the other factors it interacts with affect social security systems in different ways.

According to the ILO (International Labor Organization), the factors affecting the functioning of today's social security system and creating the need for restructuring are discussed as the changes concerning the demographic structure, the change in the labor market, international labor migration, the spread of undeclared working, globalization and economic crises caused by increasing uncertainties. In line with ILO's reformist approach to social security systems; this section aims to investigate the effects of aging of the population on social security systems, to seek an answer to the question of how social security systems will respond to this transition in the demographic structure and to suggest solutions. In addition, the weight, functions and implementation of supplementary pension schemes in pension systems differ according to the welfare regimes of countries, labor relations and the organization of labor markets. However, the common feature of all reforms is primarily to encourage the expansion of supplementary pension schemes. For this reason, the general features and functions of supplementary pension schemes are also evaluated in terms of different welfare regimes (Alper et al., 2015: 9-12).

Rapid improvements in medicine, technology and education have increased life expectancy at birth. Governments have started to allocate higher shares from their general budgets in return for the pensions to be paid to retired individuals and the health expenditures that shall be incurred for these individuals.

The rapid aging of the population is still in progress. United Nations Population Fund (UNFPA) projection estimate that approximately 22% of the world's population shall consist of individuals aged 60 and over by 2050. While the young population is concentrated in developing and underdeveloped countries, the concentration of elderly individuals in developed countries is remarkable.

THEORETICAL FRAMEWORK

Demographic Transition and the Concept of Elderly Workforce

Comprehensive reform proposals concerning social security systems have been suggested as of the second half of the 1990s under the leadership of international organizations such as WB, EU and OECD. The essence of these reform proposals is a three-pillar model based on individual pension programs. Within the scope of these reform model proposals, it is observed that the retirement age has been increased for both male and female employees, the contribution to the pension system has been increased in terms of value and duration, the pension payments have been decreased, the calculation methods of pensions has been changed, thus the share of the elderly in social welfare has been reduced (Ulukan, 2020: 99).

The impact of demographic structure on social security systems is not equally important and decisive for the whole social security system and for all social risks. The two social risks with the greatest impact are aging and health risks. In addition, two insurance branches that social security systems spend at higher rates are also old age insurance and health insurance. With a rough calculation, we can say that 60% of the total social security expenditures are related to old age and 30% are related to health insurance. The effects of demographic structure changes on unemployment and maternity insurances, along with these two insurance branches, are also determinative. However, the social risk in which this effect is most dominant is old age; its effect on social security systems is mostly related to this insurance branch (Alper et al., 2012: 27).

Demographic transition theory, which is also referred to as the aging of the population, is at the forefront of the theories explaining social aging. This theory describes the conversion of high birth and death rates to low birth and death rates. Before the demographic transition, life expectancy is short, fertility rates are higher and the share of young people in the population is higher. Accordingly, demographic transition begins as a result of the decrease in mortality rates and prolongation of life expectancy in the world. As a result of this situation, a rapid population growth is observed, and then population growth slows down again with the decrease in birth rates. At this stage, population replacement rates are clearly declining. The share of the elderly in the population begins to increase in the last phase of the demographic transition (Günaydın, 2018: 2). According to this theory, aging of the population will continue all over the world until 2050 and the transition will be completed. The demographic transition, which is estimated to be completed all over the world towards the end of the 21st century, started in the European continent as of the 19th century. Life expectancy is long and birth rates are lower in many European countries experiencing the last phase of this transition. For this reason, the share of the elderly population is high in many European countries. In recent years, decreasing birth rates have been observed in developing countries. Towards mid-21st century, this rate is estimated to fall below the threshold of

2.1 children per each fertile woman in these countries, which is necessary for the population to renew itself. Demographic transition in Turkey, which started in the 1950s, is estimated to be completed in the middle of the 21st century (Kurtkapan, 2019: 31).

The number of the population aged 65 and over in our country, which is referred to as the elderly, was 6 million 495 thousand 239 people as of 2015, whereas this figure increased by 22.5% over the last five years and reached 7 million 953 thousand 555 people as of 2020. Hence, the share of the elderly in the total population which was 8.2% as of 2015, increased to 9.5% as of 2020. As of 2020, 44.2% of the elderly population is male and 55.8% is female. Population-based projections reveal that the share of elderly population will be 11.0% by 2025, 12.9% by 2030, 16.3% by 2040, 22.6% by 2060 and 25.6% by 2080. When the elderly population is distributed by age group, 61.3% of the elderly population as of 2015 is in the 65-74 age group, 30.7% is in the 75-84 age group and 8.0% is in the 85 and over age group. In 2020, however, it has been observed that 63.8% of the elderly population is in the 65-74 age group, 27.9% is in the 75-84 age group and 8.4% is in the 85 and over age group. The share of the elderly individuals exceeding 10% of the total population is an indicator of the aging of the population. The elderly population in Turkey has increased at a higher rate than the population in other age groups. Demographic structure of the population in Turkey, experiencing the "demographic transition" process which is also referred to as the global aging process, has changed with the decrease in fertility and mortality rates, the developments in the field of health, the increase in the living standards, welfare level and life expectancy at birth. While the share of children and young people in the total population is decreasing, the share of the elderly thereof is increasing. Although Turkey still has a relatively younger population compared to countries with an elderly population structure, the number of elderly population is quite high (TURKSTAT, 2021).

"Age discrimination" is reported as the most important problem faced by elderly individuals in their work life. Age discrimination in employment is defined as acting arbitrarily without considering an individual's current or potential job performance in recruitment, promotion, dismissal, determination of working conditions as well as regarding the training offered at the workplace and similar issues. As a result of this discrimination, particularly the workforce aged 50 and over are exposed to limitations considering re-employment, working conditions and career development. It is emphasized in many international agreements that individuals should not be discriminated against in the labor market due to their age and governments are imposed important duties in this regard. ILO's Social Security (Minimum Standards) Convention dated 1952 (No. 102) contains provisions on aging and the Discrimination (Employment and Occupation) Convention dated 1958 (No. 111) requires member states to review their national policies in a way to prevents discrimination in employment and occupation. Furthermore, ILO's Older Workers Recommendation dated 1980 (No. 162) calls member states upon to ensure that older workers have equal opportunities and are treated without any discrimination due to their age and to prevent employment and occupational age discrimination. EU Council Directive 2000/78/EC establishing a general framework for Equal Treatment in Employment and Occupation also includes regulations to prevent age discrimination (Günaydın, 2018: 6).

Aging of the population in terms of demographics or demographic aging is a demographic process that is in relationship with the social, economic and cultural structures that shape the lives of societies. Demographic aging is referred to as the changes with regard to the age structure of the population as a result of the decrease in fertility and prolongation of life expectancy, subsequent decrease of the share of the young population in the total population and the relative increase in share of the elderly population. Aging and the elderly population, which makes up 9.5 percent of the country's population as of today and is estimated to reach around 20 percent of the total population by the middle of the century, is a transition that shall be felt in every aspect of individual and social life. It is also compulsory to provide information about the aging population as well as the problems and advantages that may arise regarding the elderly population in addition to produce new structures and policies. Priority programs will not only provide more qualified living conditions to the increasing number of elderly population, but also provide a facilitating ground in the context of the individual, society and administration (Republic of Turkey Ministry of Development Eleventh Development Plan, 2018a: 2).

As of July 2012, the population covered by social security in the context of social insurance programs in Turkey has reached 86% of the total population. This situation indicates the necessity of developing policies for the 14% who are out of the scope of the Turkish social security system. We may discuss the relationship between demographics and coverage for each of the social risks as well as for the overall social security system. When evaluated in terms of old-age insurance, the world average of the population who can receive a pension to the population who has passed the retirement age and entitled for retirement is 40.2%, while this rate is 92% in Western Europe, 75.6% in North America and 28.4% in North Africa. The same rate, which has reached out to 87% in Turkey, lags behind Western Europe but indicates a very high value in the context of world standards (Alper et al., 2012: 24).

United Nations Population Fund (UNFPA) and the Turkish Industrialists' and Businessmen's Association (TUSIAD) have launched a research project titled "Demography and Management towards 2050" giving reference to the demographic transition process, which takes place once throughout the history of each country and how Turkey went through this process considering that what this transition process will bring towards 2050 is of great importance in terms of decisions and practices to be taken in the public and private sectors. The project, which is planned to address the effects of demographic changes and transitions in particular on the main social policy areas, consists of a main report titled "Demography and Management Towards 2050" and industry based sub-reports titled "Education, Labor, Health and Social Security (Pension)". The project is expected to enable public and private sector managers to take advantage of the "demographic window of opportunities" that every society encounters once throughout their demographic transition process in their future plans and projects. The main report titled "Demography and Management Towards 2050" and industry based sub-report titled "An Overview of the Education System", within the scope of the project, were completed and presented to the public in October 2010. Reports on other industries, titled "An Overview of the Labor, Health and Social Security Systems" were also published in November 2012 and publicized (Alper, 2019: 344).

Aging of the population is the most serious demographic change in terms of social security systems. It is the gradual increase in the share of the 65+ age group, which is defined as the passive population, in the total population. This is referred to as the situation where the share of the elderly population in the total population increases due to the prolongation of the average life expectancy on the grounds of the decrease in birth and mortality rates as well as the improvement in life standards, particularly in health. The aging of the population is one of the demographic variables that endanger the sustainability of the system in distribution-based social security systems, to the extent that it decreases the number of population working and thus paying premiums and increases the number of pensioners (Alper et al., 2012: 25).

Demographic characteristics of Turkey clearly indicate that Turkey has entered into an aging process and the effects of demographic changes will soon lead to an increase in the elderly population. Turkey has experienced a demographic transition with the role of social and economic changes as well as global effects and has reached a position where the population growth rate slowed down and the fertility and mortality rates are lower. This process has also built the foundations of today's demographic structure.

The change in the demographic structure of Turkey has started to draw attention particularly since the beginning of the 21st century. The significant decrease in the fertility level and the prolongation of the life expectancy at birth form the basis of the increase in the elderly population in Turkey (Republic of Turkey Ministry of Development Eleventh Development Plan, 2018a: 21).

Demographic transition process, which varies from country to country, exhibited four different stages in Turkey between the years 1923-1994. The first stage, covering the years 1923-1955, refers to the period when births and deaths were high. The second stage coincides with the years 1955-1985, where the birth and death rates were jointly decreasing, however the decrease in the death rates was higher than the decrease in the birth rates. This stage represents the period when the population growth rate is highest. The third stage started after 1985, when the birth rates started to decrease rapidly. The main characteristic of the period is that there was a definite and irreversible decline in the population growth rate. Today, Turkey has entered the fourth stage, where the net renewal rate has fallen below 1.0 and the population has become almost stagnant with a little increase. This phase is expected to be completed in 2050. Some authors add a fifth stage, which is currently experienced in European countries such as Germany, France, Lithuania and Hungary, where the birth rate is lower than the death rate, the population is gradually decreasing while the elderly population is increasing rapidly (Alper, 2019: 346).

Social security systems built on premium paying regimes made significant gains based on the social welfare state understanding that developed in the post-World War II period in addition to the social security standards developed by ILO's social security agreements and recommendations. However, the crisis in the 1970s, changes in the economic, social and demographic structure and the industrial revolution necessitated the restructuring of social security systems. Since the beginning of the 1990s a new restructuring period, which may be summarized as the transition to multi-pillar social security systems brought to the agenda with the World Bank Report (1994) and not requiring radical changes has been introduced concerning social security systems. Thus, social security systems are expected to enter into a restructuring process that will simultaneously fulfill the three basic functions of social security (income redistribution, insurance and savings) and adopt a multi-pillar institutional structure and operational scheme. Such a process began after the 1990s. Modern social security systems are expected to realize their own restructuring process, while on the other hand

- To include everyone within the scope of insurance coverage against every risk,
- To reduce the rate of undeclared employment,
- To reduce financing gaps and
- To offer permanent and effective solutions to the problems faced within the scope of reducing the increase in old age and health insurance expenditures.

Only 20% of the world's population is included within a social security protection at ILO standards. 40% of the total population has almost no social security insurance. Informal/undeclared employment rate has increased and, in some countries, nearly 80% of the workforce has become informal. It is not possible to develop a minimum social security and decent work environment where there is informal/ undeclared employment. Aging of the population, which is considered among the demographic characteristics, jeopardizes the sustainability of premium based social security systems in terms of both retirement and health insurance, and the relationship between population and demographic structure starts right at this point (Alper, 2019: 353-354).

For the purpose to reduce the financial deficits of the social security system to a sustainable level, age for retirement was increased from 38 to 58 for women and from 43 to 60 for men in 1999 on the grounds of Law No. 4447, after requiring a gradual transition for those who were defined to the insurance system before 23.5.2002. Furthermore, with the regulation introduced by Law No. 5510, which entered into force in 2008, age for retirement for those who started their business life after 1.10.2008 was gradually increased to 65 years for male employees in the 2036-2044 period and for female employees between 2036-2048. In other words, individuals will have to take part in the labor market for a longer period of time by raising the age for retirement (Turkish Republic Ministry of Development Eleventh Development Plan, 2018b: 43).

Another factor that will affect the labor market, in addition to these regulations introduced in the field of social security, is the aging of the population. The share of the individuals aged 65 and over in the total population, which was 7.7% as of 2013, is expected to increase to 10.2% by 2023 and to 20.8% in 2050. Estimates indicate that the age distribution of the population will change over the next 20 years, in parallel with the decrease in population growth rate, and the share of age groups over 40 in the total population in the working age will increase accordingly. These projections indicate that the share of the population between the ages of 40-65 in the total workforce will increase in the coming years, depending on demographic factors and the increase in the age for retirement. Another fundamental problem arises at this point. The participation of the labor force aged 40 and over in the labor market and employment rates remained low in Turkey, as women and men were given the opportunity to retire at a very early age, such as 38 and 43 respectively except for a very short period of time. With the social security reform, the age for retirement was increased, taking into account the average life expectancy and the life remaining after retirement. However, the ages to which the entitlement for retirement is increased are the ages when the participation of the labor force in the labor market and employment are quite low (Republic of Turkey Ministry of Development Eleventh Development Plan, 2018b: 44).

Where qualifications rapidly lose their value due to technological developments; the workforce aged 55 and over in Turkey cannot compete with the large number of young and adult workforces in the labor market. As a result, people in this age group either remain unemployed or are willing to work in low-paid informal/undeclared jobs. Considering the rate of undeclared/informal employment in our country; it is observed that undeclared employment as of 2014 is the highest particularly among those aged 65 and over, with a rate of 83.53%. This is followed by the 60-64 age group with 72.99% and the young population in the 15-19 age group with 66.58%. There are usually two ways to discharge older individuals from the labor market. The first is the early retirement of employees who have reached their 50s, even if they are more productive than their younger colleagues. The other is to refer to the impairment benefit, which is the implicit way of eliminating the elderly workforce from the labor market. Due to the early retirement opportunity provided in our country in the past, individuals retired at a young age; however, due to insufficient pensions, these people had to return to business life (Demirbilek and Öktem Özgür, 2017: 22-23).

The reform steps taken towards the pension system over time have made the conditions for retirement from the public pension program significantly more difficult in many countries including our country; this also reduced the gains to be earned in case of retirement. Considering the increase in the number of non-standard jobs and irregular jobs due to digitalization in the labor market, it has become nearly impossible to meet the conditions to qualify for retirement after the reforms that took effect. The decrease in the retirement salary to be obtained as a result of these regulations will also adversely affect the attractiveness of the social security system by disrupting the relationship between the contributions paid for the system and the income obtained in return for the said contribution. Considering the prevalence of undeclared employment, it is possible that this effect will reduce the trust towards the system and will have a nurturing effect on undeclared employment (Demirbilek and Öktem Özgür, 2017: 23).

The pension system in Turkey was transformed into three stages between 1999 and 2008 in line with the WB's recommendations. At the first stage of this transition, which was announced as a reform, the conditions for accessing the Social Security Institution (SSI) pension based on distribution were made difficult and the pension to be earned in return was decreased. In the second stage, the Private Pension System (BES) was introduced as an alternative to compensate for the decreased income. Thirdly, with the social security reform that was initiated in 2006 and was completed in 2008, the Social Insurance Institution, State Retirement Fund (Emekli Sandığı) and Social Security Organization for Artisans and the Self-employed (Bağ-Kur) were gathered under one roof as SGK, the conditions for being entitled to retirement were made difficult and the income to be earned from the pension system was decreased through the changes introduced with respect to the calculation methods (Ulukan, 2020: 99).

Regulations such as increasing the age to qualify for retirement, reducing pension payments, making the conditions for being qualified for retirement more difficult along with the increase in the elderly population as well as the individualization and privatization of the pension systems push the elderly population to remain in labor market. The elderly population is one of the most important risk groups mostly affected by poverty. Main causes of elderly poverty are considered as inequalities in the labor market, inequalities in income transfer and insufficient social security coverage. In particular, low pension payments and the prevalence of undeclared employment increase the extent of elderly poverty. Based on the changes introduced by the laws numbered 4447 and 5510, also known as the social security reform in Turkey, the lower limit of the old-age pension and the income replacement rates have been reduced and the relationship between premiums paid and pensions earned has been strengthened (Ulukan, 2020: 100-103).

The Impact of Demographic Transition on Welfare States

The foundations of the welfare state in the modern sense go back to the legal arrangements introduced in England in the middle of the 19th century to provide basic education. Another accepted starting point regarding modern welfare state is the social insurance system introduced by Bismark in 1883. When we look at the countries that are the starting points of welfare state practices, it is observed that these practices were introduced in Germany in the 19th century, later spread to Western European countries, North America and Australia (Özdemir, 2007: 17).

Major contribution concerning the classification of welfare states was suggested by Esping-Andersen.

Esping-Andersen proposes three different welfare regime models within the scope of welfare regime classification. These models are liberal model, corporatist model and the social democratic model. Later classification studies consist of criticisms and contributions to Esping-Andersen's classification (Kol, 2014: 133-134).

Another effect of demographic change on social security systems is the changing family structure and differentiating needs. Although there are differences between countries; the changes with respect to the traditional protective family structure, the increase in the number of women employees participating in the labor force and the increase in the age of having children, the increase in the number of single-parent households neutralize the understanding of protection provided through the family; individuals' expectations from welfare states differ both in the employment period and in the retirement periods (Alper et al., 2015: 3).

Social democratic welfare regimes are also referred to as universal welfare regimes, Scandinavian model or modern welfare regimes. The reason why this regime model is also referred to as the Swedish Model is that the leading country of the model is Sweden. Other countries in this regime group are Norway, Denmark, the Netherlands and Finland (Özdemir, 2007: 140). Social democratic welfare regimes, also known as the labor-oriented society model, are the models in which social rights are most institutionalized and popularized and social needs are most frequently met from outside the market (Kol, 2014: 138).

The coverage of the public pension schemes in countries with social democratic welfare regimes are generally universal; they are residence-based, offer flat-rate benefits and financed by general tax revenues. Public pension schemes in these countries assume the function of providing all citizens with a minimum endowment assurance in elder ages. The role of maintaining living standards by compensating the income obtained during the employment is mainly fulfilled by occupational pension programs (Alper et al., 2015: 33).

Benefits provided by the state to its citizens in the liberal welfare model are minimal and is subject to an income research. State, in the liberal model, is the last resort and only intervenes for the poorest people who are in the worst situation. Minimum level social benefits are granted in accordance with the results of income surveys and in this respect, bear the characteristics of stigmatizing the citizen (Kol, 2014: 137).

The scope of public pension schemes in countries that have adopted liberal welfare regimes is quite limited and requires income surveys. A limited retirement benefit is provided exclusive to the most needy in order to reduce poverty and almost all of the working population in these countries is expected to earn endowment assurance during retirement from secondary and tertiary supplementary pension schemes (Alper et al., 2015: 36).

The conservative regime model is encountered in countries such as Germany, France, Austria, Italy and Belgium, which have historically had a corporatist structure (Özdemir, 2007: 137).

In Conservative/Corporatist welfare regimes, income from public pension schemes is determined by the contributions paid during the employment period. The fact that these programs offer more generous retirement income, often in relation to earnings over the period worked, results in a narrower coverage of occupational pension schemes compared with the other two occupational pension schemes. Parametric reforms, which lead to a reduction in the pensions earned from public pension schemes in these countries, increase the significance of the occupational pension schemes in terms of maintaining the standard of living earned during the employment throughout the retirement period. In Germany, which is the representative executor of this regime, the automatic registration system and high-rate state subsidy were introduced as a result of the Riester reform carried out in 2001 and the scope of occupational pension schemes was tried to be expanded. Conservative/corporatist occupational pension scheme bears mixed characteristics of the other two regimes and lies between these two regimes in terms of its general characteristics (Alper et al., 2015: 39).

The Concept of Elderly Workforce

Old age is a concept that corresponds to a certain period of human life. For this reason, a person who has survived until this period, which is accepted as the old age period, will attain the title of being elder. Aging causes some physical and spiritual losses in people over a certain period (aging period). Individuals can no longer maintain their former strength and abilities in terms of body and spirit and they suffer a constant loss. The concept of old age is typically divided into two as chronological old age and biological old age. Chronological old age refers to the state of having lived for certain years as of birth. An old age determined on the basis of the number of calendar years lived is mentioned here. In any case, the period beginning with the completion of 65 years is referred to as old age as per International Labor Organization norms. Apart from these definitions, people may get old physically and spiritually before they reach old age as of the known calendar age. For this reason, biological old age is a state that is expressed according to the physical and spiritual depreciation of the person (Arıcı, 2015: 362-363). Social security systems have set a certain chronological age at which payment of old-age benefits will begin for practical reasons; this is called as the age of retirement. Age of retirement varies from country to country depending on the social and demographic structure of countries, employment policies and many other factors. This age is generally determined as 65 and even higher in developed Western countries, which have faced the problem of aging of the population. In Turkish case, on the other hand, the prerequisites of reaching the age of retirement were not sought after 1969 in order to be entitled for a pension from the old-age insurance; the period of employment for a certain period of time in the insured status and paying social security premium was deemed sufficient. Insured persons were entitled to an old-age pension at an age where they could not be considered as chronologically and biologically old. Although Law No. 4447 mainly aimed to put an end to this wrong policy, it aggravated the conditions required to be qualified for retirement more than necessary. Moreover, the conditions have become a bit more difficult with Law No. 5510 (Şakar, 2017: 241-242).

Structure of the Turkish Social Security System

Premium based regimes (social insurance schemes) constitute the basic pillar of the social security system in Turkey. Therefore, the concept of social security system and its problems refers to social insurance and its problems. The payments regarding nearly 90% of those covered by social security and more than 90% of the expenditures in this context are realized through social insurance. With the right policies and the right beginnings, Turkey built a social security system based on social insurance, but failed to ensure the sustainability of this system. Many practices contrary to social insurance principles such as early retirement, amnesty of premium debts, borrowing practices has aged the developed social insurance system in terms of active/passive insured balance only 50 years after the second half of the 1940s, that is in the 1990s, and brought it to a financially unsustainable point. This has led to the search for comprehensive changes and further restructuring (reform) need as of the 1990s (Alper, 2019: 354).

Most significant outcome of the social security reform affecting people's daily lives has been to facilitate access to health services owing to the transition in health services. Pursuant to the figures as of the end of 2019, 573 million people applied to health service providers. Except for 1.2 million citizens (1.5%), 98.5% of the population is covered by general health insurance. This expansion with respect to the scope of the General Health Insurance was achieved after the premium payments of 9.08 million people was assumed by the Government. When evaluated in terms of creating an effective and easily accessible system, which is one of the primary objectives of the reform, SGK has further developed and expanded the scope of e-insurance applications that started with SSI as of the 2000s. The institution had the capacity to carry out all transactions related to the insured, employers, pension-benefit recipients and third parties through the e-insurance application (Alper, 2021: 26-27).

The institutional structure was restructured with the Social Security Institution Law No. 5502, which came into force in 2006; and the social insurance legislation was restructured on the grounds of the Social Insurance and General Health Insurance Law No. 5510, which entered into force in 2008. Financing deficits of the Turkish social insurance system prevail despite the measures put into effect in 1999 and reinforced in 2008 by Law No. 5510. It is expected that 66.2 billion TL will be transferred from the budget in 2012 for financing the social insurance institution, 25.5 billion of which will be used for financing the deficit. Despite the implementations such as insurance premium amnesties and debt restructuring in addition to the measures introduced by the reform, the ratio of total revenues to expenses remained around 70%. The opportunities and threats facing the Turkish social security system today are as follows:

- Considering Turkish social insurance system, it is nearly impossible to increase the revenues by raising premium rates and/or raising the limits of earnings subject to premium payment.
- The possibility of increasing the number of insured active employees by reducing the rate of undeclared employment, which is currently calculated at the level of 40%, is considered as an opportunity.
- Although it has been 10 years since the age of retirement was raised and the nearly half of the gradual transition period has been completed, no improvement has been achieved yet in the ratio of insured active/passive employees.
- New pension calculation method introduced by Law No. 5510 will again reduce the level of benefit and pensions in the long run. Therefore, it is no longer possible to update the pension and benefit calculation system to reduce expenses.
- The most significant opportunity is that Turkey has not yet completed the demographic transition process and still has a demographic window of opportunity. The percentage share of the 15-64 age group in the total population will continue to increase until 2020, and until 2041 in absolute terms and will continue to offer Turkey the positive effects of the demographic window of opportunity (Alper, 2019: 354-355).

Despite the decrease in the number of insured passive employees based on the gradual increase in the age of retirement, the increase in the number of registered employees based on the decrease in undeclared employment rate and the young population using the opportunities offered by demographic window of opportunity, the ratio of insured active/passive employees have deteriorated. An interesting development was experienced during the period in terms of eliminating the financing gaps of social insurance institutions, which is one of the reasons for the reform steps. While the corporate finance deficit of the SSI decreased in the narrow sense, the financing contribution of the government to the system through direct or indirect transfers have increased. The expected improvement regarding the coverage ratio of insurance premium revenues to expenses could not be achieved, and the 70% rate could not be overcome like a wall. Although the amnesty of premium debts and restructuring of premium debts with its new name gained momentum, the expected improvement in premium collection rates could not be achieved. The instability regarding the social insurance legislation still prevails although numerous amendments have been introduced in the Law No. 5510 on the grounds of 65 different laws, decrees and decisions of the Constitutional Court over the past 11 years. Palliative (temporary) solutions such as the payment of Bayram bonuses, contrary to the principles of social insurance, have been voiced against the decrease in benefits and pensions (Alper, 2021: 27-30).

The rate of pensions was reduced by Law No. 5510 after the social security reform, taking into account the actuarial balances, in order to ensure the financial sustainability of the system. This situation has raised the significance of issues such as reporting insurance premiums over real wages, encouraging staying for longer periods in work life and increasing individual savings so that individuals can maintain their standard of living even during retirement. The development of the private pension system is important in terms of reducing the pressure on the social insurance institution, especially in terms of the general level of pensions. Entry to the Private Pension System, which entered into force with Law No. 4632 in 2001, is optional and it is required to pay premiums to the system for at least 10 years and to be at 56 years old in order to qualify for earning a monthly pension from the system (Republic of Turkey Ministry of Development Eleventh Development Plan, 2018b: 18)

In addition, on the grounds of the Private Pension Savings and Investment System Law published in the Official Gazette dated 29 June 2012 and issued 28338, the tax advantage in the system was abolished and as of January 1, 2013, the principle of state contribution was adopted requiring the payment of 25% of each paid contribution to participant's account as a contribution provided by the government. Thus, with this amendment; the incentive system, which was previously available only to those subject to income tax, has been transformed into a structure that can be benefited by all segments over the age of 18, regardless of whether they are working or not. Amendments have been introduced requiring the collection of a withholding tax only over the amount of the revenue, instead of the total savings amount, which is defined as securities income and is subject to withholding tax in case of leaving the system. In addition, the upper limit of the contributions to be paid by employers to the private pension system on behalf of their employees and which can be subject to deduction in determining the tax base has been increased from 10% to 15% of the gross wage. With the Law No. 6740, the practice of Auto Enrollment System was introduced in 2017 allowing public and private sector employees under the age of 45 to be included into the Private Pension System with "automatic" participation. Throughout this transition period, private sector employees will be gradually included in the system, depending on the size of the workplace they are affiliated with (Republic of Turkey Ministry of Development Eleventh Development Plan, 2018b: 18).

The Impact of Social Security Reforms on the Elderly Workforce

Since the second half of the 2010s, the pace of pension reforms has slowed down in developed countries and narrower regulations have been introduced. The main reason for the social security crisis that has emerged in many developed countries until this stage has been the rapid aging trend that has shaped the demographic structures of the countries and the increasing trend of elderly dependency rates. Rapid aging and the increase in elderly dependency rates causing the insufficiency of premium revenues obtained from the actively working population in meeting the old age insurance expenditures as well as the prolongation of the old age period, the diversity of social demands and needs due to the increase in welfare cause a significant portion of public resources to be used to finance old age.

There are limited applications such as to gradually increase the age of retirement in parallel with the prolongation of the average human lifespan, increasing premium rates and reducing old-age payments; however new solutions are on the agenda. While efforts are sought to prevent elderly workforce from leaving the labor market due to retirement, on the other hand, "flexible retirement plans" are offered as an alternative to meet the labor shortage. Under this plan, individuals are given the flexibility to decide how and when they shall be qualified for retirement before or after the legal age, provided that they continue to work or work for fewer hours.

Bellaby (2006), in a study conducted with a sample of 5344 people in England, concluded that pension reforms strengthened gender differences and increased the rates of unemployment. It also strengthened inequalities with respect to health, increasing the rates from 13.5% to 32.6%.

Bertoni, Brunello, and Mazzarella (2018) investigated the effects of increasing the age of retirement from 57 to 60 on a sample of 9093 people aged between 42-51 who were and were not affected by the increase in retirement age. Accordingly, a one-year increase in retirement age is said to increase the rate of regular exercise by 3.2%, obesity rate by 1.6% and the individual's satisfaction with his/her health by 2.7%.

Bottazzi, Jappelli, and Padula (2006) investigated the effects of the proposal for increasing the age of retirement for male employees from 60 to 65 and female employees from 55 to 60 in private sector and for increasing the age of retirement thereof to 65 to 60 respectively in the public sector in a study conducted with 15.649 people between the ages of 20-50 who are currently either employed or self-employed. Although there are differences in terms of gender, the study revealed that pension reform is expected to increase the age of retirement by 0.686 years in the private sector, 1.110 years in the public sector and 2.285 years in the self-employed.

In a study conducted on women in the USA, Choi (2001) revealed that life satisfaction increases by 1% in workers beyond retirement.

For the purpose of a study on the increase in the retirement age in the Netherlands; De Grip, Fouarge, and Montizaan (2013) worked with a total of 3500 people consisting of public sector employees born between 1955-1959 and 1960-1964 and who were affected by the increasing retirement age and individuals born between 1950-1954 however who were not affected by the increase in the retirement age. As a result of the study, it was concluded that the pension reform is expected to increase the retirement age by 3.6 months for employees born between 1954-1959 and to increase the retirement age by 10.8 months for those born after 1959. De Grip, Lindeboom, & Montizaan (2012) also concluded that pension reforms increase depression.

Demou, Bhaskar, Xu, Mackay and Hunt (2017) concluded in their study conducted with employees working even after retirement that participation in labor force increased by 33% for women and 15.5% for men. A study conducted by Engels, Geyer & Haan (2017) on women born between 1938 and 1944, it was revealed that pension reforms increased the retirement age and employment from 4.10 months to 17.37 months.

For the purpose of a study conducted on the increase in the retirement age of women from 60 to 63; Geyer and Welteke (2019) worked with a total of 3477 people born between 1952-1962 and concluded that pension reforms increased the employment rate by 13.5%.

A study conducted by Hagen (2018) on the increase in the retirement age of public sector employees from 63 to 65 revealed that pension reforms increased the retirement age by 4.5 months however had no effect in terms of benefiting from health services.

Mein, Martikainen, Hemingway, Stansfeld and Marmot (2003) conducted a study on individuals aged 60, who are still working and are forced to retire and concluded that the effects of continuing to work after retirement on mental and physical health are unknown.

A study conducted by Montizaan and Vendrik (2014) with individuals born in 1950 and who are affected by the rising retirement age and individuals born in 1949 however who are not affected by the rising retirement age revealed that pension reforms reduced job satisfaction by 0.638 points.

Staubli and Zweimüller (2013) conducted a study on private sector employees aged between 57-64 with less than 45 years of social insurance and women aged between 52-59 working in the private sector with less than 40 years of social insurance concluded that pension reforms increased employment rates by 11% for women and 9.75% for men.

Wahrendorf, Akinwale, Landy, Matthews and Blane (2017) interviewed male and female employees aged between 65-80 and who continue to work after the age of 65 and retired men and women aged between 65-80 in a study covering 15 European Union member countries and Switzerland. They concluded that post-retirement work reduces psycho-social work stress. Lower control and reward-effort imbalance decrease accordingly. Physical health also declines in post-retirement work. Participants in the study evaluated themselves as poor in terms of health, they evaluated their mobility as restricted and their comprehension ability as reduced. Considering the effects of post-retirement work on mental health, the research revealed that the quality of life worsened and the cognitive level decreased despite the decrease in depression symptoms.

Effects of the COVID-19 Pandemic on the Social Security Rights of the Elderly Workforce

Prolongation of life expectancy increases the risk of being in need of care in the last stage of life. Care assurance and care services are also the main functions expected from the social system. Individuals can live for twenty or even thirty years after retirement. This situation brings a huge financial burden on the social security system. This increase in health expenditures is not only related to the elderly. Social security makes it necessary to act within a multidimensional system. In order for the system to perform its functions, it should be placed on various pillars. The main risk faced by individuals who are exposed to loss of income due to illness, impairment and unemployment is the possibility of being excluded from the labor market as they get older (Tufan, 2014: 100).

In Turkey, Law No. 5510 adopted the gradual increase in retirement age introduced in 1999 with Law No. 4447 in the same way and with a gradual increase starting from 2036 finalized the retirement age as 65 for men and women by 2048. As expected, individuals who completed their service period and premium payment days in a short time however required to wait to get older in order to be qualified for retirement started to give voice to their demands for "early retirement". However, the government showed a serious resistance against the demands of those waiting for retirement on the grounds that they were not old enough and did not step back from the policy of gradually raising the retirement age. Thus, the expectation in the society towards lowering the retirement age seems to have been broken (Alper, 2019: 372-373).

ILO, in its report where it discussed the improvements foreseen on national social security systems in the COVID-19 Pandemic crisis, made several recommendations concerning social security policies. Accordingly;

- All citizens should have access to health services for pandemic treatment and testing.
- Temporary wage subsidies should be provided to workers affected by the pandemic.
- Subsidizing or deferring social security contributions should be allowed as a precautionary measure to keep business running and retain employees.

- Employees whose workplaces are locked down or who are unable to work due to mandatory quarantine should be provided with sickness benefits. However, this measure has not been widely adopted.
- Unemployment benefits should be increased and assistance should be provided to workers who were not covered before.
- The amount of social assistance supports should be increased with one-time additional payments and eligibility conditions should be relaxed.
- Minimum pensions should be improved.

RESULTS AND RECOMMENDATIONS

Negative effects that occur with the aging of societies have a great impact on social insurance, which is the most common pillar of social security systems. This effect emerges in the form of a change in the balance between the active and passive insured and the increase in expenditures for the elderly. It is accepted that there is an agreement between generations in society as such: The working generation provides care for children and youth; when they get older, they are entitled to be cared for by the generation whom they had previously taken care of (Tufan, 2016: 125).

The demographic change experienced causes an increase in social assistance, social service and retirement allowances. The social security reforms implemented in various countries resulted in an increase in the age required for being qualified for retirement for achieving a sustainable pension system. The main reason for the social security crisis has been the rapid aging trend that has shaped the demographic structures of the countries and the increasing trend of elderly dependency rates. Prolongation of the old age period causing the insufficiency of premium revenues obtained from the actively working population in meeting the old age insurance expenditures as well the diversity of social demands and needs due to the increase in welfare cause a significant portion of public resources to be used to finance old age.

There are limited applications such as to gradually increase the age of retirement in parallel with the prolongation of the average human lifespan, increasing premium rates and reducing old-age payments; however new solutions are on the agenda. While efforts are sought to prevent elderly workforce from leaving the labor market due to retirement, on the other hand, “flexible retirement plans” are offered as an alternative to meet the labor shortage. Under this plan, individuals are given the flexibility to decide how and when they shall be qualified for retirement before or after the legal age, provided that they continue to work or work for fewer hours. Demou, Bhaskar, Xu, Mackay and Hunt (2017) concluded in their study conducted with employees working even after retirement that participation in labor force increased by 33% for women and 15.5% for men. Engels, Geyer, and Haan (2017) concluded that pension reforms increased the retirement age and employment rates. Increasing the retirement age also improves the participation rate of the elderly in the labor force, but on the other hand decreases economic productivity. In this sense, raising the retirement age alone is not a sufficient solution to solve the problems of the social security system (Arıcı and Alper, 2018: 221).

Raising the retirement age affects the labor force participation rates of elderly workforce as well as their well-being and health. Bottazzi, Jappelli, and Padula (2006) determined that pension reform increased the retirement age while De Grip, Lindeboom, and Montizaan (2012) concluded that increasing retirement age increases depression. On the other hand, in a study conducted on women in the USA, Choi (2001) revealed that life satisfaction increases by 1% in workers who work beyond retirement. There are also studies indicating that the increased retirement age has no effect on benefiting from health services (Hagen, 2018). Mein, Martikainen, Hemingway, Stansfeld and Marmot (2003) conducted a study on individuals aged 60, who are still working and are forced to retire and concluded that the effects of continuing to work after retirement on mental and physical health are unknown. Wahrendorf, Akinwale, Landy, Matthews and Blane (2017) interviewed male and female employees aged between 65-80 and who continue to work after the age of 65 and retired men and women aged between 65-80 in a study covering 15 European Union member countries and Switzerland. Accordingly post-retirement work reduces psycho-social work stress. Lower control and reward-effort imbalance decrease accordingly. Physical health also declines in post-retirement work. Participants in the study evaluated themselves as poor in terms of health, they evaluated their mobility as restricted and their comprehension ability as reduced. The research, considering the effects of post-retirement work on mental health, revealed a decrease in depression symptoms.

The COVID-19 Pandemic, which we can consider as environmental factors that have emerged in recent years, has influenced the whole world. Coronaviruses, the cause of many diseases especially the common cold, have emerged in the last twenty years. The Severe Acute Respiratory Syndrome (SARS) epidemic (2002-2003), the H1N influenza epidemic (2009) and the Middle East Respiratory Syndrome (MERS) epidemic (2012) are also caused by coronaviruses. The new coronavirus and the disease it causes emerged in December 2019 in Wuhan, China and was named COVID-19 by the World Health Organization (WHO) to mean Corona Virus Disease of 2019 (Cascella et al., 2020: 2-3).

Elder workers, who are already faced with the possibility of being excluded from the labor markets as they get older, have been in a difficult situation with the closure of their workplaces and a ban on leaving the house and the serious contraction in the services sector as a result of the COVID-19 Pandemic (Aydın, 2020: 185). It has been revealed that the infection is transmitted from person to person, particularly adults are susceptible to COVID-19 and the severity of the disease correlates with age. This situation not only puts the elder citizens who have to work after retirement in a difficult situation but also increases the costs of social assistance and social services. The International Labor Organization (ILO) has made several recommendations for social security policies. Accordingly, increasing minimum pensions and social benefits may provide improvements on national social security systems in the COVID-19 Pandemic crisis.

RECOMMENDATIONS FOR FURTHER RESEARCH

This study provides some suggestions that may guide future studies on the impact of the COVID-19 Pandemic on the social security rights of the elderly workforce.

- The effects of the legal regulations introduced during the COVID-19 Pandemic on the social security rights of the elderly workforce should be evaluated by taking into account the practices of different countries.
- The similarities and differences of social security reforms introduced in developed countries where the share of the elderly population is higher should be examined.
- Social security policies should be developed to address the differences with respect to active/passive insured ratios in different countries following the demographic transition process.

- The answer to the question "Should post-COVID-19 Pandemic financing gap of the social security system be assumed by the states or the private sector?" should be given taking into account the different development and welfare levels of countries.
- Active employment policies should be developed in order to ensure the elderly workforce to stay employed for longer terms and demand pensions at a later age.
- The relationship between active aging and healthy aging policies and social security reforms may be further discussed.
- What problems may social security systems face after the COVID-19 Pandemic and which solutions may be suggested for these problems?
- What allowances may be provided for the elderly workforce from the Unemployment Insurance Fund and how can these allowances be financed?
- What incentives may be implemented to encourage employers to employ and retain the elderly workforce?
- To what extent short-time working, flexible working, remote working and job-sharing policies are implemented in order to keep the elderly workforce in employment and how can the applicability of these policies be broader?
- Complementary social security schemes based on individual pension system should be encouraged.
- The coverage of social security programs should be improved in line with the principle of inclusiveness for all.
- The transition from the informal/undeclared economy to formal economy will improve the management and financing of social security programs.

CONCLUSION

Aging of the population in terms of demographics or demographic aging is a transition process that is in relationship with the social, economic and cultural structures that shape the lives of societies. Demographic aging is referred to as the changes with regard to the age structure of the population as a result of the decrease in fertility and prolongation of life expectancy, subsequent decrease of the share of the young population in the total population and the relative increase in share of the elderly population. Aging of the population is the most serious demographic change in terms of social security systems. It is the gradual increase in the share of the 65+ age group, which is defined as the passive population, in the total population. Demographic characteristics of Turkey clearly indicate that Turkey has entered into an aging process and the effects of demographic changes will soon lead to an increase in the elderly population. Regulations such as increasing the age to qualify for retirement, reducing pension payments, making the conditions for being qualified for retirement more difficult along with the increase in the elderly population as well as the individualization and privatization of the pension systems push the elderly population to remain in labor market. Social insurance schemes constitute the basic pillar of the social security system in Turkey. There are limited applications such as to gradually increase the age of retirement in parallel with the prolongation of the average human lifespan, increasing premium rates and reducing old-age payments; however new solutions are on the agenda. While efforts are sought to prevent elderly workforce from leaving the labor market due to retirement, on the other hand, "flexible retirement plans" are offered as an alternative to meet the labor shortage. Under this plan, individuals are given the flexibility to decide how and when they shall be qualified for retirement before or after the legal age, provided that they continue to work or work for fewer hours. The demographic change experienced causes an increase in social assistance, social service and retirement allowances. The social security reforms implemented in various countries resulted in an increase in the age required for being qualified for retirement for achieving a sustainable pension system. Raising the retirement age affects the labor force participation rates of elderly workforce as well as their well-being and health. The main reason for the social security crisis has been the rapid aging trend that has shaped the demographic structures of the countries and the increasing trend of elderly dependency rates. Prolongation of the old age period causing the insufficiency of premium revenues obtained from the actively working population in meeting the old age insurance expenditures as well the diversity of social demands and needs due to the increase in welfare cause a significant portion of public resources to be used to finance old age. Elder workers, who are already faced with the possibility of being excluded from the labor markets as they get older, have been in a difficult situation with the closure of their workplaces and a ban on leaving the house and the serious contraction in the services sector as a result of the COVID-19 Pandemic. It has been revealed that the infection is transmitted from person to person, particularly adults are susceptible to COVID-19 and the severity of the disease correlates with age. This situation not only puts the elder citizens who have to work after retirement in a difficult situation but also increases the costs of social assistance and social services. The International Labor Organization (ILO) has made several recommendations for social security policies. Accordingly, increasing minimum pensions and social benefits may provide improvements on national social security systems in the COVID-19 Pandemic crisis.

REFERENCES

Alper, Y. (2019). *My Writings on Social Security.* Turkish Metal Union Research and Training Center.

Alper, Y. (2021). *Social Security Reform, Administrative Autonomy and the Changing Roles of the Social Partners. In Labor Economics and Industrial Relations Congress "Social Policies and Current Discussions"*. Turk-Is Publications.

Alper, Y., Arici, K., Turcan Ozsuca, S., Aydın, U., & Gokbayrak, S. (2015). *A Success Story in Complementary Retirement: OYAK.* Turkiye Is Bankasi Cultural Publications.

Alper, Y., Deger, C., & Sayan, S. (2012). Demographics and Management Towards 2050: An Overview of the Social Security (Pension) System. Istanbul: TÜSİAD-T/2012-11/535.

Arici, K. (2015). *Turkish Social Security Law*. Gazi Bookstore Publications.

Arici, K., & Alper, Y. (2018). Social Security. Eskisehir: Anadolu University Press.

Aydın, U. (2020). Covid-19 Pandemic; Problems and solutions in the field of labor and social security law. *Journal of Istanbul Aydın University Faculty of Law*, *6*(2), 181–214.

Bellaby, P. (2006). Can they carry on working? Later retirement, health, and social inequality in an aging population. *International Journal of Health Services*, *36*(1), 1–23. doi:10.2190/EE2N-4A1Q-ARVD-XN05 PMID:16524163

Bertoni, M., Brunello, G., & Mazzarella, G. (2018). Does postponing minimum retirement age improve healthy behaviors before retirement? Evidence from middle-aged Italian workers. *Journal of Health Economics*, *58*, 215–227. doi:10.1016/j.jhealeco.2018.02.011 PMID:29550666

Bottazzi, R., Jappelli, T., & Padula, M. (2006). Retirement expectations, pension reforms, and their impact on private wealth accumulation. *Journal of Public Economics*, *90*(12), 2187–2212. doi:10.1016/j.jpubeco.2006.03.005

Cascella, M., Rajnik, M., Cuomo, A., Dulebohn, S. C., & Di Napoli, R. (2020). *Features, evaluation and treatment coronavirus (COVID-19).* StatPearls Publishing. https://www.ncbi.nlm.nih.gov/pubmed/32150360

Ceylan, H. (2015). *Aging and the Welfare State*. Istanbul: Acilim Book.

Choi, N. (2001). Relationship between life satisfaction and postretirement employment among older women. *International Journal of Aging & Human Development*, *52*(1), 45–70. doi:10.2190/2W25-DH9H-2F4D-7HWX PMID:11310574

De Grip, A., Fouarge, D., & Montizaan, R. (2013). How sensitive are individual retirement expectations to raising the retirement age? *De Economist*, *161*(3), 225–251. doi:10.100710645-013-9205-5

Demirbilek, T., & Oktem Ozgur, A. (2017). Elderly employment in the context of the silver economy and active aging. *Journal of Research on Elderly Issues*, *10*(1), 14–28.

Demou, E., Bhaskar, A., Xu, T., Mackay, D. F., & Hunt, K. (2017). Health, lifestyle and employment beyond state-pension age. *BMC Public Health*, *17*(1), 971. doi:10.118612889-017-4957-5 PMID:29262819

Geyer, J., & Welteke, C. (2019). Closing routes to retirement for women: How do they respond? *The Journal of Human Resources*, 1–46.

Gunaydin, D. (2018). The aging problem of the workforce within the framework of Turkey's demographic transformation. *Journal of Research on Elderly Issues*, *11*(1), 1–13.

Gundogan, N. (2001). Aging of the workforce and its effects on labor markets. *Journal of Ankara University Faculty of Political Sciences*, *56*(04), 95–108.

Hagen, J. (2018). The effects of increasing the normal retirement age on health care utilization and mortality. *Journal of Population Economics*, *31*(1), 193–234. doi:10.100700148-017-0664-x

Kol, E. (2014). Evaluation of health systems in terms of welfare regimes: Southern European welfare model and Turkey. *Gumushane University Electronic Journal of Social Sciences*, *5*(10), 131–168.

Kol, E., & Topgul, S. (2022). The Process Of Demographic Change in Turkey Effects On The Social Security System. In A Gift to Prof. Dr. İhsan Erkul Social Policy and Industrial Relations Articles. Eskisehir: Nisan Publication.

Kurtkapan, H. (2019). Social reflections of demographic transformation and old age in Turkey. *Social Security Journal*, *15*, 27–46.

Mein, G., Martikainen, P., Hemingway, H., Stansfeld, S., & Marmot, M. (2003). Is retirement good or bad for mental and physical health functioning? Whitehall II longitudinal study of civil servants. *Journal of Epidemiology and Community Health, 57*(1), 46–49. doi:10.1136/jech.57.1.46 PMID:12490648

Montizaan, R. M., & Vendrik, M. C. M. (2014). Misery loves company: Exogenous shocks in retirement expectations and social comparison effects on subjective well-being. *Journal of Economic Behavior & Organization, 97*, 1–26. doi:10.1016/j.jebo.2013.10.009

Ozdemir, S. (2007). *Welfare State in the Process of Globalization*. Istanbul Chamber of Commerce Publications.

Ozen, S., & Ozbek, C. (2017). Elderly workers and Human Resources Practices. *Journal of Labor and Society, 2*, 547–572.

Republic of Turkey Ministry of Development Eleventh Development Plan. (2018a). *Aging Special Commission Report*. Author.

Republic of Turkey Ministry of Development Eleventh Development Plan. (2018b). *Sustainability of the Social Security System Specialization Commission Report*. Author.

Sakar, M. (2017). *Social Insurance Application* (12th ed.). Beta Publications.

Staubli, S., & Zweimüller, J. (2013). Does raising the early retirement age increase employment of older workers? *Journal of Public Economics, 108*, 17–32. doi:10.1016/j.jpubeco.2013.09.003 PMID:24319299

Topgul, S. (2016). Ageism or Discrimination against Older Adults in Work Life. *Turkish Journal of Sociology, 36*, 385–391.

Topgul, S. (2020). Changing Foods for Elderly Individuals According to the Changing Demographic Order. *International Social Mentality and Researcher Thinkers Journal, 6*(32), 991–1005.

Topgul, S. (2021). Elderly Care and Socıal Work From Internatıonal Aspects. *The Journal of International Social Research, 14*(76), 688–696.

Tufan, I. (2014). *Structural Change of Aging in Turkey*. Koc University Publications.

Tufan, I. (2016). *Aging and Aging from Antiquity to the Present*. Nobel Publications.

Turkish Statistical Institute. (2020a). Elderly with Statistics, 2019. *Turkish Statistical Institute News Bulletin, 33712*. https://data.tuik.gov.tr/Bulten/Index?p=IstatistiklerleYaslilar201933712#:~:text=T%C3%9C%C4%B0K%20Kurumsal&text=Ya%C5%9Fl%C4%B1%20n%C3%BCfus%20olarak%20kabul%20edilen,9%2C1'e%20y%C3%BCkseldi

Turkish Statistical Institute. (2021). Elderly with Statistics, 2020. *Turkish Statistical Institute News Bulletin, 37227*. https://data.tuik.gov.tr/Bulten/Index?p=Istatistiklerle-Yaslilar-2020-37227

Ulukan, U. (2020). Demographic transformation and older workers in Turkey. *Fiscaoeconomia, 4*(1), 94–110. doi:10.25295/fsecon.2020.01.005

United Nations. (2017). *World Population Prospects*. https://esa.un.org/unpd/wpp/Publications/Files/WPP2017_KeyFindings.pdf

United Nations. (2019). *Ageing,* https://www.un.org/en/sections/issues-depth/ageing/

Wahrendorf, M., Akinwale, B., Landy, R., Matthews, K., & Blane, D. (2017). Who in Europe works beyond the state pension age and under which conditions? Results from SHARE. *Journal of Population Ageing, 10*(3), 269–285.

KEY TERMS AND DEFINITIONS

Aging: It is a universal process that is observed in every living creature over time and causes a decrease in all functions. Today, the terms "young old age" is used for 65-74 years of age, "mid old ages" is used for 75-84 years of age and "old age" is used for over 85 years of age when describing the stages of old age. It is a biological process that occurs in all organisms depending on the effect of time and is characterized by progressive loss of functions.

Corporatist Welfare Regime: It is less dependent in terms of connection with the market, but there is a gradual process in terms of benefits provided to its citizens; its re-distributing effect is negligible. In many cases these corporatist regimes are shaped by Church traditions. Affiliation with the church is determinant in their perspectives on social policy besides determining their conservative attitudes towards family and gender.

COVID-19: Coronavirus disease (COVID-19) is an infectious disease caused by a newly discovered coronavirus.

Demographic Window of Opportunity: The period during which a country's working-age population is higher than the sum of the young and elder populations. The most significant characteristic of this period is that it lasts for a certain period of time (about 30-40 years).

Elderly Workforce: While the elderly workforce is statistically defined as the workforce in the 55-64 age group, it is sometimes referred to as the individuals between 50-64 age group or even between the 45-64 age group.

Old Age: It is defined as a stage, as an extension of adulthood, in which physical and mental changes are seen in the later period of life. State grants an old-age pension to citizens aged 65 and over, who do not have any social security and are in poor financial condition.

Retirement: It is the term attributed to the situation that begins when people who pursue their lives by working quit working in a planned way, assuming that they cannot work due to old age. Pension, which is referred to as the amount of money a retired person needs to live without working, is usually paid to the retiree as a permanent income, sometimes as a lumpsum payment or sometimes as a combination of these.

Social Insurances: Workmen's insurance is the insurance made by deducting a portion of their earnings in order to secure the health and future of the employees working in return for wages.

Social Security: It is a scheme of actions assumed by the government to ensure the well-being of huge and potentially vulnerable population including children, the elderly, the sick and the unemployed through measures to ensure their access to food and shelter and to provide adequate resources to promote health and well-being for the population.

Welfare State: Welfare state or social state means the state that accepts primary responsibility for the welfare of its citizens beyond the minimum level and suggests that the State should play a main role in protecting and promoting the economic and social well-being of its citizens.

Section 3
Multigenerational Workforce

Chapter 10
Baby Boomers and Their Influence in the Colombian Organizational and Entrepreneurial Context

Rafael Ignacio Pérez-Uribe
https://orcid.org/0000-0001-9924-6657
Universidad Santo Tomas, Colombia

David Ocampo-Guzmán
Universidad EAN, Colombia

Maria Pilar Ramirez-Salazar
https://orcid.org/0000-0002-9462-0897
Universidad EAN, Colombia

ABSTRACT

The Baby Boomers were a pivotal generation (1946 – 1964) for the Third Industrial Revolution (1945 – 2010), but with ages raging from 55 to 76, many are retirees and/or have entered the last stages of their productive lives. The last official census conducted in 2018 by Colombia's National Administrative Department of Statistics (DANE) concluded that there are 48,258,494 human beings living within Colombian soil, and out of the grand total, the Boomers accounted for 16,38%, which sums 7,904,742 (4,275,703 female and 3,629,039 male) raging between 55 to 75 years of age. The underlying question, and the one that the authors intend to answer, is Are Colombian Boomers like those in Europe and the US? In trying to answer this conundrum as best they can, an adaptation of the Rokeach's Personal Values Survey is employed, which is combined with another set of questions designed by the authors that identifies personal and familiar characteristics of the respondents by means of a non-probabilistic sample technique.

DOI: 10.4018/978-1-7998-2395-7.ch010

Copyright © 2022, IGI Global. Copying or distributing in print or electronic forms without written permission of IGI Global is prohibited.

INTRODUCTION

It must not surprise anyone or anybody from any part of the world that throughout all economies, organizations are composed by human talent belonging to different generations. Baby Boomers, Generation X, Millennials, Centennials (Generation Z), they all come together within the boundaries of all types of organizations. Public, private, non-profit, SMEs, conglomerates, regardless of size, nature, and/or core activity, chances are that within one same organization a turmoil of sorts is being cooked in a cauldron of generation diversity.

This poses an enormous challenge for the Human Resources units and their experts. Long gone are the 70s and 80s, times when Baby Boomers reigned supreme amongst the entrepreneurial worlds! Now human resource management must strive to please different palates which are antagonistic in nature, and they better deliver if the organizations' goals are to be attained!

The authors (two Boomers and one Gen X, no less!) are on the same page when it comes to understand the paramount importance of not only highlighting the fact that companies' workforces are composed of different generations, but also in comprehending those generations' traits, characteristics, behaviours, and demeanours, for there is not a consensus in the confines of the academic world of these, and it would surely be an enormous handicap if there was (Díaz-Sarmiento, *et al.,* 2017).

Therefore, it is this chapter's aim to thoroughly describe the various generations that lie behind this notorious fact with the Baby Boomers being the epicentre of this characterization. Field research with 120 Colombian Boomers was conducted and the results were contrasted with what is generally depicted as Boomer behaviour around the world.

THEORICAL FRAMEWORK

The Concept of Generation

Díaz-Sarmiento *et al.,* (2017) have procured an exquisite dissertation regarding the concept of "generation", which can be observed in table 1.

Table 1. Generation: Various concepts

Authors	Concept
Kertzer (1983)	The word "generation" es commonly associated with kinship; persons who have the same age and are at the same stage in history and life, teenage years, youth, middle age, senior years, etc.
Comte cited by Leccardi, C. and Feixa, C. (2011).	This concept states that generations can be quantified and condensed within the human cycle of life and serve as measuring instruments of a society's progress. (Or lack of) Societies achieve progress by the combining efforts of old and new generations. The first ones bring stability and experience to the table, whilst the younger ones bring new inputs and fresh impetus. Comte (2011) a generation's time to shine is 30 years. Once this time has passed, it is the dawn of a new generation.
Mannheim and De la Yncera (1993)	As Comte stated, it is during its 30s that a generation begins its creativity pinnacle and that once it has reached its 60s, the inevitable twilight comes to its fruition. When a generation "overstays its welcome" and its reign lasts longer than that, a society's progress can be hampered. It is pivotal for generations to understand and accept when their time to "ride into the sunset" has come and to refrain from occupying the role of creative and innovative force when it no longer belongs to them.

Continued on following page

Table 1. Continued

Authors	Concept
Ortega & Gasset cited by Capell and Niño (2007).	Generations are composed by a "complete social body" whose constant interactions allow a society to obtain its historic purpose. There are biological cycles that allow three generations to be condensed into one; and each one of them has different traits and characteristics, and each has the ambition to have and to exercise power. The first generation consists of persons who have reached the power positions. The second one by persons who exercise and strive in keeping, and the third one who are on their way to losing it. Hence, two stages are clear, each one lasting fifteen years. From 30 to 45, power is conceived and pursued, and from 45 to 60 it is attained and used.
Marias (1955) cited by Díaz-Sarmiento *et al.,* (2017, p.194)	Generations can be described by cohorts of people that were born within a specific time range, thus sharing certain elements in their perceptions regarding life, history, and society in general.
Mill and Navarro (1969)	Generations are made up by human groups that takeover society, moulding it to their "image and likeness". Their behaviour ins heavily influenced by the events taking place during their time on top. By means of education and experience, they not only leave a mark in their time, but aim to leave a mark in the times to come, sometimes having a very hard time accepting when their time to step down has come.
Ferrari cited by Martin (2015).	Each generation has its own conception of the world and tends to mould its time based on it. Under this point of view, it is evident that every generation has been rebellious when striving to attain power, but once it has achieved it, its rebellious nature begins to fade away, giving place to the new power.
Dilthey cited in Martin (2015)	A generation is a group of people living at the same time and age, sharing the conducts and customs that identify that time and age. That is a cornerstone for building a closeness that can be enhanced or eroded as times passes by. Events, circumstances, incidents, and affairs bring them together, hence they are prone to react to these in similar fashions. Generations and their essence are more determined by their experimental time rather than their chronological time. It is what they go through as a generation what defines them, not the range of years when they were born.
Heidegger cited by Del Moral (2001)	Members of a generation share much more than a year or range of years of birth: they share a "collective fate". What brings individuals together as a generation are those "common historical topics" that are shared by a society at a specific juncture. These not only serve as the events that bring a generation together, but they are also the barriers preventing other generations wanting to "seat on the throne" to take their place.

Source. Authors

Different Generations

Howe and Strauss quoted by Rosenberg (2020) have given a very accurate definition of the different **Generation Cohorts** that have surfaced since the 1900s. These are illustrated by table 2:

Table 2. Different generations by Howe and Strauss

Years	Generation Name
1900 to 1924	Galvanized Iron (G.I.)
1925 to 1945	Silent Generation
1946 to 1964	Baby Boomers
1965 to 1979	Generation X
1980 to 2000	Millennials or Generation Y
2000 onwards	New Silent Generation or Generation Z[1]

Source. Authors

1900 to 1924: Galvanized Iron (G.I.)

During WWI, American soldiers came up with a pretty unique name for the German artillery projectiles: Galvanized Iron or GIs. As a parallel development, the term GI began to be utilised in reference to "Government Issues" and/or "General Issue", but more importantly, all articles of war, equipment, military equipment, weapons, and related articles were called "Ground Infantry". It is not clear, nor there is a general consensus as to which one of the above resulted in the common way to refer to American soldiers: GIs. It is known who made the first reference to the immensely popular name **G.I. Joe**, and that was no other than the Patriarch of de Baby Boomers, Mr. GI himself, President Dwight D. Eisenhower, who in 1945, when WWII was entering its final stages and victory for the Allies was inevitable, said:

The United Nations will greatly remember all of the Generals, but all these agree with me in the selection of the truly heroic selection in this war. He is GI Joe and his buddies

From that point onwards, GI JOE was used in all references to the Armed Forces of the United States. (Rivas-Rodríguez, 2016).

Brokaw (1998) as cited by Pumphrey (2011, paragraph 5) this generation, often quoted as "The Greatest Generation", is notable by its perseverance and manner of striving through adversity, traits that were evident during WWI and WWII, and that were the cornerstone by which the US became a better place to live in.

Furthermore, Pumphrey (2011) again cites Brokaw (1998) in explaining how it was that the Greatest Generation endured tremendous hardships and challenges, such as economic depression, unemployment, hunger, and war overseas, that led them to courage, character, discipline, and a sense of personal responsibility and duty with themselves, their families, and society in general. It was these traits that permitted the defeat of Hitler and his allies. It was these characteristics in their ethos that built the American economy and transform it into a beacon of science and development for all mankind. These traits provided the United States with the opportunity to live free and opulent, the likes of which humanity had never saw before.

Inebriated by the sweet nectar of victory, the GI Generation shepherded the American public into embracing the Founding Fathers fate, thus embarking on the most ambitious ventures, building parks, bridges, monuments, malls that were conceived and executed by commercial, civic, and governmental institutions, all functioning like clockwork. "Bigger is better" was born during those days (Sorry Hulk Hogan!).

Literally, the sky was the limit, and by means of embracing and letting technology and science roam free, everything was possible, from raising children to beating the "Russkies" in the Space Race.

The GIs were determined not only in leaving a better world for their children; they were obsessed with their children's generation being better than them (Rose, 2008).

These are the distinctive traits of the GI Generation (Brokaw, 1998; Gambone, 2005; Rose, 2008):

- Personal Responsibility: Being held accountable was perceived as an honour, and as such, leadership was built on being honourable and responsible.
- Humility: Only by being humble one could be worthy of respect. Humility was a measure of one's dignity and modesty. Absolutely no one was above the common welfare, and hence, anyone with delusions of grandeur was swiftly put in his/her place.

- Work Ethics: For the GI Generation working was not a choice: it was an obligation. Everyone was working for survival, theirs, their families', but most importantly, their countries'. Working was a reason to be proud.
- Austerity: Having endured the 1929 Stock Market Crash, the GIs were set on saving every penny they could. Frugality was the name of the game, and everyone played it.
- Compromise: Probably one of the most important values embraced by the GIs. No need to sign contracts under the presence of lawyers; a handshake was sufficient to ensure that both parties were going to honour their respective commitments.

1925 to 1945: The Silent Generation

The term **"Silent Generation"** came to prominence in 1951, when Time Magazine visualized it as the most notorious trait of that time's generation:

Opposed to the Flaming Youth of their parents, this younger generation is but a small flame

The generation's "silent" demeanour can be derived from the harsh times during which its members were born, and the fact that their coming of age took place in the middle of **McCarthyism**, certainly a most effective deterrent for the boisterous minds and mouths youngsters usually have. Yes, the Silent Generation has been notorious for intending to work along the system rather than change it, but not too few a not so silent and untraditional minds were a part of it, minds that without a doubt changed the world in a significant manner (Smith, 2020).

The eldest members of this generation were born at the beginning of the Great Depression. Their childhood was met with the appalling events that lead and took place during WWII, while their coming of age came about during the 50s and early 60s. In terms of size, the Silent Generation is smaller than its predecessor, the GI, and also smaller than its successor, the Baby Boomers. But then again, isn't the filling the best part of a sandwich and/or an OREO cookie?

The low birth rate of this generation is generally attributed to the conditions of economic adversity and war present throughout those years. Plus, many men were recruited to serve their country, either for WWI or WWII, and never made it back from the fields in Europe.

But it was not only war and economic hardship the obstacles: Mother Nature herself made her presence felt during the **"Dust Bowl"** (The Dust Bowl was a period of severe dust storms that greatly damaged the ecology and agriculture of the American and Canadian prairies during the 1930s; severe drought and a failure to apply dryland farming methods to prevent the aeolian processes caused the phenomenon).

Thusly, the Silent Generation began its existence facing dire circumstances, Great Depression, Dust Bowl, the uncertainty in politics and economics that set the stage for Hitler and the Third Reich and WWII, so it was not really a very prudent time to start a family. Those who did, bred a generation of cautious, conscientious, and meticulous human beings (Enam & Konduri, 2018).

According to Dobransky- Fasiska (2002), these are the main idiosyncrasies found in the Silent Generation:

1. Thrifty: Born and raised into economic uncertainty and restraint, surplus wasn't in their vocabulary, nor in their customs. As a consequence, Silent Generation members are all about austerity and frugality. This might explain why Paul McCarney sent his children to Public Schools.

2. Respectful: Authority was always respected. Whether it was a school's headmaster, a mother, a father, or John Lennon's Aunt Mimi, any authority figure was respected, and that became a train of thought and behaviour far and near for them, and in all walks of life.
3. Loyal: Silent Generation affiliates are loyal to the very end. They are loyal to their beliefs, their careers, their families, their friends.
4. Determined: It has often been said that few things mould your character better than adversity. Adversity became the daily bread for the Silent Generation from the get-go, hence a sheer intestinal fortitude was developed that became their drive, their will to succeed. The Beatles, The Rolling Stones, The Who, are a testament of the Silent Generation's determination.

1965 to 1979: Generation X

Just as the Silent Generation is a "sandwich" generation between the GIs and the Silent Generation, the Generation X is the buffer between the Baby Boomers and the Millennials. Generation X was not the only term coined for them, but it is the one that winded up being used the most.

In 1992, The Atlantic newspaper tried coining **"Thirteeners"** as an alternate term for Generation X, but the name never caught on and Generation X became the widely accepted term for a loosely defined generation. They are a loosely defined generation on account of not having the strong ser of beliefs and values their predecessors possess, nor do they have those delusions of grandeur that their successors have. Not being prone to be dubbed as conservative or liberal, capitalists or socialists, hippies or yuppies, the members of Generation X are exactly that: X (Thomas & Pickering, 2005).

What is not loosely about those born between 1965 and 1979 is the fact that they are the ones replacing the Boomers at the top of the organizational pyramid. Many of them are being promoted to the upper echelons of management, while Boomers are retiring, either voluntarily or not. Baby Boomers have reached the end of their productive lives and are being "send out to grass" with the representatives of Generation X occupying their places.

If Baby Boomers are a generation known to put work first and over all things, Gen X is known for being the generation that began striving to achieve a balance and equilibrium between life and work. Boomers were also known to be submissive and compliant with authority figures, whereas Gen X are not. This is in great part a consequence of being born into an era where no world-changing crises took place, while the legacy from the Silent Generation really cemented itself. The Sexual Revolution, as well as the Female Revolution, both from the 60s, resulted in a decrease in the birth rate.

They are also the children of women who began to pursue their professional fulfilment, and not mere housewives. Hence, Gen X are very independent, much more so than prior generations, and they have developed strong technical skills alongside other set of skills and competences, among which responsibility and experience stand out. As sons and daughters from **Reaganomics**, they are a generation prone to greed, self-catering, selfish persons with little regard to what others think of them, as long as they are successful economically (Martin & Prince, 2008).

Gen X is the audience that was paying attention to Gordon Gekko's infamous speech (Stone, 1987):

The point is, ladies and gentlemen, that greed, for lack of a better word, is good. Greed is right. Greed works. Greed clarifies, cuts through, and captures the essence of the evolutionary spirit. Greed, in all of its forms, greed for life, for money, for love, knowledge, has marked the upward surge in mankind and greed, you mark my words, will not only save Teldar paper, but that other malfunctioning corporation called the USA. Thank you very much.

Furthermore, Gen X is the generation were having a superior level of education became very profitable, thus changing the essence and landscape of education. Pursuing a degree for the Gen X frame of mind has nothing to do with moulding yourself as a person with an upright conscience, but rather as building yourself as a valuable asset for an organization. It is no coincidence that Gex X is the "MBA" generation (Howe & Strauss, 1992).

1981 to 1997: Millennials or Generation Y

Born from 1981 onwards, this is a generation that came of age and/or awakened in a digital, hyperconnected world. Most of them cannot fathom a world where one has to use a type-writing machine to prepare an essay, or to write a quarterly report. They woke up in a world where you did not send postcards for Christmas or Birthdays, where you didn't have to record an LP on cassette. Instant gratification is at their fingertips, literally.

Approximately 94% of Gen Y are online service users, frequent consumers of Apps such as Facebook, Instagram, Twitter, LinkedIn, among others. It is not that being on Social Media es a tool they can benefit from, is that NOT being on Social - Media is a need they must satisfy. Being "wired" is their normal status, making Gen Y prone to conditions known as "millennial diseases". And yet, "Beauty is in the eye of the beholder, and as most events, their perception varies upon being looked under different optics. Millennials have developed the capacity to manipulate several devices at the same time, something that their forerunners have serious difficulties with (Barros and Landa, 2021).

Millennials have also developed new ways of studying and have taken full advantage of living in a hyperconnected world. Most of them are bilingual, trilingual, and even polyglots. Bear in mind, they are natives in the digital language; it is their true mother language. They have transcended the Gen X desire for money, for they are aware that **Global Warming** is the leitmotiv of their very existence, and they pursue higher levels of education as means to counter its insurmountable threat. 9 to 5 jobs are not appealing to their nature, and their need for flexible hours and variety of chores make them prone to undertake and putting enterprising ideas and business projects into practice.

This entails a huge challenge for HRM in all aging organizations, for if they are unable to respond to the Gen Y's petitions and adapt themselves to this new mindset of the workforce, within a 5-year span, companies will have serious problems in retaining competent personnel to fill the voids left by the Boomers and the Gen X (Hershatter and Epstein, 2010).

Contrary to their predecessors, Gen Y do not feel money and economic success to be their masters. For them, being thirty and living in their parents' is normal, nothing to be ashamed of. Quite the opposite, Gen Y strongly believe that the current state of affairs was brought about by their predecessors' greed. Transparency, collaboration, compromise, tolerance, those are the values they strive for, and they seek to imbue the rest of the world with them once they are the ones seating in the drivers' seat (McDonald, 2015).

When it comes to their consumer patterns, Millennials are volatile, voluble, and versatile, a triple V of sorts (Eisner, 2005). Just as they are indifferent to money's charm, they are also immune to the effects of traditional publicity stunts. Want to entice a Millennial? Influencers are the key (Lippincott, 2012).

This is a generation willing and able to leave their mark in society. Their endeavour is to develop a unique personality via social media, clothing, events, cultural sessions. Gen Y is a content consumer rather than a product consumer (Graybill, 2014).

Millennials have the ability of making themselves unique through their individuality, making the constant evolution in ICTs as their main ally, not only in their personal lives, but in their professional lives as well. It is through their digital platforms that they disseminate their political and social agenda: equality and tolerance (Hayes, Parks, McNeilly & Johnson, 2018).

1998 – Present Day: New Silent Generation/Centennials/Generation Z

Today's teenagers and twenty-year-olds were born during the late-late 1990s and the Third Millenium's earlier years. Representing roughly a 23,7% of the world's population, they are an important part of any organization's **Marketing Plans**, especially when it comes to the **Digital Marketing** appendix. Centennials are the ones moving the needle in terms of social media consumption, and their consumer preferences are easy to identify there. Want to reach out to GenZ? Better learn how to use your social networks in an impeccable fashion, for **Influencer Marketing** and **YouTubers** are the right channels to do so (De Barba, 2016).

Access to the labour market does not come easy for Centennials, thus they are a generation prone to entrepreneurship and business creation. Born into a world completely absorbed by ICT use in daily chores, and having social media as a mother language, GenZ enjoys a great capacity for autonomous learning and self-instruction abilities, hence creativity and self-learning are huge traits that Centennials have taken full advantage from in this time and age (Chillakuri, 2020).

Centennials are the first generation born into the **Digital Era**. They do not have the slightest idea of how life was without Windows, Microsoft Office, Apple Computers, smart-phones, tablets, and the Cloud. Not only were they born with a superior capacity for manipulating different gadgets and the different kinds of computer language, but they also spend from 6 to 10 hours daily in honing even further those crafts (Sánchez, 2018). Different alternatives for communication are at their disposal and they learn very quickly how to use them. Virtual platforms, ecosystems, novel channels, all lead them to new professional possibilities, new ways of learning new skills to do such everyday activities as orders, purchases, and reservations (Massot, 2018).

Unlike their predecessors, centennials are not afraid to be critical, to question everything and count on their talent to take advantage of the new opportunities of the market. They are constantly on the move and evolving, easily adapting to new environments, and changing landscapes; this is probably the reason behind their irreverence (Balmes, 2018).

Having and projecting an active digital image is an enormous goal of them, and it is through their online profiles where all aspects regarding their everydayness can be found. What other cybernauts make of them is the validation they are desperately seeking for. Of course, this makes them socially awkward when look under their predecessors' eyes, but the way their predecessors mingle socially is awkward for them! (Calero, 2020).

Social media is not only used by centennials for communication, interactions, and exchanges, it is the cornerstone of their human interactions as well as their source of information and culture. Therefore, GenZ is not a well-read generation, nor is it filled with educated, cultured, and cultivated individuals. Very often, the presence of inconsistencies in both oral and written expressions is evident (Cerezo, 2017).

Immediacy is almost an addiction for the average centennial, and it is in almost every walk of life. Immediacy in their internet connections, that allows the fastest navigation possible. Immediacy in their relationships, built on their online profiles and not through trials and tribulations. Immediacy in their streaming services, which allows them to binge on an entire season of X or Y show, rather than having to endure a whole week of waiting time to watch the next episode. This leads to an impatient character, impatience that makes them prone to tantrums and fits when they do not get their way, and fast. Seems that they are not keen on Aerosmith's lyric:

Life Is a Journey, Not a Destination

Indeed, they are oblivious to the fact that short term plans and events get old quickly, and that a long-term vision of one's life and goals is way more desirable (Jiménez, 2018).

Most of their photographs are selfies, and most are an acute rendition of who they really are. Going out of their way to please someone is not on their hardware. What you see is what you get (Dolot, 2018).

Social causes are their bread and butter. All centennials have a greater social and environmental conscience far superior to their predecessors'. Diversity, respect, gender equality, climate change, global warming, all are crucial issues for GenZ, and they do not spare any effort to undertake them as top priority endeavours (Baysal, 2014).

For centennials, marriage, kids, the house with the white picket fence and German shepherd is not in the cards. They have other, more ambitious aspirations, like becoming influencers and entrepreneurs (Singh & Dangmei, 2016).

The Baby Boomers

The end of World War II brought a baby boom to many countries, especially Western ones. Nations such as the United States, Canada, New Zealand, and Australia saw a considerable growth in their birth rates which led to what is known as the "Baby Boom" phenomenon. Historians have reached a consensus in regards as the reasons behind this occurrence but is undeniable that one pivotal element was the deep and profound desire of the surviving soldiers to settle down and seize the second chance, they had been given by forming a family. Being surrounded by death and pandemonium made them come out of the war years with a newfound zest for life, thus the period between 1946 and 1964 saw an incredible surge in births (Arbeláez & Franco, 2013, p.16).

Born between those years, the Boomer generation has witnessed deep and radical changes, both geopolitical aspects as in technology. Their 30s saw them appreciating the benefits from Sony's Betamax and Walkman, only to watch them become obsolete less than a decade later. Their 20s were lived under the banner of "Peace and love" that the immortal 60s brought about, and they have been front row spectators for all major changes and transformations in the Information and Communication Technologies (ICTs) and within the financial world (ACIS, 2019).

Sons and daughters of the Silent Generation and parents of Gen X and some Millennials, it is commonplace for latter half of the Baby Boomer Generation to be referred to as the **"Generation Jones"** (Corporate finance Institute, 2021).

As years have gone by, and new generations have come of age, the manner in which the elder and senior population is perceived has been transformed radically. Senior citizens are no longer considered as a helpless, unable, uncapable and/or without resistance and vitality, but quite the opposite. A large percentage of nowadays' senior citizens are Baby Boomers, and the last thing they feel like is helpless and/or hapless, furthermore, their purchasing power is one of the most coveted prizes and rightfully so: with their housing bought and paid for, with their offspring already in its adult life and enjoying their monthly pensions, their status as elderly citizens has been rethought altogether (Denk, 2003, p. 25).

According with Arbeláez & Franco (2013, p.26), the Boomer shopping experiences contains the following characteristics 1) Many at time they enjoy a double income (pension + wage), their income allows them to have an exquisite palate, aiming at premium categories in their purchases, 2) Shopping is an extension of their social relationships. By means of shopping, the Boomers are prolonging an existing social bond, 3) A swift, top-notch service is a must to garner their loyalty, 4) They are detached from the act of searching for goods and/or services to purchase; that is something they rather have someone else do for them, or keep them company whilst doing it, at the very least, 5) While scouting for goods and services is unappealing, purchasing itself is a beseeching experience (having a solid purchasing power might explain this), 6) Regardless of their robust finances, Boomers are always on the hunt for the best "bang for their buck".

Díaz-Sarmiento *et al.*, (2017, p.196) have cited New Strategist Publication (2010) to assess Boomer behaviour. Most of them were raised by young mothers, most of which were housewives, conservatives and traditionalists to the core who transmitted those same core values to the Boomers. Those values in turn have moulded the Boomer capacity to lead, to adapt, to guide and generate changes. For them, building solid teams with high spirits, a strong social commitment, and a vocation to work in favour of the general interest is paramount (Kupperschmidt, 2000).
Zemke *et al.,* (2013) have put it best:

After all, they are the generation that lived through the Civil Rights Movement, the Empowerment movement and the search for diversity

Table 3 summarizes the Boomers general essence (Corporate Finance Institute, 2021) (Díaz-Sarmiento *et al.,* 2017).

Table 3. Essence of the Baby Boomers

Trait	Definition
Focused and determined	Hard work comes easy for the boomers. They witnessed MLK's and Malcom X's achievements, the success of women's liberation movement, Neil Armstrong's landing on the moon, all achievements that required focus and determination.
Competitive	By virtue of being conceived and born at a time when many other children were being conceived and born, competition became the name of the game for the Boomers. All throughout their lives they have had to compete with their fellow Boomers, from a position in school to a position in work, they always had to compete for their "slice of the pie".
Valuable Relations	Having a lot of kids your age forces you to be competitive, but at the same time it allows you to grow up amongst lots of children your same age with whom to play. Alongside family values, loyalty amongst friends is predominant for the Boomers.
Independent and Confident	By means of hard work, a solid and healthy self-confidence arose amongst the Boomers. Moreover, they are ingenious, witty, and self-assured enough to know if the are able to handle tricky situations by themselves or if they need help.

Continued on following page

Table 3. Continued

Trait	Definition
Excellence and Quality	Having witnessed first-hand moments of deep changes and crises, boomers value excellence and quality in all walks of life. Whether is in relations, in a meal, in a trip, or in something as pedestrian as a glass of wine, Boomers are always in the lurk for the best they can obtain and are willing to pay for it.
Work Ethics	Boomers are power-driven and demand high levels of human development. They are probably the last generation that could seriously hope to spend their entire productive life working for the same organization until retiring with their pension. There are no half measures for them when it comes to authority: they either love it or hate it. Material goods are their bread and butter, and often, they perceive and measure success by that measuring stick. Accustomed to hierarchies and competitiveness, work comes first at all costs.
Education	The Boomers were the first generation to perceive education as means to an end, not as a path that is made of principle that leads to character. Boomers are today's policy makers in many countries.
Search for new Jobs	As one of their life goals is to keep the same job for their entire work life, Boomers have found that they are not very good at selling themselves as an asset. Their social skills are dated, very useful to build meaningful relations with friends, but not so polished for presenting themselves as an organization's solution. They never thought about tempering the increasingly important presentation and social skills, for they always saw themselves getting pensioned at the same place (Van Selm & Van den Heijkant, 2021, p. 10).

Source. Authors.

Baby Boomers in Colombia

The last population census conducted by Colombia's **National Administrative Department of Statistics (DANE)** took place in 2018. It was revealed then that Baby Boomers represent more than 9% of the total population in Colombia. This generation is segmented in different age groups, with each group possessing its own traits and peculiarities (ACIS, 2019). There are pre-retired, pensioners, and late retirees/grandparents. The latter are the breadwinners and act as providers for their children and grandchildren, fact that does not come as a surprise: the Boomers are well-off, a lot of times enjoying a better, more solid financial situation than their successors represented in better incomes, more assets and equity.

During the first semester of 2016, **Kantar Ibope Media Colombia** conducted a thorough research known worldwide as **Target Group Index (TGI)**. It is a research aimed at studying consumer habits in media, brands, products, lifestyles, and attitudes. The following are the most relevant findings (Ríos, 2016):

- 12% of Colombian Boomers are web surfers.
- 41% own a Smartphone.
- 6% do not own a Smartphone but intend to purchase one within the next six (6) months.
- 30% have utilised their Smartphone as an internet router during the last 30 days.
- 40% use the Web for information and/or as a source of entertainment and amusement.
- Among the mobile applications to which more time was devoted were text messaging, social networks, e-mail, and classified ads.
- The Bible, solitary games, news sites and various video-on-demand service sites are the used the most.
- 47% regard television as their main source of entertainment, while 49% regards it as their main source of information.

- 35% consider themselves as addicted to television.
- 44% still use newspapers and magazines as source for information on a daily basis and have a current subscription to one of these.
- Radio is still a very important source of information and entertainment for the Boomers with 90% confirming that they have listened to the radio within the last 30 days and 43% stating that radio is their main source of information and divertissement.

In regards with other more personal traits, table 4 illustrates them. It is worth clarifying that these traits were included in research conducted in Spain, called **"Revolución Boomer"** and they were homologated to Colombian behaviour (Abio, 2020):

Table 4. Colombian Baby Boomers: Traits

Trait	Definition
Responsibility	While attentive to tend to every need their parents and offspring might have, Colombian Boomers strive to keep their independence and their own agenda. Very seldom do they live with their parents, and though they do enjoy spending leisure time with their offspring, they aim at maintaining a separate space from them.
Liberated and life-enjoying	As mentioned before, many Boomers enjoy the benefits of having two incomes (pension + honoraria/wages), thus having a solid financial capacity that allows them to pamper themselves.
Handling Technology	Boomers grew up during a time when typewriters were a common tool. Then came the programming boards and cards (Fortran anyone?), then the first PCs, then the first Microsoft Office and Windows, and here we are with laptops, tablets, Smart TVs, and Smartphones. Boomers have utilised them all, and up until now, tamed them all!
Fretting and inquiring	Curious minds, curious behaviour, Colombian Boomers are never afraid of learning.
Other defining traits	Colombian Boomers see themselves as selfless, unselfish beings. They are not naïve, nor social justice warriors, but they do believe in doing what is right and defending their conception of justice and fairness.

Source. Authors

METHODOLOGY

This is a research study entailing both quantitative and qualitative elements (Hernández, Fernández, Baptista, 2016) in which a convenience sample was utilised (Otzen & Manterola, 2017) by means of interviewing and surveying the lifestyles, living standards and overall expectations of **120 Baby Boomers** that are acquaintances, colleagues and/or friends with the authors. Many of the interviewed and surveyed are professors, business consultants, entrepreneurs, businessmen and women, housewives and some are retirees. Anex 1 contains the survey used, called "Baby Boomer Generation" and that took place between February and March 2021.

Findings

Age Group

Data reveals a three (3) level spectrum:

1. **48 to 56 years of age:** 31 persons responded the survey. These are yet to obtain their pensions and represent 25% of the total survey population.
2. **57 to 64 years:** 64 persons responder the survey, representing 53% of the total. These are already pensioners or well on their way of obtaining their retirement with pay.
3. **65 to 72 years:** 25 persons from this age group responded the survey, that is equivalent to 20% (figure 1)

Figure 1. Distribution by age group
Source. Authors.

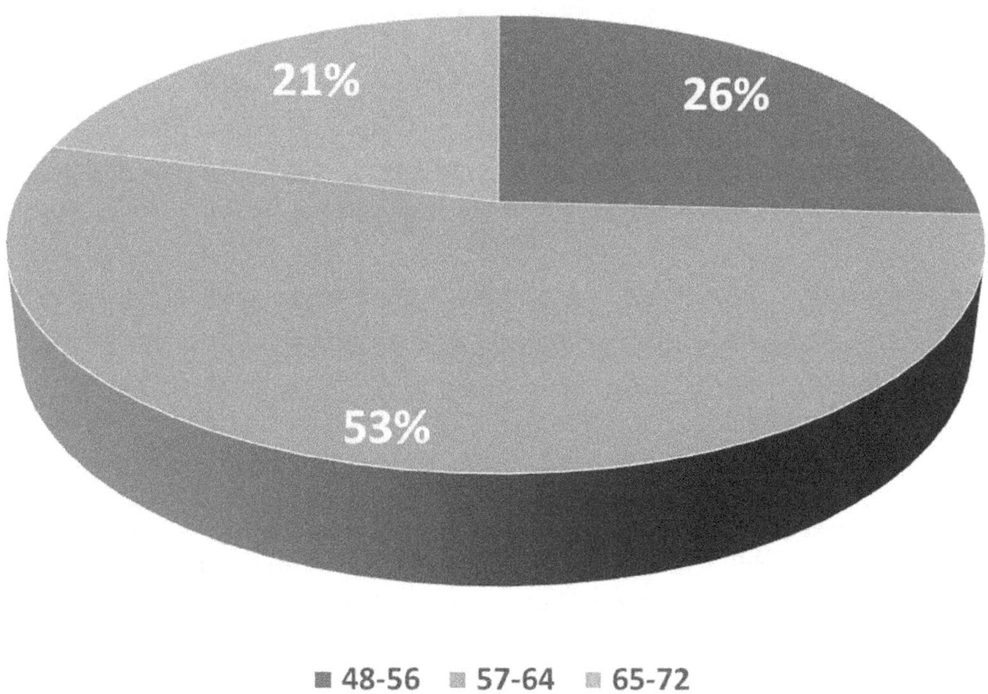

Gender

53% are female, while 48% male (figure 2).

Figure 2. Gender
Source. Authors.

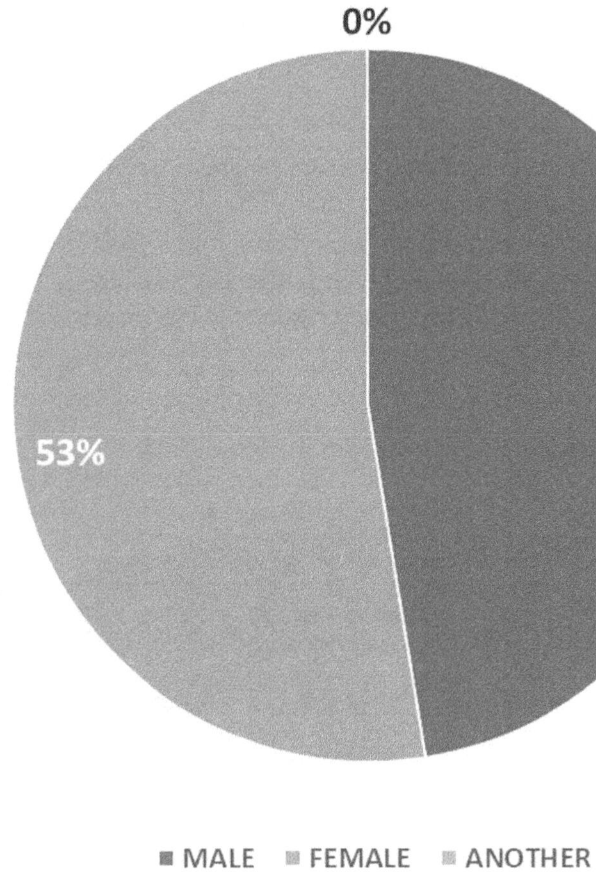

Siblings

Only 5% of the surveyed do not have siblings, which further illustrates the fact that Boomers grew up in households with several children. 95% of the respondents have strong family ties between siblings. Interviewees with 1 to 4 siblings make for 54% of the total and 41% have more than 4 siblings (figure 3).

Figure 3. Total Siblings
Source. Authors.

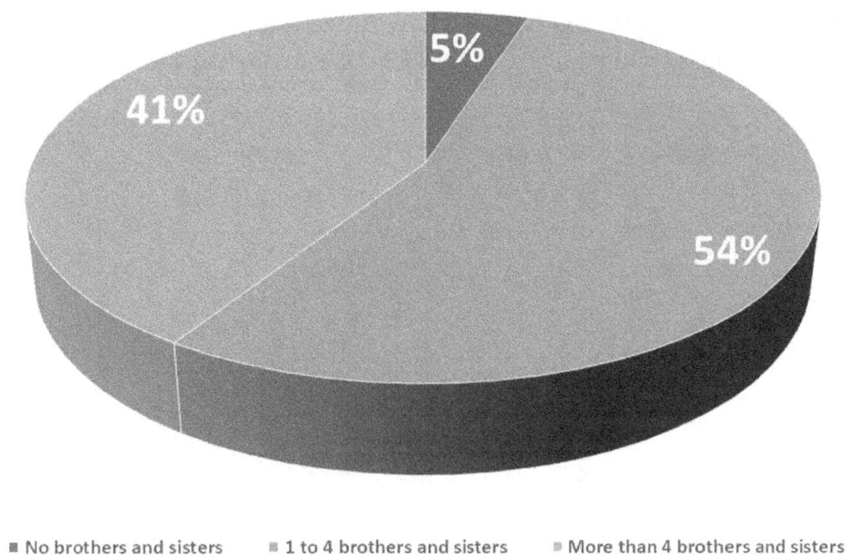

Civil Status

Most respondents are married (69%), 13% are separated or divorced and 10% are bachelorettes/bachelors. Traditional family bonds are very strong still (figure 4).

Figure 4. Civil Status
Source. Authors.

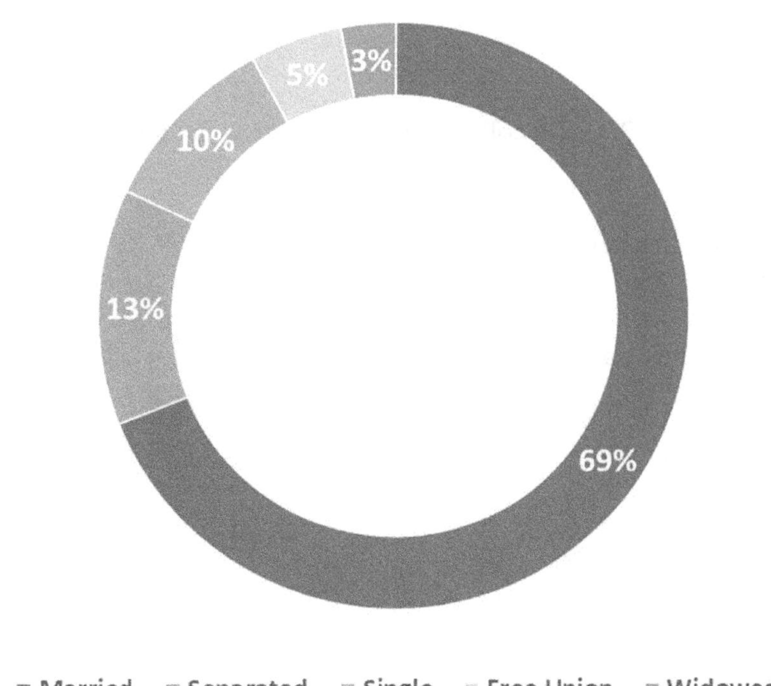

Number of Children

Data obtained shows that 51,7% of the interviewees have two (2) children, while 22,5% have one (1) child. Colombian Boomers have less children than their predecessors, who had 4 to 6 kids per family (figure 5).

Figure 5. Number of Children
Source. Authors.

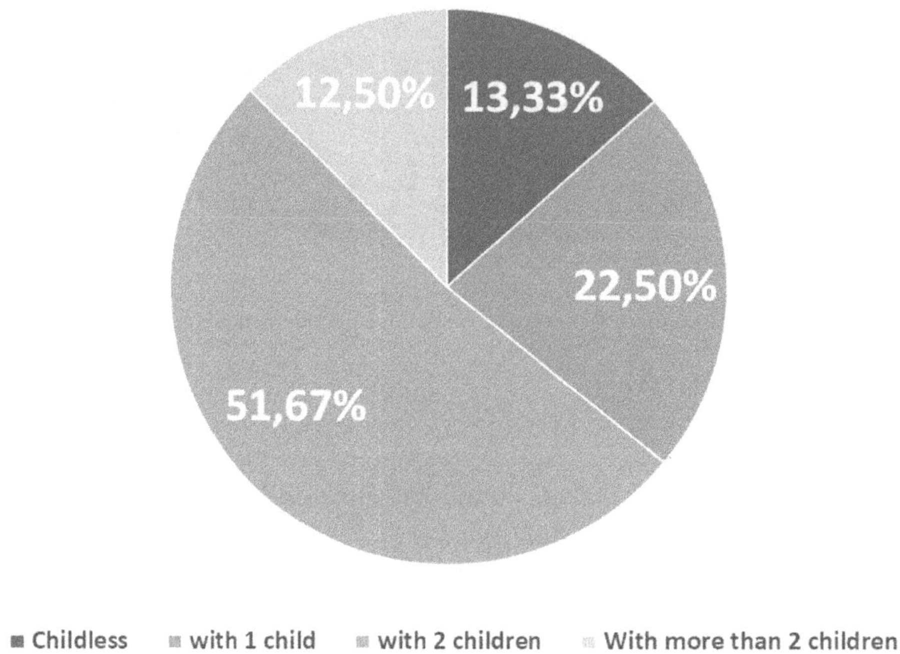

Education Level

Out of the 120 respondents, 35% have a college/university degree and 60% have postgraduate degrees, divided as follows:

- 23% have a specialization degree
- 21% have master's degree
- 13% have PhD
- 3% post-doctoral studies (figure 6).

Figure 6. Education level
Source. Authors.

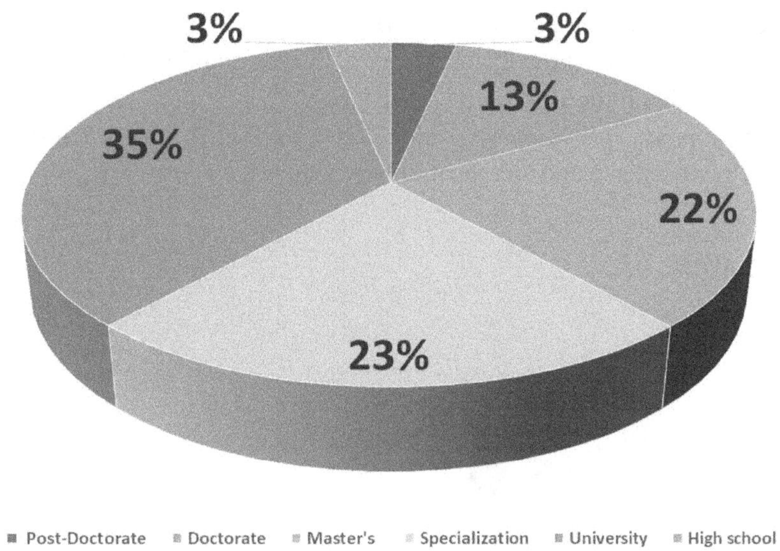

Pensioners

At the time of the survey, 35% of the respondents were enjoying the benefit of retirement with pay, meaning that 65% were yet to meet the requirements to do so and/or were in the process (figure 7).

Figure 7. Pensioners vs Not-pensioners
Source. Authors.

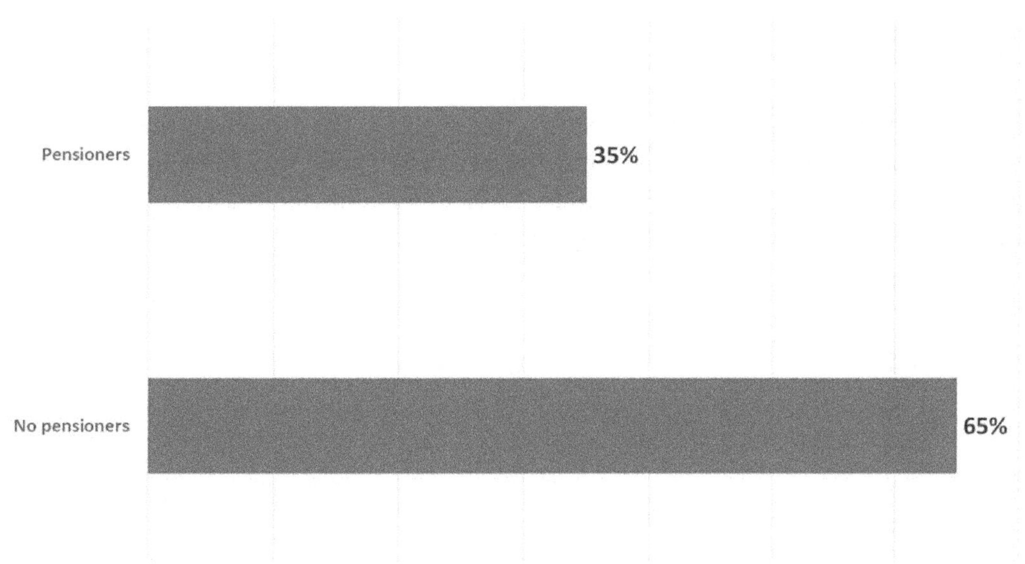

Work Activity

21% of the surveyed population is not active. As shown in figure 7, 35% is already enjoying a pension, therefore it is inferred that 14% of the pensioners are also active and working, enjoying then a double income, thus making their livelihood solid and robust.

79% of the respondents are still working, hence it is clear that Boomers are still respected and appreciated for both their experience and scholarity level (figure 8).

Figure 8. Active vs inactive
Source. Authors.

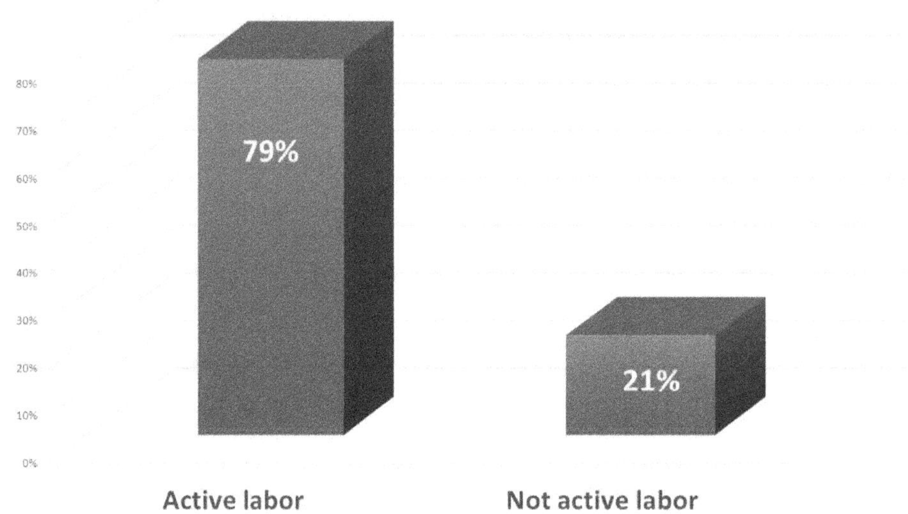

Experience in Business Creation

Data provided expounds the fact that 58% of interviewees owns or has owned an enterprise, demonstrating that entrepreneurship is present in Colombian Boomers. 42% does not have, nor have ever, owned their own business and their efforts are focused on further tempering their skills by means of studying, as question 6 of the survey reveals. Figure 9 lays out these data.

Figure 9. Experience in business creation
Source. Authors.

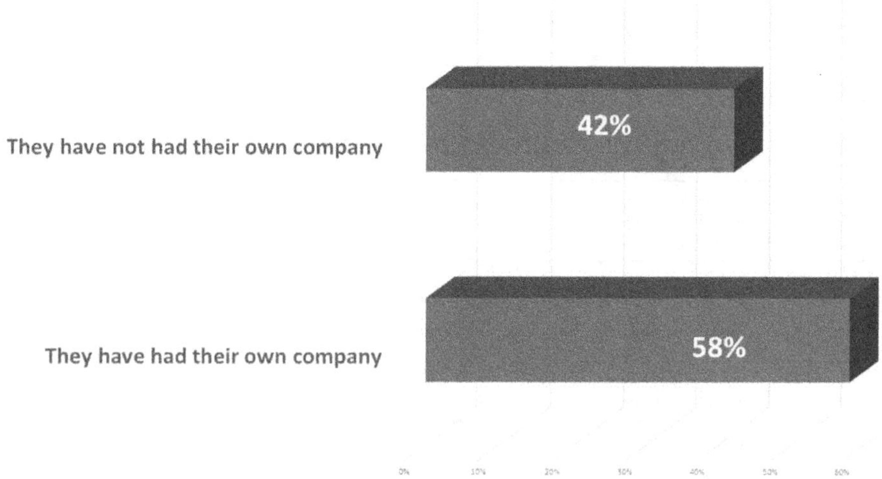

Current Activity

The answers given by the respondents to this question gave us a myriad of dispersions, but by virtue of categorizing and classifying them table 5 came to life. 25% of the surveyed work in the education sector, which explains why high levels of education are present; they are a prerequisite for such field of work. 22,5% are independent contractors and/or consultants offering specialized assessments in legal, business, and real state sectors. 21,6% are active in private or public sector companies, occupying administrative and/or managerial posts. 14% are retirees enjoying their pensions, 13% are entrepreneurs and will remain active after becoming pensioners and the remaining 3% are devoted medics, doctors and members of care services networks, all activities deeply appreciated in these pandemic times.

Table 5. Current activity classification

Current Activity	# Persons
Teaching, research, and consultancy	30
Specialized consultants and independent contractors	27
Employee (private or public sector)	26
Pensioner/retiree	17
Entrepreneur	16
Medic, doctors,	4
TOTAL	**120**

Source. Authors.

Values in Maturity

As shown in table 6, health and family are the most coveted values for our surveyed Colombian Boomers.

Table 6. Values in maturity for Colombian Baby Boomers

Value	Importance	Favourability
HEALTH (Physical and mental welfare)	1	60%
FAMILY SECURITY AND SAFETY (loved ones' wellbeing)	2	43,3%
LEADING A COMFORTABLE LIFE (a tranquil existence)	3	36,73%
FREEDOM (Independence and free choice)	4	32,5%
EQUALITY (same opportunities)	5	21,7%
LEAD AN EXCITING LIFE (active and stimulating existence)	6	20,8%
NATIONAL SECURITY (feeling embraced and protected by the State)	7	15,8%

Source. Authors.

Preferred Values

By taking a glimpse at table 7, it is clear that these 120 Colombian Boomers are invested in the following core values, in order of importance:

1. Respect.
2. Leading a peaceful, tranquil, and harmonious life.
3. True friendship.

Table 7. Preferred alues by Colombian Boomers

Value	Order of Importance	% of Favourability
RESPECT FOR ONE-SELF (Self-esteem)	1	54,2%
A WORLD IN PEACE (without conflicts and/or wars)	2	38,3%
TRUE AND MEANINGFUL FRIENDSHIP	3	32,5%
SALVATION (believing in eternal life)	4	26,7%
PLEASURE (enjoying life)	5	25,7%
SENSE OF ACHIEVEMENT (accomplishing goals)	6	20%
SOCIAL RECOGNITION (respect and admiration)	7	6,7%

Source. Authors.

Attitudes and Behaviours

As shown in table 8, the most coveted attitude and behaviour by Colombian Boomers is honesty.

Table 8. Attitudes and behaviours preferred by Colombian Boomers

Attitude and Behaviour	Order of Importance	% of Favourability
HONESTY (veracity and sincerity)	1	66,7%
CAPABLE (competent, effective)	2	24,2%
OPEN MINDED (open to different ideas)	3	23,3%
SERVICEABLE (care for others' welfare)	3	23,3%
BRAVE (stand my ground)	4	22,5%
MERCIFUL (forgiving)	5	17,5%
AMBITIOUS (still aspires to achieve)	6	10,8%

Source. Authors.

Traits

Table 9 entails the order of importance in which the 120 interviewees perceive their respective traits and hallmarks, where independence and responsibility came out on top, sharing the number one spot, while loyalty came in second.

Table 9. Most important traits and hallmarks

Traits and Hallmarks	Order of Importance	% of Favourability
INDEPENDENCE (self-sufficient)	1	45%
RESPONSIBLE (trust-worthy, compromitted)	1	45%
LOYAL	2	35%
EDUCATED (courteous and polite)	3	28,3%
LOGICAL (rational)	4	27,5%
SELF-CONTAINED (prudent)	5	23,3%
OBEDIENT (disciplined and respectful)	6	21,7%

Source. Authors.

CONCLUSION

The conducted survey allows us to conclude that Colombian Baby Boomers have the same traits, hallmarks, and behaviour of all Boomers around the world, characteristics that are mentioned in table 3 and that several studies have also detailed (Corporate finance Institute, 2021; Díaz-Sarmiento *et al.*, 2017).

In addition to those findings, our survey has enabled us to come to the following conclusions regarding Colombian Boomers when compared to Boomers all around the globe:

- 54% come from traditional families and have between 1 and 4 siblings while 41% also come from traditional families but have 4 or more siblings. Both data coincide with the trend in Boomers around the world.

- 69% of the surveyed Colombian Boomers have traditional families themselves, for they are married. 51,7% have two children, whereas 22,5% have just one. These two findings make it very clear that just as Boomers around the world, Colombian Boomers spawned far less offspring than their predecessors, who in average parented 4 – 6 children.
- A considerable percentage of Colombian Baby Boomers have a college education, and many have graduate level studies. Only 3% have remained only with a secondary school diploma. This fact explains to a large extent why Colombian Boomers enjoy a good standard of living.
- More than 50% of the interviewees have been or are entrepreneurs, evincing that for Colombian Boomers entrepreneurship and economic independence have been important, realisable goals. Moreover, some of the surveyed are still generating income throughout besides their retiree pensions, which enables them to enjoy a solid economic position as they enter their seniority.
- Regarding their set of preferred values and importance given to certain aspects of life, physical and mental health comes first, taken care of loved ones second and thirdly, leading a harmonious and tranquil life.
- Respect, true friendship, and a world in peace are the most coveted aims and goals.
- Honesty, having an open mind, their capacity to work and embracing change are the attitudes most Colombian Boomers strive for.
- The most relevant traits and hallmarks identified by means of the survey are self-reliance and sufficiency, independence and responsibility, the latter understood as being reliable, trustworthy and an undying commitment to make the best out of their lives in its current stage.

New Investigation

With the same survey that was carried out in this work, it could be sent again to a larger sample of BB, to compare the results evidenced in this research and expand the conclusions presented in this chapter.

REFERENCES

Abio, J. (2020). *The Boomer Generation: Redesigning the future with the Adultescents*. https://www.neo2.com/generacion-boomer-baby-boom/

Acis. (2019). *Baby Boomers: How the banking industry can captivate this generation?* https://www.acis.org.co/portal/content/noticiasinternacionales/baby-boomers-%C2%BFc%C3%B3mo-la-banca-puede-cautivar-esta-generaci%C3%B3n

Altman, Y., Baruch, Y., Manrique-de-Lara, P., & Viera Armas, M. M. (2020). Baby boomers at the cusp of their academic career: Storming ahead, hanging on, or Calling it a day. *Studies in Higher Education*, *45*(7), 1335–1350. doi:10.1080/03075079.2019.1610864

Arbeláez, D., & Franco, N. (2013). *Analysis of the Baby Boomers from a Colombian brand perspective and its impact in publicity*. Universidad autónoma de occidente. Facultad de comunicación social departamento de ciencias de la comunicación. Programa comunicación publicitaria. Santiago de Cali. https://red.uao.edu.co/bitstream/handle/10614/5694/T03734.pdf;jsessionid=261869EB5E72DDA251450B72DAA1663C?sequence=1

Balmes, M. (2018). *Characteristics and traits of Generation Z at work.* https://www.modelocurriculum.net/blog/caracteristicas-de-la-generacion-z-en-el-trabajo

Barros, M. E. E., & Landa, C. C. S. (2021). *Social Media and its influence in Millennials buying decision* Universidad Técnica de Ambato Facultad de Ciencias Administrativas. Trabajo de titulación en la modalidad de artículo académico previo a la obtención del Título de Licenciadas en Marketing y Gestión de Negocios. Ambato – Ecuador. Marzo 2021. http://repositorio.uta.edu.ec/bitstream/123456789/32749/1/100%20AA-MKT.pdf

Baysal, S. (2014). Working With Generations X And Y In Generation Z Period: Management of Different Generations in Business Life. *Mediterranean Journal of Social Sciences, 5*(19). DOI:.2014.v5n19p218 doi:10.5901/mjss

Brokaw, T. (1998). *The greatest generation*. Vintage.

Calero, L. (2020). *Characteristics of Generation Z.* https://www.luiscalero.com/caracteristicas-de-la-generacion-z/

Capell, H. C., & Niño, E. L. (2007). The historic method of generations: The Spanish psychology case. *Revista de Historia de la Psicología*, *28*(1), 67–86.

Cerezo, P. (2017). *Generation Z and information.* http://www.injuve.es/sites/default/files/2017/28/publicaciones/documentos_7._la_generacion_z_y_la_informacion.pdf

Chillakuri, B. (2020). Understanding Generation Z expectations for effective onboarding. *Journal of Organizational Change Management*, *33*(7), 1277–1296. doi:10.1108/JOCM-02-2020-0058

Corporate finance Institute. (2021). https://corporatefinanceinstitute.com/resources/knowledge/other/baby-boomers/

De Barba, G. (2016). *7 Characteristics of Generation Z.* https://www.entrepreneur.com/article/268023

Del Moral, J. M. (2001). Historicity and temporality in the Being and in times of M. Heidegger. *Philosophic Signs*, (5), 133-141.

Denk, H. (2003). *Sports for the elderly.* Barcelona: Editorial paidotribo.

Díaz-Sarmiento, C., López-Lambraño, M., & Roncallo-Lafon, L. (2017). Understanding generations: a revision of the concept, classification and distinctive traits of Baby Boomers, X and Millennials. Clio America Journal, 11(22), 188-204.

Dobransky-Fasiska, D. (2002). *A discriminant analysis of entrepreneurial personality characteristics for each of three generational cohorts: The Silent Generation, the Baby Boomers, and Generation X.* University of Pittsburgh. ProQuest Dissertations Publishing. 3078835. https://www.proquest.com/openview/0ce8dee68ddf8ec22aa93b4d81f8868e/1?pq-origsite=gscholar&cbl=18750&diss=y

Dolot, A. (2018). The Characteristics of Generation Z. *E-Mentor*, *74*(2), 44-50. https://www.ceeol.com/search/article-detail?id=737237

Eisner, S. (2005, Autumn). *Managing Generation Y. Advanced Management Journal*, *70*(4), 4–15.

Enam, A., & Konduri, K. C. (2018). Time Allocation Behaviour of Twentieth-Century American Generations: GI Generation, Silent Generation, Baby Boomers, Generation X, and Millennials. *Transportation Research Record: Journal of the Transportation Research Board, 2672*(49), 69–80. doi:10.1177/0361198118794710

Fingerman, K., Pillemer, K., Silverstein, M., & Suitor, J. (2012). The Baby Boomers' Intergenerational Relationships. *The Gerontologist, 52*(2), 199–209. doi:10.1093/geront/gnr139

Gambone, M. (2005). *The Greatest Generation Comes Home: The Veteran in American Society*. Texas University Press.

Graybill, J. (2014, January). Millennials among the Professional Workforce in Academic Libraries: Their Perspective on Leadership. *Journal of Academic Librarianship, 40*(1), 10–15. https://doi.org/10.1016/j.acalib.2013.09.006

Hayes, J., Parks, C., McNeilly, S., & Johnson, P. (2018, November). Boomers to Millennials: Generational Stereotypes at Work in Academic Librarianship. *Journal of Academic Librarianship, 44*(6), 845–853. https://doi.org/10.1016/j.acalib.2018.09.011

Hershatter, A., & Epstein, M. (2010). Millennials and the World of Work: An Organization and Management Perspective. *Journal of Business and Psychology, 25*, 211–223. https://doi.org/10.1007/s10869-010-9160-y

Howe, N., & Strauss, W. (1992). *The New Generation Gap*. https://yacrisishotline.tripod.com/sitebuildercontent/sitebuilderfiles/thenewgenerationgap.pdf

Jimenez, T. J. P. (2018). *Digital skills and characteristics of generations*. September 20th, 2018. https://comunicacion897672657.wordpress.com/2018/09/20/habilidades-digitales-y-caracteristicas-de-las-generaciones/

Kertzer, D. I. (1983). Generation as a sociological problem. *Annual Review of Sociology, 9*(1), 125–149.

Kupperschmidt, B. R. (2000). Tips to help you recruit, manage, and keep Generation X employees. *Nursing Management, 31*(3), 58–60.

Leccardi, C., & Feixa, C. (2011). The concept of generation within the theories of youth. *Ultima Década, 19*(34), 11–32.

Lippincott, J. K. (2012). Information Commons: Meeting Millennials' Needs. *Journal of Library Administration, 52*, 6–7, 538–548. doi:10.1080/01930826.2012.707950

Mannheim, K. y de la Yncera, I. S. (1993). The problem with generations. *Reis,* (62), 193-242.

Martin, M. (2015). Ortega & Gasset's theory of generations: a look at the XXI Century. *Tiempo y espacio,* (20), 98-110.

Martin, N., & Prince, D. (2008). Factoring for X: An Empirical Study of Generation X's Materialistic Attributes. *Journal of Management and Marketing Research*. https://www.researchgate.net/profile/Diane-Fulton/publication/228488948_Factoring_for_X_An_Empirical_Study_of_Generation_X's_Materialistic_Attributes/links/54de25c40cf2814662eda78b/Factoring-for-X-An-Empirical-Study-of-Generation-Xs-Materialistic-Attributes.pdf

Massot, D. (2018). *Generation Z: 15 traits of those born between 1995 and 2010*. Published on 09/04/18. https://es.aleteia.org/2018/04/09/generacion-z-conocen-las-15-caracteristicas-de-los-nacidos-entre-1995y-2010/

McDonald, N. (2015). Are Millennials Really the "Go-Nowhere" Generation? *Journal of the American Planning Association*, *81*(2), 90–103. doi:10.1080/01944363.2015.1057196

Mill, J. S., & Navarro, M. Á. L. (1969). *Essay on freedom*. http://www.encuentrodefilantropos.co/Textos/Ensayo%20sobre%20la%20Libertad.pdf

National Administrative Department of Statistics. (2018a). *Colombia results: National total*. https://www.dane.gov.co/files/censo2018/infografias/info-CNPC-2018total-nal-colombia.pdf

National Administrative Department of Statistics. (2018b). *Population structure, men and women. Comparative 1985 and 2018*. https://sitios.dane.gov.co/cnpv/#!/est_pob

Otzen, T., & Manterola, C. (2017). Sampling techniques on a study population. *International Journal of Morphology*, *35*(1), 227–232.

Phillipson, C. (2007). Understanding the Baby Boom Generation: Comparative Perspectives. *International Journal of Ageing and Later Life*, *2*(2), 7–11.

Pumphrey, C. (2011). *How the Greatest Generation Works*. https://people.howstuffworks.com/culture-traditions/generation-gaps/greatest-generation1.htm

Rios, A. (2016). Characteristics of Colombian Baby Boomers. *Revistapym*. https://revistapym.com.co/caracteristicas-los-baby-boomers-colombianos

Rivas-Rodriguez, M. (2016). *A Soldier's Story: World War II and the Forgotten Battle for the Aleutian Islands*. https://www.kut.org/life-arts/2016-11-11/a-soldiers-story-world-war-ii-and-the-forgotten-battle-for-the-aleutian-islands

Rokeach, M. (1973). *The Nature of Human Values*. The Free Press. http://faculty.wwu.edu/tyrank/Rokeach%20Value%20Survey.pdf

Rose, K. (2008). *Myth and the Greatest Generation: A Social History of Americans in World War II*. Routledge.

Rosenberg, M. (2020). *Generational Names in the United States: Traditionalists, Gen Zs, and Everything in Between*. https://www.thoughtco.com/names-of-generations-1435472

Sánchez, M. A. (2018). *10 facts about Generation Z*. https://www.lavanguardia.com/vivo/20180715/45818419326/dia-habilidades-juventud-generacion-z.html

Singh, A. P., & Dangmei, J. (2016). Understanding the generation Z: the future workforce. *South -Asian Journal of Multidisciplinary Studies, 3*(3). https://www.researchgate.net/profile/Jianguanglung-Dangmei/publication/305280948_UNDERSTANDING_THE_GENERATION_Z_THE_FUTURE_WORKFORCE/links/5786a11008aef321de2c6f21/UNDERSTANDING-THE-GENERATION-Z-THE-FUTURE-WORKFORCE.pdf

Smith, R. (2020). *The Silent Generation: Characteristics and History*. https://www.familysearch.org/blog/en/silent-generation-characteristics/

Stone, O. (Director) & Pressman, E. (Producer) (1987). Wall Street. [Motion Picture]

Thomas, A., & Pickering, G. (2005). X-it: Gen-X and Older Wine Drinker Comparisons in New Zealand. *International Journal of Wine Marketing, 17*(2).

Time Magazine. (1951). *People: The Younger Generation.* http://content.time.com/time/subscriber/article/0,33009,856950,00.html

Van Selm, M., & Van den Heijkant, L. (2021). In Search of the Older Worker: Framing Job Requirements in Recruitment Advertisements Work. Aging and Retirement, 1–15. doi:10.1093/worker/waaa026

Warshaw, G., Bragg, E., Thomas, D., Ho, M. L., & Brewer, D. (2006). Are Internal Medicine Residency Programs Adequately Preparing Physicians to Care for the Baby Boomers? A National Survey from the Association of Directors of Geriatric Academic Programs Status of Geriatrics Workforce Study. *Journal of the American Geriatrics Society*. doi:10.1111/j.1532-5415.2006.00895.x

Whitney Gibson, J., Greenwood, R., and Murphy, E., Jr. (2009). Generational Differences in The Workplace: Personal Values, Behaviours, And Popular Beliefs. *Journal of Diversity Management, 4*(3).

Wilton, D. (2009). *G.I.* Wordorigins.org

Zemke, R., Raines, C., & Filipczak, B. (2013). *Generations at work: Managing the clash of Boomers, Gen Xers, and Gen Years in the workplace.* AMACOM Div. American Mgmt. Assn.

KEY TERMS AND DEFINITIONS

Baby Boomer Generation: "Baby boomer" is a term used to describe a person who was born between 1946 and 1964. The baby boomer generation makes up a substantial portion of the world's population, especially in developed nations. It represents 21.19% of the population of the United States of America. As the largest generational group in U.S. history (until the millennial generation slightly surpassed them), baby boomers have had—and continue to have—a significant impact on the economy. As a result, they are often the focus of marketing campaigns and business plans.

Gender: Gender refers to the characteristics of women, men, girls, and boys that are socially constructed. This includes norms, behaviours and roles associated with being a woman, man, girl, or boy, as well as relationships with each other. As a social construct, gender varies from society to society and can change over time. Gender is hierarchical and produces inequalities that intersect with other social and economic inequalities. Gender-based discrimination intersects with other factors of discrimination, such as ethnicity, socioeconomic status, disability, age, geographic location, gender identity and sexual orientation, among others.

Rokeach Value Survey (RVS): an instrument that assesses participants' values to help them determine what is most important in their lives and make good personal choices. Two kinds of values are distinguished in the survey: instrumental, that is, modes of conduct and behavioural characteristics that are seen as socially desirable; and terminal, that is, end states of existence or ultimate modes of living that have been idealized.

ENDNOTE

1 This generation is also referred to as Centennials.

APPENDIX

Baby Boomers' Survey in Colombia

The objective of this questionnaire is to collect information pertinent to the generation of Baby Boomers in Colombia, born between 1946 and 1964, thus permitting a comparison between characteristics and behaviours amongst Colombian Boomers and their European and American counterparts

1. Age: ______
2. Gender:
   a. Male ___
   b. Female ____
   c. Other ______
3. Paternal and/or Maternal Family
   a. Number of sisters _____
   b. Number of brothers ______
4. Marital Status:
   a. Married_____
   b. Bachelor/bachelorette______
   c. Widow/Widower ______
   d. Separated/Divorced ______
   e. Consensual union ______
5. Number of children: ________ Female: _____ Male: ______
6. Education level:
   a. Primary/basic ___
   b. Secondary____
   c. University____
   d. Specialisation ____
   e. Maester's degree_____
   f. Doctorate _____
   g. Post-doctorate studies_____
7. During the course of your working life, have you established/created your own company, registered with the respective government and private entities?
   a. Yes___
   b. No____
8. Are you a pensioner?
   a. Yes____
   b. No___
9. Please, describe the last activity you engaged in and/or are currently undertaking
10. List the value that is most important to you, with 1 being the most important, 2 being the least important, and so on up to number 9:
   a. Leading a comfortable live (a quiet life) _____

b. Equality (same amount of opportunities for everyone) _____
c. Leading an exciting life (an active and stimulating life) _____
d. Family safety (the wellbeing of loved ones) _____
e. Freedom (independence and free choice) _____
f. Health (physical and mental welfare) _____
g. Interior harmony (no internal conflicts) _____
h. Mature love (sexual and spiritual intimacy) _____
i. National security (state protection) ______

11. List the value that is most important to you, with 1 being the most important, 2 being the least important, and so on up to number 9:
    a. Pleasure (life's enjoyment) _____
    b. Salvation (believe in the afterlife) _____
    c. Respect for self (self-esteem) _____
    d. Sense of achievement (satisfaction for achieving goals) _____
    e. Social recognition (respect and admiration) _____
    f. True friendship (fraternal relationship with close people) _____
    g. Wisdom (a mature approach to life) _____
    h. A world in peace (a world free from wars and conflicts) _____
    i. A world of beauty (beauty of nature and the arts) _____
12. List the value that is most important to you, with 1 being the most important, 2 being the least important, and so on up to number 8:
    a. Ambitious (aspirations) _____
    b. Open minded (embracing different ideas) _____
    c. Capable (competent; effective) _____
    d. Clean and tidy _____
    e. Brave (stand my ground) _____
    f. Merciful (forgives others) _____
    g. Helpful (cares for other's welfare) _____
    h. Honest (true and sincere) _____
13. List the value that is most important to you, with 1 being the most important, 2 being the least important, and so on up to number 10:
    a. Entrepreneur _____
    b. Independent (self-sufficient) _____
    c. Intellectual (pensive, reflexive) _____
    d. Logical (rational) _____
    e. Caring (affectionate, tender) _____
    f. Loyal (faithful) _____
    g. Obedient (disciplined, respectful) _____
    h. Polite (courteous and kind) _____
    i. Responsible (trustworthy and committed) _____
    j. Self-contained (prudent) _____

Chapter 11
Back to School:
Mid-Life Adult Perspectives About Their Graduate Education

Özge Erdemli
https://orcid.org/0000-0002-8004-020X
Ankara University, Turkey

Nihan Demirkasımoğlu
Hacettepe University, Turkey

Tuğba Güner Demir
Ankara University, Turkey

ABSTRACT

This chapter aims to gain in-depth knowledge of the doctoral experience of older graduate students. For this purpose, a phenomenological study was conducted. Ten students aged 40 and older who are studying in graduate education were interviewed. Collected data were analyzed using descriptive and content analysis techniques. Findings revealed that being a doctoral student aged 40 and over has both advantages and disadvantages. Almost all of the participants try to complete their education simultaneously with their profession. In addition, they have heavier family responsibilities than the younger doctorants. This factor leads to a distraction and division in their motivation. However, it is clear that being in the university environment, acquiring new perspectives, and producing something new gives satisfaction to the participants despite the existing difficulties. On the other hand, young doctorants' insufficient professional experience makes older PhDs advantageous in terms of integrating their professional experience with doctoral education.

INTRODUCTION

In the 21st century, education has become a vital component in many older adults' lives. Although the role of education largely focuses on investing the youth, education is a lifelong process and that is a

DOI: 10.4018/978-1-7998-2395-7.ch011

Copyright © 2022, IGI Global. Copying or distributing in print or electronic forms without written permission of IGI Global is prohibited.

worthwhile investment for all ages (Burdett, 2008). Universities and graduate education are seen as part of lifelong learning and as a result, the average age of graduate students is increasing (Lauzon, 2011). In line with the aging trend of the world, The United Nations stated that the number of people over 60 will triple from 2010 to 2050. As a result of this increase, it is expected that there will be a 300% growth in the number of older adults between 2000 and 2050 (Findsen & Formosa, 2011). For this reason, the aging population has become an important research topic that attracts the attention of researchers. Diverse needs of both aging adults and the job market directs the growing aging population to more learning opportunities and higher levels of education. Today, doctoral education is one of these opportunities that attracts the older workforce than in the past. Recently, As Poulter (2017) indicated, new ways to achieve doctoral qualification have multiplied, and with this growth and diversification, the learning identities of participants participating in doctoral programs have also expanded and diversified (Poulter, 2017). If older adults can be supported to develop their competencies, their status may turn from a burden to an opportunity (Kanter, 2006).

The median age at entry to doctoral programs is 29 on average across The Organisation for Economic Co-operation and Development (OECD) countries, with 60% of entrants aged between 26 and 37 (OECD, 2019). Therefore, it can be stated that entry to doctoral programs is generally under the age of 40 among OECD countries. However, there is an undeniable participation in doctoral programs outside these age ranges. The average age at entry to doctoral programs in Turkey is 29, which is the OECD average (OECD, 2019). According to the data of the Turkish the Council of Higher Education (CoHE), 18876 students were enrolled in doctoral programs in the 2020-2021 academic year in Turkey, and 11.13% of them are 40 years old and over (CoHE, 2021). When the statistics for 2013-2014 are analyzed, it is noteworthy that the rate of new students aged 40 and over enrolled in doctoral programs is 3.98% (CoHE, 2013). Therefore, there has been a significant increase in enrollment of adults aged 40 and over in doctoral programs in Turkey over a seven-year period. At this point, older adult learners are seen as an important human resource that needs to be encouraged, empowered, and valued (Freedman, 2011). As the doctoral students of the future will not be just young adults, graduate adults expect more from the universities. Revealing the educational expectations of older adults in graduate education will guide universities in understanding and developing supportive initiatives to meet the needs of this experienced growing population in the workforce. In Turkey, 106148 doctoral students are studying in the 2020-2021 academic year, and 19.3% of these students are 40 years old and above (CoHE, 2021). The fact that Turkey's elderly population has increased by 22.5% in the last five years (Turkish Statistical Institute, 2020), it makes worth empirically researching the phenomenon of aging workforce and graduate studentship experiences within Turkish context.

BACKGROUND

Although graduate students have a lot in common with undergraduate students, they have differentiating characteristics (Kerns, 2006). Therefore, historically, graduate students have been defined as individuals who need different attention and support from undergraduate students (Schroeder & Terras, 2015). The definition of adult learner in higher education is mostly used to cover all university students aged 18 and over. Although non-traditional older student is generally used to describe individuals who are 25 years or older, there is no common definition of older graduate student (Barker et al., 1997). The educational opportunities and support needs needed for youth and adult students coexisting in higher education differ, and there is often an increase in problematic situations for older students (Kasworm, 2003). As the population of "non-traditional" students in higher education, including older adults, increases, the demographics of the student population are changing and a wide variety of experiences emerge. Increasing numbers of adults are returning to school after a long time (Cooper, 1999).

Some students start their graduate studies right after undergraduate education, while for others, this period may take place in the middle or later stages of their career. For students in the second group, it may not be easy to find peers with whom they can easily relate, and they may have different responsibilities in their lives that challenge them. When the challenging conditions of the job market are added to this situation, different learning experiences from traditional graduate experiences may emerge (Polson, 2003). Especially after a long break from undergraduate or graduate education, new doctorates are not familiar with the traditions and requirements of the new institution when they start their education in different places from the universities they graduated from. Therefore, in both higher education and adult education literature, there is a need to recognize postgraduate students in their different aspects as a group with unique identity and needs (Kerns, 2006).

Reasons of Graduate Education for Older Students

The increase in adult participation in graduate education is a result of their beliefs about the importance of a graduate degree in achieving job stability, financial support, and relevant life opportunities. Increasing and diversifying expectations from employees in the business world require adults to access new information (Kasworm, 2003). For these reasons, many older adults seek active learning and continuing education in different areas of life. This pursuit of learning is a necessity for the individual to survive in today's global conditions (Cooper, 1999). According to Mezirow (1991), adults need to learn to change the structure of their expectations, rather than to fill their lack of knowledge. The main reasons for adult students to come to university can be expressed as better career opportunities, improving general knowledge level and improving self-esteem (Broekemier, 2002).

The learning motivations of older students are shaped by demographic, economic and technological developments. More specifically, this group continues their education life to establish and develop social friendships, serve the society better, support their professional development and pursue a new career (Broekemier, 2002). Another reason counted among the reasons for students' postgraduate education tendencies is; the uncertainty of the job market and the threat of rising unemployment since the late 1980s. More specifically, it is considered as a tool for the market to internalize the professional discourse and behavior model of graduate students (Guillory, 1996). Most studies of the graduate experience of adult students focus on the experiences of female students, as their number is increasing and they make up more than half of the graduate student ratio (Cooper, 1999). In a study examining the reasons for women to choose postgraduate education, most of the women mentioned their expectations in the job market, their desire to change jobs, a better career and pay. In addition to these, women gave reasons such as "becoming someone" or of "finding out who I am" (Taylor & Marienau, 1995).

Baker (1992), in his research on graduate students over the age of 25, states that as the age of the students increases, the number of female, part-time and married students also increases. According to the results of the Adult Skills Survey, a product of the International Adult Skills Assessment Program (PIAAC) conducted by the OECD on the competence of adults at a global level, Turkey is one of the countries where gender-based differences in information processing skills of older adults are the highest, to the detriment of women (OECD, 2016).

Challenges of Graduate Education for Older Student

In a study examining five university cohorts for a graduate degree program to learn out their good and bad learning experiences revealed that adult students think positive about if the program is meaningful, they receive feedback, group interactions and active participation. They negatively evaluated situations such as fear, anxiety, lack of respect, injustice, lack of support, unclear teacher expectations from the course and the lack of evaluation criteria, crowded groups, cold classrooms and too early class hours (Reiff & Ballin, 2008). According to the results of the research on the problems faced by teachers, administrators and inspectors who are studying in the field of educational sciences, it has been determined that the problems that are difficult for adults in graduate education are that the homework cannot be done in the desired quality due to the excess of homework, the overlapping of the course hours and the working hours, the library being open during working hours and the difficulties in reaching the counselors (Nayır, 2011). In another study, it was determined that adult female postgraduate students had difficulties such as having classes during workhours, lack of childcare support, and the institutional policies that are not sensitive to these special needs (Lewis, 1988).

In a study conducted based on interviews with nine graduate students to explain the perceived counseling needs and experiences of students from different learning environments, it was determined that all adult graduate students need quality and holistic counseling, regardless of the learning environment (Schroeder & Terras, 2015). Baker (1992), on the other hand, in his study investigating the needs of graduate students aged 25 and over, determined that all of the participants gave high priority to counseling, library and computer services. It has been determined that those over the age of 32 need orientation programs with high priority, and students between the ages of 25-32 need economic support. Sudol and Hall (1991) determined that older graduate students had to spend a significant part of their income to finance their education expenses and therefore they considered it a mistake to return to the graduate education. Further, older graduates reported the insufficient support of the university in terms of accommodation and insurance. In addition, the generational differences between graduate students and their professors may result in difficulties in understanding each other due to differences in student experiences. The conditions and attitudes of new-style graduate students may conflict with the way graduate programs run by the conservatively trained professor (Hovey, 1964). Such changing demographic realities require rethinking and restructuring student services. Today's graduate students have such diverse needs that multiple service providers need to take responsibility, including individual counselors, departments, universities, institutes and student offices (Polson, 2003).

Finally, according to the results of a recent study conducted on 1367 doctoral students from 15 different universities in Turkey, it was determined that the dissatisfaction of the students, especially at the proficiency exam stage, reached the highest level and their satisfaction with the content of the programs, the doctorate area and faculty members decreased significantly from the second year. It was determined that students in the field of social sciences mainly complained that research methods were not adequately taught (Bozkurt et al., 2021). When literature and past research presented so far are evaluated together, but no empirical analysis of the doctoral adventure of graduate students aged 40 and over as adult learners has been found focusing the Turkish context. The rich data potential of qualitative research seems appropriate in understanding the experience of such a group with a deep and thick understanding.

The Purpose of the Study

The purpose of this phenomenological research is to grasp a detailed understanding of older doctoral students of Turkish higher education aged 40 and over. To this end, research questions were formulated as follows:

1. What are the reasons for adults aged 40 and over preferring graduate programs?
2. What are the characteristics required to succeed in doctoral programs?
3. How do the PhD students aged 40 and over perceive themselves different from the younger PhDs?
4. What are the difficulties that adults aged 40 and over face in their doctoral programs?
5. What are the expectations of adults aged 40 and over for their professional development from doctoral programs?

METHOD

This study, which aims to gain in-depth knowledge of the experience of older graduate students, was conducted with a qualitative phenomenological approach. Phenomenology is focused on individuals' meaning making as the quintessential element of the human experience (Patton, 2014). In this study, the graduate experiences of individuals aged 40 and over are investigated in depth.

Study Group

Criterion sampling was used in the selection of participants. The criterion is that graduate students are 40 years or older. Also, 10 students aged 40 and older who are studying in graduate education were be selected to ensure diversity in terms of gender, age and area of study (e.g, medical sciences and educational sciences). Demographic information on the participants is presented in Table 1.

Table 1. Demographic information of the participants

Code	Gender	Age	Marital Status	Children	Area of Study	Year of Start of Doctorate	Education Period	Employment Status
P1	Female	42	Yes	Yes	Medical sciences	2018	Thesis period	Yes
P2	Male	46	Yes	Yes	Educational Sciences	2014	Thesis period	Yes
P3	Male	47	Yes	Yes	Educational Sciences	2017	Thesis period	Yes
P4	Male	54	Yes	Yes	Medical sciences	2017	Thesis period	Yes
P5	Male	51	Yes	Yes	Medical sciences	2019	Course period	Yes
P6	Male	45	Yes	Yes	Educational Sciences	2014	Thesis period	No
P7	Male	56	Yes	Yes	Medical sciences	2018	Thesis period	Yes
P8	Female	41	No	No	Educational Sciences	2019	Thesis period	Yes
P9	Female	44	Yes	Yes	Medical sciences	2018	Thesis period	Yes
P10	Male	44	Yes	Yes	Educational Sciences	2018	Thesis period	Yes

As seen in Table 1, the participants consist of three female and seven male students—their ages change from 41 to 56 years old. The marital status of one of the participants is single, while the other participants are married. All of the married participants have children. Five of the participants are studying at medical sciences, others at educational sciences. Their year of start of doctorate change from 2014 to 2019. One participant is in the course period, while the other participants are in the thesis period. As part of the research ethics, the participants were anonymized by coding as P1, P2,....P10 (Hammersly & Traianou, 2017).

Data Collection

Data were collected through a semi-structured interview form developed by the researchers. After the draft interview form is prepared, experts' views were applied for the validity of the scope. Interviews with participants were conducted online (in online media such as Skype, Google meetings, Zoom). The interviews took place in July 2021 and August 2021. All the participants were ensured anonymity, and confidentiality. An audio recording was made with permission from the participants. Ethical approval for the current study was granted by the Ethics Committee.

Data Analysis

Collected data were analyzed using descriptive and content analysis techniques with the NVivo 10 software Application. In the analysis process, transcript files were opened in NVivo, and categories and themes were created by coding the opinions of the participants. On the other hand, some themes were derived deductively in line with the pre-determined questions. For the reliability of the analyses, each researcher first analyzed the data and then compared coding schemas. According to Creswell (1998), inter-rater evaluation is one of the methods used in providing reliability. In addition, detailed descriptions were done during the data collection and analysis process (Yıldırım & Şimşek, 2018) and direct citations were included in the presentation of the data (Merriam, 2015).

RESULTS

The views of adults post graduate adults aged 40 and over were themed in line with the aims of the research and the research questions were used as pre-determined themes.

Reasons for Adults Age 40 and Over to Prefer a Doctorate

Adults aged 40 and over expressed their reasons for choosing the doctoral program from different perspectives. These reasons are explained below under the relevant sub-themes.

Personal and Professional Development

Participants stated that they preferred doctoral programs primarily to provide personal and professional development. Besides, adults prefer doctoral programs in order to be more successful in their profession and to do their work more selflessly while fulfilling their duties and in promotion situations. P6, who worked as a teacher in a school, took the job of school administrator and chose the doctorate program in the field of educational administration in order to be successful in this field. He expressed: "I decided to know the requirements of my job and to do it properly."

To Be an Academic Staff

Some of the participants related their graduate education with their long-term goals and a work transition from school to university. For example, P3 explained his motivation with the following sentences:

My goal was to focus on the main subject, to go to university, to become an academician. If this is not possible, I want to go to university part time. I don't know if it's still going on, but in the past, there was part-time work, and they were assigning people to the university for additional course fees. I am trying to be in this academic environment, in this university environment, I want it. Cause that atmosphere makes me feel comfortable.

As can be understood from the above statement, some of the adults prefer doctoral programs with the aim of becoming academicians in universities in the future. However, there are also participants who stated that they do not aim for this, but prefer these programs because they enjoy being involved in scientific studies. For example, P2 told, "Let me be an associate professor as a distant target after completing the doctorate, I did not think about it. In other words, only after completing this master's degree, let me continue in the scientific environment, this was the purpose".

Producing Original-Scientific Studies

Another reason why middle-aged adults prefer doctoral programs is the desire to produce original and scientific studies. Some adults, who enjoy producing scientific and original things in master's degree, expressed that they want to continue this situation in doctorate. A PhD candidate in the field of public health expressed his thoughts with these words:

My aim was to put my studies on a scientific basis over the years, and to share the achievements obtained in some areas that are lacking in our country, especially by doing epidemiology and field studies, with those who are interested in publications.

P8 similarly supports this view with the sentences "I wanted to be a link in the chain of the minds that read and think and produce in this country".

Friend Influence

The influence of peers is an important driving force in the preference of doctoral programs. One of the participants (P5) expressed the beginning of his doctoral story as follows: "I decided and started when some of my friends started their doctorate in 2018" (P5), while another participant (P7) stated: "In 2017, I started another program. My doctor friend, who started a different doctoral program at the university, talked about the courses and the environment in his doctoral program, and I was interested."

Finding Previous Graduations Unsatisfactory

Some participants drew attention to the fact that their current diplomas lost their value over time in their preference for graduate education programs (P3): "I realized that over time that having a bachelor's degree had lost its meaning"; He added that he did not need postgraduate education when he first graduated because even the number of teachers with undergraduate degrees was low at that time (at that time there were more teachers with undergraduate degree), but this graduation lost its meaning with time and many teachers now have graduate degrees. There are other participants with similar views from medical sciences. For example P4 said, "First of all, I realized that the Master's program was not enough. (It) should have gone further."

Characteristics Required to Succeed in a Ph.D. Program

According to adults aged 40 and over, individuals must have various characteristics in order to be successful in doctoral programs. These characteristics stated by the participants are explained below.

Foreign Language Proficiency

According to the participants who have a PhD, one of the keys to being successful is to have foreign language proficiency. P7 stated: "Foreign language is important because it is possible to benefit from a wider resource pool". One of the participants P4 told:

It is necessary to know at least one foreign language. It is better if a second foreign language is known. It is not enough to just do research in English. In the broadest sense, it is necessary to do research in German, French and Spanish. Not every information is available in the USA or England.

Being a Researcher and Interrogator

As can be understood from the statement of the P7: "It is necessary to be investigative and especially interrogative", it is important to be successful in the doctoral education. In addition, enjoying to do research and not to get tired of researching (P3) is seen important during this process.

Field Knowledge Proficiency

In order to achieve success in doctoral programs, the fact that people have knowledge in the field they are doing is another feature emphasized by the participants. For example P2 stated:

First, the person must have a good grasp of the conceptual and theoretical framework of the field in which he will do his doctorate. When you say being a judge, you are making progress in the doctoral education process, but he has to have knowledge about that field, to attract attention, so he has to have a certain competency related to that field, first of all.

It can be inferred that having a certain knowledge about the field is considered important by the participants. Another support comes from P7, signifying the importance of being knowledgeable in the field of study:

For my own doctoral program, Public Health, having worked in this field before and having a public health perspective in different fields is a plus. As I am still a general practitioner, reconciling what I learned with current practices also provides permanent knowledge.

Time Management

Participants pointed out the importance of time management in order to be successful in doctoral studies. P6's statements evidence this sub-theme as follows:

It is necessary to be multi-disciplined. It is necessary to know time management very well. You know, you need to be able to plan your duties very well, without disrupting your duties while working and without disrupting your responsibilities towards your family. Otherwise, something remains to be missing.

Be Eager to Learn

An important aspect of being successful in a doctorate is that the person doing the doctorate is eager to learn new information. P5 expressed his views as "It is important to be willing to learn new things and to have a sense of duty". P7 supports this issue and said:

I started my PhD program when I was 53 years old. I think my age is a bit older for the doctorate program. Age factor is not a factor that affects participation in this program, learning something and self-development. The intensity of the work you actually do during the doctoral program, the extra time you can spare and the desire to improve yourself are much more important. It is important to be willing.

Reading and Observing

According to the participants, in order to be successful in doctoral programs, individuals must also have good reading and observation skills. While P3 expressed his views on this subject with the sentences "Maybe it will be a classical answer, but to be successful in the doctorate, read once, read, read, read", P1 explains with the statements "To be successful in the program process, there must be reading, listening and observing". Similarly, P4 draws attention to this issue with the sentences:

It is necessary to work hard, to do very serious research, to ask many questions, to know the deficits of our country, to know its surpluses, to know what we can bring to our country, to know how to combine experience and knowledge through academic means.

Choosing the Right Student

An important component of achieving success in doctoral programs has been expressed as choosing the right student. Participant opinions on this subject are given below. Sample participant views are given below:

Our state should determine this well, why are we doing the doctorate, that is, to produce scientific studies, to produce original things, to make it useful for the country, isn't it the state allocates money for this, so it is necessary to choose people who will work for this purpose. In other words, let me do a doctorate for a job, I will cover a place, then I will sleep for the rest of my life, I will be comfortable, yes, the state provides me with funds rather than people with such a mentality, I use them, so I have to repay them with a debt to my state, to my nation, so I have to produce, I have to contribute. I need to develop people with this type of structure should choose. I don't know if we can choose, of course, this is a separate dimension, I think it would be better if it was like that (P2).

Those who really want to do the doctorate, people over the age of 35, those who have serious experience but are not aware of how to do the job and what they can do should do it, one should not get a doctorate just to get a title, to do and develop things that are not available in the world or in Turkey... Those who contribute to the desired field should do a doctorate, should be inclined to multidisciplinary and multisectoral work, those who have a rich view and are open to development should do a doctorate (P4).

As can be seen from the above views, it is important that the people who will enroll in doctoral programs are selected from those who have the awareness to contribute to the field by producing truly scientific and original studies.

Determination and Perseverance

Being determined is another characteristic that helps to achieve success in doctoral programs according to the participants of the research. P1, who started his doctoral education at the age of 39, told, "I think there should be no age restriction or preference for starting doctoral education. I think that determination and perseverance are enough to successfully complete the program process." Similarly, P8 noted, "In order to be successful, the individual must have characteristics such as perseverance and determination."

Other Features

In addition to the above-mentioned features, some of the participants mentioned the competence of self-expression, open-mindedness, and being open to interdisciplinary work. Some of the students' opinions on this subject are given below:

Even if you know more than the teachers, the way you express this is also important, you should pay attention to this, otherwise the teachers may react to you (P4).

It is necessary to be open-minded, that is, it is necessary to be open-minded about researching what is going on without prejudice, not reading and researching in order to confirm the accuracy of what you know... (P6)

For continuous improvement, in order to improve myself, to teach the new generation how to do better, it is necessary to be open to working with different sectors and disciplines (P4).

Differences With Young Doctorates

The participants were asked what they would say if they compared themselves with young doctorants, and the answers obtained from the participants were analyzed under various themes.

Experience

When the participants compare themselves with young doctorants, they especially draw attention to the issue of experience. Participants over the age of 40 emphasized that the experience they have in professional life provides them with significant benefits. Some of these opinions are given below:

I was 49 years old. Frankly, I wish I could have started earlier, but I do not think that age affects the doctoral process negatively; on the contrary, I even see the benefits of experience in working life (P5).

Age can have its advantages and disadvantages. The advantage of starting late can be that the person can choose the courses that suit his needs more with the work experience he has gained, and the things he learned in the doctorate can be more useful because it will be added to an experience (P6).

As I said before, I started the doctoral program in my 29th year in the profession. In other words, I had earned the right to retire... At my age, both my actual job and my previous working life being in primary care gives me intense experience and good manners (P7).

My experience in my profession contributes to me as it is related to my doctoral department (P9).

As can be seen, middle-aged adults stated that they had benefited from their Professional experience through gaining a certain perspective. Participants also drew attention to the fact that young doctorants can sometimes make wrong interpretations due to being inexperienced. For example, a participant (P2) stated:

There are novices among young people, for example, they suddenly learn an idea, especially in social sciences, in things where the results do not have sharp results like in positive sciences, if we do this, that's what happens. However, when you have management experience, you say, look, it does not produce such a result. In other words, age and experience give a practical perspective.

Time

Adults participating in the research think that young doctoral students are more advantageous in terms of time. As a matter of fact, P7 pointed out the importance of having more time "Young friends have more new information and time to research". P6 stressed the families responsibilities as follows: "Of course, the advantage of starting early is that there may be less factors such as family responsibilities, child responsibility, job responsibilities that will prevent from the doctorate", and that young doctorants may have more time because of the possibility that their family, child and work responsibilities may be less, and they are more likely to spare time for studying. Stating that he tried to overcome the problems he experienced in terms of time due to his responsibilities, thanks to the support of his wife and the sacrifices he made, P3's views on this subject are as follows:

For example, I have children, I have two children, I have two daughters, they have education, they have homework, etc. but my wife also has support in this regard. I mean, I couldn't take it without support, I also sacrificed myself, and for example, I sleep less.

Language Competency

Another issue that the participants emphasized when they compared themselves with young doctors is that young adults think that their language proficiency is better. While P2 of the participants expressed their thoughts on this subject with the statements "their language skills could be better", P3 expressed their opinions on this subject with the sentences "Let me say that their foreign language knowledge is better than me, they are good as a foreign language".

Another issue that the participants emphasized when older adults compared themselves to young doctorants, they think younger doctorants' language proficiency is better. While P2 expressed his views as "their language skills can be better", P3 stated that "Let me say that their foreign language is better than me, they are good in foreign language ".

Work-Productivity

Younger adults with a doctorate may be more productive, according to the opinions of adults aged 40 and over who participated in the study. One participant explains his views on this subject with the following words:

And now young friends are more productive. For example, there are young friends like you, of course, I am not in a race with them and I have never seen myself like that, but they are more productive, I can see that. For example, we have an article requirement to complete the doctorate, you know, I tried so hard to write one article myself, I was able to write one.

P8 stressed the importance of being update though self-criticism as follows: "There were also issues where I noticed my own shortcomings. These were the times when I felt that I was unfamiliar with many recent topics during the discussions during the lecture, and that my student perspective was dulled." However, there are also participants who thought the opposite and stated that young adults are less hardworking. For example, P3 noted, "There is a bit of callousness in the younger generation, there is a little less work, so if I were at that age, if I had that energy, I would work harder and do more. As it can be understood from the statements "I think they read a little less". This criticism implies that young adults do not use their energy fully.

Challenges Adults 40 and Over Face in Doctoral Programs

Adults aged 40 and over may also encounter various difficulties in doctoral programs. These difficulties expressed by the participants are described below.

Time Constraint

The difficulty mostly mentioned was the time pressure. Some of the opinions of the participants regarding this difficulty are given below:

When I started my doctorate, I was 39 years old, you are married, you have children, you have a job, I was working as an administrator, and you need to allocate time for the doctorate. You are divided, I wonder if I am neglecting my family, am I neglecting my job, these are the first things in the background. After that, you say to quit the doctorate because it really takes a lot of time (P2).

It is an important issue to encourage or at least help people in working life so that they can spare time for their academic education in their professional subjects. Especially at the beginning of working life, it is very difficult to find and maintain this opportunity with work. For these reasons, I could not think of graduate education until now (P5).

The biggest challenge in the lesson phase is that the lessons are during working hours and for this, I can spare time from my actual work. Sometimes I used my permissions for this. I was usually able to find time in the evenings and weekends to prepare assignments and presentations (P7).

As can be seen from the above opinions, participants in the doctoral program may have difficulty in finding time for attendance and homework due to their work. Moreover, they may even have to leave some of their duties due to these difficulties. Among the participants who experienced such a situation, P6 expressed their views as follows:

For example, when I first started, I had a similar difficulty. At that time, I was working as an assistant principal at a school. I asked permission from the school to continue my doctoral studies. The school said it couldn't let me. He sent my permission petition to the Provincial Directorate of National Education. The Provincial Directorate of National Education gave me a letter saying that it is not in the public interest for the school administrator to have a doctorate, so it cannot be allowed. For this reason, I had to resign from my managerial position at the school.

One participant (P3) tried to overcome these difficulties in attendance by taking unpaid leave and expressed this situation as follows:

I started my doctorate in 2017, but because I am a classroom teacher, there was a problem in attending the courses. This time, I had to take unpaid leave, civil servants who completed 5 years get 12 months of unpaid leave, what did I do, I took 8 months for one, so I passed two terms like that, summer vacation came in between, then I took 4 months and saved three terms in this way.

Challenges to the Thesis

Most of the participants included to this research are at the thesis period. Therefore, among the difficulties they have mentioned, there are thesis-related problems. First of all, some participants stated that they had difficulties in choosing a thesis topic. P7 stated: “I still have difficulties in choosing a thesis topic. The intensity of my advisor and the factors brought by the pandemic that has been experienced for more than a year led to a decrease in my motivation”. Another challenge is experienced at the thesis writing process. For example, P1 reported: “There may be difficulties in obtaining research permissions from the sectors that will cooperate in thesis research”. P2 expressed the importance of the advisor’s critical role to overcome this problem as follows:

Now this thesis is very important, the advisor is very important because now you develop a thesis proposal, write it and send it to the teacher. The advisor corrects that you will write in capital letters here and put a comma here. I’m not saying these are important or unimportant, but they are not things your advisor should check. So, could you put that scientific study model well? are there any dead ends? The advisor should be able to see the problems you will experience when you develop the proposal and research questions. Believe me when you can’t see it, you are really trying for nothing… You know, I expect this from the advisor. When I ask the question, what will be the result? The advisor should pay attention to these; the advisor should intervene in these matters.

Transportation

Adults also mentioned the transportation problem as a difficulty. For example, P6 reported his challenge because of living a different city than his doctoral study as follows:

I made a round trip from a different city to my doctorate classes. It was really challenging, I mean, going to class until the evening, leaving here at 4 or 5 pm, coming to Ankara by bus, entering the class and then returning home, it used to find 10 pm-22.30 pm. Coming back home was really tiring, it’s a hassle. During this period, I was always asking myself the following question when I was leaving Ankara for class and returning home, “Is the things I learned today worth the hardship?” and my answer was always positive so I continued with the strength from what I learned there.

As can be seen from the above view, adults participating in the program from different cities describe their fatigue as a difficulty. They try to overcome this difficulty by justifying their earnings at the end of the day.

Difficulties in Measurement and Evaluation

Some of the participants stated that they had difficulties in the measurement-evaluation processes. By stating that "I had no problems with homework, but some teachers gave standard grades. I was angry at this", P4 criticizes that assessment and evaluation is not fair and giving standard grades to everyone makes him angry. One of the participants, P5 told, "I am not very familiar with this system since the university I graduated from is not in the credit system. I had a little difficulty with this."

Budget Crunch

The budget and its size needed to finance the expenses to survive doctoral education, is another challenging point. For example, P2 reported:

You need to buy books and allocate a budget for this, which can cause difficulties from time to time. For example, if you take one day off to the classes I mentioned earlier, your additional course is cut off when you become an administrator. This creates a resource problem.

P3 complained that taking unpaid leave to continue the courses in the doctorate caused a budget problem. My wife works and I had savings, we used them at that time." expresses it in words.

The Expectations of Adults Aged 40 and Over for Their Professional Development From Doctoral Programs

Another theme of the research is the expectations of older adults regarding the contribution of doctoral programs to their professional development.

Creating a Career Advantage

Adults over the age of 40 expect to gain an advantage in their careers by developing professionally after completing their doctoral program. While P1 expressed this expectation with the phrase "I believe it can provide an advantage in terms of career," P8 said:

My biggest expectation is to be an expert in my field in a professional sense. Because in this field, first of all, myself and my teachers really put effort, time and effort. I have occupied this country's university chair to train a scientist candidate for this country. I want to give you your due.

He emphasized the importance of professional expertise for himself. On the other hand, there are also participants who think that doctoral education will not bring any benefits in terms of career advancement. Two participants, who expressed their views in this line are from the field of educational administration in social sciences and explained his views with the following words:

There is not an iota of value to do a doctorate in National Education. This happens, go to the ministry, in front of many people's names, Dr. or there are associate professors, but they did not come to these authorities with their knowledge. If these authorities are political authorities, if there are bilateral rela-

tions, you will progress in National Education, you will be the Head of the Department, you will be the general manager, but other than that, I will earn the title of doctor right now. Unfortunately, there is no such thing in National Education (P3).

I was excited about the education system, I had thoughts that I could contribute to the education system. I had thoughts that I could improve the school where I worked. But then I realized that I couldn't achieve these things in my lifetime. When I first started my doctorate, the thought that there is no public interest in the director of the Provincial Directorate of National Education killed my thoughts. After that, I don't think that anyone who has a doctorate in the national education system or who wants to make a contribution is supported, it's more of a systemic problem. I don't think it's just a me problem (P6).

Broadening the Perspective

Another expectation from these programs for adults over the age of 40 who are doing their doctorate is to broaden their perspectives. Moreover, participants with doctoral education state that this process contributes to the expansion of their perspectives even before completing the program. The opinions of the participants on this subject are given below.

It gave me a broader perspective. It allowed me to see the relationships between my PhD field and other fields. I have established relationships and bridges with other fields of interest and work in my doctoral field, and I have developed those fields as well (P4).

I realize that I approach the subjects that I need information about by researching from more sources and considering all aspects. If I am going to give information to others on a subject, I do not trust a single source; I feel the need to look at other sources (P5)

Its effect on my personal and professional development was eye-opening for me, I mean, maybe I had thoughts about events before, or I could express my opinion in the face of an event, but I learned to look at the events more objectively or to analyze the problems more deeply in the doctorate. That is, it has made significant contributions not only in my professional life but also in my personal life (P6)

Transition to University (As Academics)

It was determined that some of the participants who participated in the research had the goal of becoming an academician by going to a post-doctoral university. P4 from expressed this expectation as follows: "I want to be an academician in my field of study, because I believe that those who come from the practice or those who are both in the practice and in the academy will be more successful in the academic field". P7 explained his motivation to publish and become an academician by conducting post-doctoral scientific research with the following sentences:

After completing my doctorate, if I still feel motivated and can find a suitable environment, I would like to do research, have a higher level of knowledge on certain subjects, write articles and share them in scientific journals and media, and develop projects. Academically, if I feel competent, it will be good to have the appropriate title and staff.

Socialization

Adults aged 40 and over also stated that the doctoral process created a certain professional socialization environment for them. P4 described this situation as "I developed personal relationships" while P2 reported:

Going there, coming there, breathing the air of a university again, because you graduated in 98, 16 years have passed, so you enter the university again 16 years later. You smell the air there, there is information sharing, there is a conversation with friends.

As can be seen, returning to university allows middle-aged adults to make new friends and socialization opportunities. P7 supports this approach in that: "I have made good friendships with young friends, new colleagues and professors in the department".

DISCUSSION AND CONCLUSION

This phenomenological qualitative research focused the views of adults aged 40 and over about their Ph.D. experiences. Firstly, the reasons for preferring doctoral education were questioned. It was found that the participants doctoral education was preferred to ensure their personal and professional development, to rise in their profession or to switch to academia. However, expectations of some participants were not met during the doctoral process. The main reason why having a Ph.D. will not have a positive impact on older adults' professional careers is the prevalence of practices that do not attach importance to merit in the transition to higher positions. On the other hand, the majority of participants expect to change their professional career and become an academician after their doctorate. Green and Powell (2005) emphasize that the purpose of doctoral education in countries such as Poland, the Netherlands and England is a door to an academic career. Similarly, Karadağ's (2014) study, in which he examined the doctoral education process in Turkey, stated that the individual and organizational purpose of doctoral education is to train faculty members/scientists and to contribute to the development of disciplines.

Another theme of the research was the characteristics that ensure success in doctoral education. Participants intensely emphasized foreign language proficiency among the features that ensure success. Matas (2012) also asserted that knowing a foreign language, especially English, is a competency that doctoral students should have. Considering that most of the publications in the academic world are in English, it is possible to state that knowing a foreign language is a basic requirement beyond achieving success in doctoral education. As a matter of fact, Nerad and Tryzna (2008) stated that English has become a global language in doctoral education. In many countries, including European countries, the language of instruction for the doctorate is English. Researches and presentations are made in English. Most scientific journals are published in English. Even communication on the Internet is mostly carried out in English. In summary, the authors point out that English has become the dominant academic language at the international level. These statements are also consistent with the findings of this study.

In this study, it was revealed that one of the conditions for success in the doctoral program is personal characteristics. Findings revealed that it is important for a person to be inquisitive and questioning, observable, eager to learn, determined and determined to achieve success. As a matter of fact, Parker (2012) stated that candidates who will start their doctoral education should have critical scientific skills such as accessing new information, producing new information and thinking creatively, as well as competencies such as reading and evaluating the literature, determining the research topic, planning and conducting a scientific research, and field knowledge. While the participants stated that having these characteristics is important for success, it was emphasized that the doctoral process also played a role in acquiring these characteristics and broadened the students' perspective. As a matter of fact, Tzanakou (2014) also stated that beyond the expertise gained by the doctoral education, it provides problem solving, critical reasoning, and in-depth thinking skills from different perspectives.

In the study, the age factor was one of the variables taken into account in doctoral education. Participants stated that young doctors have better language proficiency and can be more productive. It is possible to explain this situation with the spread of language education and the increasing opportunities in language education with the developing technology. On the other hand, older Ph.D students perceived their experience to make a positive contribution to their education when compared to young doctorants. However, they stated that they had difficulty in allocating time for doctoral education compared to young doctorates due to the increase in their responsibilities in both business and family life with the advancing time. The time problem also stands out among the difficulties they encounter during the doctoral process. It has been observed that students have difficulties in attending classes, especially during the course period, since the classes are within working hours. In Sudoll and Hall's (1991) study, graduate students stated that they had problems with time. They stated that meetings, symposiums and conferences were held in the afternoon and therefore they did not attend these events due to both their work and their families. Another finding of this study was to deal with this challenge. Successful time management skills were considered to be necessary to handle this challenge.

Another difficulty that the doctoral students face is related to the thesis process. Findings implied that advisors did not meet the older students expectations satisfactorily. As a matter of fact, research on the graduate education process comes to the fore with the supervisor-student relations (Ezebilo, 2012). For example, Kehm (2006) reports that there are important problems regarding the doctoral advising process in Europe. Accordingly, despite the innovation efforts to develop the dyadic relations between student and advisor, quality issues remain problematic. Similarly, Wadesango and Machingambi (2011) stated in their study in South Africa that students in the graduate education process do not receive sufficient support from their advisors. On the other hand, Ives and Rowley (2005) emphasized that the satisfaction of doctorants in choosing their advisors and their fields of study during the doctoral process is important for them to progress in a more beneficial and successful way. In addition, it was stated that more qualified research could be conducted if the students chose an expert and experienced consultant in the field.

Measurement and evaluation practices in the doctoral process have been another subject that has been criticized. Participants stated that in some courses, the assignments were not evaluated fairly and they were skipped by giving standard grades. Finally, budget problems were one of the difficulties experienced by the participants during the doctoral process. Some participants had to temporarily leave their jobs and take unpaid leave in order to continue their classes. Similarly, in the study of Sudoll and Hall (1991) graduate students aged between 37 and 50 stated that the participants faced economic difficulties during their education. In the aforementioned study, the participants stated that large deductions were made from their salaries during their education, and that the university did not provide the economic facilities that graduate students gave to undergraduate students, so they had to borrow money or exchange their pension funds.

In conclusion, being a doctoral student aged 40 and over, has both advantages and disadvantages. Almost all of the participants try to complete their education simultaneously with their profession. In addition, they have the heavier family responsibilities than the younger doctorants. This factor leads a distraction and division in their motivation. However, it is clear that being in the university environment, acquiring new perspectives and producing something new, gives satisfaction to the participants despite the existing difficulties. On the other hand, young doctorants' insufficient professional experience makes older Ph.Ds advantageous in terms of integrating their professional experience with doctoral education. Older adults are not hopeful about their future Ph.D. degree to carry them higher positions at their careers. Perhaps, because of this, they prioritize the transition to university.

This study has important implications for the doctoral experience of PhD students aged 40 and over. Especially considering the disadvantages they have, measures can be taken to facilitate access to the doctoral process. Institutions can be more facilitating and supportive in order to support the training processes of their postgraduate employees. Universities can also make it easier to participate in events such as conferences and symposia by using online platforms, which are especially prominent with the effect of developing technology and especially the pandemic. For the purpose of improving the advisor's advising competencies, their heavy workload can be reduced and trainings can be organized to develop their skills as well. The foreign language requirement of the participants is a very important problem. Although candidates are accepted by providing certain language proficiency at the entrance to the doctoral program, it may still be insufficient. Universities should reconsider their criteria of language competencies and open up new spaces to develop supportive policies for older adults' language skills.

REFERENCES

Baker, H. K. (1992). Service needs of traditional age and adult graduate students. *NASPA Journal*, *30*(1), 20–29. doi:10.1080/00220973.1992.11072287

Barker, S., Felstehausen, G., Couch, S., & Henry, J. (1997). Orientation programs for older and delayed-entry graduate students. *NASPA Journal*, *35*(1), 57–68. doi:10.2202/1949-6605.1037

Bozkurt, V., Yalçınkaya, E., Karataş, A., Talas, M., & Şahin, A. (2021). Perceptions of doctoral students: Satisfaction, difficulties, gained skills and performance in publishing in academic journals. *Yükseköğretim Dergisi*, *11*(2), 263–275. doi:10.2399/yod.20.516442

Broekemier, G. M. (2002). A comparison of two-year and four-year adult students: Motivations to attend college and the importance of choice criteria. *Journal of Marketing for Higher Education*, *12*(1), 31–48. doi:10.1300/J050v12n01_03

Burdett, J. D. (2008). *A phenomenological study of the graduate school experience of women age 60 and older* (Doctoral dissertation). Texas State University.

CoHE. (2013). *Öğrenim düzeyine göre öğrenci sayıları*. https://istatistik.yok.gov.tr/

CoHE. (2021). *Öğrenim düzeyine göre öğrenci sayıları*. https://istatistik.yok.gov.tr/

Cooper, M. K. (1999). *The return to academics: The experience of the older graduate student* (Doctoral thesis). University of Minnesota.

Creswell, J. W. (1998). Qualitative inquiry and research design: Choosing among five traditions. *Sage (Atlanta, Ga.)*.

Ezebilo, E. E. (2012). Challenges in postgraduate studies: Assessments by doctoral students in a Swedish University. *Higher Education Studies*, *2*(4), 49–57. doi:10.5539/hes.v2n4p49

Findsen, B., & Formosa, M. (2011). *Lifelong learning in later life: A handbook on older adult learning*. Sense Publishers. doi:10.1007/978-94-6091-651-9

Freedman, M. (2011). *The big shift: Navigating the new stage beyond midlife*. Public Affairs.

Green, H., & Powell, S. (2007). *The doctorate worldwide*. McGraw-Hill Education.

Guillory, J. (1996). Preprofessionalism: What graduate students want. *Profession*, 91–99. https://www.jstor.org/stable/25595583

Hammersly, M., & Traianou, A. (2017). *Ethics in qualitative research* (S. Balcı & B. Ahi, Trans.). Anı Yayıncılık.

Hovey, R. B. (1964). Graduate students: New style: Shall we revise old-style programs to meet present needs? *The Journal of Higher Education*, *35*(8), 442–449. doi:10.1080/00221546.1964.11773567

Ives, G., & Rowley, G. (2005). Supervisor selection or allocation and continuity of supervision: Ph. D. students' progress and outcomes. *Studies in Higher Education*, *30*(5), 535–555. doi:10.1080/03075070500249161

Kanter, R. M. (2006). *Back to college at midlife. Ending a career will soon mark the start of a new life*. https://www.aarp.org/personal-growth/life-long-learning/info-2006/back_to_college_at_midlife.html

Karadağ, N. (2014). *Türkiye'de doktora eğitim süreci kapasitesinin değerlendirilmesi (Eğitim Bilimleri Enstitüsü örneği)* [Capacity assessment of doctorate degree process in Turkey (The Case of Institute of Education Sciences)] (Doctoral thesis). Gazi University.

Kasworm, C. E. (2003). Setting the stage: Adults in higher education. *New Directions for Student Services*, *2003*(102), 3–10. doi:10.1002s.83

Kehm, B. M. (2006). *Doctoral education in Europe and North America: A comparative analysis*. https://citeseerx.ist.psu.edu/viewdoc/download?doi=10.1.1.526.1332&rep=rep1&type=pdf

Kerns, L. (2006). Adult graduate students in higher education: Refocusing the research agenda. *Adult Learning*, *17*(1-4), 40–42. doi:10.1177/104515950601700114

Lauzon, A. (2011). The changing nature of graduate education: Implications for students in the second half of life. *International Journal of Lifelong Education*, *30*(3), 287–307. doi:10.1080/02601370.2011.564315

Lewis, L. H. (1988). *Addressing the needs of returning women*. JosseyBass Publishers.

Matas, C. P. (2012). Doctoral education and skills development: An international perspective. *REDU: Revista de Docencia Universitaria*, *10*(2), 163.

Merriam, S. B. (2015). *Qualitative research: A guide for design and implementation* (S. Turan, Trans.). Nobel Yayıncılık.

Mezirow, J. (1991). *Transformative dimensions of adult learning*. Jossey-Bass.

Nayır, F. (2011). Problems of postgraduate students including school principals, teachers and inspectors in educational sciences. *Ankara University Journal of Faculty of Educational Sciences*, *44*(2), 199–222. doi:10.1501/Egifak_0000001230

Nerad, M., & Trzyna, T. (2011). Globalization and doctoral education- toward a research agenda. In M. Nerad & M. Heggelund (Eds.), *Toward a global PhD?: Forces and forms in doctoral education worldwide* (pp. 300–330). University of Washington Press.

OECD. (2016). *Skills matter: Further results from the survey of adult skills, country note Turkey*. https://www.oecd.org/skills/piaac/Skills-Matter-Turkey-Turkish-version.pdf

OECD. (2019). *Education at a glance 2019 OECD indicators*. https://www.oecd-ilibrary.org/education/education-at-a-glance-2019_f8d7880d-en

Parker, R. (2012). Skill development in graduate education. *Molecular Cell*, *46*(4), 377–381. doi:10.1016/j.molcel.2012.05.003 PMID:22633484

Patton, M. Q. (2014). *Nitel araştırma ve değerlendirme yöntemleri* (M. Bütün & S. B. Demir, Trans.). Pegem.

Polson, C. J. (2003). Adult graduate students challenge institutions to change. *New Directions for Student Services*, *2003*(102), 59–68. doi:10.1002s.90

Poulter, G. D. (2017). *The learner identities of older adults engaged in higher degree programmes* (Doctoral thesis). University of Glasgow. https://eleanor.lib.gla.ac.uk/record=b3304884

Reiff, M., & Ballin, A. (2008). *What do adult graduate students want? Using the typology of cognitive/affective/psychomotor learning domains to explore good and bad learning experiences*. Adult Education Research Conference. https://newprairiepress.org/aerc/2008/papers/56

Schroeder, S. M., & Terras, K. L. (2015). Advising experiences and needs of online, cohort, and classroom adult graduate learners. *The Journal of the National Academic Advising Association*, *35*(1), 42–55. doi:10.12930/NACADA-13-044

Sudol, D., & Hall, A. M. (1991). *Back to school: Warnings and advice to the older graduate student*. https://files.eric.ed.gov/fulltext/ED332217.pdf

Taylor, K., & Marienau, C. (1995). Bridging practice and theory for women's adult development. *New Directions for Adult and Continuing Education*, *1995*(65), 5–12. doi:10.1002/ace.36719956503

Turkish Statistical Institute. (2020). *İstatistiklerle yaşlılar*. https://data.tuik.gov.tr/Bulten/Index?p=Istatistiklerle-Yaslilar-2020-37227

Tzanakou, C. (2014). *The value of the PhD in a knowledge-based economy: beyond financial and career gains*. https://era.ideasoneurope.eu/2014/03/11/the-value-of-the-phd-in-a-knowledge-based-economy-beyond-financial-and-career-gains/

Wadesango, N., & Machingambi, S. (2011). Post graduate students' experiences with research supervisors. *Journal of Sociology and Social Anthropology*, *2*(1), 31–37. doi:10.1080/09766634.2011.11885545

Yıldırım, A., & Şimşek, H. (2018). *Qualitative research methods in the social sciences*. Seçkin Yayıncılık.

KEY TERMS AND DEFINITIONS

Adult Education: It is a practice in which adults engage in systematic and continuous self-educating activities to acquire new forms of knowledge, skills, attitudes, or values.

Doctorants: Students in the thesis period of the doctoral program.

Graduate Education: It is the training conducted after the undergraduate education and aimed at specialization.

Mid-Life Adults: Mid-Life Adults refers to individuals between the ages of 40 and 65.

Older Graduates: Older graduates refers to graduate students between the ages of 40 and 65.

Older Students: Students who are older than the majority of students.

PhD Programme: Specific field of doctoral education.

Chapter 12
International Retirement Migration of European Baby Boomers:
Retiring Knowledge Worker Perspectives and the Case of Turkey

Gülçin Bilgin Turna
Recep Tayyip Erdogan University, Turkey

ABSTRACT

This chapter examines how retiring knowledge workers from Europe can carry their educational attainment, wealth, competencies, and experience with them to conduct their activities on a transnational scale. A qualitative approach is adopted consisting of observations and interviews with Dutch professors. What's more, a literature review was done about international retirement migration (IRM) and statistics about Europe and Turkey. IRM of thousands of baby boomers can be harnessed across borders through scientific, academic, volunteer, and educational (SAVE) activities, which can contribute to peace and prosperity in the host communities along with the knowledge workers' personal development and well-being. The propensity of retiring knowledge workers to engage in cross-border living, learning, and transition requires the analysis of Turkey's image as a temporary or permanent destination for IRM.

INTRODUCTION

At the dawn of the 21st century, the global demographic transformation may be both the greatest challenge and opportunity in human history. In 1969, world population was 3.6 billion. In 2019, it was 7.7 billion. Numbers will increase to 9.8 billion by 2050 and 11 billion by 2100 according to United Nations projections (Population Institute, 2020). Parallel to these findings, population over 60 years of age was 962 million in 2017 worldwide, more than twice as large as in 1980. The number of older people is expected to double again by 2050. The number of people aged 80 or over is also projected to be 425

DOI: 10.4018/978-1-7998-2395-7.ch012

Copyright © 2022, IGI Global. Copying or distributing in print or electronic forms without written permission of IGI Global is prohibited.

million by then. Thus, Europe's aging population has prompted concerns about a "demographic time bomb". Europe has so many elderly people leading to major consequences for the affordability of long-term care for older people. As populations keep growing older in the world, it is more important than ever for governments to design "innovative policies and public services specifically targeted to older persons, including policies addressing housing, employment, health care, infrastructure and social protection, among others". Increasing longevity and declining fertility are the main drivers of population aging globally. Thus, some countries are turning to "international migration as a policy response to population aging" (United Nations, 2017).

It is important to note that the aging population in the industrialized world has relatively high levels of wealth, educational attainment, skills and work experience. In contrast, the less-developed world populations continue to expand, with millions of youth entering the labor force every year, while they may have the energy, they lack skills and work experience. These two aspects are driving the globalization phenomenon of the first half of the twenty-first century.

The starting point is that the aging population provides not only great challenges but also significant opportunities, when perceived from an International Retirement Migration (IRM) perspective. IRM has great potential for international human mobility when shaped around the capabilities and aspirations of humans, such that their performance and well-being is optimized. However, the potential of IRM remains under-exploited. At least four reasons can be identified. First, many stakeholders are involved in the design, management and marketing of host destinations that could possibly provide expatriate seniors opportunity to connect, meet and work with local residents, thereby offering a highly educational experience, but may be unaware of the value proposition IRM holds and in consequence fail to exhibit a strong demand for IRM. Second, in selected situations where a demand exists for the engagement of seniors in scientific, academic, volunteer and educational (SAVE) activities (Kask et al., 2011). This could be captured, due to their temporary nature, parallel to the tourist markets.

Presently, most destinations emphasize the 'use value' orientation in tourist marketing. In contrast, SAVE activities draw on the concept of the host community linked to the 'exchange value' orientation. Also, the latter enables us to comprehend and reflect on the favorable place characteristics that expatriate retiring knowledge workers in the pursuit of a 'better life' (Balkir and Kirkulak, 2009). Third, there is a lack of knowledge about the factors affecting retiring knowledge workers' intentions to continue working. Within this realm the SAVE activities market is rather small in comparison to the 'mass tourism market'. Fourth, IRM interests people who are 'actuaries, demographers and human-service planners', because the flows might change a country's age distribution of government spending on old-age income support, health services, and their long-term care (Warnes, 2009). Its multidisciplinary nature serves both as a strength and a weakness.

The focus of the chapter, retiring knowledge workers' propensity to engage in cross-border living, learning and transition, is highly complex, yet under research in a time when businesses and government are in search of inclusive solutions to retain the skills of experienced workers whose life expectancy is lengthening. Expectations to live longer than previous generations may prompt individuals to stay in the workforce longer and reduce their savings at a later age. With the increasing life expectancy and aging population, pension policy, pension and healthcare financing, it is likely for countries to adapt the structure of regional and global economic systems (Bloom et al., 2011).

Against the backdrop of the recent commemoration of 400 years of the official relations between Turkey and the Netherlands, it was examined to what extent, if any, the enhancement of Turkey's image could contribute to raise the demand for IRM by increasing the number of European retiring knowledge workers who would commit to SAVE activities in Turkey for research. The best way to deal with demographic changes and cultural differences is to share peace and prosperity across national borders through cultural, social and economic growth and the integration, where appropriate, of trade, finance and tourism in the international marketplace.

This chapter is organized as follows: first, baby boom knowledge workers and IRM conditions in Europe are analyzed. Second, Europe's and Turkey's current conditions are discussed. Third, Turkey's image as a destination for IRM is analyzed. Forth, how retiring knowledge workers from Europe can carry their educational attainment, wealth, competencies and experience with them to conduct their activities on a transnational scale is discussed.

BACKGROUND

How Demographic Aging Is Intrinsic to Clusters of Global Risks and Europe's Baby Boom Knowledge Workers

The number of people who are 65 or older in the EU is projected to rise by 70%, from 61 million in 2000 to 103 million in 2050 (Eurostat, 2000). The EU's population is increasing, while its age structure is becoming older as (post-war) baby-boom generations reach retirement age. As Eurostat mentioned in 2012, "In the coming decades, the EU will face challenges associated with an aging society, impacting a range of areas such as labor markets, pensions, health care, housing and social services" (Eurostat Pocketbooks, 2012). In OECD countries, aging of the population will put pressure on government tax and spending systems. Major changes in existing social systems will be required. Aging populations will therefore have a major impact on the growth and living standards in all countries (Turner et al., 1998).

In 2020, the world started to cope with Covid-19 which stands for coronavirus disease and is so highly contagious that it spreads primarily through contact with an infected person when they cough or sneeze. Although all age groups are at risk of contracting Covid-19, elderly (over 60 years old) have more tendency to develop severe illness if they contract the disease due to potential underlying health conditions. Elderly diagnosed with Covid-19 may require "hospitalization, intensive care, or a ventilator to help them breathe, or they may even die" (Centers for Disease Control and Prevention, 2020). It is now more important than ever for elderly to take a good care. Some changes in the human body in the elderly and retirement after long working life cause some restrictions in daily activities and changes in lifestyle. When health problems are added to the natural changes in the human organism, the problems of the elderly even become more complex. Another phenomenon is that people (especially knowledge workers) who are accustomed to the work might get badly ill after retiring when they feel unneeded in the society.

Knowledge workers are white-collar workers such as academics, programmers, engineers, architects, scientists, accountants, lawyers, pharmacists who 'think for a living' (Davenport, 2005). The aging of the Baby Boom generation includes thousands of retiring and retired European knowledge workers. Many of these professionals will be in search for activities and health care that they perceive as relevant to their personal development and well-being. In the wake of the financial crisis and the projected decline of pensions a question of great import arises whether and to what extent values set/worldview on the one hand health and well-being on the other might influence knowledge workers to opt for taking up temporary residence across borders from their native country.

The generation of older workers in the western developed economies who is approaching retirement has enjoyed a lifetime of increasing mobility for both work and leisure purposes. The globalizing economy has increased movement of both human and material assets, in turn, resulting in a dramatic growth of leisure travel. More imminent retirees are seeking some forms of continuing economic activity and in-comers relocating from more advanced economies to lower cost environments offer a senior profile of time, money, and experience. A combination of declining personal savings and a significant proportion of retirees without pension entitlements is coupled with more positive incentives including the stimulation and sociability of working for enjoyment rather than money, enhanced opportunity for relaxation and travel, more time with family and friends, and the opportunity for volunteer and charity work.

People in the age range of 60 years old and over have different needs than their younger counterparts. They are likely to need more healthcare and rely on social pensions for the bulk of their income. As the aging population grows and gains more political weight, it will become increasingly difficult to adopt policies to reduce health and pension benefits. People in the age range of 80 years old and over also have different needs. As their health conditions deteriorate, the need for full-time care increases. As private savings decrease rapidly, the need for financial support increases. They place more demands on government resources, family resources, and personal savings. With better health and increased life expectancy, individuals can be expected to work longer. Even if individuals decide not to work longer, increased life expectancy increases the need for high standard of living in retirement (Bloom et al., 2011). Mental capacity changes with age. The aging person moves from knowledge absorption to knowledge adoption. The quality of the knowledge transfer holds the potential to move us closer to the concept of wisdom.

Including life satisfaction, happiness and sense of belonging, retirees have a set of expectations that are relevant to the decision making process. In particular, these expectations are social, personal, and financial security factors for an aging person and will impact on their 'rest of life' decisions. Expectations of retirement and own discretionary time may be shattered by health, financial, or relationship upsets. Generally, an aging population will need more support of various types such as income security and greater access to healthcare. Low birth rates, children moving away from their parents, rural-to-urban migration, and new cultural norms of adoptive obligations are increasingly depriving older people of the security they once had.

World Economic Forum (2011) had indicated that 'cross-cutting global risks economic disparity and global governance failures' have a high influence on other global risks. Territorial actors should be able to respond effectively to risks, including the increasing demand for 'food-water-energy' nexus (Go and Govers, 2011). Globalization along with individualization and developments in information and communication technologies have a huge impact on countries, regions and cities. The impact of 'global interconnectedness' on economic, social and political activities is increasingly 'stretched' across globe. The global nature of social and economic turbulences, especially after the outbreak of Covid-19 (another great example of global interconnectedness), has resulted in imbalances in the global system triggering the feelings of uncertainty. However, after the sharp recession because of the lockdowns all over the world, the global economy will increase rapidly in the normalization process offering new opportunities for some sectors such as food, artificial intelligence (Ince, 2020) as well as recreation and tourism.

The decline in the levels of trust and consumer confidence, following in the wake of territorial actors' continued struggle with 'hard power' issues such as high taxes and dwindling investments in infrastructure and education (Fraim, 2003). Dennis and Melewar (2010) mention that "in a world where the values and stability of our financial and work environments are threatened daily, one thing remains relatively stable through the years and even generations: our sense of place. The greater the chaos is, the more the people seek security of the places that they know and trust". Low birth rates and higher life expectancy causing population aging in Europe contribute to Europe's population pyramid shape which means the total number of the older population will increase within the coming decades since post-war baby-boom generations reach retirement. This will put a high burden on the working age population as they provide for the older population (Eurostat, 2000).

MAIN FOCUS OF THE CHAPTER

Methodology

A qualitative approach (observations and interviews) was adopted consisting of meetings with Prof. Dr. Frank M. Go[1] (who was a respected Dutch academic in the search of a country to live temporarily after his retirement) and his colleagues for about six months at the Rotterdam School of Management/ Erasmus University in the Netherlands in 2013. What's more, a literature review was done about IRM, and statistics about Europe and Turkey.

The design and method deployed in this chapter provides definitions in response to the questions that must be answered to develop Turkey's image within a systematic framework and is based on five steps: 1. How do selected stakeholders perceive Turkey's (inter)national reputation? 2. What is Turkey's real character (essential features)? 3. How can the content of this study contribute to changing the way service is understood and practiced by decision makers in a manner that would contribute to closing the reputation-reality gap? 4. Which stakeholders are most likely to change their beliefs and expectations to establish the critical mass needed for effective decision making? 5. Who will provide leadership to this change making process and monitoring its progress?

IRM Conditions in Europe

IRM entails the movement of older people to those places for the pursuit of a better life. Williams et al. (1997) explained four reasons for the growth of IRM. The first two refer to the increase in longevity and the decline in the legal age of retirement which together typically extend the duration of retirement. Many people anticipate longer periods of active post-work life in the "third age" to which Phillipson (1998) refers as 'the triumph of retirement'. Third, with the increase in the lifetime flow of earnings, people now have sufficient resources to consider a range of retirement strategies, including migration abroad. Fourth, lifetime mobility has provided more knowledge and experience of living in foreign countries. Repeat holiday visits transformed into seasonal or permanent immigration. Thus, Southern Europe has become attractive to Northern Europeans, because of relatively cheaper house prices, favorable fiscal and tax policies, lower costs of living and heating. Southern Europe especially the Mediterranean basin, including Costa del Sol (Spain), Algarve (Portugal), Tuscany (Italy) and Malta have been popular retiree destinations. These places offered what Northern Europeans are in search of: 'sunshine, a healthy climate, relaxed and outdoor lifestyle, free of formalities and the availability of property for purchase or rental'.

The IRM literature has heavily focused on Northern Europeans moving to Southern Mediterranean (Balkir and Kirkulak, 2009). Moving represents not only a way of managing economic risks in retirement, also improving their financial and social status (Repetti et al., 2018). Mediterranean coastal resorts have attracted millions of Northern Europeans to the Southern Europe for a short term holiday leading to the decision of retirement migration to these hot and sunny locations (Williams et al., 2000). The reasons behind the moves are the "physical setting (climate, coastal location, beautiful landscape)" and the "socio-cultural environment (food, cultural heritage, way of life)". In recent years, the IRM map has been changing. Traditional destinations have become outdated and saturated with retirement immigrants, and the prices of once relatively cheap retirement properties are now expensive due to cumulative demand. Rural properties in areas such as Tuscany and Provence, or in coastal areas in the French and Italian Riviera are no longer affordable. Therefore, new geographical frontiers such as Croatia, Bulgaria, Morocco and Turkey are opened for the lovers of the Mediterranean climate (King et al., 2021). Shorter distances involved in these migration systems, such as Switzerland to southern Italy, or Germany to Turkey make transnational living a feasible option, as long as good health and personal mobility are maintained (Fokkema et al., 2016).

Turkey as a Destination for IRM: Defining Turkey's Image in Europe

In Turkey, there is the traditional people living in poverty in Central-East Anatolia and the other modern, very 'European', urban Turkey, as represented by Istanbul and Ankara. The majority of first wave Turkish immigrants who live in Germany, the Netherlands and Austria come from the backward southeast of Turkey, not from the modern cities. They usually had not more than elementary education (Haller, 2013). They tend to stick with their traditions they brought with them since 1960s like any other immigrants. As Turkey is becoming more diverse and modern, Turkish immigrants in Europe remain traditionalist. Professionals such as politicians and journalists frequently update their perceptions of different countries and places. However, there are prejudices that the general public cannot be changed easily. People will not change their images of a place, unless they have a good reason to do so. Therefore, Turkey's enormous improvements over the years do not register with most Europeans. Turkey is a secular country and has a working democracy. Turkey has been adopting the EU norms (Euronews, 2013). Turkey is more likely to highlight its strengths and the contribution that Turkey can make to the EU's economic growth. In April 2007 Turkish government published a plan for adopting most EU laws by 2013, irrespective of the state of accession talks or the public's mood (Barysch, 2007). Improvements to the institutional framework will further strengthen Turkey's competitive position (World Economic Forum, 2013).

Turkey, which is a founding member of both OECD and the United Nations, is also active in NATO and the Council of Europe. Turkey has a unique geographic position, lying partly in Asia and Europe. Turkey has acted as a bridge between the two continents. About one-third of Turkey's land area is utilized for agriculture. Turkey's main trading partner is Germany, almost half of the trade is with Europe. Health care is provided by both state and private health services (Dewdney, 2020).

Reputation Institute[2] built 'Country RepTrak®' on a multivariate model which measures the overall appeal of a country based on three dimensions: effective government (37.1%), appealing environment (36%), and advanced economy (26.9%). It serves as a tool, which offers policy makers support in systematic decision making in the realm of country reputation management. The results of this process provide policy makers insight, first, how and why people perceive countries in a more positive or negative light; second, which attributes invite investment to improve the country's brand reputation; third, what kind of reputation management efforts regarding specific attributes are likely opportune (Reputation Institute, 2015). Figure 1 depicts the multidimensional map derived from the Country RepTrak®, which identifies some attributes that were used for measuring the relative similarity of countries. It demonstrates the respondents' perceptions from other than the ones under investigation. They situate Turkey inside the quadrant involving three attributes: beautiful, friendly and enjoyable. These attributes justify the fact that Turkey was the 6th most visited country in the world for touristic purposes in 2015 (Reputation Institute, 2015: 9) as shown in Figure 1.

Countries that score relatively high on the perceptual map in relation to the attribute "technology", e.g., the United States of America (the USA) represents a material-oriented culture, which considers the "use-value" of goods and services significant, which often leads to over-consumption. Instead, Turkish consumers lean more towards the cultural significance, expressed in the "exchange-value" accord goods and services along with their purposeful utility. There is a dearth of analyses on a wide range of stakeholders such as the business and local community, who represent the country brand concept (Trueman, 2004).

Reputation presents an economic value to countries which is mainly based on emotions. It is the product of our perceptions of a country's actions and communications, as well as stereotypes, influences and direct experiences (Tisch, 2017) with its products and/or destinations. It is difficult to predict macroeconomics, political events and technology will conspire to create new opportunities and deal with the threats. So how can Turkey prepare for an uncertain future? Learning from the experience of others can provide policy makers of the Turkish Ministry of Industry and Trade with a good set of historical patterns for managing risk and developing "reputational landscape" (Fombrun and Van Riel, 1997). Ayyildiz and Turna's (2014) research revealed that for Dutch and Swedish people, in the perception of Turkey, "media and word-of-mouth communication" were the most important sources of information.

Figure 1. Countries reputation mapping
Source: Reputation Institute, 2015.

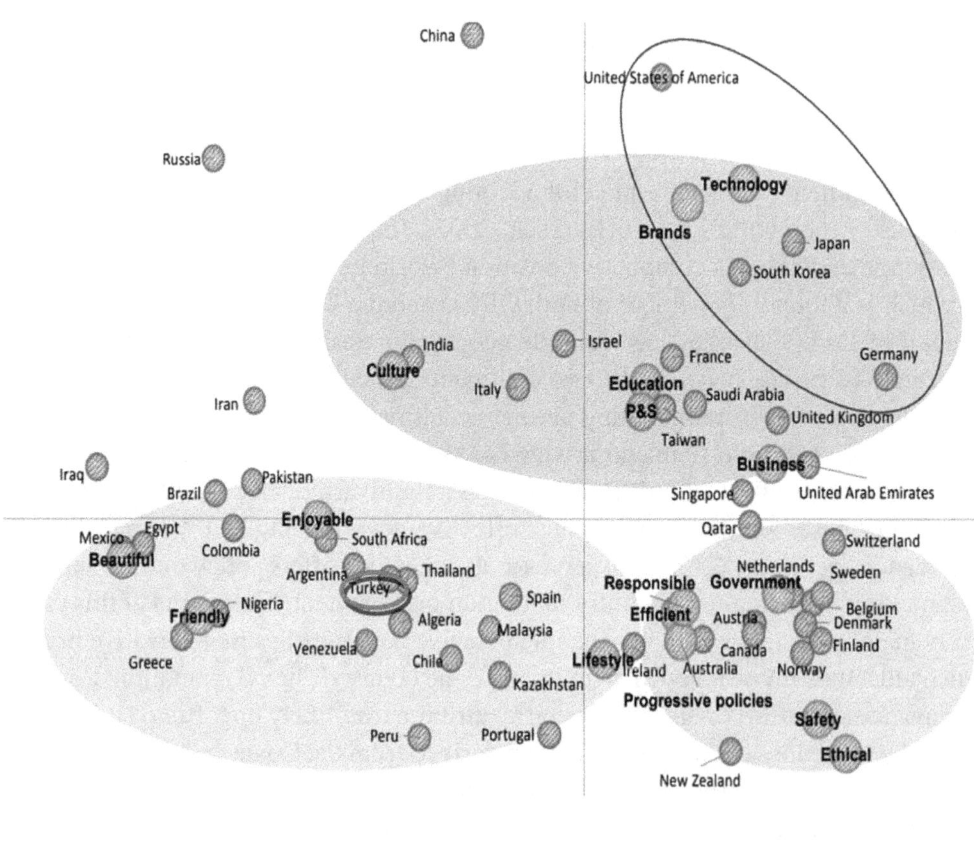

Reputation is comprised of socially-beneficial reputation systems that are shaped over time. They are based on the "reputational object" (Mahon and Wartick, 2003) which lives up to the stakeholders' "perceptual judgments" (Kowalczyk and Pawlish, 2002). Reputation serves an important role because countries always try to attract foreign investments, tourism and trade (Fernandez-Crehuet et al., 2021; Newburry, 2019; Yang et al., 2008). To what extent would Turkey be attractive in the perception of retiring knowledge workers as a country to take up (temporary) residence in the pursuit of e.g., a combination of research/publishing, work, leisure activities, and health care in comparison to other Mediterranean destinations?

Figure 2. The world's top 10 destinations by international tourist arrivals (million)
Source: UNWTO (World Tourism Organization) Tourism Highlights, 2021, p.8

	Country	2016	2017	2018	2019
1	France	82.6	86.9	89.3	89.0
2	Spain	75.6	81.8	82.8	83.5
3	United States	75.6	76.9	79.8	79.3
4	China	59.3	60.7	62.9	65.7
5	Italy	52.4	58.3	61.6	64.5
6	**Turkey**	**31,3**	**37,6**	**45,8**	**51,2**
7	Mexico	35.0	39.3	41.3	45.0
8	Germany	35.6	37.5	38.9	39.6
9	Thailand	32.6	35.4	38.2	40.0
10	United Kingdom	35.8	37.7	36.3	39.4

Turkey has been an attractive tourism destination for Europeans and migrants since 1980s (Kaiser and Friedrich, 2004). Istanbul, Ankara, İzmir are three major big cities of Turkey where the foreign population primarily intensified until 1950s. With the 1980s, there was an expansion towards the Mediterranean and Aegean coastal zone, so called the Turkish Riviera (Yakar and Sudas, 2019).

Turkey is located very close to Europe and is relatively less expensive than any other southern European countries. Turkey has a lot to offer in terms of natural beauty, historical places, hospitality especially towards foreign tourists, good climate, service quality at the hotels and restaurants, tasty food, availability of organic fruits and vegetables. That is why Turkey is the 6th most visited country in the world according to UNWTO's 2020 Edition report, published on January 2021, that gives international tourism trends for 2019 as shown in Figure 2.

Turkey is a popular European retirees' destination, particularly for British, German, Dutch and Nordic citizens. Funded by TUBITAK (National Scientific and Technological Research Council of Turkey), Balkir and Kirkulak conducted research in 2009 both with the retired migrants and with the local community in Antalya, the city located in southern Turkey, where the Mediterranean climate and relaxed lifestyle have attracted the elderly tourists. In 2010 between January and September, Antalya was visited by 2.3 million Russian, 1.8 million German and 371 thousand Dutch followed by 360 thousand British, 240 thousand Swedish, 192 thousand Norwegian, and 150 thousand Danish tourists (TUROFED, 2010).

Figure 3 shows the number of foreign tourists and their nationalities, who have visited Antalya and Mugla in Figure 4 (another popular province in Turkey for IRM) over the recent years. Figures give a general idea of which nationalities are more attracted to southern Turkey in terms of tourism, however they do not reflect the number of people who have migrated there after retirement.

Figure 3. Top 10 foreign visitors in Antalya by nationalities
Source: Turofed Tourism Report, 2019/1, page 25.

MİLLİYET NATIONALITIES	2014	2015	2016	2017	2018
RUSYA/ RUSSIAN FEDERATION	3.487.698	2.836.902	486.548	3.715.035	**4.651.709**
ALMANYA/ GERMANY	2.839.576	3.001.016	1.975.355	1.658.811	**2.292.996**
UKRAYNA/ UKRAIN	284.632	314.708	572.700	715.011	**709.074**
İNGİLTERE/ UNITED KINGDOM	430.042	438.398	333.995	361.903	**632.086**
POLONYA/ POLAND	243.549	240.641	100.824	168.702	**383.230**
HOLLANDA/ NETHERLAND	489.820	434.842	306.280	257.546	**374.237**
KAZAKİSTAN/KAZAKHSTAN	269.221	268.389	125.927	237.244	**244.528**
BELÇİKA/ BELGIUM	262.080	235.121	143.427	135.726	**185.148**
ÇEKYA/CZECHIA	151.897	135.338	46.692	83.409	**164.637**
BEYAZ RUSYA/ BELARUS	142.176	137.951	70.943	163.686	**163.677**
DİĞER/ OTHER	405.750	446.581	368.889	496.843	**699.423**
T.C./ TURKISH CITIZENS	418.143	440.366	447.506	514.475	**553.244**
GENEL TOPLAM/ GENERAL TOTAL	**11.539.522**	**10.875.464**	**6.181.913**	**9.738.962**	**12.712.603**

First-time and repeat visitor groups develop their return intention and satisfaction based on slightly different aspects of holiday destination. While both the first-time and repeat visitors commonly regard quality of food and accommodation, hospitality and safety as a reason to come back, they consider different additional services to develop their return intentions. The repeat visitors promise more future business than first-time visitors do (Yuksel, 2001). The longevity, number and form of prior connections with the adopted region are important factors for retirement (Diaz et al., 2004). Repeat tourist experiences may create emotional attachment to the place with the establishment of personal contacts (Turna, 2013). A sense of familiarity with the place can culminate with a decision of buying a second home in Turkey. With its estimated 12.832 foreign residents, Antalya (a city in the south of Turkey) is currently the most popular international tourism destination with a share of almost one-third of Turkey's total international arrivals. Therefore, tourism has played a vital role in the development of this region and many migrants experienced the area first as tourists before turning resident. Alanya (one of Antalya's districts) has become home to 38 foreigners' nationalities. It has been revealed that European retirees who settled in Turkey mostly has a positive attitude and perception of Turkey (Ozerim, 2012).

Figure 4. Top 10 foreign visitors in Mugla by nationalities (2018)
Source: Turofed Tourism Report, 2019/1, page 27.

Natonalities	Toplam/ Total
England	1.027.304
Russian Federation	398.596
Germany	218.195
Ukraine	176.871
Poland	138.948
Netherlands	128.638
Belgium	58.059
Lebanon	50.022
Israel	43.507
France	37.682
Other	46.886
Total	**2.805.115**

Researchers Balkir and Kirkulak (2009) identified several conditions that drive IRM that are relevant to the Turkish–EU Migratory relationship, these are, first, the "sunshine, climate, lower cost of living, natural beauty, good social relationships, respect for elders, security and a peaceful lifestyle" in Turkey where elderly is highly respected. Second, Europe's lower and middle class can afford to purchase and maintain a house with a swimming pool, at a relatively low cost certainly when compared to the housing costs in European countries. Third, Alanya (a district in Antalya) has been using the marketing slogan, "The same sun, the same sea, why pay more?" to convince retirees to settle in Turkey beyond the traditional Mediterranean destinations such as Spain.

In partnership with National Geographic the journalist Dan Buettner[3] identified five "Blue Zones", where people live longer and healthier than anywhere else on earth. People not only live to 90 or even 100 years but also live healthy without disability or medication in these blue zones namely: in "the Italian island of Sardinia; Okinawa, Japan; Loma Linda, California; Costa Rica's isolated Nicoya Peninsula; Ikaria, an isolated Greek island". The inhabitants of these remote islands adhere to a lifestyle that includes a healthy diet, daily exercise, and a low stress life (Singularity Hub Staff, 2009). While the citizens from the countries in Northern Europe may consider the Blue Zones romantic and attractive most would be unlikely to make the transition from the industrialized societies to an isolated island lifestyle. Instead, the majority of retiring knowledge workers would prefer to migrate to a SAVE heaven such as Turkey. That is a place situated on the continuum which ranges from the 'industrialized society' on one extreme and the Blue Zone. Retirees from Northern Europe have migrated to enjoy the quality of life in Mediterranean destinations over the years. Such enclaves of foreign residents have developed in the case of Antalya that is well positioned to attract the "SAVE" market, particularly those Northern European retiring knowledge workers in search of preventive healthcare.

Figure 5. House sales numbers to foreigners in Turkey
Source: General Directorate of Land Registry and Cadastre (GDLRC)

Province	January-October 2019	January-October 2020
Total	**36 197**	**31 423**
Istanbul	16 322	14 424
Antalya	7 169	6 053
Ankara	2 004	2 176
Bursa	1 873	1 068
Yalova	1 432	1 008
Mersin	698	994
Izmir	626	731
Samsun	672	698
Sakarya	1 027	678
Mugla	774	613
Other provinces	3 600	2 980

TurkStat, House Sales Statistics, 2020

Foreigners are allowed to buy or rent a house in Turkey. Antalya and Mugla are usually the most attractive cities in Turkey for foreigners for temporary or permanent residence. Istanbul is the most populated historic, cultural and economic center of Turkey. House sales numbers in big cities such as Istanbul, Ankara and Bursa in Figure 5 are high mainly due to expats (people residing in a country other than their native country and usually refers to professionals or skilled workers taking positions abroad).

Figure 6. Top 30 nationalities of Europeans who own a house in Turkey
Source: Turkish Address Based Population Registration System, 2020.

Country of citizenship (European countries only)	2019		2020
Total	**247 456**		**250 495**
Germany	88 539		92 284
Russian Federation	40 201		43 679
Austria	17 300		18 047
Ukraine	20 228		17 505
Bulgaria	13 474		14 195
United Kingdom	13 950		13 985
Greece	11 866		12 137
Netherlands	6 518		6 550
France	3 444		3 181
Denmark	3 067		3 148
Sweden	2 630		2 517
Belarus	2 501		2 412
Albania	3 003		2 216
Norway	2 358		2 156
Italy	2 146		1 948
Romania	1 873		1 741
North Macedonia	1 861		1 558
Belgium	1 659		1 556
Kosovo	1 852		1 516
Spain	1 320		1 140
Bosnia and Herzegovina	1 141		1 073
Switzerland	1 013		1 029
Poland	1 053		953
Finland	816		688
Ireland	668		651
Lithuania	545		512
Hungary	434		377
Montenegro	388		324
Czechia	380		308
Latvia	251		238

German and Russian seem to be, by far the most, the top two nationalities who own a house in Turkey as shown in Figure 6. Besides, top European nationalities who bought a house in Turkey between the period of January-October 2020 (which is the first period of the Covid-19 pandemic) are Russian (2.295), German (1.006), British (878), Ukrainian (598) and Swedish (414) (TurkStat, 2020).

SOLUTIONS AND RECOMMENDATIONS

As more locations develop their brand and offer towards a wider range of incomers it will be possible to monitor the degree to which they are consciously pitching in order to attract older life-cycle migrants to economic engagement with the host community. In their 'bidding' to attract these migrants, destinations are creating conditions which benefit all inhabitants, not just incomers. Policies should be developed utilizing the social marketing dimension of destination image development to maximize mutual benefit, and to provide a moral imperative for incomers to make the fullest contribution possible (Go and Little, 2013).

The perceived level of resistance among people to change their learning and support habits within working environments can be interpreted as a barrier to their re-engagement. Local community policy makers and destination marketers should accomplish the goal of enhancing both residents' quality of life and their ability to warmly welcome visitors, which in turn increase guest's behavioral intentions and their satisfaction (Ghasemi, 2016). Since Turkish culture and language is very different than the Western European countries, the adaptation process faces significant cross-cultural, infrastructural and governance gaps. Within this context, Go and Trunfio (2012) point respectively to "bridging, bonding and a sense of belonging" as crucial stages in building a "Community of Practice". For example, consumers book a hotel in Turkey (bridging) on the Internet, trust can occur when they experience the destination and communicate with local people (bonding), once people become more familiar with the area, particularly its inhabitants, they may form friendships and may even develop a "sense of belonging" leading to buy or rent properties.

The increased mobility of retiring knowledge workers brings new forms of technical literacy into host communities, with the prospects for a comfortable and complete retirement tempered in the current downturn, and more life-cycle migrants are considering some blend of retirement with part-time work. Aging population with high levels of wealth, educational attainment and skills and young population of the less developed world with the strength of youth can be beneficial to each other. Older and experienced incomers may possess the knowledge and experience to identify appropriate resources if they cannot contribute them directly themselves. With their retirement prospects altered by economic change, globalization and recession, many older workers are reconsidering their work-retirement balance. Those who choose to become life-cycle migrants represent a relatively sticky resource for their destination communities compared with other forms of inward resources. Individuals looking at life-cycle relocation can stage their relocation and build connections into a region using a variety of tools to establish a remote presence prior to committing to full relocation. This provides the opportunity for a two-way exploration of mutual compatibilities.

IRM is a significant and growing feature of Europe. As a result of increasing globalization and international mobility, destination management organizations (DMOs) are now in greater need than ever to form joint arrangements to cope with growing complexity of their environments, notably the complex problems that are beyond the capabilities of any one organization to solve single-handedly (Jamal and Getz, 1995). The success of a DMO is often determined by its ability to form and manage relations with other stakeholders (organizations, individuals etc.) operating within its environment. There are often interdependencies between DMOs and destination stakeholders because they do not possess or control such important resources as human, political, structural or symbolic, which influence their future. Undoubtedly, DMOs operate in a system which can be viewed as an integrated whole, whose essential properties arise from the relationships between its constituent parts. It comprises a set of elements, the set of relationships between these elements, and the set of relationships between those elements and the environment (Hall, 2000).

DMOS are embedded within systems, and each system has strictly defined boundaries and operates within an external environment. Systems theory recognizes that the behavior of a system is constrained by the needs and conditions of its setting. Changes in one component of the system, as the increasing presence of international retired settlers (IRS) in different regions of Turkey, and the ways in which its internal processes and subsystems are linked, influence entire system. Co-operative efforts, connectedness, dialogues, and other types of interaction between locals and this new interconnected stakeholder (namely IRS), together with their interdependencies, may offer a cutting-edge resource to smart DMOs in Turkey. DMOs in Turkey often operate in an environment of scarce resources and therefore they should exchange relations to achieve relatively predictable environments (Yuksel, 2002). One notable scarce resource is knowledge (intellectual capital, know-how, examples of best practices around the globe, etc.). Due to limited know-how, the majority of DMOs in Turkey, aiming to develop sustainable tourism management (STM), tend to form a delegation to visit/study best practices selected around the world in order to get familiarized with the concept of STM, different STM models and activities. In addition to such rewarding visits, DMOs in pursuit of STM opt for organizing seminars by inviting international experts to give government officials, private sector representative and civil society organizations a broader perspective regarding STM. In line with these endeavors, DMOs in regions where international retirees are settled may capitalize on social capital that IRSs have by developing a mechanism to exchange best practices and knowledge transfer.

Coinciding with a recent regulation fostering society-centered decision making instead of centralized council structure in Turkey, participation of IRSs, among other stakeholders, in DMOs stands out as an untapped opportunity for improving quality of public services. While IRSs do not have right to vote in Turkey, since Turkey is not an EU country, there are some examples. During a referendum about moving local town hall offices to a neighboring, bigger city, all foreign residents who have a fixed abode in that location could cast their ballots. The exchange of such intangible resources as knowledge and social capital among varied stakeholders at a destination can improve DMOs performance. However, knowledge and social capital exchange can hardly take place when stakeholders in a given setting know nothing about one another.

The future success of a DMO is likely to be determined by its ability to conceive its role and position within mobile networks and place making in cultural tourism (Baerenholdt and Haldrup, 2006); and challenges its conventional understandings of territorial learning within a system of networks or a network of systems, including internal and external networks. Against that backdrop destinations can be understood as fulcrums of international networks and global dynamics of industrial countries' economic development, and then there is the rise of pervasive computing: The Internet and social media to exploit the qualities of geographical context, and the sociability or the human context of information. How will social and physical infrastructures of the cyber-nomadic experience aid destinations to define and reach new market segments and create and sustain new cooperative organizational forms?

Within the emerging environment wherein the physical and the digital are fusing, we anticipate that 'smart' destinations will take advantage of both the advantages of their physical assets (e.g., climate, culture, etc.) and the sociability of information, particularly the sharing of knowledge between stakeholders (organizations, individuals etc.) across national boundaries. This study pinpoints the 'cognitive surplus', creativity and potential generosity (Shirky, 2010) of the Baby Boom generation characterized by high levels of wealth, educational attainment, skill, and experience for transfer to emerging economies with populations marked by the strength of youth, but often lacking the resources, knowledge and skills.

In business and higher education, big restructuring operations have been followed by internationalization strategies and strategic alliances, which got accompanied by new forms of individualized 'regulation'. Within this more dynamic framework, not only the destination's internal logic, but also increasingly its collaboration with a variety of stakeholders along the value chain has proven significant in developing successful change strategies. This implies that DMOs should be viewed less as an integrated whole, and more as a node within the international value chain wherein managing relationships with the knowledge network (e.g. SAVE) has become the critical task on which the destination's existence falls or stands. Websites and the growth of social media has become an important tool for IR migrant in the search for reliable sources of data about places to retire (Gursoy and McCleary, 2004). Destination stakeholders must consider creating awareness of the destination through WOM (word-of-mouth), trustworthy websites and government channels. Migrants evaluate a destination based on pre-retirement visits that create attachment and emotions for the place towards the decision-making processes of short stay, semi-permanent or permanent migrants (Ashton et al., 2019).

The devastating impact of the Covid-19 pandemic on global tourism started in early 2020 and carried into 2021. All the countries experienced large drops in tourist arrivals as they have tightened travel restrictions in response to new variants of the virus. Quarantines and mandatory testing, and in some cases the complete closure of borders, have prevented the resumption of international travel. In addition, the speed and distribution of the vaccination roll-out have been slower than expected, further delaying the restart of tourism. As Covid-19 vaccines become more applicable around the world, international tourism along with IRM will accelerate.

FUTURE RESEARCH DIRECTIONS

Future work may benefit from a destination management perspective in which knowledge and experience of migrants may pave the way for improved quality of life in the settled area for hosts and learning institutions of the region. An empirical study can be conducted on the intellectual capital of immigrant settlers and their tendency to share this capital with institutions and people in their region within the framework of the theory of social change.

CONCLUSION

The authorities and policy makers should lever the 'exchange value' model, which remains under research, for focusing on attracting retired knowledge workers to engage in SAVE activities, thereby making a potentially valuable contribution to translating the intention referred to in the Turkish 2023 Industry and Technology Strategy (2019-2023) towards celebrating the 100th anniversary of the foundation of Turkish Republic. Collaboration with independent international experts, companies from various industries, exchanging ideas with stakeholders (Turna, 2022) and transformational strategy to attract retiring knowledge workers from Europe will provide benefits both for Turkey and Europeans.

Country and city brands can be placed on a continuum in this case how much retired and retiring baby boomers decide to carry their national rights of legal citizenship, the benefits of their educational attainment, wealth, competencies and experience with them to conduct their activities in Turkish that appeal and matter to them. This paradigm shifts from destination management based on the 'use value' model, which enables serial reproduction of industrial society holiday images implying substantial challenges for Turkish policymakers. In this context the 'use value' model plays an essential role for 'translating' the strategic intention at the operational scale by 'swapping' scientific, academic, volunteer and educational activities in a 'SAVE Heaven' environment thereby contributing to the host communities' peace and prosperity on the one hand and the knowledge worker 'in-residence' personal development and well-being on the other.

It stands to reason that the 'exchange value model' deserves due consideration for Turkey to achieve, simultaneously, a harmonious economic success and a sense of societal well-being. For instance, retired European academics can contribute to universities in Turkey where they take up temporary/permanent residence across borders from their native country. Likewise, other knowledge workers can also make contributions to the countries according to their area of expertise. In this way they feel needed and valuable as they keep contributing to the society.

In international trade and investment, policies that seek to contribute to diversity of trade goods must become underpinned by a redefined foreign economic relations and foreign direct investments structure that represents a value proposition for local companies and investors alike. As Turkey's economy is transforming from an industrial to a service economy, its workplace will need to mine, paradoxically, the human expression, which is built on personal interests outside the workplace, e.g. to develop creative hotspots.

Turkey is a developing country that adopted tourism not only as an economic growth strategy, but also a tool for favorable image on an international platform (Tosun and Timothy, 2001). Almost 30 million international tourists go back to their country happily after experiencing destinations in Turkey and they tell other people. Especially Europeans, whose expectations about Turkey are low before visiting, tend to be impressed by the objects, artefacts Turkey has to offer. Through word of mouth, they recommend Turkey to their acquaintances spreading the country's positive image. In 2011, Turkey became the sixth most visited country in the world with 29 million international tourists. By the year 2019, Turkey still held the same position as the sixth most visited country (after France, Spain, the USA, China, Italy) in the world with 46 million international tourists (UNWTO, 2021:8).

Turkey has successfully followed the traditional Mediterranean destinations such as Spain to attract tourists. Policymakers draw on the 'use value' model, which results in serial reproduction of holiday images and un-reflexive host-guest relationships to compete head on with rivals. The main lesson learned can be that the approach used by the traditional Mediterranean destinations ignores the propensity of retiring knowledge workers to engage in cross-border living, learning and transition. Same justifies the analysis of the perceived attractiveness of Turkey as a destination for knowledge workers 'in-residence' in pursuit of SAVE activities, which represent within a landscape of well-being perspective, a preventive health care lifestyle.

The blurring boundaries between retirement and work and the blurring boundaries between countries, taking the mobility of retirement, require a ditto transformational strategy to sustain Turkish differential competitive advantage. However, this paradigm shifts present substantial challenges for policymakers, businesses, government, higher education/university their respective objectives, agenda, interests, etc. With health care costs spiraling out of control in Northern European countries, a growing number of retired and retiring knowledge workers will be in search for a cultural climate of enjoyment as a means of preventive health care treatment. Therefore, to overcome fragmentation necessary for capitalizing on the emerging opportunities future, research should give serious consideration of an integrated approach based on the 'exchange value model', to co-create the images and reflexive host-guest relationships.

REFERENCES

Ashton, A. S., Scott, N., & Choibamroong, T. (2019). Place development for international retirement migrants: A decision-making process model. *Journal of Place Management and Development*, *12*(3), 449–468. doi:10.1108/JPMD-05-2018-0035

Ayyildiz, H., & Turna, G. B. (2014). Turkey's image as a tourist destination in Northern Europe. *International Journal of Advances in Management, Economics and Entrepreneurship*, *1*(4), 1–8.

Baerenholdt, J. O., & Haldrup, M. (2006). Mobile networks and place making in cultural tourism: Staging viking ships and rock music in roskilde. *European Urban and Regional Studies*, *13*(3), 209–224. doi:10.1177/0969776406065431

Balkir, C., & Kirkulak, B. (2009). Turkey, the new destination for international retirement migration, migration and mobility in Europe. In Migration, Mobility and Europe. Edward Elgar Publishing, MPG Books Group.

Barysch, K. (2007). *What Europeans think about Turkey and why, Essay partly based on the CER Seminar on Europe's public opinion on Turkish EU accession.* Centre for European Reform Essays. https://www.cer.eu/sites/default/files/publications/attachments/pdf/2011/essay_turkey_barysch_25sept07-1392.pdf

Bloom, D. E., Canning, D., & Fink, G. (2011). *Implications of population aging for economic growth. Harvard University Program on the Global Demography of Aging.* NBER Working Paper No 16705, National Bureau of Economic Research. https://www.nber.org/system/files/working_papers/w16705/w16705.pdf

Centers for Disease Control and Prevention. (2020, September 11). *Older Adults.* https://www.cdc.gov/coronavirus/2019-ncov/need-extra-precautions/older-adults.html

Davenport, T. H. (2005). *Thinking for a living: How to get better performance and results from knowledge workers.* Harvard Business School Press.

Dennis, C., & Melewar, T. C. (2010). Place marketing and branding in a turbulent world. *Place Branding and Public Diplomacy*, *6*(2), 76. doi:10.1057/pb.2010.17

Dewdney, J. C. (2020, November 8). Turkey. *Britannica.* https://www.britannica.com/place/Turkey/Demographic-trends#ref44475

Diaz, M. A. C. (2004). Northern European retired residents in nine southern European areas: Characteristics, motivations and adjustment. *Ageing and Society*, *24*(3), 353–381. doi:10.1017/S0144686X04001898

Euronews. (2013, June 3). *Is this the Turkish Spring? The view from The Euronews Istanbul Correspondent.* https://www.euronews.com/2013/06/03/is-this-the-turkish-spring-the-view-from-the-euronews-istanbul-correspondent-/

Eurostat Pocketbooks. (2012). *The European Union and the BRIC countries.* Eurostat European Commission. https://ec.europa.eu/eurostat/web/products-pocketbooks/-/ks-31-11-414

Fernandez-Crehuet, J. M., Rosales-Salas, J., & Cogollos, S. D. (2021). Country's international reputation index. *Corporate Reputation Review*, *24*(1), 14–30. doi:10.105741299-019-00088-8

Fokkema, T., Cela, E., & Witter, Y. (2016). Pendular migration of older adults: Misconceptions and nuances. In V. Horn & C. Schweppe (Eds.), *Transnational Aging: Current Insights and Future Challenges* (pp. 141–161). Routledge. doi:10.4324/9781315756394

Fombrun, C., & Van Riel, C. (1997). The reputational landscape. *Corporate Reputation Review*, *1*(1-2), 5–13. doi:10.1057/palgrave.crr.1540008

Fraim, J. (2003). *Battle of symbols global dynamics of advertising, entertainment and media*. Daimon Verlag.

Ghasemi, V., Del Chiappa, G., & Correia, A. (2016). Host-Guest interactions: Conceptualising and testing the role of apathy. *8th World Conference for Graduate Research in Tourism Hospitality and Leisure. Proceedings Book*, 497-502.

Go, F. M., & Govers, R. (2011). *Introduction to the international place branding yearbook managing reputational risk*. Palgrave MacMillan.

Go, F. M., & Little, S. (2013). Older workers in a global economy – Life cycle migration and knowledge transfer. In P. Taylor (Ed.), *Older Workers in an Aging Society: Critical Topics in Research and Policy* (pp. 817–819). Edward Elgar.

Go, F. M., & Trunfio, M. (2012). A paradigm shift from tourism destination management to democratic governance of place branding: The cases of Pompei and Campi Flegrei. *Journal of Travel and Tourism Research*, (Spring), 4–17.

Gursoy, D., & McCleary, K. W. (2004). An integrative model of tourists' information search behavior. *Annals of Tourism Research*, *31*(2), 353–373. doi:10.1016/j.annals.2003.12.004

Hall, P. (2000). Creative cities and economic development. *Urban Studies (Edinburgh, Scotland)*, *37*(4), 639–649. doi:10.1080/00420980050003946

Haller, M. (2013). The image of Turkey in Europe today. *European Review (Chichester, England)*, *21*(3), 327–335. doi:10.1017/S106279871300029X

Ince, F. (2020). The effects of Covid-19 pandemic on the workforce in Turkey. *Social Mentality and Researcher Thinkers Journal*, *6*(32), 1125–1134. doi:10.31576mryj.546

Jamal, T. B., & Getz, D. (1995). Collaboration theory and community tourism planning. *Annals of Tourism Research*, *22*(1), 186–204. doi:10.1016/0160-7383(94)00067-3

Kaiser, C., & Friedrich, K. (2004). Migration decisions, living environments and adjustments to changing needs of elderly Germans on Mallorca. In A. M. Warnes (Ed.), *Final Report ESF-Network*. doi:10.1017/S0144686X04001898

Kask, S. B., Kline, C., & Lamoureux, K. (2011). Modeling tourist and community decision making, The SAVE Market. *Annals of Tourism Research*, *38*(4), 1387–1409. doi:10.1016/j.annals.2011.03.011

King, R., Cela, E., & Fokkema, T. (2021). New frontiers in international retirement migration. *Aging and Society: An Interdisciplinary Journal*, *41*(6), 1205–1220. doi:10.1017/S0144686X21000179

Kowalczyk, S. J., & Pawlish, M. J. (2002). Corporate branding through external perception of organizational culture. *Corporate Reputation Review*, *5*(2-3), 159–174. doi:10.1057/palgrave.crr.1540172

Mahon, J. F., & Wartick, S. L. (2003). Dealing with stakeholders: How reputation, credibility and framing influence the game. *Corporate Reputation Review*, *6*(1), 19–35. doi:10.1057/palgrave.crr.1540187

Newburry, W., Deephouse, D. L., & Gardberg, N. A. (2019). Global Aspects of Reputation and Strategic Management. In *Global Aspects of Reputation and Strategic Management (Research in Global Strategic Management, 18)*. Emerald Publishing Limited. doi:10.1108/S1064-485720190000018009

Ozerim, M. G. (2012). Turkey on the Route of Retirement Migration: The Motivations of European Retirement Migrants to Prefer Turkey and Their Perception of Turkey. *Journal of Yasar University*, *28*(7), 4766–4787.

Phillipson, C. (1998). *Reconstructing Old Age: New Agendas in Social Theory and Practice*. Sage Books.

Population Institute. (2020). *Population Clock*. https://www.populationinstitute.org/resources/

Repetti, M., Phillipson, C., & Calasanti, T. (2018). Retirement migration in Europe: A choice for a better life? *Sociological Research Online*, *23*(4), 780–794. doi:10.1177/1360780418782243

Reputation Institute, Country RepTrak. (2015). *The World's Most Reputable Countries. The World's View on Countries: An Online Study of the Reputation of 55 Countries*. Author.

Shirky, C. (2010). *Cognitive Surplus: How Technology Makes Consumers into Collaborators*. The Penguin Press.

Singularity Hub Staff. (2009). *Blue Zones – Places in the World Where People Live to 100 and Stay Healthy*. https://singularityhub.com/2009/07/20/blue-zones-places-in-the-world-where-people-live-to-100-and-stay-healthy/

Tisch, D. (2017). *What gives a nation great reputation?* https://policyoptions.irpp.org/magazines/july-2017/what-gives-a-nation-a-great-reputation/

Tosun, C., & Timothy, D. J. (2001). Shortcomings in planning approaches to tourism development in developing countries: The case of Turkey. *International Journal of Contemporary Hospitality Management*, *13*(7), 352–359. doi:10.1108/09596110110403910

Trueman, M., Klemm, M., & Giroud, A. (2004). Can a city communicate? Bradford as a corporate brand. *Corporate Communications*, *9*(4), 317–330. doi:10.1108/13563280410564057

TurkStat. (2020). *House Sale Statistics*. General Directorate of Land Registry and Cadastre.

Turna, G. (2022). How "Dieselgate" Changed Volkswagen: Rushing to Erase the Traces of Greenwashing. In Socially Responsible Consumption and Marketing in Practice. Springer. doi:10.1007/978-981-16-6433-5_16

Turna, G. B. (2013). *The effects of product-country image and tourism destination image on international consumer behavior: Comparative analysis of Turkey, Spain, Germany, Sweden and the Netherlands.* Black Sea Technical University.

Turner, D., Giorno, C., De Serres, A., Vourc'h, A., & Richardson, P. (1998). *The macroeconomic implications of aging in a global context.* OECD Economics Department Working Papers, 193, OECD Publishing. doi:10.1787/18151973

TUROFED-Turkish Hotelier Federation. (2010). *Tourism Report 2.* http://www.turofed.org.tr/PDF/DergiTr/Turofed_Dergi-Turofed50.pdf

TUROFED-Turkish Hotelier Federation. (2019). *Tourism Report.* https://www.turofed.org.tr//panel/upload_system/pages_file/f0d8ac64de76e795a84a98a188b926b1.pdf

United Nations, Department of Economics and Social Affairs. (2017). *World Population Aging 2017 Highlights.* https://www.un.org/en/development/desa/population/publications/pdf/aging/WPA2017_Highlights.pdf

UNWTO-World Tourism Organization. (2021). *International Tourism Highlights, 2020 Edition.* https://www.e-unwto.org/doi/epdf/10.18111/9789284422456

Warnes, T. (2009). International Retirement Migration. In P. Uhlenberg (Ed.), *International Handbook of Population Aging. International Handbooks of Population* (Vol. 1). Springer. doi:10.1007/978-1-4020-8356-3_15

Williams, A. M., King, R., Warnes, A., & Patterson, G. (2000). Tourism and international retirement migration: New forms of an old relationship in southern Europe. *Tourism Geographies*, *2*(1), 28–49. doi:10.1080/146166800363439

Williams, A. M., King, R., & Warnes, T. (1997). A place in the sun: International retirement migration from Northern to Southern Europe. *European Urban and Regional Studies*, *4*(2), 115–134. doi:10.1177/096977649700400202 PMID:12292969

World Economic Forum. (2011). *Global Risks 2011* (6th ed.). https://www3.weforum.org/docs/WEF_GlobalRisks_Report_2011.pdf

World Economic Forum. (2013). *The Global Competitiveness Report 2012-2013.* https://www3.weforum.org/docs/WEF_GlobalCompetitivenessReport_2012-13.pdf

Yakar, M., & Sudas, I. (2019). The New Geographies of Foreign Population in Turkey. *Aegean Geographical Journal*, *28*(2), 129–164.

Yang, S. U., Shin, H., Lee, J. H., & Wrigley, B. (2008). Country reputation in multidimensions: Predictors, efects, and communication channels. *Journal of Public Relations Research*, *20*(4), 421–440. doi:10.1080/10627260802153579

Yuksel, A. (2001). Managing customer satisfaction and retention: A case of tourist destinations, Turkey. *Journal of Vacation Marketing*, 7(2), 153–168. doi:10.1177/135676670100700205

Yuksel, F. (2002), *Inter-Organisational Relations and Central-Local Interactions in Tourism Planning in Belek, Turkey* (Doctoral Thesis). Sheffield University.

KEY TERMS AND DEFINITIONS

Baby Boomers: The living generation that was born between 1946 and1964, are currently the largest group in the workforce, and many of them are either preparing to retire or already retired.

Country Image: It is the total beliefs a person has about a specific country.

COVID-19: A pandemic causing respiratory illness with symptoms such as a cough, fever, muscle pain and difficulty breathing.

Destination Management Organization (DMO): It is an organization that aims to attract visitors in order to enhance the local economy through engaging local communities to ensure that tourism development is mutually beneficial for both tourism stakeholders and local residents.

Destination Marketing: It is a form of marketing in which a destination is promoted to potential visitors by increasing awareness of a certain destination with the aim of raising demand for the destination and improving its positive image.

Expats: Skilled workers or professionals who take positions outside their home country.

International Retired Settlers (IRS): They are the people who are foreign retirees beyond retirement age and who are granted the right to stay over a long period or indefinitely in the territory of a country other than their own provided that they have sufficient independent income and do not become a charge to that country.

International Retirement Migration (IRM): It is the notion of retirees who decide to move, either permanently or seasonally, to Mediterranean Europe from Northern Europe.

Knowledge Workers: They are the workers whose main capital is knowledge such as engineers, academics, architects, lawyers, and scientists whose job is to "think for a living."

SAVE Tourism: It is a tourism concept combining the supply and demand of "scientific, academic, volunteer and education" tourism.

Sustainable Tourism Marketing (STM): It is a tourism concept that takes full account of economic, social and environmental impacts which are the main three pillar of sustainability while addressing the needs of stakeholders for both today and the future.

ENDNOTES

1 Frank M. Go was Emeritus Endowed Professor of Event and Tourism Marketing in the Department of Marketing Management at Rotterdam School of Management, Erasmus University (RSM). He joined RSM in September 1996 and established the Centre for Tourism Marketing. As an internationally well-known and respected scholar, he taught event and tourism marketing to bachelor and master students until his retirement in 2014.

[2] Reputation Institute is a global private consulting firm based in Boston and Copenhagen, founded by Dr. Charles Fombrun and Dr. Cees van Riel in 1997.

[3] Dan Buettner is an explorer, National Geographic Fellow, award-winning journalist and producer, and a New York Times bestselling author. He discovered the five places in the world—dubbed Blue Zones—where people live the longest, healthiest lives, https://www.bluezones.com/dan-buettner/.

Chapter 13
The Human Resources Perspective on the Multigenerational Workforce

Fatma Ince
https://orcid.org/0000-0002-0628-5858
Mersin University, Turkey

ABSTRACT

It is a key issue how different generations coming together for a specific purpose of the business evaluate critical information. In information processing, HRM has critical roles in adapting to the diversity of the multigenerational workforce and fostering creativity. While managing a multigenerational workforce can provide a competitive advantage, ignoring the process can cause sustainability matters for the business. From this point of view, it is useful to consider the multigenerational workforce from different perspectives in terms of HRM. All efforts to understand employees are substantial as they contribute to creating an effective and synergic organization.

INTRODUCTION

Basic demographic factors such as gender and age can lead to differences in social life as well as in organizational life. In today's organizational structures, where the importance of the individual has increased, intense efforts are made to motivate employees in line with individual and organizational goals. As with all organizational concepts, to understand a subject it is necessary to classify it and then identify the characteristics of each group. Only in this way can motivational tools be developed for a particular group. As businesses become increasingly globalized, it has become inevitable for them to understand and manage differences. Every culture, even every subculture, has its characteristics and every age group has its perceptions. Considered in more detail, there may even be differences between an individual born in the winter and an individual born in the summer or born in the Northern Hemisphere and an individual born in the Southern Hemisphere. According to Ince (2022a), as a social being, the individual is affected by the cultural structure of society and other environmental conditions. Since the

DOI: 10.4018/978-1-7998-2395-7.ch013

Copyright © 2022, IGI Global. Copying or distributing in print or electronic forms without written permission of IGI Global is prohibited.

complex mental process of individuals takes into account many variables at the same time, it can produce different results even if the conditions are the same. For this reason, it is seen as quite normal that the technological, economic, and social conditions of the period in which they grew up affect the emotions, thoughts, and behavior tendencies of the individual.

The number and level of influence of internal and external factors affecting the individual can be further increased. However, the real issue is how to use this information in organizational settings that require different individuals to work together for a specific purpose. Multinational organizations that can work in harmony with each other to achieve strategic goals but need to keep creativity alive have to exhibit successful Human Resources Management (HRM) practices in this regard. While diversity in the workplace is a factor that can provide a competitive advantage if managed well, ignoring or not following the process can create problems that cause sustainability problems for the business. Therefore, tasks such as getting to know individuals, and making their presence in the business meaningful with career plans in line with their personal goals have critical importance for the business. Furthermore, the importance of perceptions of the individuals in a workplace should consider with a clear focus on the values, mission, and vision of organizational structure, which is relevant to HRM functions. However, the issue of managing multigenerational employees may require a detailed consideration of HRM functions influenced by organizational culture. This cannot only provide a direct focus on business purpose but can also convince target groups of the business by providing insight into the context that influences corporate decision making. Thus, this chapter of the book discusses generational classifications and presents some organizational applications for understanding different age groups in the workplace.

METHODOLOGY

To understand the state of the future of Human Resource Management, it is necessary to search the variables that affect the nature of individuals in an organization. Environmental factors such as economy, technology, social culture, and other life conditions that affect people are variables that also have the potential to affect the future of the HRM practices, as well as organizational structures. One of the concepts that explain the change of individuals in light of all these factors is generations. Thereby, the idea of this chapter is to provide a basic theoretical framework for generations and their impacts on HRM. According to this idea, it is aimed to provide a practical, and comprehensive guide for practices of future HRM within the scope of the generations. This literature search is based on the general scanning model also known as the qualitative research method by using secondary data to draw attention to new generations in the workplace. Following the theoretical structure, a hypothetical scenario that is based on an HRM case study is discussed within the scope of critical theory.

AGE DIFFERENCES IN THE WORKPLACE

Although the main starting point is age, some differences can be seen in the classification of generations. While some researchers start the age groups from the post-war period, others consider the later period, and also some age differences emerge when classifying the last generations. In this section, the generally accepted five-point classification will be included as the Silent, Baby Boomers, Generation X, Y, and Z. Because this classification appeals to all age groups, considering the important events affecting people. In this title, generations and their distinctive features will be discussed in general terms before workplace practices. Thus, it is thought that the human characteristics reflected in the organizational structure will be realized more clearly.

Common Characteristics of Generations

The individual, who has different roles in business and social life, is not only affected by environmental factors but also affects the existing cultural structure. This mutual relationship between the individual and the environment requires knowing the cultural values of the employees as well as the characteristics of the business. This situation is seen as one of the requirements of directing the individual towards common goals. New studies that will help professionals better understand human nature are invaluable to an effective management process. For this reason, approaches such as generations that classify individuals provide information that serves effective management tools such as communication, orientation, coordination, and harmony.

Since it is not possible to easily use an unknown or newly discovered device, it will not be effective to try to guide a person with a complex cognitive structure without understanding it. This requirement can be observed quite clearly in some areas. In the field of marketing, serious statistical analyzes are carried out with high costs to know the consumer. The main purpose of these studies is to analyze consumers and guide their consumption behavior better. For this reason, businesses that value people and offer opportunities to reveal their potential are seen as more attractive for qualified personnel. For this reason, it is recommended that businesses consider classifications such as generation when working with different age groups. Looking at the classifications, it is seen that there are some minor age differences and name differences. One of these classifications is Generation XYZ as follows (Wiedmer, 2015; Bravo et al., 2020):

- Generation X: Also known as the Latchkey kids, MTV Generation, and 13th Generation, this group was born in 1965-1979 and consists of people who are expected to hold managerial positions in existing businesses.
- Generation Y: Those born between 1980-1996 are also called Millennials, Echo Boomers, and Boomerang Generation and are currently mid-level in their careers.
- Generation Z: Those born between 1997-2015, are also known as the iGeneration, Post-Millenials, Homeland Generation. The youngest employees of this classification are in this generation.

In the XYZ classification, it is seen that Generation Y is called the Millennials in some sources. Looking at the information on the birth interval of the generations, few changes in the age range are striking. However, the general lines of the classification were preserved, since the differences between one or two years of age would not affect the events that marked the period and the sociocultural structure. Another classification of generations, which are considered to be five, can be summarized as follows (Taylor et al., 2014; Stewart et al., 2017):

- Silent: Born between 1928 and 1945, this generation is also known as Traditionalist, Builders, Lucky Few.
- Boomers: Born between 1946 and 1964, this generation is also known as the Baby Boomers or Me Generation.

- Generation X: Born between 1965 and 1980, this generation is also known as the Baby Bust.
- Millennials: This generation was born between 1981 and 1996, also known as Generation Y, Gen Next, or Net Generations.
- Generation Z: This generation was born after 1997, also known as the iGen, Linkster Generation, Zoomers, or Gen 2020.

This classification can be made in six groups by considering the previous generation born up to 1925 in some sources. The previous generation born during the war is called the Greatest Generation or G.I. Generation. In this classification, it is seen that those born between 1890 and 1915 are called the Lost Generation. In some articles, those born between 1901 and 1913 are called the Interbellium Generation; those born between 1910 and 1924 are called the Greatest Generation (Connaway et al., 2008). However, the reflections on business life after the Silent Generation will be discussed in this section. Therefore, The Gen Alpha classification, which was born after 2012, will not be evaluated under the following titles for the same reason, they were not actively involved in business life.

Cultures of Generations

When the elements that make up the culture are examined, it is understood why the culture should be handled in terms of generations. The interactive components of the culture can be listed as follows; socio-economic status, sexual orientation, age, race, religion, ethnicity, education, gender, nationality, family, language, and generation. It is known that there are local cultures and even subcultures besides the national culture (Özdevecioğlu & İnce, 2011). In addition, it should not be forgotten that every organization has a unique organizational culture. For this reason, culture is one of the issues that should be emphasized for every workplace for efficiency. It is known that culture has many direct and indirect effects on personality. Like a set of shared values, beliefs, and norms, culture influences an individual's learning style, lifestyle, and even behavioral patterns. So, it can be said that culture is one of the powerful factors that shape personality. The importance of culture for HRM lies at this point. The learning process, perception style, and interpretation of the world of an individual trained during the war will be affected by all developments. Thus, knowing the methods in which the individuals learn better and which features they seek as a leader will facilitate the manager's work. Learning and development is a crucial part of the HRM process to enhance an employee's skills, knowledge, and competency, resulting in better performance in an organization. In addition, skills and competencies are required for an employee to perform certain tasks and procedures according to a required job standard (Banfield et al., 2018). Employee learning and development is linked to a business's ability to achieve strategic goals, as an evolving workforce provides decision-making authority, shares information, minimizes incivility, and provides performance feedback (Spreitzer & Porath, 2012). So, it would be valuable to describe the generational differences in the workforce in terms of HRM functions such as recruitment, training and development, motivation, and so on.

Considering the period in which the Silent Generation lived, there seem to be great events that are profoundly shocking such as World War II and the Bombing of Darwin. This generation, which also saw the effect of communism, lived its childhood in the presence of events that shook the world (Robinson et al., 2013). Living in an uneasy society during wartime would have psychological consequences as well as physical harm. Even people who are not involved in war see immigrant societies and share the suffering of the world. In a study conducted on the mental effects of war in adults, and children, it was determined that especially the belief system and social relations of the children were damaged and they were forced to deal with high-stress levels (Lustig et al., 2004; McCrindle & Wolfinger, 2009). Therefore, the conditions in which the society is located, and the cultural perspective formed according to these conditions also affect the attitudes of individuals. The Silent Generation prefers military-style disciplined learning because of all cultural factors. Rules and orders should be clear, precise, and unambiguous. In addition to these learning environments, they prefer formal and didactic learning for education. Also, the training focus is from top to down, traditional, and on-the-job style. This fondness for traditional methods is also seen in other habits (Shen, 2019). The generation that likes face-to-face communication prefers to be informed in person, and in advance in practices such as promotion, dismissal, relocation, or additional remuneration.

Secondly, the Baby Boomers went beyond the radio limited life of the previous generation to meet television. The critical events of this period can be listed as follows; the Vietnam War, Decimal Currency, Neil Armstrong, and Cyclone Tracy. Studies on the effects of war and cyclone events that affect human psychology have found that women are more prone to fear. In addition, individual characteristics such as anxiety, nervous fears, and habits may change in a stressful environment (Milne, 1977). While the impact of war and cyclones on gender is not true in all situations, it is one of the saddening truths that is accepted whenever families are more stressed, overly anxious, or hysterical. In this period when seeing means believing, the most basic method of persuasion is to talk with evidence. Therefore, the focus has been on documents prepared with technical data and evidence. Since this generation prefers a quiet environment, they learn comfortably in a structured classroom environment. This generation, acting according to long-term needs, attaches importance to informing the authorities while working in an organization (Palmatier & Crecelius, 2019). Unlike the previous generation, in addition to using cash, multiple payment methods such as split or partial payment can also be used.

As in previous generations, natural and economic events that shaped the century were experienced during the X Generation period. The Challenger Explodes, Stock Market Crash of 1987, Halley's Comet, Berlin Wall, and the Newcastle Earthquake are the most important events that attract the most attention in this term. More than simply separating East and West Berlin, the Berlin Wall was like the dividing line between capitalism and socialism. After the Second World War, one of the divided parts of the country flourished with capitalism, while the other fell under the influence of socialism and oppressive rule. This process, including the other countries around it, and the destruction of the wall took place among influential events all over the world. Those born during this period were raised by parents who knew the effects of capitalism and socialism, and they feel the universal effects of the 1987 Stock Market Crash. This event also as known Black Monday forces the countries to international financial integration. On the other hand, all domestic investors saw the economic interdependence of international financial markets in such a large scope (Hamao et al., 1991). Not only the investors but also the consumers and households were affected by this global-scale event. Due to the sociological, and psychological effects of all these events, seeing is believing. After all, seeking expert opinion, one of the knowledge sources of different ways of persuasion, is valid for this generation. The financial values of this generation include the medium-term goals takes to accomplish. These goals can be taken into account as practices in incentives. They volunteer for using credit savvy and life-stage debt to achieve financial aims. On the other hand, the learning style of Gen X beyond the case studies, practical methods, and similar applications (Beck & Garris, 2019). Hence, creating a round-table discussion, and a relaxed atmosphere could be suitable in the workplace. Especially spontaneous or interactive training gives positive and productive results for employee training and development.

The Millennials or Generation Y experienced these events; The Columbine High School massacre, Thredbo Disaster, New Millennium, September 11, and Bali Bombing. The psychological effects of such events, which endanger the sense of security of individuals, can continue for a long time. Depression and post-traumatic disorder can be seen even in psychologically strong individuals. The way people perceive the outside world after their disasters changes according to safety perception. After all, it can be said that they love the emotional and participative styles for training and the stories make it easy to learn a new concept. Therefore, multi-sensory, and visual technics should be preferred for workplace training. For the best learning atmosphere, new methods such as the cafe-style with music, and multi-modals can be used. Because these technics are also capable to fill missing modalities given the observed ones and they are ideal for deep learning for this generation (Kamalia et al., 2019). Otherwise, unlike other generations, the financial values of Gen Y are based on the short-term wants, they live with credit-dependent and choose the lifestyle debt to achieve financial aims. They consider the comments of their friends more than loyalty, so changing jobs is not as dramatic as previous generations, but more normal. One of the consequences of this landscape in the light of current advancements and the emergence of the gig economy is the changing jobs. These could be useful points for HRM professionals as knowing the environment in which employees are more prone to learn and practice can encourage desired behavior.

The last generation of this classification is Gen Z which was born with the Iraq and Afghanistan War, Asian Tsunami, WikiLeaks, Global Financial Crisis (GFC), and the Arab Spring. The Asian Tsunami is also known as the 2004 Indian Ocean Tsunami is the deadliest tsunami on record, because it caused more than 230.000 deaths. After the disaster, the towns and villages have been rebuilding to maintain the immense destruction. Also, in 2008 the world economy faced its most dangerous crisis called GFC since the Great Depression of the 1930s. This is the most significant economic shock in the post-war period and it affects all economic activity in every country, and region from the US to the World (Martin, 2015; Tudoran, 2020). Although the effects of all these developments on the people living in that period differ, they still provide general information in terms of social psychology. These disasters and their repercussions help to understand the change in the attitude of people living in that period and what happened afterward. Considering the issue in terms of the application of HRM practices in a multigenerational context, it is necessary to understand the workplace organizational behaviors of Gen Z.

One of the factors that should not be forgotten is advanced technology and its effects on business life. Advanced technology is increasingly evident in many aspects of business life, helping to make learning fun, exciting, and richly rewarding. Whence it is seen that the multi-modal technics and e-learning with interactive styles can be more successful (Ince, 2021b). For this generation, kinesthetic learning and student-centered approach should be preferred in applications such as increasing participation, problem-solving, communication skills, critical thinking. According to Wagner (2014), the lounge room style, and multi-stimulus atmosphere are recommended for this learning environment. On the other hand, the needs of each generation should be determined by taking into account the digital gaps based on individual and socio-cultural differences in the accelerated digital learning process (Ince, 2021c). The financial values of this generation include digital solutions such as e-stores, e-commerce, and life-long debt (Ince, 2020b). This means that flexible and open to change interactive applications can be used as motivators for HRM professionals. Keeping up with the digital world is one of the most important points for this generation, both in business and non-business conditions.

CHALLENGES OF THE MULTIGENERATIONAL WORKFORCE

The communication process is defined as the transfer or exchange of information, ideas, or messages. From this point of view, communication in the workplace can be defined as the process of exchanging information and ideas, both verbal and non-verbal, within an organization. Working efficiently and being productive is based on organizational communication skills, which have strategic importance for all organizations. When the psychological concepts related to the organization are examined in detail, it is seen that each term is the result of interpersonal communication under the name of employees, colleagues, managers, stakeholders (Ince, 2018a). Therefore, all perception terms, which are considered from a managerial perspective, emerge or develop as a result or reflection of organizational communication. Besides that, the sensitivity of organizational activities to technology will also affect perceptions as a part of organizational atmosphere and climate. Thus, the communication styles and technology preferences of generations are discussed in this title of the chapter.

Types of Generational Communication

Communication is one of the most basic elements of organizations because interpersonal relations begin and develop with the exchange of information. It is not merely a transfer of information, it is also about sharing the workplace atmosphere as it is a cultural interaction. Effective communication requires focusing on the real message and emotion to achieve the goal adequately. This exchanging process is about the presentation of views or messages by the sender in a way best understood by the receiver. So, a successful organizational communication strategy has the potential to create an obvious difference in the incentive structure resulting from the motivation between parties (DeCenzo et al., 2016). It is one of the factors that motivate employees in the implementation of innovative ideas (Dulaimi & Hartman, 2006). This is because poor communication and misunderstanding are generally linked to social distancing and poor emotional connection (Neeley, 2015).

The actual message transfer, called effective or empathetic communication, is not limited to the skills of the sender, but the target must also be a good listener. This basic information about communication shows that this concept, which is a part of the culture, is shaped as a result of mutual interaction. Therefore, the perception of the individual will be affected by many variables such as the communication style, culture, close friends, working environment, communication habits within and outside the family during the growth period. So, it can be said that socio-cultural, individual, and environmental factors, which are the basic elements of all cultures, affect the communication style as well as the individual's age, childhood, and generation. This situation makes the communication preferences of different generations an increasingly important organizational issue. Knowing individual differences in communication, which is very important in business life, will make an organizational contribution in a multigenerational workplace. So, The HR manager should consider the communication tools as an opportunity to maintain loyalty and commitment.

The Silent Generation, the first generation in the classification, had the habit of using formal letters in their youth. The Baby Boomers saw the first TV, and they became part of the first mass advertisement in parallel. Also, the communication media of this generation is the telephone because they grew up with pre cell phone mobile technology, such as the radio, television, and landline telephones (North, 2019). Secondly, Generation X was introduced to personal computers due to advanced technology and as a result, the e-mail and text message system are entered their life as new communication tools. So, they are comfortable with smartphones, e-mail, laptops, PDAs, tablets, and other technology in the workplace. Gen X as known as the middle child of generations has better educated than previous generations (Berge & Berge, 2019). Besides all these, they live and work in a more ethnically diverse atmosphere, making them more resilient to alternative lifestyles as well as better adapting to change. These values make this generation a good listener and an effective communicator in an organization.

Thirdly, the Millennial or Gen Y enjoys the tablets and smartphones as the technological toys allow text or social media communications effortlessly. This generation, which already gives importance to the recommendations of their friends in investment and shopping decisions, prefers to use social media and comments very effectively. However, the preferred social media tool for communication and shopping can change over time. Because previous generations seem to have moved away from some applications, such as Meta, where they started to trend more. There are also differences between social media or internet usage and the timing of it. Lastly, the Gen Z child of high technology prefers handheld devices to communicate. After this generation, it is thought that technological solutions such as 3D printers, google glass, wearable technology, and other fashion technology devices are thought to be the main signature products of future generations. Gen Z grew up during the most accelerated periods in terms of technological change (TC) and economic growth. And they have witnessed a period in which the unprecedented rapid growth in technology in human history. They have the opportunity to use the internet 24/7 by accessing the global information network for activities such as problem-solving, networking, communication, learning, and purchasing. They do not even know the world without smart devices and the internet, so they are text-specific and look for on-demand content everywhere (Dimock, 2019). Because of the nature of early mobile adopters, the basic communication channels are shaped via the internet or Wi-Fi.

While technology has made it easier for people to communicate with others, it has also shaped the way of life. In particular, the emergence of electronic communication devices facilitates one-way technology communication with a wide range of products such as mobile phones, e-mails, and social networking sites. On the other hand, the coronavirus disease (COVID) pandemic, which is still in effect, shows that telecommunication tools are working successfully and sustainably. Recent events have accelerated the trend of working remotely and could permanently change the way of work (Ince, 2020a). So, using the internet for distance working exposes the organization to new approaches or new ways of doing business. Especially in multinational companies, HR professionals have already used applications such as distance education or online interview in processes such as recruitment and training activities. However, technology-oriented change is expected in other functions of human resources. Since the interrelationship between technology and communication cannot be ignored, the next topic focuses on the impact of technology on generations.

Technology Preferences of Different Generations

A deeper understanding of technological choices opens HRM to possibilities hidden from a more restricted view. Looking at the developments in technology, robotics, and Artificial Intelligence (AI) in recent years, it is seen that the inventions that changed the world came from the Baby Boomer Generation. The inventions of the 21st century from the synthetic cell to the World Wide Web (WWW) have reshaped the world. The most interesting technological and scientific innovations of this generation target a wide variety of needs. Research to visualize individual atoms has aided this progress and has given scientists the chance to develop the smallest nanotechnology.

After the invention of the scanning tunneling microscope, DNA fingerprinting was invented in the 1950s and is used to separate people, identify criminals, and interpret historical ruins. The Jarvik 7 artificial heart, Apple II - the first personal computer, Segway self-balancing personal transporter, Optical character recognition (OCR), and text-to-speech technology are some of the inventions in this period (Kiger, 2010). The importance of all these inventions and more for HRM is that it helps professionals interpret the cultural conditions, needs, and technological influences that drive people. So, it can be said that The relationships between HRM and technology can define the context of solutions that contribute to an understanding of the objectives set by the organization's competitive strategy.

When the stories of the emergence of these inventions are examined in detail, it is seen that adults who have spent childhood in the postwar period need to find answers to the problems they observe. Besides, all these developments include the perspective of the Baby Boomers, but also show the place of technology in people's life. Accidental, unintended, or intended scientific discoveries that changed the world have created the infrastructure of technological developments and brought technology to an indispensable position in the center of human life. As mentioned before, the life perspectives and tendency to use technology may vary depending on the person's growing conditions, age, education, and other factors. In simple terms, it does not mean that every individual uses available technology at the same rate because individual differences must be respected. However, intergenerational classification is often preferred as a powerful tool as it gives insight into age groups and preferences.

In the modern age, the iconic technology begins with the radio, motor vehicle, so on and continues to the Android, İpad, Google, Wi-Fi, and other similar inventions. The TV, audio cassette, and transistor radio are used in the 1950s, while the VCR, Walkman, and IBM PC are used in the 1970s. The progress of technology continues and takes a huge step with the Internet, e-mail, SMS, DVD, PlayStation, Xbox, and iPod (Tidd & Bessant, 2018). While the endless development of technology continues to progress day by day, it also offers opportunities for discoveries.

Domestic technology, new web, and mobile applications show that technology is rapidly renewing itself in a short time. In addition to looking at the technological developments witnessed by the oldest generation, it is seen that there have been very high developments in the last century. With the spread of Meta among grandparents or older generations, they started to make their life easier by adapting to technology (Chugh & Ruhi, 2018). The use of computers to assist communication and production processes is also a clear indicator of these trends. The emergence of human-computer interaction technologies is making IT an integral part of projects in all businesses, from small to large. So, it can be said that IT plays a critical role in the business world for whole generations. A single e-mail can reach any business interest group in the world. Not only communication systems, but also business systems such as inventory management, data management, customer relations management, and management information systems are developing technology-oriented.

From capital to labor-intensive businesses, organizations become more flexible and diversified with new organizational structures or global-scale applications. Also, the entrepreneurs strive for developments that capture age as well as personal preferences. It is necessary to think more innovatively to meet the needs of technology-oriented new generations. Because ignoring the different characteristics of new generations will not be a sustainable approach. The technology-heavy multitasking is seen as some of the new habits that shape the future. Thereby, if new generations cannot imagine a world without it by putting the internet at the center of their life and growing up with role models that build their future, it is necessary to provide a workplace accordingly. Organizational conditions and career opportunities should be diversified according to personal preferences and technology compatibility. The harmony between technology, individuals, and organizations is seen as one of the important sources of motivation. From this point of view, some critical factors that motivate generations will be discussed in the next title.

Motivation and Workplace Culture

The Baby Boomers feel comfortable with face-to-face communication, while Gen X chooses e-mail or instant messaging (IM). Furthermore, the Millennials and other new generations prefer text messages to phone calls. On the other hand, while the Silent Generation's ideal leader is an authoritative and commanding style, Baby Boomers prefer thinkers who give orders. The style that performs with coordination is preferred by Gen X, while collaboration and empowerment are seen as the favorite of the Millennials. Additionally, Gen Z wants the inspiring or co-creator style in their work life. Consequently, the influencers of the generations are varied due to the role model effect. Discipline and arrangement are what the Silent Generations look for in the workplace, that is why they are considering the authorities. But the Baby Boomers value experts and seek evidence-based reasoning. Gen X tends to be pragmatic, so they follow the practitioners while the Millennials put excessive emphasis on peers because they care about experiences, and Gen Z prefers to use the user-generated forums to reach information and make a decision (Prawitasari, 2018).

Reaching information in the workplace is a process that requires a printer and output for the Silent Generation. Because they prefer to read the information from a paper or a copy, while Gen Z and other new generations will google the information they need to know. Old generations in the workplace wait for respect from others. Because they consider the job title to be a position to be respected, Gen X thinks that the ideas should be respected and other next generations are focusing on the involvement. Also, the priorities of life are changing from work to family and friends (Rodriguez et al., 2019). It is very important to choose the appropriate motivation tool to motivate the generations with different habits, business values and to work in harmony with each other in the same work environment. Because the workplace energy, which is an indicator of the employee's effort towards work, can be increased depending on motivation tools (Ince, 2018b). This situation can be observed quite clearly in family businesses. Since the perspectives of the first generation who are the founders of the business and the young generation are different, their perspectives on concepts such as leadership, management or motivation will also be different. While the founding generation sees work as a very valuable and almost part of the family, the younger generation may want to improve themselves in different areas (Ince, 2022c). Therefore, the life experience and motivation of the individual who was born as the son of the company owner, and the efforts of individuals who risk everything and start an enterprise will be diverse.

For the motivation of the young generations, the last technology can be used, because they look for innovations slowly, while older ones simply accept it. The latest technology and new devices are part of the planning, meeting, and decision-making process in modern organizations. Many technology applications are used even in daily routine works. Thereby, technology has not only developed new types of products and inventions but also significantly improved the way it works. Technology management needs to provide advanced decision-making systems and implementation tools to meet organizational needs. The promotion opportunities in the workplace and the methods of reaching the target group are also affected by these factors. Thus, it is necessary to consider the priority and expectation of an employee while planning a career.

The lifelong or traditional career path is the best way of the work for the Silent Generation. Also, the Baby Boomers have job commitment with the values of loyalty, self-driven, and high work ethic. The tenure average of Gen X is 15 years, while the Boomers and Silent Generation have more than 15 years. Furthermore, these years are getting short for the Millennials and Gen Z from year to month. Because Gen X evaluates work-life balance as opposed to commitment. Work and life integration is the key factor for the Millennials due to their idealistic, fair, and flexible values. The goal of advancement is the main reason for working in an organization. Similarly, Gen Z looks for learning opportunities with a purpose in an organization. They have realistic and multicultural fluency values with technology native skills but the work aim of this generation will be determined in the future clearly (Lim et al., 2019; Rodriguez et al., 2019). All these developments show that organizational practices such as determining the organizational communication channels and career management process should be suitable for generations, their values, and expectations.

MANAGING GENERATIONAL DIFFERENCES IN HR

The management style, known as the art of directing the employees to a specific purpose, emerges and is shaped depending on the current workforce and organizational conditions. The strategic structure that includes the target, mission, and vision should be prepared for the future with a structure that includes employees in all positions. In a few years, 5 generations are expected to be a part of business life in the same organization (Ince, 2018a). They have already started working together shoulder to shoulder in some businesses.

The preferred style of management and leadership of the generations is explained before. Therefore, it can be said that the shift of the management style and behaviors expected from the manager from the authoritarian structure to a more participatory and instructive structure. Management levels are shifting from hierarchical structure to teamwork in parallel with organizational structures that have become simpler and flatter. Due to the expectations of new generations, the gap between management and employees is gradually closing. As mentioned earlier, young workers also pay attention to learning and development opportunities in the workplace. It is not just about working but more so about personal growth, and individual talents. Thereby, especially in developed countries where the living conditions are better, new generations may choose diversity in their careers while looking for a job suitable for their self-realization goals (Rodriguez, et al., 2003). As it is known, the family, friends and themselves are taking more priority in the next generation, while the main concern of retiring employees is work. Promoting openness and action orientation in these priorities are important for building a (HPO) high performance organization (DeWaal, 2020). So, it can be said that these are important implications for the performance management of generations.

The Baby Boomers place great emphasis on career advancement as they grew up in a famine economy and poverty. As a manager or an employee, they expect authority to be respected. Also, they are very sensitive to feedback as a team member. They live to work, so job security is the main motivation tool for them. The ideal management style should include power, authority, and business-oriented goals. As a result of the reduction of the effects of the war and the re-establishment of countries, the new generation that emerged from the psychology of scarcity has become a generation that focuses more on entrepreneurial values. Gen X focuses its career on a lack of job security and work-life balance. They adopt a more informal approach to work than previous (Suomäki et al., 2019). Hence, managers of this generation must be goal-oriented and give them the chance to be more flexible, creative, and multi-tasking.

Integrity, diversity, honesty, and responsibility are some of the values of the Gen Y. These values lead them to feel more social, confident, optimistic, altruistic, and practical. As good team workers, these employees tend to be collaborative and achievement-oriented. A helpful management style should include mentoring and feedback with career-focused opportunities. They prefer meaningful and flexible work because they also want to spend time with their friends or family (Patil & Peshave, 2020). Thus, the business should not cover the whole life. So, It would be unreasonable to expect employees to live constantly thinking about their work. Career options that go beyond living a permanent life by purchasing a house or car with lifetime employment must offer increasingly flexible options. Because career orientation preferences change from lifelong work in a flexible job to freedom. People are increasingly focusing on making themselves happy rather than focusing on work and career.

For retirees, career management is a stable path that includes lifelong work. Afterward, the values of loyalty to the employer and commitment to work began to gain importance. However, the middle generation gives importance to work-life balance rather than the happiness of the boss and wants to feel more independence in business life. So, they always want to know the career options and they can change the firm more easily than previously. As freedom and flexibility become more important, managerial job changing is increasingly an option for today's mid-level managers. Furthermore, future generations will prefer multitasking and a variety of career paths to constantly change jobs. After successful applications, it is useful to take a closer look at the common mistakes made in the next issue.

Successful Implications and Harmony

Generally, when successful managers are asked about diversity, they will say that they are open-minded and do not care about diversity. However, in real life, it is quite possible to come across examples where even basic differences such as gender and ethnicity cannot be completely overcome. Therefore, The first condition of working together with different generations as an effective team is not to evaluate anyone with your truths. Some companies like IBM, Google, and General Mills are doing their best to increase the differences and take advantage of this situation. Some practices, such as on-the-job training opportunities, career counseling, and mentoring programs, help employees learn from each other. According to Abraham & Dao (2019), taking individual differences into account while adapting to the environment is an important part of sustainability innovation systems (SIS). In other words, the subject is a strategic issue that is important for the future of the enterprise.

Understanding generations and balancing their needs with organizational goals should be one of the values that guide business strategy and should be reflected in the entire structure from a managerial perspective. New approaches such as management by objectives (MBO), high-performance work practices (HPWPs) can be seen as a powerful tool in evaluating performance by ensuring the harmony of the employee and the organization in terms of generations (Nguyen, 2020). According to MBO, the evaluation process involves aligning the individual's personal development goals with those of the organization, thereby helping to achieve high self-motivation.

As mentioned earlier, each employee's perception of trust and support may depend on different circumstances. Keeping the lines of communication open can be a useful way to be aware of the changing situations, possible challenges and address them.

While older generations adapt to technology in the workplace, new generations are already used to it. Hence, the manager should allow the employee to develop and sometimes accept learning from the employee. Because it is an important point for developing organizational design, learning culture, and strategy. Organizational culture expresses the system of meaning shared by group members and distinguishes the business from other organizations (Becker, 2008). In addition, organizational culture expresses goals through values, beliefs, and guides activities through shared assumptions or group norms (Groysberg et al., 2018).

Since the working style of the aging workforce and the perspective of the youth are different, clear policies need to be established to avoid potential conflicts among employees. In a workplace where different generations work together, it can be helpful to identify conflict and problem-solving methods in advance. Both theoretical and practical training on various subjects should be organized in certain periods to eliminate the differences in intergenerational technology approaches and ways of doing business (Hassan et al., 2019). This training will not only make the employee feel valued but will also allow them to improve themselves. A common set of values should be established where employees can share their perspectives, cultures, and habits. Some small celebrations or parties can facilitate the integration of different groups of employees by seeing each other in a different environment. It can be said that strategic awareness is based on diversity, synergy, and creative thinking and therefore it is necessary to be sensitive to the differences between generations. Because cultural synergy is one of the powerful tools in providing sustainability and competitive advantage (Ince, 2018c). So, the generations and their potential contributions must be considered to make a difference as a manager.

Common Mistakes and Negative Stereotypes

Awareness is a key point in the organization as it removes limitations on the general validity of the discussed managerial implications or results. So, one of the biggest mistakes made in a multigenerational workplace is to assume that all values begin to become universal with globalization. Some eating or fashion habits may converge, but the way employees perceive the world and their moral norms will continue to reflect the influences of their time. This is how the synergy effect, which is the most important contribution expected from working in the same environment with different generations, emerges (Ince, 2021a). It should be considered that the factors in each individual's psychological contract are different from each other, and therefore the management approach should be adjusted to meet the expectations of each employee.

The second common mistake is to act with confidence or common sense, which is bound together by shared experiences within a social group. Therefore, it is not right for the manager or employees to evaluate their environment and colleagues with their cultural values (Fratrièová & Kirchmayer, 2018). Because the culture that forms the list of common behaviors can vary according to each group's qualifications and upbringing. It is previously discussed that many global events have marked each period, but their impacts on people are different. Thus, it may be insufficient to evaluate the search for a guarantee of a life of a person born in the war period and the search for an adventure of a person born in the internet age from the same point of view.

On the other hand, generalizing to employees based on ethnicity, gender or age can be harmful if biased. Generational classification can be a good guide for understanding employees of different age groups. However, this guide will do more harm than good if used in a biased way. So, individual differences should always be taken into account. Because even identical twins raised in the same family can have various career options by adopting different value systems. Since human psychology is affected by many factors at the same time, evaluating it from a single point of view can create a vicious circle. In addition, it should not be forgotten that organizational and other external environmental factors have many direct and indirect effects on individual perceptions. Thus, within the context of the contingency approach, each event should be evaluated in its context.

Since communication is the most basic information transfer method of social and organizational structure, all deficiencies in this field can lead to undesirable results. In addition to choosing the wrong method in organizational communication, the illusion that communication takes place correctly is one of the mistakes made. For effective communication, just conveying the message is never enough (Kitchen & Daly, 2002). In this way, transmitting a message at the decoding level of the target is a more functional solution. Functional and empathic communication includes elements that take into account all the parties involved. Aging employees may prefer to talk to people face to face rather than look at their e-mails. Younger generations may prefer to use a phone or other smart device rather than writing in a notebook. For this reason, the meetings should be communicated not only in writing but also verbally, and the way employees attend the meeting should not be interpreted as not being taken seriously. It should be always considered that all generations have their work values and job habits due to behavioral patterns (Ince, 2018a). The entry of the new generation into business life, technological developments, and extraordinary situations such as pandemics show that new and different ways of working can emerge in business life. It should not be forgotten that there is no golden rule of directing people, and each individual is a unique value.

HRM CASE STUDY: CHALLENGES OF MANAGING THE GENERATIONS

This is a hypothetical scenario-based case study that is written for training or setting up discussions. It is not the primary purpose to show that managerial decisions are handled effectively or ineffectively or to question a managerial situation. Published materials and other academic resources are used in the preparation of the case study. Before the detail of a case, critical management studies (CMS) approaches will be included, and the role of generations in critical management in terms of HRM will be revealed.

SETTING THE STAGE

Negative organizational outcomes such as turnover intention, burnout, and conflict have the potential to directly or indirectly affect the performance of the business. There are different reasons for such perceptions, both individualistic and environmental. The former emphasizes personal characteristics, while the latter emphasizes organizational characteristics and work environment. The frequency and continuity of these perceptions create results ranging from serious anxiety disorders to stress and even physical ailments and affect individual and organizational performances (Buick & Thomas, 2001; Liang, 2012). Work-related psychological problems lead to negative organizational perceptions and consequences such as increased absenteeism, job dissatisfaction, low organizational commitment, low employee energy, and effort (Maslach et al., 2001; Maslach & Leiter, 2005).

To direct the individual to the determined goals, it is necessary to avoid negative organizational perceptions, to provide a positive atmosphere and organizational support. Even successful managers experience burnout from time to time, so they are fired and less experienced individuals who have not yet learned the intricacies of the job are hired during these periods (Krone, et al., 1989). While management experience in another industry can be judged by the knowledge of an educated workforce, training inexperienced employee means time and cost to the business. So there are also long-term harms that can result from ineffective decisions. Therefore, it can be said that there are indirect effects as well as direct performance decreases. For this reason, the studies which are aimed at defining the employees and their characteristics are very valuable. Critical management studies can support the search for identity in this sense.

Critical theory contributes to expanding the perspectives of areas such as management by considering individual differences from various aspects. Individual differences are associated with the challenge of asymmetrical power within the organization, regardless of their origin. According to Alvesson & Deetz (2006), differences in the workplace can be seen as a tool for freedom or one side to become dominant. Therefore, CMS addresses individual differences in the workplace in terms of their potential to lead to exclusionary practices (Alvesson & Willmott, 2002). Bhabha (1994), while examining the subject in terms of culture, also touched on the results of marginalization and hybridization. As a result of the dominant side putting pressure on the other culture, an obligatory hybrid culture emerges from the union of the old and the new. The ontological and agential issues statuses of identity are conceptualized to understand an ongoing process and dynamic relationship between individuals and others. There are many sociological and psychological studies on individuals and organizations, such as the self-concept, social identity theory, and socially constructed self (Cooley, 1902; Tajfel & Turner, 1979). In contemporary theorizing, interest in individual characteristics has continued in terms of CMS. While these studies serve the individual, they also address collectives (Hardy 2004). Therefore, examining such studies in the field of HRM will contribute to the efficiency of the functions to understand group dynamics as well as individual behaviors in the workplace. Thus, the topic is seen as important for both professionals and trainers.

CASE DESCRIPTION

iFitam Inc. has been serving the plastic manufacturing industry for more than 30 years. The company states that its target is to provide excellent workmanship, quality plastic products, and a competitive price with a fast turnaround time. The company, which wants to make new investments and expand its existing activities in different regions with its growth strategy, tries to manage this process correctly. Mr. Morex, one of the company's oldest employees, is asked to form a new team and work to open a new branch in a different region. Mr. Morex, who prefers to continue his business life with intense shifts, states that he cannot live without working despite his retirement and that he has a lot of work in this business. The thoughts of Mr. Morex, whom the trainees see as an old and grumpy man, are as follows:

"Compliance with working hours is very important. It is good to be disciplined, for example, when you go to meetings, you need to have an agenda and a pen. Behaviors such as taking notes, arriving on time, finishing work on time are indicators of discipline. After all, you're making money out of this business, so it should be rewarded. I have come across many financial and economic crises in my career. Therefore, I know the difficulties of making money very well. Today's youth want to get rich the easy way and do not know how to use money efficiently due to a lack of knowledge. If they get some money, they either spend it or deposit it in the bank because they don't know how to deposit it. They state that they come to the interviews with their phones and record the conversations on their phones. But for me, it means that they are very careless about meetings and working hours. Even while listening to you, they are interested in something else on their phones, not paying their full attention. They need to be constantly monitored as they are inexperienced and prone to making mistakes. This business is too precious for me to be handed over to young and unqualified people. Thus, I must continue to support my business as much as possible. Young workers tend to avoid work and think more about themselves than work".

It is seen that the company, whose workforce turnover rate has increased by 4% in recent years, has difficulty in finding qualified personnel while filling this gap. For this reason, while the pressure to replace these employees, at least 3% of whom are qualified personnel, leads to a decrease in the number of qualified personnel, the employment rate cannot fill this gap. For this reason, Mr. Morex thinks that new staff should be recruited first from within the organization and then from outside. This situation requires him to work in coordination with the HR department. However, due to the workload, the HR department sometimes cannot wait for Mr. Morex to attend and has to move forward. While job interviews continue for different positions within the company, HR does not only conduct job interviews for the new branch. However, Mr. Morex creates difficulties because he does not want to accept this situation.

Newly recruited students frequently state that they do not want to work with Mr. Morex. He also does not want to work with beginners who have not yet completed the adaptation process. It has been learned that some young employees even endure this situation to learn the job, they do not have the opportunity to rise due to former employees and also they do not think of staying in the business for a long time because there is no current career or retirement plan. There is no other way to learn on the work yet, as practices such as orientation or on-the-job training are not kept up to date. Sometimes an unexpected position change is made before the job is fully learned and the deficiencies are tried to be eliminated. When this change coincided with the marketing unit, it would not be possible to receive additional incentives due to aging premium policies despite heavy selling pressure. Mr. Morex's stern demeanor and insistence on doing things his way begin to affect the commitment of these young people who want to rise and advance in their careers. Mr. Morex, who has used the advantage of being in the business for a long time and knows almost all employees, maintains this attitude even in units outside his authority. Because he is controlling, oppressive, and meticulous, the top management supports this attitude by keeping quiet about the situation. With a manager like Mr. Morex, it will not be possible for anyone to slack off from work. In this way, although the costs were kept under control, there were also successful cases where serious mistakes were returned early thanks to this meticulousness.

Because he is not very good with technology, he likes to supervise people at work rather than sitting at a desk. For this reason, Mr. Morex misses e-mail announcements if not told face-to-face and holds other employees responsible for this. According to him, if a meeting or announcement is to be made, it should be spoken face to face and notified in advance. Events such as appointments, meetings, interviews should be planned. But the growing business can no longer afford the cumbersomeness of communicating with written documents. Changes such as new international connections, new branches, and new employees require remote meetings and electronic expediting of transactions.

On top of all that, while employees try to find shortcuts to get their work done on time, they sometimes have to neglect their managers and choose ways to communicate with them and make quick decisions. Because it took a long time to try to persuade some executives who resisted change, like Mr. Morex, there was a risk of missing out on immediate opportunities. Even if they managed to persuade Mr. Morex, they were not appreciated and their success was attributed to others. Some employees quit their jobs and went to a rival company just because of it.

As the unit manager also contributes to performance evaluation systems, Mr. Morex avoids appreciating young employees because he thinks they should not be pampered. He has even been seen to deter people he finds untrustworthy and to have others do their work. According to him, a reliable employee comes first. Therefore, it is safer to outsource the job to a trusted long-established person rather than a novice employee. Young employees and senior managers, who reported this situation to the HR department, have not yet been offered a solution while the work continues.

Seen as one of the best employees of the company and reliable in the eyes of senior management, Morex does not hesitate to use this image against the HR department. Employees with no hope of promotion also find themselves working in a competitive work environment. Due to the culture of competition between departments, each department blames the other when there is an incomplete or faulty transaction in the company. For this reason, although the works are progressing, full coordination cannot be achieved.

CURRENT CHALLENGES FACING THE ORGANIZATION

Undefined business processes and generational conflicts are some of the challenges and issues faced by the organization during its growth phase. Lack of communication undermines employee confidence and can lead to poor performance levels and poor teamwork. Such organizations have a weak workplace culture that has to face the growing problem of employment. Regardless of staffing shortages, completing tasks and working with difficult managers are some of the main challenges for the organization's HR functions.

Different expectations and working styles of each generation increase the need for effective communication and open and flexible structures. So, senior management should support processes such as recruitment, orientation and training of the HR department and should be open to innovations in these processes.

The HRM department, which deals with the entire service of an employee from hiring to retirement, needs to analyze the current situation well. The next steps should be determined according to the results of the analysis, the career map and the necessary motivation tools for this map should be updated. Problems experienced in such matters lead to situations such as one-man authority in the organization, the inability of different groups to work effectively, lack of authority, and dysfunctional conflicts. In the case study, HRM plays a key role in communication between managers and young employees.

SOLUTIONS AND RECOMMENDATIONS

First of all, looking at the current situation in the workplace, it is seen that different age groups and therefore different generations have to work in the same environment. As understood from the company and manager story in the case study, Mr. Morex belongs to Baby Boomer Generation. It is known that the Boomer Generation is deeply committed to their work, as they see very difficult financial conditions and economic instability. This generation, which is hard-working, determined, dedicated to working, ability to forge their career upward, strong commitment in the workplace, is now working together with more open-minded but competitive Gen X, as well as Gen Y, which is very open to mobility and role change, and the technology intuitive, career multi-tasker and critical Gen Z. It is seen that young interns and graduates who have just started work are Gen Z. First of all, the problems arising from the coexistence of different situations can be mentioned, while evaluating the current situation. Here, the conflict between the Boomer, which adopts the classical management approach, and Gen Z, which prefers technology-oriented progress, is seen. When the issue is discussed in terms of HRM, it is beneficial to evaluate the processes due to the functions of the department.

Motivating Factors: Lower-level employees may have trouble seeing the big picture about their business strategy or vision. Therefore, managers must understand the frustrations of lower-level employees who do less interesting work and find it difficult to adapt to the current management style. While responsibilities are constantly increasing, the interests of the employees must also be considered. Thus, various primary research methods can be used to analyze employee expectations, and then these analysis results can be used as a motivation tool. For quality results and professional commitment, motivational tools need to be tailored to the individual.

Employee Growth and Employment Process: Developing employees and providing new employment in line with the basic objectives of the enterprise are among the duties of HRM. For this purpose, it should be aimed primarily to determine the development needs of the existing employees and to provide the necessary training on time. Methods such as fishbone diagrams, job analysis, or job enlargement models should be applied to determine how many employees are needed and appropriate training should be obtained. Employee growth stages such as training, recognition, or promotion should be carefully monitored and effective communication should be ensured in all these processes.

Qualified Staff Retention and Business Attractiveness: In the employment policy, it is necessary to increase this rate by giving importance to the current employee retention rate. In addition to preventing wear and tear, a suitable working environment should be created where they can devote their energies to their work, not people. Therefore, opportunities such as participatory management, teamwork, various bonus applications, flexible working hours, job security, learning opportunities, and effective communication should be offered especially to the younger generation. In addition, creating a career development plan is both a motivation and a basic requirement for all employees. Employees should be given problem-solving opportunities so that organizational communication can be affected. So, HR activities can help inspire employees in a multi-generational workplace.

Career Management and Promotion Opportunities: Employees should be able to predict their future with updated career maps. There is a need for the identification and analysis of training at all levels and in all areas of assigned work. Since the training needs will change according to the position and job description of the employee, they should be followed up to date. Employees should be prepared for their future responsibilities as well as their current knowledge and skills.

Job Descriptions and Training Need Analysis at Different Levels of the Organization: Effective training needs analysis (TNA) helps employees to do their current job with existing skills, knowledge, and attitudes. Practices such as job enrichment also help employees prepare for their future responsibilities. However, it should be taken into account that every new business area needs detailed job descriptions and job analyzes. The organizational structure needs to be clear to ensure that responsibilities are completed by those assigned and to define the boundaries of each employee. For this reason, job descriptions should be prepared in a way that everyone can understand and should be adopted by all employees, including management.

Improving Communication and Employee Engagement: Different analyzes can be used to identify employee expectations and evaluate available reward opportunities. As a result of these analyzes, the promotion opportunity of each generation within the framework of their priorities makes it easier to gain loyalty. In addition, rewarding high performance, the suitability of insurance and pension systems, and the implementation of remuneration policies that will prevent the employee's future anxiety will also contribute. At this stage, the HRM department can benefit from the training and development plans as well as the performance improvement policy and employee engagement activities. Providing a flexible organizational culture that can be changed according to individual needs facilitates the implementation of the HR business model for desired outputs.

Business Strategy: Supporting the HRM function at a strategic level and not flexing the decisions taken by this department by the senior management will also facilitate consistency in the operation. Besides, establishing a communication and control network that will make it easier to stay away from stereotypes for generations will contribute to the rapid progress of works and facilitate the destruction of some psychological barriers.

CONCLUSION AND FUTURE RESEARCH

Understanding interpersonal differences have always been one of the important issues in both organizational and social life. Some classifications have been made to understand and interpret the inner world of humans, who is social entity that transmits information through communication. Factors such as gender, age, culture, education are called demographic factors and are analyzed as the main variable of almost every research. The only way to achieve the set organizational goals is to observe, understand and guide people appropriately. Therefore, the more individual variables are known, the easier it will be to understand and guide behavior since unknown variables cannot be managed. This is the main reason why employees are classified and interpreted in an organization.

One of the classifications made to understand current and future employees is the generations made according to the ages and cultures of individuals. According to this classification, each individual develops a perception by being affected by the cultural elements of the age. For this reason, it may be easier to understand certain age groups if the critical factors that constitute the basic values of individuals are known. Accordingly, those born in and after 1928 are called Silent Generation, while those born in and after 1946 are called Baby Boomers. The next generations are classified as Gen X, Millennials (Gen Y), and Gen Z, and finally, those who are children now are called Alpha. For organizations, this classification includes clues about how the manager should behave in situations where there are five different generations in the same work environment. Only in this way can organizational synergy be developed smoothly. Thus, this classification based on age differences generally reflects the thought system that underlies all perceptions of the employees.

To understand the differences, it is helpful to examine the reasons underlying the possible consequences of these variables. In addition to developments such as global events, wars, crises, natural events, technological developments also offer different conditions to people. Therefore, understanding key cultural variables means seeing the dynamics that drive the human network that supports the organizational structure. From this point of view, firstly the basic features that make up the generational differences, then the cultural elements and the communication patterns developed in the light of these variables are mentioned in this chapter. After mentioning the forms of perception developed with the effect of technology, the motivation and management elements are also mentioned. After the theoretical structure, the scenario-based HRM case study is discussed within the scope of critical theory. The main purpose of the study is to raise awareness about business life and to emphasize the importance of evaluating individuals according to their conditions. Because each individual is different from their point of view these differences are valuable because they are the main source of synergy.

In light of the above information, it can be suggested to the HR manager and other researchers to be objective and free from stereotypes. To achieve the goals based on increasing the competitive advantage of the business, creativity, and innovation obtained by the combination of differences are needed (Ince, 2022b). For this reason, it will be very useful to conduct large-scale studies addressing generations in terms of HRM functions. Comparisons on a global scale will help to understand different cultures and other environmental impacts of generations. Besides, HR practices, which are gradually changing with the effect of technology, must continue to maintain their success in offering new solutions to different problems of generations. Only in this way will personal expectations and organizational goals harmonize and the performance of the employees will reach the desired levels. The coexistence of 5 different generations should be considered as an opportunity for synergy and sustainability, and this process should be closely monitored by the managers.

REFERENCES

Abraham, T., & Dao, V. T. (2019). A Longitudinal Exploratory Investigation of Innovation Systems and Sustainability Maturity Using Case Studies in Three Industries. *Journal of Enterprise Information Management*, *32*(4), 668–687. doi:10.1108/JEIM-07-2018-0149

Alvesson, M., & Deetz, S. (2006). Critical Theory and Postmodernism Approaches to Organization Studies. In S. R. Clegg, C. Hardy, T. B. Lawrence, & W. R. Nord (Eds.), *The Sage Handbook of Organization Studies* (2nd ed.). Sage. doi:10.4135/9781848608030.n8

Alvesson, M., & Willmott, H. (2002). Identity Regulation as Organizational Control: Producing The Appropriate Individual. *Journal of Management Studies*, *39*(5), 619–644. doi:10.1111/1467-6486.00305

Banfield, P., Kay, R., & Royles, D. (2018). *Introduction to Human Resource Management* (3rd ed.). Oxford University Press.

Beck, J. J., & Garris, R. O. III. (2019). Managing Personal Finance Literacy in the United States: A Case Study. *Education Sciences*, *9*(2), 129–140. doi:10.3390/educsci9020129

Becker, H. S. (2008). *Art Worlds: 25th Anniversary Edition, Updated, and Expanded*. University of California Press. doi:10.1525/9780520934870-014

Berge, Z. L., & Berge, M. B. (2019). The Economic ABCs of Educating and Training Generations X, Y, and Z. *Performance Improvement*, *58*(5), 44–53. doi:10.1002/pfi.21864

Bhabha, H. (1994). *The Location of Culture*. Routledge. doi:10.4324/9780203820551

Bravo, R., Catalán, S., & Pina, J. M. (2020). Intergenerational Differences in Customer Engagement Behaviours: An analysis of Social Tourism Websites. *International Journal of Tourism Research*, *22*(2), 182–191. doi:10.1002/jtr.2327

Buick, I., & Thomas, M. (2001). Why Do Middle Managers in Hotels Burn Out? *International Journal of Contemporary Hospitality Management*, *13*(6), 304–309. doi:10.1108/EUM0000000005968

Chugh, R., & Ruhi, U. (2018). Social Media in Higher Education: A Literature Review of Facebook. *Education and Information Technologies*, *23*(2), 605–616. doi:10.100710639-017-9621-2

Connaway, L. S., Radford, M. L., Dickey, T. J., Williams, J. D. A., & Confer, P. (2008). Sense-making and Synchronicity: Information-seeking Behaviors of Millennials and Baby Boomers. *Libri*, *58*(2), 123–135. doi:10.1515/libr.2008.014

Cooley, C. H. (1983). *Human Nature and the Social Order*. Transaction Books.

DeCenzo, D. A., Robbins, S. P., & Verhulst, S. L. (2016). *Fundamentals of Human Resource Management*. John Wiley & Sons.

DeWaal, A. (2020). Creating High-Performance Organizations in Asia: Issues to Consider. *International Journal of Management and Applied Research*, *7*(2), 86–103. doi:10.18646/2056.72.20-007

Dimock, M. (2019). Defining Generations: Where Millennials End and Generation Z Begins. *Pew Research Center*, *17*, 1–7.

Dulaimi, M., & Hartmann, A. (2006). The Role of Organizational Culture in Motivating Innovative Behaviour in Construction Firms. *Construction Innovation*, *6*(3), 159–172. doi:10.1108/14714170610710712

Fratrièová, J., & Kirchmayer, Z. (2018). Barriers to Work Motivation of Generation Z. *Journal of Human Resource Management*, *21*(2), 28–39.

Groysberg, B., Lee, J., Price, J., & Cheng, J. (2018). The Leader's Guide to Corporate Culture. *Harvard Business Review*, *96*(1), 44–52.

Hamao, Y., Masulis, R. W., & Ng, V. (1991). *The Effects of the 1987 Stock Crash on International Financial Integration*. Working Paper No.55, Columbia University.

Hardy, C. (2004). Scaling Up and Bearing Down in Discourse Analysis: Questions Regarding Textual Agencies and their Context. *Organization*, *11*(3), 415–425. doi:10.1177/1350508404042000

Hassan, S., DeHart-Davis, L., & Jiang, Z. (2019). How Empowering Leadership Reduces Employee Silence in Public Organizations. *Public Administration*, *97*(1), 116–131. doi:10.1111/padm.12571

Ince, F. (2018a). *Effective Communication and Behavior Across Generations*. Eğitim Publisher.

Ince, F. (2018b). *Different Aspects of Employee' Energy*. Eğitim Publisher.

Ince, F. (2018c). The Effect of Synergic Management on Human Resources Management Performance, 459-468. In H. Babacan, T. Soldatovi, & D. N. Delobegovi (Eds.), *Academic Research in Social, Human and Administrative Sciences-I*. Gece Publisher.

Ince, F. (2020a). The Effects of Covid-19 Pandemic on The Workforce In Turkey. *Social Mentality and Researcher Thinkers Journal*, *6*(32), 1125–1134. doi:10.31576mryj.546

Ince, F. (2020b). Financial Literacy in Generation Z: Healthcare Management Students. *Smart Journal*, *6*(36), 1647–1658. doi:10.31576mryj.616

Ince, F. (2021a). Creating Synergic Entrepreneurship as Support of Sustainability: Opportunities and Challenges. In R. Perez-Uribe, D. Ocampo-Guzman, N. Moreno-Monsalve, & W. Fajardo-Moreno (Eds.), Handbook of Research on Management Techniques and Sustainability Strategies for Handling Disruptive Situations in Corporate Settings (pp. 464-486). IGI Global. doi:10.4018/978-1-7998-8185-8.ch022

Ince, F. (2021b). Opportunities and Challenges of E-Learning in Turkey. In B. Khan, S. Affouneh, S. Hussein Salha, & Z. Najee Khlaif (Eds.), *Challenges and Opportunities for the Global Implementation of E-Learning Frameworks* (pp. 202–226). IGI Global. doi:10.4018/978-1-7998-7607-6.ch013

Ince, F. (2021c). COVID-19 Pandemic Made Me Use It: Attitude Of Generation Z Towards E-Learning. *Smart Journal*, *7*(54), 3489–3494. doi:10.31576mryj.1215

Ince, F. (2022a). Digital Literacy Training: Opportunities and Challenges. In M. Taher (Ed.), *Handbook of Research on the Role of Libraries, Archives, and Museums in Achieving Civic Engagement and Social Justice in Smart Cities* (pp. 185–199). IGI Global. doi:10.4018/978-1-7998-8363-0.ch009

Ince, F. (2022b). Creative Leadership: A Multidisciplinary Approach to Creativity. In Z. Fields (Ed.), *Achieving Sustainability Using Creativity, Innovation, and Education: A Multidisciplinary Approach* (pp. 30–49). IGI Global. doi:10.4018/978-1-7998-7963-3.ch002

Ince, F. (2022c). Leadership and Sustainability: From the First to the Second Generation of SMEs Ownership. In Research Anthology on Strategies for Maintaining Successful Family Firms (pp. 639-660). IGI Global. doi:10.4018/978-1-6684-3550-2.ch029

Kamalia, S., Indartono, S., & Islamiah, R. (2019). The Role of Families on Internalization of the Tolerance Values for Millennial Generation to Decrease the Potential of Intolerant Conflict and Radicalism Behavior within the Multi Religion Society. *Advances in Social Science, Education and Humanities Research*, *323*, 316–325. doi:10.2991/icossce-icsmc-18.2019.57

Kiger, P. J. (2010). *Baby Boomer Inventions That Changed the World.* https://www.reuters. com/article /idUS182429596720101222

Kitchen, P. J., & Daly, F. (2002). Internal Communication During Change Management. *Corporate Communications*, *7*(1), 46–53. doi:10.1108/13563280210416035

Krone, C., Tabacchi, M., & Farber, B. (1989). Manager Burnout. *The Cornell Hotel and Restaurant Administration Quarterly*, *30*(3), 58–63. doi:10.1177/001088048903000317

Liang, Y. W. (2012). The Relationships Among Work Values, Burnout, and Organizational Citizenship Behaviors: A Study From Hotel Front-Line Service Employees in Taiwan. *International Journal of Contemporary Hospitality Management*, *24*(2), 251–268. doi:10.1108/09596111211206169

Lim, D. H., Oh, E., Ju, B., & Kim, H. N. (2019). Mediating Role of Career Coaching on Job-Search Behavior of Older Generations. *International Journal of Aging & Human Development*, *88*(1), 82–104. doi:10.1177/0091415017743009 PMID:29345142

Lustig, S. L., Kia-Keating, M., Knight, W. G., Geltman, P., Ellis, H., Kinzie, J. D., & Saxe, G. N. (2004). Review of Child and Adolescent Refugee Mental Health. *Journal of the American Academy of Child and Adolescent Psychiatry*, *43*(1), 24–36. doi:10.1097/00004583-200401000-00012 PMID:14691358

Martin, G. (2015). *Understanding Social Movements*. Routledge. doi:10.4324/9780203837092

Maslach, C., & Leiter, M. P. (2005). Stress and Burnout: The Critical Research. In C. L. Cooper (Ed.), *Handbook of Stress Medicine and Health*. CRC Press.

Maslach, C., Schaufeli, W. B., & Leiter, M. P. (2001). Job Burnout. *Annual Review of Psychology*, *52*(1), 397–422. doi:10.1146/annurev.psych.52.1.397 PMID:11148311

McCrindle, M., & Wolfinger, E. (2009). *The ABC of XYZ: Understanding the Global Generations*. McCrindle Research.

Milne, G. (1977). Cyclone Tracy: II the Effects on Darwin Children. *Australian Psychologist*, *12*(1), 55–62. doi:10.1080/00050067708255860

Neeley, T. (2015). Global Teams That Work. *Harvard Business Review*, *93*(10), 74–81. doi:10.2469/dig.v45.n12.5

Nguyen, N. T., & Pham, L.-H.-T. (2020). How to Motivate Employees? Special Case of Millennial Generation in Vietnam. *Journal of Southwest Jiaotong University*, *55*(2), 1–13. doi:10.35741/issn.0258-2724.55.2.40

North, M. S. (2019). A Gate to Understanding "Older" Workers: Generation, Age, Tenure, Experience. *The Academy of Management Annals*, *13*(2), 414–443. doi:10.5465/annals.2017.0125

Özdevecioğlu, M., & İnce, F. (2011). Cultural Synergy Management: Conceptual Framework. *Erciyes University Journal of Economics and Administrative Sciences*, (38), 27–45.

Palmatier, R. W., & Crecelius, A. T. (2019). The "First Principles" of Marketing Strategy. *AMS Review*, *9*(1-2), 5–26. doi:10.100713162-019-00134-y

Patil, N., & Peshave, M. A. (2020). Millennial Employees: Professional Expectations and Challenges at Working Place. *UGC Care Journal*, *19*(22), 356–370.

Prawitasari, G. (2018). The Influence of Generations on Career Choice: Social Cognitive Career Theory Perspective. *Konselor*, *7*(1), 15–20. doi:10.24036/02018718464-0-00

Robinson, W. R., Utz, R. L., Keyes, K. M., Martin, C. L., & Yang, Y. (2013). Birth Cohort Effects on Abdominal Obesity in the United States: The Silent Generation, Baby Boomers and Generation X. *International Journal of Obesity*, *37*(8), 1129–1134. doi:10.1038/ijo.2012.198 PMID:23229734

Rodriguez, M., Boyer, S., Fleming, D., & Cohen, S. (2019). Managing the Next Generation of Sales, Gen Z/Millennial Cusp: An Exploration of Grit, Entrepreneurship, and Loyalty. *Journal of Business-To-Business Marketing*, *26*(1), 43–55. doi:10.1080/1051712X.2019.1565136

Rodriguez, R. O., Green, M. T., & Ree, M. J. (2003). Leading Generation X: Do The Old Rules Apply? *Journal of Leadership & Organizational Studies*, *9*(4), 67–75. doi:10.1177/107179190300900406

Shen, A. (2019). Marketing Preventive Health to Baby Boomers: What if Unhealthy Lifestyles are Attributable to the Counterculture? *Journal of Macromarketing*, *39*(2), 151–165. doi:10.1177/0276146719835290

Spreitzer, G., & Porath, C. (2012). Creating Sustainable Performance. *Harvard Business Review*, *90*(1), 92–99. PMID:22299508

Stewart, J. S., Oliver, E. G., Cravens, K. S., & Oishi, S. (2017). Managing Millennials: Embracing Generational Differences. *Business Horizons*, *60*(1), 45–54. doi:10.1016/j.bushor.2016.08.011

Suomäki, A., Kianto, A., & Vanhala, M. (2019). Work Engagement Across Different Generations in Finland: A Qualitative Study of Boomers, Yers and Xers. *Knowledge and Process Management*, *26*(2), 140–151. doi:10.1002/kpm.1604

Tajfel, H., & Turner, J. (1979). An Integrative Theory of Intergroup Conflict. In W. G. Austin & S. Worchel (Eds.), *The Social Psychology of Intergroup Relations. Monterey*. Brooks/Cole Publishing Company.

Taylor, P., Parker, K., Morin, R., Patten, E., & Brown, A. (2014). *Millennials in Adulthood*. Washington, DC: Pew Research Center. http://www. pewsocialtrends. org/2014/03/07/millennials-inadulthood

Tidd, J., & Bessant, J. R. (2018). *Managing Innovation: Integrating Technological, Market and Organizational Change*. John Wiley & Sons.

Tudoran, C. (2020). New Training Trends in High-Risk Technology Fields. *Proceedings of the International Conference on Business Excellence, Sciendo*, *14*(1), 474-489. 10.2478/picbe-2020-0045

Wagner, E. A. (2014). Using a Kinesthetic Learning Strategy to Engage Nursing Student Thinking, Enhance Retention, and Improve Critical Thinking. *The Journal of Nursing Education*, *53*(6), 348–351. doi:10.3928/01484834-20140512-02 PMID:24814353

Wiedmer, T. (2015). Generations do Differ: Best Practices in Leading Traditionalists, Boomers, and Generations X, Y, and Z. *Delta Kappa Gamma Bulletin*, *82*(1), 51–58.

KEY TERMS AND DEFINITIONS

AI: Artificial intelligence is a field which human intelligence processes are stimulated by computer systems to enable problem solving.

CMS: Critical management studies offers a number of alternatives to mainstream management theory with the aim of radically transforming existing practices.

GFC: Global financial crisis is a severe worldwide economic crisis that represents a period of extreme stress in global financial markets and banking systems.

HPO: High performance organization is a conceptual framework developed to create a highly efficient organization in which roles are clearly defined, leading to sustainable organizational performance.

HPWP: High performance work practices are a set of human resources practices aimed at improving the overall performance and effectiveness of the organization by making better use of skills.

HRM: Human resources management is a strategic approach to the effective and efficient management of employees in an organization in order to gain sustainable competitive advantage and outperform their competitors.

MBO: Management by objectives is a strategic process in which objectives are communicated to organizational members by arranging organizational structures aimed at achieving each objective.

OCR: Optical character recognition or reader is a business solution for automating data extraction from physical text with the use of technology to distinguish printed or handwritten text characters.

TNA: Training needs analysis is a systematic process that determines what type of training is required and includes details on training implementation to help employees work efficiently.

Compilation of References

Aaltio, I., Salminen, H. M., & Koponen, S. (2014). Ageing employees and human resource management–evidence of gender-sensitivity? *Equality, Diversity and Inclusion*, *33*(2), 160–176. doi:10.1108/EDI-10-2011-0076

Abdel-Ghany, M., & Sharpe, D. L. (1997). Consumption patterns among the young-old and old-old. *The Journal of Consumer Affairs*, *31*(1), 90–112. doi:10.1111/j.1745-6606.1997.tb00828.x

Abio, J. (2020). *The Boomer Generation: Redesigning the future with the Adultescents*. https://www.neo2.com/generacion-boomer-baby-boom/

Aborg, C., Fernström, E., & Ericson, M. (2002). *Telework Work Environment and Well-Being: Longitudinal Study*. Technical Report 2002-031, Uppsala University, Department of Information Technology, Uppsala, Sweden.

Abraham, T., & Dao, V. T. (2019). A Longitudinal Exploratory Investigation of Innovation Systems and Sustainability Maturity Using Case Studies in Three Industries. *Journal of Enterprise Information Management*, *32*(4), 668–687. doi:10.1108/JEIM-07-2018-0149

Açıkgöz, Ö., & Günay, A. (2021). Short-term impact of the Covid-19 pandemic on the global and Turkish economy. *Turkish Journal of Medical Sciences*, *51*(SI-1), 3182–3193. doi:10.3906ag-2106-271 PMID:34365782

Acis. (2019). *Baby Boomers: How the banking industry can captivate this generation?* https://www.acis.org.co/portal/content/noticiasinternacionales/baby-boomers-%C2%BFc%C3%B3mo-la-banca-puede-cautivar-esta-generaci%C3%B3n

Adioetomo, S. M., & Mujahid, G. (2014). *Indonesia on the threshold of population ageing (monograph series no. 1)*. UNFPA Indonesia. https://indonesia.unfpa.org/sites/default/files/pub-pdf/BUKU_Monograph_No1_Ageing_03_Low-res.pdf

Ajzen, I. (1991). The theory of planned behavior. *Organizational Behavior and Human Decision Processes*, *50*(2), 179–211. doi:10.1016/0749-5978(91)90020-T

Alper, Y., Deger, C., & Sayan, S. (2012). Demographics and Management Towards 2050: An Overview of the Social Security (Pension) System. Istanbul: TÜSİAD-T/2012-11/535.

Alper, Y. (2019). *My Writings on Social Security*. Turkish Metal Union Research and Training Center.

Alper, Y. (2021). *Social Security Reform, Administrative Autonomy and the Changing Roles of the Social Partners. In Labor Economics and Industrial Relations Congress "Social Policies and Current Discussions"*. Turk-Is Publications.

Alper, Y., Arici, K., Turcan Ozsuca, S., Aydın, U., & Gokbayrak, S. (2015). *A Success Story in Complementary Retirement: OYAK*. Turkiye Is Bankasi Cultural Publications.

Altig, D., Baker, S., Barrero, J. M., Bloom, N., Bunn, P., Chen, S., Davis, S. J., Leather, J., Meyer, B., Mihaylov, E., Mizen, P., Parker, N., Renault, T., Smietanka, P., & Thwaites, G. (2020). Economic uncertainty before and during the COVID-19 pandemic. *Journal of Public Economics*, *191*, 104274. doi:10.1016/j.jpubeco.2020.104274 PMID:32921841

Altman, Y., Baruch, Y., Manrique-de-Lara, P., & Viera Armas, M. M. (2020). Baby boomers at the cusp of their academic career: Storming ahead, hanging on, or Calling it a day. *Studies in Higher Education, 45*(7), 1335–1350. doi:10.1080/03075079.2019.1610864

Altunöz, U. (2014). Tüketim Fonksiyonu ve Türkiye için Gelir-Tüketim İlişkisinin Ampirik Analizi. International Conference of Eurasian Economies.

Alvesson, M., & Deetz, S. (2006). Critical Theory and Postmodernism Approaches to Organization Studies. In S. R. Clegg, C. Hardy, T. B. Lawrence, & W. R. Nord (Eds.), *The Sage Handbook of Organization Studies* (2nd ed.). Sage. doi:10.4135/9781848608030.n8

Alvesson, M., & Willmott, H. (2002). Identity Regulation as Organizational Control: Producing The Appropriate Individual. *Journal of Management Studies, 39*(5), 619–644. doi:10.1111/1467-6486.00305

Al-Wakel, E. (2014). *Ontology-based recommendation of academic papers* (Doctoral dissertation). University of New Brunswick.

Amâncio, A., & Cavalcanti, P. C. U. (1975). *Clínica Geriátrica* [Geriatric Clinic]. Atheneu Publisher.

Amit, R., & Muller, E. (1995). "Push" and "pull" entrepreneurship. *Journal of Small Business and Entrepreneurship, 12*(4), 64–80. doi:10.1080/08276331.1995.10600505

Analoui, F., Labbaf, H., & Noorbakhsh, F. (2000). Identification of clusters of managerial skills for increased effectiveness: The case of the steel industry in Iran. *International Journal of Training and Development, 4*(3), 217–234. doi:10.1111/1468-2419.00109

Anderson, A. R. (2015). Conceptualising entrepreneurship as economic "explanation" and the consequent loss of "understanding.". *International Journal of Business and Globalisation, 14*(2), 145–157. doi:10.1504/IJBG.2015.067432

Anderson, K. H., & Burkhauser, R. V. (1985). The retirement-health nexus: A new measure of an old puzzle. *The Journal of Human Resources, 20*(3), 315–330. doi:10.2307/145884

Arbeláez, D., & Franco, N. (2013). *Analysis of the Baby Boomers from a Colombian brand perspective and its impact in publicity*. Universidad autónoma de occidente. Facultad de comunicación social departamento de ciencias de la comunicación. Programa comunicación publicitaria. Santiago de Cali. https://red.uao.edu.co/bitstream/handle/10614/5694/T03734.pdf;jsessionid=261869EB5E72DDA251450B72DAA1663C?sequence=1

Argimon, I. L., & Stein, L. M. (2005). Habilidades Cognitivas em Indivíduos Muito Idosos: Um Estudo Longitudinal [Cognitive Skills in Very Elderly Individuals: A Longitudinal Study]. *Cadernos de Saude Publica, 21*(1), 64–72. doi:10.1590/S0102-311X2005000100008 PMID:15692639

Arici, K., & Alper, Y. (2018). Social Security. Eskisehir: Anadolu University Press.

Arici, K. (2015). *Turkish Social Security Law*. Gazi Bookstore Publications.

Arione, E., Barone, G., Holsten, M., & Weber, F. (1999). *Capitalisation of Existing Approaches*. Academic Press.

Arshad, M. N. M., & Malik, Z. (2015). Quality of human capital and labor productivity: A case of Malaysia. *International Journal of Economics, Management and Accounting, 23*(1), 37-55. https://journals.iium.edu.my/enmjournal/index.php/enmj/article/view/289

Ashton, A. S., Scott, N., & Choibamroong, T. (2019). Place development for international retirement migrants: A decision-making process model. *Journal of Place Management and Development, 12*(3), 449–468. doi:10.1108/JPMD-05-2018-0035

Astrayuda, I. (2017, May 18). Mencermati fenomena aging population. *Investor.id.* https://investor.id/archive/mencermati-fenomena-aging-population

Atanasoff, L., & Venable, M. A. (2017). Technostress: Implications for adults in the workforce. *Career Development, 65*(4), 326–338. doi:10.1002/cdq.12111

Autor, D. H., Frank, L., & Richard, J. M. (2003). The skill content of recent technological change: An empirical exploration. *The Quarterly Journal of Economics, 118*(4), 1279–1333. doi:10.1162/003355303322552801

Avolio, B. J., Barrett, G. V., & Sterns, H. L. (1984). Alternatives to age for assessing occupational performance capacity. *Experimental Aging Research, 10*(2), 101–105. doi:10.1080/03610738408258551 PMID:6499889

Axelson, M. L., & Penfield, M. P. (1983). Factors associated with food expenditures of elderly persons living alone. *Home Economics Research Journal, 12*(2), 228–236. doi:10.1177/1077727X8301200213

Aydın, U. (2020). Covid-19 Pandemic; Problems and solutions in the field of labor and social security law. *Journal of Istanbul Aydın University Faculty of Law, 6*(2), 181–214.

Ayyildiz, H., & Turna, G. B. (2014). Turkey's image as a tourist destination in Northern Europe. *International Journal of Advances in Management, Economics and Entrepreneurship, 1*(4), 1–8.

Badan Perencanaan Pembangunan Nasional, Badan Pusat Statistik, United Nations Population Fund. (2018). *Proyeksi penduduk Indonesia 2015-2045.* https://www.bps.go.id/publication/download.html?nrbvfeve=NzhkMjRkOTAyMDAyNmFkOTVjNmI1OTY1&xzmn=aHR0cHM6Ly93d3cuYnBzLmdvLmlkL3B1YmxpY2F0aW9uLzIwMTgvMTAvMTkvNzhkMjRkOTAyMDAyNmFkOTVjNmI1OTY1L3Byb3lla3NpLXBlbmR1ZHVrLWluZG9uZXNpYS0yMDE1LTItwNDUtaGFzaWwtc3VwYXMtMjAxNS5odG1s&twoadfnoarfeauf=MjAyMS0xMS0wOCAyMTozMzowMQ%3D%3D

Badan Pusat Statistik. (2013). *Sensus pertanian 2013.* https://st2013.bps.go.id/dev2/index.php

Badan Pusat Statistik. (2020). *Statistik penduduk lanjut usia 2020.* https://www.bps.go.id/publication/download.html?-nrbvfeve=MGZjMDIzMjIxOTY1NjI0YTY0NGMxMTEx&xzmn=aHR0cHM6Ly93d3cuYnBzLmdvLmlkL3B1YmxpY2F0aW9uLzIwMjAvMTIvMjEvMGZjMDIzMjIxOTY1NjI0YTY0NGMxMTExL3N0YXRpc3Rpay1wZW5kdWR1ay1sYW5qdXQtdXNpYS0yMDIwLmh0bWw%3D&twoadfnoarfeauf=MjAyMS0xMS0wOCAyMTowMzoyNQ%3D%3D

Baerenholdt, J. O., & Haldrup, M. (2006). Mobile networks and place making in cultural tourism: Staging viking ships and rock music in roskilde. *European Urban and Regional Studies, 13*(3), 209–224. doi:10.1177/0969776406065431

Bai, L. (2006). Graduate unemployment: Dilemmas and challenges in China's move to mass higher education. *The China Quarterly, 185*, 128–144. doi:10.1017/S0305741006000087

Baker, H. K. (1992). Service needs of traditional age and adult graduate students. *NASPA Journal, 30*(1), 20–29. doi:10.1080/00220973.1992.11072287

Balkir, C., & Kirkulak, B. (2009). Turkey, the new destination for international retirement migration, migration and mobility in Europe. In Migration, Mobility and Europe. Edward Elgar Publishing, MPG Books Group.

Balmes, M. (2018). *Characteristics and traits of Generation Z at work.* https://www.modelocurriculum.net/blog/caracteristicas-de-la-generacion-z-en-el-trabajo

Baltes, M. M., & Carstensen, L. L. (1999). Social-psychological theories and their applications to aging: From individual to collective. Handbook of Theories of Aging, 1, 209-226.

Banfield, P., Kay, R., & Royles, D. (2018). *Introduction to Human Resource Management* (3rd ed.). Oxford University Press.

Barbuto, A., Gilliland, A., Peebles, R., Rossi, N., & Shrout, T. (2020). *Telecommuting: smarter workplaces.* http://hdl.handle.net/1811/91648

Barclays Economic Reports. (2001). *Third Age Entrepreneurs – Profiting from Experience.* Barclays PLC.

Barker, S., Felstehausen, G., Couch, S., & Henry, J. (1997). Orientation programs for older and delayed-entry graduate students. *NASPA Journal, 35*(1), 57–68. doi:10.2202/1949-6605.1037

Baron, R. A., & Tang, J. (2011). The role of entrepreneurs in Firm-level innovation: Joint effects of Positive affect, Creativity, and environmental dynamism. *Journal of Business Venturing, 26*(1), 49–60. doi:10.1016/j.jbusvent.2009.06.002

Barros, M. E. E., & Landa, C. C. S. (2021). *Social Media and its influence in Millennials buying decision* Universidad Técnica de Ambato Facultad de Ciencias Administrativas. Trabajo de titulación en la modalidad de artículo académico previo a la obtención del Título de Licenciadas en Marketing y Gestión de Negocios. Ambato – Ecuador. Marzo 2021. http://repositorio.uta.edu.ec/bitstream/123456789/32749/1/100%20AA-MKT.pdf

Bartsch, S., Weber, E., Büttgen, M., & Huber, A. (2021). Leadership matters in crisis-induced digital transformation: How to lead service employees effectively during the COVID-19 pandemic. *Journal of Service Management, 32*(1), 71–85. doi:10.1108/JOSM-05-2020-0160

Baruch, Y., & Nicholson, N. (1997). Home, sweetwork: Requirements for effective homeworking. *Journal of General Management, 23*(2), 15–30. doi:10.1177/030630709702300202

Barysch, K. (2007). *What Europeans think about Turkey and why, Essay partly based on the CER Seminar on Europe's public opinion on Turkish EU accession.* Centre for European Reform Essays. https://www.cer.eu/sites/default/files/publications/attachments/pdf/2011/essay_turkey_barysch_25sept07-1392.pdf

Baucus, D. A., & Human, S. E. (1994). Second-career entrepreneurs: A multiple case study analysis of entrepreneurial processes and antecedent variables, Entrepreneurship. *Theory into Practice, 19*(2), 41–71.

Baysal, S. (2014). Working With Generations X And Y In Generation Z Period: Management of Different Generations in Business Life. *Mediterranean Journal of Social Sciences, 5*(19). DOI:.2014.v5n19p218 doi:10.5901/mjss

Becker, H. S. (2008). *Art Worlds: 25th Anniversary Edition, Updated, and Expanded.* University of California Press. doi:10.1525/9780520934870-014

Beck, J. J., & Garris, R. O. III. (2019). Managing Personal Finance Literacy in the United States: A Case Study. *Education Sciences, 9*(2), 129–140. doi:10.3390/educsci9020129

Beck, V. (2009). *Older Workers–Older Learners: The Perspectives of Employers in the East Midlands.* Learning and Skills Council.

Behan, B. A., Kirschner, J., & Snyder, S. M. (2009). Succession in PRACTICE. *Chief Executive, 239*(Mar/Apr), 28.

Bellaby, P. (2006). Can they carry on working? Later retirement, health, and social inequality in an aging population. *International Journal of Health Services, 36*(1), 1–23. doi:10.2190/EE2N-4A1Q-ARVD-XN05 PMID:16524163

Bellante, D., & Foster, A. C. (1984). Working wives and expenditure on services. *The Journal of Consumer Research, 11*(2), 700–707. doi:10.1086/209006

Berge, Z. L., & Berge, M. B. (2019). The Economic ABCs of Educating and Training Generations X, Y, and Z. *Performance Improvement, 58*(5), 44–53. doi:10.1002/pfi.21864

Bernardes, A., & Pinheiro, S. (2014). Anatomia do Envelhecimento [Anatomy of Aging]. In M. T. Veríssimo (Ed.), *Geriatria Fundamental, Saber e Praticar* [Fundamental Geriatrics, Know & Practice] (pp. 41–47). Ed. Técnicas, Lda.

Bertoni, M., Brunello, G., & Mazzarella, G. (2018). Does postponing minimum retirement age improve healthy behaviors before retirement? Evidence from middle-aged Italian workers. *Journal of Health Economics*, *58*, 215–227. doi:10.1016/j.jhealeco.2018.02.011 PMID:29550666

Bhabha, H. (1994). *The Location of Culture*. Routledge. doi:10.4324/9780203820551

Bloom, D. E., Canning, D., & Fink, G. (2011). *Implications of population aging for economic growth. Harvard University Program on the Global Demography of Aging*. NBER Working Paper No 16705, National Bureau of Economic Research. https://www.nber.org/system/files/working_papers/w16705/w16705.pdf

Bloom, D. E., Canning, D., & Fink, G. (2010). Implications of population ageing for economic growth. *Oxford Review of Economic Policy*, *26*(4), 583–612. doi:10.1093/oxrep/grq038

Bobbio, N. (1996). *De Senectute*. Einaudi Publisher.

Bodur, F. B., & Avcı, G. M. (2015). Household Expenditure Patterns: Evidence from Working-Couple Households in Turkey. *International Review of Economics and Management*, *3*(2), 85–108. doi:10.18825/irem.23503

Bonacini, L., Gallo, G., & Scicchitano, S. (2021). Working from home and income inequality: Risks of a 'new normal' with COVID-19. *Journal of Population Economics*, *34*(1), 303–360. doi:10.100700148-020-00800-7

Botham, R., & Graves, A. (2009). *The Grey Economy: How Third Age Entrepreneurs Are Contributing to Growth*. National Endowment for Science, Technology and the Arts (NESTA).

Bottazzi, R., Jappelli, T., & Padula, M. (2006). Retirement expectations, pension reforms, and their impact on private wealth accumulation. *Journal of Public Economics*, *90*(12), 2187–2212. doi:10.1016/j.jpubeco.2006.03.005

Boubakri, H. (2013). *Revolution and international migration in Tunisia*. Robert Schuman Centre for Advanced Studies. (MPC RR 2013/01)

Boyatzis, R. (1993). Beyond competence: The choice to be a leader. *Human Resource Management Review*, *3*(1), 1–14. doi:10.1016/1053-4822(93)90007-Q

Boyatzis, R. (2006). Using tipping points of emotional intelligence and cognitive competencies to predict financial performance of leaders. *Psicothema*, *18*(SUPPL.1), 124–131. PMID:17295969

Boyatzis, R. (2008). Competencies in the 21st century. *Journal of Management Development*, *27*(1), 5–12. doi:10.1108/02621710810840730

Boyatzis, R. (2009). Competencies as a behavioral approach to emotional intelligence. *Journal of Management Development*, *28*(9), 749–770. doi:10.1108/02621710910987647

Boyatzis, R. (2011). Managerial and Leadership Competencies: A Behavioral Approach to Emotional, Social and Cognitive Intelligence. *Vision: The Journal of Business Perspective*, *15*(2), 91–100. doi:10.1177/097226291101500202

Boyatzis, R., Goleman, D., & Rhee, K. (2000). Clustering competence in emotional intelligence: Insights from the Emotional Competence Inventory (ECI). In R. Bar-On & J. D. A. Parker (Eds.), *Handbook of Emotional Intelligence* (pp. 343–362). Jossey-Bass.

Boyatzis, R., & Kolb, D. (1995). From learning styles to learning skills the exec skills profile. *Journal of Managerial Psychology*, *10*(5), 3–17. doi:10.1108/02683949510085938

Bozkurt, V., Yalçınkaya, E., Karataş, A., Talas, M., & Şahin, A. (2021). Perceptions of doctoral students: Satisfaction, difficulties, gained skills and performance in publishing in academic journals. *Yükseköğretim Dergisi*, *11*(2), 263–275. doi:10.2399/yod.20.516442

Brant, J., Dooley, R., & Iman, S. (2008). Leadership succession: An approach to filling the pipeline. *Strategic HR Review*, *7*(4), 17–24. doi:10.1108/14754390810880499

Bravo, R., Catalán, S., & Pina, J. M. (2020). Intergenerational Differences in Customer Engagement Behaviours: An analysis of Social Tourism Websites. *International Journal of Tourism Research*, *22*(2), 182–191. doi:10.1002/jtr.2327

Brito, F. C., & Litvoc, J. (2004). Conceitos Básicos [Basic Concepts]. In F. C. Brito & J. Litvoc (Eds.), *Envelhecimento: Prevenção e Promoção de Saúde* [Aging: Prevention and Health Promotion]. Atheneu Publisher.

Broekemier, G. M. (2002). A comparison of two-year and four-year adult students: Motivations to attend college and the importance of choice criteria. *Journal of Marketing for Higher Education*, *12*(1), 31–48. doi:10.1300/J050v12n01_03

Brokaw, T. (1998). *The greatest generation*. Vintage.

Brunetti, M. J. (2006). The estate tax and the demise of the family business. *Journal of Public Economics*, *90*(10-11), 1975–1993. doi:10.1016/j.jpubeco.2006.05.012

Bryant, W. K. (1988). Durables and wives' employment yet again. *The Journal of Consumer Research*, *15*(1), 37–47. doi:10.1086/209143

Bueno, C. M., & Tubbs, S. L. (2004). Identifying Global Leadership Competencies: An Exploratory Study. *The Journal of American Academy of Business, Cambridge*, *5*(1/2), 80–87.

Buheji, M., & Buheji, A. (2020). Planning competency in the new normal– employability competency in post- covıd-19 pandemic. *International Journal of Human Resource Studies*, *10*(2), 237–251. doi:10.5296/ijhrs.v10i2.17085

Buick, I., & Thomas, M. (2001). Why Do Middle Managers in Hotels Burn Out? *International Journal of Contemporary Hospitality Management*, *13*(6), 304–309. doi:10.1108/EUM0000000005968

Bui, T., Button, P., & Picciotti, E. G. (2020). Early evidence on the impact of coronavirus disease 2019 (COVID-19) and the recession on older workers. *The Public Policy and Aging Report*, *30*(4), 154–159. doi:10.1093/ppar/praa029 PMID:34191898

Burdett, J. D. (2008). *A phenomenological study of the graduate school experience of women age 60 and older* (Doctoral dissertation). Texas State University.

Burnett, M., & Dutsch, J. (2006). Competency-based training and assessment center: Strategies, technology, process, and issues. *Advances in Developing Human Resources*, *8*(2), 141–143. doi:10.1177/1523422305279687

Burns, E., Smith, L., & Ulrich, D. (2012). Competency Models with Impact. *People & Strategy*, *35*(3), 16–23.

Byham, W. (1996). *Developing dimension / competency based Human Resource Systems*. Development Dimensions International, Inc.

Byham, W., & Moyer, R. (1996). *Using competencies to build a successful organization*. Development Dimensions International, Inc.

Çağlayan, E., & Astar, M. (2012). A microeconometric analysis of household consumption expenditure determinants for both rural and urban areas in Turkey. *American International Journal of Contemporary Research*, *2*(2), 27–34.

Calero, L. (2020). *Characteristics of Generation Z*. https://www.luiscalero.com/caracteristicas-de-la-generacion-z/

Cannon, T. (2008). Silver entrepreneurship: New days, new ways. *Working with Older People (Brighton, England)*, *12*(2), 30–33. doi:10.1108/13663666200800029

Capell, H. C., & Niño, E. L. (2007). The historic method of generations: The Spanish psychology case. *Revista de Historia de la Psicología*, *28*(1), 67–86.

Carstensen, L. L., Fung, H. H., & Charles, S. T. (2003). Socioemotional selectivity theory and the regulation of emotion in the second half of life. *Motivation and Emotion*, *27*(2), 103–123. doi:10.1023/A:1024569803230

Carstensen, L. L., Isaacowitz, D. M., & Charles, S. T. (1999). Taking time seriously: A theory of socioemotional selectivity. *The American Psychologist*, *54*(3), 165–181. doi:10.1037/0003-066X.54.3.165 PMID:10199217

Cascella, M., Rajnik, M., Cuomo, A., Dulebohn, S. C., & Di Napoli, R. (2020). *Features, evaluation and treatment coronavirus (COVID-19)*. StatPearls Publishing. https://www.ncbi.nlm.nih.gov/pubmed/32150360

Castells, M. (2002). A Era da Informação: Economia [The Information Age: Economy, Society and Culture - Volume I]. *Society and Culture, I.*

Çebi Karaaslan, K., Oktay, E., & Alkan, Ö. (2022). Determinants of Household Saving Behaviour in Turkey. *Sosyoekonomi*, *30*(51), 71–90. doi:10.17233osyoekonomi.2022.01.04

CEDEFOP. (2010). *Future skill supply in Europe. Medium-term forecast up to 2020.* Luxembourg: Publications Office of the European Union. https://www.cedefop.europa.eu/files/3052_en.pdf

CEDEFOP. (2015). *Matching skills and jobs in Europe: Insights from Cedefop's European skills and jobs survey*. Luxembourg: Publications Office. https://www.cedefop.europa.eu/files/8088_en.pdf

Centers for Disease Control and Prevention. (2020, September 11). *Older Adults.* https://www.cdc.gov/coronavirus/2019-ncov/need-extra-precautions/older-adults.html

Cerezo, P. (2017). *Generation Z and information.* http://www.injuve.es/sites/default/files/2017/28/publicaciones/documentos_7._la_generacion_z_y_la_informacion.pdf

Ceylan, H. (2015). *Aging and the Welfare State*. Istanbul: Acilim Book.

Chalise, H. N. (2019). Aging: Basic Concept. *American Journal of Biomedical and Life Sciences*, *1*(1), 8–10.

Chang, H. T., Liu, S. W., & Mishra, N. (2015). A tracking and summarization system for online Chinese news topics. *Aslib Journal of Information Management*, *67*(6), 687–699. doi:10.1108/AJIM-10-2014-0147

Chang, H. T., Li, Y. W., & Mishra, N. (2016). mCAF: A multi-dimensional clustering algorithm for friends of social network services. *SpringerPlus*, *5*(1), 1–15. doi:10.118640064-016-2420-1 PMID:27386242

Chang, H. T., Mishra, N., & Lin, C. C. (2015). IoT big-data centred knowledge granule analytic and cluster framework for BI applications: A case base analysis. *PLoS One*, *10*(11), e0141980. doi:10.1371/journal.pone.0141980 PMID:26600156

Chang, H., & Yen, S. T. (2011). Full-time, part-time employment and life satisfaction of the older people. *Journal of Socio-Economics*, *40*(6), 815–823. doi:10.1016/j.socec.2011.08.008

Chan, S. J., & Lin, J. W. (2016). Aiming for better employment: A holistic analysis from admission to labor market. *Journal of Higher Education Policy and Management*, *38*(3), 282–296. doi:10.1080/1360080X.2016.1174405

Charness, N., & Czaja, S. J. (2006). *Older Worker Training: What We Know and Don't Know. #2006-22*. AARP.

Chen, J. K. C., & Sriphon, T. (2021). Perspective on COVID-19 pandemic factors impacting organizational leadership. *Sustainability*, *13*(3230), 1–21. doi:10.3390u13063230

Chillakuri, B. (2020). Understanding Generation Z expectations for effective onboarding. *Journal of Organizational Change Management*, *33*(7), 1277–1296. doi:10.1108/JOCM-02-2020-0058

Choi, N. (2001). Relationship between life satisfaction and postretirement employment among older women. *International Journal of Aging & Human Development, 52*(1), 45–70. doi:10.2190/2W25-DH9H-2F4D-7HWX PMID:11310574

Chouhan, V. S., & Srivastava, S. (2014). Understanding Competencies and Competency Modeling— A Literature Survey. *IOSR Journal of Business and Management, 16*(1), 14–22. doi:10.9790/487X-16111422

ChristelisD.FonsecaR. (2016). Labor market policies and self-employment transitions of older workers. *Available at* SSRN 2837804. doi:10.2139/ssrn.2837804

Christensen, K., Doblhammer, G., Rau, R., & Vaupel, J. W. (2009). Ageing populations: The challenges ahead. *Lancet, 374*(9696), 1196–1208. doi:10.1016/S0140-6736(09)61460-4 PMID:19801098

Chugh, R., & Ruhi, U. (2018). Social Media in Higher Education: A Literature Review of Facebook. *Education and Information Technologies, 23*(2), 605–616. doi:10.100710639-017-9621-2

Chung, Y. S., & Magrabi, F. M. (1990). Age-related changes in expenditure patterns. In *The 36th Annual Conference of the American Council on Consumer Interests* (pp. 200-206). Academic Press.

Čiutienė, R., & Railaitė, R. (2014). Challenges of Managing an Ageing Workforce. *Procedia: Social and Behavioral Sciences, 156*(April), 69–73. doi:10.1016/j.sbspro.2014.11.121

Clark, S. C. (2000). Work/Family border theory: A new theory of work/family balance. *Human Relations, 53*(6), 747–770. doi:10.1177/0018726700536001

CoHE. (2013). *Öğrenim düzeyine göre öğrenci sayıları.* https://istatistik.yok.gov.tr/

CoHE. (2021). *Öğrenim düzeyine göre öğrenci sayıları.* https://istatistik.yok.gov.tr/

Cohn, R. M. (1979). Age and the satisfactions from work. *Journal of Gerontology, 34*(2), 264–272. doi:10.1093/geronj/34.2.264 PMID:438481

Coll, C., Marchesi, A., & Palacios, J. (2004). *Desenvolvimento Psicológico e Educação* [Psychological Development and Education]. Artmed Publisher.

Conger, J., & Ready, D. (2004). Rethinking leadership competencies. *Leader to Leader, 2004*(Spring), 41–48. doi:10.1002/ltl.75

Connaway, L. S., Radford, M. L., Dickey, T. J., Williams, J. D. A., & Confer, P. (2008). Sense-making and Synchronicity: Information-seeking Behaviors of Millennials and Baby Boomers. *Libri, 58*(2), 123–135. doi:10.1515/libr.2008.014

Cook, F. L., & Settersten, R. A. (1995). Expenditure Patterns by Age and Income Among Mature Adults: Does Age Matter? *The Gerontologist, 35*(1), 10–23. doi:10.1093/geront/35.1.10 PMID:7890194

Cooley, C. H. (1983). *Human Nature and the Social Order.* Transaction Books.

Cooper, M. K. (1999). *The return to academics: The experience of the older graduate student* (Doctoral thesis). University of Minnesota.

Corporate finance Institute. (2021). https://corporatefinanceinstitute.com/resources/knowledge/other/baby-boomers/

Costa, E. M. S. (1998). *Gerontodrama: A Velhice em Cena: Estudos Clínicos e Psicodramáticos sobre o Envelhecimento e a Terceira Idade* [Gerontodrama: Old Age on Stage - Clinical and Psychodramatic Studies on Aging and the Third Age]. Ágora Publisher.

Creswell, J. W. (2009). Research Design: Qualitative, Quantitative and Mixed Approaches. In Research Design: Qualitative, Quantitative, and Mixed Methods Approaches (3rd ed.). Sage Publication, Inc.

Creswell, J. W. (1998). Qualitative inquiry and research design: Choosing among five traditions. *Sage (Atlanta, Ga.).*

Curran, J., & Blackburn, R. A. (2001). Older people and the enterprise society: Age and self-employment propensities. *Work, Employment and Society*, *15*(4), 889–902. doi:10.1177/095001701400438279

Dandu, S., Rage, K., Sundar Raj, M., Mishra, N., Sivakumar, D., & Mohan, S. (2021). Practical Approach to the Defect Prediction Model for Software Testing. *J Nucl Ene Sci Power Generat Techno, 10*(9), 2.

Dardengo, C. F. R., & Mafra, S. C. T. (2018). Os Conceitos de Velhice e Envelhecimento ao Longo do Tempo: Contradição ou Adaptação? [The Concepts of Old Age and Aging over Time: Contradiction or Adaptation?]. *Revista de Ciências Humanas*, *18*(2), 1–23.

Darmawan, K., Saleh A., Subagjo, H., Masunaga, T., & Wakatsuki, T. (2006). The effect of green revolution technology during the period of 1970-2003 on sawah soils properties in Java, Indonesia; I. Carbon and nitrogen distribution under different land management practice and soils types. *Soil Science and Plant Nutrition, 52*(5), 634 - 644. doi:10.1111/j.1747-0765.2006.00075.x

Davenport, T. H. (2005). *Thinking for a living: How to get better performance and results from knowledge workers.* Harvard Business School Press.

De Barba, G. (2016). *7 Characteristics of Generation Z.* https://www.entrepreneur.com/article/268023

De Grip, A., Fouarge, D., & Montizaan, R. (2013). How sensitive are individual retirement expectations to raising the retirement age? *De Economist*, *161*(3), 225–251. doi:10.100710645-013-9205-5

de Lange, A. H., Taris, T. W., Jansen, P. G. W., Smulders, P., Houtman, I. L. D., & Kompier, M. A. J. (2006). Age as a factor in the relation between work and mental health: results from the longitudinal TAS study. In J. Houdmont & S. McIntyre (Eds.), *Occupational Health Psychology: European Perspectives on Research, Education and Practice* (Vol. 1, pp. 21–45). ISMAI Publications.

DeatonA. (2005). Franco Modigliani and the life cycle theory of consumption. *Available at* SSRN 686475. doi:10.2139/ssrn.686475

DeCenzo, D. A., Robbins, S. P., & Verhulst, S. L. (2016). *Fundamentals of Human Resource Management*. John Wiley & Sons.

Del Moral, J. M. (2001). Historicity and temporality in the Being and in times of M. Heidegger. *Philosophic Signs*, (5), 133-141.

Delamare-Le Deist, F., & Winterton, J. (2005). What Is Competence? *Human Resource Development International*, *8*(1), 27–46. doi:10.1080/1367886042000338227

Deloitte. (2020, 1 August). *COVID-19: Çalışanlara ve Çalışma Hayatına Olası Etkileri.* https://www2.deloitte.com/content/dam/Deloitte/tr/Documents/human-capital/covid-19-calisanlara-vecalisma-hayatina-olasi-etkileri.pdf

Demirbilek, T., & Oktem Ozgur, A. (2017). Elderly employment in the context of the silver economy and active aging. *Journal of Research on Elderly Issues*, *10*(1), 14–28.

Demou, E., Bhaskar, A., Xu, T., Mackay, D. F., & Hunt, K. (2017). Health, lifestyle and employment beyond state-pension age. *BMC Public Health*, *17*(1), 971. doi:10.118612889-017-4957-5 PMID:29262819

Denk, H. (2003). *Sports for the elderly.* Barcelona: Editorial paidotribo.

Dennis, C., & Melewar, T. C. (2010). Place marketing and branding in a turbulent world. *Place Branding and Public Diplomacy*, *6*(2), 76. doi:10.1057/pb.2010.17

Denton, F. T., Mountain, D. C., & Spencer, B. G. (2002). *Age, retirement and expenditure patterns: An econometric study of older Canadian households* (No. 82). McMaster University.

DeRue, D., & Myers, C. (2009). Leadership Development: A Review and Agenda for Future Research. *Journal of Selection and Assessment*, 832–855.

DeWaal, A. (2020). Creating High-Performance Organizations in Asia: Issues to Consider. *International Journal of Management and Applied Research*, *7*(2), 86–103. doi:10.18646/2056.72.20-007

Dewan, S., & Ernst, E. (2020). Rethinking the world of work. *Finance & Development*, *57*(4), 22–25.

Dewdney, J. C. (2020, November 8). Turkey. *Britannica*. https://www.britannica.com/place/Turkey/Demographic-trends#ref44475

Diaz, M. A. C. (2004). Northern European retired residents in nine southern European areas: Characteristics, motivations and adjustment. *Ageing and Society*, *24*(3), 353–381. doi:10.1017/S0144686X04001898

Díaz-Sarmiento, C., López-Lambraño, M., & Roncallo-Lafon, L. (2017). Understanding generations: a revision of the concept, classification and distinctive traits of Baby Boomers, X and Millennials. Clio America Journal, 11(22), 188-204.

Dictionary, O. (2020, April 11). *Meaning of the New Normal in English*. https://www.lexico.com/definition/the_new_normal

Dimock, M. (2019). Defining Generations: Where Millennials End and Generation Z Begins. *Pew Research Center*, *17*, 1–7.

Dirani, K. M., Abadi, M., Alizadeh, A., Barhate, B., Garza, R. C., Gunasekara, N., Ibrahim, G., & Majzun, Z. (2020). Leadership competencies and the essential role of human resource development in times of crisis: A response to Covid-19 pandemic. *Human Resource Development International*, *00*(00), 1–15. doi:10.1080/13678868.2020.1780078

Dobransky-Fasiska, D. (2002). *A discriminant analysis of entrepreneurial personality characteristics for each of three generational cohorts: The Silent Generation, the Baby Boomers, and Generation X*. University of Pittsburgh. ProQuest Dissertations Publishing. 3078835. https://www.proquest.com/openview/0ce8dee68ddf8ec22aa93b4d81f8868e/1?pq-origsite=gscholar&cbl=18750&diss=y

Dolado, J. J., Felgueroso, F., & Jimeno, J. F. (2000). Youth labor markets in Spain: Education training and crowding-out. *European Economic Review*, *44*(4-6), 943–956. doi:10.1016/S0014-2921(99)00050-1

Dolot, A. (2018). The Characteristics of Generation Z. *E-Mentor*, *74*(2), 44-50. https://www.ceeol.com/search/article-detail?id=737237

Dreze, J., & Sen, A. (1999). India: Economic Development and social opportunity. Oxford University Press.

Dulaimi, M., & Hartmann, A. (2006). The Role of Organizational Culture in Motivating Innovative Behaviour in Construction Firms. *Construction Innovation*, *6*(3), 159–172. doi:10.1108/14714170610710712

Dulewicz, V., & Higgs, M. (2003). Leadership at the top: The need for emotional intelligence in organizations. *The International Journal of Organizational Analysis*, *11*(3), 193–210. doi:10.1108/eb028971

Dulewicz, V., & Higgs, M. (2004). Can Emotional Intelligence be developed? *International Journal of Human Resource Management*, *15*(1), 95–111. doi:10.1080/0958519032000157366

Duxbury, L., & Halinski, M. (2014). When more is less: An examination of the relationship between hours in telework and role overload. *Work (Reading, Mass.)*, *2014*(48), 91–103. doi:10.3233/WOR-141858 PMID:24763352

Eisner, S. (2005, Autumn). *Managing Generation Y. Advanced Management Journal*, *70*(4), 4–15.

Ekstrand, M. D., Riedl, J. T., & Konstan, J. A. (2011). *Collaborative filtering recommender systems*. Now Publishers Inc. doi:10.1561/9781601984432

Elgin, C., & Tumen, S. (2010). Can sustained economic growth and declining population coexist? Barro-Becker children meet Lucas. *Economic Modelling*, *29*(5), 1899–1908. doi:10.1016/j.econmod.2012.06.004

El-Sappagh, S. H., & Elmogy, M. (2015). Case based reasoning: Case representation methodologies. *International Journal of Advanced Computer Science and Applications*, *6*(11), 192–208.

Enam, A., & Konduri, K. C. (2018). Time Allocation Behaviour of Twentieth-Century American Generations: GI Generation, Silent Generation, Baby Boomers, Generation X, and Millennials. *Transportation Research Record: Journal of the Transportation Research Board*, *2672*(49), 69–80. doi:10.1177/0361198118794710

Ennis, M. (2008). *Competency models: A review of the literature and the role of the Employment and Training Administration (ETA)*. Academic Press.

Entrust, J. G. (2021). Securing the remote workforce in the new normal. *Computer Fraud & Security*, *2*, 8–11.

Erişen, M. A., & Yılmaz, F. Ö. (2020). COVID-19 Pandemisi Döneminde Bireylerin Harcamalarının İncelenmesi. *Gaziantep Üniversitesi Sosyal Bilimler Dergisi, 19*, 340-353. doi:10.21547/jss.787849

Erminda, J. G. (1999). Processo de Envelhecimento [The Aging Process]. In *O Idoso: Problemas e Realidade* [The Elderly: Problems and Reality]. Formasau Publisher.

Eurobarometer, S. (2012). Active Ageing–Report. European Commission, (378).

Euronews. (2013, June 3). *Is this the Turkish Spring? The view from The Euronews Istanbul Correspondent*. https://www.euronews.com/2013/06/03/is-this-the-turkish-spring-the-view-from-the-euronews-istanbul-correspondent-/

European Union. (2005). *Livro Verde - "Uma nova solidariedade entre gerações face às mutações demográficas"* [Green Paper - "Confronting demographic change: a new solidarity between the generations"]. Academic Press.

Europeia, C. (2013). *Entrepreneurship 2020 action plan*. Communication from the Commission to the European Parliament, The Council, The European Economic and Social Committee and the Committee of the Regions.

Eurostat Pocketbooks. (2012). *The European Union and the BRIC countries*. Eurostat European Commission. https://ec.europa.eu/eurostat/web/products-pocketbooks/-/ks-31-11-414

Eurostat. (2011). *Active ageing and solidarity between generations: A statistical portrait of the European Union 2012*. Publications office of the European Union.

Evans, D. S., & Leighton, L. S. (1989). The determinants of changes in US self-employment, 1968–1987. *Small Business Economics*, *1*(2), 111–119. doi:10.1007/BF00398629

Eversole, B., Gloeckner, G., & Banning, J. H. (2007). Understanding differential organizational responses to work/life issues: The role of beliefs and decision-making styles of chief executive officers. *Journal of European Industrial Training*, *31*(4), 259–273. doi:10.1108/03090590710746423

Ezebilo, E. E. (2012). Challenges in postgraduate studies: Assessments by doctoral students in a Swedish University. *Higher Education Studies*, *2*(4), 49–57. doi:10.5539/hes.v2n4p49

Fabisiak, J., & Prokurat, S. (2012). Age management as a tool for the demographic decline in the 21st century: An overview of its characteristics. *Journal of Entrepreneurship Management and Innovation*, *8*(4), 83–96.

Farr, J. L., Tesluk, P. E., & Klein, S. R. (1998). Organizational structure of the workplace and the older worker. *Impact of Work on Older Adults*, 143-185.

Federal Interagency Forum on Aging-Related Statistics. (2020). *Older Americans 2020: Key indicators of well-being.* https://agingstats.gov/docs/LatestReport/OA20_508_10142020.pdf

Feeser, H. R., & Dugan, K. W. (1989). Entrepreneurial motivation: a comparison of high and low growth high tech founders. *Frontiers of Entrepreneurship Research, 9*(1), 13-27.

Fernandes, A. (2008). *Questões Demográficas* [Demographic Issues]. Colibri Publisher.

Fernandez-Crehuet, J. M., Rosales-Salas, J., & Cogollos, S. D. (2021). Country's international reputation index. *Corporate Reputation Review*, *24*(1), 14–30. doi:10.105741299-019-00088-8

Ferreira, A. J. (2014). Demografia e Epidemiologia do Envelhecimento [Demography and Epidemiology of Aging]. In M. T. Veríssimo (Ed.), *Geriatria Fundamental, Saber e Praticar* [Fundamental Geriatrics, Know & Practice] (pp. 59–64). Ed. Técnicas, Lda.

Figueiredo, P. (2019). *Competências para uma liderança percebida como eficaz - Líderes e liderados* [PhD Thesis in Management]. Universidade Europeia.

Figueiredo, E., & Paiva, T. (2019). Senior entrepreneurship and qualified senior unemployment: The case of the Portuguese Northern region. *Journal of Small Business and Enterprise Development*, *26*(3), 342–362. doi:10.1108/JSBED-01-2018-0006

Figueiredo, P., & Sousa, M. J. (2016). Leaders and followers: The leadership style perceived in modern organizations. In G. L. Jamil, J. Poças-Rascão, F. Ribeiro, & A. Malheiro da Silva (Eds.), *Handbook of Research on Information Architecture and Management in Modern Organizations*. IGI Global. doi:10.4018/978-1-4666-8637-3.ch009

Findsen, B., & Formosa, M. (2011). *Lifelong learning in later life: A handbook on older adult learning*. Sense Publishers. doi:10.1007/978-94-6091-651-9

Fingerman, K., Pillemer, K., Silverstein, M., & Suitor, J. (2012). The Baby Boomers' Intergenerational Relationships. *The Gerontologist*, *52*(2), 199–209. doi:10.1093/geront/gnr139

Fiorini, A. (2016). *The Protection of the Best Interests of Migrant Children-Private International Law Perspectives. Migrant Children in the XXI Century. Selected Issues of Public and Private International Law, Series" La ricerca del diritto*. Editoriale Scientifica.

Flood, F. (2019). Leadership in the remote, freelance, and virtual workforce era. *Global Encyclopedia of Public Administration, Public Policy, and Governance*. https://link.springer.com/referenceworkentry/10.1007%2F978-3-319-31816-5_3825-1

Fokkema, T., Cela, E., & Witter, Y. (2016). Pendular migration of older adults: Misconceptions and nuances. In V. Horn & C. Schweppe (Eds.), *Transnational Aging: Current Insights and Future Challenges* (pp. 141–161). Routledge. doi:10.4324/9781315756394

Fombrun, C., & Van Riel, C. (1997). The reputational landscape. *Corporate Reputation Review*, *1*(1-2), 5–13. doi:10.1057/palgrave.crr.1540008

Fonseca, R., & Parker, S. C. (2019). Entrepreneurship among older workers: International evidence. Handbook of Research on Entrepreneurship and Aging, 23–51. doi:10.4337/9781788116213.00007

Fossum, J. A., Arvey, R. D., Paradise, C. A., & Robbins, N. E. (1986). Modeling the skills obsolescence process: A psychological/economic integration. *Academy of Management Review*, *11*(2), 362–374. doi:10.2307/258466

Fougère, M., Harvey, S., Mercenier, J., & Mérette, M. (2009). Population ageing, time allocation and human capital: A general equilibrium analysis for Canada. *Journal Economic Modeling*, *26*(1), 30–39. doi:10.1016/j.econmod.2008.05.007

Fowell, T. (2021). *Hybrid work: What is hybrid work and why do employees want it?* https://envoy.com/blog/what-is-a-hybrid-work-model/

Fraiman, A. P. (1995). *Coisas da Idade* [Things of the Age]. Editora Gente.

Fraim, J. (2003). *Battle of symbols global dynamics of advertising, entertainment and media*. Daimon Verlag.

Fratrièová, J., & Kirchmayer, Z. (2018). Barriers to Work Motivation of Generation Z. *Journal of Human Resource Management*, *21*(2), 28–39.

Freedman, M. (2011). *The big shift: Navigating the new stage beyond midlife*. Public Affairs.

Gajendran, R. S., & Harrison, D. A. (2007). The good, the bad, and the unknown about telecommuting: Meta-analysis of psychological mediators and individual consequences. *The Journal of Applied Psychology*, *92*(6), 1524–1541. doi:10.1037/0021-9010.92.6.1524 PMID:18020794

Galloway, L., & Cooney, T. M. (2012). Introduction. *International Journal of Entrepreneurship and Innovation*, *13*(2), 77–79. doi:10.5367/ijei.2012.0080

Gambone, M. (2005). *The Greatest Generation Comes Home: The Veteran in American Society*. Texas University Press.

Garcia, L. (2015). *Why do older entrepreneurs face unique challenges?* Academic Press.

Gatimu, S. M., Milimo, B. W., & San Sebasti, M. (2016). Prevalence and determinants of diabetes among older adults in Ghana. *BMC Public Health*, *16*(1), 1174. doi:10.118612889-016-3845-8 PMID:27871259

Geyer, J., & Welteke, C. (2019). Closing routes to retirement for women: How do they respond? *The Journal of Human Resources*, 1–46.

Ghasemi, V., Del Chiappa, G., & Correia, A. (2016). Host-Guest interactions: Conceptualising and testing the role of apathy. *8th World Conference for Graduate Research in Tourism Hospitality and Leisure. Proceedings Book*, 497-502.

Giambatista, R., Rowe, W., & Riaz, S. (2005). Nothing succeeds like succession: A critical review of leader succession literature since 1994. *The Leadership Quarterly*, *16*(6), 963–991. doi:10.1016/j.leaqua.2005.09.005

Gist, M., Rosen, B., & Schwoerer, C. (1988). The influence of training method and trainee age on the acquisition of computer skills. *Personnel Psychology*, *41*(2), 255–265. doi:10.1111/j.1744-6570.1988.tb02384.x

Glossary, G. (2021, 23 August). *Remote work*. https://www.gartner.com/en/information-technology/glossary/remote-work

Goda, G. S., Jackson, E., Nicholas, L. H., & Stith, S. S. (2021). *The impact of Covid-19 on older workers' employment and social security spillovers*. NBER Working Paper, 29083. https://www.nber.org/papers/w29083

Go, F. M., & Govers, R. (2011). *Introduction to the international place branding yearbook managing reputational risk*. Palgrave MacMillan.

Go, F. M., & Little, S. (2013). Older workers in a global economy – Life cycle migration and knowledge transfer. In P. Taylor (Ed.), *Older Workers in an Aging Society: Critical Topics in Research and Policy* (pp. 817–819). Edward Elgar.

Go, F. M., & Trunfio, M. (2012). A paradigm shift from tourism destination management to democratic governance of place branding: The cases of Pompei and Campi Flegrei. *Journal of Travel and Tourism Research*, (Spring), 4–17.

Goleman, D, Boyatzis, R., & Mckee, A. (2007). *Os Novos Líderes – A Inteligência Emocional nas Organizações* (3ª edição). Gradiva.

Goleman, D. (1998). What makes a leader? *Harvard Business Review*, 82–91. PMID:10187249

Goleman, D., Boyatzis, R., & Mckee, A. (2001). Primal Leadership: The Hidden Driver of Great Performance. *Harvard Business Review*, (December), 42–51.

Goos, M., Manning, A., & Salomons, A. (2014). Explaining job polarization: Routine-biased technological change and offshoring. *The American Economic Review*, *104*(8), 2509–2526. doi:10.1257/aer.104.8.2509

Gopal, A. (2003). Disengaged employees cost Singapore $4.9 Billion. *Gallup Management Journal*. https://gmj.gallup.com/content/default.aspx?ci=1207

Graybill, J. (2014, January). Millennials among the Professional Workforce in Academic Libraries: Their Perspective on Leadership. *Journal of Academic Librarianship*, *40*(1), 10–15. https://doi.org/10.1016/j.acalib.2013.09.006

Green, H., & Powell, S. (2007). *The doctorate worldwide*. McGraw-Hill Education.

Grossmann, V., & Strulik, H. (2010). Should continued family firms face lower taxes than other estates? *Journal of Public Economics*, *94*(1-2), 87–101. doi:10.1016/j.jpubeco.2009.10.005

Groves, K. S. (2007). Integrating leadership development and succession planning best practices. *Journal of Management Development*, *26*(3), 239–260. doi:10.1108/02621710710732146

Groysberg, B., Lee, J., Price, J., & Cheng, J. (2018). The Leader's Guide to Corporate Culture. *Harvard Business Review*, *96*(1), 44–52.

Gruenfeld, L. W. (1962). A study of the motivation of industrial supervisors. *Personnel Psychology*, *15*(3), 303–315. doi:10.1111/j.1744-6570.1962.tb01625.x

Guillemard, A. (2003). *L'Âge de l'Emploi. Les Sociétés à l'Épreuve du Vieillissement* [The Age of Employment. The Societies to the Test of the Ageing]. Armand Colin Publisher.

Guillory, J. (1996). Preprofessionalism: What graduate students want. *Profession*, 91–99. https://www.jstor.org/stable/25595583

Gunaydin, D. (2018). The aging problem of the workforce within the framework of Turkey's demographic transformation. *Journal of Research on Elderly Issues*, *11*(1), 1–13.

Gundogan, N. (2001). Aging of the workforce and its effects on labor markets. *Journal of Ankara University Faculty of Political Sciences*, *56*(04), 95–108.

GuptaS.MontenovoL.NguyenT. D.Lozano-RojasF.SchmutteI. M.SimonK. I.WeinbergB. A.WingC. (2020). *Effects of social distancing policy on labor market outcomes*. NBER Working Paper, w27280. https://ssrn.com/abstract=3615476

Gursoy, D., & McCleary, K. W. (2004). An integrative model of tourists' information search behavior. *Annals of Tourism Research*, *31*(2), 353–373. doi:10.1016/j.annals.2003.12.004

Guzmán, V. E., Muschard, B., Gerolamo, M., Kohl, H., & Rozenfeld, H. (2020). Characteristics and Skills of Leadership in the Context of Industry 4.0. *Procedia Manufacturing*, *43*, 543–550. doi:10.1016/j.promfg.2020.02.167

Hagen, J. (2018). The effects of increasing the normal retirement age on health care utilization and mortality. *Journal of Population Economics*, *31*(1), 193–234. doi:10.100700148-017-0664-x

Hair, J. Jr, Black, W., Babin, B., & Anderson, R. (2010). *Multivariate Data Analysis* (7th ed.). Pearson Education Inc.

Hall, D. T., & Nougaim, K. E. (1968). An examination of Maslow's need hierarchy in an organizational setting. *Organizational Behavior and Human Performance*, *3*(1), 12–35. doi:10.1016/0030-5073(68)90024-X

Haller, M. (2013). The image of Turkey in Europe today. *European Review (Chichester, England)*, *21*(3), 327–335. doi:10.1017/S106279871300029X

Hall, P. (2000). Creative cities and economic development. *Urban Studies (Edinburgh, Scotland)*, *37*(4), 639–649. doi:10.1080/00420980050003946

Hamao, Y., Masulis, R. W., & Ng, V. (1991). *The Effects of the 1987 Stock Crash on International Financial Integration*. Working Paper No.55, Columbia University.

Hamblin, H. (2001). Employees' perspectives on one dimension of labour flexibility: Working at a distance. *Work, Employment and Society*, *9*(3), 473–498. doi:10.1177/095001709593003

Hamlin, R. (2002). *Towards a Generic Theory of Managerial Effectiveness: a meta-level analysis from organisations within the UK public sector*. Academic Press.

Hammersly, M., & Traianou, A. (2017). *Ethics in qualitative research* (S. Balcı & B. Ahi, Trans.). Anı Yayıncılık.

Hardy, C. (2004). Scaling Up and Bearing Down in Discourse Analysis: Questions Regarding Textual Agencies and their Context. *Organization*, *11*(3), 415–425. doi:10.1177/1350508404042000

Harms, R., & Ehrmann, T. (2003). The performance implications of entrepreneurial management: linking Stevenson's and Miller's conceptualization to growth. In *Babson Kauffman Research Conference on Entrepreneurship*. Babson College.

Harms, R., Luck, F., Kraus, S., & Walsh, S. (2014). On the motivational drivers of gray entrepreneurship: An exploratory study. *Technological Forecasting and Social Change*, *89*, 358–365. doi:10.1016/j.techfore.2014.08.001

Hart, M., Anyadike-Danes, M., & Blackburn, R. (2004). Entrepreneurship and age in the UK: Comparing third age and prime age new venture creation across the regions. REnT xvIII, 25-26.

Harvey, L. (2001). Defining and measuring employability. *Quality in Higher Education*, *7*(2), 97–109. doi:10.1080/13538320120059990

Hassanien, H. (2019). Web Scraping Scientific Repositories for Augmented Relevant Literature Search Using CRISP-DM. *Applied System Innovation*, *2*(4), 37. doi:10.3390/asi2040037

Hassan, S., DeHart-Davis, L., & Jiang, Z. (2019). How Empowering Leadership Reduces Employee Silence in Public Organizations. *Public Administration*, *97*(1), 116–131. doi:10.1111/padm.12571

Hatak, I., Harms, R., & Fink, M. (2015). Age, job identification, and entrepreneurial intention. *Journal of Managerial Psychology*, *30*(1), 38–53. doi:10.1108/JMP-07-2014-0213

Hawkins, J., & Dulewicz, V. (2007). *The relationship between performance as a leader and emotional intelligence, intellectual and managerial competences*. Academic Press.

Hayes, J., Parks, C., McNeilly, S., & Johnson, P. (2018, November). Boomers to Millennials: Generational Stereotypes at Work in Academic Librarianship. *Journal of Academic Librarianship*, *44*(6), 845–853. https://doi.org/10.1016/j.acalib.2018.09.011

Hayflick, L. (1996). *Como e Por Que Envelhecemos* [How and Why We Get Old]. Campus Publisher.

Hayward, M. D., Grady, W. R., Hardy, M. A., & Sommers, D. (1989). Occupational influences on retirement, disability, and death. *Demography*, *26*(3), 393–409. doi:10.2307/2061600 PMID:2529146

Helming, S., Ungermann, F., Hierath, N., Stricker, N., & Lanza, G. (2019). Development of a training concept for leadership 4.0 in production environments. *Procedia Manufacturing*, *31*, 38–44. doi:10.1016/j.promfg.2019.03.007

Helyer, R., & Lee, D. (2012). The twenty-first century multiple generation workforce: Overlaps and differences but also challenges and benefits. *Education + Training*, *54*(7), 565–578. doi:10.1108/00400911211265611

Henkens, K., & Tazelaar, F. (1997). Explaining retirement decisions of civil servants in the Netherlands: Intentions, behavior; and the discrepancy between the two. *Research on Aging*, *19*(2), 139–173. doi:10.1177/0164027597192001

Henseke, G., & Felstead, A. (2017). Assessing the growth of remote working and its consequences for effort, well-being and work-life balance. *New Technology, Work and Employment*, *32*(3), 195–212. doi:10.1111/ntwe.12097

Hershatter, A., & Epstein, M. (2010). Millennials and the World of Work: An Organization and Management Perspective. *Journal of Business and Psychology*, *25*, 211–223. https://doi.org/10.1007/s10869-010-9160-y

Hershkowitz, M. (2020). *The new normal balancing act. How to manage both remote and on premises teams*. https://www.cio.com/article/3587592/the-new-normal-balancing-act-how-to-manage-both-remote-and-on-premises-teams.html

Hertel, G., & Zacher, H. (2018). Managing the Aging Workforce. In C. Viswesvaran, N. Anderson, D. S. Ones, & H. K. Sinangil (Eds.), The SAGE Handbook of Industrial, Work and Organizational Psychology: Personnel Psychology and Employee Performance (2nd ed., vol. 3). SAGE Publications Ltd. doi:10.4135/9781473914964.n19

Higgs, P., Mein, G., Ferrie, J., Hyde, M., & Nazroo, J. (2003). Pathways to early retirement: Structure and agency in decision-making among British civil servants. *Ageing and Society*, *23*(6), 761–778. doi:10.1017/S0144686X03001326

Hirsch, J. E., & Buela-Casal, G. (2014). The meaning of the h-index. *International Journal of Clinical and Health Psychology*, *14*(2), 161–164. doi:10.1016/S1697-2600(14)70050-X

Hogan, R., & Warrenfeltz, R. (2003). Educating the Modern Manager. *Academy of Management Learning & Education*, *2*(1), 74–84. doi:10.5465/amle.2003.9324043

Holahan, C. K. (1988). Relation of life goals at age 70 to activity participation and health and psychological well-being among Terman's gifted men and women. *Psychology and Aging*, *3*(3), 286–291. doi:10.1037/0882-7974.3.3.286 PMID:3268271

Hood, W. W., & Wilson, C. S. (2001). The literature of bibliometrics, scientometrics, and informetrics. *Scientometrics*, *52*(2), 291–314. doi:10.1023/A:1017919924342

Host, A., McMahon, A. T., Walton, K., & Charlton, K. (2016). Factors influencing food choice for independently living older people—A systematic literature review. *Journal of Nutrition in Gerontology and Geriatrics*, *35*(2), 67–94. doi:10.1080/21551197.2016.1168760 PMID:27153249

House, R., Javidan, M., Hanges, P., & Dorfman, P. (2002). Understanding cultures and implicit leadership theories across the globe: An introduction to project GLOBE. *Journal of World Business*, *37*(1), 3–10. doi:10.1016/S1090-9516(01)00069-4

Hovey, R. B. (1964). Graduate students: New style: Shall we revise old-style programs to meet present needs? *The Journal of Higher Education*, *35*(8), 442–449. doi:10.1080/00221546.1964.11773567

Howe, N., & Strauss, W. (1992). *The New Generation Gap*. https://yacrisishotline.tripod.com/sitebuildercontent/sitebuilderfiles/thenewgenerationgap.pdf

Hoyer, W. J., & Roodin, P. A. (2003). *Adult Development and Aging*. McGraw Hill Publisher.

Hristoski, I., & Sotiroski, K. (2012). Conceptual data modelling of modern human migration. *Management Information Systems*, *7*(4), 3–12.

Huber, P. J. (1981). *Robust Statistics*. John Wiley. doi:10.1002/0471725250

ILO. (2014). *Skill mismatch in Europe: Statistics Brief.* International Labor Organisation.

ILO. (2021a). *ILO monitor: COVID-19 and the world of work. Seventh edition.* https://www.ilo.org/global/topics/coronavirus/impacts-and-responses/WCMS_767028/lang--en/index.htm

ILO. (2021b). *World employment and social outlook. Trends 2021.* https://www.ilo.org/global/research/global-reports/weso/trends2021/WCMS_795453/lang--en/index.htm

Ince, F. (2021a). Creating Synergic Entrepreneurship as Support of Sustainability: Opportunities and Challenges. In R. Perez-Uribe, D. Ocampo-Guzman, N. Moreno-Monsalve, & W. Fajardo-Moreno (Eds.), Handbook of Research on Management Techniques and Sustainability Strategies for Handling Disruptive Situations in Corporate Settings (pp. 464-486). IGI Global. doi:10.4018/978-1-7998-8185-8.ch022

Ince, F. (2022c). Leadership and Sustainability: From the First to the Second Generation of SMEs Ownership. In Research Anthology on Strategies for Maintaining Successful Family Firms (pp. 639-660). IGI Global. doi:10.4018/978-1-6684-3550-2.ch029

Ince, F. (2018a). *Effective Communication and Behavior Across Generations*. Eğitim Publisher.

Ince, F. (2018b). *Different Aspects of Employee' Energy*. Eğitim Publisher.

Ince, F. (2018c). The Effect of Synergic Management on Human Resources Management Performance, 459-468. In H. Babacan, T. Soldatovi, & D. N. Delobegovi (Eds.), *Academic Research in Social, Human and Administrative Sciences-I*. Gece Publisher.

Ince, F. (2020). The effects of Covid-19 pandemic on the workforce in Turkey. *Social Mentality and Researcher Thinkers Journal*, *6*(32), 1125–1134. doi:10.31576mryj.546

Ince, F. (2020b). Financial Literacy in Generation Z: Healthcare Management Students. *Smart Journal*, *6*(36), 1647–1658. doi:10.31576mryj.616

Ince, F. (2021b). Opportunities and Challenges of E-Learning in Turkey. In B. Khan, S. Affouneh, S. Hussein Salha, & Z. Najee Khlaif (Eds.), *Challenges and Opportunities for the Global Implementation of E-Learning Frameworks* (pp. 202–226). IGI Global. doi:10.4018/978-1-7998-7607-6.ch013

Ince, F. (2021c). COVID-19 Pandemic Made Me Use It: Attitude Of Generation Z Towards E-Learning. *Smart Journal*, *7*(54), 3489–3494. doi:10.31576mryj.1215

Ince, F. (2022a). Digital Literacy Training: Opportunities and Challenges. In M. Taher (Ed.), *Handbook of Research on the Role of Libraries, Archives, and Museums in Achieving Civic Engagement and Social Justice in Smart Cities* (pp. 185–199). IGI Global. doi:10.4018/978-1-7998-8363-0.ch009

Ince, F. (2022b). Creative Leadership: A Multidisciplinary Approach to Creativity. In Z. Fields (Ed.), *Achieving Sustainability Using Creativity, Innovation, and Education: A Multidisciplinary Approach* (pp. 30–49). IGI Global. doi:10.4018/978-1-7998-7963-3.ch002

India-Age dependency ratio. (n.d.). *Indexmundi*. https://www.indexmundi.com/facts/india/age-dependency-ratio

International Labour Organization. (2014). *World of work 2014: Developing with jobs.* https://www.ilo.org/wcmsp5/groups/public/@dgreports/@dcomm/documents/publication/wcms_243961.pdf

Iqbal, N., & Ashraf, M. H. (2006). *Evaluation of jCOLIBRI. Master*. Malardalen University.

Ives, G., & Rowley, G. (2005). Supervisor selection or allocation and continuity of supervision: Ph. D. students' progress and outcomes. *Studies in Higher Education*, *30*(5), 535–555. doi:10.1080/03075070500249161

Jacobs, E., Shipp, S., & Brown, G. (1989). Families of working wives spending more on services and nondurables. *Monthly Labor Review*, *112*, 15–23.

Jamal, T. B., & Getz, D. (1995). Collaboration theory and community tourism planning. *Annals of Tourism Research*, *22*(1), 186–204. doi:10.1016/0160-7383(94)00067-3

James, W. & Grantham, C. (2010). Managing a remote workforce: proven practices from successful leaders. *The Work Design Collaborative*, 1-23.

Jiang, J., Woosnam, K., & Draper, J. (2014). Structural Elements of Articles and Diachronous Citation Analysis Among Top-ranking Tourism Journals (1990-2010). *Tourism Management Perspectives*, *12*, 48–56. doi:10.1016/j.tmp.2014.06.004

Jimenez, T. J. P. (2018). *Digital skills and characteristics of generations.* September 20th, 2018. https://comunicacion897672657.wordpress.com/2018/09/20/habilidades-digitales-y-caracteristicas-de-las-generaciones/

Junaidi., E., & Prihanto, P.H. (2017). Faktor-faktor sosial ekonomi yang mempengaruhi keterlibatan penduduk lanjut usia dalam pasar kerja di Provinsi Jambi. *Jurnal Masyarakat, Kebudayaan dan Politik, 30*(2), 197-205. doi:10.20473/mkp.V30I22017.197-205

Kalwij, A., Kapteyn, A., & Vos, K. (2010). Retirement of Older Workers and Employment of the Young. *The Economist, 158*(4), 341-359.

Kamalia, S., Indartono, S., & Islamiah, R. (2019). The Role of Families on Internalization of the Tolerance Values for Millennial Generation to Decrease the Potential of Intolerant Conflict and Radicalism Behavior within the Multi Religion Society. *Advances in Social Science, Education and Humanities Research*, *323*, 316–325. doi:10.2991/icossce-icsmc-18.2019.57

Kanfer, R., & Ackerman, P. L. (2004). Aging, Adult Development, and Work Motivation. *Academy of Management Review*, *29*(3), 440–458. doi:10.2307/20159053

Kanter, R. M. (2006). *Back to college at midlife. Ending a career will soon mark the start of a new life.* https://www.aarp.org/personal-growth/life-long-learning/info-2006/back_to_college_at_midlife.html

Karadağ, N. (2014). *Türkiye'de doktora eğitim süreci kapasitesinin değerlendirilmesi (Eğitim Bilimleri Enstitüsü örneği)* [Capacity assessment of doctorate degree process in Turkey (The Case of Institute of Education Sciences)] (Doctoral thesis). Gazi University.

Kask, S. B., Kline, C., & Lamoureux, K. (2011). Modeling tourist and community decision making, The SAVE Market. *Annals of Tourism Research*, *38*(4), 1387–1409. doi:10.1016/j.annals.2011.03.011

Kasworm, C. E. (2003). Setting the stage: Adults in higher education. *New Directions for Student Services*, *2003*(102), 3–10. doi:10.1002s.83

Kato, S., & Wiklund, J. (2011). Doing Good to Feel Good—A theory of entrepreneurial action based in Hedonic Psychology. *Frontiers of Entrepreneurship Research*, *31*(4), 123–137.

Kautonen, T., Down, S., & Minniti, M. (2014). Ageing and entrepreneurial preferences. *Small Business Economics*, *42*(3), 579–594. doi:10.100711187-013-9489-5

Kautonen, T., Kibler, E., & Minniti, M. (2017). Late-career entrepreneurship, income and quality of life. *Journal of Business Venturing*, *32*(3), 318–333. doi:10.1016/j.jbusvent.2017.02.005

Kautonen, T., Luoto, S., & Tornikoski, E. T. (2010). Influence of work history on entrepreneurial intentions in 'prime age' and 'third age': A preliminary study. *International Small Business Journal, 28*(6), 583–601. doi:10.1177/0266242610368592

Kautonen, T., Tornikoski, E. T., & Kibler, E. (2011). Entrepreneurial intentions in the third age: The impact of perceived age norms. *Small Business Economics, 37*(2), 219–234. doi:10.100711187-009-9238-y

Kehm, B. M. (2006). *Doctoral education in Europe and North America: A comparative analysis.* https://citeseerx.ist.psu.edu/viewdoc/download?doi=10.1.1.526.1332&rep=rep1&type=pdf

Kelly, R., Hayward, C., Avolio, A., & O'rourke, M. (1989). Noninvasive determination of age-related changes in the human arterial pulse. *Circulation, 80*(6), 1652–1659. doi:10.1161/01.CIR.80.6.1652 PMID:2598428

Kenton, W. (2021). *Satellite Operation, Investopedia.* https://www.investopedia.com/terms/s/satellite-operation.asp

Kerns, L. (2006). Adult graduate students in higher education: Refocusing the research agenda. *Adult Learning, 17*(1-4), 40–42. doi:10.1177/104515950601700114

Kertzer, D. I. (1983). Generation as a sociological problem. *Annual Review of Sociology, 9*(1), 125–149.

Kertzman, O. F. (2005). Responsabilidade Social e Envelhecimento: O Que as Empresas Têm a ver com Isso? [Social Responsibility and Aging: What's in it for Companies?]. *A Terceira Idade*, 16.

Keynes, J. M. (2018). *The general theory of employment, interest, and money.* Springer. (Original work published 1936) doi:10.1007/978-3-319-70344-2

Kiger, P. J. (2010). *Baby Boomer Inventions That Changed the World.* https://www.reuters. com/article / idUS182429596720101222

Kim, S., & Lee, J. H. (2006). Changing facets of Korean higher education: Market competition and the role of the state. *Higher Education, 52*(3), 557–587. doi:10.100710734-005-1044-0

King, R., Cela, E., & Fokkema, T. (2021). New frontiers in international retirement migration. *Aging and Society: An Interdisciplinary Journal, 41*(6), 1205–1220. doi:10.1017/S0144686X21000179

Kırpık, G. (2020). COVID-19 pandemisinin insan kaynakları üzerindeki etkisinin akademi, medya ve iş dünyası perspektifinden incelenmesi. *Manas Sosyal Araştırmalar Dergisi, 9*(4), 2393–2406. doi:10.33206/mjss.757777

Kitchen, P. J., & Daly, F. (2002). Internal Communication During Change Management. *Corporate Communications, 7*(1), 46–53. doi:10.1108/13563280210416035

Kline, R. B. (2011). Principles and practice of structural equation modeling. In Structural Equation Modeling (3rd ed.). The Guilford Press.

Kniffin, K. M., Narayanan, J., Anseel, F., Antonakis, J., Ashford, S., Bakker, A. B., Bamberger, P., Bapuji, H., Bhave, D. P., Choi, V. K., Creary, S. J., Demerouti, E., Flynn, F. J., Gelfand, M. J., Greer, L. L., Johns, G., Kesebir, S., Klein, P. G., Lee, S. Y., ... Vugt, M. (2020). COVID-19 and the workplace: Implications, issues, and insights for future research and action. *The American Psychologist, 76*(1), 63–77. doi:10.1037/amp0000716 PMID:32772537

Koelln, K., Rubin, R. M., & Picard, M. S. (1995). Vulnerable elderly households: Expenditures on necessities by older Americans. *Social Science Quarterly*, 619–633.

KoiralaJ.AcharyaS. (2020). Dimensions of Human Resource Management Evolved with the Outbreak of COVID-19. https://ssrn.com/abstract=3584092or doi:10.2139/ssrn.3584092

Kol, E., & Topgul, S. (2022). The Process Of Demographic Change in Turkey Effects On The Social Security System. In A Gift to Prof. Dr. İhsan Erkul Social Policy and Industrial Relations Articles. Eskisehir: Nisan Publication.

Kol, E. (2014). Evaluation of health systems in terms of welfare regimes: Southern European welfare model and Turkey. *Gumushane University Electronic Journal of Social Sciences*, *5*(10), 131–168.

Kooij, D., de Lange, A., Jansen, P., & Dikkers, J. (2008). Older workers' motivation to continue to work: Five meanings of age: A conceptual review. *Journal of Managerial Psychology*, *23*(4), 364–394. doi:10.1108/02683940810869015

Kowalczyk, S. J., & Pawlish, M. J. (2002). Corporate branding through external perception of organizational culture. *Corporate Reputation Review*, *5*(2-3), 159–174. doi:10.1057/palgrave.crr.1540172

Kowalewski, S., Moretti, L., & McGee, D. (2011). Succession Planning: Evidence from "Best Companies in New York.". *International Journal of Management and Marketing Research*, *4*(2).

Krone, C., Tabacchi, M., & Farber, B. (1989). Manager Burnout. *The Cornell Hotel and Restaurant Administration Quarterly*, *30*(3), 58–63. doi:10.1177/001088048903000317

Kupperschmidt, B. R. (2000). Tips to help you recruit, manage, and keep Generation X employees. *Nursing Management*, *31*(3), 58–60.

Kurland, N. B., & Bailey, D. E. (1999). Telework: The advantages and challenges of working here, there, anywhere, and anytime. *Organizational Dynamics*, *28*(2), 53–68. doi:10.1016/S0090-2616(00)80016-9

Kurtkapan, H. (2019). Social reflections of demographic transformation and old age in Turkey. *Social Security Journal*, *15*, 27–46.

Kwon, D. B. (2009). *Human capital and its measurements.* OECD World Forum. https://www.oecd.org/site/progresskorea/44109779.pdf

Lanchimba, C., Quisnancela, J., & Méndez, Y. S. (2020). The choice of elderly labor: Evidence from Ecuador. *Revista de Análisis Económico*, *35*(1), 75–97. doi:10.4067/S0718-88702020000100075

Langevin, A. (1998). A Construção Social das Idades: Mulheres Adultas de Hoje e Velhas de Amanhã [The Social Construction of Ages: Today's Adult Women and Tomorrow's Older Women]. *Caderno CRH*, *29*, 129–149.

Lang, F. R., & Carstensen, L. L. (2002). Time counts: Future time perspective, goals, and social relationships. *Psychology and Aging*, *17*(1), 125–139. doi:10.1037/0882-7974.17.1.125 PMID:11931281

Larson, B. Z., Vroman, S. R., & Makarius, E. E. (2020). A Guide to managing your (newly) remote workers. *Harvard Business Review.* https://hbr.org/2020/03/a-guide-to-managing-your-newly-remote-workers

Lauder, H., & Mayhew, K. (2020). Higher education and the labor market: An introduction. *Oxford Review of Education*, *46*(1), 1–9. doi:10.1080/03054985.2019.1699714

Lauzon, A. (2011). The changing nature of graduate education: Implications for students in the second half of life. *International Journal of Lifelong Education*, *30*(3), 287–307. doi:10.1080/02601370.2011.564315

Laverde-Rojas, H., & Correa, J. C. (2019). Can Scientific Productivity Impact the Economic Complexity of Countries? *Scientometrics*, *120*(1), 267–282. doi:10.100711192-019-03118-8

Law on Health (Law No. 36 / 2009). https://peraturan.bpk.go.id/Home/Details/38778/uu-no-36-tahun-2009

Law on Welfare of the Elderly (Law No. 13 / 1998). https://peraturan.bpk.go.id/Home/Details/45509/uu-no-13-tahun-1998

Leccardi, C., & Feixa, C. (2011). The concept of generation within the theories of youth. *Ultima Década*, *19*(34), 11–32.

Lee, S., Schmidt-Klau, D., & Verick, S. (2020). The labor market impacts of Covid-19: A global perspective. *Indian Journal of Labor Economics*, *63*(1), 11–15. doi:10.100741027-020-00249-y

Lester, R. (2020), *Support Remote Work During The Pandemic & Beyond*. https://blog.bold360.com/ai-insights/the-new-normal-4-steps-to-support-remote-work-during-the-pandemic-beyond/

Levenson, A. (2020). A long time until the economic new normal, leaders must learn from the pandemic now to position their companies to thrive in the next crisis. *Sloan Review*. https://sloanreview.mit.edu/article/a-long-time-until-the-economic-new-normal/McArdle

Lévesque, M., & Minniti, M. (2006). The effect of aging on entrepreneurial behavior. *Journal of Business Venturing*, *21*(2), 177–194. doi:10.1016/j.jbusvent.2005.04.003

Lewis, S. (2021). *Why age inclusive workforces play a crucial role in building back a better society post-COVID*. https://www.weforum.org/agenda/2021/09/why-age-inclusive-workforces-play-a-crucial-role-in-building-back-a-better-society-post-covid/

Lewis, K., & Walker, E. (2013). Third age self-employment: A business assistance perspective. *Journal of Small Business and Enterprise Development*, *20*(2), 399–419. doi:10.1108/14626001311326798

Lewis, L. H. (1988). *Addressing the needs of returning women*. JosseyBass Publishers.

Liang, J., Wang, H., & Lazear, E. P. (2018). Demographics and entrepreneurship. *Journal of Political Economy, 126*, S140–S196. doi:10.1086/698750

Liang, Y. W. (2012). The Relationships Among Work Values, Burnout, and Organizational Citizenship Behaviors: A Study From Hotel Front-Line Service Employees in Taiwan. *International Journal of Contemporary Hospitality Management*, *24*(2), 251–268. doi:10.1108/09596111211206169

Lim, D. H., Oh, E., Ju, B., & Kim, H. N. (2019). Mediating Role of Career Coaching on Job-Search Behavior of Older Generations. *International Journal of Aging & Human Development*, *88*(1), 82–104. doi:10.1177/0091415017743009 PMID:29345142

Lippincott, J. K. (2012). Information Commons: Meeting Millennials' Needs. *Journal of Library Administration*, *52*, 6–7, 538–548. doi:10.1080/01930826.2012.707950

Lisenkova, K., Mérette, M., & Wright, R. (2012). Population ageing and the labour market: Modelling size and age-specific effects. *Economic Modelling*, *35*, 981–989. doi:10.1016/j.econmod.2013.09.007

Liu, Y., Green, A., & Pensiero, N. (2016). Expansion of higher education and inequality of opportunities: A cross-national analysis. *Journal of Higher Education Policy and Management*, *38*(3), 242–263. doi:10.1080/1360080X.2016.1174407

Logan, J., Hendry, C., Brown, J., & Courtney, N. (2009). *Barriers and pathways to entrepreneurship and innovation*. Academic Press.

Logan, J., Hendry, C., Courtney, N., & Brown, J. (2008). *Unlocking the potential of the UK's Hidden Innovators*. Cass Business School.

London, M. (1990). Enhancing career motivation in late career. *Journal of Organizational Change Management*, *3*(2), 58–71. doi:10.1108/09534819010001351

Lopes, A., & Gonçalves, C. M. (2012). Envelhecimento Ativo e Dinâmicas Sociais Contemporâneas [Active Aging and Contemporary Social Dynamics]. In C. Paúl & O. Ribeiro (Eds.), *Manual de Gerontologia* [Gerontology Manual]. Ed. Técnicas, Lda.

Lustig, S. L., Kia-Keating, M., Knight, W. G., Geltman, P., Ellis, H., Kinzie, J. D., & Saxe, G. N. (2004). Review of Child and Adolescent Refugee Mental Health. *Journal of the American Academy of Child and Adolescent Psychiatry, 43*(1), 24–36. doi:10.1097/00004583-200401000-00012 PMID:14691358

Luz, H. R. A. (2014). Sociologia do Envelhecimento [Sociology of Aging]. In M. T. Veríssimo (Ed.), *Geriatria Fundamental, Saber e Praticar* [Fundamental Geriatrics, Know & Practice] (pp. 65–74). Ed. Técnicas, Lda.

Magalhães, D. N. (1989). *A Invenção Social da Velhice* [The Social Invention of Old Age]. Papagaio Publisher.

Mahon, J. F., & Wartick, S. L. (2003). Dealing with stakeholders: How reputation, credibility and framing influence the game. *Corporate Reputation Review, 6*(1), 19–35. doi:10.1057/palgrave.crr.1540187

Mannheim, K. y de la Yncera, I. S. (1993). The problem with generations. *Reis,* (62), 193-242.

Manxhari, M., Veliu, L., & Jashari, J. (2017). Developing Models of Managerial Competencies of Managers : A Review. *International Journal of Economics. Commerce and Management, V*(4), 186–200.

Maritz, A, Zolin, R., De Waal, G., Fisher, R., Perenyi, A., & Eager, B. (2015, Sept.). Senior entrepreneurship in Australia: Active ageing and extending working lives. *International Journal of Organizational Innovation,* 1–39.

Maritz, A., Perenyi, A., de Waal, G., & Buck, C. (2020). Entrepreneurship as the unsung hero during the current COVID-19 economic crisis: Australian perspectives. *Sustainability (Switzerland), 12*(11), 4612. Advance online publication. doi:10.3390u12114612

Market Business News (MBN). (2021, July 23). *Hub – definition and meaning*. https://marketbusinessnews.com/financial-glossary/hub-definition-meaning/

Markus, L. H., Cooper-Thomas, H., & Allpress, K. N. (2005). Confounded by Competencies? An Evaluation of the Evolution and Use of Competency Models. *New Zealand Journal of Psychology, 34*(2), 117–126.

Marôco, J. (2011). *Análise Estatística com o SPSS Statistics* (5ª ed.). ReportNumber, Lda.

Marsh, K., & Musson, G. (2008). Men at work and at home: Managing emotion in telework. *Gender, Work and Organization, 15*(1), 31–48.

Martin, M. (2015). Ortega & Gasset's theory of generations: a look at the XXI Century. *Tiempo y espacio,* (20), 98-110.

Martin, N., & Prince, D. (2008). Factoring for X: An Empirical Study of Generation X's Materialistic Attributes. *Journal of Management and Marketing Research.* https://www.researchgate.net/profile/Diane-Fulton/publication/228488948_Factoring_for_X_An_Empirical_Study_of_Generation_X's_Materialistic_Attributes/links/54de25c40cf2814662eda78b/Factoring-for-X-An-Empirical-Study-of-Generation-Xs-Materialistic-Attributes.pdf

Martin, G. (2015). *Understanding Social Movements.* Routledge. doi:10.4324/9780203837092

Maslach, C., & Leiter, M. P. (2005). Stress and Burnout: The Critical Research. In C. L. Cooper (Ed.), *Handbook of Stress Medicine and Health.* CRC Press.

Maslach, C., Schaufeli, W. B., & Leiter, M. P. (2001). Job Burnout. *Annual Review of Psychology, 52*(1), 397–422. doi:10.1146/annurev.psych.52.1.397 PMID:11148311

Massot, D. (2018). *Generation Z: 15 traits of those born between 1995 and 2010.* Published on 09/04/18. https://es.aleteia.org/2018/04/09/generacion-z-conocen-las-15-caracteristicas-de-los-nacidos-entre-1995y-2010/

Matas, C. P. (2012). Doctoral education and skills development: An international perspective. *REDU: Revista de Docencia Universitaria, 10*(2), 163.

Mayhew, W. (2014). Seniorpreneurs are the fastest growing segment of entrepreneurship. *PivotMagazine.* http://www.pivotmagazine.ca/2014/seniorpreneurs/

Mayhew, K., Deer, C., & Dua, M. (2004). The move to mass higher education in the UK: Many questions and some answers. *Oxford Review of Education, 30*(1), 65–82. doi:10.1080/0305498042000190069

McClave, J., Benson, P., & Sincich, T. (2014). *Statistics for Business and Economics* (12th ed.). Pearson Education Inc.

McClelland, D. C. (1973). Testing for competence rather than for "intelligence". *The American Psychologist, 28*(1), 1–14. doi:10.1037/h0034092 PMID:4684069

McCrindle, M., & Wolfinger, E. (2009). *The ABC of XYZ: Understanding the Global Generations.* McCrindle Research.

McDonald, N. (2015). Are Millennials Really the "Go-Nowhere" Generation? *Journal of the American Planning Association, 81*(2), 90–103. doi:10.1080/01944363.2015.1057196

Mcevoy, G. M., Hayton, J. C., Warnick, A. P., Mumford, T. V., Hanks, S. H., & Blahna, M. J. (2005). A competency-based model for developing human resource professionals. *Journal of Management Education, 29*(3), 383–402. doi:10.1177/1052562904267538

McGreevy, K. M., Lipsitz, S. R., Linder, J. A., Rimm, E., & Hoel, D. G. (2009). Using median regression to obtain adjusted estimates of central tendency for skewed laboratory and epidemiologic data. *Clinical Chemistry, 55*(1), 165–169. doi:10.1373/clinchem.2008.106260 PMID:19028825

McGuinness, S., & Pouliakas, K. (2017). Deconstructing theories of overeducation in Europe: A wage decomposition approach. In S. W. Polachek, K. Pouliakas, G. Russo, & K. Tatsiramos (Eds.), *Research in labor economics, skill mismatch in labor markets* (pp. 81–127). Emerald Publishing Ltd. doi:10.1108/S0147-912120170000045003

Mein, G., Martikainen, P., Hemingway, H., Stansfeld, S., & Marmot, M. (2003). Is retirement good or bad for mental and physical health functioning? Whitehall II longitudinal study of civil servants. *Journal of Epidemiology and Community Health, 57*(1), 46–49. doi:10.1136/jech.57.1.46 PMID:12490648

Meister, J. (2020). The impact of the coronavirus on HR and the new normal of work. *Forbes.* https://www.forbes.com/sites/jeannemeister/2020/03/31/the-impact-of-the-coronavirus-on-hrand-the-new-normal-of-work/#178b9d232b60

Merriam, S. B. (2015). *Qualitative research: A guide for design and implementation* (S. Turan, Trans.). Nobel Yayıncılık.

Mezirow, J. (1991). *Transformative dimensions of adult learning.* Jossey-Bass.

Mill, J. S., & Navarro, M. Á. L. (1969). *Essay on freedom.* http://www.encuentrodefilantropos.co/Textos/Ensayo%20sobre%20la%20Libertad.pdf

Milne, G. (1977). Cyclone Tracy: II the Effects on Darwin Children. *Australian Psychologist, 12*(1), 55–62. doi:10.1080/00050067708255860

Mingers, J., & Leydesdorff, L. (2015). A Review of Theory and Practice in Scientometrics. *European Journal of Operational Research, 246*(1), 1–19. doi:10.1016/j.ejor.2015.04.002

Misachi, J. (2021). The population of India. *Worldatlas.* https://www.worldatlas.com/geography/the-population-of-india-an-overview.html

Mishra, N. (2017). In-network distributed analytics on data-centric IoT network for BI-service applications. *International Journal of Scientific Research in Computer Science, Engineering and Information Technology.*

Mishra, N. (2018). Internet of Everything Advancement Study in Data Science and Knowledge Analytic Streams. *International Journal of Scientific Research in Computer Science and Engineering, 6*(1), 30-36.

Mishra, N. (2019). Data Science and Knowledge Analytic Contexts on IoE Data for E-BI Application Case. In Edge Computing and Computational Intelligence Paradigms for the IoT (pp. 100-126). IGI Global. doi:10.4018/978-1-5225-8555-8.ch007

Mishra, N., & Samuel, J. M. (2021). Towards Integrating Data Mining With Knowledge-Based System for Diagnosis of Human Eye Diseases: The Case of an African Hospital. In Handbook of Research on Disease Prediction Through Data Analytics and Machine Learning (pp. 470-485). IGI Global.

Mishra, N. (2010). *Art of Software Defect Association & Correction Using Association Rule Mining. Academic Press.*

Mishra, N. (2011). A Framework for associated pattern mining over Microarray database. *Journal of Global Research in Computer Science*, *2*(2).

Mishra, N., Alebachew, K., & Patnaik, B. C. (2018). Data Organization and Knowledge Inference from Sensor Database for Smart Wear. International Journal of Scientific Research in Computer Science. *Engineering and Information Technology*, *3*(1), 1039–1044.

Mishra, N., Alebachew, K., & Patnaik, B. C. (2018). Knowledge Analytics in Cloud Centric IoT Vicinities. *International Journal on Computer Science and Engineering*, *6*(1), 385–390.

Mishra, N., Chang, H. T., & Lin, C. C. (2014). Data-centric knowledge discovery strategy for a safety-critical sensor application. *International Journal of Antennas and Propagation*, *2014*, 2014. doi:10.1155/2014/172186

Mishra, N., Chang, H. T., & Lin, C. C. (2015). An Iot knowledge reengineering framework for semantic knowledge analytics for BI-services. *Mathematical Problems in Engineering*, *2015*, 2015. doi:10.1155/2015/759428

Mishra, N., Chang, H. T., & Lin, C. C. (2018). *Sensor Data Distribution and Distributed Knowledge Inference Systems.* LAP LAMBERT Academic Publishing.

Mishra, N., Chang, H. T., & Lin, C. C. (2018). Sensor data distribution and knowledge inference framework for a cognitive-based distributed storage sink environment. *International Journal of Sensor Networks*, *26*(1), 26–42. doi:10.1504/IJSNET.2018.088387

Mishra, N., Lin, C. C., & Chang, H. T. (2014). Cognitive inference device for activity supervision in the elderly. *TheScientificWorldJournal*, *2014*, 2014. doi:10.1155/2014/125618 PMID:25405211

Mishra, N., Lin, C. C., & Chang, H. T. (2014, December). A cognitive oriented framework for IoT big-data management prospective. In *2014 IEEE International Conference on Communiction Problem-solving* (pp. 124-127). IEEE. 10.1109/ICCPS.2014.7062233

Mishra, N., Lin, C. C., & Chang, H. T. (2015). A cognitive adopted framework for IoT big-data management and knowledge discovery prospective. *International Journal of Distributed Sensor Networks*, *11*(10), 718390. doi:10.1155/2015/718390

Mishra, N., Thangavel, G., & Samuel, J. M. (2020). A Case Assessment Of Knowledge-Based Fit In Frame For Diagnosis Of Human Eye Diseases. *Journal of Critical Reviews*, *7*(6), 754–763.

Moehrle, T. (1990). Expenditure Patterns of the Elderly Workers and Nonworkers. *Monthly Labor Review*, *113*, 34–41.

Mok, K. H., & Jiang, J. (2018). Massification of higher education and challenges for graduate employment and social mobility: East Asian experiences and sociological reflections. *International Journal of Educational Development*, *63*, 44–51. doi:10.1016/j.ijedudev.2017.02.003

Mok, K. H., & Wu, A. (2016). Higher education, changing labor market and social mobility in the era of Massification in China. *Journal of Education and Work*, *29*(1), 77–97. doi:10.1080/13639080.2015.1049028

Molino, M., Cortese, C. G., & Ghislieri, C. (2019). Unsustainable working conditions: The association of destructive leadership, use of technology, and workload with workaholism and exhaustion. *Sustainability*, *11*(2), 446. doi:10.3390u11020446

Molino, M., Ingusci, E., Signore, F., Amelia, M., Amelia, G., Maria, L., Russo, V., Zito, M., & Cortese, C. G. (2020). Wellbeing costs of technology use during covid-19 remote working: An investigation using the italian translation of the technostress creators scale. *Sustainability*, *12*(5911), 1–20. doi:10.3390u12155911

Montizaan, R. M., & Vendrik, M. C. M. (2014). Misery loves company: Exogenous shocks in retirement expectations and social comparison effects on subjective well-being. *Journal of Economic Behavior & Organization*, *97*, 1–26. doi:10.1016/j.jebo.2013.10.009

Moore, C. J., Lehane, M. S., & Price, C. J. (1994, March). Case based reasoning for decision support in engineering design. In *IEE Colloquium on Case Based Reasoning: Prospects for Applications* (Digest No. 1994/057) (pp. 4-1). IET.

Morel, A., Joly, B., & Maigne, M. (2004). *Rapport sur la Gestion des Âges et les Politiques de l'Emploi dans l'Union Européenne* [Report on Labour Management and Employment Policies in the European Union]. IGAS.

Moulton, J. G., & Scott, J. C. (2016). Opportunity or necessity? Disaggregating self-employment and entry at older ages. *Social Forces*, *94*(4), 1539–1566. doi:10.1093fow026

Mouraviev, N., & Avramenko, A. (2020). Senior Entrepreneurship: Ageing, Entrepreneurial Identity, Behaviour and Challenges. *Entrepreneurship for Deprived Communities*, 67–93. doi:10.1108/978-1-78973-985-520201005

Muijnck, J. A., & Zwinkels, W. S. (2002). Older Employees in SME's: A Literature Review on the Use of Older Employees. In Onderzoek voor Bedrijf & Beleid, Zoetermeer. EIM.

Mulder, M., & Collins, K. (2007). Competence Development in Organisations : Its Use in Practice. Paper Presented at the *Annual Meeting of the AERA*.

Mumford, M., Marks, M., Connelly, M., Zaccaro, S., & Reiter-Palmon, R. (2000). Development of leadership skills: Experience and timing. *The Leadership Quarterly*, *11*(1), 87–114. doi:10.1016/S1048-9843(99)00044-2

Mumford, M., Zaccaro, S., Connelly, M., & Marks, M. (2000). Leadership skills: Conclusions and future directions. *The Leadership Quarterly*, *11*(1), 155–170. doi:10.1016/S1048-9843(99)00047-8

Mumford, M., Zaccaro, S., Harding, F., Jacobs, T., & Fleishman, E. (2000). Leadership skills for a changing world: Solving complex social problems. *The Leadership Quarterly*, *11*(1), 11–35. doi:10.1016/S1048-9843(99)00041-7

Mumford, T., Campion, M., & Morgeson, F. (2007). The leadership skills strataplex: Leadership skill requirements across organizational levels. *The Leadership Quarterly*, *18*(2), 154–166. doi:10.1016/j.leaqua.2007.01.005

Nasir, Z. M., Ali, S. M., & Chaudhry, M. A. (2000). Labour market participation of the older people. *Pakistan Development Review*, *39*(4), 1075–1086. doi:10.30541/v39i4IIpp.1075-1086

National Administrative Department of Statistics. (2018a). *Colombia results: National total*. https://www.dane.gov.co/files/censo2018/infografias/info-CNPC-2018total-nal-colombia.pdf

National Administrative Department of Statistics. (2018b). *Population structure, men and women. Comparative 1985 and 2018*. https://sitios.dane.gov.co/cnpv/#!/est_pob

Nayır, F. (2011). Problems of postgraduate students including school principals, teachers and inspectors in educational sciences. *Ankara University Journal of Faculty of Educational Sciences*, *44*(2), 199–222. doi:10.1501/Egifak_0000001230

Neeley, T. (2015). Global Teams That Work. *Harvard Business Review, 93*(10), 74–81. doi:10.2469/dig.v45.n12.5

Nerad, M., & Trzyna, T. (2011). Globalization and doctoral education- toward a research agenda. In M. Nerad & M. Heggelund (Eds.), *Toward a global PhD?: Forces and forms in doctoral education worldwide* (pp. 300–330). University of Washington Press.

Neri, A. L. (2001). *Memória e Sociedade: Lembranças de Velhos* [Memory and Society: Remembrances of Old People]. Companhia das Letras Publisher.

Neri, A. L., & Cachioni, M. (1999). Velhice Bem-sucedida e Educação [Successful Old Age and Education]. In A. L. Neri & G. G. Debert (Eds.), *Velhice e Sociedade* [Elderly and Society] (pp. 113–140). Papirus Publisher.

Netto, M. (2002). *Gerontologia: A velhice e o Envelhecimento em Visão Globalizada* [Gerontology: Old Age and Aging in a Global View]. Atheneu Publisher.

Newburry, W., Deephouse, D. L., & Gardberg, N. A. (2019). Global Aspects of Reputation and Strategic Management. In *Global Aspects of Reputation and Strategic Management (Research in Global Strategic Management, 18).* Emerald Publishing Limited. doi:10.1108/S1064-485720190000018009

Nguyen, N. T., & Pham, L.-H.-T. (2020). How to Motivate Employees? Special Case of Millennial Generation in Vietnam. *Journal of Southwest Jiaotong University, 55*(2), 1–13. doi:10.35741/issn.0258-2724.55.2.40

Ningrum, V., Subroto, A., Widodo, Y. B., Aji, G. B., Harfina, G., Wiratri, A., & Suryanto, J. (2016). *Rural youth aspiration in agriculture: support or threaten food security?* [Presented Paper]. The 3rd Asia Future Conference.

Noe, R. A., Noe, A. W., & Bachhuber, J. A. (1990). An investigation of the correlates of career motivation. *Journal of Vocational Behavior, 37*(3), 340–356. doi:10.1016/0001-8791(90)90049-8

Noone, J., Knox, A., O'Loughlin, K., McNamara, M., Bohle, P., & Mackey, M. (2018). An analysis of factors associated with older workers' employment participation and preferences in Australia. *Frontiers in Psychology, 9*(2524), 1–16. doi:10.3389/fpsyg.2018.02524 PMID:30618949

North, M. S. (2019). A Gate to Understanding "Older" Workers: Generation, Age, Tenure, Experience. *The Academy of Management Annals, 13*(2), 414–443. doi:10.5465/annals.2017.0125

Nyiri, L. (2002). Knowledge-based society and its impact on labor-market values. *Society and Economy, 24*(2), 201–218. doi:10.1556/SocEc.24.2002.2.3

Oberer, B., & Erkollar, A. (2018). Leadership 4.0: Digital Leaders in the Age of Industry 4.0. *International Journal of Organizational Leadership, 7*(4), 404–412. doi:10.33844/ijol.2018.60332

OECD. (1996). *The knowledge-based economy*. OECD Publishing.

OECD. (1998). *Maintaining Prosperity in an Ageing Society*. OECD Publishing.

OECD. (2016). *Skills matter: Further results from the survey of adult skills, country note Turkey*. https://www.oecd.org/skills/piaac/Skills-Matter-Turkey-Turkish-version.pdf

OECD. (2016). *Skills matter: Further results from the survey of adult skills*. Paris: OECD Publishing. https://www.oecd.org/skills/piaac/Skills_Matter_Further_Results_from_the_Survey_of_Adult_Skills.pdf

OECD. (2017). *Social security contributions (indicator)*. doi:10.1787/3ebfe901-en

OECD. (2018). *Transformative technologies and jobs of the future*. Paris: OECD Publishing. https://www.oecd.org/innovation/transformative-technologies-and-jobs-of-the-future.pdf

OECD. (2019). *Education at a glance 2019 OECD indicators*. https://www.oecd-ilibrary.org/education/education-at-a-glance-2019_f8d7880d-en

OECD. (2019a). *Skills matter: Additional results from the survey of adult skills*. OECD Publishing., doi:10.1787/1f029d8f-

OECD. (2019b). *Speech at launch of OECD's: Education at a glance 2019: OECD indicators*. https://www.hepi.ac.uk/2019/09/10/hepi-hosts-the-launch-of-education-at-a-glance-2019-oecd-indicators%EF%BB%BF-the-worlds-best-source-of-education-data/

OECD. (2020). *OECD economic outlook 2020*. OECD Publishing. doi:10.1787/0d1d1e2e-

OECD. (2021a). *Education at a glance 2021: OECD indicators*. OECD Publishing. doi:10.1787/b35a14e5-

OECD. (2021b). *OECD economic outlook 2021*. OECD Publishing., doi:10.1787/edfbca02-

OECD. (2021c). *OECD employment outlook 2021: Navigating the Covıd-19 crisis and recovery*. OECD Publishing. doi:10.1787/5a700c4b-

Oliveira, C. R., & Pinto, A. M. (2014). Biologia e Fisiopatologia do Envelhecimento [Biology and Pathophysiology of Aging]. In M. T. Veríssimo (Ed.), *Geriatria Fundamental, Saber e Praticar* [Fundamental Geriatrics, Know & Practice] (pp. 17–28). Ed. Técnicas, Lda.

Ong, F. S. (2012). Older consumers in Malaysia: Spending pattern, leisure activities and consumption preferences. *International Journal of Ageing and Later Life*, *2*(1), 85–117. doi:10.3384/ijal.1652-8670.072185

Ong, F. S., Kitchen, J. P., & Jama, A. T. (2008). Consumption patterns and silver marketing: An analysis of older consumers in Malaysia. *Marketing Intelligence & Planning*, *26*(7), 682–698. doi:10.1108/02634500810916663

Otzen, T., & Manterola, C. (2017). Sampling techniques on a study population. *International Journal of Morphology*, *35*(1), 227–232.

Ozdemir, S. (2007). *Welfare State in the Process of Globalization*. Istanbul Chamber of Commerce Publications.

Özdevecioğlu, M., & İnce, F. (2011). Cultural Synergy Management: Conceptual Framework. *Erciyes University Journal of Economics and Administrative Sciences*, (38), 27–45.

Ozen, S., & Ozbek, C. (2017). Elderly workers and Human Resources Practices. *Journal of Labor and Society*, *2*, 547–572.

Ozerim, M. G. (2012). Turkey on the Route of Retirement Migration: The Motivations of European Retirement Migrants to Prefer Turkey and Their Perception of Turkey. *Journal of Yasar University*, *28*(7), 4766–4787.

Pakdel, F., Gharebaghi, R., & Ghazavi, R. (2019). Effect of Selenium on Thyroid Disorders: Scientometric Analysis. *Iranian Journal of Public Health*, *48*(3), 410–420. doi:10.18502/ijph.v48i3.883 PMID:31223567

Palmatier, R. W., & Crecelius, A. T. (2019). The "First Principles" of Marketing Strategy. *AMS Review*, *9*(1-2), 5–26. doi:10.100713162-019-00134-y

Parker, R. (2012). Skill development in graduate education. *Molecular Cell*, *46*(4), 377–381. doi:10.1016/j.molcel.2012.05.003 PMID:22633484

Parker, S. C., & Rougier, J. C. (2007). The retirement behaviour of the self-employed in Britain. *Applied Economics*, *39*(6), 697–713. doi:10.1080/00036840500447807

Patel, S. H., & Grey, C. (2006). *Grey Entrepreneurs in the UK; IKO Working Paper No. 18*. Open University Research Centre on Innovation, Knowledge and Development. Milton Keynes: Open University.

Patil, N., & Peshave, M. A. (2020). Millennial Employees: Professional Expectations and Challenges at Working Place. *UGC Care Journal*, *19*(22), 356–370.

Patil, R., & Gopalakrishnan, G. (2020). A study on employee experience with respect to remote working during the covid 19-pandemic. *Journal of Critical Reviews*, *7*(11), 3910–3918.

Patnaik, B. C., & Mishra, N. (2016). A Review on Enhancing the Journaling File System. *Imperial Journal of Interdisciplinary Research, 2*(11).

Patton, M. Q. (2014). *Nitel araştırma ve değerlendirme yöntemleri* (M. Bütün & S. B. Demir, Trans.). Pegem.

Paúl, C., Teixeira, L., & Ribeiro, O. (2017). Active Aging in Very Old Age and the Relevance of Psychological Aspects. *Frontiers in Medicine*, *4*(181), 1–7. doi:10.3389/fmed.2017.00181 PMID:29164117

Paulin, G. D. (2000). Expenditure patterns of older Americans, 1984-97. *Monthly Labor Review*, *123*, 3–28.

Peace, J. (2021). *Hybrid work model: 4 best practices for fairness, The Enterprisers Project.* https://enterprisersproject.com/article/2021/6/hybrid-work-model-4-best-practices

Pedro, D., Fracasso, N. V., Costa, R. G., Rossaneis, M. Â., Aroni, P., & Haddad, M. (2020). Age Management Practices Toward Workers Aged 45 years or Older: An Integrative Literature Review. *Revista Brasileira de Medicina do Trabalho*, *18*(2), 194–202. doi:10.47626/1679-4435-2020-536 PMID:33324461

Perenyi, A., Zolin, R., & Maritz, A. (2018). The perceptions of Australian senior entrepreneurs on the drivers of their entrepreneurial activity. *International Journal of Entrepreneurial Behaviour & Research*, *24*(1), 81–103. doi:10.1108/IJEBR-12-2016-0424

Pestana, M. H., & Gageiro, J. N. (2014). Análise de dados para ciências sociais - A complementaridade do SPSS (6a ed.). Academic Press.

Petzer, M. (2020). *Coronavirus and the Workforce: How Can We Limit Redundancies?* http://researchonline.ljmu.ac.uk/iFd/eprint/12960/1/coronavirus-workforce redundancies _2020 0402T170659.pdf 31.

Phillipson, C. (1998). *Reconstructing Old Age: New Agendas in Social Theory and Practice.* Sage Books.

Phillipson, C. (2007). Understanding the Baby Boom Generation: Comparative Perspectives. *International Journal of Ageing and Later Life*, *2*(2), 7–11.

Phillips, S. (2020). Working through the pandemic: Accelerating the transition to remote working. *Business Information Review*, *37*(3), 129–135. doi:10.1177/0266382120953087

PIAAC Expert Group in Problem Solving in Technology-Rich Environments. (2009). PIAAC problem solving in technology rich environments: A conceptual framework. *OECD Education Working Papers*, 36. doi:10.1787/19939019

Pinder, C. (1998). *Work motivation in organizational behavior.* Prentice Hall.

Pinto, A., Ramos, S., & Nunes, S. (2015). Managing an Aging Workforce: What is the Value of Human Resource Management Practices for Different Age Groups of Workers? *TÉKHNE - Review of Applied Management Studies*, *12*, 58-68. doi:10.1016/j.tekhne.2015.01.007

Polson, C. J. (2003). Adult graduate students challenge institutions to change. *New Directions for Student Services*, *2003*(102), 59–68. doi:10.1002s.90

Population Institute. (2020). *Population Clock.* https://www.populationinstitute.org/resources/

Pouliakas, K. (2012). The skill mismatch challenge in Europe. *Employment and Social Developments in Europe*, 351-394.

Poulter, G. D. (2017). *The learner identities of older adults engaged in higher degree programmes* (Doctoral thesis). University of Glasgow. https://eleanor.lib.gla.ac.uk/record=b3304884

Prahalad, C., & Hamel, G. (1990). The core competence of the corporation. *Harvard Business Review*, (May-June), 1–15.

Prasad, K. D. V., & Mangipudi, M. R. (2020). Post-Covid19 pandemic back to workplace policies and procedures: A case study with reference to agricultural research sector. *Hyderabad. European Journal of Business and Management Research*, *5*(4), 1–5. doi:10.24018/ejbmr.2020.5.4.421

Pratt, M. W., Norris, J. E., Arnold, M. L., & Filyer, R. (1999). Generativity and moral development as predictors of value-socialization narratives for young persons across the adult life span: From lessons learned to stories shared. *Psychology and Aging*, *14*(3), 414–426. doi:10.1037/0882-7974.14.3.414 PMID:10509696

Prawitasari, G. (2018). The Influence of Generations on Career Choice: Social Cognitive Career Theory Perspective. *Konselor*, *7*(1), 15–20. doi:10.24036/02018718464-0-00

Priyadarsini, K., Mishra, N., Prasad, M., Gupta, V., & Khasim, S. (2021). Detection of malware on the internet of things and its applications depends on long short-term memory network. *Journal of Ambient Intelligence and Humanized Computing*, 1–12. doi:10.100712652-020-02823-0

Pumphrey, C. (2011). *How the Greatest Generation Works*. https://people.howstuffworks.com/culture-traditions/generation-gaps/greatest-generation1.htm

Pusat Studi Kependudukan dan Kebijakan Universitas Gajah Mada. (2014). *Tinggi, angka pekerja lansia di Indonesia*. https://cpps.ugm.ac.id/ tinggi-angka-pekerja-lansia-di-indonesia/

PwC. (2020, May 8). *TMT companies well-prepared for hybrid work model*. https://www.pwc.com/us/en /industries/tmt/library/companies-prepared-for-hybrid-work-model.html

PwC. (2021, January 12). *PwC's US Remote Work Survey. It's time to reimagine where and how work will get done*. https://www.pwc.com/us/en/library/covid-19/us-remote-work-survey.html

Radl, J. (2013). Labour market exit and social stratification in western Europe: The effects of social class and gender on the timing of retirement. *European Sociological Review*, *29*(3), 654–668. doi:10.1093/esr/jcs045

Ramirez, M. C., Armando, R., & Devesa, R. (2019). A Scientometric Look at Mathematics Education from Scopus Database. *The Mathematics Enthusiast*, *16*(1), 37–46. doi:10.54870/1551-3440.1449

Ratnawat, R. K. (2018). Competency Based Human Resource Management : Concepts, Tools, Techniques, and Models : A Review. *International Journal of Multidisciplinary*, *3*(5), 119–124.

Ratten, V. (2019). Older entrepreneurship: A literature review and research agenda. *Journal of Enterprising Communities: People and Places in the Global Economy*, *13*(1/2), 178–195. doi:10.1108/JEC-08-2018-0054

Reiff, M., & Ballin, A. (2008). *What do adult graduate students want? Using the typology of cognitive/affective/psychomotor learning domains to explore good and bad learning experiences*. Adult Education Research Conference. https://newprairiepress.org/aerc/2008/papers/56

Repetti, M., Phillipson, C., & Calasanti, T. (2018). Retirement migration in Europe: A choice for a better life? *Sociological Research Online*, *23*(4), 780–794. doi:10.1177/1360780418782243

Republic of Turkey Ministry of Development Eleventh Development Plan. (2018a). *Aging Special Commission Report*. Author.

Republic of Turkey Ministry of Development Eleventh Development Plan. (2018b). *Sustainability of the Social Security System Specialization Commission Report*. Author.

Reputation Institute, Country RepTrak. (2015). *The World's Most Reputable Countries. The World's View on Countries: An Online Study of the Reputation of 55 Countries*. Author.

Rios, A. (2016). Characteristics of Colombian Baby Boomers. *Revistapym*. https://revistapym.com.co/caracteristicas-los-baby-boomers-colombianos

RitchieH.RoserM. (2019). *Age Structure*. https://ourworldindata.org/age-structure

Rivas-Rodriguez, M. (2016). *A Soldier's Story: World War II and the Forgotten Battle for the Aleutian Islands*. https://www.kut.org/life-arts/2016-11-11/a-soldiers-story-world-war-ii-and-the-forgotten-battle-for-the-aleutian-islands

Robinson, E. (2015). Perceived social norms and eating behaviour: An evaluation of studies and future directions. *Physiology & Behavior*, *152*, 397–401. doi:10.1016/j.physbeh.2015.06.010 PMID:26072177

Robinson, W. R., Utz, R. L., Keyes, K. M., Martin, C. L., & Yang, Y. (2013). Birth Cohort Effects on Abdominal Obesity in the United States: The Silent Generation, Baby Boomers and Generation X. *International Journal of Obesity*, *37*(8), 1129–1134. doi:10.1038/ijo.2012.198 PMID:23229734

Robson, C., & McCartan, K. (2016). *Real World Research* (4th ed.). John Wiley & Sons Ltd.

Rodrigues, L. S., & Soares, G. A. (2006). Velho, Idoso e Terceira Idade na Sociedade Contemporânea [Old, Elderly and Senior Citizens in the Contemporary Society]. *Revista Ágora*, *4*, 1–29.

Rodriguez, D., Patel, R., Bright, A., Gregory, D., & Gowing, M. K. (2002). Developing competency models to promote integrated human resource practices. *Human Resource Management*, *41*(3), 309–324. doi:10.1002/hrm.10043

Rodriguez, M., Boyer, S., Fleming, D., & Cohen, S. (2019). Managing the Next Generation of Sales, Gen Z/Millennial Cusp: An Exploration of Grit, Entrepreneurship, and Loyalty. *Journal of Business-To-Business Marketing*, *26*(1), 43–55. doi:10.1080/1051712X.2019.1565136

Rodriguez, R. O., Green, M. T., & Ree, M. J. (2003). Leading Generation X: Do The Old Rules Apply? *Journal of Leadership & Organizational Studies*, *9*(4), 67–75. doi:10.1177/107179190300900406

Roehrich, J. K., Lewis, M. A., & George, G. (2014). Are public–private partnerships a healthy option? A systematic literature review. *Social Science & Medicine*, *113*, 110–119. doi:10.1016/j.socscimed.2014.03.037 PMID:24861412

Rokeach, M. (1973). *The Nature of Human Values*. The Free Press. http://faculty.wwu.edu/tyrank/Rokeach%20Value%20 Survey.pdf

Rose, K. (2008). *Myth and the Greatest Generation: A Social History of Americans in World War II*. Routledge.

Rosenberg, M. (2020). *Generational Names in the United States: Traditionalists, Gen Zs, and Everything in Between*. https://www.thoughtco.com/names-of-generations-1435472

Rosencrance, L. (2021). *Hybrid Workforce*. https://whatis.techtarget.com/definition/hybrid-workforce

Rouco, C. (2015). Identification of Leadership Competences in the Different Organizational Levels: Military Context. *Journal of Business and Economics*, *6*(4), 709–721. doi:10.15341/jbe(2155-7950)/04.06.2015/008

Rouco, C., & Sarmento, M. (2012). Development model of leadership skills in the military context. *Proceedings of the 13th UFHRD International Conference on Human Resource Development Research and Practice across Europe*, 1–17.

Rowan, L. (2021). *Remote Work: The New Normal?* https://www.15five.com/blog/remote-work-the-new-normal/

Rubin, R. M., & Koelln, K. (1996). Elderly and nonelderly expenditures on necessities in the 1980s. *Monthly Labor Review*, *119*, 24–31. PMID:10162467

Rudolph, C. W., Allan, B., Clark, M., Hertel, G., Hirschi, A., Kunze, F., Shockley, K., Shoss, M., Sonnentag, S., & Zacher, H. (2020). Pandemics: Implications for research and practice in industrial and organizational psychology. *Industrial and Organizational Psychology: Perspectives on Science and Practice*, 1–82.

Saba, T., & Guerin, G. (2005). Extending employment beyond retirement age: The case of health care managers in Quebec. *Public Personnel Management*, *34*(2), 195–214. doi:10.1177/009102600503400205

Sakar, M. (2017). *Social Insurance Application* (12th ed.). Beta Publications.

Saleh, S. D., & Otis, J. L. (1964). Age and level of job satisfaction. *Personnel Psychology*, *17*(4), 425–430. doi:10.1111/j.1744-6570.1964.tb00077.x

Salem, A. B. M., Roushdy, M., & HodHod, R. A. (2005). A case based expert system for supporting diagnosis of heart diseases. *AIML Journal, 5*(1), 33-39.

Salem, A. B. M. (2007). Case based reasoning technology for medical diagnosis. *World Academy of Science, Engineering and Technology*, *31*, 9–13.

Salgado, M. A. (2007). Os Grupos e a Ação Pedagógica do Trabalho Social com Idosos [The Groups and the Pedagogical Action of Social Work with the Elderly]. *A Terceira Idade, 18*(39), 1-96.

Sánchez, M. A. (2018). *10 facts about Generation Z.* https://www.lavanguardia.com/vivo/20180715/45818419326/dia-habilidades-juventud-generacion-z.html

Sardeshmukh, S. R., Sharma, D., & Golden, T. D. (2012). Impact of telework on exhaustion and job engagement: A job demands and job resources model. *New Technology, Work and Employment*, *27*(3), 193–207. doi:10.1111/j.1468-005X.2012.00284.x

Saunders, M., Lewis, P., & Thornhill, A. (2019). *Research Methods for Business Students* (8th ed.). Pearson Education Limited.

Schawbel, D. (2020). How to put people at the heart of your company's COVID-19 response, *World Economic Forum*. https://www.weforum.org/agenda/2020/10/covid19-remote-working-burnout-business-response/

Schepers, J., Voordeckers, W., Steijvers, T., & Laveren, E. (2014). The entrepreneurial orientation-performance relationship in private family firms: The moderating role of socioemotional wealth. *Small Business Economics*, *43*(1), 39–55. doi:10.100711187-013-9533-5

Schippmann, J. S., Ash, R. A., Carr, L., & Hesketh, B. (2000). The practice of competency modeling. *Personnel Psychology*, *53*(3), 703–740. doi:10.1111/j.1744-6570.2000.tb00220.x

Schneider, R. H., & Irigaray, T. Q. (2008). O Envelhecimento na Atualidade: Aspectos Cronológicos, Biológicos e Sociais [Aging in the Modern World: Chronological, Biological and Social Aspects]. *Estudos de Psicologia*, *25*(4), 585–593. doi:10.1590/S0103-166X2008000400013

Schøtt, T., Rogoff, E., Herrington, M., & Kew, P. (2017). *GEM Special Report on Senior Entrepreneurship 2017*. Global Entrepreneurship Research Association.

Schroeder, S. M., & Terras, K. L. (2015). Advising experiences and needs of online, cohort, and classroom adult graduate learners. *The Journal of the National Academic Advising Association*, *35*(1), 42–55. doi:10.12930/NACADA-13-044

Schwab, D. P., & Heneman, H. G. III. (1977). Age and satisfaction with dimensions of work. *Journal of Vocational Behavior, 10*(2), 212–220. doi:10.1016/0001-8791(77)90058-6

Scopus. (2021). *Why choose Scopus.* https://www.elsevier.com/solutions/scopus/why-choose-scopus

Seeley, R. R., Stephens, T. D., & Tate, P. (2008). *Anatomia e Fisiologia - 8ª Edição* [Anatomy and Physiology - 8th Edition]. Lusociência Publisher.

Sekhampu, T., & Niyimbanira, F. (2013). Analysis Of The Factors Influencing Household Expenditure In A South African Township. *International Business & Economics Research Journal, 12*(3), 279–284. doi:10.19030/iber.v12i3.7671

Sengupta, S., Sahay, A., & Croce, F. (2018). Conceptualizing social entrepreneurship in the context of emerging economies: An integrative review of past research from BRIICS. *The International Entrepreneurship and Management Journal, 14*(4), 771–803. doi:10.100711365-017-0483-2

Settersten, R. A. Jr, & Mayer, K. U. (1997). The measurement of age, age structuring, and the life course. *Annual Review of Sociology, 23*(1), 233–261. doi:10.1146/annurev.soc.23.1.233

Shapero, A., & Sokol, L. (1982). *The social dimensions of entrepreneurship. University of Illinois at Urbana-Champaign's Academy for Entrepreneurial Leadership Historical Research Reference in Entrepreneurship.* Prentice Hall.

Sharpe, A. (2011), Is ageing a drag on productivity growth? A review article on ageing, health and productivity: The economics of increased life expectancy, *International Productivity Monitor, 21*, 82-94. http://www.csls.ca/ipm/21/IPM-21-Sharpe.pdf

Shen, A. (2019). Marketing Preventive Health to Baby Boomers: What if Unhealthy Lifestyles are Attributable to the Counterculture? *Journal of Macromarketing, 39*(2), 151–165. doi:10.1177/0276146719835290

Sheynkman, A. (2021). *SpaceIQ.* https://spaceiq.com/blog/what-is-shared-workspace/

Shirky, C. (2010). *Cognitive Surplus: How Technology Makes Consumers into Collaborators.* The Penguin Press.

Simpson, S. (2021). Writing a hybrid working policy: A guide for HR. *Personnel Today.* https://www.personneltoday.com/hr/hybrid-working-policy-hr-guide/

Singh, A. P., & Dangmei, J. (2016). Understanding the generation Z: the future workforce. *South -Asian Journal of Multidisciplinary Studies, 3*(3). https://www.researchgate.net/profile/Jianguanglung-Dangmei/publication/305280948_UNDERSTANDING_THE_GENERATION_Z_THE_FUTURE_WORKFORCE/links/5786a11008aef321de2c6f21/UNDERSTANDING-THE-GENERATION-Z-THE-FUTURE-WORKFORCE.pdf

Singh, R. (2009). The aging population and mature entrepreneurs: Market trends and implications for entrepreneurship. *New England Journal of Entrepreneurship, 12*(1), 45–53. doi:10.1108/NEJE-12-01-2009-B004

Singularity Hub Staff. (2009). *Blue Zones – Places in the World Where People Live to 100 and Stay Healthy.* https://singularityhub.com/2009/07/20/blue-zones-places-in-the-world-where-people-live-to-100-and-stay-healthy/

Smith, R. (2020). *The Silent Generation: Characteristics and History.* https://www.familysearch.org/blog/en/silent-generation-characteristics/

Smith, D. B., & Moen, P. (1998). Spousal influence on retirement: His, her, and their perceptions. *Journal of Marriage and Family, 60*(3), 734–744. doi:10.2307/353542

Soberon-Ferrer, H., & Dardis, R. (1991). Determinants of household expenditures for services. *The Journal of Consumer Research, 17*(4), 385–397. doi:10.1086/208565

SongL. (2008). In search of gender bias in household resource allocation in rural China. *Available at* SSRN 1136265. doi:10.2139/ssrn.1136265

Souza, J. A. V., Freitas, M. C., & Queiroz, T. A. (2007). Violência Contra os Idosos: Análise Documental [Violence Against the Elderly: A Documentary Analysis]. *Revista Brasileira de Enfermagem*, *60*(3), 268–272. doi:10.1590/S0034-71672007000300004 PMID:17684902

Spreitzer, G., & Porath, C. (2012). Creating Sustainable Performance. *Harvard Business Review*, *90*(1), 92–99. PMID:22299508

Staubli, S., & Zweimüller, J. (2013). Does raising the early retirement age increase employment of older workers? *Journal of Public Economics*, *108*, 17–32. doi:10.1016/j.jpubeco.2013.09.003 PMID:24319299

Sterns, H. L., & Alexander, R. A. (1987). Industrial gerontology: the aging individual and work. In K. W. Schaie (Ed.), *Annual Review of Gerontology and Geriatrics* (Vol. 7, pp. 243–264). Springer Publishing Company.

Sterns, H. L., & Doverspike, D. (1989). Aging and the retraining and learning process in organizations. In I. Goldstein & R. Katze (Eds.), *Training and Development in Work Organizations* (pp. 299–332). Jossey-Bass.

Sterns, H. L., & Miklos, S. M. (1995). The aging worker in a changing environment: Organizational and Individual Issues. *Journal of Vocational Behavior*, *47*(3), 248–268. doi:10.1006/jvbe.1995.0003

Stevens, G. W. (2012). A Critical Review of the Science and Practice of Competency Modeling. *Human Resource Development Review*, *12*(1), 86–107. doi:10.1177/1534484312456690

Stewart, J. S., Oliver, E. G., Cravens, K. S., & Oishi, S. (2017). Managing Millennials: Embracing Generational Differences. *Business Horizons*, *60*(1), 45–54. doi:10.1016/j.bushor.2016.08.011

Stirzaker, R. J., & Galloway, L. (2017). Ageing and redundancy and the silver lining of entrepreneurship. *International Journal of Entrepreneurship and Innovation*, *18*(2), 105–114. doi:10.1177/1465750317706441

Stone, O. (Director) & Pressman, E. (Producer) (1987). Wall Street. [Motion Picture]

Strober, M. H., & Weinberg, C. B. (1977). Working wives and major family expenditures. *The Journal of Consumer Research*, *4*(3), 141–147. doi:10.1086/208689

Stypińska, J., Franke, A., & Myrczik, J. (2019, April). Senior Entrepreneurship: The Unrevealed Driver for Social Innovation. *Frontiers in Sociology*, *4*, 1–16. doi:10.3389/fsoc.2019.00030 PMID:33869354

Sudol, D., & Hall, A. M. (1991). *Back to school: Warnings and advice to the older graduate student.* https://files.eric.ed.gov/fulltext/ED332217.pdf

Sumarsono, F. S. (2015). Analisis partisipasi kerja penduduk lanjut usia di Indonesia. *Jurnal Ilmiah Mahasiswa FEB*, *4*(1). https://jimfeb.ub.ac.id/index.php/jimfeb/article/view/2435/2217

Sum, N. L., & Jessop, B. S. (2013). Competitiveness, the knowledge-based economy, and higher education. *Journal of the Knowledge Economy*, *4*(1), 24–44. doi:10.100713132-012-0121-8

Sun, S. H., & Chen, J. L. (2007, June). *Knowledge representation and reasoning methodology based on CBR algorithm for modular fixture design. Journal of the Chinese Society of Mechanical Engineers.*

Suomäki, A., Kianto, A., & Vanhala, M. (2019). Work Engagement Across Different Generations in Finland: A Qualitative Study of Boomers, Yers and Xers. *Knowledge and Process Management*, *26*(2), 140–151. doi:10.1002/kpm.1604

Super, D. E. (1984). Career and life development. In D. Brown & L. Brooks (Eds.), *Career Choice Development*. Jossey-Bass.

Tajfel, H., & Turner, J. (1979). An Integrative Theory of Intergroup Conflict. In W. G. Austin & S. Worchel (Eds.), *The Social Psychology of Intergroup Relations. Monterey*. Brooks/Cole Publishing Company.

Taylor, P., Parker, K., Morin, R., Patten, E., & Brown, A. (2014). *Millennials in Adulthood*. Washington, DC: Pew Research Center. http://www. pewsocialtrends. org/2014/03/07/millennials-inadulthood

Taylor, K., & Marienau, C. (1995). Bridging practice and theory for women's adult development. *New Directions for Adult and Continuing Education*, *1995*(65), 5–12. doi:10.1002/ace.36719956503

Taylor, P. (2004). Age and Work: International Perspectives. *Social Policy and Society*, *3*(2), 163–170. doi:10.1017/S1474746403001623

Teichler, U. (1997). Graduate employment: Challenges for higher education in the twenty-first century. *Higher Education in Europe*, *22*(1), 75–84. doi:10.1080/0379772970220109

Teixeira, S. (2011). *Gestão Estratégica* [Strategic Management]. Escolar Publisher.

Thomas, A., & Pickering, G. (2005). X-it: Gen-X and Older Wine Drinker Comparisons in New Zealand. *International Journal of Wine Marketing*, *17*(2).

Thulin, E., Vilhelmson, B., & Johansson, M. (2020). New telework, time pressure, and time use control in everyday life. *Sustainability*, *11*(11), 3067. doi:10.3390u11113067

Tidd, J., & Bessant, J. R. (2018). *Managing Innovation: Integrating Technological, Market and Organizational Change*. John Wiley & Sons.

Time Magazine. (1951). *People: The Younger Generation*. http://content.time.com/time/subscriber/article/0,33009,856950,00.html

Ting, H., Ling, J., & Cheah, J. H. (2020). Editorial: It Will Go Away!? Pandemic crisis and business in asia. *Asian Journal of Business Research*, *10*(1), 1–7. doi:10.14707/ajbr.200072

Tisch, D. (2017). *What gives a nation great reputation?* https://policyoptions.irpp.org/magazines/july-2017/what-gives-a-nation-a-great-reputation/

Topal, K., & Çağlayan Akay, E. (2021). Hanehalkı Tüketim Harcamalarının Mikroekonometrik Analizi: LAD-LASSO Yöntemi. *Ekoist: Journal of Econometrics and Statistics*, (33), 13–31. doi:10.26650/ekoist.2020.33.843564

Topgul, S. (2016). Ageism or Discrimination against Older Adults in Work Life. *Turkish Journal of Sociology*, *36*, 385–391.

Topgul, S. (2020). Changing Foods for Elderly Individuals According to the Changing Demographic Order. *International Social Mentality and Researcher Thinkers Journal*, *6*(32), 991–1005.

Topgul, S. (2021). Elderly Care and Socıal Work From Internatıonal Aspects. *The Journal of International Social Research*, *14*(76), 688–696.

Torraco, R. J. (2005). Writing integrative literature reviews: Guidelines and examples. *Human Resource Development Review*, *4*(3), 356–367.

Tosun, C., & Timothy, D. J. (2001). Shortcomings in planning approaches to tourism development in developing countries: The case of Turkey. *International Journal of Contemporary Hospitality Management*, *13*(7), 352–359. doi:10.1108/09596110110403910

Tranfield, D., Denyer, D., & Smart, P. (2003). Towards a methodology for developing evidence-informed management knowledge by means of systematic review. *British Journal of Management*, *14*(3), 207–222.

Trueman, M., Klemm, M., & Giroud, A. (2004). Can a city communicate? Bradford as a corporate brand. *Corporate Communications*, *9*(4), 317–330. doi:10.1108/13563280410564057

Tubbs, S., & Schulz, E. (2006). Exploring a taxonomy of global leadership competencies and meta-competencies. *The Journal of American Academy of Business, Cambridge*, *8*(2), 29–35.

Tudoran, C. (2020). New Training Trends in High-Risk Technology Fields. *Proceedings of the International Conference on Business Excellence, Sciendo*, *14*(1), 474-489. 10.2478/picbe-2020-0045

Tufan, I. (2014). *Structural Change of Aging in Turkey*. Koc University Publications.

Tufan, I. (2016). *Aging and Aging from Antiquity to the Present*. Nobel Publications.

TUİK. (n.d.). *Household Budget Survey*. Retrieved March 3, 2021, from https://www.tuik.gov.tr/Kurumsal/Mikro_Veri

Tulasi, D., Sigit, R., Pradana, D. W., & Ellitan, L. (2019). The Role of Leadership in Industrial Revolution 4.0. *International Journal of Trend in Research and Development*, *6*(5), 97–100.

Türkay, H. (2004). Doğrusal Regresyon Analizinde M Tahminciler ve Ekonometrik Bir Uygulama. *Doğu Anadolu Bölgesi Araştırmaları*, 106-115.

Türkbal, A. (2005). *Makro İktisat*. Aktif Yayınevi.

Turkish Statistical Institute. (2020). *İstatistiklerle yaşlılar*. https://data.tuik.gov.tr/Bulten/Index?p=Istatistiklerle-Yaslilar-2020-37227

Turkish Statistical Institute. (2020a). Elderly with Statistics, 2019. *Turkish Statistical Institute News Bulletin, 33712*. https://data.tuik.gov.tr/Bulten/Index?p=IstatistiklerleYaslilar201933712#:~:text=T%C3%9C%C4%B0K%20Kurumsal&text=Ya%C5%9Fl%C4%B1%20n%C3%BCfus%20olarak%20kabul%20edilen,9%2C1'e%20y%C3%BCkseldi

Turkish Statistical Institute. (2021). Elderly with Statistics, 2020. *Turkish Statistical Institute News Bulletin, 37227*. https://data.tuik.gov.tr/Bulten/Index?p=Istatistiklerle-Yaslilar-2020-37227

TurkStat. (2020). *House Sale Statistics*. General Directorate of Land Registry and Cadastre.

Turna, G. (2022). How "Dieselgate" Changed Volkswagen: Rushing to Erase the Traces of Greenwashing. In Socially Responsible Consumption and Marketing in Practice. Springer. doi:10.1007/978-981-16-6433-5_16

Turna, G. B. (2013). *The effects of product-country image and tourism destination image on international consumer behavior: Comparative analysis of Turkey, Spain, Germany, Sweden and the Netherlands*. Black Sea Technical University.

Turner, D., Giorno, C., De Serres, A., Vourc'h, A., & Richardson, P. (1998). *The macroeconomic implications of aging in a global context*. OECD Economics Department Working Papers, 193, OECD Publishing. doi:10.1787/18151973

TUROFED-Turkish Hotelier Federation. (2010). *Tourism Report 2*. http://www.turofed.org.tr/PDF/DergiTr/Turofed_Dergi-Turofed50.pdf

TUROFED-Turkish Hotelier Federation. (2019). *Tourism Report*. https://www.turofed.org.tr//panel/upload_system/pages_file/f0d8ac64de76e795a84a98a188b926b1.pdf

Tuscia, U. (2008). *The generational turnover in agriculture : The ageing dynamics and the eu support policies to young farmers Anna Carbone and Giovanna Subioli* [Paper presentation]. 109th EAAE Seminar. https://www.researchgate.net/publication/23509051_The_Generational_Turnover_In_Agriculture_The_Ageing_Dynamics_And_The_Eu_Support_Policies_To_Young_Farmers

Tusianti, E. (2019). Penuaan penduduk dan tantangannya di masa depan dalam sudut pandang ketenagakerjaan. In W. Winardi & E. Tusianti (Eds.), *Analisis isi terkini 2019: penuaan penduduk dan tantangannya di masa depan dalam sudut pandang ketenagakerjaan*. https://www.bps.go.id/publication/2019/12/11/6749d130c7369027fd21df8c/analisis-isu-terkini-2019-.html

Tzanakou, C. (2014). *The value of the PhD in a knowledge-based economy: beyond financial and career gains*. https://era.ideasoneurope.eu/2014/03/11/the-value-of-the-phd-in-a-knowledge-based-economy-beyond-financial-and-career-gains/

Uchôa, E., Firmo, J., & Lima-Costa, M. F. F. (2002). Envelhecimento e Saúde: Experiência e Construção Cultural [Aging and Health: Experience and Cultural Construction]. In M. C. S. Minayo & C. E. A. Coimbra (Eds.), *Antropologia, Saúde e Envelhecimento* [Anthropology, Health and Aging]. Fiocruz Publisher.

Ulukan, U. (2020). Demographic transformation and older workers in Turkey. *Fiscaoeconomia*, *4*(1), 94–110. doi:10.25295/fsecon.2020.01.005

UNESCO. (2021). *Institute of statistics*. http://data.uis.unesco.org/

United Nations Population Fund. (2014). *Indonesia on the Threshold of Population Ageing*. UNFPA Indonesia.

United Nations, Department of Economic and Social Affairs, Population Division. (2019). *World population ageing 2019: Highlights* (ST/ESA/SER.A/430). https://www.un.org/en/development/desa/population/publications/pdf/ageing/WorldPopulationAgeing2019-Report.pdf

United Nations, Department of Economics and Social Affairs. (2017). *World Population Aging 2017 Highlights*. https://www.un.org/en/development/desa/population/publications/pdf/aging/WPA2017_Highlights.pdf

United Nations. (2017). *World Population Prospects*. https://esa.un.org/unpd/wpp/Publications/Files/WPP2017_KeyFindings.pdf

United Nations. (2019). *Ageing*, https://www.un.org/en/sections/issues-depth/ageing/

UNWTO-World Tourism Organization. (2021). *International Tourism Highlights, 2020 Edition*. https://www.e-unwto.org/doi/epdf/10.18111/9789284422456

Vakola, M., Soderquist, K. E., & Prastacos, G. P. (2007). Competency management in support of organisational change. *International Journal of Manpower*, *28*(3/4), 260–275. doi:10.1108/01437720710755245

Valentine, S., Valentine, W. R., & Dick, J. (1998). Intrinsic and extrinsic motivators and older employees' attitudes towards their current jobs. *Perceptual and Motor Skills*, *87*(2), 407–410.

Vallerand, R. J., O'Connor, B. P., & Hamel, M. (1995). Motivation in later life: Theory and assessment. *International Journal of Aging & Human Development*, *41*(3), 221–238.

Van Meteren, R., & Van Someren, M. (2000, May). Using content-based filtering for recommendation. In *Proceedings of the machine learning in the new information age: MLnet/ECML2000 workshop* (Vol. 30, pp. 47-56). Academic Press.

Van Selm, M., & Van den Heijkant, L. (2021). In Search of the Older Worker: Framing Job Requirements in Recruitment Advertisements Work. Aging and Retirement, 1–15. doi:10.1093/worker/waaa026

Vandemaele, S., & Vancauteren, M. (2015). Nonfinancial goals, governance, and dividend payout in private family firms. *Journal of Small Business Management, 53*(1), 166–182.

Vedder, R., Denhart, C., & Robe, J. (2013). *Why are recent college graduates underemployed? University enrollments and labor-market realities.* https://files.eric.ed.gov/fulltext/ED539373.pdf

Vibriyanti, D., Harfina, D., & Widayatun. (2017). Pemetaan kondisi lansia dalam keluarga di era globalisasi. In *Keluarga dan globalisasi di Indonesia: Pemetaan data terkait remaja, ibu dan anak, serta penduduk lanjut usia (lansia).* Pustaka Sinar Harapan.

Vibriyanti, D., Harfina, D., Seftiani, S., & Sitohang, M. Y. (2019). *Lansia sejahtera tanggung jawab siapa?* Obor.

Vranaková, N., Gyurák Babel'ová, Z., & Chlpeková, A. (2021). Sustainable Human Resource Management and Generational Diversity: The Importance of the Age Management Pillars. *Sustainability, 13*(15), 1–18. doi:10.3390u13158496 PMID:34804601

Wadesango, N., & Machingambi, S. (2011). Post graduate students' experiences with research supervisors. *Journal of Sociology and Social Anthropology, 2*(1), 31–37. doi:10.1080/09766634.2011.11885545

Wagner, E. A. (2014). Using a Kinesthetic Learning Strategy to Engage Nursing Student Thinking, Enhance Retention, and Improve Critical Thinking. *The Journal of Nursing Education, 53*(6), 348–351. doi:10.3928/01484834-20140512-02 PMID:24814353

Wahrendorf, M., Akinwale, B., Landy, R., Matthews, K., & Blane, D. (2017). Who in Europe works beyond the state pension age and under which conditions? Results from SHARE. *Journal of Population Ageing, 10*(3), 269–285.

Wainwright, T., Kibler, E., Blackburn, R., & Kautonen, T. (2011). Who are you calling old?: revisiting notions of age and ability amongst older entrepreneurs. *34th Institute for Small Business and Entrepreneurship (ISBE) Annual Conference: Sustainable futures: enterprising landscapes and communities.*

Walker, P. (2007). System transition in Japanese short-term higher education: What future for the Japanese junior college in crisis? *Compare: A Journal of Comparative Education, 37*(2), 239–255. doi:10.1080/03057920601165603

Wang, Z., Shepley, M., & Rodiek, S. (2012). Aging-inplace at home through environmental support of 654physical activity—An interdisciplinary conceptual framework and analysis. *Journal of Housing for the Elderly, 26*(4), 338–354. doi:10.1080/02763893.2011.625289

Ware, J., & Grantham, C. (2010). Managing a remote workforce: proven practices from successful leaders. *The Work Design Collaborative*, 1-27. https://pdfslide.net/reader/f/managing-a-remote-workforce-proven-practices-from-successful-leaders

Warnes, T. (2009). International Retirement Migration. In P. Uhlenberg (Ed.), *International Handbook of Population Aging. International Handbooks of Population* (Vol. 1). Springer. doi:10.1007/978-1-4020-8356-3_15

Warshaw, G., Bragg, E., Thomas, D., Ho, M. L., & Brewer, D. (2006). Are Internal Medicine Residency Programs Adequately Preparing Physicians to Care for the Baby Boomers? A National Survey from the Association of Directors of Geriatric Academic Programs Status of Geriatrics Workforce Study. *Journal of the American Geriatrics Society.* doi:10.1111/j.1532-5415.2006.00895.x

Watkins-Mathys, L. (2012). Age and grey entrepreneurship. In *Lessons on Profiting from Diversity* (pp. 94–113). Palgrave Macmillan.

Watson, I. (1998). *Applying case-based reasoning: techniques for enterprise systems.* Morgan Kaufmann Publishers Inc.

We Work Remotely (WWR). (2021, July 15). *Hybrid Work From Home Work Model: Here's How to Make it Work.* https://weworkremotely.com/hybrid-wfh-work-model-here-s-how-to-make-it-work

Weber, P., & Schaper, M. (2004). Understanding the grey entrepreneur. *Journal of Enterprising Culture*, *12*(2), 147–164.

Webster, J., & Watson, R. T. (2002). Analyzing the past to prepare for the future: Writing a literature review. *Management Information Systems Quarterly*, xiii–xxiii.

WEF. (2020a). *The future of jobs report 2020.* Geneva: World Economic Forum https://www3.weforum.org/docs/WEF_Future_of_Jobs_2020.pdf

WEF. (2020b). *The global competitiveness report 2020.* Geneva: World Economic Forum. https://www.weforum.org/reports/the-global-competitiveness-report-2020

WEF. (2021). *Davos Lab: Youth Recovery Plan.* Geneva: World Economic Forum https://www3.weforum.org/docs/WEF_Davos_Lab_Youth_Recovery_Plan_2021.pdf

Weinberg, C. B., & Winer, R. S. (1983). Working wives and major family expenditures: Replication and extension. *The Journal of Consumer Research*, *10*(2), 259–263. doi:10.1086/208965

West, J. (2000). Higher education and employment: Opportunities and limitations in the formation of skills in a mass higher education system. *Journal of Vocational Education and Training*, *52*(4), 573–588. doi:10.1080/13636820000200148

Whitney Gibson, J., Greenwood, R., and Murphy, E., Jr. (2009). Generational Differences in The Workplace: Personal Values, Behaviours, And Popular Beliefs. *Journal of Diversity Management, 4*(3).

WHO. (2021). *WHO coronavirus (Covid-19) dashboard.* https://covid19.who.int/

Wiedmer, T. (2015). Generations do Differ: Best Practices in Leading Traditionalists, Boomers, and Generations X, Y, and Z. *Delta Kappa Gamma Bulletin*, *82*(1), 51–58.

Wiklund, J., & Shepherd, D. (2003). Knowledge-based resources, entrepreneurial orientation, and the performance of small and medium-sized businesses. *Strategic Management Journal*, *24*(13), 1307–1314. https://doi.org/10.1002/smj.360

Williams, A. M., King, R., Warnes, A., & Patterson, G. (2000). Tourism and international retirement migration: New forms of an old relationship in southern Europe. *Tourism Geographies*, *2*(1), 28–49. doi:10.1080/146166800363439

Williams, A. M., King, R., & Warnes, T. (1997). A place in the sun: International retirement migration from Northern to Southern Europe. *European Urban and Regional Studies*, *4*(2), 115–134. doi:10.1177/096977649700400202 PMID:12292969

Wilton, D. (2009). *G.I.* Wordorigins.org

Wirakartakusumah, M.D., & Evi, H.A. (1994). *Aging in Indonesia: Demographic Characteristic.* Departement of Geography University of Adelaide.

Wiratri, A. (2017). Relasi petani, negara, dan swasta di Indonesia. In V. Ningrum & A. Wiratri (Eds.), *Pemuda & pertanian berkelanjutan: Dependensi, strategi, dan otonomi petani.* Pustaka Sinar Harapan.

Wolf, G., London, M., Casey, J., & Pufahl, J. (1995). Career experience and motivation as predictors of training behaviors and outcomes for displaced engineers. *Journal of Vocational Behavior*, *47*(3), 316–331.

Woltereck, H. (1959). *Vida Nova Para os Velhos* [New Life for Old People]. IBRASA – Instituição Brasileira de Difusão Cultural S. A.

World Economic Forum. (2011). *Global Risks 2011* (6th ed.). https://www3.weforum.org/docs/WEF_GlobalRisks_Report_2011.pdf

World Economic Forum. (2013). *The Global Competitiveness Report 2012-2013.* https://www3.weforum.org/docs/WEF_GlobalCompetitivenessReport_2012-13.pdf

World Health Organization. (2002). *Active Aging: A Policy Framework.* World Health Organization.

World Health Organization. (2005). *Envelhecimento Ativo: Um Projeto de Política de Saúde* [Active Aging: A Health Policy Project]. World Health Organization.

Wu, C. C. (2011). High graduate unemployment rate and Taiwanese undergraduate education. *International Journal of Educational Development*, *31*(3), 303–310. doi:10.1016/j.ijedudev.2010.06.010

Xiao, F., Barnard-Brak, L., Lan, W., & Burley, H. (2019). Examining problem solving skills in technology-rich environments as related to numeracy and literacy. *International Journal of Lifelong Education*, *38*(3), 327–338. doi:10.1080/02601370.2019.1598507

Yakar, M., & Sudas, I. (2019). The New Geographies of Foreign Population in Turkey. *Aegean Geographical Journal*, *28*(2), 129–164.

Yamashita, K. (2008). *The Perilous Decline of Japanese Agriculture.* The Tokyo Foundation. http://www.tokyofoundation.org/en/articles/2008/the-perilous-decline-of-japanese-agriculture-1

Yang, S. U., Shin, H., Lee, J. H., & Wrigley, B. (2008). Country reputation in multidimensions: Predictors, efects, and communication channels. *Journal of Public Relations Research*, *20*(4), 421–440. doi:10.1080/10627260802153579

Yemisrach, F. (2015). *Experience of eight deported women Ethiopians who returned from Kingdom of Saudi Arabia* (Unpublished Master's thesis). Addis Ababa University. Retrieved from http://hdl. handle. net/123456789/8056

Yen, S. T. (1993). Working wives and food away from home: The Box-Cox double hurdle model. *American Journal of Agricultural Economics*, *75*(4), 884–895. doi:10.2307/1243976

Yıldırım, A., & Şimşek, H. (2018). *Qualitative research methods in the social sciences*. Seçkin Yayıncılık.

Yin, R. (2009). *Case study research: Design and methods* (4th ed.). Sage Publication, Inc.

Yukl, G. (1989). Managerial Leadership : A Review of Theory and Research. *Journal of Management*, *15*(2), 251–289. doi:10.1177/014920638901500207

Yukl, G., Gordon, A., & Taber, T. (2002). A Taxonomy of Leadership Behavior: Integrating a Half Century of Behavior Research. *Journal of Leadership & Organizational Studies*, *9*(1), 15–32. doi:10.1177/107179190200900102

Yuksel, F. (2002), *Inter-Organisational Relations and Central-Local Interactions in Tourism Planning in Belek, Turkey* (Doctoral Thesis). Sheffield University.

Yuksel, A. (2001). Managing customer satisfaction and retention: A case of tourist destinations, Turkey. *Journal of Vacation Marketing*, *7*(2), 153–168. doi:10.1177/135676670100700205

Yvoire, A. (2010). *Les Systèmes de Retraite en Europe* [Retirement Systems in Europe]. https://www.futuribles.com/fr/revue/365/les-systemes-de-retraite-en-europe/

Zandi, S., Nemati, B., Jahanianfard, D., Davarazar, M., Sheikhnejad, Y., Mostafaie, A., Kamali, M., & Aminabhavi, T. M. (2019). Industrial Biowastes Treatment Using Membrane Bioreactors (MBRs) - A Scientometric Study. *Journal of Environmental Management*, *247*, 462–473. doi:10.1016/j.jenvman.2019.06.066 PMID:31254761

Zeegen, E. N., Yates, A. J., & Jevsevar, D. S. (2020). COVID-19 pandemic: Returning to normalcy or returning to a new normal. *The Journal of Arthroplasty*, *35*(7), 537–541. doi:10.1016/j.arth.2020.04.040 PMID:32376171

Zemke, R., Raines, C., & Filipczak, B. (2013). *Generations at work: Managing the clash of Boomers, Gen Xers, and Gen Years in the workplace.* AMACOM Div. American Mgmt. Assn.

Zhao, H., O'Connor, G., Wu, J., & Lumpkin, G. T. (2021). Age and entrepreneurial career success: A review and a meta-analysis. *Journal of Business Venturing*, *36*(1), 106007. https://doi.org/10.1016/j.jbusvent.2020.106007

Zwick, T. (2012). Training effectiveness - Differences between younger and older employees. In Working and ageing - The benefits of investing in an ageing workforce (pp. 36–55). Academic Press.

About the Contributors

Fatma İnce received her Ph.D. degree in Management and Organization. Currently, she is an Associate Professor of Organization at Mersin University in Turkey, where she teaches Organizational Behavior, Entrepreneurship, Creative Thinking, Leadership, and Teamwork at undergraduate and graduate levels. Her research interests consist of entrepreneurship, leadership, creativity, synergy, generations, and learning organizations. And besides, she serves as Assistant Director at the University Career Center to provide strategic oversight and management for the students' careers as they enhance their skills.

* * *

Shikha Aggarwal is Assistant Professor with the Management Department of Institute of Technology and Science. She has been in academic teaching and research for more than 6 years. She is pursuing Ph.D. in the area of knowledge management. She has diverse experience of teaching export import documentation, international business, business research methods. She has published papers in national and international journals of repute.

Vanessa Amorim is a Business and Economics Ph.D. student at the University of Aveiro - Portugal. She has a master's in Organizational Management - Specialization: Business Management and a Post-Graduation in Management Tools for Business Competitiveness from Institute Polytechnic of Porto - Portugal. Her main research interests are Innovation, Entrepreneurship, Marketing, and Business Management.

Oscar Bernardes has a PhD in Management from the University of Beira Interior, Portugal (UBI) since 2013, currently he is Assistant Professor at the ISCAP IPP, and ISEP IPP and University of Aveiro. He started lecture, since 2008, on various subjects linked to management, such as Innovation and Technology, Entrepreneurship, Marketing, Strategy and Competitiveness. Previous work experience includes collaborations with several companies, since 2003, having performed the following roles: CEO, consultant, and leadership trainer. His main research interests are Innovation and Technology, Entrepreneurship, Marketing and Strategy.

Gülçin Bilgin Turna studied Business Administration at Yeditepe University in Istanbul. She earned the scholarship from "Scientific and Technological Research Council of Turkey" and received a PhD in Business Administration from Black Sea Technical University after getting an MBA from Yeditepe University. She took some courses from Halmstad University in Sweden as a part of her PhD education.

She served as a visiting researcher for one semester at Rotterdam School of Management, Erasmus University in the Netherlands where she worked with Professor Frank Go. Her studies are mainly in the area of Marketing: sustainable marketing, consumer behavior, measurement and improvement of an image. She works as an assistant professor at Recep Tayyip Erdogan University in Rize/Turkey.

Kübranur Çebi Karaaslan got her bachelor's, master's and doctorate degrees in the department of econometrics. In 2017, she started to work as a Research Assistant at Erzurum Technical University, Department of Econometrics. She was appointed as an assistant professor in the Department of Econometrics. Her main research interests are categorical data analysis, discrete choice model, count data model, microeconometrics, happiness economics, household expenditures, consumer behavior, energy, public health and saving.

Nihan Demirkasımoğlu has earned her Master and doctoral degrees in the Educational Administration at Ankara University. She is working for Hacettepe University at the Department of Educational Sciences. Her research interests include ethics in education, qualitative research, organizational behavior, academic writing and issues in higher education. She teaches qualitative research, academic writing, organization theories, introduction to management and academic writing styles at graduate level. She has published numerous national and international articles in the field of educational administration and co-authored several books and book translations.

Özge Erdemli is a research assistant at the department of Educational Administration, Ankara University at the Department of Educational Sciences. She has earned her Master and doctoral degrees in the Educational Administration at Ankara University. Her research interests include ethics in education, qualitative research, organizational behavior, educational administration, teacher professional development. She has published numerous national and international articles in the field of educational administration.

Dilek Esen was born in 1982 in Izmir, Turkey. She completed her university education at Gazi University Faculty of Commerce and Tourism Education between 2000-2004. She get master's degree from Gazi University Institute of Educational Sciences in the Department of Office Management Education, and Kocaeli University, Institute of Social Sciences in the Department of Business Administration. She completed the Dokuz Eylul University Business Administration Doctorate program in 2018 and get a doctorate degree. She worked at Kocaeli University, Izmir Dokuz Eylul University and Izmir Democracy Universities . She has been working atDokuz Eylul University in Izmir Vocational School since 2013. She teaches Organizational Behavior, Strategic Human Resources Management, Business Management courses. She works in the field of Management and Organization and conducts academic studies on sustainable human resources management, career management, sustainability.

Paula Figueiredo has a degree in Economics with a specialization in Human Resources Economics, a Master in Human Resources Management and a PhD in Management. She is currently a Professor and Researcher at Universidade Lusófona, and she has also been the Director of an institution since 2019. Paula has 20 years of experience in the business area with functions of direction, coordination, and consultancy. Throughout her professional experience, she has collaborated on leadership development projects. At the research level, she has developed research on Human Resource Development, more specifically Leadership Development in organizations, with some publications in scientific journals and conferences.

Aslı Günay currently works as an Assistant Professor of Economics at the Social Sciences University of Ankara, Ankara, Turkey. She received her Ph.D. from Suleyman Demirel University, Isparta, Turkey. Her research interests are public economics, applied macroeconomics, education economics, and higher education. She's also served as an academic consultant for the Turkish Council of Higher Education in Ankara, Turkey. Her work has been published in some national and international scientific journals including Applied Economics, Open Economies Review, and Turkish Journal of Medical Sciences.

Tuğba Güner Demir is a research assistant at the Faculty of Educational Sciences, Department of Educational Administration at Ankara University, Ankara-Turkey. She has earned her doctoral degrees in Educational Administration at Ankara University. She is teaching Educational Administration, Turkish Education System and School Management, Ethics in Education in undergraduate levels. Her research interests include educational administration, teacher professional development, higher education.

Inayah Hidayati is a researcher in social demography at the Research Center for Population, National Research and Innovation Agency – BRIN since 2010. She has educational background in Human Geography from Universitas Gadjah Mada and Universitas Indonesia. Her research focuses on demography, population mobility and human geography studies. She started her career as an academic and has more than 20 peer-reviewed journal articles, book, proceeding paper and technical reports to her credit. Her latest publication is available in internationally rated impact journals with title 'Move backward to make a step forward": Understanding the migration of the highly educated to Sorong City, West Papua, Indonesia (Asian and Pacific Migration Journal, 2021)'. Her Research ID is https://orcid.org/0000-0002-6646-6212.

Luh Kitty Katherina has been working as a researcher at the LIPI Population Research Center since 2014 with the main focus of study in the field of urbanization and environmental change. In the last few years, he has begun to pursue the field of family resilience studies. She completed her bachelor's and master's degree in Planology Engineering at the Bandung Institute of Technology in 2005 and 2011. Several of his writings related to his field have been published in national and international books and scientific proceedings as well as in accredited national journals.

Emre Kol has PhD in Labour Economics and Industrial Relations at the Anadolu University (2014). He is studied Labour Economics and Industrial Relations as an undergraduate (2004) at Kocaeli University and earned a M.Sc. at Anadolu University (2009). He started to work a Research Assistant at Anadolu University in 2005. At the end of PhD studies, he was appointed as an Assistant Professor in the same program in 2015. Recently he works as Assistant Professor at the Department of Labour Economics and Industrial Relations in Anadolu University. He has 9 book chapters, sevearal published articles and 10 international conference papers. He has published widely in the areas of health policies and welfare systems. Kol's research and teaching focus on health policies, welfare systems and social policies, long-term care services, health policies in relation to the changing welfare regime, social work studies and social work practices in health care institutions.

Kishore Kumar Krishnan is a Doctorate in Mathematics with a specialization in Fuzzy Graph theory from Bharathiar University, Coimbatore, India. He completed his M.Sc., Mathematics from the University of Madras, India, M. Phil Mathematics from Alagappa University, India and M.E., in Systems Engineering and Operations Research from Anna University, Chennai, India. He has 15+ years of Academic Teaching & Research experience across recognized Indian and Oman Universities. He has over 20 publications in SCIE, SCOPUS indexed and other peer-reviewed journals; ISBN Book & Chapters and IEEE Conference proceedings. He has also been a Reviewer in various SCIE, Scopus and peer-reviewed Journals and Conferences. He has significant research contributions in Vague graphs, Vague networks, and Neuromorphic graph theory. He is a member of professional bodies like MTA, ISPS. His research areas include Data analysis, Data mining, Fuzzy graphs, Neutrosophic graphs and Vague graphs.

Maria Lamas is a professor at the School of Health | IPP (ESS IPP), in the technical and scientific area of Clinical Analysis and Public Health. Member of the Center for Research in Health and Environment (CISA), ESS IPP, and collaborator of the Research Center in Technologies and Health Services (CINTESIS) - University of Porto (UP), Portugal, in the line of research on aging. She is author and co-author of several scientific papers. Graduated in Clinical Analysis and Public Health, Master in Hydrobiology from the Faculty of Sciences, UP, and is a doctoral student in Gerontology at the Institute of Biomedical Sciences Abel Salazar (ICBAS), UP, Portugal.

Bruno Lopes is a Business and Economics Ph.D. student at the University of Aveiro - Portugal. He has a master's in Human Resource Management and Development and a bachelor degree in Human Resources from Institute Polytechnic of Porto - Portugal. His main research interests are: Human Resources, Ageing, Career Management and Business Management.

Nilamadhab Mishra is a Doctorate in Computer Science & Information Engineering with a specialization in Data Science & Machine Learning from Chang Gung University (CGU), Taiwan. He completed his MCA from Utkal University, India, and M.Tech in Computer Science & Engineering from Biju Patnaik University of Technology, India. He has 18+ years of Academic Teaching & Research experience across recognized Indian, Taiwan, and African Universities. He has over 30 publications in SCI/SCIE & SCOPUS indexed and other peer-reviewed journals; ISBN Book & Chapters; Indian and Australian Patents; and IEEE Conference proceedings. He has also been a Reviewer, Associate Editor, and Editorial Board Member in various peer-reviewed Journals and Conferences. He has significant research contributions in IoT Network-Centric Data Science & Analytics Blend in with Cognitive Apps Policy & Explorations. He is a Senior member of professional bodies like CSI, ORCID, IAENG, ISROSET, ISRD, ASR, IEDRC, and IEEE Collaborate. His research areas include Network Centric Data Analytics, Data Science & Machine Learning: Analytics and Applications, IoT Big-Data Applications, and Cognitive Apps Policy Assessments.

Vanda Ningrum is a Researcher with 12 years of experience in a government institution. She holds a Master's Degree in Management and Social welfare. Her specialist in demographic and social welfare studies. Expertise in field research, data collection/analysis, and project management. She has extensive experience working with cross-functional scientific and research teams in foreign countries. She has a track record of delivering some new concepts for academic and policy government during her work. Her latest publications cover Community Resilience, Rural Development, Farmer's Sovereignty, Youth and Agriculture, and Human Ecology.

Rafael Pérez-Uribe is a Doctor of Business Sciences, U. Nebrija. Diploma of Advanced Studies in applied economics, U. Nebrija. Master's Degree in Organizational Management, EAN University.

Maître es Sciences, University of Quebec to Chicoutimi. Specialist in Evaluation and Construction of Management Indicators for Higher Education, School of Business Administration. Postgraduate Studies as Kenkyusei (Associate Researcher) in Total Quality Control and Quality Circles, Fukushima University, Japan. Business Administrator, Universidad Jorge Tadeo Lozano. Professor and senior researsher attached to the Human Resources Master in Santo Thomas University.

Intan Adhi Perdana Putri holds master's degree in Tropical Marine Resource Economics from the Department of Resources and Environmental Economics, Bogor Agricultural University. Meanwhile, her bachelor's degree in Aquatic Water Resource Management was obtained from Padjajaran University, Indonesia. Working as researcher at Research Centre for Population, The National Research and Innovation Agency, Intan has wide experience in conducting research on population, human and environment, coastal areas, and Sustainable natural resources management. Further, she has accumulated the knowledge and skills by attending some international prestigious courses. She has published her works in various journals and conference proceedings in Indonesia and abroad.

Maria Ramirez is a Ph.D. in Management at Universidad EAN.2015. Ph.D. in Entrepreneurial Sciences at Universidad Nebrija- España. Master in Business Management at Universidad de Quebec. Consultant in Collaborative Open Innovation topics, expert in design, management, implementing, monitoring and assessment of innovation projects to optimize resources and processes in organizations. Researcher of group G3Pymes in topics such as: [1] Innovation Management, developing business modernization plans; [2] University – business – government the triple helix model, designing programs to strenghten regional innovation ecosystems.[3] Education, matching the Millenials profile with Innovation in Education and Online learning. On-campus and off-campus University professor teaching entrepreneurship, management and innovation. Leader of the EAN-BIZLAB Program, aimed at developing Intrapreneurship Challenges as Collaborative Open Innovation.

Sari Seftiani has been a researcher at Research Center for Population – National Research and Innovation Agency (PR Kependudukan-BRIN) since 2010. She studied in Sociology, Faculty of Social Political Science, Gadjah Mada University for her bachelor in 2008. In 2016, she received a scholarship from StuNed to obtain her Master of Sciences in Population Studies at the University of Groningen, the Netherland. Her research has focused on population issues such as family, older people and health issues. Her thesis about the health of older people in Indonesia based on access to health care. In BRIN, she involved in various research about family and older people, family resilience and health security. Her current research is about the COVID-19 pandemic from a social demographic perspective.

Vidhi Tyagi is currently working with Amity University, Noida. She has been into academics from past 15 years and has teaching experience for Graduate and Undergraduate students. She has done PhD in Human Resource from Jiwaji University, Madhya Pradesh and qualified NET in HR, Labour Laws and Industrial Relations. Her specialization area is Human Resource Management, Organization Behavior and Industrial Relations. Along with it, she has keen interest in the research and her area of research is employee engagement and Talent Management. She has guided many BBA and MBA students for completing their projects. She has presented many research papers in National and International Conferences at IIM and IIT level and has various publications in the Journals of repute. She has also conducted Faculty Development Programs and Webinars at National level.

Deshinta Vibriyanti is a researcher at the Research Center for Population – National Research and Innovation Agency (PR Kependudukan-BRIN) since 2006. She completed her undergraduate education at the Faculty of Psychology at Gadjah Mada University (2003) and a master's degree in the Postgraduate Study Program of Population and Employment at the University of Indonesia (2012). She used to be heavily involved in research on employment and education issues. In 2015, she received a Research Grant from the Sumitomo Foundation to conduct a study in Japan entitled Japanese Government Policy for the Elderly Population and Its Implementation: Lessons Learned for Indonesia. However, since 2015 until now, she has focused on studies on family and health, especially at aging issues, and family resilience.

Baye Yemataw is a professor in Information Systems, Debre Berhan University at Ethiopia, Africa. He has completed a master's in science with a specialization in information systems and sciences from the same university. He has 5 years of experience in teaching and research in DBU as a professor and researcher. His area of research includes machine learning, data mining, and recommender system design.

Index

A

active aging 1-2, 5-7, 21-23, 195, 197
Adult Education 230, 232, 250-251
age dependency ratio 43, 52, 66
age management 1-2, 8-9, 12, 21-22, 57-58, 61
aging workers 49-50, 133
aging workforce 8, 11-12, 18-19, 22, 32, 34, 44-46, 48, 57-59, 66, 115, 137, 178, 231, 286
Artificial Intelligence 84, 113, 121, 170, 255, 281, 297

B

Baby Boomer Generation 116, 209, 212, 226, 281, 290
Baby Boomers 201-202, 204-206, 209-212, 220-226, 228, 252, 266, 272, 275-276, 278, 280, 282-284, 292, 294, 296

C

Case Base System 113
CMS 274, 287-288, 297
competence management 115-116, 118-119, 140
Conceptual Knowledge Modelling 101, 113
consumption 27, 68-71, 80-81, 83, 208, 271, 276
Corporatist Welfare Regime 199
Country Image 272
COVID-19 49, 51, 55, 63, 71, 81, 115, 135-136, 144-147, 154-156, 158-163, 165-166, 168, 170-178, 192, 194-197, 199, 254-255, 263, 266, 269, 272, 294-295
Covid-19 pandemic 51, 55, 71, 115, 135-136, 144-147, 154-155, 158-163, 165-166, 171-172, 177-178, 192, 194-196, 263, 266, 269, 294-295
Critical Theory 274-275, 288, 292-293
cross-border living 252-253, 267
cross-sectional data 83

D

Data Elicitations 113
Data Mining 95, 112-113
demographic aging 1-2, 7, 182, 195, 254
demographic transition 26, 178, 181-184, 186, 189, 194
demographic window of opportunity 189, 199
dependent variable 69, 71-72, 80, 83
Destination Management Organizations (DMO) 272
Destination Marketing 252, 272
digital skills 144, 146, 150-151, 153-155, 158-159, 224
doctorants 230, 240-241, 247-248, 251

E

elder ages 178, 187
elderly workforce 178, 180-181, 185, 187, 190, 192-196, 199
Expats 262, 272

G

GEM Report 57, 67
Gen X 202, 206-207, 209, 274, 278, 281, 283-284, 290, 292
Gen Y 207-208, 274, 279, 281, 285, 290, 292
Gen Z 274, 279, 281, 283-284, 290, 292, 296
gender 6, 12-13, 16, 18, 25, 28, 31, 36, 40, 43, 68, 70-72, 78-79, 82, 85, 94, 96-97, 102-103, 106, 176, 191, 199, 209, 213-214, 226-228, 234, 274, 277-278, 285-286, 292
GFC 279, 297
government schemes 42, 47
graduate education 230-234, 236-237, 242, 247, 249-251
gray entrepreneurship 47, 62

H

Healthy Life Expectancy 6, 23
heteroscedasticity 77, 83
higher education 10, 93, 144-149, 151-159, 175, 222, 231-232, 234, 248-249, 266-267, 293
Household Budget Survey 68-69, 71, 82
household expenditure 68-69, 74, 78-80, 82-83
HPO 284, 297
HPWP 297
HRM 1, 8, 57, 67, 116, 139, 207, 274-275, 277, 279, 281-282, 287-288, 290-293, 297
human migration 84-88, 92, 111
Human Resource Management 12, 16-17, 22, 59, 67, 115, 118, 134-136, 139-140, 161, 170, 176, 202, 275, 293-294
hybrid working 160, 164-165, 169, 173-174, 177

I

independent variable 75, 83
informal sector 24-25, 33-36, 38
International Organization for Migration 84
International Retired Settlers (IRS) 265, 272
International Retirement Migration (IRM) 252-253, 272

K

KBRF 84, 88, 90-91, 94, 96, 99, 101, 103-104, 108-110, 113
knowledge base 51, 90, 93, 100, 108, 113
knowledge workers 252-254, 259, 262, 264, 266-268, 272

L

labor market 7, 13, 18-19, 25, 28, 31-33, 36, 38, 48-49, 60, 88, 133, 144-150, 153-157, 159, 180, 182, 185-186, 190, 192-193, 195
Leader Competence 115, 120, 130, 132-133, 140
leadership effectiveness 115, 134
Least Absolute Deviation Regression 68, 83
lifespan 23, 51, 190, 193, 195

M

Managing Remote Workforce 160
MBO 285, 297
microeconometric 81
Mid-Life Adults 230, 251
Millennials 202, 206-209, 223-225, 274, 276-277, 279, 283-284, 292, 294, 296-297
motivation 9, 13, 38, 42, 46-51, 56, 60-64, 66, 69, 117, 119, 131, 134, 161-162, 168, 171-174, 230, 236, 243, 245, 248, 274, 277, 280, 283-284, 290-292, 294

N

Normal Distribution Assumption 77, 83
Northern Europe 252, 262, 268, 272

O

OCR 282, 297
OECD 7, 21, 40, 50, 59, 64, 67, 85, 144-146, 148-149, 151-155, 157, 181, 231-232, 250, 254, 257, 271
old age 2, 20-21, 25-26, 29, 34-36, 38, 50, 181, 184, 187-188, 190, 193, 196-197, 199, 270
older entrepreneurship 42, 44, 47, 64
Older Graduates 230, 233, 251
older people 2, 5, 24-40, 49, 56, 58-60, 81, 179, 252-253, 255-256
Older Students 230, 232, 247, 251
Ordinary Least Squares Method 75, 83
organizational 7-8, 18, 44, 50-51, 56-57, 59, 61, 63-65, 115-119, 134, 136-139, 165, 167-168, 170-173, 176-177, 201, 206, 223, 246, 265, 270, 274-277, 279-280, 282-287, 291-297

P

pandemic 43, 45, 51-52, 55, 57-58, 71, 115-116, 135-136, 144-151, 153-155, 158-166, 169-174, 176-178, 192, 194-196, 219, 243, 248, 263, 266, 269, 272, 281, 294-295
PhD Programme 230, 251
PIACC 144, 151, 159
population aging 2, 4, 19, 23, 25, 27, 30, 51, 253, 256, 268, 271
Problem Solving in Technology-Rich Environments 151, 157, 159

Q

quality of life 1, 5-6, 19, 23, 31, 34, 36, 45, 62, 192, 262, 264, 266

R

recommender system 88-89, 93-94, 110, 113

remote workforce 160, 175, 177
remote working 57, 160-163, 165-176, 195
Retired Settlers 252, 265, 272
retirement 7-8, 11-13, 16-17, 20, 23, 25, 27, 35-36, 40, 48, 51-52, 56-57, 59, 62, 64-65, 81, 118, 178-181, 183-199, 213, 217, 226, 252-257, 260, 264, 267-268, 270-272, 288-290
Rokeach Value Survey (RVS) 227
rule-based 84, 90, 93, 104, 113

S

SAVE Tourism 252, 272
Scientometrics 1, 9, 20-21
self- employment 42, 45, 47-49, 51, 57-59
social insurance 178-179, 183, 186, 188-190, 192-193, 195, 198
Social Insurances 199
social security 6-7, 13, 19, 25-28, 34-35, 38, 64, 148, 156, 178-186, 188-190, 192-199
SST 46, 67
Survey data 34, 68-70
sustainable tourism management 265
Sustainable Tourism Marketing (STM) 272

T

Theory of planned behavior 46, 59, 67
TNA 291, 297

U

unemployment 43, 48, 51, 61, 92, 145-149, 154-155, 158-159, 181, 191-193, 195, 204, 232

W

web-scraping 1, 9-10, 23
Welfare State 45, 184, 186, 197-199
workforce 1-2, 7-8, 11-12, 18-19, 22-23, 30, 32, 34, 37, 43-46, 48-49, 52, 56-60, 62, 66, 115, 118, 136-137, 139, 146-147, 150, 160-161, 165, 168-169, 172, 174-182, 184-185, 187, 190, 192-197, 199, 207, 224, 226, 231, 253, 269, 272, 274, 277, 280, 284, 286-287, 289, 294

Recommended Reference Books

IGI Global's reference books are available in three unique pricing formats:
Print Only, E-Book Only, or Print + E-Book.

Shipping fees may apply.

www.igi-global.com

ISBN: 978-1-7998-1048-3
EISBN: 978-1-7998-1049-0
© 2020; 605 pp.
List Price: US$ **285**

ISBN: 978-1-5225-8933-4
EISBN: 978-1-5225-8934-1
© 2020; 667 pp.
List Price: US$ **295**

ISBN: 978-1-7998-0357-7
EISBN: 978-1-7998-0359-1
© 2020; 451 pp.
List Price: US$ **235**

ISBN: 978-1-7998-0070-5
EISBN: 978-1-7998-0071-2
© 2020; 144 pp.
List Price: US$ **175**

ISBN: 978-1-5225-6980-0
EISBN: 978-1-5225-6981-7
© 2019; 339 pp.
List Price: US$ **235**

ISBN: 978-1-5225-5390-8
EISBN: 978-1-5225-5391-5
© 2018; 125 pp.
List Price: US$ **165**

Do you want to stay current on the latest research trends, product announcements, news, and special offers?
Join IGI Global's mailing list to receive customized recommendations, exclusive discounts, and more.
Sign up at: **www.igi-global.com/newsletters.**

Publisher of Peer-Reviewed, Timely, and Innovative Academic Research

IGI Global
PUBLISHER of TIMELY KNOWLEDGE

www.igi-global.com Sign up at www.igi-global.com/newsletters facebook.com/igiglobal twitter.com/igiglobal linkedin.com/igiglobal

Ensure Quality Research is Introduced to the Academic Community

Become an Evaluator for IGI Global Authored Book Projects

The overall success of an authored book project is dependent on quality and timely manuscript evaluations.

Applications and Inquiries may be sent to:
development@igi-global.com

Applicants must have a doctorate (or equivalent degree) as well as publishing, research, and reviewing experience. Authored Book Evaluators are appointed for one-year terms and are expected to complete at least three evaluations per term. Upon successful completion of this term, evaluators can be considered for an additional term.

If you have a colleague that may be interested in this opportunity, we encourage you to share this information with them.

IGI Global Author Services

Providing a high-quality, affordable, and expeditious service, IGI Global's Author Services enable authors to streamline their publishing process, increase chance of acceptance, and adhere to IGI Global's publication standards.

Benefits of Author Services:

- **Professional Service:** All our editors, designers, and translators are experts in their field with years of experience and professional certifications.
- **Quality Guarantee & Certificate:** Each order is returned with a quality guarantee and certificate of professional completion.
- **Timeliness:** All editorial orders have a guaranteed return timeframe of 3-5 business days and translation orders are guaranteed in 7-10 business days.
- **Affordable Pricing:** IGI Global Author Services are competitively priced compared to other industry service providers.
- **APC Reimbursement:** IGI Global authors publishing Open Access (OA) will be able to deduct the cost of editing and other IGI Global author services from their OA APC publishing fee.

Author Services Offered:

English Language Copy Editing
Professional, native English language copy editors improve your manuscript's grammar, spelling, punctuation, terminology, semantics, consistency, flow, formatting, and more.

Scientific & Scholarly Editing
A Ph.D. level review for qualities such as originality and significance, interest to researchers, level of methodology and analysis, coverage of literature, organization, quality of writing, and strengths and weaknesses.

Figure, Table, Chart & Equation Conversions
Work with IGI Global's graphic designers before submission to enhance and design all figures and charts to IGI Global's specific standards for clarity.

Translation
Providing 70 language options, including Simplified and Traditional Chinese, Spanish, Arabic, German, French, and more.

Hear What the Experts Are Saying About IGI Global's Author Services

"Publishing with IGI Global has been ***an amazing experience*** *for me for sharing my research. The* ***strong academic production*** *support ensures quality and timely completion."* – **Prof. Margaret Niess, Oregon State University, USA**

"The service was ***very fast, very thorough, and very helpful*** *in ensuring our chapter meets the criteria and requirements of the book's editors. I was* ***quite impressed and happy*** *with your service."* – **Prof. Tom Brinthaupt, Middle Tennessee State University, USA**

Learn More or Get Started Here:

For Questions, Contact IGI Global's Customer Service Team at cust@igi-global.com or 717-533-8845

IGI Global
PUBLISHER of TIMELY KNOWLEDGE
www.igi-global.com

IGI Global
PUBLISHER of TIMELY KNOWLEDGE
www.igi-global.com

Celebrating Over 30 Years of Scholarly Knowledge Creation & Dissemination

InfoSci®-Books

A Database of Nearly 6,000 Reference Books Containing Over 105,000+ Chapters Focusing on Emerging Research

InfoSci®-Books Database

The **InfoSci®-Books** is a database of nearly 6,000 IGI Global single and multi-volume reference books, handbooks of research, and encyclopedias, encompassing groundbreaking research from prominent experts worldwide that spans over 350+ topics in 11 core subject areas including business, computer science, education, science and engineering, social sciences, and more.

Open Access Fee Waiver (Read & Publish) Initiative

For any library that invests in IGI Global's InfoSci-Books and/or InfoSci-Journals (175+ scholarly journals) databases, IGI Global will match the library's investment with a fund of equal value to go toward **subsidizing the OA article processing charges (APCs) for their students, faculty, and staff** at that institution when their work is submitted and accepted under OA into an IGI Global journal.*

INFOSCI® PLATFORM FEATURES

- Unlimited Simultaneous Access
- No DRM
- No Set-Up or Maintenance Fees
- A Guarantee of No More Than a 5% Annual Increase for Subscriptions
- Full-Text HTML and PDF Viewing Options
- Downloadable MARC Records
- COUNTER 5 Compliant Reports
- Formatted Citations With Ability to Export to RefWorks and EasyBib
- No Embargo of Content (Research is Available Months in Advance of the Print Release)

**The fund will be offered on an annual basis and expire at the end of the subscription period. The fund would renew as the subscription is renewed for each year thereafter. The open access fees will be waived after the student, faculty, or staff's paper has been vetted and accepted into an IGI Global journal and the fund can only be used toward publishing OA in an IGI Global journal. Libraries in developing countries will have the match on their investment doubled.*

To Recommend or Request a Free Trial:
www.igi-global.com/infosci-books

eresources@igi-global.com • Toll Free: 1-866-342-6657 ext. 100 • Phone: 717-533-8845 x100

IGI Global
PUBLISHER of TIMELY KNOWLEDGE
www.igi-global.com

IGI Global
PUBLISHER of TIMELY KNOWLEDGE
www.igi-global.com

Publisher of Peer-Reviewed, Timely, and Innovative Academic Research Since 1988

IGI Global's Transformative Open Access (OA) Model: **How to Turn Your University Library's Database Acquisitions Into a Source of OA Funding**

Well in advance of Plan S, IGI Global unveiled their OA Fee Waiver (Read & Publish) Initiative. Under this initiative, librarians who invest in IGI Global's InfoSci-Books and/or InfoSci-Journals databases will be able to subsidize their patrons' OA article processing charges (APCs) when their work is submitted and accepted (after the peer review process) into an IGI Global journal.

How Does it Work?

Step 1: **Library Invests in the InfoSci-Databases:** A library perpetually purchases or subscribes to the InfoSci-Books, InfoSci-Journals, or discipline/subject databases.

Step 2: **IGI Global Matches the Library Investment with OA Subsidies Fund:** IGI Global provides a fund to go towards subsidizing the OA APCs for the library's patrons.

Step 3: **Patron of the Library is Accepted into IGI Global Journal (After Peer Review):** When a patron's paper is accepted into an IGI Global journal, they option to have their paper published under a traditional publishing model or as OA.

Step 4: **IGI Global Will Deduct APC Cost from OA Subsidies Fund:** If the author decides to publish under OA, the OA APC fee will be deducted from the OA subsidies fund.

Step 5: **Author's Work Becomes Freely Available:** The patron's work will be freely available under CC BY copyright license, enabling them to share it freely with the academic community.

Note: *This fund will be offered on an annual basis and will renew as the subscription is renewed for each year thereafter. IGI Global will manage the fund and award the APC waivers unless the librarian has a preference as to how the funds should be managed.*

Hear From the Experts on This Initiative:

"I'm very happy to have been able to make one of my recent research contributions **freely available** along with having access to the **valuable resources** found within IGI Global's InfoSci-Journals database."

– **Prof. Stuart Palmer**, Deakin University, Australia

"Receiving the support from IGI Global's OA Fee Waiver Initiative **encourages me to continue my research work without any hesitation**."

– **Prof. Wenlong Liu**, College of Economics and Management at Nanjing University of Aeronautics & Astronautics, China

For More Information, Scan the QR Code or Contact:
IGI Global's Digital Resources Team at eresources@igi-global.com.

IGI Global
PUBLISHER of TIMELY KNOWLEDGE

Are You Ready to **Publish Your Research?**

IGI Global
PUBLISHER of TIMELY KNOWLEDGE

IGI Global offers book authorship and editorship opportunities across 11 subject areas, including business, computer science, education, science and engineering, social sciences, and more!

Benefits of Publishing with IGI Global:

- Free one-on-one editorial and promotional support.
- Expedited publishing timelines that can take your book from start to finish in less than one (1) year.
- Choose from a variety of formats, including: Edited and Authored References, Handbooks of Research, Encyclopedias, and Research Insights.
- Utilize IGI Global's eEditorial Discovery® submission system in support of conducting the submission and double-blind peer review process.
- IGI Global maintains a strict adherence to ethical practices due in part to our full membership with the Committee on Publication Ethics (COPE).
- Indexing potential in prestigious indices such as Scopus®, Web of Science™, PsycINFO®, and ERIC – Education Resources Information Center.
- Ability to connect your ORCID iD to your IGI Global publications.
- Earn honorariums and royalties on your full book publications as well as complimentary copies and exclusive discounts.

Join Your Colleagues from Prestigious Institutions, Including:

Australian National University
Massachusetts Institute of Technology
Johns Hopkins University
Harvard University
Tsinghua University
Columbia University in the City of New York

Learn More at: www.igi-global.com/publish

or Contact IGI Global's Aquisitions Team at: acquisition@igi-global.com

Purchase Individual IGI Global InfoSci-OnDemand Book Chapters and Journal Articles

InfoSci®-OnDemand

Pay-Per-View Articles and Chapters from IGI Global

For More Information, Visit: www.igi-global.com/e-resources/infosci-ondemand

Browse through nearly 150,000+ articles/chapters to find specific research related to their current studies and projects that have been contributed by international researchers from prestigious institutions, including MIT, Harvard University, Columbia University, and many more.

Easily Identify, Acquire, and Utilize Published Peer-Reviewed Findings in Support of Your Current Research:

Accurate and Advanced Search: Utilize the advanced InfoSci-OnDemand search engine to identify research in your area of interest.

Affordably Acquire Research: Provide an affordable alternative to purchasing an entire reference book or scholarly journal.

Fast and Easy One-Click Shopping: Simply utilize the OnDemand "Buy Now" button on the webpage.

Instantly Download/Access Your Content: Receive an immediate link to download your InfoSci-OnDemand content to your personal computer and device.

Access Anywhere, Anytime, and on Any Device: Additionally, receive access to your OnDemand articles and chapters through a personal electronic library.

Benefit from the InfoSci Platform Features: Providing formatted citations, full-text PDF and HTML format, no embargo of content, no DRM, and more.

"It really provides **an excellent entry into the research literature of the field**. *It presents a manageable number of* **highly relevant sources** *on topics of interest to a wide range of researchers. The sources are* **scholarly, but also accessible** *to 'practitioners'."*

- Ms. Lisa Stimatz, MLS, University of North Carolina at Chapel Hill, USA

Interested in Additional Savings and Acquiring Multiple Articles and Chapters Through InfoSci-OnDemand?

Subscribe to InfoSci-OnDemand Plus

Learn More

www.ingramcontent.com/pod-product-compliance
Lightning Source LLC
LaVergne TN
LVHW080635011026
849160LV00014B/1231
* 9 7 8 1 6 6 8 4 4 8 9 0 8 *